The Nonprofit Organization
Essential Readings

BROOKS/COLE SERIES IN PUBLIC ADMINISTRATION

The Nonprofit Organization
Essential Readings

David L. Gies
Anschutz Family Foundation

J. Steven Ott
University of Maine

Jay M. Shafritz
University of Pittsburgh

Brooks/Cole Publishing Company
Pacific Grove, California

Brooks/Cole Publishing Company
A Division of Wadsworth, Inc.

Printed in the United States of America

10 9 8 7 6 5 4 3 2 1

Library of Congress Cataloging in Publication Data

The Nonprofit organization: essential readings / [edited] by David L.
  Gies, J. Steven Ott, Jay M. Shafritz.
      p.   cm.
  Includes bibliographical references.
  ISBN 0-534-12588-3
  1. Corporations, Nonprofit—United States. I. Gies, David L.
II. Ott, J. Steven. III. Shafritz, Jay M.
HD62.6.N665 1989
658'.048—dc19   89-17373
                                                      CIP

Sponsoring Editor: *Cynthia C. Stormer*
Editorial Assistant: *Mary Ann Zuzow*
Production Editor: *Linda Loba*
Manuscript Editor: *Barbara Kimmel*
Permissions Editor: *Carline Haga*
Interior Design: *Vernon T. Boes*
Cover Design: *Erin Mauterer, Bluewater A & D*
Art Coordinator: *Lisa Torri*
Typesetting: *ExecuStaff*
Printing and Binding: *Malloy Lithographing, Inc.*

Dedicated to
Fred B. Anschutz

Foreword

E. D. Hirsch's bestseller, *Cultural Literacy,* argues that there is a core of shared knowledge—words, ideas, events—that gives form and meaning to the vast diffusion of a society's culture. He argues further that some grasp of that core is necessary if people are going to learn efficiently.

There is an equivalent that might be called *philanthropic literacy.* The editors of this volume believe that it is contained in the collection of readings they have brought together in this volume. Amidst the *Essential Readings* there is a lexicon of essential facts, concepts, principles, and actions that are essential to an understanding of this field. Dr. Hirsch's *Cultural Literacy* brings together a list of about 5000 terms that he and his colleagues have prepared; they have even written a *Dictionary of Cultural Literacy* that defines the 5000 terms.

Our field has not yet reached that point. It is a bold step for the editors of this volume to declare that there is a body of essential readings, much less to propose a list of essential terms.

All these are devices to help people learn—in this case, to learn more about the "non-profit sector." The editors believe, as I do, that the subject-matter of this volume is essential to an understanding of American society and how it works. The vast majority of Americans is deficient in its knowledge of the philanthropic tradition. Until very recently, the subject has not been taught—in school, in college, in professional education. Most people do not know what is meant when someone refers to "the third sector." Most people have only a fuzzy notion of what difference there is between "nonprofit" enterprise and any other kind.

Although organized philanthropy was present in this country before there was a country, and then was brought in by the new settlers, and although philanthropy is organized and conducted on a larger scale by far than is true of any other nation or society in the history of the world—more people are employed full-time in this sector than in the federal and state governments combined—despite these rather dramatic historical facts, Americans know little about it except to have a vague notion that it is probably a good thing.

This collective ignorance has serious consequences. Major changes in tax policy are implemented in general ignorance of their impact on nonprofit and charitable organizations. Economists and public policy experts are at the beginning of their study of the subtle connections between tax policy and gifts of money. Fiscal pressures inspire measures that would remove tax exemption from some organizations, or prevent them from earning income from commercial activities. There are important arguments on both sides of such issues, but often the debaters themselves rely on shaky evidence and primitive analysis. Even so, the consequences are still important. ("A billion here and a billion there," as Senator Dirksen is supposed to have said, "and the next thing you know you're talking about real money.")

The editors provide a rationale for the third sector that is based on the inadequacy of the other two sectors. Government (the first sector) provides public goods but only in categorical ways; the marketplace (the second sector) provides for the exercise of individual choice but fails to provide public goods; the third sector lacks the coercive power of government and the driving self-interest of the marketplace but it provides for individual choice and it provides public goods. This rationale is a *defect model,* if you will; philanthropy works in many important situations because other ways fail.

Is there anything else at work? Is there something powerfully altruistic deep in human nature that underlies organized philanthropy? There is perhaps more than wishful thinking behind the question. On one side there are the arguments of sociobiologists who contend that altruism is necessary to explain human evolution; on the other side there is the role of philanthropy in organized religion, clearly the dominant philanthropic force in the American tradition. As Dennis Young asks, *If not for profit, for what?* Young is looking at the role of entrepreneurs in the nonprofit sector and trying to understand what makes them tick. It is not fashionable to talk about the power of nonmaterial values but such values are undeniably present in the third sector. One should be as alert to them as to more fashionable (and in my opinion *naive*) interpretation based on narrow self-interest.

Most of the people who are attracted to careers in philanthropy bring deeper motivations and values than simple self-interest. They are often "called" to their work out of a commitment to a cause or to a value. Some other people find themselves charged with the responsibility of managing nonprofit organizations—charged with what used to be called the "stewardship" of resources. In both cases the requirement is to balance the claims of the economic and the spiritual; it is simple foolishness to concentrate on the one and to pretend that the other is not important.

Readers of this volume are among the first of a new generation of educated Americans. Read this volume carefully and you will join the small but growing elite who have become philanthropically literate. The editors guide you both by their choice of material and by the helpful introductory texts. You will be visiting with some of my favorite people: Tocqueville (the subject of a major new biography, by the way; a Frenchman of profound importance to Americans); Merle Curti (the social historian before social history was popular, who is probably the only general historian of philanthropy we have yet produced); and the sociologists Peter Berger and Richard John Neuhaus. You will also meet the names that I have become so familiar with over the past decade or so as philanthropic studies has begun to emerge as a field: John Filer, Burton Weisbrod, Virginia Hodgkinson, Lester Salamon, Philip Kotler. There are other names: INDEPENDENT SECTOR is high among them, the umbrella organization for the field that has finally given the third sector a strong national voice.

No one can predict the future of the study of philanthropy in the university. It will be difficult to develop the conceptual structure that now exists as a makeshift shanty.

If the profession of medicine is based on biology and chemistry and anatomy and physiology, what is the profession of philanthropy to be based on? If biology and chemistry and anatomy and physiology are absolute requirements of the practice of medicine, what are the absolute requirements of the practice of philanthropy?

That returns us to the opening of this foreword: What does it mean to be philanthropically literate? Read this book carefully, and study it and think about it, and you'll have begun to formulate your own answer to that question.

Robert L. Payton
Director, Center on Philanthropy
Professor of Philanthropic Studies
Indiana University

Preface

The Nonprofit Organization: Essential Readings is a collection of what we, the editors, consider to be the most important and informative articles, chapters, and papers written to date about the nonprofit organization. In making our selections, we used several criteria. The two most important were:

1. "Should a thoughtful manager of a nonprofit organization or serious graduate student be expected to be able to identify this author and his or her basic themes?" If the answer was affirmative, then it was so because the contribution is being increasingly recognized as an important theme by an important writer.

2. Each article, paper, or chapter had to make a fundamental statement that has been echoed or attacked repeatedly. As such, the selection had to be seen as significant in the sense that it must be (or will be) an integral part of the foundation for the future building of the field of nonprofit organization.

Thus, *The Nonprofit Organization: Essential Readings* attempts to present a balanced picture of the essential philosophical underpinnings, concepts, and principles that are essential to the serious student's understanding of the essence of the modern nonprofit organization.

Several pervasive themes or conceptual threads are woven throughout this anthology. These themes represent the theoretical core of the volume or, if you will, the authors' conceptual biases.

1. Mediating structures (voluntary associations and "those [other] institutions standing between the individual in his private life and the large institutions [*megastructures*] of public life" [Berger & Neuhaus, 1977, p. 2]) are absolutely essential component elements of our society. Neither government agencies nor private-for-profit sector firms can function as effective mediating structures. The mediating structure role filled by nonprofit organizations provides one important explanation for the ongoing vitality of the nonprofit sector.

2. People behave with some degree of economic rationality. Their actions reflect demands for certain goods and services. Many goods are acquired and consumed by individuals who purchase them for a predetermined cost (for example, hamburgers). Economists call these *private goods*. A second type of goods is consumed by groupings of people who are not conscious parties to the acquisition and/or consumption decisions (for example, beneficiaries of clean air and rivers, and national defense), or are consumed by people who do not pay for them directly (for example, for most people, health care). In the language of economics, these are *public goods, social goods,* or *collective goods* (Musgrave & Musgrave, 1980, chapters 3 & 4; Rose-Ackerman, 1986, pp. 4–7; Weisbrod, 1988, pp. 25–27). When public goods are involved *or* when there are informational inequalities in the market, the private marketplace fails and resources are not allocated efficiently. Government or nonprofit sector organizations are better solutions (alternative institutions to private firms) when the marketplace fails (Weisbrod, 1988, pp. 6, 8). For some purposes, government is the obvious choice; however, there are arenas in which it is not. Thus, marketplace failure coupled with limits on government provide a second major justification and explanation for the pervasiveness of nonprofit organizations in the United States. Such failure, in a

free enterprise/market-oriented economy, provides a second major explanation for the pervasiveness of nonprofit organizations in the United States.

3. Open, multiple, conflicting, and competing—but responsive and caring—groups preserve traditional democratic values. A single-dimensional helping sector cannot be effective in a heterogeneous society consisting of many ethnic, cultural, and religious groups.

4. The human acts of charity and philanthropy are woven into our cultural fabric. Alexis de Tocqueville (1840), the insightful Frenchman who traveled the vast new land of America in the 1830s, was in awe of the almost instinctive nature and ease with which associations were formed to meet almost every variety of community need. This associate-to-meet-needs propensity has many theoretical and motivational roots. Several of the articles reprinted here by, for example, Andrew Carnegie, Merle Curti, and Elizabeth Boris, document the diversity of motivations and forms of philanthropy, but they speak equally eloquently to our seemingly never-ending propensity to be philanthropic.

Beyond these themes we could find no single, theoretical framework that would yield a coherent anthology. There is no such thing as *the* theory of nonprofit organizations. Rather, there are many theories that attempt to explain the existence, behavior, structure, purpose, and place in society of third sector organizations.

We decided to approach the book's organization as though we were preparing an outline, or syllabus, for a course on managing in the nonprofit sector. Our prototypical students were to be experienced first and second-level managers of nonprofit organizations who were enrolled in their first of several courses about nonprofit organizations and management. This not totally hypothetical class of seasoned student managers provided the basis for the organization of this text. With a clear vision of them in front of us, we set out to design and sequence the chapters to explain and interpret *for them* the vital functions, institutions, issues, traditions, and values that shape the environments surrounding them in their work. The composition of the class dictated that our primary task was to help develop peoples' ability to understand *why* things are as they are—to interpret, without any fiction, fables, or mythology. They also kept reminding us to limit the amount of purely descriptive information and "how-to tools" we included: These could be picked up at workshops. Most importantly, the sequence of chapters and articles had to communicate our understanding of the complex cognitive and normative realities that face practicing nonprofit managers. This proved to be a tall order. We hope that what follows satisfies the challenge that we set for ourselves, and our class.

Topics Covered

Chapter I—The Nonprofit Sector: Its History, Essence, and Philosophy introduces important themes and issues involving the traditions, theoretical justifications, and ideologies of the world of voluntarism and nonprofit organizations. Why is it here? Why not absorb the study of its organizations and functions into schools of business or public administration? Are nonprofit board members right in saying that an organization should be run like a business? Isn't this overlooking something important? Do voluntarism and the nonprofit sector warrant separate study? Is managing in it worth all of the hassle and headaches?

Chapter II—Impacts of Public Policy on Nonprofit Organizations requires explanation. Although all organizations are affected by changes in governmental policy shifts, nonprofit organizations are impacted dramatically. Changes in government tax policy, funding priorities, service delivery strategies, and regulations restricting tax exempt activities and income, predetermine many policy decisions for nonprofit organizations. Changes in government policy alter nonprofit organizations' income sources and streams, the nature of their activities, organizational structure, and relationships among central stakeholders. Thus, Chapter II precedes the chapter on planning and policy formation (Chapter III), because public policy and its shifts define the parameters for strategic planning and policy formulation in nonprofit organizations. Only after government establishes the shape of the playing field can nonprofits begin their policy formulation and planning processes.

Chapter III—Planning and Policy Formulation explores the processes managers use to decide fundamental questions of nonprofit organizational purpose, mission, and direction: Who and what an organization is and is not, how it fits into its particular environment, and how it fits into and attempts to shape its environment.

Chapter IV—Governance: The Roles and Functions of Boards of Directors examines the formal legal and functional roles and mechanisms by which nonprofit organizations are governed. Thus, this chapter addresses the formal linkages between the internal workings of a nonprofit organization (authority and accountability) and its external environment (organizational adaptation to the world around it).

All organizations require management, but *Chapter V—Managing Nonprofit Organizations* highlights why managing in the nonprofit sector warrants attention as a subject in its own right. The managerial roles and functions are affected by the unique contexts, philosophies, ethical codes, governance structures, value systems, and legal ground rules under which organizations in the nonprofit sector operate. The chapter speaks to the inherent ethical problems and the deep tensions and paradoxes of working as managers in nonprofit organizations.

Chapter VI—Entrepreneurship and Promotional Management is about an essential frame of mind in the 1980s; the willingness of nonprofit organization managers, staff, and boards to create and to be receptive to opportunities. It is a positive orientation toward risk-taking ventures. The chapter emphasizes entrepreneurial business enterprise-type ventures and the marketing of goods and services, and the ramifications for nonprofit organizations as the sector boundaries become less well defined.

Chapter VII—Philanthropy and Voluntarism in American Society brings the subject of nonprofit organizations full-circle, back to the most fundamental reasons why the sector exists: to the benevolent donation of money, property, and time or effort to eliminate or prevent the causes of social problems and injustices. It is about the pros and cons of our society's chosen ways to "form a more perfect union" and to "secure the blessings of liberty to ourselves and our posterity."

Criteria for Selection

Obviously, the thirty-one articles that follow are not the only essential readings in the field of nonprofit organizations. Although academic interest in nonprofit organizations is in its infancy, many primary and secondary sciences with long and distinguished traditions have provided important concepts and understandings. Major contributions to the sector's intellectual foundation have come from such diverse disciplines and fields as economics, history, religion, organization theory, sociology, social work, psychology, philosophy, political science, economics, business administration, public administration, hospital administration, and educational administration. The world of nonprofit organizations is so diverse that there cannot be—and should not be—a single definitive list of essential readings.

We readily admit that some important contributors and contributions to the field have not found their way into this collection. Omitting some was difficult. However, considerations of space and balanced perspectives necessarily prevailed.

Several criteria were employed when we made our final selections. First, we asked ourselves: "Does the article provide the serious student of nonprofit organizations a reason for the existence of the sector?" "Does it help to explain where the sector came from, how it fits into the broad context of society, its uniqueness, and how its organizations are managed?"

The second criterion is related to the first: Each article or portion of the anthology had to make a basic statement that has been consistently echoed or represents a particular line of thinking over the years. Some articles, like Alfred Stern's "Instilling Activism in Trustees," have been included because they describe a point of view demonstrating the difference between managing in the nonprofit sector versus managing in the public and private sectors.

Finally, the article had to be readable. Those students who have already had reason to peruse the literature of nonprofit organizations will appreciate the importance of this criterion.

Acknowledgments

We wish we could acknowledge everyone who has contributed ideas, insights, stimulation, challenges, and constructive criticisms during the development of this volume. However space and propriety require that we limit our statements of appreciation to those who played primary roles in shaping our preliminary ideas into a cohesive anthology. Among those whom we absolutely must acknowledge are Jacquelyn Wolf, University of Toronto; Elizabeth T. Boris, Council on Foundations; E. Samuel Overman, University of Colorado, Denver; Leo A. G. Wiegman, formerly with The Dorsey Press; Jon Van Til, Rutgers University, Camden; Albert C. Hyde, University of Pittsburgh; Daniel Oran, Foresight, Inc.; Carol Matteson, University of Maine at Augusta; Sue Anschutz Rodgers and Karen Tucker, Anschutz Family Foundation; Versa Clark, Cathleen Cortelyou, and Terry Galpin-Plattner, Center for Nonprofit Excellence; Jackie Compton, Frost Foundation; and Phil Panun, Denver Public Library.

In addition, we would like to express our appreciation to the reviewers of this book, for their helpful comments and suggestions: Dr. Mary Anna Colwell, University of San Francisco; Professor Roger Kahn, Metro State College, Denver, Colorado; Professor Hank Rubin, Roosevelt University, Chicago, Illinois; and Professor Jon Van Til, Rutgers University, Camden, New Jersey.

Robert L. Payton, Director of the Indiana University Center on Philanthropy not only wrote the thoughtful *Foreword* but also has been a substantive force in shaping our philosophical perspective on the sector for many years. Finally, deep appreciation and admiration to the students at Pitt's Graduate School of Public and International Affairs, who made PIA 224 in summer 1988 such an exciting experience and, in the process, helped us make crucial decisions about *Essential Readings*.

David L. Gies
J. Steven Ott
Jay M. Shafritz

References

Berger, P., & Neuhaus, R. J. (1977). *To empower people: The role of mediating structures in public policy.* Washington, DC: American Enterprise Institute.

Musgrave, R. A., & Musgrave, P. B. (1980). *Public finance in theory and practice.* New York: McGraw-Hill.

Rose-Ackerman, S. (1986). *The economics of nonprofit institutions.* New York: Oxford University Press.

Tocqueville, A. de. (1840). *Democracy in America,* Vol. II. New York: Alfred A. Knopf, Inc.

Weisbrod, B. A. (1988). *The nonprofit economy.* Cambridge, MA: Harvard University Press.

About the Authors of Original Articles

The Foreword

Robert L. Payton is Director of the Center on Philanthropy at Indiana University. Previously he was Scholar-in-Residence in Philanthropic Studies at the University of Virginia, President of Exxon Education Foundation, President of Hofstra University, President of C. W. Post College, U. S. Ambassador to Cameroon, and Vice Chancellor of Washington University in St. Louis. He is a member of the boards of the Independent Sector, Technoserve, and the Cultural Literacy Foundation. Mr. Payton has published numerous articles, monographs, and books, most recently *Philanthropy* (1988). Educated at the University of Chicago, from which he holds a master's degree in history, Mr. Payton was awarded an honorary doctorate in literature by Adelphi University in 1988. In 1984 he received the Distinguished Service to Education Award from the Council for Advancement and Support of Education.

Chapter I

Stephen R. Block is Executive Director of the Institute for Nonprofit Organization Management, a Colorado nonprofit organization that provides educational, training, and consulting services to voluntary and philanthropic organizations. He consults in the development of foundations and in corporate giving. His writings have appeared in books and professional journals such as *Nonprofit and Voluntary Sector Quarterly, Journal of Social Work, Clinical Social Work Journal, Journal of Voluntary Action Research, Journal of Sociology and Social Welfare, Arete,* and *Journal of Psychiatric Treatment and Evaluation.* He is Consulting Editor to the *Nonprofit and Voluntary Sector Quarterly,* serves on the Nonprofit Concentration Curriculum Review Board at the University of Pittsburgh, and is on the National Association of Schools of Public Affairs and Administration's Committee for Nonprofit Management. He has been an adjunct faculty member at San Francisco State University, Indiana University, and Colorado State University. Dr. Block received a Bachelor of Arts degree from Brooklyn College, City University of New York; a Master's degree in Social Work from Indiana University; and a Doctor of Public Administration concentrating in nonprofit organization management from the University of Colorado.

Chapter II

Gary N. Scrivner, CPA, is Chief Financial Officer of the University of Arizona Foundation. Previously he spent twelve years with "Big Eight" public accounting firms, most recently Coopers & Lybrand. His articles have appeared in Prentice-Hall's *Tax Exempt Organizations,* the *Journal of Accountancy, Philanthropy Monthly,* and others. Mr. Scrivner has served on numerous boards and committees of nonprofit organizations. He has consulted with many types of tax exempt organizations on organizational and exemption issues, public charity status, private foundation taxes, related and unrelated income, grant management, fundraising and development, lobbying and political action, split interest trusts, reorganizations, mergers, strategic planning, and volunteerism. He is a doctoral student in nonprofit organization management at the University of Colorado at Denver.

Chapter IV

Michael R. Ostrowski is the Executive Director of Child and Family Services of New Hampshire, a statewide nonprofit human service organization that provides child welfare, residential, family, and elderly services as well as advocacy. He is active with the Child Welfare League of America and the national accrediting body for child welfare, family service, and residential programs. Before moving to New Hampshire, Mr. Ostrowski was Executive Director of a family service agency in Michigan, directed a substance abuse program, and helped to develop employee assistance programs. He is a past President of the Michigan Chapter of the National Association of Social Workers and has served on many boards of nonprofit organizations. Mr. Ostrowski received his bachelors and masters degrees from Wayne State University and is a doctoral candidate at the University of Colorado, Graduate School of Public Affairs. He resides in Bedford, New Hampshire.

Chapter V

Hank Rubin is Associate Professor of Public Administration at Roosevelt University in Chicago. Dr. Rubin is a practitioner, researcher, and writer in the field of nonprofit administration. He has been executive director of two nonprofit organizations and an officer and board member in more than a dozen civic and professional nonprofits. He consults internationally in nonprofit administration, planning, and curriculum development for teaching nonprofit administrators. He has served on the ASPA Committee on Professional Standards and Ethics, as Treasurer of the Chicago Ethics Project, and as a member of the NASPAA Committee on Nonprofit Administration. He has administered civil rights and public education programs. Dr. Rubin created a degree program and a certificate program in nonprofit administration and has taught in both. His bachelor's and master's degrees are from the University of Chicago, his Ph.D. from Northwestern University.

E. Samuel Overman is an Associate Professor and Director of Doctoral Studies at the Graduate School of Public Affairs, University of Colorado at Denver. He has published books on *Public Management Research in the United States* (Praeger, 1983) and *Methodology and Epistemology for Social Science* (University of Chicago Press, 1988). Professor Overman's numerous journal articles are primarily on information management and policy, including studies in computing at NASA's Johnson Space Center and nonprofit organizations. His articles appear in such journals as *Public Administration Review, Computing in Human Services, Public Productivity Review,* and *Management Science and Policy Analysis.* Professor Overman received his Ph.D. from the University of Pittsburgh.

Jacquelyn Wolf is Director of the School of Continuing Studies at the University of Toronto, Canada, and is on the faculty of the Voluntary Sector Management Program at York University. Previously she was on the Faculty of Management and headed management continuing education at the University of Manitoba. Ms. Wolf was city editor of a major metropolitan newspaper and senior editor of the national wire service bureau in Vancouver, B.C. She has consulted with nonprofit, business, and government organizations for more than 10 years with respect to major change strategies. Ms. Wolf has an M.B.A. from the University of Manitoba and did her undergraduate work at the University of Kansas. She is a doctoral candidate in public administration, specializing in nonprofit organization policy at the University of Colorado.

Chapter VI

Theodore R. Kauss is Vice President and Executive Director of The Frost Foundation, a Denver, Colorado philanthropic organization. Before joining Frost, Dr. Kauss held administrative posts at Centenary College of Louisiana, including Executive Vice President and Acting President; was a senior associate with Cresap, McCormick and Paget, Inc., management consultants; and was director of the Master of Arts in Teaching Program and professor at Northwestern University. He has published numerous articles in education and business journals; authored the fastback book, *Leaders Live with Crises* (1974), published by the Phi Delta Kappa Foundation; and served on the boards of cultural, community, and professional organizations. Dr. Kauss received his B.S. and M.S. degrees at the University of Wisconsin and completed his Ph.D. at Northwestern University.

Randall J. Kauss is a writer and consultant with Northern Telecon in Richardson, Texas. Prior to his present position, he was a technical writer and editorial assistant with Geomath in Denver, Colorado and the Tandy Corporation in Fort Worth, Texas. He has served as a proposal writer and free lance editor with nonprofit organizations in several states. Mr. Kauss graduated from Texas Christian University with degrees in journalism and history.

Chapter VII

Elizabeth T. Boris is Vice President for Research for the Council on Foundations. Previously she directed a program on Business Ethics and Social Responsibility for the Council of Better Business Bureaus. She chairs a committee of the National Center for Charitable Statistics, and is a public member of the Committee on Accreditation for the American Library Association. Dr. Boris is an advisory board member of the Center for Nonprofit Organization Management, the Center for the Study of Philanthropy at the City University of New York, *Giving USA,* the Independent Sector Research Group, and others. Author of many articles and reports, she also coauthored a book on foundation careers and is a contributor to several others. Dr. Boris received her B.A. degree from Douglass College, Rutgers University, and her M.A. and Ph.D. from Rutgers University. She is an adjunct Associate Professor at the University of Colorado.

The Authors/Editors

David L. Gies is currently the Director of the Anschutz Family Foundation and has extensive nonprofit organization experience. Previously, Mr. Gies was Chief Financial Officer of the Institute for Nonprofit Organization Management, which provides management consultation to nonprofit organizations throughout the United States. He has also served as Executive Director of the Las Animas County Rehabilitation Center and at one time was employed by the State of Colorado to establish and expand nonprofit community rehabilitation programs across the state. Mr. Gies has published numerous articles in the

Journal of Voluntary Action Research and the *Journal of Rehabilitation Administration.* He earned his master's degree from DePaul University, Chicago, Illinois, and his bachelor's degree from Colorado State University.

J. Steven Ott is on the faculty and is Director of Graduate Programs in Public Administration at the University of Maine, where he teaches courses in nonprofit organization management, public management, health care policy and administration, and organization theory, behavior, and change. Previously Dr. Ott was executive vice-president of a management consulting firm where he accumulated more than twenty years experience working with nonprofit organizations both as a member of boards of directors and as a consultant. He has taught courses at the University of Colorado at Denver and the University of Pittsburgh. Dr. Ott's degrees are from the Pennsylvania State University, the Sloan School of Management at M.I.T., and the University of Colorado. He has written or cowritten recent books on nonprofit organization management, organization theory, organizational culture, organizational behavior, and health care management. With Shafritz, he coauthored *The Facts on File Dictionary of Nonprofit Organization Management.*

Jay M. Shafritz is a professor at the Graduate School of Public and International Affairs at the University of Pittsburgh. Previously he taught at the University of Colorado at Denver, Rensselaer Polytechnic Institute, the University of Houston, and the State University of New York at Albany. He earned his bachelor's degree from Temple University, his master's from the City University of New York, and his Ph.D. from Temple University. Professor Shafritz is the author, coauthor, or editor of more than two dozen other books on subjects related to the management of nonprofit organizations, including *The Facts on File Dictionary of Nonprofit Organization Management.*

Contents

CHAPTER SEVEN
Philanthropy and
Voluntarism in American Society   335
Introduction

Introduction

This book is about voluntarism. It is about the American nature of giving freely, giving of oneself—one's time, money, and free association—for mutual benefit. Thus, our subject is not limited to the study of nonprofit organizations or even to the nonprofit sector: Rather, it is about the unique ways we have chosen to organize ourselves in this country to "form a more perfect union, establish justice, insure domestic tranquillity, . . .promote the general welfare, and secure the blessings of liberty for ourselves and our posterity." We have decided collectively to accomplish these goals, to achieve these individualistic and shared ends through the voluntary actions, the nonprofit efforts, of "we the people." Daily, we implement programs for youth, contribute food and shelter to the poor, support the arts, provide for education, protect the environment, promote dirt bike racing, fight to bear arms, lobby for gun control, become "right to life" spokespeople, and advocate for the right of women to make basic choices, all through nonprofit organizations. Promoting justice, domestic tranquillity, and the general welfare for all is *the* central raison d'être for the nonprofit sector.

It was not until 1894 that Congress formally recognized the vital roles that nonprofit organizations fill in enhancing our way of life. In the Tariff Act of 1894, Congress granted tax exemption to nonprofit charitable, religious, educational, and fraternal associations. From this inauspicious genesis, the nonprofit sector has become an enormous producer and distributor of an unparalleled array of ideas and services. In 1984,* 821,000 third sector (or nonprofit) organizations employed 11.4 million people who together earned $157.1 billion. Nonprofit organizations accounted for 5.6 percent of the 1984 national income ($176.3 billion), and current operating expenditures approached $210 billion—18 percent of all services in the personal consumption expenditures component of the gross national product (Hodgkinson & Weitzman, 1986, pp. 3,4).

The nonprofit sector is a particularly unique democratic phenomenon. In some respects it is the most capitalistic of our economic responses, reacting to marketplace failure by filling economic voids with volunteer time and charitable contributions. In contrast, more socialistic economies tend to meet similar types of community needs through tax-supported government programs and services. Nonprofits provide a flexible alternative to tax-supported government action.

People of the world respond to problems by coming together out of mutual caring, organizing their efforts in an effective way, and implementing strategies in the name of specific causes. Over time, worldwide efforts and international programs evolve demonstrating a common association response that frequently is cited as a phenomenon unique to the United States. But voluntarism is strong in some nations and is evolving in others. The myriad examples of international voluntary associations—the International Red Cross, the World Wildlife Fund, international service clubs, and worldwide religious affiliation organizations—all suggest that the often-quoted observation by Alexis de Tocqueville (1840) that Americans "of all ages, all conditions, and all dispositions constantly form associations," is generous. Clearly, however, people in democratic/capitalistic societies do have

---

* The most recent year for which data are available from the INDEPENDENT SECTOR.

more at stake that encourages them to provide direct support to the charitable organizations of primary choice than do people in nations without marketplace economies.

Repeatedly through history, citizens have recognized a need and then built a nonprofit constituency dedicated to ameliorating or eliminating it, even though the issue or its targeted people often were socially undesirable (at the time). In instance after instance over the years, this voluntary process has led to eventual public policy changes and government support (or tolerance) for what was originally a politically unacceptable cause, case, or issue.

This phenomenon of nonprofit sector leadership for unpopular causes and cases has been observed in community after community on issue upon issue. The provision of services to people with mental retardation is one of many typical examples. Prior to the 1960s, very little was done for people with developmental disabilities beyond the efforts of parents and relatives who struggled through mazes of limited, disconnected, and segregated services. Large state institutions, or *warehouses* (depending on one's point of view) were the dubious exceptions. What few community services there were typically were established by or through parent organizations. Some programs were initiated by religious groups, often in response to the pleas of their membership. Over time, parents who shared concerns about the lack of services and access to them established organizations for mutual support, advocacy, and public information. These organizations, such as the Association for Retarded Citizens or, more simply, the Concerned Parents of XYZ County, gave the members strength and power to speak their views of "the general welfare" and "domestic tranquillity" needs of their children and themselves.

Primarily as a result of the grassroots campaigns conducted by parents of people with mental retardation, all state legislatures passed laws in the early 1960s establishing and funding systems of services. In most states, nonprofit organizations became the leading providers of direct community-based services, working in the seams, or crevices, between government agencies and for-profit enterprises. Similar sagas could be told about services for people who have chronic mental illness or Alzheimer's disease; who have suffered strokes or physical, psychological, and/or sexual abuse; who are poor, near-poor, or homeless. The same is true for myriad art appreciation programs, symphony orchestras, museums, zoos, and botanical gardens. Each of these public assets was started by citizens who first formed nonprofit associations to address their cause or case.

In the nineteenth century, Alexis de Tocqueville (1840) was impressed by this nation's shared control and responsibility of efforts to meet community needs. He observed that throughout Europe, in contrast with the experience in the United States, the *secondary power*—the ability of the nobility, cities, and provincial bodies to represent local affairs—had been relinquished to the centralized authority. Such centralization eliminated the need for the development of philanthropy in European nations. Tocqueville wrote:

> My object is to remark that all these various rights which have been successively wrested, in our time, from classes, guilds, and individuals have not served to raise new secondary powers on a more democratic basis, but have uniformly been concentrated in the hands of the sovereign. Everywhere the state acquires more and more direct control over the humblest members of the community and a more exclusive power of governing each of them in his smallest concerns.
>
> Almost all the charitable establishments of Europe were formerly in the hands of private persons or of guilds; they are now almost all dependent on the supreme government, and in many countries are actually administered by that power. The state almost

exclusively undertakes to supply bread to the hungry, assistance and shelter to the sick, work to the idle, and to act as the sole reliever of all kinds of misery (1840, pp. 303–304).

Tocqueville's "secondary power" is what we refer to today as activities that serve the public good. Indeed, the current context of Tocqueville's discussion is focused on concepts of public and private good. Who is responsible for what? What is to be held as a common good? What are the limits of self-interest?

There is no supreme government responsible for services to homeless people. Services to homeless people became a national topic only after local groups, often church related, recognized the need and organized to address it. As the means to meet new needs becomes more apparent to volunteers (nonprofit organizers), grant applications are submitted to foundations; programs develop and community awareness of problems expands; communities respond with new or adapted public social programs. Often, the need is redefined and articulated as communities gain experience in dealing with it. In time, new patterns of services are created. Thus, secondary power impacts on community and national consciousness, philosophy, and programs. This is pluralism at its very best; freedom helping to preserve social order (Bellah, Madsen, Sullivan, Swider, & Tipon, 1985).

From 1982 through 1988, the administration of President Ronald Reagan refocused the nation's emphasis on the power of "we the people" and on individual, voluntary, nongovernmental responses to community problems. The Reagan agenda was predicated on the assumption that issue identification and action responsibility should be returned to local communities, thus increasing community reliance on nonprofits at a time when the government was simultaneously decreasing the size of, and the sector's access to, its traditional funding sources. Never in our history had the third sector been called upon to do so much more with so much less. The impact of the myriad aspects of the *Reagan Revolution* on nonprofits and those who would manage them in the 1980s were unprecedented, particularly since Reagan's emphasis on voluntary action proved to be more rhetoric than substance.

The early signs emanating from the George Bush administration did not signal the arrival of less complex times for the nonprofit sector. In fact, President Bush's 1988 campaign may be most remembered for its "thousand points of light," a reference to voluntarism and Bush's belief that a new, more altruistic age had begun in Washington. And Congress was quick to join in. Senate Majority Leader George Mitchell (D.–ME) and House Speaker Jim Wright (D.–TX) pledged to make national service a top priority for legislative action in 1989. Numerous national and community service bills were introduced. Among those receiving the most attention was a bill introduced by Senator Sam Nunn (D.–GA) and Representative Dave McCurdy (D.–OK) that would make eligibility for federally guaranteed college tuition loans dependent on providing community service for one or two years through a proposed "Citizens Corp."

Now is the time for all good men and women—everyone who is associated with nonprofit organizations—to come to the aid of the sector; to learn more about how to make nonprofit organizations more effective instruments for social benefit.

References

Bakal, C. (1979). *Charity U.S.A.* New York: Times Books.

Bellah, R. N., Madsen, R., Sullivan, W. M., Swider, A., & Tipon, S. M. (1985). *Habits of the heart: Individualism and commitment in American life.* Berkeley: University of California Press.

Belknap, C. M. (1984). *The federal income tax exemption of charitable organizations: Its history and underlying policy.* New York: The Rockefeller Foundation.

Berger, P., & Neuhaus, R. J. (1977). *To empower people: The role of mediating structures in public policy.* Washington, DC: American Enterprise Institute.

Bethune, J. (1843). *The power of faith of the late Mrs. Isabella Graham.* New York: American Tract Society.

Brooks, H., Liebman, L., & Schelling, C. S. (Eds.). (1984). *Public–private partnership: New opportunities for meeting social needs.* Cambridge, MA: Ballinger.

Buchanan, J. M. (1968). *The demand and supply of public goods.* Chicago: Rand McNally.

Clotfelter, C. T. (1985). *Federal tax policy and charitable giving.* Chicago: University of Chicago Press.

Cuninggim, M. (1972). *Private money and public service: The role of foundations in American society.* New York: McGraw-Hill.

Davis, K. (1973). The case for and against business assumption of social responsibilities. *Academy of Management Journal, 16,* 312–32.

Douglas, J. (1983). *Why charity? The case for a third sector.* Beverly Hills, CA: Sage Publications.

Hartogs, N., & Weber, J. (1978). *Impact of government funding on the management of voluntary agencies.* New York: Greater New York Fund/United Way.

Hodgkinson, V. A., & Weitzman, M. S. (1986). *Dimensions of the independent sector: A statistical profile* (2nd ed.). Washington, DC: Independent Sector.

Layton, D. N. (1987). *Philanthropy and voluntarism.* Washington, DC: The Foundation Center.

Musgrave, R. A., & Musgrave, P. B. (1980). *Public finance in theory and practice.* New York: McGraw-Hill.

Nielson, W. A. (1979). *The endangered sector.* New York: Columbia University Press.

O'Connell, B. (1983). *America's voluntary spirit.* New York: The Foundation Center.

O'Neill, M. (1989). *The third America.* San Francisco: Jossey-Bass.

Ott, J. S., & Shafritz, J. M. (1986). *Dictionary of nonprofit organization management.* New York: Facts on File.

Payton, R. L., Novak, M., O'Connell, B., & Hall, P. D. (1988). *Philanthropy: Four views.* New Brunswick, NJ: Transaction Books.

Rose-Ackerman, S. (1986). *The economics of nonprofit institutions.* New York: Oxford University Press.

Smith, D. H. (1966). The importance of formal voluntary organizations for society. *Sociology and Social Research, 50,* 483–492.

Tocqueville, A. de. (1840). *Democracy in America,* Vol. II. New York: Knopf.

Weisbrod, B. A. (1988). *The nonprofit economy.* Cambridge, MA: Harvard University Press.

Wolf, J. (1985). A comparison of the role of the voluntary sector in Canada and the United States. *The Philanthropist, 5*(3), 3–16.

Young, D. R. (1983). *If not for profit, for what?.* Lexington, MA: Lexington Books.

CHAPTER ONE
The Nonprofit Sector:
Its History, Essence, and Philosophy

Introduction

Kenneth Boulding describes doing good as "a difficult art" (Boulding, 1965). In this chapter, we attempt to provide the reader with a sense of why this is so, a task that requires us to articulate what the nonprofit sector and its organizations are all about. In order to do so, we will explore the history, essence, philosophy, and values of voluntarism. For example, the readings that follow present the nonprofit sector from the perspectives of historians, research statisticians, and economists.

The sector's first philosophical pillar is that of the applied philosophers. The study of voluntarism is, in fact, the study of applied ethics or applied moral philosophy. Voluntary action for the public good begins with an individual taking the initiative to improve the lives of others: This is by definition an ethical act. The second philosophical pillar is market failure economics, a concept that explains the existence of nonprofit organizations based on the failure of the private market system to provide for the public good.

Why should we bother with all of this? The answer is not academic. This sector of the economy in the United States has become the object of high expectations in the eyes of many public policy decision makers, expectations that it has (or will) become our primary —and rightful—vehicle for righting myriad societal wrongs. It is the nonprofit sector that represents the *thousand points of light* that George Bush so often alluded to during his 1988 presidential campaign.

The voluntary sector is increasingly important as an area of study. Nonprofit management, third sector organizations, and independent sector programs are only new articulations of the old concepts of charity, philanthropy, and social action. The notions of charity and philanthropy are old, but how they are influencing today's society is new.

In a country where the profit motive is supreme, it is both curious and inevitable that we have a pervasive nonprofit sector. In most other societies voluntarism does not play as significant a role in the lives of people as it does in ours. Indeed, some serious students of the nonprofit sector, including, for example, Robert L. Payton, Director of the Center on Philanthropy at Indiana University, believe that voluntarism (or philanthropy in its broad sense) is, "the best thing one can say about the United States. We have inherited a tradition of voluntary action for the public good." Few other societies have developed such extensive organized systems or approached the magnitude of voluntary action that we have in this nation. We have legalized, protected, and encouraged our voluntary sector in ways that most other societies have not.

The essence of the sector is its voluntary nature. The essential purpose of the sector is, as Boulding puts it, "to do good." Therefore, we begin with a brief historical review of the tradition of "doing good." Since the Reformation, two predominant forms of sharing, assisting, and cooperating for the benefit of others are evident in western civilizations: individual and associational. The focus of this book is on associational voluntarism. Although accounts of collaborative voluntary action can be found dating back to the origins of record-keeping, our modern forms of institutionalized associational voluntary action trace their lineage to the Reformation's stimulation of freedom of association; increased interdependence (reduced self-sufficiency) caused by the Industrial Revolution's need for specialization (division of labor) and urbanization; and rapid expansion during the 1900s (Cass & Manser, 1976). Also, one cannot overlook the influence of the growth of liberal democratic theory following the Industrial Revolution. The writings of philosophers such as Locke and Mill provided articulate rationales for the development of associations to counterbalance dictatorial power. The western tradition of voluntarism has roots in two diverse ideological streams:

1. The Greco-Roman heritage of emphasis on community, citizenry, and social responsibility. The Greco-Roman ideology rests on a foundation of social reform to relieve community social problems; to improve the quality of life for all in the community.

2. The Judeo-Christian belief that relationships with a higher power affect our choices; our decision making. Thus, our purpose is not to change peoples' lots but rather to alleviate the (preordained) suffering of others, particularly the poor. Under the Judeo-Christian tradition, one does not help others solely from concern for oneself or one's neighbors, but because a deity has given instructions to do so. We have been told to love our neighbor as we love ourself: One loves one's neighbor because one loves God first and thus seeks to obey.

These two distinct, historical, ideological themes remain clearly evident today in fundamental roles of nonprofit organizations. For example, Ott and Shafritz (1986) distinguish between: *cause advocacy*, or leadership for social reform; and *case advocacy*, or individual service to a person or a limited group of persons in need.

The influence of the two ideologies has been replayed countless times and in countless ways through the history of the American nonprofit sector, and is reflected in the following definitions of two types of voluntarism.

- *Philanthropy* is the giving of money or self to solve social problems; it is developmental, an investment in the future, an effort to prevent future occurrences or recurrences.
- *Charity* is relieving or alleviating specific instances of suffering; it is acts of mercy or compassion.

We tend to view the two forms of voluntary action as complementary elements in a nonprofit system. We need philanthropy as well as charity. However, this is not always the case. For example, Andrew Carnegie, an ardent philanthropist, abhorred charity. "It were better for mankind that the millions of the rich were thrown into the sea than so spent as to encourage the slothful, the drunken, the unworthy. . . .so spent, indeed, as to produce the very evils which it hopes to mitigate or cure" (Carnegie, 1900, p. 26). Yet from the Judeo-Christian charitable tradition, almshouses, charitable hospitals, orphan homes, and charitable organizations such as the Little Sisters of the Poor, the Salvation Army, the International Red Cross, and countless others, have helped relieve untold instances of human suffering in the United States over the last 150 years.

As this nation was founded on the democratic ideals of both individualism and pluralism, our fundamental notion of how domestic problems (such as poverty, health, child raising, housing, mental illness, homelessness, and inequitable access to employment opportunities) should be addressed is returning in the 1980s to its historical stable state: community-level problem solving. Our basic approach to dealing with domestic problems and issues in the United States has progressed from individual and family-level resolution, to community problem solving (as the country urbanized), to massive state intervention, and back toward community problem solving. In part this return to the past has been a negative reaction to the perceived failure of the New Deal/Great Society's "generous revolution" of the decades from the 1930s to the 1980s. During these years, federal expenditures for social welfare increased by twenty times while the U.S. population increased by only one half (Murray, 1984). Thus, in the second half of the 1980s the nexus of responsibility for charity and social action once again showed signs of shifting from a national orientation back to one of local control.

Clearly *change* is the single word that best describes the environment around non-profit organizations during the 1980s. President Ronald Reagan's administration and his personal communicative abilities combined to help change the nation's basic vision about how social problems and community needs should be addressed, and how remedial and ameliorating activities should be funded. From the provision of social services to the support of metropolitan symphonies, local structures now provide for the continued survival or decide the final fate of many nonprofit organizations. The role and responsibilities of the public sector has indeed contracted, in perception if not in fact. It even has become popular to advocate the privatization of human services previously provided by the public sector (Sundquist, 1984).

The pioneer barn-raising spirit of neighbors helping each other in good times and bad has become the foundation for domestic public policy reform. Returning responsibility to the people, allowing and requiring communities to decide which local problems should be addressed, has become vogue. In the short span of one decade, programs for people have moved a great distance from what they had been for more than fifty years. What stream of events and philosophical currents led to such radical change in social policy? A nation that was committed to—and believed it could—win the "War on Poverty" through "Great Society programs" only two decades ago, now must attempt to cope with the reality of having a seemingly never-ending need for "head start" programs and health care and housing for the poor.

Change and uncertainty characterize much that is happening in communities in the 1980s. There are never-ending needs to be met without the will (some would say the ability) to fund solutions or to alleviate the suffering of individuals. Yet there is a sense of hope, perhaps even positive indicators, that charity and philanthropy will continue to expand to fill pressing needs. It appears to those of us who are attempting to understand the nonprofit sector that a new way of conceptualizing social action and private charitable activity is evolving. Critically positioned between the business sector's profit motive and the governmental sector's drive to delegate responsibility and control for meeting social needs, nonprofit sector organizations stand to be of even greater utility in the 1990s.

The dilemma of our time is balance. How can we regain our international trade competency, while at the same time control governmental growth and national debt, and deal with our most pressing domestic social problems? The United States has elected to achieve this balance through creative interplay among its three socio-economic sectors. The future will be replete with tensions and solutions among these sectors. The priority to demonstrate a profit in the private sector will be compromised by the realization that the marketplace is a complicated blend of conflicting attitudes and beliefs. Corporate success must be defined as a blending of bottom-line earnings and social responsibilities. Recognition of the substantive value of individual time contributed to children in need, or the time a professional contributes to a nonprofit board of directors, is becoming commonplace. "In an age of alienating megasystems, impersonal technology, and forced mobility, whether we can expand democracy depends on the success of that search for community. The ideology that promotes greed and beggar-thy-neighbor individualism is rapidly becoming less relevant to both individual and national survival" (Alperovitz & Faux, 1984, p. 275).

Our individual and collective ability to establish and employ effective structures of mediation (Berger & Neuhaus, 1977) seems to be more crucial than ever before. We have more people, more imperatives to be economically productive, more reasons to doubt our country's economic and military invincibility, and more reasons for the assimilation of diverse cultures. These prevalent conditions, perhaps requirements, of citizenship must be tempered. The tempering or mediating institutions that are being described most frequently today are the family, neighborhood voluntary associations, and churches; that is, our community nonprofit organizations.

This chapter's first reading is "The Gospel of Wealth" by Andrew Carnegie, the turn-of-the-century steel baron whose personal saga is one of the greatest of all rags-to-riches models of industrial opportunity in the new world. Actually, this article was published orginally in two 1889 journal articles under the simpler title, "Wealth." It was renamed and republished as "The Gospel of Wealth" in 1900.

"The Gospel of Wealth" was the first compelling justification for a philosphy of philanthropy in the United States. It was eminently influential in establishing an early conceptual basis for philanthropy and against charity in the United States. Carnegie himself was a premier philanthropist, giving away most of his wealth to colleges and community libraries.

Concerned about communism, Carnegie viewed the democratic ideals of individualism, the right to hold private property, and the right to accumulate wealth, as essential for humankind and the country to evolve into a higher form. Carnegie was pragmatic as well as philosophical. He advocated maintaining a spirit of competition and the higher result of human experience (thereby preventing the spread of communism) through (1) redistribution of wealth by those who achieved it, (2) living a moderate lifestyle, and (3) not spoiling heirs by leaving them vast sums. Carnegie insisted that money should be used to help people help themselves. Not even a quarter should be wasted on a passing beggar to encourage "slothful behavior." Carnegie truly was concerned about possible struggles between the haves and have nots. The rich, he believed, bear the obligation to "even things out" in society.

The second article in this chapter about the philosophical and values bases of the sector was written almost 80 years after Carnegie but is generally regarded as equally important: "To Empower People: The Role of Mediating Structures in Public Policy," by Peter Berger and Richard Neuhaus (1977). Berger and Neuhaus provided the Reagan administration with the philosophical justification for divesting public social programs to the nonprofit sector. In a complex society such as ours, individuals need mediating structures, buffers to help them cope with large public and private bureaucracies in attempting to resolve social problems. Community needs thus can be met best through neighborhood, family, and church voluntary associations. The conservative agenda for the 1980s was ripe for the Berger and Neuhaus concept of mediating structures as an alternative to ever-growing government and private agencies. Not only did divestiture of governmental social programs to small community-based organizations make good fiscal sense, it also was a preferable solution for the individuals involved. Berger and Neuhaus were cited repeatedly by Reagan administration officials who favored privatization. (For more detail, see Lester Salamon's article, "Nonprofit Organizations, The Lost Opportunity," in Chapter Two.)

The economist, Burton A. Weisbrod, is generally credited with popularizing the view that voluntary organizations result from government market failure, in "Toward a

Theory of the Voluntary Non-Profit Sector in a Three-Sector Economy," a 1975 article that is reprinted here. Weisbrod provides a strong theoretical framework for justifying non-profits as nongovernmental instruments for the provision of collective goods. Along with Berger and Neuhaus, Weisbrod's concepts have provided theoretical justification and impetus toward an expanded role for the nonprofit sector. Weisbrod provides a framework where the dynamics between public sector and nonprofit sector choices, choices between services and goods provided as collective goods or individual goods, are played out. In our democratic/pluralistic society, dissatisfied "consumers" react to governmental marketplace failures by creating nonprofit sector alternatives.

Virginia Hodgkinson and Murray Weitzman's (1986) statistical profile, "The Independent Sector: An Overview" is included here for perspective. Hodgkinson and Weitzman provide an overview of the dimensions of the nonprofit sector as well as its growth and increasing influence in recent years. They analyze the sector and its development in relation to national income, earnings, employment, and other leading socio-economic indicators. Their research shows, for example, that the nonprofit sector expanded faster than other sectors of the national economy between 1977 and 1982. The total share of earnings in the third sector grew from 6.7 percent ($75.9 billion) to 7.5 percent ($139.2 billion). During the same years, employment in the sector increased at an annual rate of 3.7 percent. While the growth of the sector has been impressive, the rate of growth slowed, both absolutely and in relation to the other sectors, between 1982 and 1984 (1984 is the most recent year for which hard data are available).

The final article in the chapter, Stephen R. Block's "A History of the Discipline," provides a comprehensive historical review and analysis of the sector's development from the Babylonian Code of Hammurabi, through the English Poor Laws, and into modern society. "A History of the Discipline" is organized around Milofsky's (1979) six "influential traditions of American participation": Protestant patrician, urban ethnic, free professional, organizational professional, interorganizational coordination, and corporate philanthropic. Block also offers a historical look at the often-argued question of whether tax laws impact on peoples' propensity to give.

Block concludes that a distinct management type is emerging from unique needs and circumstances in the nonprofit sector. Management of nonprofit organizations, he argues, deserves new consideration and perhaps, recognition as a separate management field.

References

Addams, J. (1902). *Democracy and social ethics* (Ed. by A. F. Scott). Reprinted 1964. Cambridge, MA: Harvard University Press/Belknap Press.

Allen, K. K., Chapin, I., Keller, S., & Hill, D. (1979). *Volunteers from the workplace*, Washington, DC: National Center for Voluntary Action.

Alperovitz, G., & Faux, J. (1984). *Rebuilding America: A blueprint for a new economy.* New York: Pantheon.

Anderson, R. T. (February, 1971). Voluntary associations in history. *American Anthropologist*, *73*(1), 209–219.

Berger, P., & Neuhaus, R. J. (1977) *To empower people: The role of mediating structures in public policy.* Washington, DC: American Enterprise Institute.

Boulding, K. E. (Winter, 1965). The difficult art of doing good. *Colorado Quarterly*, *13*(3), 197–211.

Bremner, R. H. (1980). *The public good.* New York: Knopf.

Carnegie, A. (June, 1889, and December, 1889). Wealth. *North American Review*, *CXLVII*, 653-664, and *CXLIX*, 682–698.

Carnegie, A. (1900). *The gospel of wealth: And other timely essays.* New York: The Century Company.

Cass, R. H., & Manser, G. (1976). *Voluntarism at the crossroads*. New York: Family Service Association of America.

Clotfelter, C. T. (1980). Tax incentives and charitable giving. *Journal of Public Economics, 13*, 319–340.

Dickinson, F. G. (Ed.). (1962). *Philanthropy and public policy*. Washington, DC: National Bureau of Economic Research.

Franklin, B. (1772). On the institution in Holland to prevent poverty. In A. H. Smyth (Ed.) (1970), *The writings of Benjamin Franklin*. New York: Haskell House.

Gardner, J. W. (1980). *Toward a pluralistic but coherent society*. New York: Institute for Humanistic Studies.

Gladden, W. (1895). Tainted money. *Outlook, 52*, 886–887.

Hodgkinson, V. A., & Weitzman M. S. (1986). *Dimensions of the independent sector*. Washington, DC: Independent Sector.

James, E. (1983). Comparisons of nonprofit sectors abroad. In *Working papers for spring research forum: Since the Filer Commission*. Washington, DC: Independent Sector.

Kramer, R. M. (1981). *Voluntary agencies in the welfare state*. Berkeley, CA: University of California Press.

Meyer, J. (1982). *Meeting human needs: Toward a new public philosophy*. Washington, DC: American Enterprise Institute.

Milofsky, C. (1979). *Not for profit organizations and community: A review of the sociological literature* (PONPO working paper no. 6). New Haven, CT: Yale University.

Murray, C. (1984). *Losing ground: American social policy 1950–1980*. New York: Basic Books.

Nielsen, W. A. (1980). *The third sector: Keystone of a caring society* (Occasional paper, no. 1). Washington, DC: Independent Sector.

O'Connell, B. (1989). What voluntary action can and cannot do for America. *Public Administration Review, 49*(5), 486–491.

O'Neill, M. (1989). *The third America: The emergence of the nonprofit sector in the United States*. San Francisco: Jossey-Bass.

Ott, J. S., & Shafritz, J. M. (1986). *The Facts on File dictionary of nonprofit organization management*. New York: Facts on File.

Payton, R. L., Novak, M., O'Connell, B., & Hall, P. D. (1988). *Philanthropy: Four views*. New Brunswick, NJ: Transaction Books.

Phelps, E. S. (Ed.). (1975). *Altruism, morality, and economic theory*. New York: Russell Sage Foundation.

Rockefeller, J. D. (1908). The difficult art of giving. *The world's work*. (Reprinted in 1984. New York: Sleepy Hollow Press.)

Silver, M. (1980). *Affluence, altruism, and atrophy: The decline of welfare states*. New York: New York University Press.

Sundquist, J. L. (1984). Privatization: No panacea for what ails government. In H. Brooks, L. Liebman, & C. Schelling (Eds.), *Public-private partnership: New opportunities for meeting social needs* (p. 306). Cambridge, MA: Ballinger Publishing.

Trattner, W. H. (1974). *From poor law to welfare state*. New York: Free Press.

Van Til, J. (1980). Volunteering and democractic theory. In J. D. Harman (Ed.), *Volunteerism in the eighties* (pp. 199–220). Washington, DC: University Press of America.

Van Til, J. (1988). *Mapping the third sector: Voluntarism in a changing social economy*. New York: The Foundation Center.

Vonhoff, H. (1971). *People who care, an illustrated history of human compassion*. Philadelphia, PA: Fortress Press.

Weisbrod, B. A. (1975). Toward a theory of the voluntary non-profit sector in a three-sector economy. In E. S. Phelps (Ed.), *Altruism, morality, and economic theory*. New York: Russell Sage Foundation.

Weisbrod, B. A. (1977). *The voluntary non-profit sector: An economic analysis*. Lexington, MA: D. C. Heath.

Wolf, T. (1984). *The nonprofit organization*. Englewood Cliffs, NJ: Prentice-Hall.

ARTICLE 1
The Gospel of Wealth
Andrew Carnegie

The problem of our age is the proper administration of wealth, so that the ties of brotherhood may still bind together the rich and poor in harmonious relationship. The conditions of human life have not only been changed, but revolutionized, within the past few hundred years. In former days there was little difference between the dwelling, dress, food, and environment of the chief and those of his retainers. The Indians are to-day where civilized man then was. When visiting the Sioux, I was led to the wigwam of the chief. It was just like the others in external appearance, and even within the difference was trifling between it and those of the poorest of his braves. The contrast between the palace of the millionaire and the cottage of the laborer with us to-day measures the change which has come with civilization.

This change, however, is not to be deplored, but welcomed as highly beneficial. It is well, nay, essential for the progress of the race, that the houses of some should be homes for all that is highest and best in literature and the arts, and for all the refinements of civilization, rather than that none should be so. Much better this great irregularity than universal squalor. Without wealth there can be no Maecenas. The "good old times" were not good old times. Neither master nor servant was as well situated then as to-day. A relapse to old conditions would be disastrous to both—not the least so to him who serves—and would sweep away civilization with it. But whether the change be for good or ill, it is upon us, beyond our power to alter, and therefore to be accepted and made the best of. It is a waste of time to criticise the inevitable.

It is easy to see how the change has come. One illustration will serve for almost every phase of the cause. In the manufacture of products we have the whole story. It applies to all combinations of human industry, as stimulated and enlarged by the inventions of this scientific age. Formerly articles were manufactured at the domestic hearth or in small shops which formed part of the household. The master and his apprentices worked side by side, the latter living with the master, and therefore subject to the same conditions. When these apprentices rose to be masters, there was little or no change in their mode of life, and they, in turn, educated in the same routine succeeding apprentices. There was, substantially, social equality, and even political equality, for those engaged in industrial pursuits had then little or no political voice in the State.

But the inevitable result of such a mode of manufacture was crude articles at high prices. To-day the world obtains commodities of excellent quality at prices which even the generation preceding this would have deemed incredible. In the commercial world similar causes have produced similar results, and the race is benefited thereby. The poor enjoy what the rich could not before afford. What were the luxuries have become the necessaries of life. The laborer has now more comforts than the farmer had a few generations ago. The farmer has more luxuries than the landlord had, and is more richly clad and better housed. The landlord has books and pictures rarer, and appointments more artistic, than the King could then obtain.

The price we pay for this salutary change is, no doubt, great. We assemble thousands of operatives in the factory, in the mine, and in the counting-house, of whom the employer can know little or nothing, and to whom the employer is little better than a myth. All intercourse between them is at an end. Rigid Castes are formed, and, as usual, mutual ignorance breeds mutual distrust. Each Caste is without sympathy for the other, and ready to credit anything disparaging in regard to it. Under the law of competition, the employer of thousands is forced into the strictest economies, among which the rates paid to labor figure prominently, and often there is friction between the employer and the employed, between capital and labor, between rich and poor. Human society loses homogeneity.

The price which society pays for the law of competition, like the price it pays for cheap comforts and luxuries, is also great; but the advantages of this law are also greater still, for

SOURCE: "Wealth," by Andrew Carnegie, *1889, North American Review, June,* pp. 653–664. Reprinted by permission.

it is to this law that we owe our wonderful material development, which brings improved conditions in its train. But, whether the law be benign or not, we must say of it, as we say of the change in the conditions of men to which we have referred: It is here; we cannot evade it; no substitutes for it have been found; and while the law may be sometimes hard for the individual, it is best for the race, because it insures the survival of the fittest in every department. We accept and welcome, therefore, as conditions to which we must accommodate ourselves, great inequality of environment, the concentration of business, industrial and commercial, in the hands of a few, and the law of competition between these, as being not only beneficial, but essential for the future progress of the race. Having accepted these, it follows that there must be great scope for the exercise of special ability in the merchant and in the manufacturer who has to conduct affairs upon a great scale. That this talent for organization and management is rare among men is proved by the fact that it invariably secures for its possessor enormous rewards, no matter where or under what laws or conditions. The experienced in affairs always rate the MAN whose services can be obtained as a partner as not only the first consideration, but such as to render the question of his capital scarcely worth considering, for such men soon create capital; while, without the special talent required, capital soon takes wings. Such men become interested in firms or corporations using millions; and estimating only simple interest to be made upon the capital invested, it is inevitable that their income must exceed their expenditures, and that they must accumulate wealth. Nor is there any middle ground which such men can occupy, because the great manufacturing or commercial concern which does not earn at least interest upon its capital soon becomes bankrupt. It must either go forward or fall behind: to stand still is impossible. It is a condition essential for its successful operation that it should be thus far profitable, and even that, in addition to interest on capital, it should make profit. It is a law, as certain as any of the others named, that men possessed of this peculiar talent for affairs, under the free play of economic forces, must, of necessity, soon be in receipt of more revenue than can be judiciously expended upon themselves; and this law is as beneficial for the race as the others.

Objections to the foundations upon which society is based are not in order, because the condition of the race is better with these than it has been with any others which have been tried. Of the effect of any new substitutes proposed we cannot be sure. The Socialist or Anarchist who seeks to overturn present conditions is to be regarded as attacking the foundation upon which civilization itself rests, for civilization took its start from the day that the capable, industrious workman said to his incompetent and lazy fellow, "If thou dost not sow, thou shalt not reap," and thus ended primitive Communism by separating the drones from the bees. One who studies this subject will soon be brought face to face with the conclusion that upon the sacredness of property civilization itself depends—the right of the laborer to his hundred dollars in the savings bank, and equally the legal right of the millionaire to his millions. To those who propose to substitute Communism for this intense Individualism the answer, therefore, is: The race has tried that. All progress from that barbarous day to the present time has resulted from its displacement. Not evil, but good, has come to the race from the accumulation of wealth by those who have the ability and energy that produce it. But even if we admit for a moment that it might be better for the race to discard its present foundation, Individualism,—that it is a nobler ideal that man should labor, not for himself alone, but in and for a brotherhood of his fellows, and share with them all in common, realizing Swedenborg's idea of Heaven, where, as he says, the angels derive their happiness, not from laboring for self, but for each other,—even admit all this, and a sufficient answer is, This is not evolution, but revolution. It necessitates the changing of human nature itself—a work of aeons, even if it were good to change it, which we cannot know. It is not practicable in our day or in our age. Even if desirable theoretically, it belongs to another and long-succeeding sociological stratum. Our duty is with what is practicable now; with the next step possible in our day and generation. It is criminal to waste our energies in endeavoring to uproot, when all we can profitably or possibly accomplish is to bend the universal tree of humanity a little in the direction most favorable to the production of good fruit under existing circumstances. We might as well urge the destruction of the highest existing type of man because he failed to reach our ideal as to favor the destruction of Individualism, Private Property, the Law of Accumulation of Wealth, and the Law of Competition; for these are the highest results of human experience, the soil in which society so far has produced the best fruit. Unequally or unjustly, perhaps, as these laws sometimes operate, and imperfect as they appear to the Idealist, they are, nevertheless, like the highest type of man, the best and most valuable of all that humanity has yet accomplished.

We start, then, with a condition of affairs under which the best interests of the race are promoted, but which inevitably gives wealth to the few. Thus far, accepting conditions as they exist, the situation can be surveyed and pronounced good. The question then arises,—and, if the foregoing be correct, it is the only question with which we have to deal,—What is the proper mode of administering wealth after the laws upon which civilization is founded have thrown it into the hands of the few? And it is of this great question that I believe I offer the true solution. It will be understood that *fortunes* are here spoken of, not moderate sums saved by many years of effort, the returns from which are required for the comfortable maintenance and education of families. This is not *wealth*, but only *competence*, which it should be the aim of all to acquire.

There are but three modes in which surplus wealth can be disposed of. It can be left to the families of the decedents; or it can be bequeathed for public purposes; or, finally, it can be administered during their lives by its possessors. Under the first and second modes most of the wealth of the world that has reached the few has hitherto been applied. Let us in turn consider each of these modes. The first is the most injudicious. In monarchical countries, the estates and the greatest portion of the wealth are left to the first son, that the vanity of the parent may be gratified by the thought that his name and title are to descend to succeeding generations unimpaired. The condition of this class in Europe to-day teaches the futility of such hopes or ambitions. The successors have become impoverished through their follies or from the fall in the value of land. Even in Great Britain the strict law of entail has been found inadequate to maintain the status of an hereditary class. Its soil is rapidly

passing into the hands of the stranger. Under republican institutions the division of property among the children is much fairer, but the question which forces itself upon thoughtful men in all lands is: Why should men leave great fortunes to their children? If this is done from affection, is it not misguided affection? Observation teaches that, generally speaking, it is not well for the children that they should be so burdened. Neither is it well for the state. Beyond providing for the wife and daughters moderate sources of income, and very moderate allowances indeed, if any, for the sons, men may well hesitate, for it is no longer questionable that great sums bequeathed oftener work more for the injury than for the good of the recipients. Wise men will soon conclude that, for the best interests of the members of their families and of the state, such bequests are an improper use of their means.

It is not suggested that men who have failed to educate their sons to earn a livelihood shall cast them adrift in poverty. If any man has seen fit to rear his sons with a view to their living idle lives, or, what is highly commendable, has instilled in them the sentiment that they are in a position to labor for public ends without reference to pecuniary considerations, then, of course, the duty of the parent is to see that such are provided for *in moderation*. There are instances of millionaires' sons unspoiled by wealth, who, being rich, still perform great services in the community. Such are the very salt of the earth, as valuable as, unfortunately, they are rare; still it is not the exception, but the rule, that men must regard, and, looking at the usual result of enormous sums conferred upon legatees, the thoughtful man must shortly say, "I would as soon leave to my son a curse as the almighty dollar," and admit to himself that it is not the welfare of the children, but family pride, which inspires these enormous legacies.

As to the second mode, that of leaving wealth at death for public uses, it may be said that this is only a means for the disposal of wealth, provided a man is content to wait until he is dead before it becomes of much good in the world. Knowledge of the results of legacies bequeathed is not calculated to inspire the brightest hopes of much posthumous good being accomplished. The cases are not few in which the real object sought by the testator is not attained, nor are they few in which his real wishes are thwarted. In many cases the bequests are so used as to become only monuments of his folly. It is well to remember that it requires the exercise of not less ability than that which acquired the wealth to use it so as to be really beneficial to the community. Besides this, it may fairly be said that no man is to be extolled for doing what he cannot help doing, nor is he to be thanked by the community to which he only leaves wealth at death. Men who leave vast sums in this way may fairly be thought men who would not have left it at all, had they been able to take it with them. The memories of such cannot be held in grateful remembrance, for there is no grace in their gifts. It is not to be wondered at that such bequests seem so generally to lack the blessing.

The growing disposition to tax more and more heavily large estates left at death is a cheering indication of the growth of a salutary change in public opinion. The State of Pennsylvania now takes—subject to some exceptions—one-tenth of the property left by its citizens. The budget presented in the British Parliament the other day proposes to increase the death-duties; and, most significant of all, the new tax is to be a graduated one. Of all forms of taxation, this seems the wisest. Men who continue hoarding great sums all their lives, the proper use of which for public ends would work good to the community, should be made to feel that the community, in the form of the state, cannot thus be deprived of its proper share. By taxing estates heavily at death the state marks its condemnation of the selfish millionaire's unworthy life.

It is desirable that nations should go much further in this direction. Indeed, it is difficult to set bounds to the share of a rich man's estate which should go at his death to the public through the agency of the state, and by all means such taxes should be graduated, beginning at nothing upon moderate sums to dependents, and increasing rapidly as the amounts swell, until of the millionaire's hoard, as of Shylock's, at least

" ——— The other half
Comes to the privy coffer of the state."

This policy would work powerfully to induce the rich man to attend to the administration of wealth during his life, which is the end that society should always have in view, as being that by far most fruitful for the people. Nor need it be feared that this policy would sap the root of enterprise and render men less anxious to accumulate, for to the class whose ambition it is to leave great fortunes and be talked about after their death, it will attract even more attention, and, indeed, be a somewhat nobler ambition to have enormous sums paid over to the state from their fortunes.

There remains, then, only one mode of using great fortunes; but in this we have the true antidote for the temporary unequal distribution of wealth, the reconciliation of the rich and the poor—a reign of harmony—another ideal, differing, indeed, from that of the Communist in requiring only the further evolution of existing conditions, not the total overthrow of our civilization. It is founded upon the present most intense individualism, and the race is prepared to put it in practice by degrees whenever it pleases. Under its sway we shall have an ideal state, in which the surplus wealth of the few will become, in the best sense, the property of the many, because administered for the common good, and this wealth, passing through the hands of the few, can be made a much more potent force for the elevation of our race than if it had been distributed in small sums to the people themselves. Even the poorest can be made to see this, and to agree that great sums gathered by some of their fellow-citizens and spent for public purposes, from which the masses reap the principal benefit, are more valuable to them than if scattered among them through the course of many years in trifling amounts.

If we consider what results flow from the Cooper Institute, for instance, to the best portion of the race in New York not possessed of means, and compare these with those which would have arisen for the good of the masses from an equal sum distributed by Mr. Cooper in his lifetime in the form of wages, which is the highest form of distribution, being for work done and not for charity, we can form some estimate of the possibilities for the improvement of the race which lie embedded in the present law of the accumulation of wealth. Much of this sum, if distributed in small quantities among the people, would have been wasted in the indulgence of appetite, some of it in excess, and it may be doubted whether even the part put to the best use, that of adding to the comforts of the home, would have yielded results for the race, as a race, at all comparable to those which are flowing and are to flow from the Cooper Institute from generation to generation. Let the advocate of violent or radical change ponder well this thought.

We might even go so far as to take another instance, that of Mr. Tilden's bequest of five millions of dollars for a free library in the city of New York, but in referring to this one cannot help saying involuntarily, How much better if Mr. Tilden had devoted the last years of his own life to the proper administration of this immense sum; in which case neither legal contest nor any other cause of delay could have interfered with his aims. But let us assume that Mr. Tilden's millions finally become the means of giving to this city a noble public library, where the treasures of the world contained in books will be open to all forever, without money and without price. Considering the good of that part of the race which congregates in and around Manhattan Island, would its permanent benefit have been better promoted had these millions been allowed to circulate in small sums through the hands of the masses? Even the most strenuous advocate of Communism must entertain a doubt upon this subject. Most of those who think will probably entertain no doubt whatever.

Poor and restricted are our opportunities in this life; narrow our horizon; our best work most imperfect; but rich men should be thankful for one inestimable boon. They have it in their power during their lives to busy themselves in organizing benefactions from which the masses of their fellows will derive lasting advantage, and thus dignify their own lives. The highest life is probably to be reached, not by such imitation of the life of Christ as Count Tolstoï gives us, but, while animated by Christ's spirit, by recognizing the changed conditions of this age, and adopting modes of expressing this spirit suitable to the changed conditions under which we live; still laboring for the good of our fellows, which was the essence of his life and teaching, but laboring in a different manner.

This, then, is held to be the duty of the man of Wealth: First, to set an example of modest, unostentatious living, shunning display or extravagance; to provide moderately for the legitimate wants of those dependent upon him; and after doing so to consider all surplus revenues which come to him simply as trust funds, which he is called upon to administer, and strictly bound as a matter of duty to administer in the manner which, in his judgment, is best calculated to produce the most beneficial results for the community—the man of wealth thus becoming the mere agent and trustee for his poorer brethren, bringing to their service his superior wisdom, experience, and ability to administer, doing for them better than they would or could do for themselves.

We are met here with the difficulty of determining what are moderate sums to leave to members of the family; what is modest, unostentatious living; what is the test of extravagance. There must be different standards for different conditions. The answer is that it is as impossible to name exact amounts or actions as it is to define good manners, good taste, or the rules of propriety; but, nevertheless, these are verities, well known although undefinable. Public sentiment is quick to know and to feel what offends these. So in the case of wealth. The rule in regard to good taste in the dress of men or women applies here. Whatever makes one conspicuous offends the canon. If any family be chiefly known for display, for extravagance in home, table, equipage, for enormous sums ostentatiously spent in any form upon itself,—if these be its chief distinctions, we have no difficulty in estimating its nature or culture. So likewise in regard to the use or abuse of its surplus wealth, or to generous, free-handed cooperation in good public uses, or to unabated efforts to accumulate and hoard to the last, whether they administer or bequeath. The verdict rests with the best and most enlightened public sentiment. The community will surely judge, and its judgments will not often be wrong.

The best uses to which surplus wealth can be put have already been indicated. Those who would administer wisely must, indeed, be wise, for one of the serious obstacles to the improvement of our race is indiscriminate charity. It were better for mankind that the millions of the rich were thrown into the sea than so spent as to encourage the slothful, the drunken, the unworthy. Of every thousand dollars spent in so called charity to-day, it is probable that $950 is unwisely spent; so spent, indeed, as to produce the very evils which it proposes to mitigate or cure. A well-known writer of philosophic books admitted the other day that he had given a quarter of a dollar to a man who approached him as he was coming to visit the house of his friend. He knew nothing of the habits of this beggar; knew not the use that would be made of this money, although he had every reason to suspect that it would be spent improperly. This man professed to be a disciple of Herbert Spencer; yet the quarter-dollar given that night will probably work more injury than all the money which its thoughtless donor will ever be able to give in true charity will do good. He only gratified his own feelings, saved himself from annoyance,—and this was probably one of the most selfish and very worst actions of his life, for in all respects he is most worthy.

In bestowing charity, the main consideration should be to help those who will help themselves; to provide part of the means by which those who desire to improve may do so; to give those who desire to rise the aids by which they may rise; to assist, but rarely or never to do all. Neither the individual nor the race is improved by alms-giving. Those worthy of assistance, except in rare cases, seldom require assistance. The really valuable men of the race never do, except in cases of accident or sudden change. Every one has, of course, cases of individuals brought to his own knowledge where temporary assistance can do genuine good, and these he will not overlook. But the amount which can be wisely given by the individual for individuals is necessarily limited by his lack of knowledge of the circumstances connected with each. He is the only true reformer who is as careful and as anxious not to aid the unworthy as he is to aid the worthy, and, perhaps, even more so, for in alms-giving more injury is probably done by rewarding vice than by relieving virtue.

The rich man is thus almost restricted to following the examples of Peter Cooper, Enoch Pratt of Baltimore, Mr. Pratt of Brooklyn, Senator Stanford, and others, who know that the best means of benefiting the community is to place within its reach the ladders upon which the aspiring can rise—parks, and means of recreation, by which men are helped in body and mind; works of art, certain to give pleasure and improve the public taste, and public institutions of various

kinds, which will improve the general condition of the people;—in this manner returning their surplus wealth to the mass of their fellows in the forms best calculated to do them lasting good.

Thus is the problem of Rich and Poor to be solved. The laws of accumulation will be left free; the laws of distribution free. Individualism will continue, but the millionaire will be but a trustee for the poor; intrusted for a season with a great part of the increased wealth of the community, but administering it for the community far better than it could or would have done for itself. The best minds will thus have reached a stage in the development of the race in which it is clearly seen that there is no mode of disposing of surplus wealth creditable to thoughtful and earnest men into whose hands it flows save by using it year by year for the general good. This day already dawns. But a little while, and although, without incurring the pity of their fellows, men may die sharers in great business enterprises from which their capital cannot be or has not been withdrawn, and is left chiefly at death for public uses, yet the man who dies leaving behind him millions of available wealth, which was his to administer during life, will pass away "unwept, unhonored, and unsung," no matter to what uses he leaves the dross which he cannot take with him. Of such as these the public verdict will then be: "The man who dies thus rich dies disgraced."

Such, in my opinion, is the true Gospel concerning Wealth, obedience to which is destined some day to solve the problem of the Rich and the Poor, and to bring "Peace on earth, among men Good-Will."

ARTICLE 2 ──────────────

To Empower People: The Role of Mediating Structures in Public Policy
Peter L. Berger and Richard John Neuhaus

Mediating Structures and the Dilemmas of the Welfare State

Two seemingly contradictory tendencies are evident in current thinking about public policy in

SOURCE: *To Empower People,* by P. L. Berger and R. Neuhaus. © 1977 by American Enterprise Institute for Public Policy Research. Reprinted by permission.

America. First, there is a continuing desire for the services provided by the modern welfare state. Partisan rhetoric aside, few people seriously envisage dismantling the welfare state. The serious debate is over how and to what extent it should be expanded. The second tendency is one of strong animus against government, bureaucracy, and bigness as such. This animus is directed not only toward Washington but toward government at all levels. Although this essay is addressed to the American situation, it should be noted that a similar ambiguity about the modern welfare state exists in other democratic societies, notably in Western Europe.

Perhaps this is just another case of people wanting to eat their cake and have it too. It would hardly be the first time in history that the people wanted benefits without paying the requisite costs. Nor are politicians above exploiting ambiguities by promising increased services while reducing expenditures. The extravagant rhetoric of the modern state and the surrealistic vastness of its taxation system encourage magical expectations that make contradictory measures seem possible. As long as some of the people can be fooled some of the time, some politicians will continue to ride into office on such magic.

But this is not the whole story. The contradiction between wanting more government services and less government may be only apparent. More precisely, we suggest that the modern welfare state is here to stay, indeed that it ought to expand the benefits it provides—but that *alternative mechanisms are possible to provide welfare-state services.*

The current anti-government, anti-bigness mood is not irrational. Complaints about impersonality, unresponsiveness, and excessive interference, as well as the perception of rising costs and deteriorating service—these are based upon empirical and widespread experience. The crisis of New York City, which is rightly seen as more than a fiscal crisis, signals a national state of unease with the policies followed in recent decades. At the same time there is widespread public support for publicly addressing major problems of our society in relieving poverty, in education, health care, and housing, and in a host of other human needs. What first appears as contradiction, then, is the sum of equally justified aspirations. The public policy goal is to address

human needs without exacerbating the reasons for animus against the welfare state.

Of course there are no panaceas. The alternatives proposed here, we believe, can solve *some* problems. Taken seriously, they could become the basis of far-reaching innovations in public policy, perhaps of a new paradigm for at least sectors of the modern welfare state.

The basic concept is that of what we are calling mediating structures. The concept in various forms has been around for a long time. What is new is the systematic effort to translate it into specific public policies. For purposes of this study, mediating structures are defined as *those institutions standing between the individual in his private life and the large institutions of public life.*

Modernization brings about an historically unprecedented dichotomy between public and private life. The most important large institution in the ordering of modern society is the modern state itself. In addition, there are the large economic conglomerates of capitalist enterprise, big labor, and the growing bureaucracies that administer wide sectors of the society, such as in education and the organized professions. All these institutions we call the *megastructures.*

Then there is that modern phenomenon called private life. It is a curious kind of preserve left over by the large institutions and in which individuals carry on a bewildering variety of activities with only fragile institutional support.

For the individual in modern society, life is an ongoing migration between these two spheres, public and private. The megastructures are typically alienating, that is, they are not helpful in providing meaning and identity for individual existence. Meaning, fulfillment, and personal identity are to be realized in the private sphere. While the two spheres interact in many ways, in private life the individual is left very much to his own devices, and thus is uncertain and anxious. Where modern society is "hard," as in the megastructures, it is personally unsatisfactory; where it is "soft," as in private life, it cannot be relied upon. Compare, for example, the social realities of employment with those of marriage.

The dichotomy poses a double crisis. It is a crisis for the individual who must carry on a balancing act between the demands of the two spheres. It is a political crisis because the megastructures (notably the state) come to be devoid of personal meaning and are therefore viewed as unreal or even malignant. Not everyone experiences this crisis in the same way. Many who handle it more successfully than most have access to institutions that *mediate* between the two spheres. Such institutions have a private face, giving private life a measure of stability, and they have a public face, transferring meaning and value to the megastructures. Thus, mediating structures alleviate each facet of the double crisis of modern society. Their strategic position derives from their reducing both the anomic precariousness of individual existence in isolation from society and the threat of alienation to the public order.

Our focus is on four such mediating structures—neighborhood, family, church, and voluntary association. This is by no means an exhaustive list, but these institutions were selected for two reasons: first, they figure prominently in the lives of most Americans and, second, they are most relevant to the problems of the welfare state with which we are concerned. The proposal is that, if these institutions could be more imaginatively recognized in public policy, individuals would be more "at home" in society, and the political order would be more "meaningful."

Without institutionally reliable processes of mediation, the political order becomes detached from the values and realities of individual life. Deprived of its moral foundation, the political order is "delegitimated." When that happens, the political order must be secured by coercion rather than by consent. And when that happens, democracy disappears.

The attractiveness of totalitarianism—whether instituted under left-wing or right-wing banners—is that it overcomes the dichotomy of private and public existence by imposing on life one comprehensive order of meaning. Although established totalitarian systems can be bitterly disappointing to their architects as well as their subjects, they are, on the historical record, nearly impossible to dismantle. The system continues quite effectively, even if viewed with cynicism by most of the population—including those who are in charge.

Democracy is "handicapped" by being more vulnerable to the erosion of meaning in its institutions. Cynicism threatens it; wholesale cynicism can destroy it. That is why mediation is so crucial to democracy. Such mediation cannot be sporadic and occasional; it must be institutionalized in *structures*. The structures we have chosen to study have demonstrated a great capacity for adapting and innovating under changing conditions. Most important, they exist where people are, and that is where sound public policy should always begin.

This understanding of mediating structures is sympathetic to Edmund Burke's well-known claim: "To be attached to the subdivision, to love the little platoon we belong to in society, is the first principle (the germ as it were) of public affections." And it is sympathetic to Alexis de Tocqueville's conclusion drawn from his observation of Americans: "In democratic countries the science of association is the mother of science; the progress of all the rest depends upon the progress it has made." Marx too was concerned about the destruction of community, and the glimpse he gives us of post-revolutionary society is strongly reminiscent of Burke's "little platoons." The emphasis is even sharper in the anarcho-syndicalist tradition of social thought.

In his classic study of suicide, Emile Durkheim describes the "tempest" of modernization sweeping away the "little aggregations" in which people formerly found community, leaving only the state on the one hand and a mass of individuals, "like so many liquid molecules," on the other. Although using different terminologies, others in the sociological tradition—Ferdinand Toennies, Max Weber, Georg Simmel, Charles Cooley, Thorstein Veblen—have analyzed aspects of the same dilemma. Today Robert Nisbet has most persuasively argued that the loss of community threatens the future of American democracy.

Also, on the practical political level, it might seem that mediating structures have universal endorsement. There is, for example, little political mileage in being anti-family or anti-church. But the reality is not so simple. Liberalism—which constitutes the broad center of American politics, whether or not it calls itself by that name—has tended to be blind to the political (as distinct from private) functions of mediating structures. The main feature of liberalism, as we intend the term, is a commitment to government action toward greater social justice within the existing system. (To revolutionaries, of course, this is "mere reformism," but the revolutionary option has not been especially relevant, to date, in the American context.)

Liberalism's blindness to mediating structures can be traced to its Enlightenment roots. Enlightenment thought is abstract, universalistic, addicted to what Burke called "geometry" in social policy. The concrete particularities of mediating structures find an inhospitable soil in the liberal garden. There the great concern is for the individual ("the rights of man") and for a just public order, but anything "in between" is viewed as irrelevant, or even an obstacle, to the rational ordering of society. What lies in between is dismissed, to the extent it can be, as superstition, bigotry, or (more recently) cultural lag.

American liberalism has been vigorous in the defense of the private rights of individuals, and has tended to dismiss the argument that private behavior can have public consequences. Private rights are frequently defended *against* mediating structures—children's rights against the family, the rights of sexual deviants against neighborhood or small-town sentiment, and so forth. Similarly, American liberals are virtually faultless in their commitment to the religious liberty of individuals. But the liberty to be defended is always that of privatized religion. Supported by a very narrow understanding of the separation of church and state, liberals are typically hostile to the claim that institutional religion might have public rights and public functions. As a consequence of this "geometrical" outlook, liberalism has a hard time coming to terms with the alienating effects of the abstract structures it has multiplied since the New Deal. This may be the Achilles heel of the liberal state today.

The left, understood as some version of the socialist vision, has been less blind to the problem of mediation. Indeed the term alienation derives from Marxism. The weakness of the left, however, is its exclusive or nearly exclusive focus on the capitalist economy as the source of this evil, when in fact the alienations of the socialist states, insofar as there are socialist states, are much more severe than those of the capitalist states. While some theorists of the New Left have addressed this problem by using elements from the anarcho-syndicalist tradition, most socialists see mediating structures as something that may be relevant to a post-revolutionary future, but that in the present only distracts attention from the struggle toward building socialism. Thus the left is not very helpful in the search for practical solutions to our problem.

On the right of the political broad center, we also find little that is helpful. To be sure, classical European conservatism had high regard for mediating structures, but, from the eighteenth century on, this tradition has been marred by a romantic urge to revoke modernity—a prospect that is, we think, neither likely nor desirable. On the other hand, what is now called conservatism in America is in fact old-style liberalism. It is the laissez-faire ideology of the period before the New Deal, which is roughly the time when liberalism shifted its faith from the market to government. *Both* the old faith in the market *and* the new faith in government share the abstract thought patterns of the Enlightenment. In addition, today's conservatism typically exhibits the weakness of the left in reverse: it is highly sensitive to the alienations of big government, but blind to the analogous effects of big business. Such one-sidedness, whether left or right, is not helpful.

As is now being widely recognized, we need new approaches free of the ideological baggage of the past. The mediating structures paradigm cuts across current ideological and political divides. This proposal has met with gratifying interest from most with whom we have shared it, and while it has been condemned as right-wing by some and as left-wing by others, this is in fact encouraging. Although the paradigm may play havoc with the conventional political labels, it is hoped that, after the initial confusion of what some social scientists call "cognitive shock," each implication of the proposal will be considered on its own merits.

The argument of this essay—and the focus of the research project it is designed to introduce—can be subsumed under three propositions. The first proposition is analytical: *Mediating structures are essential for a vital democratic society.* The other two are broad programmatic recommendations: *Public policy should protect and foster mediating structures,* and *Wherever possible, public policy should utilize mediating structures for the realization of social purposes.* The research project will determine, it is hoped, whether these propositions stand up under rigorous examination and, if so, how they can be translated into specific recommendations.

The analytical proposition assumes that mediating structures are the value-generating and value-maintaining agencies in society. Without them, values become another function of the megastructures, notably of the state, and this is a hallmark of totalitarianism. In the totalitarian case, the individual becomes the object rather than the subject of the value-propagating processes of society.

The two programmatic propositions are, respectively, minimalist and maximalist. Minimally, public policy should cease and desist from damaging mediating structures. Much of the damage has been unintentional in the past. We should be more cautious than we have been. As we have learned to ask about the effects of government action upon racial minorities or upon the environment, so we should learn to ask about the effects of public policies on mediating structures.

The maximalist proposition ("utilize mediating structures") is much the riskier. We emphasize, "wherever possible." The mediating structures paradigm is not applicable to all areas of policy. Also, there is the real danger that such structures might be "co-opted" by the government in a too eager embrace that would destroy the very distinctiveness of their function. The prospect of government control of the family, for example, is clearly the exact opposite of our intention. The goal in utilizing mediating structures is to expand government services without producing government oppressiveness. Indeed it might be argued that the achievement of that goal is one of the acid tests of democracy.

It should be noted that these propositions differ from superficially similar proposals aimed at decentralizing governmental functions. Decentralization is limited to what can be done *within* governmental structures; we are concerned with the structures that stand *between* government and the individual. Nor, again, are we calling for a devolution of governmental responsibilities that would be tantamount to dismantling the welfare state. We aim rather at rethinking the institutional means by which government exercises its responsibilities. The idea is not to revoke the New Deal

but to pursue its vision in ways more compatible with democratic governance.

Finally, there is a growing ideology based upon the proposition that "small is beautiful." We are sympathetic to that sentiment in some respects, but we do not share its programmatic antagonism to the basic features of modern society. Our point is not to attack the megastructures but to find better ways in which they can relate to the "little platoons" in our common life.

The theme is *empowerment.* One of the most debilitating results of modernization is a feeling of powerlessness in the face of institutions controlled by those whom we do not know and whose values we often do not share. Lest there be any doubt, our belief is that human beings, whoever they are, understand their own needs better than anyone else—in, say, 99 percent of all cases. The mediating structures under discussion here are the principal expressions of the real values and the real needs of people in our society. They are, for the most part, the people-sized institutions. Public policy should recognize, respect, and, where possible, empower these institutions.

A word about the poor is in order. Upper-income people already have ways to resist the encroachment of megastructures. It is not their children who are at the mercy of alleged child experts, not their health which is endangered by miscellaneous vested interests, not their neighborhoods which are made the playthings of utopian planners. Upper-income people may allow themselves to be victimized on all these scores, but they do have ways to resist if they choose to resist. Poor people have this power to a much lesser degree. The paradigm of mediating structures aims at empowering poor people to do the things that the more affluent can already do, aims at spreading the power around a bit more—and to do so where it matters, in people's control over their own lives. Some may call this populism. But that term has been marred by utopianism and by the politics of resentment. We choose to describe it as the empowerment of people. . . .

Voluntary Association

. . .There is a history of debate over what is meant by a voluntary association. For our present purposes, a voluntary association is a body of people who have voluntarily organized themselves in pursuit of particular goals. (Following common usage, we exclude business corporations and other primarily economic associations.) Important to the present discussion is the subject of volunteer service. Many voluntary associations have both paid and volunteer staffing. For our purposes, the crucial point is the free association of people for some collective purpose, the fact that they may pay some individuals for doing work to this end not being decisive.

At least since de Tocqueville the importance of voluntary associations in American democracy has been widely recognized. Voluntarism has flourished in America more than in any other Western society and it is reasonable to believe this may have something to do with American political institutions. Associations create statutes, elect officers, debate, vote courses of action, and otherwise serve as schools for democracy. However trivial, wrongheaded, or bizarre we may think the purpose of some associations to be, they nonetheless perform this vital function.

Apart from this political role, voluntary associations are enormously important for what they have actually done. Before the advent of the modern welfare state, almost everything in the realm of social services was under the aegis of voluntary associations, usually religious in character. Still today there are about 1,900 private colleges and universities, 4,600 private secondary schools, 3,600 voluntary hospitals, 6,000 museums, 1,100 orchestras, 5,500 libraries and no less than 29,000 nongovernmental welfare agencies. Of course not all of these are equally important as mediating structures. Orchestras and groups promoting stamp-collecting or the preservation of antique automobiles are, however important in other connections, outside our focus here. We are interested in one type within the vast array of voluntary associations—namely, associations that render social services relevant to recognized public responsibilities.

Assaults on voluntary associations come from several directions, from both the right and left of the political spectrum. Some condemn them as inefficient, corrupt, divisive, and even subversive. Many subscribe to the axiom that public services should not be under private control. From the far left comes the challenge that such associations supply mere palliatives, perpetuate the notion of charity, and otherwise manipulate people into acceptance of the status quo.

Such assaults are not merely verbal. They reflect a trend to establish a state monopoly over all organized activities that have to do with more than strictly private purposes. This trend has borne fruit in outright prohibition, in repressive taxation, and in the imposition of licensing and operating standards that have a punitive effect on nongovernmental agencies.

Of course there are instances of corruption and inefficiency in voluntary agencies. A comparison of governmental and nongovernmental social services on these scores, however, hardly supports the case for governmental monopoly. It should be obvious that government bureaucrats have a vested interest in maintaining and expanding government monopolies. Similarly, politicians have an interest in setting up services for which they can claim credit and over which they can exercise a degree of power. In short, social services in the modern welfare state are inescapably part of the political pork barrel.

Pork barrels may be necessary to political democracy. The problem confronting us arises when the vested interests in question use coercive state power to repress individual freedom, initiative, and social diversity. We are not impressed by the argument that this is necessary because voluntary associations often overlap with the functions of government agencies. Overlap may in fact provide creative competition, incentives for performance, and increased choice. But our more basic contention is against the notion that anything public must *ipso facto* be governmental. That notion is profoundly contrary to the American political tradition and is, in its consequences, antidemocratic. It creates clients of the state instead of free citizens. It stifles the initiative and responsibility essential to the life of the polity.

Our present problem is also closely linked with the trend toward professionalization. Whether in government or nongovernment agencies, professionals attack allegedly substandard services, and substandard generally means nonprofessional. Through organizations and lobbies, professionals increasingly persuade the state to legislate standards and certifications that hit voluntary associations hard, especially those given to employing volunteers. The end result is that the trend toward government monopoly operates in tandem with the trend toward professional monopoly over social services. The connection between such monopoly control and the actual quality of services delivered is doubtful indeed.

Professional standards are of course important in some areas. But they must be viewed with robust skepticism when expertise claims jurisdiction, as it were, over the way people run their own lives. Again, ordinary people are the best experts on themselves. Tutelage by certified experts is bad enough when exercised by persuasion—as, for example, when parents are so demoralized that they feel themselves incapable of raising their children without ongoing reference to child-raising experts. It is much worse, however, when such tutelage is imposed coercively. And, of course, lower-income people are most effectively disfranchised by the successful establishment of expert monopolies.

Professionalization is now being exacerbated by unionization of professionals. In principle, employees of nongovernment agencies can be unionized as readily as government employees. In practice, large unions prefer to deal with the large and unified management that government offers. Standards and certification become items of negotiation between union and management, thus reinforcing the drive toward professional monopolies. In addition, unions would seem to have an intrinsic antagonism toward volunteer work. It is alleged that the volunteer is an unpaid laborer and is therefore exploited. This argument has been recently advanced also by some feminists, since many volunteers are women.

In protesting the use of labor and feminist rhetoric to camouflage the establishment of coercive monopolies and the disfranchisement of people in the running of their own lives, our position is neither anti-union nor anti-feminist. Who defines exploitation? We trust people to know when they are being exploited, without the benefit of instruction by professionals, labor organizers, or feminist authors. So long as voluntary work is genuinely voluntary—is undertaken by free choice—it should be cherished and not maligned. It is of enormous value in terms of both the useful activity offered to volunteers and the actual services rendered. In addition, because of their relative freedom from bureaucratic controls, voluntary associations are important laboratories of innovation in social services; and, of course, they sustain the expression of the rich pluralism of American life.

Attacks on the volunteer principle also aid the expansion of the kind of capitalist mentality that would put a dollar sign on everything on the grounds that only that which has a price tag has worth. We believe it proper and humane (as well as "human") that there be areas of life, including public life, in which there is not a dollar sign on everything. It is debilitating to our sense of the polity to assume that only private life is to be governed by humane, nonpecuniary motives, while the rest of life is a matter of dog-eat-dog.

An additional word should be said about the development of paraprofessional fields. To be sure, people who make their living in any socially useful occupation should be given respectful recognition and should be paid a decent wage. However, much of the paraprofessional development is in fact empire-building by professional and union monopolists who would incorporate lower-status occupations into their hierarchy. At least in some instances, the word that best describes this development is exploitation. This is the case, for example, when parents and other lay people can no longer hold professionals to account because they have themselves been co-opted into the vested interests of the professionals.

With the immense growth of knowledge and skills in modern society, professions are necessary and it is inevitable that there be organizations and unions to defend their interests. This development cannot be, and should not be, reversed. It can, however, be redirected. The purpose of the professions is to serve society—not the other way around. Too often professionals regard those they serve as clients in the rather unfortunate sense the Latin word originally implied. The clients of a Roman patrician were one step above his slaves in the social hierarchy, not entirely unlike some of today's servile dependents upon professionals. Such a notion has no place in democratic society.

Professionals should be ancillary to the people they serve. Upper-income people refer to "our" doctor or "my" doctor, and whatever patterns of dependency they develop are largely of their own choosing. It should be possible for lower-income people to use the possessive pronoun in referring to professionals.

The policy implications of our approach touch also on the role of nonprofit foundations in our society. Technically, there are different kinds of foundations—strictly private, publicly supported, operating, and so on—but the current assault applies to all of them. The argument is summed up in the words of the late Wright Patman whose crusade against foundations led to Title I of the Tax Reform Act of 1969:

> Today I shall introduce a bill to end a gross inequity which this country and its citizens can no longer afford: the tax-exempt status of the so-called privately controlled charitable foundations, and their propensity for domination of business and accumulation of wealth. . . . Put most bluntly, philanthropy —one of mankind's more noble instincts— has been perverted into a vehicle for institutionalized deliberate evasion of fiscal and moral responsibility to the nation. (*Congressional Record*, August 6, 1969)

Of course, foundations have engaged in abuses that need to be curbed, but the resentment and hostility manifested by the curbers also needs to be curbed if we are not to harm the society very severely. The curbers of foundations make up an odd coalition. Right-wing forces are hostile to foundations because of their social experimentation (such as the Ford Foundation's programs among inner-city blacks), while others are hostile because of the role of big business ("the establishment") in funding foundations. The most dangerous part of the 1969 legislation is the new power given to the Internal Revenue Service to police foundation activities. The power to revoke or threaten to revoke tax exemption is a most effective instrument of control. (In recent years such threats have been made against religious organizations that opposed the Vietnam War and advocated sundry unpopular causes.) More ominous than the prospect that a few millionaires will get away with paying less taxes is the prospect of government control over officially disapproved advocacy or programs.

Directly related to this concern is the relatively new concept of tax expenditure that has been infiltrated into public policy. It is calculated,

for example, that a certain amount of revenue is lost to the government because a private college is tax exempt. The revenue lost is called a tax expenditure. This may seem like an innocuous bit of bookkeeping, but the term expenditure implies that the college is in fact government-subsidized (a tax expenditure is a kind of government expenditure) and therefore ought to be governmentally controlled. This implication, which is made quite explicit by some bureaucrats, is incipiently totalitarian. The logic is that all of society's wealth *really* belongs to the government and that the government should therefore be able to determine how all wealth—including the wealth exempted from taxation—should be used. The concept of tax expenditure should be used, if at all, as a simple accounting device having no normative implications.

While large foundations would seem to be remote from the mediating structures under discussion, in fact they are often important to such structures at the most local level, especially in the areas of education and health. Were all these institutions taken over by the government, there might be a more uniform imposition of standards and greater financial accountability than now exists (although the monumental corruption in various government social services does not make one sanguine about the latter), but the price would be high. Massive bureaucratization, the proliferation of legal procedures that generate both public resentment and business for lawyers, the atrophying of the humane impulse, the increase of alienation—these would be some of the costs. Minimally, it should be public policy to encourage the voluntarism that, in our society, has at least slowed down these costs of modernity.

As always, the maximalist side of our approach—that is, using voluntary associations as agents of public policies—is more problematic than the minimalist. One thinks, for example, of the use of foster homes and half-way houses in the treatment and prevention of drug addiction, juvenile delinquency, and mental illness. There is reason to believe such approaches are both less costly and more effective than using bureaucratized megastructures (and their local outlets). Or one thinks of the successful resettlement of more than 100,000 Vietnam refugees in 1975, accomplished not by setting up a government agency but by working through voluntary agencies (mainly religious). This instance of using voluntary associations for public policy purposes deserves careful study. Yet another instance is the growth of the women's health movement, which in some areas is effectively challenging the monopolistic practices of the medical establishment. The ideas of people such as Ivan Illich and Victor Fuchs should be examined for their potential to empower people to reassume responsibility for their own health care. Existing experiments in decentralizing medical delivery systems should also be encouraged, with a view toward moving from decentralization to genuine empowerment.

We well know that proposals for community participation are not new. The most obvious example is the Community Action Program (CAP), a part of the War Against Poverty of the 1960s. CAP led to much disillusionment. Some condemned it as a mask for co-opting those who did, or might, threaten local power elites. Thus, community organizations were deprived of real potency and turned into government dependents. From the other side of the political spectrum, CAP was condemned for funding agitators and subversives. Yet others charged that CAP pitted community organizations against the institutions of representative government. To some extent these criticisms are mutually exclusive—they cannot all be true simultaneously. Yet no doubt all these things happened in various places in the 1960s.

That experience in no way invalidates the idea of community participation. First, the peculiar developments of the 1960s made that decade the worst possible time to try out the idea (and the same might be said about experiments in the community control of schools during the same period). Second, and much more important, the institutions used to facilitate community participation were not the actual institutions of the community but were created by those in charge of the program. This was especially true in inner-city black areas—the chief focus of the program—where religious institutions were, for the most part, neglected or even deliberately undercut. So, to some extent, were the family structures of the black community. In short, the program's failures resulted precisely from its failure to utilize existing mediating structures.

This said, it remains true that mediating structures can be co-opted by government, that they can become instruments of those interested in destroying rather than reforming American society, and that they can undermine the institutions of the formal polity. These are real risks. On the other side are the benefits described earlier. Together they constitute a major challenge to the political imagination.

Empowerment Through Pluralism

The theme of pluralism has recurred many times in this essay. This final section aims simply to tie up a few loose ends, to anticipate some objections to a public policy designed to sustain pluralism through mediating structures, and to underscore some facts of *American* society that suggest both the potentials and limitations of the approach advanced here.

It should be obvious that by pluralism we mean much more than regional accents, St. Patrick's Day, and Black Pride Days, as important as all these are. Beyond providing the variety of color, costume, and custom, pluralism makes possible a tension within worlds and between worlds of meaning. Worlds of meaning put reality together in a distinctive way. Whether the participants in these worlds see themselves as mainline or subcultural, as establishment or revolutionary, they are each but part of the cultural whole. Yet the paradox is that wholeness is experienced through affirmation of the part in which one participates. This relates to the aforementioned insight of Burke regarding "the little platoon." In more contemporary psychological jargon it relates to the "identity crisis" which results from "identity diffusion" in mass society. Within one's group—whether it be racial, national, political, religious, or all of these—one discovers an answer to the elementary question, "Who am I?", and is supported in living out that answer. Psychologically and sociologically, we would propose the axiom that any identity is better than none. Politically, we would argue that it is not the business of public policy to make value judgments regarding the merits or demerits of various identity solutions, so long as all groups abide by the minimal rules that make a pluralistic society possible. It is the business of public policy not to undercut, and indeed to enhance, the identity choices available to the American people (our minimalist and maximalist propositions throughout).

This approach assumes that the process symbolized by "E Pluribus Unum" is not a zero-sum game. That is, the *unum* is not to be achieved at the expense of the *plures*. To put it positively, the national purpose indicated by the *unum* is precisely to sustain the *plures*. Of course there are tensions, and accommodations are necessary if the structures necessary to national existence are to be maintained. But in the art of pluralistic politics, such tensions are not to be eliminated but are to be welcomed as the catalysts of more imaginative accommodations. Public policy in the areas discussed in this essay has in recent decades, we believe, been too negative in its approach to the tensions of diversity and therefore too ready to impose uniform solutions on what are perceived as national social problems. In this approach, pluralism is viewed as an enemy of social policy planning rather than as a source of more diversified solutions to problems that are, after all, diversely caused and diversely defined.

Throughout this paper, we have emphasized that our proposal contains no animus toward those charged with designing and implementing social policy nor any indictment of their good intentions. The reasons for present pluralism-eroding policies are to be discovered in part in the very processes implicit in the metaphors of modernization, rationalization, and bureaucratization. The management mindset of the megastructure—whether of HEW, Sears Roebuck, or the AFL-CIO—is biased toward the unitary solution. The neat and comprehensive answer is impatient of "irrational" particularities and can only be forced to yield to greater nuance when it encounters resistance, whether from the economic market of consumer wants or from the political market of organized special interest groups. The challenge of public policy is to anticipate such resistance and, beyond that, to cast aside its adversary posture toward particularism and embrace as its goal the advancement of the multitude of particular interests that in fact constitute the common weal. Thus, far from denigrating social planning, our proposal challenges the policy maker with a much more complicated and exciting task than today's approach. Similarly, the self-esteem of the professional in all areas of social service is elevated when he or she defines the professional task in terms of being helpful and ancillary to people rather than in terms of creating a power monopoly whereby people become dependent clients.

Of course, some critics will decry our proposal as "balkanization," "retribalization," "parochialization," and such. The relevance of the Balkan areas aside, we want frankly to assert that tribe and parochial are not terms of derision. That they are commonly used in a derisive manner is the result of a worldview emerging from the late eighteenth century. That worldview held, in brief, that the laws of Nature are reflected in a political will of the people that can be determined and implemented by rational persons. Those naive notions of Nature, Will, and Reason have in the last hundred years been thoroughly discredited in almost every discipline, from psychology to sociology to physics. Yet the irony is that, although few people still believe in these myths, most social thought and planning continues to act as though they were true. The result is that the enemies of particularism ("tribalism") have become an elite tribe attempting to impose order on the seeming irrationalities of the real world and operating on premises that most Americans find both implausible and hostile to their values. Social thought has been crippled and policies have miscarried because we have not developed a paradigm of pluralism to replace the discredited assumptions of the eighteenth century. We hope this proposal is one step toward developing such a paradigm.

Throughout this essay we have frequently referred to democratic values and warned against their authoritarian and totalitarian alternatives. We are keenly aware of the limitations in any notion of "the people" actually exercising the *kratein*, the effective authority, in public policy. And we are keenly aware of how far the American polity is from demonstrating what is possible in the democratic idea. The result of political manipulation, media distortion, and the sheer weight of indifference is that the great majority of Americans have little or no political will, in the sense that term is used in democratic theory, on the great questions of domestic and international policy. Within the formal framework of democratic polity, these questions will perforce be answered by a more politicized elite. But it is precisely with respect to mediating structures that most people do have, in the most exact sense, a political will. On matters of family, church, neighborhood, hobbies, working place, and recreation, most people have a very clear idea of what is in their interest. If we are truly committed to the democratic process, it is *their* political will that public policy should be designed to empower. It may be lamentable that most Americans have no political will with respect to U.S. relations with Brazil, but that is hardly reason to undercut their very clear political will about how their children should be educated. Indeed policies that disable political will where it does exist preclude the development of political will where it does not now exist, thus further enfeebling the democratic process and opening the door to its alernatives.

As difficult as it may be for some to accept, all rational interests do not converge—or at least there is no universal agreement on what interests are rational. This means that public policy must come to terms with perduring contradictions. We need not resign ourselves to the often cynically invoked axiom that "politics is the art of the possible." In fact politics is the art of discovering *what* is possible. The possibility to be explored is not how far unitary policies can be extended before encountering the backlash of particularity. Rather, the possibility to be explored is how a common purpose can be achieved through the enhancement of myriad particular interests. This requires a new degree of modesty among those who think about social policy—not modesty in the sense of lowering our ideals in the search for meeting human needs and creating a more just society, but modesty about *our* definitions of need and justice. Every world within this society, whether it calls itself a subculture or a supraculture or simply the American culture, is in fact a subculture, is but a part of the whole. This fact needs to be systematically remembered among those who occupy the world of public policy planning and implementation.

The subculture that envisages its values as universal and its style as cosmopolitan is no less a subculture for all that. The tribal patterns evident at an Upper West Side cocktail party are no less tribal than those evident at a Polish dance in Greenpoint, Brooklyn. That the former is produced by the interaction of people trying to transcend many particularisms simply results in a new, and not necessarily more interesting, particularism. People at the cocktail party may think of themselves as liberated, and indeed they may have elected to leave behind certain particularisms into which they were born. They

have, in effect, elected a new particularism. *Liberation is not escape from particularity but discovery of the particularity that fits.* Elected particularities may include life style, ideology, friendships, place of residence, and so forth. Inherited particularities may include race, economic circumstance, region, religion, and, in most cases, politics. Pluralism means the lively interaction among inherited particularities and, through election, the evolution of new particularities. The goal of public policy in a pluralistic society is to sustain as many particularities as possible, in the hope that most people will accept, discover, or devise one that fits.

It might be argued that the redirection of public policy proposed here is in fact naive and quixotic. A strong argument can be made that the dynamics of modernity, operating through the megastructures and especially through the modern state, are like a great leviathan or steamroller, inexorably destroying every obstacle that gets in the way of creating mass society. There is much and ominous evidence in support of that argument. While we cannot predict the outcome of this process, we must not buckle under to alleged inevitabilities. On the more hopeful side are indications that the political will of the American people is beginning to assert itself more strongly in resistance to "massification." In contradiction of social analysts who describe the irresistible and homogenizing force of the communications media, for example, there is strong evidence that the media message is not received uncritically but is refracted through myriad world views that confound the intentions of would-be manipulators of the masses. (Happily, there are also many often-contradictory media messages.) New "Edsels" still get rejected (though the Edsel itself is a collector's item). The antiwar bias of much news about the Vietnam War (a bias we shared) was, studies suggest, often refracted in a way that reinforced support of official policy. Promotion of diverse sexual and lifestyle liberations seems to be doing little empirically verifiable damage to devotion to the family ideal. Thirty years of network TV English (not to mention thirty years of radio before that) has hardly wiped out regional dialect. In short, and to the consternation of political, cultural, and commercial purveyors of new soaps, the American people demonstrate a robust skepticism toward the modern peddlers of new worlds and a remarkable inclination to trust their own judgments. We do not wish to exaggerate these signs of hope. Counter-indicators can be listed in abundance. We do suggest there is no reason to resign ourselves to the "massification" that is so often described as America today.

America today—those words are very important to our argument. While our proposal is, we hope, relevant to modern industrialized society in general, whether socialist or capitalist, its possibilities are peculiarly attuned to the United States. (We might say, to North America, including Canada, but some aspects of particularism in Canada—for example, binationalism between French- and English-speaking Canadians —are beyond the scope of this essay.) There are at least five characteristics of American society that make it the most likely laboratory for public policy designed to enhance mediating structures and the pluralism that mediating structures make possible. First is the immigrant nature of American society. The implications of that fact for pluralism need no elaboration. Second, ours is a relatively affluent society. We have the resources to experiment toward a more humane order—for example, to place a floor of economic decency under every American. Third, this is a relatively stable society. Confronted by the prospects of neither revolution nor certain and rapid decline, we do not face the crises that call for total or definitive answers to social problems. Fourth, American society is effectively pervaded by the democratic idea and by the sense of tolerance and fair play that make the democratic process possible. This makes our society ideologically hospitable to pluralism. And fifth, however weakened they may be, we still have relatively strong institutions—political, economic, religious, and cultural—that supply countervailing forces in the shaping of social policy. Aspirations toward monopoly can, at least in theory, be challenged. And our history demonstrates that the theory has, more often than not, been acted out in practice.

Finally, we know there are those who contend that, no matter how promising all this may be for America, America is very bad for the rest of the world. It is argued that the success of America's experiment in democratic pluralism is at the expense of others, especially at the

expense of the poorer nations. It is a complicated argument to which justice cannot be done here. But it might be asked, in turn, whether America would in some sense be better for the world were we to eliminate any of the five characteristics mentioned above. Were the American people more homogeneous, were they as poor as the peasants of Guatemala, were their institutions less stable and their democratic impulses less ingrained—would any of these conditions contribute concretely to a more just global order? We think not.

Neither, on the other hand, are we as convinced as some others seem to be that America is the "advance society" of human history, or at least of the modern industrialized world. Perhaps it is—perhaps not. But of *this* we are convinced: America has a singular opportunity to contest the predictions of the inevitability of mass society with its anomic individuals, alienated and impotent, excluded from the ordering of a polity that is no longer theirs. And we are convinced that mediating structures might be the agencies for a new empowerment of people in America's renewed experiment in democratic pluralism.

ARTICLE 3 ⸻

Toward a Theory of the Voluntary Non-Profit Sector in a Three-Sector Economy*

Burton A. Weisbrod

This paper is an exploratory effort to examine the role of a voluntary, "philanthropic" sector

* This research has received a variety of support: from the Institute for Research on Poverty, pursuant to the Economic Opportunity Act of 1964; from the University of Wisconsin Graduate School; and from Guggenheim Foundation and Ford Foundation fellowships. In connection with various parts of the research I have been very fortunate to be assisted by Jennifer Gerner, A. James Lee, Donna Beutel, and Marc Bendick, Jr. Eugene Smolensky, Mark Menchik, and Donald Nichols provided helpful comments on an earlier draft of this paper. SOURCE: "Toward a Theory of Voluntary Nonprofit Sector in a Three Sector Economy" by Burton A. Weisbrod. Reprinted from ALTRUISM, MORALITY, AND ECONOMIC THEORY, Edmund S. Phelps, editor. © Russell Sage Foundation, 1975. Used with permission of the Russell Sage Foundation.

in an economy with public and private (for-profit) sectors and with collective-consumption and private-consumption goods. More generally, it seeks an answer to the questions what factors determine which goods will be provided governmentally, which privately in for-profit markets, and which in voluntary markets. The approach is primarily positive, attempting particularly to predict the circumstances under which the voluntary sector will develop, grow and decline. A model will be fashioned in which certain behavioral and organizational constraints limit public-sector and for-profit sector activities and stimulate the voluntary sector; and in which the existence of collective-consumption goods is not sufficient to ensure governmental production or provision. The existence of such voluntary organizations will thus be explained with a minimum of institutional assumptions. In effect, we set forth the logic behind a hypothesis that there are non-governmental, voluntary organizations providing collective goods. Some normative judgments will be reached regarding efficient public policy toward certain types of voluntary organizations.

The analysis presented here is essentially static. There is some consideration, however, of the effects on the distribution of economic activity among the three sectors—government, for-profit, and voluntary—that result from changes in population characteristics and in the level and inequality of income.

The interest that is now developing in organizations variously referred to as voluntary, non-profit, collective, charitable, non-market or philanthropic is overdue, for there is no doubt that a wide array of economic activity is undertaken outside the private profit-seeking sector and outside the public sector. Contemporary economics includes a long-established theory of the private (profit) sector, the rationale for its existence and the mode of its equilibrium behavior; more recently a theory of the public (government) sector has evolved, emphasizing the existence of "public," "collective-consumption" goods for which the private sector is an unsatisfactory production vehicle that is likely to produce suboptimal quantities.[1] Yet the reality of goods and services that are provided neither governmentally, in the sense of being financed through taxation, nor privately, in the sense of being financed through user charges and operated for "profit," confronts us with a gap in our theories.

But my goal is less ambitious than to explain the existence, let alone the behavior, of all of the many kinds of organizations that are found outside the private-profit and the public sectors. Rather I wish to identify one class of such activities—the provision (financing) of public-type, collective-consumption goods by non-governmental enterprises. Thus, this paper will examine some interrelations between the public sector, the private sector, and the voluntary sector, focusing on the provision of collective-consumption goods outside the government.

We begin with an analysis of governmental behavior. The existence of certain constraints on governments will be seen to create what might be termed government market failure, analogous to the conditions causing private market failures. Development of a voluntary sector will then be posited as an adjustment to the restricted capabilities of these other two sectors.

The Elements of a Simple Model of Output Determination in the Government Sector

To begin with let us assume a society in which

—People behave rationally in pursuit of their individual objectives of utility maximization;

—A given state of technology and set of production possibilities exists, and these permit production of some collective-consumption and some private-consumption goods;

—Each person's utility is a function of both his private goods and the collective-consumption goods that are available to him;

—Utility functions are not the same for all people.

One question with which we want a behavioral model to deal is: how much of the demand for collective-consumption goods will be satisfied by government. "Satisfied" by a government is defined as financed by a government, no distinction being made between government production (ownership) of some good and provision via purchase or contracting-out—that is, paying a private producer to supply it.[2] Henceforth, the term government *provision* will be used to describe both types of arrangements.

A rule or behavioral assumption is needed for determining how government will finance any given level of output for a specified good, and a rule is also required for specifying how voter demands will influence the level of government provision. Both of these are important and, given the present state of economic understanding, controversial issues. While particular assumptions will be stated shortly, it is desirable to relax the assumptions in order to determine the sensitivity of our results to the particular assumptions. Now, regarding the finance mechanism we postulate:

—any tax (any perhaps user-charge) system may be used by government to finance a particular expenditure program, subject to the constraint that the system does not permit every, or nearly every, consumer to equate the tax he pays with the marginal benefit of the good to him. Such a relatively weak assumption will not permit strong statements about government output levels, and more attention should be given to the implications of more specific requirements, but some interesting conclusions can nonetheless be reached. It should be noted, however, that the assumption is less innocuous than it might appear. It rules out vote trading, selling, or logrolling *if* the effect would be to leave each person with a *net* tax price—net or "bribe" — that is equal to his valuation of marginal output. While such trading activities do occur to some extent and do tend to reduce divergencies between marginal benefit and marginal price among consumers, the combination of information costs, strategic behavior (transaction costs) and, in most instances, legal prohibition (against "selling" votes) sustains significant divergencies.

We turn now to the need for a rule regarding how consumer-voter demands influence decisions by government to supply a good. This has received growing attention in recent years but a consensus has not yet been reached.[3] In this paper, however, we begin with the assumption that

—government will supply a quantity and quality of any commodity that is determined by a political voting process. One such process would involve majority vote, according to which the demands of the median voter would determine the outcome.[4] One alternative would be a *weighted-*majority decision rule in which the weight attached to each person's "vote" is some function of the "loudness" of his "squawk" (intensity of dissatisfaction with a given tax-and-provision decision).[5] The latter model might predict that mean, rather than median, demand, determines levels of government provision, and that the dispersion to the right and to the left of the mean might have asymmetrical effects. But these are little more than plausible speculations concerning political processes. For our present purpose we require only that the political process leaves significant numbers of voters dissatisfied with government output and taxation levels.

Summing up: If consumer-voters know the rule by which government will allocate costs among them, their utility functions will generate a set of demand functions for governmentally provided goods which, with the government-supply decision-rule, will determine a level of government provision.

While each of our assumptions may reasonably be questioned as to its realism, there is particular reason to question whether consumer-voters know how the cost of any increased government output provision will be distributed among taxpayers.[6] Nevertheless, it is perhaps reasonable to believe that whatever cost-distribution rule taxpayers expect to be used, few persons expect a rule that (even roughly) equates tax liability with the value of benefits from a marginal unit of the good. This is especially true for the host of governmentally provided goods for which there are no user charges.

The assumption of *non*-benefit-principle tax-pricing is critical to the argument that follows. The reason is that a tax-pricing system that does not equate, for each voter, his marginal tax with the marginal benefit he receives from each collective-consumption good will produce, in general, a level of government provision that exceeds what some voters demand and that falls short of what others demand. Not only is such a result non-optimal, as is well known,[7] but as we shall see, its occurrence can be expected to set in motion forces that will influence the aggregate allocation of resources among the three economic sectors. The assumption of non-benefit tax-pricing is quite general, permitting a wide range of tax systems. It rules out only a system that is, in reality, not available anyway, given that little is known about individuals' marginal valuations of particular public goods, and given that the free-rider problem leads people to hide their true valuations, even if they know them, when a benefit-based tax system is known to be used for financing a collective-consumption good.

Figure 1 illustrates a situation in which (a) voter demands for public provision of a specific good vary among the seven persons portrayed, and (b) the tax-finance price rule specifies that costs are borne equally by all,[8] with each taxpayer paying P per unit of output provided by the government. This simple, but unrealistic tax rule is used for its simplicity only; it is not implied by our assumptions. The good may be thought of as a collective-consumption good, although it need not be. Later we will consider briefly the demand for governmental provision of non-collective-consumption goods.

It is apparent from the diagram that, with each consumer-taxpayer paying the same tax, P, per unit of output, a majority of consumers (persons 4–7) would prefer to increase output to the level Q_1. At that level, consumers 1, 2, and 3 prefer to reduce the total tax and the quantity of output, while consumers 5, 6, and 7 prefer to increase both the total tax and the quantity supplied, but they are in the minority. Assuming a majority-vote rule, person 4, the median voter, has his way. In general, however, whether a majority vote or some other rule is operative, in the absence of marginal-benefit taxation the political process of determining an output level is likely to leave some consumers dissatisfied because they are receiving and paying too much of the good, while others are dissatisfied because they are receiving too little—that is, they would prefer to have the total tax payment and output level increased.[9] The relative numbers of the two dissatisfied groups depend, of course, on the particular tax-pricing system and the political decision process. The simple majority-vote rule, for example, would satisfy only the median consumer, and so the population would be split evenly between those who demand more and those who demand less at the prevailing marginal tax-prices.

The *intensities* of individuals' dissatisfactions will also generally vary; for a person who demands *more* than the quantity supplied, the intensity can be measured by the area under his demand curve, above the tax-price curve and to the right of the quantity supplied. For person 7 in Figure 1, this is the area ABC. For a person who demands *less* than the quantity supplied, the intensity of dissatisfaction may be measured, in corresponding fashion, by the area above the demand curve, below the tax-price curve, and to the left of the quantity supplied (PAGFH in Figure 1, for person 3).

Reactions of Dissatisfied Consumers

With many consumers being either undersatisfied or oversatisfied, adjustments can be expected to occur.[10] Before turning to the nature of the adjustment possibilities, note that the relative numbers of persons who desire any adjustment, and the degree of adjustment desired, depend on the variation in demands at the tax price(s) that each consumer assumes he confronts. Thus, of major importance, in addition to the tax system, is the degree of demand homogeneity of the population. The greater the homogeneity within a political unit—that is, the greater the similarity in income, wealth, religion, ethnic background, education level, and other characteristics influencing demand for any collective-consumption good—the smaller the expected variation in individual demands, and, hence, the smaller the likely degree of dissatisfaction with the politically determined level and quality of output.

There are several adjustment possibilities available to the dissatisfied consumers, including migration, formation of lower-level governments, resort to private market alternatives and to voluntary organizations. Each will be discussed in turn, but the attempt is to describe not a sequential process but rather a general equilibrium adjustment process in which all of these organizational forms for satisfying consumer demands are simultaneously operative.[11]

One option for the dissatisfied consumer is *migration* to another governmental unit in which output and tax-pricing systems lead to an improvement in his economic welfare. The viability of this adjustment option is, of course, considerably greater if local governmental units are being considered than it is if higher-level governments are the focus.[12] In any case, since moving is not costless and since locational decisions reflect many considerations other than governmental outputs and taxes, we can think of the type of situation portrayed in Figure 1 as reflecting

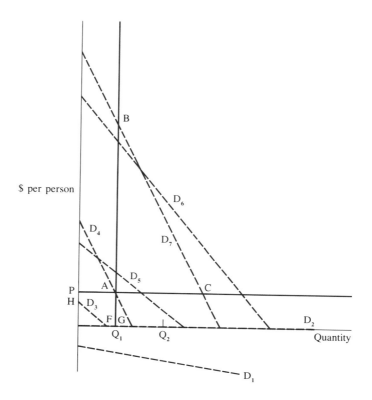

FIGURE 1

the likely situation even after migration adjustments—diverse demands, some "oversatisfied" consumers, and some "undersatisfied."

Beyond migration, the undersatisfied and the oversatisfied consumers do confront somewhat different options. The oversatisfied consumers (persons 1–3 in Figure 1), if they do not move out, will have few options except to bear the burden or else to exert political pressure to alter either the tax-price system or the output-determination system. The undersatisfied consumers, however, have other alternatives, and this paper directs attention to them.

A second adjustment outlet, open to all those who want and are willing to pay for added output, is *to form lower-level governments*. Thus persons 5, 6, and 7 in Figure 1 might organize an additional governmental unit including only themselves, to provide additional units of the commodity in question. They could not entirely

avoid the free-rider problem, of course—other persons would use some of their output if they could do so without paying (or paying less than *P*). Neither could the undersatisfied demanders avoid the cost of organizing the new governmental unit. We can expect, therefore, that while (1) some lower-level government supplementation of output will take place—and this is illustrated by parks and libraries, which are provided by federal, state, county, and local governments—at the same time, (2) some undersatisfied demand will remain.

As we consider adjustments in the several economic sectors, it should be noted that because we are considering collective goods, which benefit more than one person simultaneously, the provision of such goods in any one sector may well reduce the demand for it in the other sectors. If the good were a "pure" collective good—involving no "congestion" whatever—then an increment of output of the good in one sector would presumably bring about an *equal* decrement in another sector, at least in equilibrium. When the collective good is anything short of pure, however, the provision of an additional unit of output in one sector will not lead to an equal decrease in the level of output provided in another sector.

In addition to migration and formation of lower-level government units, the third and fourth adjustment outlets for the undersatisfied demanders, and the two on which I will focus, are the *private* (for-profit) market and the *voluntary* ("non-profit") markets.

Consider, first, the private market. The currently prevailing view among economists regarding the role of private markets in the provision of public, collective-consumption goods is simply that those markets will produce suboptimal quantities of such goods, and that, therefore, governments may be, and from an allocative-efficiency standpoint should be, called upon to take steps to see that the output level is increased. Implicit in this view is an assumption that the private and the public markets are two alternate organizational mechanisms for providing the *same* good.

Public- and Private-Good Substitutes

This, I believe, is an invalid assumption. As an alternative I suggest that we think of the production-possibility set at a given point in time as including collective-consumption goods and private-good *substitutes* for them, as well as "ordinary" private goods. Thus, for example, the collective good, lighthouse, has a private-good substitute, shipboard radar; the collective good, provision of clean air, has private-good substitutes in air filters and purifiers for home, automobile and place of work; the collective good, stand-by fire department, has a private-good substitute, sprinkler systems; the collective good, generic information (e.g., on drugs), has a private-good substitute, brand-name advertising; and the collective good, police department, has private-good substitutes that include alarms, locks, guards, and dogs.[13]

To observe that there are often private-good substitutes for collective goods by no means says, however, that they are perfect substitutes. In fact, as the examples just given suggest, these substitutes are generally different in a particular and

important way, to be discussed shortly, and this difference has a notable implication for any attempt to understand and predict the degree of public sector involvement in the provision of a good.[14]

Observing that there are private-good substitutes for collective goods suggests that it would be useful to study the "industry" comprising (1) each good or service provided by the public sector, plus (2) the substitutes provided by the private sector, plus—for the reason to be explored below—(3) the substitutes provided by the voluntary sector. In a later section of this paper I will report on some early empirical work on such industry studies.

It is presumably true that there is no technological constraint that prevents the private sector from producing collective goods. If that is so, then any observed differences in the "type" of goods provided by the private and the government sectors of an industry are likely to reflect consumers preferences and/or relative prices. From the consumer-preference viewpoint a collective-consumption good is likely to have one important disadvantage compared with a private-good substitute. The disadvantage of the collective good—whether it is governmentally or privately operated—is the lesser degree of individual control that each consumer can exercise over its form, quality and utilization or deployment. Even the classical lighthouse and national defense activities must take particular forms, must be located in particular places, and must be activated and deactivated at particular times and under particular circumstances. Rarely, if ever, will all consumers agree about how any of these decisions should be made, and yet, by the very nature of collective goods, the decisions once made affect all persons. A given lighthouse cannot be located differently for different users, nor can it be turned on and off at different times to satisfy conflicting preferences. (This is to observe once again the heterogeneity portrayed in Figure 1.)

Why, in the face of this disadvantage inherent in sharing, should a good be demanded of government when a private-good substitute exists? One answer is that the private-good substitute may be a very poor substitute—as is the case with national defense, where handguns (private goods) are poor substitutes for such collective goods as hydrogen bombs, and where a social judgment has apparently been made that devastating weapons should not be purchasable by private consumers at any price. In many, perhaps most, other cases, however, where private goods are available that can achieve virtually the same objective as the public-good version, the only significant advantage of the public good would seem to be its relative price. That is, some people may prefer to pay for a marginal unit of the public-good version at its associated tax price rather than a unit of the private-good version at its market price. (The particular tax-price system that is used will, thus, affect the number of persons who opt for the public-good or the private-good substitute.)

We can now return to an analysis of the choices open to consumers whose demands for any collective good are undersatisfied through government markets. The consumer who turns to the private-market option is, in effect, choosing an option that often involves a different form of the good in question. He may be expected to select a form which, while providing its owner with greater individual control, does so by providing smaller external benefits to other consumers. After all, if a consumer must bear the total cost rather than share the cost with others, then he will presumably tend to choose a form of the good that maximizes internal benefits, including his individual control, paying little attention to the external benefits that might be provided in greater measure by some other, collective-consumption form of the good.

The point to emphasize is that such a choice may be socially non-optimal, albeit privately optimal in an economy with only two sectors—private and public—and with output in the public sector being constrained. Purchases of private-good substitutes may reflect not simply the interaction of preferences and production costs; rather they can reflect, and, in the situation depicted in Figure 1 actually do reflect, an adjustment to the non-optimal level of provision of the collective good by government.[15] The analysis suggests, at this point, that consumers are likely to be left in non-optimal positions in both private and government markets, being over- or undersatisfied in government markets and making socially inefficient choices in private markets.

The Voluntary Sector

This brings us to a rationale for the development of voluntary non-profit organizations.[16] The reasoning above suggests the hypothesis that a class of voluntary organizations will come into existence as *extra-governmental providers of collective-consumption goods*.[17] They will "supplement" the *public* provision (which can be zero) and provide an alternative to the *private*-sector provision of private-good substitutes for collective goods.[18]

If the voluntary organizations do in fact provide collective goods, they may be expected to confront financial problems, given the free-rider problem. However, since all the alternatives available to undersatisfied demanders also involve inefficiencies, it may be worthwhile (that is, efficient) to form and maintain voluntary organizations as a "second best" solution.[19]

This exposition has seemingly implied that the initial response to demands for collective-consumption goods is sought in the public sector, with subsequent adjustments reflecting dissatisfaction with that response. Such a sequence may or may not be accurate as a description of real-world behavior—although a little evidence on this will be cited later—but in any case the sequencing is only an expositional convenience. Although the public sector has some clear advantage in the provision of collective goods, it may also have a disadvantage in the form of organizational costs.[20] When the differential costs of organizing economic activity in the various sectors (and at various governmental levels) are considered—a factual matter about which little is known—it is no longer apparent in which sector the initial response to collective-good demand will occur. It is likely, however, that the government sector will *not* be the first to respond to consumer demands for collective goods. The reason is that demands by all consumers do not generally develop simultaneously, and so the political-decision rule will at first determine a zero level of government provision, leading the undersatisfied demanders to non-governmental markets.

Not all governmentally provided goods and services have a significant collective-consumption component. Publicly provided employment services and library provision of current best-seller novels (but not research materials), for example, are not easily explainable as responses to this source of market failure.[21] Why governments provide non-collective goods is a matter deserving further scrutiny, and we will only touch on the question here. One potential justification for public provision of a private-consumption good is the saving in private-market transaction costs (or enforcement costs) in cases where there is widespread agreement regarding the quantity of an individual-consumption good that each consumer wishes to consume (or wishes others to consume). As long as tax bills are being paid to finance government provision of collective goods, there may be advantages to adding to the bill a sum to finance the "minimum" level of a private good that the political majority prefers. While more study is needed of the rationale for government provision of goods with little or no collective character, it is important to note that governments do provide them. For if this is the case, then the voluntary sector, if it is indeed providing collective-consumption goods, as has been hypothesized in this paper, will be found to be more prominent in supplementing those government activities having the "largest" collective-consumption component. By contrast, we may expect that the *private*-good activities of government will be supplemented to a relatively greater extent in the private for-profit sector.

With a collective-consumption good and substitutes for it being provided in two or even three economic sectors, there is no easy answer to the question of whether such a good is likely to be provided in optimal, sub-optimal, or super-optimal total quantities. What is needed is a more general theory that goes beyond the *private* market's tendency to underprovide collective-consumption goods and explains the public and voluntary markets' supplemental activities.

Private- and Public-Good Substitutes, Some Dynamics

Up to this point we have assumed that the set of collective-consumption and individual-consumption goods from which consumers could choose was given exogenously. Now we will drop the static assumption of a predetermined set of goods, instead examining some determinants of

what is included in the set. Specifically, is there a basis for predicting that in the course of time the menu of collective-consumption goods will expand more, or less, rapidly than the menu of private goods? What determines such changes?

It was stated above that a major distinction between public goods and their private-good substitutes is the greater individual control offered by the latter and preferred by consumers generally. Granted such a difference it would seem likely that if consumers at a given level of income are found to be purchasing a particular ratio of a public good to its private-good substitute, then at sufficiently higher income levels that ratio is likely to fall, as demand shifts in favor of the private goods. This is not to say that the income elasticity of demand for any collective good is necessarily negative at some income levels. We suggest the following hypotheses: at "very low" income levels the income elasticity of demand for a given collective good is positive and large; as income increases people shift expenditures from a pattern in which *neither* a collective good *nor* a private-good substitute is purchased to a pattern that includes *some* collective goods. And as incomes rise further, the demand for collective goods rises, but at some point the private-good substitutes will come to be bought instead of the collective good. (This point may differ, of course, for different goods.) That is, the income elasticity of demand for collective goods may be positive but lower than that for private-good substitutes at sufficiently high levels of income. Thus, the relationship between the level of per capita income and the relative size of the government sector is likely to be that of an inverted U.[22]

Some Bits of Evidence

This brief section provides a number of scraps of "evidence" on the notions presented above. None of the evidence, individually or in total, is offered as "proof" of the propositions we have discussed. Rather, they are intended to be suggestive of the types of research that would be useful in order to better understand the role of voluntary organizations in a three-sector economy that also includes government and private for-profit sectors.

1. Private-Good Substitutes for Collective Goods

We now consider the effects of relaxing the initial assumption of an exogenously determined set of collective and of private goods. If the hypothesis is correct that beyond some level of income for any given person collective goods are demanded in preference to private goods, then, as such an income level is approached by increasing numbers of persons, we should expect an increase in the amount of private-market resources devoted to research and development on private-good substitutes. Thus, the set of private, individual-consumption goods that are available would expand in response to increased incomes. This may be one of the factors explaining (a) the growing number of inventions to provide home and business security—in addition to the expanded provision of the traditional collective good, police protection; (b) the development of home garbage disposers, incinerators and, now, trash compactors as substitutes for the more collective good, trash collection; and (c) the development of electronic air filters as substitutes for cleaner air in the environment.

In more general terms, there are many other examples of how increased incomes are reducing consumers' relative demands for "shared" goods, which they can utilize only under particular conditions and at particular times—e.g., urban mass transit and public libraries—and are increasing demands for non-shared goods that are fully under the individual's control—e.g., private autos and paperback books. I do not suggest that the distinction between shared and non-shared goods is synonymous with the distinction between collective-consumption and individual-consumption goods. Nevertheless, there is a relationship: collective-consumption goods, except for the pure case, do require sharing.

2. A Fragment of Historical Evidence on Voluntary Provision of Public Goods

Our analysis concerning undersatisfied demanders of collective goods and their relationship to voluntary organizations portrays the latter as non-governmental providers of collective goods that are normally identified with governments.

Historical events provide one test of our view, which implies that before a political majority comes to demand government provision, the minority that demands governmental provision of a good will be undersatisfied and will turn to voluntary organizations. Thus, *provision by voluntary* (non-profit) *organizations is hypothesized to precede governmental provision historically.* It is noteworthy, therefore, that in 16th-century England, where governmental provision of any civilian goods or services was very modest, private "philanthropies" (voluntary organizations) were providing funds for such wide-ranging public, collective activities as schools, hospitals, non-toll roads, fire fighting apparatus, public parks, bridges, dikes and causeways, digging of drainage canals, water-works, wharves and docks, harbor cleaning, libraries, care of prisoners in jails, and charity to the poor[23]—in short, for the gamut of non-military goods that we identify today as governmental responsibilities. Such voluntary-sector giving even included support for such noble charitable causes as "houses for young women convinced of their folly." [24] At the same time we are told that private interests "sought to prod the central government to carry forward needed projects. . ."[25]—behavior that we would anticipate since collective-type goods were involved.

The relationship between governmental and voluntary provision of goods has also been noted by historians of Elizabethan England. "The various philanthropic activities, which we have been reviewing [including highways, police charity, hospitals and schools] were supplemented in some important respects by the corporate action of the towns."[26] Whether the public sector "supplemented" the voluntary, or vice versa, is, I believe, an insignificant distinction.

Note that it is quite consistent with our theoretic model that the level of politically determined governmental provision of a collective good can be zero even though a large minority (or even a majority, if a political-decision rule other than majority vote is used) has positive demands. If the undersatisfied demanders turn to the voluntary sector, as is likely, then this sector will develop first. Later, perhaps in response to economic development, the number of positive demanders might increase and so the government sector would become a provider of the good involved. Thus, in general, we might expect the voluntary sector to precede the government sector in the provision of collective goods.

A historical perspective on public-sector activities raises the question of to what extent any observed changes in the relative size or scope of government are the results of changes in the magnitudes of variables—e.g., incomes—or changes in the magnitudes of parameters—such as those mirroring attitudes toward the "appropriate" role of government. Both, of course, may be important. The view (hypothesis) being set forth here, however, is that the varying roles of government over time, as well as across countries, are not a consequence of exogenously determined "attitudes" toward government; rather that such attitudes are themselves endogenously determined by changes in incomes, in other demand variables and in the state of technology and factor prices. Depending on stages of development and on population demand characteristics, a different role for government can be expected.

3. Financing Voluntary Provision of Collective Goods

If our identification of voluntary organizations with the provision of public, collective goods is valid, we should expect these organizations to confront finance problems. Indeed, because they share with private-sector firms ". . .the absence of the coercive and compulsive powers of government," Buchanan and Tullock have grouped those two types of organizations, terming them "voluntary groups" and distinguishing them from governments.[27]

It is important, however, to distinguish between any differences among organizations in the types of their *outputs*, and differences in the methods of their *finance*, although the two are not entirely independent. Our emphasis here is on the nature of outputs, and on this basis the similarity of government and voluntary organizations is significant, as is the difference between both of these and the private for-profit organizations. The free-rider problem associated with collective goods does lead us to expect that nongovernmental providers of such goods face a financial obstacle.

Upon further study, however, it turns out that voluntary organizations do employ "coercive and compulsive powers," just as do governments, although the penalties are social rather than governmentally sanctioned fines or imprisonment. While pressures to "donate" to the United Fund, Red Cross, Cancer Society, or private colleges are (sometimes) somewhat more subtle than the pressure to pay one's taxes, the difference is one of degree, not of kind.[28]

There are several plausible reasons why people may give to a voluntary organization when there is neither compulsion of law nor any apparent *quid pro quo*. One is the social pressure just noted.[29] A second, very closely related to the first, is captured by the recent conception of Pareto optimal redistribution—individuals' utility functions may be such that they derive benefit from either the act of giving or from seeing someone else benefited.[30] That is, the *apparent* lack of a *quid pro quo* may be misleading. A "donor" to a voluntary organization may derive satisfaction from the act of giving to a "worthy" cause. Also he may benefit from the gratitude, esteem and plaudits of his neighbors and fellow citizens—rewards which to some extent even show up as financial returns and act to internalize what would otherwise be external benefits to the donor.

Sometimes the benefit from giving is quite direct and in a private-good form; thus a giver may receive a tangible gift in return for his "donation." One organization offers a "free" road atlas for a $3 donation; in other cases the donor may have his name inscribed on a plaque or even on a college library or hospital wing.[31]

The question of *why* people like such social reinforcement rewards and, hence, are willing to pay for them is an important matter of utility-function determination that economists have avoided too long. Utility functions are not determined entirely by forces exogenous to the economic system, and even if they were, economic analysis could still contribute to understanding the process of their formation. In any case, there can be no doubt that there are very many transactions in the economy that involve no binding *quid pro quo*—there are many things that people do which, like supporting voluntary organizations, bring little or no clear and certain reward. One example is truly voluntary giving to charity or to a blood bank.[32]

Another is the support by young people for old age pensions through the social security system, support which appears to hinge on the hope and faith that future generations of young people will be willing to finance the retirement of the aged just as the current generation of young people is doing. It is by no means obvious why young people have such faith, but apparently it is a real force influencing actions. It seems to apply not only to retirement pensions, but also to the support for public education. There appears to be a "social compact" such that each generation of adults agrees to support the education of the younger generation.

4. The Logic of Public Subsidy for Voluntary Giving

We have seen in Figure 1 that of the seven (groups of) people portrayed, only three demand more than Q_1 level of provision at the price P. A fourth, however, consisting of people such as person 4, would derive *some* positive benefit from additional output. It might be expected, therefore, that a majority of voters would favor a government program that financed, in addition to Q_1, a *part* of the cost of output in excess of that quantity. Given consumer awareness of the free-rider problem and its likely resolution in diversion of non-government resources from collective goods to private-good substitutes, a political majority of voters would be rational to agree not only to *full governmental* financing of some output but also to *partial* government subsidy for some additional *non*-governmental provision of collective goods.

Such a subsidy could take various forms, being an explicit grant or a tax subsidy. Both, in fact, are employed. The voluntary hospital industry in the United States, for example, receives *partial* government support through outright cash grants from the federal government for construction, through the Hill-Burton Act, and also benefits from the income-tax deductibility of private contributions to voluntary non-profit hospitals. By contrast, the public hospitals are financed *fully* by government.

It is noteworthy that such governmental subsidies, and in particular the income-tax deductibility subsidies, are extended only to some of the non-governmental organizations that

provide goods that are also provided governmentally. In general, only organizations in the health, education, charity, and religious areas can qualify for such government subsidies—not, by contrast, the non-governmental organizations that either do, or might, provide trash collection, roads, fire or security services, or other services that have counterparts in the public sector. It would seem that the magnitude of the subsidy ought to depend—from the standpoint of allocative efficiency—on the severity of the free-rider problem—that is, on the magnitude of external benefits that would be generated by individuals' private decisions to purchase (or supply) the good. If we were correct in arguing above that governments provide some non-collective-consumption goods, it would follow that subsidies would be widely supported (and would be efficient) only for the non-governmental providers of *collective* goods, and not for the non-governmental providers of private goods that substitute for collective goods.

Under current federal income-tax law, there are only two "levels" of such subsidization through the deductibility route: either zero, with gifts and grants to the organization not qualifying for tax deductibility, or full deductibility. (Of course, the importance of the latter from the *giver's* viewpoint depends on his marginal tax rate and whether he itemizes his deductions.) While a binary subsidy schedule would surely not be economically efficient under conditions of perfect information, it *could* be a reasonably good rule-of-thumb basis for setting subsidies to stimulate non-governmental provision of public goods.

How good is it? How effective is it? I make no attempt here to answer these questions carefully. While further study is needed, it seems that the kinds of activities for which private giving does qualify for tax deductibility do have a larger public-good component than is the case for other activities—that is, they enter the utility functions of more persons and enter more "importantly." If this is so, then there is at least some efficiency basis for the voluntary-donations deductibility feature of our tax system.

5. Heterogeneity of Demand

Just as the model sketched above predicts that there will often be private-market or voluntary-market supplementation of governmental provision of goods, so it also predicts that there will be little or no undersatisfied demand—and, hence, little or no extra-governmental provision —if all consumer demands are essentially the same. One testable implication of this proposition is that if two political units (e.g., countries) differ in the degree of "heterogeneity" of their populations—in the degree of income inequality, diversity of cultural heritage or other demand-determining variables—the unit with the lesser heterogeneity will, *ceteris paribus*, have a lower level of private and voluntary-sector provision of collective-type goods or their substitutes.[33] In short, that country will tend to have a relatively larger public sector. Conversely, in a country, or smaller political unit, with great *in*equality in the level of individuals' demands for collective goods, the level of private and voluntary-sector supplementation of public-sector provision will be larger and the public sector will be relatively small.[34]

It follows that one should not be surprised to find that the governmental "provision" (that is, support) of, say, church activities—which have a significant public-good component for persons of that faith but not for others—is apparently great in countries where virtually the entire population shares one religion (e.g., Spain and Ireland). Similarly, it is not surprising that the public provision (financing) is far lower in a country such as the United States, where religious preferences (including atheism) are far more diverse; it seems likely that no religion in the U.S. could win the support of a majority of voters to the cause of substantial public financing of its activities.

If our hypothesis is correct and the heterogeneity of demand for collective goods influences the degree of supplementation in private and voluntary markets, then the relative size of the government sector would be expected to be a function of that heterogeneity. As one test of this hypothesis an analysis has been undertaken of determinants of the changing relative size of the total non-defense government sector (federal, state, and local) in the U.S. for various years over the time period 1929–1969.[35] Explanatory variables in the model include, as proxies for heterogeneity of demand, the variances in income, age, and education, and measures of diversity of religion, race, and urban-ness; *mean*

or other average values (e.g., percent of population that is urban) for these six variables were also included. Of particular interest are the variance measures, for our model suggests negative signs for them. That is, it predicts that government (non-defense) expenditures as a percentage of total GNP will be a negative function of the variation in demand for collective-consumption goods, and we are taking heterogeneity of population characteristics to reflect such variation.

The regression model we used is handicapped by having only 10 degrees of freedom (24 observations and 13 independent variables); nonetheless, our findings, while not overwhelming, are rather encouraging. First, inclusion of the heterogeneity measures actually increases the significance levels of the variables reflecting mean values. Second, the F-ratio is extremely significant (.0000 level). Third, of the six heterogeneity variables, five were negative, as hypothesized. Only two of the five—religion and race—were significant, however, a result that may reflect the multi-collinearity and the relatively small number of degrees of freedom. Variance in income, for example, had the anticipated negative relationship with the relative size of the government sector, but the coefficient was significant at only the .33 level.

Further analysis of time-series data would be useful in order to test for the impact of population heterogeneity. Similarly, cross-country comparisons of the size of the government sector would be useful. Lack of data on dispersions of demand variables, however, is an obstacle to such studies.

6. Industry Analyses—the Market Niches of the Public, Private, and Voluntary Sectors

The emphasis on the respective roles of the private and voluntary sectors vis-à-vis the public sector has led me to a new type of "industry study." Each service provided by governments (at this stage no distinctions between *levels* of government are being made) can be usefully thought of as a portion of an industry that also may include a voluntary and a private for-profit sector.

One principal hypothesis is that in such industries in which the government is providing essentially a *private* good, the undersatisfied demand will be manifest principally in the private for-profit sector, and the voluntary sector will be comparatively small. Similarly, if the government services are substantially *collective*, then supplementation will tend to be in the voluntary sector, with the private for-profit sector being relatively small.

Several small-scale industry studies for the U.S. are now under way to shed light on this hypothesis—the hospital industry, the library industry, and the employment-service industry. Findings to date will be briefly summarized below. Other studies are planned for the education, fire, police-security, information-research and possible other industries.

The hospital industry is a very complex, multi-product industry. Measured by expenditures, it is 22% public, 73% voluntary, and 5% private for-profit. Much of what any hospital does involves provision of *private* services, but some outputs—such as medical care for the indigent, cancer research programs, and the stand-by availability of intensive-care units, open heart surgery facilities, and 24-hour emergency rooms that charge prices below profit-maximizing levels —appear to be of a collective-good type, benefiting many potential users simultaneously.[36] I have attempted to test the propositions that public and voluntary hospitals provide essentially identical services, while for-profit hospitals less commonly provide the kinds of collective goods just noted.[37] Data are limited but our tentative conclusion is quite supportive of our hypotheses regarding the roles of the three sectors. Consider emergency departments in small hospitals (under 50 beds), for example: in 1969, 80.3% of public hospitals and 78.5% of non-profit hospitals had such a department (a statistically insignificant difference), but only 58.7% of the private hospitals (less than the public and voluntary percentages at the .05 level of significance). In general, for all of the six hospital-size classes, each of the 21 hospital services that we had previously identified as of the collective type were provided predominantly in public and voluntary hospitals, as expected, while each of the nine services identified as private-type were provided predominantly in the private, for-profit hospitals, again as expected.[38]

We have found that private hospitals are significantly less likely than public or voluntary hospitals of similar size to have a social work department, a family-planning service, an organized outpatient department, a teacher-internship program or a cancer research program, to name some of the collective-type services studied. If there were no difference between the "collective" (government plus voluntary non-profit) and the for-profit hospitals with respect to frequency of provision of these various services, we would have expected to find that each service was equally likely to be found in either class of hospitals. In fact, however, this was decidedly not the case. Thus, our findings to date do tend to confirm the hypothesis that the collective and for-profit hospital sectors do differ in the extent of their provision of "collective-type" services.

Similarly, we have compared the relative frequency with which various services are found in the governmental and the voluntary hospitals. The hypothesis is that there will be no difference between these two sectors. We have found, after controlling for hospital size (as was also done above), that 60 percent of the services were provided with greater relative frequency in the government hospitals and 40 percent in the voluntary hospitals. This 60-40 split is significantly smaller than the 78-22 split found between the combined government-voluntary hospitals and the for-profit hospitals; this suggests that, as expected, the governmental and voluntary hospitals are more like each other than they are like the for-profit hospitals. Nevertheless, the 60-40 split is still significantly different from 50-50 (at the .05 level) and this does not support the hypothesis that the governmental and the voluntary hospitals are the same.

Further study and the search for better data seem to be warranted. We have barely scratched the surface of the research effort that is required to discern the differences in outputs by type of hospital, since we have not considered community size, the *total* supply of hospital services in the "market area," or a variety of demand-side variables.

In the case of libraries, data have thus far been exceedingly difficult to find concerning the relative size of the three sectors.[39] One might guess, *a priori*, that the stand-by services of a research library have a significant collective-good component, whereas the provision of current best sellers is essentially a private good, entering the utility function of only the person who holds it at the moment. This being so, we would expect the bulk of the *public* library services—which do *not* consist of current best sellers—to be supplemented in the *voluntary* sector, while the private-good services of the public libraries are supplemented in the *private* sector. Both appear to be the case. There are, in addition to libraries of "private" universities (voluntary, in our terms), various "non-profit" libraries such as the John Crerar Library in Chicago and the Pierpont Morgan Library in New York City. There is a private for-profit sector, too; small and diffuse, it consists of the rental libraries that specialize in the private good, current best sellers; these libraries can be thought of as supplementing the level of public provision for persons who do not want to wait weeks or months to obtain today's favorite books.

The most appropriate way to define any industry is always a problem, given the availability of close substitutes, and this is certainly the case for libraries. There is a question as to whether it is useful to define an industry to include only *rental* activities; the availability of books for outright purchase is, of course, a close substitute for library books—a private-good substitute.

Turn now to the employment-service industry.[40] Government employment services appear to provide an essentially private service in matching a worker with an employer. This being so, we would expect that persons seeking to supplement this government service, seeking a higher-quality or faster service, would turn to the *private* market, there being little rationale for attempting to organize in the voluntary sector. Indeed, given the apparently small collective-component of employment services, and the variation in the extent to which people wish to use formal employment services, we expect the size of the public sector to be small. Again, our early findings support the expectation. In a study of hiring by 75 Chicago firms in the period 1960–63, it was found that among both blue-collar and white-collar workers, almost 98 percent found their jobs through *private*-market channels—including referrals by other workers, direct firm applications, advertisements and employment agencies; nearly 2 percent found their jobs through the *public* employment

service; and only about one-half of one percent, through the *voluntary* sector, including agencies of churches and charities.[41]

Our hypothesized difference between the types of good provided publicly and privately—between the collective-consumption good and the private-good substitute—is confirmed again in the employment-service industry. *All* employment agencies obtain job-market information as part of their activities. "Unlike a public intermediary, however, private agencies quite naturally endeavour to keep this information on vacancies and workers confidential . . . . Thus, . . . private agencies *restrict* the flow of information in the market."[42] By so doing, they can convert a collective good, of the type provided by government employment services, into a private-good substitute. Such information restriction, however, while privately rational, is socially inefficient.

Conclusion

To summarize: first, the expectation is that supplementation of public-sector provision of any good will either be overwhelmingly voluntary or overwhelmingly private, depending on whether the publicly provided good is primarily a collective or an individual good. In addition to the extent of "collectiveness" of the governmentally provided good, the relative size of the voluntary and private sectors in any industry will depend on the state of technology—specifically on the closeness of private-good substitutes for collective goods and on the relative production costs.

Second, in a model attempting to explain the relative size of the government sector in some industry or for some country, a significant variable is likely to be the heterogeneity of demand—the smaller the heterogeneity the smaller the non-governmental sector. In a simple majority-vote model without vote-selling, the greater the undersatisfied demand—that is, the demand in excess of the median—the larger will be the combined private and voluntary-sector outputs, and, hence, the smaller the proportion of industry output that is governmentally provided, for that is determined solely by the median. In another model that, for example, weighted voters by intensity of preference, the resulting predictions would differ quantitatively;

yet we would still expect that greater variation in consumers' demand would lead to relatively greater extra-governmental provision and a relatively smaller role for the public sector.

The analytic approach suggested here points to a number of testable propositions, involving historical, international, and three-sector industry studies (governmental, for-profit, and voluntary). While a number of suggestive pieces of evidence from preliminary studies have been presented in this paper, much more study is needed, both positive and normative, of the interrelated roles of the governmental, private, and voluntary sectors of the economy.

Notes

1. For a useful survey of the varied conceptions of "public" goods, see Peter O. Steiner, "Public Expenditure Budgeting" (Washington, D.C.: The Brookings Institution, 1969).

2. This is not to suggest that the distinction is an insignificant one, but it is not examined in this paper. Indeed, there does not appear to be an accepted theory of the choice between government production and purchase.

3. See Anthony Downs, *An Economic Theory of Democracy* (New York: Harper and Row, 1957); Duncan Black, *The Theory of Committees and Elections* (Cambridge, U.K.: Cambridge University Press, 1958); James Buchanan and Gordon Tullock, *The Calculus of Consent* (Ann Arbor: University of Michigan Press, 1962); Jerome Rothenberg, "A Model of Economic and Political Decision-Making," in Julius Margolis, ed., *The Public Economy of Urban Communities* (Wash., D.C.: Resources for the Future, Inc., 1965); Roland N. McKean, *Public Spending* (New York: McGraw-Hill, Inc., 1968), especially ch. 9; and Hirschel Kasper, "On Political Competition, Economic Policy, and Income Maintenance," *Public Choice*, Spring 1971, pp. 1–19.

4. The majority rule approach may produce intransitive orderings. Moreover, since specific issues are generally decided by political representatives, not by voters—at least not *directly* by voters— ". . .the link between individual utility functions and social actions is tenuous, though by no means completely absent." [Kenneth Arrow, "The Organization of Economic Activity: Issues Pertinent to the Choice of Market Versus

Non-Market Allocation," in Robert Haveman and Julius Margolis, eds., *Public Expenditures and Policy Analysis* (Chicago: Markham Publishing Company, 1971), p. 70.]

5. Albert Breton posits that individuals are more likely to engage in political activity the greater the difference between their actual and their desired position. ("A Theory of the Demand for Public Goods," *Canadian Journal of Economics and Political Science*, November 1966, pp. 455–467.)

6. For a recent discussion of the issue, see W. Lee Hansen and Burton A. Weisbrod, "Who Pays for a Public Expenditure Program?," *National Tax Journal*, December 1971, pp. 515–17.

7. Paul A. Samuelson, "The Pure Theory of Public Expenditure," *Review of Economics and Statistics*, November 1954, pp. 350–56.

8. The horizontal price function assumes implicitly that the cost of supplying marginal quantities of the good (national defense, a park, or anything else) is constant, but this is simply for convenience of exposition and is in no way required.

9. In this model each consumer is seen essentially as a price taker and quantity adjuster; the tax-price rule, although a variable, is constrained. For a related discussion see Leif Johansen, "Some Notes on the Lindahl Theory of Determination of Public Expenditures," *International Economic Review*, September 1963, pp. 346–58.

10. The emphasis in the public goods literature has been on the quantity of the good *supplied* being equal for all consumers. (P. Samuelson, *op. cit.*; J. Buchanan, "Notes for a Theory of Socialism," *Public Choice*, Spring 1970, pp. 29–43, esp. p. 30.) The comparative lack of attention to inequality in *demands* (as portrayed in Figure 1) is, in my view, unfortunate. If some particular national defense expenditure, or some lighthouse—to use two favorite examples of public goods—were demanded by only one person while all other persons were indifferent to them, these goods would presumably be provided in optimal quantities in the private sector. The point is not that such examples are realistic, but only that insofar as the key concern of analysts is the efficiency of private markets— the market-failure issue—the crucial characteristic of a "public" (collective-consumption) good

is *not* its technical *availability* to many persons simultaneously, but the number of simultaneous *beneficiaries*—persons into whose utility functions it actually enters.

In Figure 1, for example, the good is, I suggest, *not* a "public good" for person 2, and is not a public good for person 3 in quantities greater than Q_1. Rather than regard a particular good as simply a public good, it is useful to think of women's public goods, water-sports enthusiasts' public goods, Catholic public goods, "hawks" and "doves" public goods, etc. [Cf. Albert Breton, "Theory of Government Grants," *Canadian Journal of Economics and Political Science*, May 1965, pp. 175–87, who refers to local, metropolitan, state, national, and world goods, but not to the aggregations of consumers (beneficiaries) discussed here.] The figure also illustrates that a commodity can be a public good for some persons—entering all of their utility functions simultaneously—and also a public "bad" for others, such as person 1, entering negatively into their utility functions.

In a recent paper Samuelson has also come to the conclusion that a public good is most usefully defined in utility terms, not in terms of "technological" characteristics of a good. See his "Pure Theory of Public Expenditure and Taxation," in J. Margolis and H. Guitton, eds., *Public Economics*, Proceedings of a Conference Held by the International Economic Association, St. Martin's Press, New York, 1969, pp. 98–123.

The *extent* of benefits to each consumer is a second determinant of the degree of private-market failure. If, for example, a lighthouse entered positively into the utility functions of a number of consumers, but was of trivial value to most, the "few" large demanders might well reach a bargain that led to essentially an optimal level of provision.

11. This paper does not explore the possible game-theoretic aspects of decision-making in the three sectors when collective-consumption goods are involved.

12. This was discussed at the theoretic level by Charles Tiebout, "A Pure Theory of Local Government Expenditure," *Journal of Political Economy*, October 1956, pp. 416–24. See Wallace Oates, "The Effects of Property Taxes and Local Public Spending on Property Values: An Empirical Study of Tax Capitalization and the Tiebout Hypothesis," *Journal of Political Economy*, November-December 1969, pp. 957–71, for a recent empirical examination of the Tiebout model of choice among local governmental units. Jerome Stein, in an analysis of optimal policy toward environmental pollution, has assumed away the issue of heterogeneous demands among consumers by assuming that. . .each locality is composed of identical households. . . .'" ("Micro-Economic Aspects of Public Policy," *American Economic Review*, September 1971, p. 534).

13. Discussing the exclusion principle with regard to collective goods, Kenneth Arrow illustrates the problem with the example of pollution: ". . .it would have to be possible in principle to supply [clean air or water] to one [person] and not the other. . . .But this is technically impossible." (In Haveman and Margolis, *op. cit.*, p. 65.)

But it is *not* impossible. Air and water filters, air conditioning, and bottled water perform precisely this exclusionary function, as do vacations to places "where the sky is not cloudy (or smoggy) all day."

14. A striking illustration of the difference between a public-good solution to a problem and a private-good solution is the adjustment to environmental hazards in less-developed areas. Where malaria-carrying mosquitos breed, the public goods, area-wide DDT spraying and swamp drainage, might be used; and among the private-good substitutes are mosquito nets and migration away from the area.

An incisive analysis of the difference between public sector and private sector rationing policies, involving money prices and waiting-time prices, is in Donald Nichols, Eugen Smolensky, and Nicholas Tiedeman, "Discrimination by Waiting Time in Merit Goods," *American Economic Review*, June 1971, pp. 312–23.

15. A vertical summation of the seven demand curves in the diagram would intersect with the commodity cost curve, *7P*, at quantity Q_2, the output level that would be Pareto optimal if tax prices were set equal to marginal valuations of each consumer. While the optimal output exceeds the "actual" in this illustration, this would not be the case under some other political-decision rule.

16. For a useful introduction to some issues in this area, see William Vickrey, "One Economist's View of Philanthropy," in *Philanthropy and Public Policy* (New York: National Bureau of Economic Research, 1962).

17. Eli Ginzberg, *et al.*, discuss a wide range of "non-profit" organizations. The authors observe that "Many non-profit organizations perform functions that are identical or closely allied to those performed by government. In fact, many governments weigh carefully whether to establish or expand certain activities under their own aegis; whether to seek to accomplish their goals by relying on non-profit organizations; or whether, as frequently happens, to do part of the work themselves and to look to non-profit organizations to do the rest." [Eli Ginzberg, Dale L. Hiestand and Beatrice J. Reubens, *The Pluralistic Economy* (New York: McGraw-Hill Book Co., 1965), p. 23.]

On the relationship between the activities of non-profit and private for-profit organizations, however, Ginzberg, *et al.*, are not in agreement with the analysis in this paper. They state: "The key difference between the private sector and the not-for-profit sector is not in the economic activities which they undertake, but in whether they are organized in order to seek a profit from their efforts." (*Ibid.*, p. 30.) These authors make no distinction between collective-consumption goods and their private-good substitutes.

18. If it is true that there exists a non-public voluntary sector that provides collective-consumption goods, as do governments, then it really is "...a shame that public goods are called 'public'." (Otto A. Davis and Andrew B. Whinston, "On the Distinction Between Public and Private Goods," *American Economic Review*, May 1967, p. 372.)

19. Our emphasis on the similarity of outputs of the government and voluntary sectors, and on the qualitatively different outputs of the private-sector substitutes, may be contrasted with the dichotomization presented by James Buchanan and Gordon Tullock. They emphasize the distinction between *government* provision and "private," where the latter includes both for-profit and "voluntary, but cooperative" organizations (Buchanan and Tullock, *op. cit.*, p. 50). The

similarity of voluntary, "philanthropic" activities and the activities of the "free market" is also expressed by Robert A. Schwartz who states that individual philanthropic efforts "supplement the functioning of the free-market system....," rather than supplementing the outputs of public markets, the emphasis suggested in the present paper. (Schwartz, "Personal Philanthropic Contributions," *Journal of Political Economy*, Nov.-Dec. 1970, p. 1291.)

20. For a theoretical analysis of organizational costs, related to both population heterogeneity and the nature of political decision rules, see J. Buchanan and G. Tullock, *op. cit.*, esp. p. 115.

21. James M. Buchanan has recently focused attention on "the effects generated by governmental organization of the supply of goods and services that are largely if not wholly 'private,' that is, fully divisible into separate and distinguishable units of consumption." "Notes for an Economic Theory of Socialism," *Public Choice*, Spring 1970, p. 29.

22. Cf. "Wagner's Law" which, though variously interpreted, predicts that the public sector will grow with per capita income. For the original exposition, see Adolf Wagner, *Finanzwissenschaft*, Leipzig, 3rd edition, 1890; for discussions in English see Richard M. Bird, "Wagner's Law of Expanding State Activity," *Public Finance*, No. 1, Vol. 26, 1971; and Bernard P. Herber, *Modern Public Finance: The Study of Public Sector Economics* (Homewood Ill.: Richard D. Irwin, Inc., 1971), pp. 371–81.

23. W. K. Jordan, *Philanthropy in England, 1480–1660* (London: George Allen and Unwin, Ltd.), 1959, *passim*.

24. Robert Nelson, "An Address to Persons of Quality and Estate, Ways and Methods of Doing Good," published in 1715, cited by B. Kirkman Gray, *A History of English Philanthropy* (London: Frank Cass and Company Limited, 1905), p. 95.

25. Jordan, *op. cit.*

26. Gray, *op. cit.*, p. 25.

27. James Buchanan and Gordon Tullock, *op. cit.*, p. 49.

28. At the theoretical level this similarity has been discussed by Thomas R. Ireland and David B. Johnson, *The Economics of Charity*

(Blacksburg, Virginia: Center for the Study of Public Choice, 1970).

29. John Stuart Mill recognized that societal reinforcement could serve as a possible inducement to people to incur costs for which there was otherwise little or no private benefit. Although arguing that "...it is a proper office of government to build and maintain lighthouses...[since] no one would build lighthouses from motives of personal interest....," and that few people would undertake scientific research without government support, he also mentioned the possibility that "great public spirit" might motivate some persons to undertake activities that are "of great value to a nation." [John Stuart Mill, *Principles of Political Economy*, Vol. III, (Toronto: University of Toronto Press, 1965), p. 968.]

30. See Harold Hochman and James Rodgers, "Pareto Optimal Redistribution," *American Economic Review*, Sept. 1969, pp. 542–57; Robert A. Schwartz, "Personal Philanthropic Contributions," *Journal of Political Economy*, Nov.-Dec. 1970, pp. 1264–91; and T. Ireland and D. Johnson, *op. cit.*

31. Note that income-tax deductibility of such "donations" would never be a sufficient inducement for giving, as long as marginal tax rates confronting an individual were less than 100 percent.

32. The market for human blood is discussed in the most thought-provoking book by Richard Titmuss, *The Gift Relationship* (London: George Allen and Unwin, 1971).

33. The influence of "subcultures," defined by homogeneity of ethnicity and income, on voting behavior is examined in James Q. Wilson and Edward C. Banfield, "Public-Regardingness as a Value Premise in Voting Behavior," *American Political Science Review*, December 1964, pp. 876–87.

34. The relationship between population heterogeneity and degree of public-sector activity has also been considered in terms of the costs of organization; the greater the heterogeneity, the larger the prospective costs of organizing through political markets relative to the costs of organizing private firms. (See Buchanan and Tullock, *op. cit.*, especially Ch. 8.)

For an interesting paper describing the variation in size of public sectors among a number of countries, and attempting to explain it by "ideological differences," see Anthony King, "Ideologies as Predictors of Public Policy Patterns: A Comparative Analysis," paper presented at Meeting of American Political Science Association, Chicago, September 1971.

35. In this work I have been aided by Jennifer Gerner.

36. This form of "option demand" was discussed by Burton Weisbrod, "Collective-Consumption Services of Individual-Consumption Goods," *Quarterly Journal of Economics*, August 1964, pp. 471–77. See also subsequent comments in the *Quarterly Journal of Economics* by M. Long, May 1967, pp. 351–52; C. Lindsay, May 1969, pp. 344–46; D.R. Byerlee, August 1971, pp. 523–27; and C. Cicchetti and A.M. Freeman, III, August 1971, pp. 528–39. Much of the debate has concentrated on whether an option demand would be present if the seller were a perfectly discriminating monopolist. Since real-world sellers are limited, however, in the knowledge required for such discrimination, and in addition seldom have substantial monopoly power, the option demand (or consumer surplus, in the case of zero uncertainty or of risk neutrality) will tend to be greater than zero for such stand-by services as those considered in the hospital industry.

37. In this hospital study I have been assisted by A. James Lee.

38. For further discussion and analysis of our findings concerning the three sectors of the hospital industry, see Burton A. Weisbrod and A. James Lee, "A Model of Demand for Collective Goods, as Applied to the Hospital Industry," paper presented at the Conference on Medical Economics from an Industrial Organization Viewpoint, Northwestern University, May 19-20, 1972 (mimeo).

39. In the library work I am being assisted by Donna Beutel.

40. In the employment-service project I am being assisted by Marc Bendick, Jr.

41. Computed from data in Eaton H. Conant, "An Evaluation of Private Employment Agencies as Sources of Job Vacancy Data," in *The Measurement and Interpretation of Job Vacancies*, A Conference of the National Bureau of Economic Research (New York: National Bureau of Economic Research, 1966), pp. 519–47.

42. *Economic Council of Canada, Eighth Annual Report*, Ottawa, September 1971, p. 189.

ARTICLE 4 ————————————
The Independent Sector: An Overview
Virginia Ann Hodgkinson and Murray S. Weitzman

The independent sector encompasses what has been called the third, or voluntary, sector of American life. It is a diverse sector including a wide range of institutions such as religious organizations, private colleges and universities, foundations, hospitals, day care centers, youth organizations, advocacy groups, and neighborhood organizations, to name but a few. But its community transcends sectors and includes millions of individual donors and volunteers, as well as the social responsibility programs of corporations.

For the purposes of this profile, the independent sector consists of those nonprofit organizations that are defined as 501(c)(3) and 501(c)(4) organizations under the federal tax code for tax-exempt organizations. These organizations include educational, scientific, religious, and other charitable organizations, as well as private foundations, corporate and community organizations, and civic and social welfare organizations. These organizations represent a major part of all nonprofit organizations. Social responsibility programs of corporations are described and counted as contributors to the sector, but tables [not included here] giving trends in numbers, programs, and finances for the independent sector refer only to those organizations that have the particular tax-exempt status as just defined.

The purpose of this statistical profile is to describe the dimensions and scope of the independent sector. In order to reveal the dimensions of the independent sector in relation to other nonprofit organizations, however, some of the tables

presented in this profile show totals for all non-profit organizations [not included here].

Since colonial times, the independent sector has been an important part of American life and, accordingly, of the economy. The purpose of this chapter is to estimate the dimensions of this sector within the context of the American economy. The independent sector interacts with both the for-profit and the government sectors in many ways, but especially through its contributions to the quality of life and community development. This chapter provides an overall description of the size of the independent sector in terms of its share of national income, its share of total U.S. employment and earnings from work, and the number of organizations it encompasses. The final section of this chapter addresses significant trends in the independent sector in relation to other sectors of the U.S. economy. Hence, this chapter summarizes the major findings about this sector, which are detailed in the chapters that follow.

National Income Originating in the Independent Sector

One way to determine the size and scope of the independent sector is to estimate its proportion of national income. The national income of the United States for a given year is the measure of the total factor costs, including labor and property earnings, associated in the production of the goods and services of the economy. The figure excludes depreciation allowances and indirect business taxes that are included in the larger aggregate figure of the gross national product. For all private, nonprofit organizations and government, only compensation of employees (including wages and salaries and supplements to wages and salaries, such as employer contributions for social insurance, pension plans, and health insurance) is counted in estimates of national income. Returns from capital are included only for the for-profit sector.

In 1984, the total national income, including the assigned or imputed value for volunteer time and unpaid family workers, was $3.144 trillion. The independent sector's share of national income was 5.6 percent, $176.3 billion. In comparison, in 1984, the for-profit sector's share of national income was 79.3 percent and the government's share was 14.5 percent.

From 1977 to 1982, the independent sector grew faster than business or government. Total national income originating in the independent sector increased 85 percent in current dollars, from $84.4 billion to $155.8 billion. In comparison, total national income originating from business increased 62 percent and that from government, 65 percent. As a result of this differential growth, the independent sector increased its proportion of national income from 5.2 percent in 1977 to 5.8 percent in 1982.

From 1982 to 1984, the rate of growth in the independent sector declined relative to the rate for business and government. During these two years, total national income in current dollars increased 13 percent in the independent sector, 19 percent in business, and 14 percent in government. In 1984, as a result of this decline in growth, the independent sector's share of national income declined to 5.6 percent.

Imputing the assigned value of volunteer time is important in calculating this unique contribution to the independent sector and, accordingly, to American society. In 1984, the value of volunteer time increased the independent sector's share of national income by $74.4 billion (2.4 percent). If the value of volunteer time had not been imputed, the independent sector's proportion of national income would have been only 3.2 percent, $101.9 billion.

nonprofit organizations' total earnings from work. Of this $157.1 billion, $90.6 billion (approximately 4.2 percent of total earnings from work) represented earnings contributed through work by volunteers to the independent sector. In 1984, business accounted for 75.3 percent of total earnings from work, and government accounted for 16.8 percent.

Between 1977 and 1982, total earnings from work in the independent sector increased 83 percent, from $75.9 billion to $139.2 billion. Earnings of paid employees increased 73 percent, and earnings contributed by volunteers increased 100 percent. Total earnings from work increased 64 percent in the business sector and 53 percent in government. Because total earnings from work grew faster in the independent sector than in other sectors of the economy, the independent sector increased its share of total earnings from work from 6.7 percent in 1977 to 7.5 percent in 1982. From 1982 to 1984, the trend was reversed. Total earnings from work increased 12.9 percent in current dollars, from $139.2 billion to $157.1 billion. Earnings of paid employees increased to 12.3 percent, and earnings contributed by volunteers increased by 13.7 percent. During these two years, total earnings from work increased 18.7 percent in business and 13.3 percent in government. As a result of a slower rate of growth in the independent sector, its share of total earnings from work declined from 7.5 percent in 1982 to 7.2 percent in 1984.

Earnings from Work in the Three Sectors of the Economy

In 1984, Americans earned approximately $2.169 trillion. Wages and salaries accounted for $1.835 trillion (84.6 percent); $233.7 billion (10.8 percent) came from self-employed workers; $93.5 billion (4.3 percent) was contributed by volunteers; and $6.8 billion (0.3 percent) was contributed by unpaid family workers. In other words, in 1984, earnings from work in this nation would have been $2.069 trillion rather than $2.169 trillion were it not for the assigned value of $100 billion in unpaid earnings.

In 1984, the independent sector accounted for $157.1 billion of total earnings from work (7.2 percent). This represented 90.8 percent of

Employment in the Independent Sector Compared with Employment in Other Sectors of the Economy

Employment is defined as paid wage and salary workers working either full-time or part-time, self-employed workers, and persons working without pay, including volunteers and unpaid family workers. In 1984, an estimated 119.80 million people worked and 112.65 million (94.0 percent) received pay. Another 6.0 percent contributed work for no pay. Of this group 5.5 percent, the equivalent of 6.6 million, were volunteers and 0.5 percent were unpaid family workers. Volunteer employment was found primarily in the independent sector. In 1984, volunteers accounted for 4.7 million full-time equivalent employees in the independent sector, 514,000 in other nonprofit organizations, 191,000 in business, and 1.2 million in government.

Between 1977 to 1982, employment grew at a faster rate in the independent sector than in business or government. The total number of paid employees increased 18.5 percent and full-time equivalent volunteers, 37.0 percent. Total employment—both paid and volunteer—increased 25.4 percent. During this period, the total number of employees in business increased 9.8 percent and the number in government, 6.9 percent. As a result of this rate of growth, the independent sector's share of total employment increased from 8.6 percent in 1977 to 9.7 percent in 1982.

From 1982 to 1984, growth in total employment was slower in the independent sector than in business. During this period, paid employees increased 2.1 percent and full-time equivalent workers increased 4.8 percent, for an overall increase of 3.2 percent in total employees. During this same period, the total number of employees in business increased 6.5 percent and in government, 2.2 percent. Had total volunteer employment not increased almost 5 percent from 1982 to 1984, the decline in the rate of growth in employment in the independent sector would have been more severe. From 1982 to 1984, the independent sector's share of total employment declined from 9.7 percent to 9.5 percent.

The Size of the Independent Sector Compared with the Size of Business and Government

Counting the number of institutions in the independent sector is a challenge, for their number includes nonprofit, tax-exempt organizations as determined by tax law and religious institutions, which by law do not have to report to the federal government. But the independent sector also includes several thousand organizations defined as public charities which had annual revenues of less than $5,000 and are not required to apply for tax-exempt status; the social responsibility programs of corporations which file different tax forms; and nonprofit organizations that file omnibus tax forms covering many separate organizations nationwide, such as the Boy Scouts. In other words, one tax form can cover several hundred separately incorporated Boy Scout Councils.

Of the estimated 1.2 million nonprofit organizations in 1984, the U.S. Department of the Treasury reported approximately 838,000 on its Master File. The number of nonprofit organizations included in the independent sector are covered in the 501 series of the tax code for tax-exempt organizations. The Internal Revenue Service reported that 352,884 organizations in 1984 had 501(c)(3) tax-exempt status. These organizations engaged in all types of educational, research, scientific, religious, philanthropic, and other charitable activities. Other tax-exempt organizations serving primarily charitable purposes also are included in the definition of independent sector organizations in this profile. There were 130,344 organizations in the 501(c)(4) category (composed primarily of civic leagues and social welfare organizations) reported by the Internal Revenue Service in 1984. By law, 501(c)(3) organizations are eligible to receive contributions that are tax-deductible for both individuals and corporations. Although 501(c)(4) organizations are tax-exempt, generally these organizations cannot receive tax-deductible contributions.

Churches are tax-exempt by statute and do not have to file for tax-exempt status with the Internal Revenue Service. About 50,000 religious organizations are included among the 483,000 independent sector organizations reported in 1984, but they are primarily social welfare organizations or schools run by the various denominations. If a church does apply for tax-exempt status, it receives blanket coverage for all its units. Because of such rulings, and because many small organizations with less than $5,000 in revenues do not have to apply for tax exemption, the number of organizations in the independent sector is greatly understated.

The most recent estimate of the number of churches, synagogues, and other religious organizations was 338,244 for 1983-84, as reported in the annual *Yearbook of American and Canadian Churches* and the *Statistical Abstract of the United States*. Adding independent sector organizations together with churches brings the total number of independent sector organizations estimated in 1984 to approximately 821,000. All told, there were approximately 19.4 million such entities. In 1984, the independent sector accounted for 4.2 percent of all organizations operating in the United States. Private, nonprofit organizations represented about 6 percent of all organizations. In comparison, the 18.1 million business organizations that filed federal income tax forms represented approximately 94 percent of total U.S. organizations, while all government entities (federal, state, and local) accounted for 82,000 units—less than 1 percent of all organizations. In terms of numbers of entities, the independent sector's share declined from 4.6 percent in 1977 to 4.2 percent in 1984, indicating that the rate of establishment of new organizations was slower in this sector than in business.

Selected Indicators for the Independent Sector in Relation to Those for Other Sectors of the Economy

A quantitative indicator of the independent sector's commitment and contribution to improving the quality of life for individuals and communities can be conceived as the relationship between its total expenditures and the total American population. Because the data are not available solely for the independent sector, expenditure estimates have been developed which refer to all private, nonprofit organizations. However, more than 90 percent of both employment and earnings from work of all private, nonprofit organizations are estimated to be attributable to the independent sector.

Current operating expenditures for all nonprofit organizations are estimated to have increased from approximately $18.2 billion in 1960 to $209.8 billion in 1984. In constant 1972 dollars, these expenditures ranged from $36.2 billion in 1960 to $80.7 billion in 1984, an increase of 123 percent. During this period, the American population increased from 181 million to 238 million, 31 percent. Therefore, in 1972 dollars, nonprofit organizations expended $200 in 1960 and $341 in 1984 for every man, woman, and child in the United States, which amounts to an increase of 71 percent for the period. However, from 1981 to 1984, per capita expenditures showed no real increase.

The previous total and per capita expenditure estimates for all nonprofit organizations

did not include assigned dollar value of time contributed by volunteers, but such estimates can be made by adding to total expenditures the assigned dollar value estimates for volunteer contributions. When these computations are made, per capita expenditures in current dollars for all nonprofit organizations increase from $451 to $616 in 1977 and from $886 to $1,235 in 1984. The inclusion of assigned dollar values for time contributed by volunteers increases the per capita expenditures by 37 percent in 1977 and by 39 percent in 1984.

Another quantitative indicator of the independent sector's relationship to American society is a comparison of its absolute and relative share of services (in terms of expenditures stemming from nonprofit organizations) compared with total personal consumption expenditures and total services. In current dollars from 1960 to 1984, expenditures for nonprofit organizations increased from 13.9 percent of total services in 1960 to a high of 19.1 percent for a three-year period extending from 1973 and ending in 1975, a year in which a trough in the business cycle was recorded in March. After 1975, expenditures of nonprofit organizations as a percentage of all services tended to decline; the next peak was 18.5 percent in 1982, a year in which that recession bottomed out in November. The estimate for 1984 is 18.0 percent, which is the lowest percentage since 1968, when it was 17.5 percent.

Personal consumption expenditures on services from nonprofit organizations rose from 5.6 percent in 1960 to a high of 9.2 percent in 1983, and declined slightly, to 9.0 percent, in 1984. As a percentage of the gross national product, expenditures on services in nonprofit organizations rose from 3.6 percent in 1960 to a high of 6.0 percent in 1983, and declined to 5.7 percent in 1984. Essentially, the trend for consumption of services originating in the nonprofit sector as a percentage of all personal consumption expenditures has continued upward with few interruptions along the way. However, for the past four years (on the basis of the revised series for 1982 through 1985), the trend at best shows no change in the consumption of services originating in the nonprofit sector either as a percentage of personal consumption expenditures or as a percentage of the gross national product.

Another quantitative indicator of any enterprise is its capacity to increase employment. This is particularly true in the independent sector, which is highly labor-intensive. Overall, employment in the independent sector grew faster than all employment from 1972 to 1982. From 1982 to 1984, employment grew faster in other sectors than in the independent sector. The annual rates of change in employment in the independent sector were 3.6 percent from 1972 to 1977, 3.5 percent from 1977 to 1982, and 1.0 percent from 1982 to 1984. In comparison, the annual rates of change for all nonagricultural employees were 2.3 percent from 1972 to 1977, 1.7 percent from 1977 to 1982, and 2.7 percent from 1982 to 1984. Employment for all nonagricultural employees increased 22 percent from 1972 to 1982 and 5.5 percent from 1982 to 1984, while the number of total employees in the independent sector increased 43 percent from 1977 to 1982 and 2.1 percent from 1982 to 1984.

The rate of growth in employment in the independent sector varied by subsector. The major growth from 1972 to 1982 was in health services, up 59 percent, and social services, up 99 percent. During this period, employment in arts and cultural organizations increased 75 percent, but from a much smaller base. But employment at colleges and universities; religious organizations; and civic, social, and fraternal organizations increased at a slower rate than all employment in nonagricultural jobs.

When cost-containment measures for health care and federal funding cuts for many social service programs were instituted in the early 1980s, employment growth in these subsectors slowed down. The annual growth rate of 4.6 percent between 1977 and 1982 in the health services subsector declined to less than 1 percent between 1982 and 1984, and total employment in hospitals declined slightly from 1982 to 1984. The trend was similar in social services. The total annual increase in employees declined from 5.2 percent between 1977 and 1982 to 3.5 percent between 1982 and 1984.

Finally, the summary of these various indicators provides an overview of the independent sector in comparison with business and government from 1977 to 1984. The independent sector grew faster than other sectors of the economy between 1977 and 1982, but this trend reversed from 1982 to 1984. National income in the independent sector increased as a proportion of total national income from 5.2 percent in 1977 to a high of 5.8 percent in 1982, and then declined

to 5.6 percent in 1984. Total earnings from work in the independent sector grew from 6.7 percent as a proportion of total earnings from work in 1977 to 7.5 percent in 1982, and declined to 7.2 percent in 1984. The total number of employees in the independent sector increased from 8.6 percent in 1977 as a proportion of total employment to 9.7 percent in 1982, and declined to 9.5 percent in 1984. The number of organizations in the independent sector declined as a proportion of all organizations from 4.6 percent in 1977 to 4.2 percent in 1984.

Essentially, the rate of growth that typified the independent sector throughout the 1970s came to a halt in 1982. By 1984, the independent sector was declining in comparison with other sectors of the economy on most national indicators. If these trends continue, they could indicate a weakening of this sector's ability to meet the demand for services.

The organizations and people who constitute the independent sector contribute significantly to the welfare of the American people in such important areas as health, education, social services, culture, and philanthropy. The various dollar estimates for the sector presented in this chapter, as well as the comparisons that have been made with the general economy, do not always accurately reflect the independent sector's value to individuals, families, and communities. Nonetheless, these estimates do generally indicate the size, scope, and importance of the independent sector to American society.

References

Commission and Chief Counsel, Internal Revenue Service. *1985 Annual Report.* Washington, D.C.: Government Printing Office, 1986.

Council of Economic Advisers. *Economic Report of the President.* Various editions. Washington, D.C.: Government Printing Office.

The Gallup Organization, Inc. *Americans Volunteer 1985.* Washington, D.C.: INDEPENDENT SECTOR, 1986.

——— . *Americans Volunteer 1981.* Washington, D.C.: INDEPENDENT SECTOR, 1982.

Jacquet, Constant H., Jr., ed. *Yearbook of American and Canadian Churches,* annual. National Council of the Churches of Christ in the U.S. Nashville: Abingdon Press.

Rudney, Gabriel, and Weitzman, Murray. "Significance of Employment and Earnings in the Philanthropic Sector, 1972–1982." Working Paper No. 77. New Haven: Program on Non-Profit Organizations, Yale University, 1983.

U.S. Department of Commerce. Bureau of the Census. *Statistical Abstract of the United States.* Various editions. Washington, D.C.: Government Printing Office.

———. Bureau of Economic Analysis. *Survey of Current Business.* Various issues, but particularly the July issues. Washington, D.C.: Government Printing Office.

U.S. Department of Labor. Bureau of Labor Statistics. *Employment and Earnings.* Various issues. Washington, D.C.: Government Printing Office.

ARTICLE 5
A History of the Discipline
Stephen R. Block

The discourse of any intellectual field of study is built upon its history. Nonprofit management is both a new and old discipline. Unlike the study of political science which can more easily be traced to Plato and Aristotle, or the field of medicine capable of being traced to Hippocrates of Cos, the lineage of nonprofit management is not as clear-cut and precise. The ancestry of nonprofit management descends from several areas. To understand the historical development of the discipline of nonprofit management, it will be essential to trace four of the field's major origins: (a) the roots of charity and philanthropy; (b) the development of the role of the volunteer; (c) the evolution of tax exemption; and (d) the adaptation of management technologies into the nonprofit sector. In addition to these four major areas, the nonprofit sector is steeped in the traditions of Americans' associating and joining in order to further a cause, to become integrated into a community or to form social and business

ties. On this subject, Milofsky (1979) proposes that nonprofit organizations are rooted in at least six traditions of American participation. An examination of the philosophical and contextual differences between the six participatory traditions may shed some additional light on the foundation of nonprofit management knowledge, in addition to gaining an understanding of the remarkable fortitude of today's nonprofit organizations. Knowledge about the organizations' historical participatory roots may also help us understand the contemporary nonprofit organization's management policy preferences, in addition to explaining why the nonprofit organization can become what Max Lerner (1983) has called a "collective expression which belies the outward atomism of American life" (p. 82).

The goal of this chapter is to see how the roots of the discipline have an impact on what scholars have done and what they may do. Without a historical perspective, research in the field lacks continuity and cumulative relevance. There has been little, if any, self-scrutiny as a discipline and a dearth of information about the evolution of this emerging profession as a whole. However, there are many signs to suggest that charity, philanthropy, and volunteerism fit squarely in the evolutionary design of the discipline. There is less clarity or evidence of events that historically led to management technology transfers or the significance of tax exemption in the development of a nonprofit curriculum. Nevertheless, attention will be given to these areas as a "kind" of conceptual bridge leading from a vast arena of activities and interest in charity, philanthropy, and volunteerism to a new "promised land" marked by books, courses, degree programs, and research.

While it is important to describe the developmental phases that have helped shape the discipline, one limitation must be acknowledged. There do not appear to be clean boundaries, no clear line at which one stops and another begins, between these fields of concern. But the new discipline of nonprofit management did start from somewhere. Indeed, as we stand in the midst of volumes of books, courses, training programs, and development of university degree programs, it is possible to look back and trace the emergence of a discipline from the relative dominance of these core areas.

The Roots of Charity and Philanthropy

Ideologically, nonprofit organization management is derived quite centrally from the historical ethos of charity and philanthropy. Early precepts of giving and taking care of community needs are part of the evolutionary development of today's nonprofit organization (Academy for Educational Development, 1979). Even if a contemporary nonprofit organization is not directly concerned with the compassionate service program interests of charity and philanthropy, it cannot deny, as part of the voluntary sector, that its heritage includes accumulated contributions of those that served and gave to others in need.

Sir Arthur Keith (1949) suggests that the concept of charitable giving may have biological aspects. According to Keith, the concept of altruism is "both inborn and instinctive" (p. 451). While Keith's evolutionary notion is quite interesting, there is no biological human trait known as altruism. Perhaps Keith's idea is not too far afield, however, given the innate altruistic qualities which are known to exist among certain insect and animal groups (Kalmus, 1963). Nevertheless, it is more likely that the origins of charity and philanthropy began with early human civilizations. For pragmatic reasons, primitive societies were the first to develop and exhibit the concept of charity or philanthropy (Bakal, 1979). In these early societies, the welfare and preservation of individuals and families required the community to share in the tasks of food gathering, hunting, and providing shelter.

As ancient societies became more complex, the idea of sharing in order to help, protect, and preserve the community was also advanced through the incorporation of rules and structure. It is known, for example, that the Babylonians were instructed through their Code of Hammurabi to protect the less fortunate of the community (Harper, 1904). This Code instructed the community to care for the poor, the widows, and the orphans. In addition to the instructive charitable nature of the Code, George (1972) indicates that the Code is one of the earliest illustrations of management thought which is characterized by a set of inscribed laws relating to a variety of business practices.

Religious doctrines, ideology, and influences on giving, compassion, and personal sacrifice are a significant part of the heritage of charity and philanthropy which eventually resulted in the development of the nonprofit sector. The notion of blessed giving existed in ancient Egypt at least 2,300 years before the Christian era (Weaver, 1967). At that time, the Egyptian aristocracy would be buried with rich gifts for the gods as well as with records of gifts that were given to the poor and needy during the aristocrat's lifetime. Propitiating the gods with gifts and records of good deeds was an attempt to satisfy the gods and assure the preservation of a restful afterlife for the giver. On the other hand, charity in the pre-Christian Greek tradition was exemplified by a different type of giving. The Greek philosophy of charitable giving aimed to fortify the community by giving community-oriented gifts rather than to help individuals who were poor. In this respect, Weaver (1967) suggests that the Greek concept of giving is closer to the guiding philosophy of modern philanthropic foundations than to the Judeo-Christian concept of charity. For example, Greek benefactors were known to have given their cities gifts of theaters and stadiums, and modern philanthropists have similarly donated large community-oriented structures such as libraries, universities, and museums.

Ancient roots also appear to extend to Biblical and religious concepts of charity. The Old Testament, for example, in the Book of Deuteronomy, commands individuals to tithe a portion of their produce and share it with the widows and hungry children in one's own community and with transients. Similar to the early Jewish concept of community giving (Frisch, 1969), as outlined by Maimonides, the early Christian communities valued the idea of helping the infirm and the poor. In fact, the scriptures of Matthew detail the Christian expectation of sharing. These Christian expectations to help the poor and needy were exacerbated during a crisis period brought on by the Bubonic Plague, and also in response to the period of the Reformation. In fact, during the period of the Reformation, individual begging was looked on askance and organized community responses were developed not only to assist the poor and homeless, but also to deter individual alms-begging and almsgiving.

In England, the influence of the Reformation and the breakup of the feudal system were among the social changes that led to an organized response to the plight of the poor. Municipalities, responding to the discontent caused by the social instability of unemployment and vagrancy, created ordinances about begging and work expectations (Leonard, 1965). As problems controlling the begging behavior of the indigent poor and the able-bodied poor increased and were not fully deterred by the laws in the townships, the Parliament responded by the creation of the English Poor Laws in 1601. The Poor Laws of 1601 codified the following three principles for overseeing the plight of the poor: public responsibility, local responsibility, and relatives' responsibility (Leiby, 1978). The fundamental element in the poor laws was the expectation that individuals should work and take care of their individual needs and the needs of their families. In the event that an individual could not fulfill this work ethic, the community was obliged and responsible for providing, at least minimally, for the needs of these poor individuals. While the English Parliament was the first to establish these laws (Rose, 1971), the early colonial settlers adopted similar principles. The advance of the poor laws in the United States became guiding principles for the development of both charitable and philanthropic activity. In addition, the poor laws set a philosophy and community ethos for the eventual creation of government intervention in problems of welfare and American statutes on social welfare.

The early implementation of poor laws in the United States were mainly at the state level. In different communities, responsibility for looking after the poor was delegated to county officials. In some situations, local churches assumed this responsibility. As the population of the country grew, the ability to monitor the poor became unwieldy. This led to the development of almshouses (also known as the "poorhouse" or sometimes referred to as "the workhouse"). These early prototypes to the modern concept of work-relief programs were intended to discourage loafers, and simultaneously to provide some adequate support to the real needy.

By the latter half of the nineteenth century, urban centers began to become overpopulated as a result of the industrial revolution and immigration of millions of people from Europe. During this period, the responsibility to oversee the poor was overwhelming and the ability to provide adequate care, services, or almshouse shelters was beginning to come under scrutiny. For example, members of the Conference of Charities and Correction reported on a variety of concerns and difficulties found in the state's role and ability to administer the almshouse. In many cases, admissions were made to the deplorable and harsh living condition in the almshouses (Bruno, 1957). In response to the recognition that there was a significant contrast in the quality of life for the rich and the poor, the charity organization and settlement movement began to flourish.

As with the poor laws, the concept of the settlement house was an English invention. In fact, many American settlement houses were modeled after the Toynbee House settlement in England, including Hull House in Chicago (Addams, 1910), the Neighborly Guild in New York, South End House in Boston, and Northwestern University Settlement House in Chicago (Bruno, 1957). The settlement house consisted of a home situated in poor neighborhoods whose residents consisted of more fortunate individuals, committed to working with community members and helping them to improve their situation. In fact, the goal of the settlement house was to provide social change through a community center of hope and opportunities, and to improve one's condition in life (Trolander, 1975). For example, many settlement houses offered day nurseries, playgrounds, lecture series, meeting places, and advice on civic matters. In addition, some settlement houses offered counseling services to promote the growth of individuals and families.

Concurrent with the settlement house movement, the Charity Organization Society movement, again an English invention, took hold in the United States. Originally, the advocates of this secular movement were inspired by clergymen who were committed to an effective system of private charity (Leiby, 1978). The framers of this movement advanced the concept of indiscriminate almsgiving to a rationalized approach where conscientious thought was given to long term consequences and outcomes. Indeed, this movement appears to have been the forerunner of the modern philanthropic foundation or corporate contribution, based on a rationale of purpose or philosophy to achieve a prescribed outcome. Furthermore, this movement attempted to be scientific by both collecting data about charitable agencies and by coordinating the effects of several of the charities. Members of a Charitable Organization Society, like the modern foundation, would review applications for financial assistance. In addition to providing some emergency relief, the society might arrange for a host of individuals to provide professional services to the poor, such as legal advice, spiritual guidance, and medical care. This movement became stronger after the turn of the twentieth century with growing interest and financial support among businessmen and chambers of commerce in addition to the traditional support of wealthy family contributors.

Support for the organized charities interested businessmen because they expected that private charities would be better administered than public charities. Following from this expectation, donors began to push for the development of a federated organization of charities that would regulate fundraising efforts and the distribution of monies. In addition, the federation would be able to oversee the quality of management of the charitable organizations. The development of the Cleveland Federation for Charity and Philanthropy in 1913 was one such example and also was a pioneering model for financial federations in other cities (Waite, 1960). The development of federations was also a critical step toward the creation of paid staff positions to manage the federations and the charitable organizations.

During the same developmental period, the creation of periodicals devoted to furthering knowledge about the charitable interests and the settlement house interests appeared. In 1909, Paul Kellogg produced *The Survey* with the financial underwriting of the Russell Sage Foundation. *The Survey* was a national magazine directed toward both the paid and volunteer charitable worker; it was intended that this magazine should envelop earlier periodicals which had a local, not a national, constituency. *The Survey* supplanted at least three periodicals: the Boston magazine *Lend-A-Hand*; the New York City publication, *Charities Review*; and the Chicago publication, *The Commons* (Chambers, 1971).

The Development of the Volunteer Role and Its Importance

While volunteerism has been said to be a very American tradition (Commission on Private Philanthropy and Public Needs, 1975), the rise and development of the concept and the practice of volunteerism parallels the evolution of charity and philanthropy. One way of viewing the Americanization of volunteerism is that it springs from the phenomena of early American community participation. In 1835, Tocqueville (1969), among the earliest observers of America's rich tradition of volunteerism, described voluntary association as uniquely American and influential for promoting America's democratic character. Tocqueville's astonishment with the Americans' propensity toward volunteerism is evident in his following quote:

> Americans of all ages, all stations in life, and all types of disposition are forever forming associations. There are not only commercial and industrial associations in which all take part, but others of a thousand different types—religious, moral, serious, futile, very general and very limited, immensely large and very minute. Americans combine to give fêtes, found seminaries, build churches, distribute books, and send missionaries to the antipodes. Hospitals, prisons, and schools take shape in that way. Finally, if they want to proclaim a truth or propagate some feeling by the encouragement of a great example, they form an association. In every case, at the head of any new undertaking, where in France you would find the government or in England some territorial magnate, in the United States you are sure to find an association. (Tocqueville, 1969, p. 513)

While its American heritage and evolvement may be similar to charity and philanthropy, volunteerism reflects some different and special aspects that deserve separate attention. Indeed, volunteers may be philanthropic or charitable but there is a wide range of voluntary activity open to individuals that goes beyond the intentions of charity. Manser and Cass (1976) define volunteerism as follows:

. . .those activities and agencies arising out of a spontaneous, private (as contrasted with governmental) effort to promote or advance some aspect of the common good, as this good is perceived by the persons participating in it. These people are volunteers —persons who, motivated by varying degrees of altruism and self-interest, choose to give their time and talents freely. (p. 42)

To differentiate the role of volunteerism from acts of charity or philanthropy is a difficult task. While all three activities require some form of action, the actions of charity and philanthropy may require little, if any, direct involvement with the beneficiaries. Volunteerism, on the other hand, is a very active process that requires active involvement with either the beneficiaries directly or an organization or group that serves a specific population. Unlike the action of charity or philanthropy, however, the activities in volunteerism do not necessarily benefit an underprivileged, poor, or needy group. In fact, many associations, agencies, or groups that utilize the volunteer may be far from experiencing financial deprivation.

Clarification of this concept and role of volunteer is useful for a broader understanding of the role of the volunteer and its importance to nonprofit organization management. In fact, an examination of the role of the volunteer has an important place in the study of nonprofit organization management because voluntary action undergirds the foundation of leadership of the nonprofit organization through the volunteer's legal/public commitment of the board of directors role. In addition to the governance aspect, quite often there are other critical and valuable areas in which the volunteer has impact on the management of the nonprofit organization, such as the development of financial resources, or in some cases, assistance in the service delivery of programs.

Smith and Freedman (1972) report that sociologists have written the most about the subject of the volunteer and the activity of joining or associating to fulfill a group objective. Looking at this source of literature, one finds it speaks mainly to the distinction between types and functions of voluntary groupings, reasons for joining, and personal satisfaction, and success

in volunteering. For example, in an early work, Rose (1954) distinguished between two types of voluntary associations, "expressive groups" and "social influence associations" (pp. 50–71). Expressive groups are defined as volunteers who band together to fulfill a personal interest such as involvement in a hobby or sport. In contrast, the social influence association is comprised of volunteers who are interested in creating political or social changes that impact on the broader society. The settlement house movement of the early twentieth century would be characteristic of this type of social influence association. Merton (1976), on the other hand, examined the internal structure of the voluntary association, particularly the leadership role of the volunteer versus the skilled professional. Likewise, Sills (1957, 1968) and Zald (1970) were concerned with the internal processes of the voluntary association. While Sills (1957, 1968) suggests that conscious controls over positions or responsibilities of the volunteers will influence the satisfaction and success levels of the volunteers, Zald (1970) believes that a written protocol or standard for tasks and responsibilities can attribute to voluntary action success.

On the issue of why individuals join voluntary associations, Jacoby and Babchuk (1963) suggested that individuals join because of the level of personal agreement they have with the organization's objectives. However, in a survey of individuals graduating from a professional school of social work, Judd, Block and Jain (1985) found that an individual's agreement with a professional association's organizational policy or objectives actually had minor bearing on whether the individual joined that professional voluntary association. Instead, these researchers found that individuals joined a voluntary professional organization because of the tangible benefits that were available to them in addition to a sense of professional identity that was derived from belonging.

Were it not for a long-standing American tradition of volunteerism, it would seem odd that, in an economic democracy that promotes capitalism, there are individuals who are willing to work for a voluntary cause/organization without financial compensation (Jones & Herrick, 1976). Marts (1966) suggests that the generosity and willingness of volunteers to give their time and energy is a result of the experiences and inspiration of American freedoms. This same concept was undoubtedly behind O'Connell's (1983) collection of readings entitled *America's Voluntary Spirit*. Bremner's (1960) view is a bit more sober. According to Bremner, the Americanization of volunteerism had its start in the colonization of the New World. The number of activities involved in the colonization required a variety of personal acts of benevolence: conversion of natives to Christianity, taming the wilderness, the cultivation of land and crops. Likewise, Max Weber spoke of the American tendency to participate in voluntary activities as a socially constructive process for bridging the Old World's hierarchical society to the New World's rugged individualism (Lerner, 1983). The joining process permitted individuals to form ties and develop positions of status in the community. Indeed, the idea of an individual joining and actually belonging to a voluntary association serves very important sociological and psychological needs.

Participation and Its Influences on the Nonprofit Sector

According to Hougland and Shepard (1985), the extent to which participation in voluntary organizations is in reality a voluntary response has been unresolved in the voluntary action literature. In fact, Palisi (1972) suggests that cultural factors such as group values, social influences, and opportunity may account more accurately for why individuals participate in voluntary organizations.

Whether one has been completely autonomous in deciding to "volunteer" is, in part, an important sociological question for understanding the dynamics of participation. A more important concern for this study, however, is the implication that participation in voluntary organizations has had a modifying influence on the culture of America. Related to this point, Milofsky (1979) suggests that an examination of six American traditions of participation will reveal how their influences on America have rooted the nonprofit sector and nonprofit organizations. The six traditions of American participation include the Protestant patrician, urban ethnic, free professional, organizational professional, interorganizational coordination, and corporate philanthropic traditions.

The Protestant Patrician Influence

The Protestant tradition was first influential in America in the mid-1800s, during the development of a strong Protestant middle class. Protestant followers were interested in community reforms as reflected in their belief in the "Protestant Ethic." One aspect of this ethic was that individuals are responsible for developing their own Christian character and for assisting other individuals to develop as well. Furthermore, ecclesiastical authority associated with this ethic asserted that individuals have a moral responsibility to contribute their own personal skills and monies to help others in need. This resolve, or philosophy, created a framework and a sense of moral obligation for an individual to participate in voluntary efforts.

According to Seeley, Junker, Jones, Jenkins, Haugh, and Miller (1957), the Protestant tradition draws certain social boundaries around an individual's willingness to volunteer. Generally, individuals are willing to donate money or services that will assist others in need, but the volunteers would prefer not to become directly involved with those they assist. Verba and Nie (1972) explain this ideology as a typical expression of wealthy or upwardly mobile, powerful individuals. In other words, voluntary leadership in nonprofit organizations preserves or creates a civic leadership position consistent with Protestant ideas about civic association.

Milofsky (1979) characterizes the influences of the Protestant patrician tradition on nonprofit organization management to include a distinctive style of leadership. Leadership in this mode is strongly committed to a community-based model with an emphasis on resource development and concrete services to those in need, such as providing hot meals and shelter. In addition, this style of leadership is weakest in responding to organizational crises and will tend to replace managers rather than revise program services.

The Urban Ethnic Influence

Unlike the Protestant influences of concern for helping others, the urban ethnic tradition evolved as a reactive response by ethnic groups who believed they were being poorly treated in American society. To protect themselves, ethnic groups began forming their own nonprofit organizations in the form of mutual aid societies. In addition to preserving cultural traditions, mutual aid organizations were helpful in assisting community members with recreational events, religious celebrations, and personal crises, such as death or illness. The development of these ethnic-related nonprofit organizations appears to have been greatest during a surge of refugee resettlement after the turn of the century through the 1920s.

The emphasis on ethnic-related community development nonprofit organizations continues to play an important role in culturally diverse communities. Interestingly, the recognition that ethnic communities have played a valuable support and assimilation role in America accounts for more recent federal incentive grants to establish mutual assistance associations for America's newest pool of refugees from Southeast Asia (Office of Refugee Resettlement, 1986). However, there is a down side to ethnic-related service organizations. By providing services to members of only one type of cultural heritage or religious system, these organizations may unwittingly reinforce cultural separation and isolation from other ethnic groups. This may also account for a vast duplication of social services in a community.

In the ethnically oriented organization, management decisions may be strongly influenced by ethnic beliefs rather than by commonly held management principles. Even with the introduction of the professionally educated nonprofit manager into this work setting, the cultural traditions of the organization may still have prevailing influence on service delivery. This is surely the case with religion-affiliated nonprofit organizations that grew out of the ethnic urban tradition, such as Jewish Family Services, Lutheran Social Services, and Catholic Community Services. In addition, Berger and Neuhaus (1977) suggest that organized ethnic/cultural groups have a strong mediating role in society which can have a strong influence on the type of policy and services developed and offered by nonprofit and governmental entities.

The Free Professional Influence

Unlike the religious and sociopolitical needs of individuals, which influenced the Protestant tradition, or the need to protect cultural and ethnic identities, evidenced in the urban ethnic tradition, the free professional tradition extends beyond these distinctive dimensions and is characterized by individuals sharing similar professional interests. This tradition is representative of controls over educational and technical skills that have been defined as critical for entering into, belonging to, and practicing within a particular profession. For example, all attorneys must attend a law school and pass a bar exam and all physicians must attend medical school and serve an internship and residency in addition to passing exams.

As a response to the acquired skills and achievements that must be attained in order to become a member of a profession, many nonprofit organizations have been spawned to protect the distinctive interests of their professional members. In fact, many professionals join trade associations to protect the values of their discipline, to assist in their own definition of being a professional, and to receive special support and tangible products like journals and continuing education programs (Judd, Block, & Jain, 1985). The National Association of Social Workers, the American Society for Public Administration, and the American Medical Association are just three examples of nonprofit organizations that exist to protect the practice domain of its members. In addition to the influence on standards and policies that professionals have over their own professions, Milofsky (1979) suggests that professionals also have an influencing effect on the norms and policies of society by controlling reports of professional research and determining what will be considered acceptable performance criteria for delivering professional services.

The Organizational Influence

This participatory tradition is a direct outgrowth of the professionalization of occupations and is characterized by many of the larger nonprofit organizations that have had both staff and volunteer involvement. Furthermore, the organizations that can be described by this tradition are church organizations or sect-like groups that have a large constituency, such as the "Y." In this situation, professional staff are oriented toward their job out of professional/occupational and career interests. In contrast, volunteers affiliate with an organization based on a personal ideology or belief system. Frequently, policy decisions or management styles are reflected by the influences of the constituency served by the organization rather than by the leadership of the organization.

The Interorganizational Influence

After World War I, the successful development of the urban ethnic tradition's ability to create community support and social services organizations found itself in a conflict. Many organizations with similar service delivery missions were in competition with one another for funding. Rather than create a situation that could discourage "giving," the concept of the community chest was introduced. The community chest movement permitted agencies to focus on service delivery while the community chest organizers would specialize in the task of fundraising.

In the 1960s and 1970s, many specialized service delivery organizations embarked on their own resource development programs relying largely on government funded grant programs. In the 1980s, with severe cuts in federally funded grant-in-aid programs, the reliance on a community-based fundraising effort has become, once again, more predominant and necessary for many nonprofit organizations to survive.

The Corporate Philanthropic Influence

There are three important influencing factors that led to the development of American corporate philanthropy. One factor is represented by the personal giving philosophy of Andrew Carnegie (1900), who believed that philanthropic giving was a social obligation, akin to the Protestant patrician tradition, rather than a religious obligation.

Carnegie's personal point of view is illustrated through his often cited remark that "The man who dies rich, dies disgraced." He was an adherent of providing philanthropic support to programs and special projects that would benefit and provide strength to the community. A second factor is characterized by the philanthropic philosophy of John D. Rockefeller, I (1908). Unlike Carnegie, Rockefeller followed a traditional, religious doctrine of giving. Both Carnegie and Rockefeller paved the way for large, organized, corporate giving.

The third important influencing factor was the development of tax credits and tax deductions which led to corporate incentives to give to tax-exempt nonprofit organizations. The practice of giving to nonprofit organizations benefits both the nonprofit organizations and the corporate giver (Galaskiewicz, 1986). The corporation gains important public relations and community benefits, while the nonprofit's financial capacity to deliver services is improved.

The Evolution and Impact of Tax-Exempt Status

Tax exemption is an essential element of the American economy and the advantages of obtaining the 501(c)(3) tax-exempt status for the nonprofit organization is an integral part of forming and maintaining charitable, educational, scientific, as well as religious organizations. In fact, the review provided by Clotfelter (1983) demonstrates the importance of tax deductions as incentives to giving to charitable causes. The relationship between tax credits and charitable giving is so strong that the contemporary nonprofit organization would adversely suffer if not for the benefit of not having to pay income taxes, as well as the incentives of the tax deduction given to its contributors (Clotfelter, 1983). While tax exemption is a popular inducement for present day charitable giving, the concept of tax exemption is not a twentieth-century phenomenon. In fact, Lashbrooke (1985) dates at least the implementation of tax exemption to the Old Testament in Ezra 7:24:

> . . .also we certify you, that touching any of the priests and Levites, singers, porters,

Nethinim, or Ministers of this House of God, it shall not be lawful to impose toll, tribute, or customs upon them. (p. 3)

In the modern era, government-endorsed tax exemption in the United States has been a common practice since the nation's founding (Hopkins, 1983). In fact, religious organizations have been spared the burden of paying taxes by statutory omission at all levels of government, and this practice was sustained during the first federal income tax that spanned 10 years from 1862 to 1872. It was not until 1894, however, that expressed tax exemption was defined in tax legislation and became the official policy of the United States (Smith & Chiechi, 1974). Section 32 of the Revenue Act of 1894, imposed a flat 2% tax on profitable income and complete tax exemption on charitable income. The 1894 statute also provided for the tax exemption of charitable, religious, educational, fraternal organizations, as well as certain savings and insurance institutions.

The 1894 act was overturned by a constitutional challenge to the rental income tax portion of the law which was not apportioned by population. Although the 1894 act was repealed, its influence on subsequent revenue legislation was measurable. Every revenue act since 1894 has bestowed tax-exempt status to religious, charitable, and educational organizations.

In addition to the historical precedent that established an unwritten rationale for tax exemptions for nonprofit organizations, Congress articulated a supporting rationale in its Revenue Act of 1909, exempting organizations which by their nature could not generate sufficient income. In seven revenue acts, Congress identified the many different types of organizations, noted in Table 3.1, which would be protected from tax liabilities. According the Gelb (1971), the Federal Government was concerned about the possible reduction of gifts to charitable organizations following the 1917 increase in individual income taxes to pay for the expenses of World War I. In response to their concern, the tax law was expanded to permit the deduction for an individual's gift to charitable organizations.

Another rationale that has supported the existence of tax exemption is the government's recognition that without tax-exempt organizations, the burden for many social programs undertaken by the nonprofit sector would need to be assumed by the government. On the other hand, Hansmann (1981) suggests that there are not sufficient arguments for justifying the exemption of taxes for the range of nonprofit organizations that Congress has allowed. Weisbrod (1977), for example, determined that the nonprofit sector often imitates the governmental sector's services to the general public.

Since 1954, tax exemption has been described best in the Internal Revenue Code 501(c)(3). Organizations that fit into this category agree to devote their net earnings to the mission

TABLE 3.1 Organizations Protected from Tax Liabilities

Revenue Act by Year	Tax Exemption by Type of Organization
1894	Charitable, educational and religious organizations
1909	Labor, horticulture, agriculture
1913	Business leagues, chambers of commerce, scientific organizations, social welfare organizations, mutual cemetery companies
1916	Public utilities, social clubs, land banks, title holding companies, farming associations
1918	Societies for prevention of cruelty to animals
1921	Foundations, community chest funds
1976	Homeowner associations, fishing associations, organizations promoting national and international sporting competition

SOURCE: E. C. Lashbrooke, *Tax Exempt Organizations*. (Westport, CT: Quorum Books, 1985.)

of the organization and they further agree that individual directors and officers will not receive any part of the net earnings. Another common thread in all organizations with the 501(c)(3) status is the advantage of attracting deductible contributions. It is largely this "benefit" that adds to the unique management characteristic of the nonprofit organization and sometimes its preoccupation with fundraising events and grant proposal writing. In fact, in 1984, the nonprofit sector received $68 billion from private contributions and approximately an equivalent amount from all levels of government sources. Clearly, the incentive for both the individual and corporate giver has been tied to the deductibility of tax-exempt gifts.

The nature of the giving/tax-exempt relationship is such an important phenomenon it can only gain increased importance as an area for research and study within the nonprofit discipline. More recently, Harvard Professor Lawrence Lindsey (Independent Sector, 1986b) has studied the potential impact of the Tax Reform Act of 1986 and its consequences on the nonprofit sector. Lindsey projects an $11 billion loss in charitable giving as a result of tax reform:

1. $6 billion from the expiration of the charitable deduction for non-itemizers.
2. $1 billion from inclusion of gifts of appreciated property on the alternative minimum tax.
3. $4 billion from lowered marginal tax rates.

The implications of a large financial shift in the nonprofit sector is another consideration for the need for nonprofit managers to be astute managers. According to the Independent Sector, the financial losses due to the Tax Reform Act of 1986 will be distributed among the subsectors (fields of practice) in the following way (see Table 3.2).

In addition to Lindsey's projections, there is agreement among nonprofit tax policy researchers that the level of an individual's after-tax income will have an important consequence on whether the individual gives, and how much, to charitable organizations in very active fundraising campaigns. In the situation of severe losses in charitable donations as projected by Lindsey, nonprofit organizations could point out to potential contributors the increased need for contributions as a result of drastic reforms. The outcome of such appeals is, of course, unpredictable. Beyond this, the impact on the creation or maintenance of private foundations is another area that is potentially affected by shifting tax liabilities. On this point, Odendahl (1985) reported that since the Tax Reform Act of 1969, there has been a decline in both the number of new grant-making foundations and the number of grant awards over $10,000.

In summary, a history exists that interweaves the development of the field of nonprofit management with the history of tax exemption and other tax policies that impact propensities toward charitable giving. In addition, there is a continued need for data collection to study the ongoing patterns of giving and its relationship to the effective management of nonprofit organizations.

TABLE 3.2 Projected Loss of Charitable Giving: A Result of the Tax Reform Act of 1986

Type of Organization	Amount of Loss	Percent Change
Religion	−5.24	−12.9
Education	−1.58	−16.5
Social	−1.18	−15.5
Health	−1.58	−15.5
Cultural	−.68	−16.5
Other	−.68	−14.3

SOURCE: Independent Sector, "Projected Loss of Charitable Giving." (Memo to Members, Attachment #7, October 8, 1986b.)

From Management to the Emergence of Nonprofit Management

A common thread among the three sectors (business, government, and the nonprofit sector) is the necessity for organizational management. There are, however, distinguishing features in each sector's orientation to the practice and study of management. In fact, the distinctive characteristics of each sector have given rise to the three types of professional fields of management practice and disciplines: business, public administration, and now, in emergent form, nonprofit management. The term "nonprofit management" is a singularly difficult one. It denotes a function of management in the nonprofit sector and implies a different type of "management" than the type found in business or in government. To understand the critical differences between nonprofit management, business management, and public management, and to learn more about the emergence of this younger (nonprofit management) practice field and discipline, it is imperative to trace its management roots beginning with the development of management as a professional field of business practice and as an academic discipline that grants degrees, such as the MBA and DBA. There is also a kinship to the field of public administration that requires identification.

Although the evolution of management is difficult to reconstruct (George, 1972), the activity of management is ubiquitous throughout the history of humankind. Some forms of management activities were a likely part of prehistoric civilization. When men hunted in bands, traveled in groups or developed tribes and villages, some form of division of labor and leadership surely marked the arrangement of management functions. According to George (1972), the imposition of taxes, the amassing of wealth, the management of major construction projects, such as pyramids, and the creation of city governments are examples of traceable practices of management during ancient civilizations.

Clearly, the advance of management tasks, functions, and management tools evolved over time. At the end of the Dark Ages, financial management and control tools such as record keeping and double entry bookkeeping were developed in response to the growth of commerce in the Mediterranean (Drucker, 1974).

Shipbuilding and outfitting the ships during the Middle Ages also saw the development of business-related activities such as warehousing, assembly line practices, and personnel supervision. But it was the period of the Industrial Revolution, predominantly in England, that witnessed the introduction of improved manufacturing technologies and improved methods of production. These improvements were largely responsible for the shift from home-based production activities to the factory system and its need for a large labor pool. The need for factory employees influenced a shift from an agrarian society to an industrial one.

The development of the capitalistic system and a growing interest in economics were highlights of this era (Massie, 1979). Adam Smith stressed economic concepts in his 1776 publication *The Wealth of Nations* and contributed greatly to the fundamental management concept of "division of labor." There were other important economic and management concepts and practices that resulted from the boom in manufacturing. One such important practice included the idea of incorporating a business for the purpose of raising capital through the sale of shares in the business. This development in entrepreneurism also paved the way for later thinking about the functions of ownership as separate from the functions of management.

The impact of the new industrial methods was also felt in the United States by the mid-nineteenth century. America's growing reliance on a railroad system provided an opportunity for railroad investors to pursue profits, while engineers pursued the mastery of management over complex organizations. The administration of complex railroad organizations became the focus of information sharing and the subject of papers presented at meetings of the American Society of Mechanical Engineers (ASME).

At one of the ASME meetings in 1886, Henry R. Towne, president of the Yale and Towne Manufacturing Company, presented his paper on "The Engineer as Economist." Towne called for the recognition of industrial management as a science and equal in importance to that of engineering. Towne emphasized the need for management to be an independent field of study with its own professional literature and professional membership society. Towne's comments marked the beginning search for a science of management and is the one event that is most often referenced as the pioneering inspiration for the development of the scientific management movement (Bedeian, 1978).

While Towne called for an independent field of study, an interesting and related development occurred just 5 years prior to his eventful address. A Philadelphia manufacturer, Joseph Wharton, recognized the need for a special management curriculum to educate and prepare individuals for a career in management. Acting on his belief, Wharton financed America's first school of management, the Wharton School, at the University of Pennsylvania. In 1898, 17 years after the Wharton School was started, the University of California and the University of Chicago launched their own business schools. A little more than a decade later the idea of business management education was becoming well institutionalized with at least 30 schools of business management in the country.

The promulgation of ideas about management as a profession inspired another Philadelphian, Frederick Taylor, to seriously question the role and responsibilities of management. As an engineer, Taylor became very interested in the idea of maximizing the performance of workers with a minimal level of stewardship. Taylor envisioned a system of cooperation and improved production through appropriate standards and rewards, a system also based on the harmonious relationship between worker and management. The development of these pioneering ideas gave Taylor recognition as the "father of Scientific Management" (Massie, 1979). Taylor's four major concepts and philosophy of management appeared in his 1911 book, *The Principles of Scientific Management*. Taylor (1911) stressed the following:

1. Develop a science for each element of a man's work, which replaces the rule-of-thumb method.
2. Scientifically select and then train, teach, and develop the workman.
3. Heartily cooperate with the men so as to insure all of the work being done in accordance with the principles of science which have been developed.
4. There is an almost equal division of the work and the responsibility between the management

and the workmen. The management should take over all the work for which they are better fitted than the workmen. (pp. 36–37)

Aside from Taylor, the insight of other supporters of scientific management figured predominantly in the development of management thought, especially in areas of efficiency (Brandeis, 1914) and motion studies (Gilbreth, 1911). Henry L. Gantt (1916, 1919), for example, contributed to the ideas of pay plans and managerial leadership, but is probably best known for his development of a charting system (the Gantt Chart) for the planning and controlling of production tasks. Another staunch advocate of the scientific method was Harrington Emerson, best known for his book *The Twelve Principles of Efficiency* (1913). Emerson was among America's first management consultants (George, 1972) who attempted to guide managers to focus on the creation of wealth through the fulfillment of company objectives while preserving company resources through the use of conservation policies. Henry Fayol, a French industrialist, who also focused his study and writing on management principles, was among the first writers to classify different management functions. In 1916, he published *Administration Industrielle et Generale*, which was later translated into English in 1930 and 1949. In Fayol's schema, management was divided into five major functions, including planning, organizing, commanding, coordination, and control. In addition, Fayol developed fourteen management principles to emphasize the managerial functions (Fayol, 1949).

The first twenty years following the turn of the twentieth century were critically important for the development of management as a field of professional practice and as an emerging academic discipline. It was during this era that Towne's earlier dream of the creation of professional societies, books, and university programs was fulfilled. In 1911, for example, approximately 300 educators and practitioners assembled at Dartmouth College's Amos Tuck School of Administration and Finance. This meeting marked the first formal attempt to pave an academic direction for the field of management. Another academic first came in 1915, when Horace B. Drury of Columbia University published *Scientific Management: A History and*

Criticism. This publication is considered to be the first doctoral dissertation in management (Mee, 1963), and, therefore, a hallmark for the fledgling academic discipline. During this same period, in 1914, the first professional management society was founded as the Society to Promote the Science of Management, later evolved into the Taylor Society, and eventually became the Society for Advancement of Management. The American Management Association, another bastion in the management field, was also formed during this developmental period.

Although the scientific management movement contributed greatly to the growth of management practice and thought, it was not without criticism. Critics claimed that the application of scientific management was a dehumanizing process because its primary concern was production and not the needs of the individual worker. As a response to the criticism of scientific management, the behavioral school of management emerged. Advocates of the behavioral school believed that management must focus on the individual worker and his/her relationship to other workers and the work environment.

One of the most important developments in this behavioral management movement was a research project launched in 1924 at the Hawthorne Plant of the Western Electric Company. The original study intended to examine the relationship between changes in environmental illumination on worker productivity. Worker productivity was not adversely affected by changing the level of illumination, and, surprisingly, worker productivity increased. In 1927, Elton Mayo was invited to conduct another experiment to further examine and explain the unanticipated worker reactions of the previous experiment. Five years of various testing procedures and manipulating the working environment conditions did not adequately explain increases in worker productivity. In retrospect, Mayo and his colleagues were able to determine that the workers were responding to improved morale, supportive supervision, and other conditions that enhanced interpersonal relationships (Mayo, 1933; Roethlisberger & Dickson, 1939).

The decade between 1930 and 1940 witnessed further advances in management's understanding of human behavior in the work environment, including the psychological needs of the individual, the effect of motivation, and

the role of executive leadership. This era was marked by the contributions of Follett on the motivating desires of the individual and the influences of the group (Metcalf & Urwick, 1942). Another major contributor was Chester Barnard (1938) whose insight into the organization as a system led him to introduce a system's orientation to management with his concept of the cooperative system. Bernard saw the organization consisting of an individual's willingness to serve, having a common purpose, and communication as a linking force. Attention to the social organization and the work of an organization's chief executive was also the concern of Luther Gulick (1937). Gulick expanded Fayol's five managerial functions into seven. The seven managerial functions have become widely identified by the mnemonic POSDCORB, which represents planning, organizing, staffing, directing, coordinating, reporting, and budgeting.

Movement away from the physical factors of scientific management continued between 1940 and the 1960s. The period marked the refinement of management techniques and principles that emerged during and following World War II. Drucker (1974) suggests that interest in management as a field of practice and an academic discipline was triggered by the performance of American manufacturing industry during World War II. It was during the mid-1950s that a significant increase in the number of professional management books and periodicals unfolded (Bedeian, 1978). In fact, *Management Science*, one of the field's major journal publications, started in 1954. The journal reflected the field's direction into management science and operations research.

The cumulative development of the management field from the turn of the twentieth century into the 1970s eventually blended the concerns of the founders of scientific management efficiency and the concerns of the human relations behavioralists with the needs of the workers. Thus, the focus of the 1960s gave rise to organizational behavior and theory (Thompson, 1967), including matters of supervision (McGregor, 1960), leadership (Fielder, 1967), and motivation (Herzberg, 1959).

In the 1970s, two particular trends were identified as important to the development of management thought. The two integrative trends include the contingency approach and the systems approach (Huse, 1979). According to George (1972),

> The concepts of management have shifted today from the level of gang bosses to the systems concept because growing complexities in our society have moved management from a relatively simple task to that of evolving information systems into patterns of management. (pp. 187–188)

The complexities of today's organizations also have required its managers to be more flexible and discriminating in applying management theory into practice. Thus, the contingency approach in management allows managers to be more eclectic in their style and to adapt to changing organizational needs and environments.

Management of the 1980s is characterized by future-oriented thinking and planning for future courses of action. This approach to planning has changed dramatically since Fayol recognized planning as a critical task of management (Radford, 1980). The newer brand of management operates within a scope of complex activities and concerns. The modern organization has many competing interests and must pay attention to several conditions besides profit. These developments have led to an emphasis on learning about different management styles in order to maximize opportunities for success (Peters & Waterman, 1982). In addition, modern organizations have been primarily concerned about responding to the social pressures of the organization's internal and external environments. In the internal environment, management has attempted to satisfy the needs of employees through the management of benefits and creating satisfying working conditions. In the external environment, management is sometimes practiced to influence the opinions of consumers as well as the need to prevent circumstances that might lead to potential litigation against the company. Management in the modern organization has also been shaped by the demands of governmental regulatory agencies and the power of the mass media.

Management Technologies Applied to the Nonprofit Sector

Because of a lack of solid data, any attempt to suggest when the management technologies of the business (for-profit) sector or the management technologies of the public sector were first adapted into the nonprofit sector is fraught with some difficulty. However, review of the historical development of management practice can provide an important context for understanding how management thought and practice has evolved over time. Examination of the development of management thought and practice provides the basis for at least speculating about the development of management practice in the nonprofit sector.

Scientific management was just beginning to develop at the time that Congress passed legislation in 1894 creating a public policy supporting the tax exemption of nonprofit organizations. Although charitable and voluntary activity has always been a fundamental part of the history of the United States, it was this formal Congressional action on behalf of the nonprofit sector that can be considered a landmark for the beginning development of the contemporary practice of nonprofit management.

It was also during the early twentieth century that the establishment of foundations and national service organizations concerned with charitable activities were on the rise (Bakal, 1979). During this period, efficiency management influenced both the activities of the business sector and public administration (Hill & Hebert, 1979). Since attention to techniques and procedures characterized the administration of the day, the nonprofit sector was undoubtedly influenced by this (Taylor's) pragmatic approach to management.

An outgrowth of the scientific management movement was the development of management principles. The principles approach was also generalized to public sector management. It was hoped that the study of important public administration activities would yield the best way or "principles" of administrative practice. Perhaps the principles approach also influenced the operations of charitable and voluntary organizations. By 1946, however, Herbert Simon (1946) demonstrated that the principles of public administration were no more than proverbs, or good, general "rules of thumb." Simon's work along with that of Dahl (1947) and Waldo (1948) seemed to create more interest in describing organizational behavior than in theorizing about it. The objections of these scholars to the notion that administrative management was a generic process of management, equally applicable in all settings and sectors, was an early recognition of the special process of management that is required in the three sectors.

The disillusionment of the administrative management approach assisted the rise of the behavioral science approach, also known as the human relations movement, which evolved next in both the business and public sectors, and the nonprofit sector as well. The experience of the business sector in the 1950s was marked by the integration of social science into management practice. The business sector did so for purposes of increasing profitability. The involvement of the social sciences was also an important development for the public sector, which recognized the powerful influences of the informal structures or social side of the organization. The public sector was struggling with its formal bureaucratic role and beginning to experiment with the idea that public administrators should assert their values into the formulation of policy. The fact that organizations appeared concerned about the humanistic needs and reactions of the individual may explain the climate of the period which supported the creation of tax-exempt legislation that gave definition to the contemporary charitable, 501(c)(3), organization.

In the 1954 establishment of Section 501 of the Internal Revenue Code, the statutory provisions for recognizing tax-exempt organizations were firmly put into place. In addition, certain collateral benefits were created through the adoption of Code 501(c)(3). By imposing certain requirements for recognition as a charitable organization, the boundaries between the three sectors became clarified, and management responsibilities were also further distinguished between organizations located in the nonprofit sector with those in the business or public sectors.

For the first time, the nonprofit organization was subject to meeting two different types of tests to either qualify or maintain the tax-exempt status of the 501(c)(3) organization—the organizational test and the operational test. First, the organizational test is one in which the organization's articles of incorporation and bylaws clearly limit the activities of the organization to one or more tax-exempt activities, such as educational, charitable, scientific, or religious activities. The second test, known as the operational test, is demonstrated by the organization's resources being primarily devoted to the activities that were outlined in the organizational test. Furthermore, the net earnings of the organization may not inure to the board of directors. Together, the operational and organizational tests provide quasi-guidelines concerning the administration of the nonprofit organization. In other words, the use of management technologies from the business or public sector must be adapted for use to further the tax-exempt mission of the nonprofit organization. In this context, the concepts that envelop management ideas of governance, marketing, financial management, planning, among other management tools, are applied to achieve different ends in the three sectors: In business, the aim of management practice is the achievement of profit; in government, the administration of laws and public policy are the end product; and, in the nonprofit sector, management is focused on the satisfactory accomplishment of the organization's service mission. Another distinction of management in the three sectors can be drawn from the target groups shown below in Table 3.3 to be served by the three sectors. In the private sector, organizations are managed in the interest of their stockholders. In the public sector, governmental entities are managed for the interest of the general public. In the nonprofit sector, organizations are managed to sometimes serve the public interest and sometimes to serve only the interests of an unfortunate (or, sometimes, even an unpopular) few who are the clients or constituents that benefit from the organizational mission.

TABLE 3.3 Management Aims and Major Target Groups in the Three Sectors

Sector	Target Group	Aim
Public	General public	Administration of laws and public policy
Business	Stockholders	Generate profit
Nonprofit	General public or minority	Organizational mission

A little more than 30 years ago, IRS Code 50I(c)(3) was created. Since that time more than two-thirds of all nonprofit organizations have been incorporated (Salamon, 1984). Following the rise in the number of new nonprofit organizations, the adaptation of management technologies have become evident in the nonprofit sector and identified in a blossoming professional literature on nonprofit management. The trend in the literature has shown that recognized management tools are being widely used in the nonprofit sector and applications of those tools are being modified to achieve different goals and objectives than in the business or public sectors.

References

Academy for Educational Development. (1979). *The voluntary sector in brief.* New York: Academy for Educational Development.

Addams, J. (1910). *Twenty years at Hull House.* New York: MacMillan.

Bakal, C. (1979). *Charity USA.* New York: Times Books.

Barnard, C. I. (1938). *The functions of the executive.* Cambridge: Harvard University Press.

Bedeian, A. G. (1978). Historical development of management. In L. R. Bittel (Ed.), *The encyclopedia of professional management* (pp. 645–650). New York: McGraw-Hill.

Berger, P. L., & Neuhaus, R. J. (1977). *To empower people: The role of mediating structure in public policy.* Washington, DC: American Enterprise Institute for Public Policy Research.

Brandeis, L. D. (1914). *Business: A profession.* Boston: Small, Maynard.

Bremner, R. H. (1960). *American philanthropy.* Chicago: University of Chicago Press.

Bruno, F. J. (1957). *Trends in social work, 1874–1956.* New York: Columbia University Press.

Carnegie, A. (1900). *The gospel of wealth and other timely essays.* New York: Century.

Chambers, C. A. (1971). *Paul U. Kellogg and the survey.* Minneapolis: University of Minnesota Press.

Clotfelter, C. T. (1983, May 3). Tax incentives and disincentives for charitable giving. In Independent Sector, *Working papers for spring research forum: Since the Filer commission* (pp. 347–367). Washington, DC: Independent Sector.

Commission on Private Philanthropy and Public Needs (Filer Commission). (1975). *Giving in America.* Washington, DC: Department of the Treasury.

Dahl, R. A. (1947, Winter). The science of public administration: Three problems. *Public Administration Review, 7,* 1–11.

Drucker, P. F. (1974). *Management-Tasks-Responsibilities-Practices.* New York: Harper & Row.

Emerson, H. (1913). *The twelve principles of efficiency.* New York: The Engineering Magazine.

Fayol, H. (1949). *General and industrial management.* Trans. C. Storrs. London: Sir Isaac Pitman & Sons.

Fielder, F. E. (1967). *A theory of leadership effectiveness.* New York: McGraw-Hill.

Frisch, E. (1969). *An historical survey of Jewish philanthropy.* New York: Cooper Square Publishers.

Galaskiewicz, J. (1986). The environment and corporate giving behavior. In Independent Sector, *Working papers for spring research forum: Philanthropy, voluntary action, and the public good* (pp. 141–154). Washington, DC: Independent Sector.

Gantt, H. L. (1916). *Industrial leadership.* New Haven: Yale University Press.

Gantt, H. L. (1919). *Organizing for work.* New York: Harcourt, Brace & Howe.

Gelb, B. A. (1971). *Tax-exempt business enterprise.* New York: The Conference Board.

George, C. S. (1972). *The history of management thought.* Englewood Cliffs, NJ: Prentice-Hall.

Gilbreth, F. B. (1911). *Motion study.* New York: Van Nostrand.

Gulick, L. (1937). Notes on the theory of organization. In L. Gulick & L. Urwick (Eds.), *Papers on the science of administration* (pp. 3–13). New York: Institute of Public Administration.

Hansmann, H. (1981). *The rationale for exempting nonprofit organizations from*

corporate income taxation. PONPO
Working Paper 23. New Haven: Yale
University Press.

Harper, R. F. (1904). *The code of Hammurabi,
king of Babylon.* Chicago: University of
Chicago Press.

Herzberg, F. (1959). *Work and the nature of
man.* New York: John Wiel & Sons.

Hill, L. B., & Hebert, F. T. (1979). *Essentials of public administration.* North
Scituate, MA: Suxbury Press.

Hopkins, B. R. (1983). *The law of tax-
exempt organizations.* New York: Wiley.

Hougland, J. G., & Shepard, J. M. (1985,
April–September). Voluntarism and the
manager: The impacts of structural
pressure and personal interest on community participation. *Journal of Voluntary Action Research, 14* (2–3), 65–78.

Huse, E. F. (1979). *The modern manager.*
St. Paul, MN: West.

Independent Sector. (1986b, October 8).
Projected loss of charitable giving.
Memo to Members, Attachment #7.

Jacoby, A., & Babchuk, N. (1963, July).
Instrumental and expressive voluntary
associations. *Sociology and Social
Research, 47,* 461–471.

Jones, J. F., & Herrick, J. M. (1976).
*Citizens in service: Volunteers in social
welfare during the depression,
1929–1941.* Detroit: Michigan State
University Press.

Judd, P., Block, S. R., & Jain, A. K. (1985,
Fall). Who joins NASW: A study of
graduating MSWs. *Arete, 10*(2), 41–44.

Kalmus, H. (1963, November 28). The evolution of altruism. *New Scientist,* London.

Keith, A. (1949). *New theory of human
evolution.* London: Watts.

Lashbrooke, E. C. (1985). *Tax exempt organizations.* Westport, CT: Quorum Books.

Leiby, J. (1978). *A history of social welfare
and social work in the United States.*
New York: Columbia University Press.

Leonard, E. M. (1965). *The early history of
English poor relief.* London, England:
Frank Cass.

Lerner, M. (1983). The joiners. In B. O'Connell
(Ed.), *America's voluntary spirit* (pp.
81–89). New York: The Foundation
Center.

Manser, G., & Cass, R. H. (1976). *Volunteerism at the crossroads.* New York:
Family Service Association of America.

Marts, A. C. (1966). *The generosity of
Americans.* Englewood Cliffs, NJ:
Prentice-Hall.

Massie, J. L. (1979). *Essentials of management.* Englewood Cliffs, NJ:
Prentice-Hall.

Mayo, G. E. (1933). *The human problems of
an industrial civilization.* Boston:
Harvard Business School.

McGregor, D. (1960). *The human side of
enterprise.* New York: McGraw-Hill.

Mee, J. F. (1963). *Management thought in a
dynamic economy,* New York: New York
University Press.

Merton, R. K. (1976). *Sociological ambiv-
alence and other essays.* New York:
Free Press.

Metcalf, H. C., & Urwick, L. (1942).
*Dynamic administration: The collected
papers of Mary Follett.* New York:
Harper & Bros.

Milofsky, C. (1979). Not for profit organizations and community: A review of the
sociological literature. PONPO Working
Paper No. 6. New Haven: Yale University Press.

O'Connell, B. (Ed.). (1983). *America's
voluntary spirit.* New York: The Foundation Center.

Odendahl, T. J. (1985, March 15). Private
foundation formation, growth, and
termination: A report on work in
progress. In Independent Sector, *Giving
and volunteering: New frontiers of
knowledge, 1985 spring research forum*
(pp. 513–524). Washington, DC:
Independent Sector.

Office of Refugee Resettlement. (1986, January).
*Assessment of the MAA incentive grant
initiative.* Final Report, Contract
Number 600-84-0231. Office of Refugee
Resettlement, U.S. Department of
Health and Human Services.

Palisi, B. J. (1972). A critical analysis of
the voluntary association concept. In
D. H. Smith, R. D. Reddy, & B. R.
Baldwin (Eds.), *Voluntary action
research: 1972.* Lexington, MA: D. C.
Heath.

Peters, T. J., & Waterman, R. H. (1982). *In search of excellence.* New York: Harper & Row.

Radford, K. J. (1980). *Strategic planning: An analytical approach.* Reston, VA: Reston Publishing.

Rockefeller, J. D. (1908). The difficult art of giving. *The world's work.*

Roethlisberger, F. J., & Dickson, W. J. (1939). *Management and the worker.* Cambridge: Harvard University Press.

Rose, A. (1954). *Theory and method in the social sciences.* Minneapolis: The University of Minnesota Press.

Rose, M. E. (1971). *The English Poor Law: 1789–1930.* Newton Abbott, UK: David and Charles, Publishers.

Salamon, L. M. (1984, Autumn). The invisible partnership, government and non-profit sector. *Bell Atlantic Quarterly, 1.*

Seeley, J. R., Junker, B. H., Jones, W. R., Jenkins, N. C., Haugh, M. T., & Miller, I. (1957). *Community chest.* Toronto: University of Toronto.

Sills, D. (1957). *The volunteers.* Glencoe, IL: Free Press.

Sills, D. (1968). Voluntary associations: Sociological aspects. In D. Sills (Ed.), *International encyclopedia of the social sciences,* Vol. 16. New York: MacMillan and Free Press.

Simon, H. (1946, Winter). The proverbs of administration. *Public Administration Review, 6,* 53–67.

Smith, C., & Freedman, A. (1972). *Voluntary associations.* Cambridge, MA: Harvard University Press.

Smith, W. H., & Chiechi, C. P. (1974). *Private foundations: Before and after the tax reform act of 1969.* Washington, DC: American Enterprise Institute for Public Policy Research.

Taylor, F. W. (1911). *The principles of scientific management.* New York: Harper & Bros.

Thompson, J. D. (1967). *Organizations in action.* New York: McGraw-Hill.

Tocqueville, A. de (1969). On the use which the Americans make of associations in civil life. In *Democracy in America,* Vol. 2 (pp. 513–517). New York: Doubleday, Anchor Books.

Trolander, J. A. (1975). *Settlement houses and the great depression.* Detroit: Wayne State University.

Verba, S., & Nie, N. (1972). *Participation in America: Political democracy and social equality.* New York: Harper and Row.

Waite, F. T. (1960). *A warm friend for the spirit.* Cleveland: Family Service Association of Cleveland.

Waldo, D. (1948). *The administrative state.* New York: Ronald Press.

Weaver, W. (1967). *U.S. philanthropic foundations: Their history, structure, management and record.* New York: Harper & Row.

Weisbrod, B. A. (1977). *The voluntary non-profit sector.* Lexington, MA: D. C. Heath.

Zald, M. N. (1970). *Organizational change.* Chicago: The University of Chicago Press.

CHAPTER TWO
Impacts of Public Policy on Nonprofit Organizations

Introduction

Public policy is never static. It changes with the moods and wishes of the governed and the governing. When public policy shifts, the impacts are felt across wide segments of society. Nonprofit organizations are affected regularly and profoundly by such shifts.

Shafritz (1985, p. 452) describes David Easton's definition of public policy as the result of public opinion and democratic processes leading to new public laws, administrative rules, and regulations. It is "policy made by certain 'occupants' who are 'authorities' in a system of government; those who 'engage in the daily affairs of a political system,' and are 'recognized by most members of the system as having the responsibilities for these matters,' and whose actions are 'accepted as binding most of the time by most of the members as long as they act within the limits of their roles'" (Shafritz, 1985, p. 452).

Nonprofit organizations have more exposure to public policy shifts than do most private enterprises because they are impacted by public policy changes of four broad types:

1. *What, Who, and How Government Taxes* (changes in income tax and inheritance tax laws and codes). For example:
   - reductions in the maximum income tax rate;
   - elimination of certain deductions for charitable giving; and
   - passage of the generation skipping tax in 1976, which eliminated a major tax advantage that accrued from making gifts to one's second generation offspring (grandchildren).
2. *What Government Permits Nonprofit Organizations to Do* (changes in the limits on the activities of nonprofit organizations). For example:
   - relaxation of prohibitions against certain types of political/educational activities;
   - new rules that define *private inurement* even more stringently;
   - tightened rules about treatment of unrelated business income [UBI];
   - increases in the percentage of private foundations' corpus (essentially, its assets) that must be distributed annually; and
   - increasing or decreasing the excise tax foundations must pay on corpus earnings.
3. *What Services Government Will Fund for Whom* (changes in the targets of public funding). For example:
   - decreases in funding for services for people with chronic mental illness and developmental disabilities;
   - increases in funding for alcohol and drug education and for support of young artists; and
   - consideration for child care and preschool training.
4. *Who Government Will Pay to Deliver Services for It* (changes in the government's form of service delivery). For example:
   - contracts with nonprofit organizations to provide services that historically were provided directly by government;
   - exclusive franchises or licenses to nonprofit organizations, or to for-profit corporations for monopoly trash hauling, ambulance service, or ferry boat operations; and
   - switching from public housing or public schools to a voucher system.

Obviously, for-profit companies also feel the impacts of changes in public policy. Nonprofits are not alone. However, most private firms are not as integrally intertwined with government in as many ways as are third sector organizations. Chapter One addresses the characteristics of the third sector that make it so susceptible to shifts in public policy. Thus, changing public policy provides a fertile field for examining shifts in this critically important element of the external environment for virtually all nonprofit organizations (Morgan, 1988). These shifts affect almost everything in and about nonprofits: their policy, management, clientele, organizational structure, affiliations, programs, finances, reporting, and even the types of tasks performed by volunteers. This chapter primarily addresses the impacts of government policy changes in taxation and funding regulation. Chapter Four continues this discussion into topics related to governance.

Public social services provide an excellent example. Like so many other humanistic government programs, public social services began expanding in the 1960s. In 1967, amendments to the Social Security Act permitted government to purchase the delivery of social services from voluntary sector organizations. This initiated a virtual explosion in the systematic use of public funds to purchase social services provided by nonprofit sector organizations. Purchase of social service dollars increased by a multiple of four between 1963 and 1971 alone. By the middle of the 1970s, privatization was becoming a popular public notion; an alternative to ever-growing government. Nonprofits thus began benefiting from expanding social service expenditures and from a higher government propensity (policy) to purchase services from nonprofit organizations. Nonprofit social service agencies flourished as never before.

As the decade of the 1970s started to wind down, social welfare spending continued to grow but at a slower pace (Abramovitz, 1986). The portion of the expenditures used to purchase services from nonprofit agencies continued to grow. During the period from about 1960 to 1975, a pattern evolved of government reliance on nonprofits to implement public policy using mostly public funds (Salamon, 1987). By the end of the 1970s, the public mood shifted again, and public policy soon followed. The administration of President Ronald Reagan was philosophically committed to the performance of public tasks by private enterprises (Abramovitz, 1986), and its drive to reduce federal taxes and deficits unmistakably signaled a new policy goal: Voluntary agencies should assume more financial as well as programmatic responsibility for social services (Demone & Gibelman, 1984).

Thus, in 30 years the nation's nonprofit social service agencies experienced a public policy cycle of:

1. Minimal public social services activities;
2. Substantial public funding and delivery of services;
3. A literal explosion of monies for services purchased from nonprofit agencies;
4. Slowed funding growth with continuing increases in purchases of services; and
5. Sharply diminished public funding with the expectation that nonprofits would absorb overhead costs as well as provide programs.

Consequently, a primary purpose of this chapter is to demonstrate the fundamental need for a nonprofit organization to have a clear sense of identity and purpose so that it can maintain direction and focus when confronted with massive changes in its external environment. Government is used here as the focus for analysis because of the magnitude—the breadth and depth—of its influence on most nonprofit organizations. In addition to being a topic of substantial importance in and of itself, this chapter also: (1) serves as preparation for Chapter Three's discussion of strategic planning and policy formulation in nonprofit organizations (the primary management tools available to nonprofits for anticipating and influencing changes in their external environments); (2) sets the stage for Chapter Four's focus on governance, particularly the boundary-spanning role played by members of boards of directors; and (3) provides the historical context and progression of legislation enacted to control abusive practices by nonprofit organizations.

The first article in this chapter, "The Filer Commission Report" (1975), is one of the three or four best known and most influential treatises on philanthropy and the nonprofit sector in the United States. The report is more than important enough to warrant inclusion in this volume on its own right, as an influential force in raising public consciousness of the nonprofit sector. (For an analysis of its impacts, see, for example, the article in this chapter by Lester Salamon.) However, we have included it here to emphasize the impact of public policy on nonprofit sector organizations: It vividly demonstrates and underscores the significance of this chapter's subject.

The official title of the "Filer Commission Report" is "The Report of the Commission on Private Philanthropy and Public Needs," but it is referred to most often by its shorter title. The Filer Commission was established in 1973 to study the roles of philanthropic giving and the voluntary sector in the United States. The Filer Commission's 1975 Report (the Commission's primary report—it also sponsored 91 research studies that were published as *Research Papers* in 1977) argued that by passing the Tax Reform Act of 1969, Congress had seriously weakened and jeopardized the future of private foundations and the entire nonprofit sector.

Prior to 1969, there was no definition of a private foundation in the Internal Revenue Service Tax Code. In fact, the IRS did not even have any way of knowing what organizations were claiming tax-exempt status. But from 1950 through 1969, the U.S. Congress became increasingly worried about the potential for foundation abuses (Edie, 1987; Hall, 1987). The pressure for government regulation mounted as congressional investigatory hearings through the 1960s brought repeated founded and unfounded reports of foundation abuses into public view. Some nonprofits (most notably in higher education and health care) also raised public ire for their failure to accept federal affirmative action guidelines (sexual as well as racial). The general public began to demand effective tax reform and control of private foundations. The pressure culminated in the Tax Reform Act of 1969, truly the watershed legislation for regulating private foundations.

The act established distinctions between private foundations and public charitable organizations, placed new restrictions and taxes on private foundations, and gave the IRS expanded strength to obtain information from foundations and other nonprofits. The Tax Reform Act of 1969 redefined the entire playing field and the rules of the philanthropy game in the United States.

By 1973, the effects of the Tax Reform Act of 1969 were unmistakably evident. The nonprofit sector appeared to be in very serious danger. Public opinion once again began to shift. Several studies were spawned in attempts to reestablish a sense of balance, a perspective, about the roles and functions of private foundations in particular and nonprofits in general. The nation's public was not ready to permit the demise of the third sector. The most notable of the study groups was the Filer Commission. Its 1975 report concluded that the nonprofit sector is extremely important to the structure of U.S. society. Among other valuable functions of the nonprofit sector are: (1) It initiates new ideas that government and business are unwilling to support; (2) It develops public policy leadership; and,

(3) It helps decrease feelings of alienation and powerlessness caused by interactions with ever larger, more impersonal, public and private institutions. The Filer Commission Report was an eloquent statement that more than caught the attention of the public and Congress.

The chapter's second article is a condensed version of "Unfair Competition by Nonprofit Organizations with Small Business: An Issue for the 1980s," by the U.S. Small Business Administration, Office of Advocacy. It analyzes the extent to which tax-exempt nonprofit organizations have entered the commercial market and are competing with for-profit, tax-paying small businesses. The laws and tax codes that established tax-exempt organizations were founded on the rationale that tax-exempt nonprofits produce what economists call *public goods* (Hansmann, 1987; Savas, 1982) or *collective goods* (Krashinsky, 1987; Weisbrod, 1988). However, this article argues that nonprofits are moving aggressively and extensively into the production of *private goods* in head-to-head competition with private enterprise. Some are taking unfair advantage of their tax-exemption. The article concludes with a loud call for more expansive government regulation and controls of commercial activities by nonprofit organizations. The obviously controversial position taken in this article by the Small Business Administration has been vigorously and repeatedly countered on numerous grounds.

Susan Rose-Ackerman's *Stanford Law Review* article, "Competition and Corporate Income Taxation," which is reprinted here, extends the Small Business Administration's argument into the field of micro-economics. Rose-Ackerman provides a comprehensive review of the debate over unfair competition by nonprofit organizations. She suggests that taxing unrelated business income (UBI) of nonprofit organizations is less fair to the missions of voluntary organizations than it is beneficial to for-profit firms' profits and productivity.

Lester Salamon's contribution to this chapter, "Nonprofit Organizations, The Lost Opportunity" insightfully assesses the contradiction between the Reagan administration's verbalized commitment to voluntarism and support for privatization of government programs and its record of actions to undermine the strength of the nonprofit sector. Salamon explains that the 1975 Filer Commission Report (Article 6 in this chapter) together with Peter Berger and Richard Neuhaus's seminal conservative 1977 treatise, "To Empower People: The Role of Mediating Structures in Public Policy" (Article 2, in Chapter One) had provided the Reagan administration with the philosophical basis for redirecting national policy on the delivery of human services. The administration had the opportunity to institutionalize the shift of human services out from government operation to the private nonprofit sector. The public mood was supportive of privatization, the administration was enjoying very high public approval, a well-articulated intellectual/philosophical basis for the redefinition was receiving wide acclaim, and a relatively strong network of nonprofit service delivery agencies already existed because they had been built during the 1970s.

Salamon's "lost opportunity" was a national human service delivery arrangement using nonprofit organizations as mediating structures (Berger & Neuhaus, 1977) coordinated through an expanded network of public–private partnerships. However, not only did the Reagan administration miss the opportunity to forge this new coalition between government and the nonprofit sector, but its "tax and budget actions had serious negative implications—apparently never thought out—for the overall health of the nonprofit sector" (Salamon, 1984, p. 271). These actions included the well-known spending cuts, but the deepest resentment among members of the nonprofit community was caused by the administration's all-consuming drive for tax reduction which took priority over its commitment to voluntarism. Specifically, the administration's tax reform package contained provisions that had significantly negative impacts on charitable giving, and the administration actively "opposed the proposals advanced by the philanthropic community to offset some of the potentially harmful effects (of income tax reform) by instituting an above-the-line charitable deduction for nonitemizers and liberalizing the foundation pay-out requirement" (Salamon, 1984, p. 273).

At almost the same time, the Office of Management and Budget began a highly publicized rewriting of the accounting principles applicable to nonprofit organizations, specifically those related to political advocacy. The Reagan administration's verbal commitment to voluntarism had lost out to two stronger motives: a compulsive drive for tax reduction and a fear that tax-exempt nonprofit resources were being used to support political advocacy on behalf of liberal causes. Salamon concludes: "The administration may have set back its own private-sector agenda for some time to come and discredited voluntarism further as a serious policy alternative."

Gary Scrivner's "100 Years of Tax Policy Changes Affecting Charitable Organizations" concludes Chapter Two. Scrivner's article is more than a comprehensive overview of the history of tax change impacts on nonprofit organizations: It also attempts to explain how "heritage, morality, and special interests help to form and affect changes in the very nature of charitable organizations." Scrivner traces these impacts and their likely causes—tradition, public policy, and special interests—from their beginnings in the United States with the Tariff Act of 1894 (the first major tax legislation in the United States to specify the organizations that were subject to taxation) through the Revenue Act of 1987 and subsequent congressional hearings. Scrivner concludes by using the causes (or bases) of tax policy changes to predict several areas of possible future legislative action.

References

Abramovitz, M. (1986). The privatization of the welfare state: A review. *Social Work*, 257.

Beckwith, E. J., & DeSirgh, J. S. (1987). Tax law and private foundations. In T. Odendahl (Ed.), *America's wealthy and the future of foundations* (pp. 267–293). Washington, DC: The Council on Foundations.

Berger, P., & Neuhaus, R. J. (1977). *To empower people: The role of mediating structures in public policy*. Washington, DC: American Enterprise Institute.

Clotfelter, C. T., & Salamon, L. M. (1982). The impact of the 1981 Tax Act on individual charitable giving. *National Tax Journal, 35,* 171–187.

Demone, H., & Gibelman, M. (1984). Reaganomics: Its impact on the voluntary not-for-profit sector. *Social Work,* 421.

Easton, D. (1965). *A systems analysis of political life*. New York: Wiley.

Edie, J. A. (1987). Congress and foundations: Historical summary. In T. Odendahl

(Ed.), *America's wealthy and the future of foundations* (pp. 43–64). Washington, DC: The Council on Foundations.

Filer, J. H. (1975). The Filer Commission report. In *Giving in America: Toward a stronger voluntary sector*. Washington, DC: National Commission on Private Philanthropy and Public Needs.

Hall, P. D. (1987). A historical overview of the private nonprofit sector. In W. W. Powell (Ed.), *The nonprofit sector: A research handbook* (pp. 3–26). New Haven, CT: Yale University Press.

Hansmann, H. (1981). The rationale for exempting nonprofit organizations from corporate income taxation. *Yale Law Journal, 91,* 54–100.

Hansmann, H. (1985). The effect of tax exemption and other factors on competition between nonprofit and for-profit enterprise. New Haven, CT: Yale University, Program on Nonprofit Organizations. Working Paper number 65.

Hansmann, H. (1987). Economic theories of nonprofit organization. In W. W. Powell

(Ed.), *The nonprofit sector: A research handbook* (pp. 27–42). New Haven, CT: Yale University Press.

Hochman, H. M., & Rodgers, J. D. (1977). The optimal treatment of charitable contributions. *National Tax Journal, 30,* 1–19.

Krashinsky, M. (1987). Transaction costs and a theory of the nonprofit organization. In S. R. Ackerman (Ed.), *The economics of nonprofit institutions* (pp. 114–132). New York: Oxford University Press.

Lee, A. J., & Weisbrod, B. A. (1977). Collective goods and the voluntary sector: The case of the hospital industry. In B. A. Weisbrod (Ed.), *The voluntary nonprofit sector.* Lexington, MA: Lexington Books.

McGovern, J. J. (April, 1986). The changing character of exempt organizations. *Philanthropy Monthly,* 19–24.

Morgan, G. (1988). *Riding the waves of change.* San Francisco: Jossey-Bass.

Ott, J. S., & Shafritz, J. M. (1986). *The Facts on File dictionary of nonprofit organization management.* New York: Facts on File.

Rose-Ackerman, S. (May, 1982). Competition and corporate income taxation. *Stanford Law Review, 34,* 1017–1039.

Salamon, L. M. (1984). Nonprofit organizations, the lost opportunity. In J. L.

Palmer, & I. V. Sawhill, *The Reagan record* (pp. 261–284). Cambridge, MA: Ballinger.

Salamon, L. M. (1987). Partners in the public service: The scope and theory of government–nonprofit relations. In W. W. Powell, (Ed.), *The nonprofit sector: A research handbook* (pp. 99–117). New Haven, CT: Yale University Press.

Salamon, L. M. (Spring 1989). The voluntary sector and the future of the welfare state. *Nonprofit and Voluntary Sector Quarterly, 18*(1), 11–24.

Savas, E. S. (1982). *Privatizing the public sector: How to shrink government.* Chatham, NJ: Chatham House Publishers.

Shafritz, J. M. (1985). *The facts on file dictionary of public administration.* New York: Facts on File.

U.S. Small Business Administration. (June, 1984). *Unfair competition by nonprofit organizations with small business: An issue for the 1980s* (3rd ed.). Washington, DC: U.S. Government Printing Office.

Weisbrod, B. A. (1975). Toward a theory of the voluntary non-profit sector in a three-sector economy. In E. S. Phelps, (Ed.), *Altruism, morality, and economic theory* (pp. 171–195). New York: Russell Sage Foundation.

Weisbrod, B. A. (1988). *The nonprofit economy.* Cambridge, MA: Harvard University Press.

ARTICLE 6 _____

The Filer Commission Report [Report of the Commission on Private Philanthropy and Public Needs]

John H. Filer

Introduction and Summary

Few aspects of American society are more characteristically, more famously American than the nation's array of voluntary organizations, and the support in both time and money that is given to them by its citizens. Our country has been decisively different in this regard, historian Daniel Boorstin observes, "from the beginning." As the country was settled, "communities existed before governments were there to care for public needs." The result, Boorstin says, was that "voluntary collaborative activities" were set up to provide basic social services. Government followed later.

The practice of attending to community needs outside of government has profoundly shaped American society and its institutional framework. While in most other countries, major social institutions such as universities, hospitals, schools, libraries, museums and social welfare agencies are state-run and state-funded, in the United States many of the same organizations are privately controlled and voluntarily supported. The institutional landscape of America is, in fact, teeming with nongovernmental, noncommercial organizations, all the way from some of the world's leading educational and cultural institutions to local garden clubs, from politically powerful national associations to block associations—literally millions of groups in all. This vast and varied array is, and has long been widely recognized as, part of the very fabric of American life. If reflects a national belief in the philosophy of pluralism and in the profound importance to society of individual initiative.

Underpinning the virtual omnipresence of voluntary organizations, and a form of individual initiative in its own right, is the practice—in the case of many Americans, the deeply ingrained habit—of philanthropy, of private giving, which provides the resource base for voluntary organizations. Between money gifts and the contributions of time and labor in the form of volunteer work, giving is valued at more than $50 billion a year, according to Commission estimates.

These two interrelated elements, then, are sizable forces in American society, far larger than in any other country. And they have contributed immeasurably to this country's social and scientific progress. On the ledger of recent contributions are such diverse advances as the creation of noncommerical "public" television, the development of environmental, consumerist and demographic consciousness, community-oriented museum programs, the protecting of land and landmarks from the often heedless rush of "progress." The list is endless and still growing; both the number and deeds of voluntary organizations are increasing. "Americans are forever forming associations," wrote de Tocqueville. They still are: tens of thousands of environmental organizations have sprung up in the last few years alone. Private giving is growing, too, at least in current dollar amounts.

Changes and Challenges

Yet, while the value of philanthropy and voluntary organizations, their past and present achievements, is hardly questioned by Americans, and while by international comparisons these two expressions of the voluntary spirit are of unmatched dimensions, a major overall conclusion of this Commission must be that there are profound, and in some areas troubling, shifts happening in the interrelated realms of voluntary organization and philanthropy, changes that reflect, as these quintessential elements in American society must, broader churnings in the society as a whole. These changes present both practical and philosophical challenges to established patterns of voluntary activity and philanthropy.

The practical challenges are suggested by the stark fact that while many new organizations are being born in the voluntary sector, since 1969 nearly 150 private colleges—representing one of the oldest and largest areas of voluntary activity throughout American history—have closed down. Among the philosophical challenges are those facing the main governmental encouragement of private giving—the charitable deduction in the federal income tax—which is being questioned on grounds of equity.

Findings

The Commission's findings—about both the enduring virtues of nonprofit activity and philanthropic giving and about current challenges to established patterns within these areas—can be summarized in four broad observations:

1. The voluntary sector is a large and vital part of American society, more important today than ever. But the sector is undergoing economic strains that predate and are generally more severe than the troubles of the economy as a whole.

According to recent extrapolations, there may be as many as six million organizations in America's voluntary sector (also referred to in this report as the third sector—third after government and business—and as the private nonprofit sector, or simply nonprofit sector for short). One out of every ten service workers in the United States is employed by a nonprofit organization, one out of every six professional workers. One ninth of all property is owned by voluntary organizations.

The last estimate encompasses groups such as labor unions and chambers of commerce, which serve primarily the economic interests of their members. The somewhat smaller part of the voluntary sector that has been the focus of the Commission's attention is defined for most Commission purposes by Section 501(c)(3) of the Internal Revenue Code, which covers organizations that are both tax exempt and eligible to receive tax-deductible gifts. The code specifically designates charitable, religious, scientific, literary and educational organizations.

The Commission estimates that revenues in these areas, including both government and private funds, add up to around $80 billion a year. This amount does not include non-money resources, such as volunteer work and free corporate services. When these are added in, it

is estimated that the voluntary sector accounts for over $100 billion in money and other resources annually.

These are impressive figures, but the significance of the third sector in today's society is found ultimately in less quantifiable dimensions.

Recent tremors in the nation's governance have strengthened the deeply rooted American conviction that no single institutional structure should exercise a monopoly on filling public needs, that reliance on government alone to fill such needs not only saps the spirit of individual initiative but risks making human values subservient to institutional ones, individual and community purposes subordinate to bureaucratic conveniences or authoritarian dictates. Thus, the third sector's role as an addition to government and, in many areas, an alternative and even counterbalance to government, has possibly never been more important; the basic rationale of the third sector in the philosophy of pluralism has possibly never been more pertinent. Also, in a society increasingly dominated by giant and impersonal institutions of business and government, voluntary organizations, generally less giant and more personal, provide arenas within which the individual can exercise personal initiative and influence on the course of events around him or her.

Economic Strains

The vital role of the voluntary sector in today's society must be viewed, however, against a background of mounting financial and economic strains that threaten the sector's ability to adequately perform this role.

The recent economy-wide pressures of inflation and recession have intensified strains that have been felt by the voluntary sector for a number of years. Even in the late 1960's, when the economy was booming, one major survey of the philanthropic landscape found matters bad and getting worse. "Without important new sources of funds amounting to many billions of dollars," the report concluded, "our society will feel the full force of what can be called the charitable crisis of the 1970's."

Acute crisis describes the state of many parts of the nonprofit sector today. The existence of whole areas within the sector may be threatened.

One Commission study asserts that it is not "idle speculation to talk of the disappearance of the liberal arts college." Another study says that "in the long run, if the economic trends continue, the vast majority of nonpublic schools seem doomed, the exceptions being schools enjoying the support of the well-to-do or heavy subsidies from a few remaining religious groups with conservative theologies or strong ethnic emphasis." Social service organizations have been slashing their budgets and reducing their staffs in order to stay afloat. In a number of cases, they have gone out of business entirely. And nonprofit arts organizations, in many cases, are surviving only through large infusions of government funds.

The problems arise on both the income and expense sides of the ledger.

Extraordinary increases in costs, many of them beyond the control of nonprofit causes, are a major factor. Costs for many nonprofit organizations have been going up far more rapidly than in the economy as a whole for a number of years. Since 1960, medical care prices have risen half again as fast as consumer prices in general. Higher education costs rose about 76 per cent between 1963–64 and 1973–74, as compared with 49 per cent for the economy-wide cost-of-living index.

The prevailing financial pattern of the nonprofit sector has become one not only of uncommonly higher costs, but of more resources required for old problems and new solutions, and of more users needing greater aggregate subsidies for the nonprofit services that they consume. In addition, new and less traditional groups, such as those oriented toward urban and racial problems, environmental and consumer organizations, and other politically and legally activist groups, have been adding their claim for pieces of the philanthropic pie. And the pie has not been growing in terms of the real purchasing power of private contributions.

2. Giving in America involves an immense amount of time and money, is the fundamental underpinning of the voluntary sector, encompasses a wide diversity of relationships between donor, donations and donee, and is not keeping pace.

Most giving—79 per cent in 1974—comes from living individuals, and the main focus of the Commission's research has been on such giving. The Commission's largest single research effort was a Commission-sponsored sample survey of 2,917 taxpayers conducted jointly by the University of Michigan's Survey Research Center and by the U.S. Census Bureau. Extensive questioning of respondents was conducted in 1974, covering giving for the previous year. In 1973, according to projections based on the respondents' answers, individuals may have given as much as $26 billion.

In addition, nearly six billion womanhours and manhours of volunteer work were contributed to nonprofit organizations in 1973, the survey indicates, and the total value placed on this contributed labor is another $26 billion. (Bequests accounted for $2.07 billion in 1974, foundations for $2.11 billion and corporations for $1.25 billion in direct dollar giving.)

Estimating the sources of giving by individuals is still more art than science, but even by conservative reckonings, $50 billion a year is the very large round-number total of the value of contributed time and money in the mid-1970's. A disproportionate amount of giving comes from contributors with the highest income, at least 13 per cent of individual giving from this 1 per cent of the population. Yet at the same time the bulk of giving, more than half, comes from households with incomes below $20,000.

Other Commission findings: college graduates give six times as much on the average as do those with only high school educations. Small town residents give more than city dwellers. The married give more than the single, the old more than the young. The giving of time was also found to correlate closely with the giving of money; the contributor of one is likely to be a contributor of the other.

Where the Giving Goes

Where does the giving go? The largest single recipient area is religion. Studies by the Interfaith Research Committee of the Commission indicate that religious giving may be larger than generally estimated, and at the same time the committee found that a sizable share of religious giving—one out of five dollars—is ultimately given in turn by religious organizations to other, non-sacramental categories of recipient. The estimated breakdown of giving in terms of ultimate recipient, in 1973, was: religion,

$10.28 billion; education, $4.41 billion; health, $3.89 billion; social welfare, $2.07 billion; arts, humanities, civic and public causes, $1.67 billion; and all other, $3.19 billion.

When incomes of givers and kinds of recipients are looked at together, a pronounced pattern is evident. Lower-income contributors give even more predominantly to religion than do Americans as a whole; higher incomes give mainly to education, hospitals and cultural institutions.

Not Keeping Pace

While philanthropy plays a far larger role in the U.S. than in any other country, a disturbing finding is that the purchasing power of giving did not keep pace with the growth of the economy through the expansive years of the 1960's and early 1970's and that in recent years it has fallen off absolutely when discounted for inflation.

The American Association of Fund-Raising Counsel estimates that giving has dropped from 1.98 per cent of the gross national product in 1969 to 1.80 per cent in 1974. A Commission-sponsored study by economist Ralph Nelson concludes that, as a proportion of personal income, giving by individuals dropped by about 15 per cent between 1960 and 1972. The relative sluggishness of giving has been even more pronounced when looked at alongside the growth of government spending. In 1960, private giving amounted to one ninth of expenditures by all levels of government (not counting defense spending); in 1974, giving added up to less than one fourteenth of government spending. The Commission's studies indicate, significantly, that it is in the $10,000 to $25,000 range that giving has fallen off the most in recent years.

The dropoff in giving is by no means uniform. Giving to religion has declined most of all, falling from 49 to 43 per cent of all giving between 1964 and 1974, paralleling a drop in church attendance and in parochial school enrollments. Meantime, giving to civic and cultural causes has actually risen. And volunteer work has gone up markedly according to government surveys conducted in 1965 and in 1974. The success of some causes in regularly raising large sums suggests that the spirit of giving may not be fading so much as shifting its focus, even if the level of giving, of money at least, clearly has declined, by virtually every barometer.

3. Decreasing levels of private giving, increasing costs of nonprofit activity and broadening expectations for health, education and welfare services as basic entitlements of citizenship have led to the government's becoming a principal provider of programs and revenues in many areas once dominated by private philanthropy. And government's growing role in these areas poses fundamental questions about the autonomy and basic functioning of private nonprofit organizations and institutions.

As a direct supporter of nonprofit organizations and activities, government today contributes almost as much as all sources of private philanthropy combined. In 1974, Commission studies indicate, government contributed about $23 billion to nonprofit organizations, compared to $25 billion from private giving. In addition, government has absorbed many philanthropic functions or services, either through the spread of public institutions and agencies that are counterparts of private organizations or through social programs that render philanthropic services and functions obsolete or redundant.

The growing role of government in what have been considered philanthropic activities is evident at every turn in the nonprofit sector. In medical and health spending, for example, the federal government was spending only 15 per cent more than private philanthropy in 1930. In 1973, it was spending nearly seven times as much. In 1960 about two thirds of all institutions of higher learning were private; today the proportion is closer to one half. In 1950 more than one half of all higher-education students were enrolled in private institutions; today the ratio is around one quarter.

The most massive change has occurred in relation to the poor, the unemployed, the aged, the infirm—largely because of Social Security legislation enacted in the 1930's. The impact of this legislation can be seen in the fact that in 1974 more than $90 billion was dispensed in old-age, survivors, disability and health insurance, and various forms of welfare assistance. Private philanthropy, by comparison, distributed around $2.3 billion in the whole "social welfare" category.

Along with this change has come an ever increasing involvement of government in the finances of nonprofit organizations themselves. The nonprofit sector has, in fact, become an increasingly mixed realm—part private, part public—in much the same sense that the profit-making sector has; and this trend poses a major dilemma. On the one hand, government money is needed and may even be a matter of life or death for many organizations as the amount of their private funding has advanced slowly or even declined. On the other hand, government money comes with strings attached, however invisible or unintentional they may be. The more an organization depends on government money for survival, the less "private" it is, and the less immune to political processes and priorities.

Various methods have evolved in recent years to "buffer" government funds from political purse-string influence. But, as many studies made for the Commission suggest, perhaps the most effective, and most possible, safeguard of autonomy is to have more than one purse to draw from. The presence of a firm core of private support, however small, in a private organization that gets major public funding can be of crucial importance in determining whether the managers of the organizations regard themselves, and behave, as independent operators or as civil servants.

In stressing the importance of private giving, however, the Commission recognizes that giving itself is influenced by government through the tax system and that some of the most debated issues concerning relations of government and the voluntary sector revolve around how the tax system is structured and how it affects donors and donees.

4. Our society has long encouraged "charitable" nonprofit activity by excluding it from certain tax obligations. But the principal tax encouragement of giving to nonprofit organizations—the charitable deduction in personal income taxes—has been both challenged from some quarters in recent years on grounds of equity and eroded by expansion of the standard deduction.

The charitable deduction has been part of the tax law since 1917, four years after the income tax itself became a basic fixture of American life. It was instituted to sustain the level of giving in the face of new steep tax rates and because it was held that personal income that went to charitable purposes should not be taxed because it did not enrich the giver. These remain the two principal rationales of the charitable deduction, under which a contributor can subtract the amount of yearly giving from income upon which income taxes are computed. In recent years, however, partly as a result of a growing tendency to look at tax immunities as forms of government subsidy, the charitable deduction has been criticized, along with other personal income tax deductions, as inequitable. This is because, under the progressive income tax, the higher the deductor's tax bracket, the greater the tax savings he or she receives from taking a deduction. Thus, high tax bracket contributors have a significantly greater incentive to give than those at the other end of the income scale.

At the same time that the charitable deduction is being challenged philosophically, it is being eroded, in very concrete terms, by liberalizations of the standard deduction, the income tax provision that allows taxpayers to deduct a set amount or a proportion of their income in lieu of taking specific, itemized deductions. The maximum standard deduction has increased greatly in recent years—from $1,000 for a couple in 1970 to $2,600 in 1975. This has so diminished the advantage of taking itemized deductions that as of 1975's returns less than one third of all taxpayers are expected to be taking the charitable deduction.

Recommendations

Such are the main dimensions, trends and issues that the Commission's extensive research has uncovered or illuminated. These findings provide the background for the Commission's recommendations, among the major ones of which are those below. They fall into three categories: proposals involving taxes and giving; those that affect the "philanthropic process," the interaction between donors, donees and the public; and a proposal for a permanent commission on the nonprofit sector.

I. Taxes and Giving

The Commission examined the existing governmental inducement to giving and considered several proposed alternatives, including tax credits for giving and matching grant systems. In doing so, it kept these six objectives in mind:

—To increase the number of people who contribute significantly to and participate in non-profit activities.

—To increase the amount of giving.

—To increase the inducements to giving by those in low- and middle-income brackets.

—To preserve private choice in giving.

—To minimize income losses of nonprofit organizations that depend on the current pattern of giving.

—To be as "efficient" as possible. In other words, any stimulus to giving should not cost significantly more in foregone government revenue than the amount of giving actually stimulated.

A. Continuing the Deduction

In light of these criteria, the Commission believes that the charitable deduction should be retained and added onto rather than replaced by another form of governmental encouragement to giving. The Commission affirms the basic philosophical rationale of the deduction, that giving should not be taxed because, unlike other uses of income, it does not enrich the disburser. Also, the deduction is a proven mechanism familiar to donor and donee, easy to administrate and less likely than credits or matching grants to run afoul of constitutional prohibitions as far as donations to religious organizations are concerned.

The deduction has been shown, furthermore, to be a highly "efficient" inducement. Computerized econometric analyses based on available tax and income data were made for the Commission and they indicate that for every dollar of taxes uncollected because of the charitable deduction, more than one dollar in giving is stimulated. The Commission's sample survey of taxpayers also indicates that itemizers who take the charitable deduction give substantially more, at every income level, than nonitemizers.

The deduction is seen as inviting the least amount of government involvement in influencing the direction of giving. And, finally, eliminating the deduction or replacing it with a tax credit or matching grant system would significantly shift giving away from several current recipient areas

at a time when these areas are already undergoing severe economic strains.

B. Extending and Amplifying the Deduction

The Commission recognizes that the charitable deduction is used by fewer and fewer taxpayers—now fewer than one third—because of the liberalized standard deduction. So, to broaden the reach of the charitable deduction and to increase giving, the Commission recommends:

That all taxpayers who take the standard deduction should also be permitted to deduct charitable contributions as an additional, itemized deduction.

This extension of the deduction would, it is calculated, provide an inducement to give to nearly 60 million nonitemizers, and would thereby result in increased giving, according to econometric projections, of $1.9 billion in 1976 dollars.

This amount is still relatively modest in terms of the amount of giving that would be needed to restore giving to its level in 1960 before its decline in relative purchasing power set in—an increase in giving, in current dollars, of around $8 billion would be required. Moreover, while extending the deduction to nonitemizers would provide many millions of taxpayers with some inducement to give, the inducement would still be tied to the progressive rate structure of the income tax and would be markedly lower at low- and middle-income levels than it is at upper levels. Therefore, the Commission recommends as an additional new incentive for low- and middle-income contributors:

That families with incomes below $15,000 a year be allowed to deduct twice the amount of their giving, and those with incomes between $15,000 and $30,000 be allowed to deduct 150 per cent of what they contribute.

The "double deduction" and the 150 per cent deduction would have the effect of doubling the proportion of tax savings for charitable giving for low-income families and increasing the proportion by one half for middle-income families and would thus appreciably narrow the range in savings between these brackets and high-income taxpayers. The amount of giving induced and the efficiency of inducing it might, moreover, be impressive. According to econometric projections, $9.8 billion more in giving would be stimulated, at a cost of only $7.4 billion in tax revenue lost.

C. Increasing Corporate Giving

Corporate giving is still a relatively new element in American philanthropy; the corporate charitable deduction itself has been in effect only for forty years. And there are those on both the left and right who question whether corporations should be involved in philanthropy at all. While recognizing that such giving can only be a minor element in the corporation's role in society, the Commission also notes that only 20 per cent of corporate taxpayers in 1970 reported any charitable contributions and only 6 per cent made contributions of over $500. The record of corporate giving is an unimpressive and inadequate one, the Commission believes. Therefore, the Commission recommends:

That corporations set as a minimum goal, to be reached no later than 1980, the giving to charitable purposes of 2 per cent of pre-tax net income, and that further studies of means to stimulate corporate giving be pursued.

II. Improving the Philanthropic Process

The social benefit that flows from giving and nonprofit activity results from a process of interaction—between donors and donees and between both and the society at large. In order to function properly—and to reassure a public grown skeptical of its institutions—this "philanthropic process" requires considerable openness between donors and donees and the public; it requires open minds as well as open doors. The tax-exempt status of nonprofit organizations, moreover, entails an obligation to openness, an accountability to the public for actions and expenditures.

Yet the Commission's research, including meetings with and reports from representatives of donee organizations, indicates that the process is operating imperfectly at best. So a number of recommendations were decided upon with the aim of improving the philanthropic process; the following are among the major ones. They fall into four categories: accountability, accessibility,

personal or institutional self-benefiting, and influencing legislation.

A. Accountability

Demands for accountability that have been heard in the business and government worlds of late are also being sounded in the voluntary sector, reflecting the haphazard procedures for accountability that exist in the sector, the increasing use of public funds by nonprofit organizations, and the perception by some that private nonprofit organizations are too private. The Commission agrees that, with notable individual exceptions, the overall level of accountability in the voluntary sector is inadequate, and the Commission therefore recommends:

That all larger tax-exempt charitable organizations except churches and church affiliates be required to prepare and make readily available detailed annual reports on their finances, programs and priorities.

Annual reporting requirements that now apply to private foundations would, in effect, be extended to tax-exempt organizations with annual budgets of more than $100,000—including corporate giving programs but excluding religious organizations. These reports would have to be filed with appropriate state and federal agencies and be made readily available to interested parties upon request. Uniform accounting measures for comparable types of nonprofit organizations are recommended, and an accounting model is provided in the compendium of Commission research, which is published separately.

That larger grant-making organizations be required to hold annual public meetings to discuss their programs, priorities and contributions.

This requirement would apply mainly to foundations, corporations and federated fundraising groups such as United Ways, those with contribution budgets of $100,000 or more. Like the above requirement it would not apply to churches or church affiliates.

B. Accessibility

Greater accessibility by potential donees to donor institutions has frequently been espoused as a goal in the nonprofit sector, yet the evidence suggests that it has been a goal honored more in preachments than in practical pursuit. The Commission believes that greater accessibility can only enrich the philanthropic process, and it is concerned that because of insufficient accessibility, the process may not be fluid enough to respond to new needs. So, with the aim of encouraging and facilitating wider access to and greater venturesomeness by institutional philanthropy, the Commission recommends:

That legal responsibility for proper expenditure of foundation grants, now imposed on both foundations and recipients, be eliminated and that recipient organizations be made primarily responsible for their own expenditures.

The 1969 Tax Reform Act places on foundations and their officers "expenditure responsibility" for any grant that a foundation makes. This provision serves as a restraint on the openness and venturesomeness of foundations. It also puts foundations in a policing and surveillance role and thus undermines the autonomy of grantees. The provision creates both an unnecessary and undesirable duplication of responsibility, and should be repealed.

That tax-exempt organizations, particularly funding organizations, recognize an obligation to be responsive to changing viewpoints and emerging needs and that they take steps such as broadening their boards and staffs to insure that they are responsive.

All exempt organizations, especially those that serve to channel funds to other nonprofit groups, have a public obligation to be aware of and responsive to new attitudes and needs of all segments of society, and each organization should periodically broaden its board and staff if need be so that a wide range of viewpoints is reflected in the organization's governance and management.

The Commission rejects the notion that all voluntary organizations should be "representative" but observes that as more government funds flow into or through voluntary organizations they may have to consider inviting "public" members on their boards as an element of public access and control.

In addition to broadening existing organizations the Commission urges the establishment of new funding organizations and structural changes

to broaden the spectrum of institutional philanthropy in general. An example is the "People's Trust" plan currently being explored in Atlanta; it would raise money in modest monthly pledges for projects close to the donors' homes.

C. Personal or Institutional Self-Benefiting

While tax-exempt charitable organizations are not allowed to make profits, situations have been uncovered in which personal money-making appeared to be the main purpose of the organization or of certain transactions made by the organization. Most notorious, perhaps, have been discoveries of instances where fund-raising and administrative costs have used as much as four out of every five dollars raised. The 1969 tax reform law placed stringent restrictions on self-benefiting by foundation personnel. The Commission believes that other tax-exempt organizations may be as open to such abuses, however, and it therefore favors extending the 1969 restriction to all exempt organizations, with appropriate modifications. Other remedies and restraints are considered desirable as well to insure public confidence that charitable nonprofit organizations do indeed serve only charitable nonprofit causes. The Commission recommends:

That all tax-exempt organizations be required to maintain "arms-length" business relationships with profit-making organizations or activities in which any principal of the exempt organization has a financial interest.

That a system of federal regulation be established for interstate charitable solicitations and that intrastate solicitations be more effectively regulated by state governments.

The Commission believes that the vast majority of charitable solicitations are conscientiously and economically undertaken. Nonetheless, cases of unduly costly or needless fund raising point to the absence of any focused mechanism for overseeing such activity and, if need be, applying sanctions. State regulation is weak and should be strengthened, but because many solicitations are spread over a number of states at once, federal regulation is needed.

The Commission recommends fuller disclosure requirements on solicitation costs and proposes that a special federal office be established to oversee solicitations and to take legal actions against improper, misleading or excessively costly fund raisings.

D. Influencing Legislation

Since 1934, organizations that are eligible to receive tax-deductible gifts have been prohibited from devoting a "substantial part" of their activities to "attempting to influence legislation."

Yet, since 1962, any business organization has been able to deduct costs of influencing legislation that affects the direct interest of the business. The anti-lobbying restriction operates unevenly among charitable groups themselves because of the vagueness that surrounds the term, "substantial part." Large organizations can lobby amply, smaller ones risk treading over some ill-defined line. Furthermore, constitutional questions are raised by what can be viewed as an infringement on free speech and on the right to petition government.

The Commission feels that the restriction inhibits a large and growing role of the voluntary sector. As government has expanded in relation to the nonprofit sector, the influencing of government has tended to become an ever more important function of nonprofit organizations. For many "public interest" and "social action" groups, it is a principal means of furthering their causes. Therefore, the Commission recommends:

That nonprofit organizations, other than private foundations, be allowed the same freedom to attempt to influence legislation as are business corporations and trade associations, that toward this end Congress remove the current limitation on such activity by charitable groups eligible to receive tax-deductible gifts.

III. A Permanent Commission

The Commission's studies have, it feels, significantly advanced the state of knowledge about America's third sector and its philanthropic underpinnings. Yet such is the immensity and diversity of this area of American life and such has been the scarcity of information that has faced the Commission that it inevitably has had to leave depths unfathomed.

A new organization of recognized national stature and authority is needed, the Commission believes, to further chart and study, and ultimately to strengthen the nonprofit sector and the practice of private giving for public purposes. In a time when the sector is subject to both economic strains and political and philosophical questioning, when profound changes are taking place in its role and relationship to government, and when philanthropy has failed to keep pace with society, in economic and financial terms at least, the Commission believes that such an entity is necessary for the growth, perhaps even the survival, of the sector as an effective instrument of individual initiative and social progress.

This Commission, in terminating its own work, puts forward as one of its major recommendations:

That a permanent national commission on the nonprofit sector be established by Congress.

Several major tasks of any new organization already await it. Among these is examining philanthropic priorities in light of America's changing social perceptions, of government's growing role in traditional philanthropic areas, and of the inevitably limited resources of private giving. Also, examining and advancing means of insulating voluntary organizations from the political and bureaucratic pressures that tend to accompany public funds.

Among other purposes and roles of the commission would be continuous collection of data on the sources and uses of the resources of the nonprofit sector; exploring and proposing ways of strengthening private giving and nonprofit activity; providing a forum for public discussion of issues affecting, and for commentary concerning, the nonprofit sector; studying the existing relationships between government and the nonprofit sector and acting as an ombudsman in protecting the interests of the sector as affected by government.

It is proposed that half the commission's membership be named by the President, subject to senatorial confirmation, the other half by the presidential appointees themselves. Funding for the commission would come half from government, half from private sources. The commission would be established as a permanent body, subject, of course, to periodic congressional review and the commission's demonstration of its benefit to society.

The Third Sector

On the map of American society, one of the least charted regions is variously known as the voluntary, the private nonprofit or simply the third sector. Third, that is, after the often overshadowing worlds of government and business. While these two other realms have been and continue to be microscopically examined and analyzed and while their boundaries are for the most part readily identified by experts and laymen alike, the third sector—made up of nongovernmental, nonprofit associations and organizations—remains something of a terra incognita, barely explored in terms of its inner dynamics and motivations, and its social, economic and political relations to the rest of the world. As on ancient maps, its boundaries fade off into extensions of the imagination, and a monster or two may lurk in the surrounding seas.

Yet it is within this institutional domain that nearly all philanthropic input—giving and volunteering—is transformed into philanthropic output—goods and services for ultimate beneficiaries. So the Commission has attempted to take the measure of this area, both quantitatively and qualitatively, and has examined the sector's roles and rationales, past, present and future.

The sector as a whole is most broadly defined by what it is not. It is not government—that is, its component organizations do not command the full power and authority of government, although some may exercise powerful influences over their members and some may even perform certain functions of government. Educational accrediting organizations, for instance, exercise aspects of the governmental power of licensing. For that matter, political parties can be considered to be a part of this sector although their relationship to government is pervasive and in many cases—congressional party caucuses, for instance—inextricable.

On the other hand, the third sector is not business. Its organizations do not exist to make profit and those that enjoy tax immunities are specifically prohibited from doing so, although near the boundaries of the sector many groups do serve primarily the economic interests of their members. Chambers of commerce, labor unions, trade associations and the like hardly pretend to be principally altruistic.

The World of Philanthropy

Inside these negative boundaries is a somewhat narrower domain within which the world of philanthropy generally operates, a domain made up of private groups and institutions that are deemed to serve the public interest rather than a primarily self-benefiting one, and it is this narrower area that has been the principal focus of the Commission. This area is legally defined by laws that determine which types of organizations should be immune from income taxes and eligible to receive tax-deductible contributions from individuals and corporations. Under the Internal Revenue Code, twenty categories of organizations are exempt from federal income tax, but most of those that are eligible to receive tax-deductible gifts as well fall in one category of the code, Section 501(c)(3). To qualify for exemption under this section, whose "501(c)(3)" designation has become for the nonprofit world virtually synonymous with tax deductibility, an organization must operate exclusively for one or more of these broad purposes: charitable, religious, scientific, literary, educational. Two narrower aims are specified as well: testing for public safety and prevention of cruelty to children or animals. The code further states that no "substantial" part of such an organization's activities may be devoted to attempting to influence legislation and that the organization may not participate at all in candidates' political campaigns.

But even these boundaries, though narrower than those set by the nongovernment, nonprofit definition, are immensely broad and vague. What is charitable, what educational, what religious? In a time in which new and unconventional religious sects are being born, it seems, almost monthly, which are genuine expressions of the religious impulse that are legitimately protected from both taxes and governmental scrutiny? Which are essentially secular cults, which outright frauds? The Internal Revenue Service, for one, wishes it had an all-purpose definition of religion to work with. When is an activity educational rather than primarily propagandistic (and thus barred from tax-deductible gifts under the current law)? Considerable litigation and administrative judgement has been devoted to answering such questions. Philosophical as well as legal arguments can be and are raised, moreover, as to whether whole groups of organizations within the tax-exempt categories are truly oriented to the public interest—their justification for tax privilege—or whether they serve primarily to further the interests of a select group.

The Commission has not attempted to establish a definition or principle by which nonprofit, nongovernmental organizations can be judged to be in the public interest and thus a proper concern of and channel for philanthropy. Others have tried to form such a definition, but none has unquestionably succeeded. In any case, a certain flexibility is seen as desirable, both philosophically and legally, in defining the public interest. One of the main virtues of the private nonprofit sector lies in its very testing and extension of any definition of the public interest, so it would be counter-productive to try to establish boundaries in more than a general, expandable sense. Similarly, although this Commission has operated under the rubric of "public needs," no attempt has been made to catalogue, let alone establish any priority scale of, such needs. Like the public interest, the closely related concept of public needs is itself fluid and shifting. A constant and transcendent public need by which the voluntary sector and philanthropy may perhaps be ultimately judged is how effectively they keep abreast of this shifting and how well they are deemed to meet whatever new public needs are perceived.

Likewise, no attempt has been made to attach, and certainly none has succeeded in attaching, a new, better name to the territory under examination, even though none of the existing names is universally admired. Here, and throughout the report, the terms voluntary sector, private nonprofit sector (or simply nonprofit sector for short) or third sector are used interchangeably and in all cases except where otherwise indicated are meant to exclude organizations that primarily serve the interests of their own members.

Dimensions of the Voluntary Sector

What are the dimensions of this sector? To the extent that they have been measured at all, the measurement has usually been only a partial one that looks at the amount of private giving and

volunteer activity that goes into nonprofit organizations. Even on this incomplete scale, however, it is clear that the nonprofit sector accounts for a very large amount of time and money. According to estimates based on surveys made for the Commission . . . at least $25 billion annually is given to various causes and organizations, and an equal amount worth of volunteer work is devoted to philanthropic activity. Yet these figures require some subtraction, and a good deal of addition. For one, a small but significant and growing amount of private giving goes to public institutions, mainly state colleges and universities. On the other hand, a sizable share of the funding of the nonprofit sector comes from the government nowadays, and considerable additional funds come from endowment and other investment income and from operating revenues, including payments to nonprofit organizations by those who use their services—students' tuitions, medical patients' fees and the like. Government funding, endowment income and service charges must be added to the overall ledger of the voluntary sector. When they are, a rough extrapolation from available data indicates the total annual receipts of the private nonprofit sector to be in the range of $80 billion, or half as much as Americans spend on food in a year. [Following] . . . is an approximate breakdown, again based on rough estimations, of what the major areas within the nonprofit sector receive and spend. (Only money inputs are indicated; volunteer work, free corporate services and the like are not included.)

Another measure of the dimensions of the nonprofit sector is the employment it accounts for. Approximately 4.6 million wage and salary workers are estimated to have worked in the nonprofit sector in 1974, or 5.2 per cent of the total American workforce for that year. One out of every ten service workers in the United States is employed by a nonprofit organization. The proportion of professional workers is even higher—nearly one out of six.

For a physical count of nonprofit organizations, the Commission has turned to a number of sources. The Internal Revenue Service lists, as of June, 1975, 691,627 exempt organizations, groups that have formally filed for and been accorded exemption from federal income taxes. But that number does not include a great many

Revenues of the Voluntary Sector

Estimates of Amounts of Private and Government Funds Received by Private Nonprofit Organizations in Major Recipient Areas, 1974 (in billions of dollars)

	Private Funds			Government Funds	Total
	Philanthropy	Service Charges and Endowment Income	Total		
Health	$ 4.0	$17.8	$21.8	$15.7	$37.5
Education	4.2	7.5	11.7	1.6	13.3
Other (Welfare, Culture, etc.)	5.4	6.0	11.4	5.9	17.3
Total (except Religion)	$13.6	$31.3	$44.9	$23.2	$68.1
Religion	11.7	0.8	12.5	—	12.5
Grand Total	$25.3	$32.1	$57.4	$23.2	$80.6

SOURCE: Commission on Private Philanthropy and Public Needs

church organizations which automatically enjoy exemption from federal income taxes without filing, nor does it include numerous small organizations that never feel the need to file for tax exemption. On the other hand, it does include a large number of groups that fall outside the philanthropic part of the nonprofit sector, such as labor unions and fraternal organizations, and it also counts a good many groups that are only active for a short time. One Commission report calculates that a "core group" of traditional philanthropic organizations includes 350,000 religious organizations, 37,000 human service organizations, 6,000 museums, 5,500 private libraries, 4,600 privately supported secondary schools, 3,500 private hospitals, 1,514 private institutions of higher education, and 1,100 symphony orchestras. Some other recent calculations: There are 1,000 national professional associations. New York City alone has around 6,000 block associations. And a study of voluntary groups in the town of Arlington, Mass., identified some 350 such groups there, serving a population of around 52,000. This last finding confirms earlier estimates of proportions between community size and the number of voluntary groups, and gives support to the extrapolation that in all, counting local chapters of regional or national groups, there may be as many as six million private voluntary organizations in the United States. A purely intuitive indication that this very large number is feasible can be glimpsed in a minute sample of nonprofit groups. To name a few:

Bedford-Stuyvesant Restoration Corporation, Phillips Exeter Academy, American Acupuncture and Herbs Research Institute, Senior Citizens Association of Wausau (Wisc.), Talmudic Research Institute, New Alchemy Institute, Aspen Institute for Humanistic Studies, Chapin School Ltd., Citizens Committee on Modernization of Maryland Courts and Justice, Bethlehem (Pa.) Public Library, Visiting Nurse Association of Milwaukee, YMCA Railroad Branch of Toledo, Chinatown (N.Y.) Day Care Center, Zen Center of Los Angeles, Big Brothers of Rapid City, World Affairs Council of Syracuse, N.Y., American Parkinson Disease Association, Bethel Temple of Evansville (Ind.), Metropolitan Opera Company, Fathers Club of Mt. St. Mary's Academy (Watchung, N.J.), Mothers Club of Stanford University, Sons and Daughters of Idaho Pioneers, Family Planning Committee of Greater Fall River (Mass.).

Ultimate Beneficiaries

The arithmetic of the nonprofit sector finds much of its significance in less quantifiable and even less precise dimensions—in the human measurements of who is served, who is affected by nonprofit groups and activities. In some sense, everybody is: the contributions of voluntary organizations to broadscale social and scientific advances have been widely and frequently extolled. Charitable groups were in the forefront of ridding society of child labor, abolitionist groups in tearing down the institution of slavery, civic-minded groups in purging the spoils system from public office. The benefits of nonprofit scientific and technological research include the great reduction of scourges such as tuberculosis and polio, malaria, typhus, influenza, rabies, yaws, bilharziasis, syphilis and amoebic dysentery. These are among the myriad products of the nonprofit sector that have at least indirectly affected all Americans and much of the rest of the world besides.

Perhaps the nonprofit activity that most directly touches the lives of most Americans today is noncommercial "public" television. A bare concept twenty-five years ago, its development was underwritten mainly by foundations. Today it comprises a network of some 240 stations valued at billions of dollars, is increasingly supported by small, "subscriber" contributions and has broadened and enriched a medium that occupies hours of the average American's day.

More particularly benefited by voluntary organizations are the one quarter of all college and university students who attend private institutions of higher education. For hundreds of millions of Americans, private community hospitals, accounting for half of all hospitals in the United States, have been, as one Commission study puts it, "the primary site for handling the most dramatic of human experiences—birth, death, and the alleviation of personal suffering." In this secular age, too, it is worth noting that the largest category in the nonprofit sector is still very large indeed, that nearly two out of three Americans belong to and evidently find comfort and inspiration in the nation's hundreds of thousands of religious organizations. All told, it would be hard to imagine American life without voluntary nonprofit organizations and associations, so entwined are they in the very fabric of our society, from massive national organizations to the local Girl Scouts, the parent-teachers association or the bottle-recycling group.

Government and Voluntary Association

Ultimately, the nonprofit sector's significance, and any measure of its continuing importance, lies in its broader societal role, as seen in the long history of voluntary association and in what signs can currently be glimpsed of new or continuing directions. To talk of the sector's role in society inevitably means looking at voluntary activity and association alongside of government. Both are expressions of the same disposition of people to join together to achieve a common end, and in much of the United States' experience they have been complementary expressions. But in global terms they often have functioned and do function as mutually competitive forces. No government tolerates all forms of voluntary association; groups that are seen as threatening a country's security or that pursue common criminal purposes are routinely suppressed. The tensions between voluntary association and government run broader and deeper in many parts of the world, however, and have done so through many periods of history.

Sociologist Robert A. Nisbet has written of the "momentous conflicts of jurisdiction between the political state and the social associations lying intermediate to it and the individual." These have been, he writes, "of all the conflicts in history, the most fateful." Such conflicts can be traced at least as far back as democratic Greece and imperial Rome, in both of which societies governments were at times hostile to voluntary association. Imperial Rome, wrote Gibbon, "viewed with the utmost jealousy and distrust any association among its subjects."

The Middle Ages witnessed a flourishing in Europe of more or less autonomous groupings —guilds, churches, fiefdoms—within weak central governments. But modern history can be seen at least in part as being patterned by the return to Greek and Roman affinities for the central, dominant state, with an accompanying discouragement of nongovernmental groups. The foremost philosophers of this monism of the state in modern times were Thomas Hobbes and Jean Jacques Rousseau, and the French Revolution was one of its most exuberant expressions. Charitable, literary, educational and cultural societies were banned in the brittle course of the revolution. "A state that is truly free," declared a legislator of revolutionary France, "ought not to suffer within its bosom any association, not even such as, being dedicated to public improvement, has merited well of the country."

"Americans Are Forever Forming Associations"

In spite of this inhospitable historical and philosophical setting, "association dedicated to public improvement" found fertile territory in the New World, a land colonized far from the reach of central governments, a vast land that did not lend itself well to strong central government of its own and in frontier areas was slow to adopt even minimal local governments. As historian Daniel Boorstin has observed, America evidenced a profound tendency to rely on voluntary, nongovernmental organizations and associations to pursue community purposes "from the beginning." As this country was settled, he writes, "communities existed before governments were there to care for public needs." The result was that "voluntary collaborative activities" were set up first to provide basic social services. Government followed later on.

It is no historical accident that one of the Founding Fathers is nearly as famous for his development of nongovernmental means to public ends as he is for his role in shaping and representing the fledgling republic. Benjamin Franklin's institutings outside of government compose a major portion of the index of the voluntary sector. He was the leading force in founding a library, a volunteer fire department, a hospital, a university and a research institution. An historical survey of philanthropy made for the Commission notes: "Franklin did not invent the principle of improving social conditions through voluntary association, but more than any American before him he showed the availability, usefulness and appropriateness to American conditions."

"The principle of voluntary association accorded so well with American political and economic theories," the survey observes further, "that as early as 1820 the larger cities had an embarrassment of benevolent organizations." Fifteen years later, this propensity to organize became the subject of one of Alexis de Tocqueville's most famous of many famous observations about the new nation:

"Americans of all ages, all stations in life, and all types of disposition are forever forming associations. There are not only commercial and industrial associations in which all take part, but others of a thousand different types—religious, moral, serious, futile, very general and very limited, immensely large and very minute. Americans combine to give fetes, found seminaries, build churches, distribute books and send missionaries to the antipodes. Hospitals, prisons and schools take shape that way. Finally, if they want to proclaim a truth or propagate some feeling by the encouragement of a great example, they form an association. In every case, at the head of any new undertaking, where in France you would find the government or in England some territorial magnate, in the United States you are sure to find an association."

Evolutions within the Third Sector

This observation applies to the United States almost as fully 140 years later. Today, in fact, private association appears to be so deeply embedded and to exist on so much broader a scale in the United States than in other parts of the world as to represent one of the principal distinguishing characteristics of American society. Yet the purposes of voluntary organization have hardly remained stationary or of the same relative significance within the voluntary sector over the years.

In a pattern of evolution that has repeated itself in different areas of society, government has taken over many services and functions of the nonprofit sector, and new focuses of nonprofit activity and organization have emerged . . . . Schools, as de Tocqueville observed, were generally founded and run by nongovernmental organizations, often churches, in early America. But soon after de Tocqueville's observations were published in 1835, the public school system began to take hold in the United States, and today only one out of ten primary and secondary school students goes to nonpublic schools. Higher education and aid to the poor correspondingly accounted for more and more nonprofit activity as the nineteenth century progressed. Then, beginning in the late nineteenth century, many of today's giant state universities got their start, and public institutions began to challenge the primacy of private institutions in higher education as well. The private nonprofit sector was the chief dispenser of "charity" well into this century, but in recent decades this function has increasingly been absorbed by government welfare and social insurance programs.

Today we appear to be on the threshold of yet another major expansion by government in an area that until a few years ago was dominated by private nonprofit (and profit) organizations, the health field. A Commission study of philanthropy in this area anticipates that by the mid-1980's, more than half of all spending on health in the United States will be accounted for by government programs, with much of the rest flowing through government-regulated private insurance plans.

Underlying Functions of Voluntary Groups

The end purposes of nonprofit activity have changed considerably over the course of American history, therefore, and unquestionably will continue to change. Yet certain basic functions— underlying social roles that have been characteristic of much or all nonprofit activity regardless of the particular service or cause involved—have endured throughout the changes that have taken place. This is not to say, of course, that all nonprofit organizations are performing these functions optimally or even adequately. Indeed...expert research the Commission has received and informal testimony it has listened to suggest that many organizations in the sector fall well short of their capabilities. Yet the same research and testimony is virtually unanimous in finding distinctive functions for the nonprofit sector and in asserting that these functions are today as important as they ever have been to the health and progress of American society, more important in some cases than ever. Among these basic functions are the following:

—Initiating new ideas and processes.

"...There are critical reasons for maintaining a vital balance of public and private support for human services," asserts a Commission report by Wilbur J. Cohen, former Secretary of Health, Education and Welfare, "not the least of which is the continuing task of innovating in areas where public agencies lack knowledge or are afraid to venture....The private sector is adept at innovation, and at providing the models government needs."

"A new idea stands a better chance of survival in a social system with many kinds of initiative and decision," observes a Commission study of the health field. Government undoubtedly provides the most fertile arena for certain kinds of initiative and innovation, but certain new ideas, these and other Commission reports indicate, stand a better chance of survival and growth in the nonprofit sector than in the corridors of government.

"The development of the early types of both health maintenance organizations and the physicians' assistance [paramedical aides] programs would never have surfaced if they had required prior public sector consensus and support," says the Commission's health study. Another study— on the role of philanthropy in the environmental field—finds: "The perspective of governmental agencies, even in the research-only...agencies..., tends to be limited and dominated by existing and agency views of the problems and alternative strategies for 'solving' the problem...It is difficult to induce...governmental agencies ...to undertake new directions of research and analysis." The "pioneering" role of nonprofit organizations has long been recognized. More than half a century ago, Beatrice and Sidney Webb, writing on the "Sphere of Voluntary Agencies," found these agencies capable of "many kinds...of...treatment...the public authorities are not likely themselves to initiate." Nongovernmental organizations, precisely because they are nongovernmental and need not be attuned to a broad and diverse constituency, can take chances, experiment in areas where legislators and government agencies are hesitant to tread.

Once successfully pioneered by nonprofit groups, and having established their legitimacy and worthiness, new ideas and processes can be, and often have been, supported and expanded by government. Birth-control technology, to take a relatively recent example, was pioneered by the nonprofit world in its more controversial beginnings and today is heavily underwritten by many governments throughout the world.

—Developing public policy. Standing outside of government, voluntary organizations not only can try out new ideas, initiate services, that may be too controversial for government bodies to deal with at early stages, but can exercise a direct influence on shaping and advancing government policy in broad areas in which the government is already involved. Groups specializing in certain policy areas are continually producing research and analysis, information and viewpoints, especially on long-range policy matters, that may be lacking at times in government circles themselves, preoccupied as they often are with day-to-day operating concerns. A major function of nonprofit groups in public policy development has been to help clarify and define issues for public consideration, both at local and regional levels, as the Regional Plan Association does through its studies and proposals for the New York metropolitan area, or as The Brookings Institution does at the national level. Privately sponsored special commissions and boards of inquiry have been frequently formed at both levels to focus analysis and attention on issues as diverse as hunger, cable communication and legalized gambling.

—Supporting minority or local interests. For many of the same reasons the nonprofit world can experiment with new ideas less cautiously than government, voluntary groups can support causes and interests that may be swept aside by majoritarian priorities or prejudices. The civil rights movement grew out of the initiatives of nonprofit organizations such as the NAACP; the consumer and environmental movements, once the concerns of only a few perceptive or single-minded people, also found their early nourishment in private groups. But the causes need not be—or may not ever come to be regarded as—so large and socially significant. William S. Vickrey, an economist at Columbia University, has written of the "cumbersomeness of public agencies in dealing with relatively small-scale

activities," of the impediments facing "high-level decision-making bodies on matters of small magnitude in which they have relatively little basis for judgment." More specialized private agencies may be able to operate efficiently and intelligently within their spheres, may be more sensitive to small-scale problems than government. In the health field, for example, a Commission report notes that nonprofit organizations "can assist in support of health programs for religious and ethnic groups, migratory workers, and racial minority groups which the public sector cannot often address. . . Private philanthropy will be needed in the future to even out some of the inequities which will invariably occur between different communities, and to respond to the health needs of groups too culturally different to gain adequate public support."

—Providing services that the government is constitutionally barred from providing. In the United States, the government is proscribed from entering the broadest area of the nonprofit sector, religion. So there is simply no alternative to the nonprofit sector if religious functions are to be filled at all in this country. Similarly, as the Council on Foundations points out in its report to the Commission, the establishment in 1973 of a private nonprofit National News Council to oversee the news media "is an experiment that, if not totally off-limits to the government because of the First Amendment, is clearly not the kind of function that it should or would undertake."

—Overseeing government. Alongside government's constitutional inhibitions are its institutional ones. Despite its own internal checks and balances, government can hardly be counted on to keep a disinterested eye on itself. In his historical perspective on philanthropy written for the Commission, historian Robert H. Bremner observes: "A marked tendency of American philanthropy has been to encourage, assist and even goad democratic government—and democratic citizens—toward better performance of civic duties and closer attention to social requirements." The Nathan Committee, which looked at philanthropy in Great Britain a quarter century ago, saw much the same role for voluntary groups. "They are able to stand aside from and criticize state action, or inaction, in the interests of the inarticulate man-in-the-street." As government's role in many areas formerly dominated by nongovernmental groups grows ever larger, and the voluntary role grows correspondingly smaller, the monitoring and influencing of government may be emerging as one of the single most important and effective functions of the private nonprofit sector.

—Overseeing the market place. While most of the third sector's activity relates more closely to government than to the business sector because of the nonprofit, public-interest common denominator of government and voluntary organizations, the sector does play a role, and perhaps a growing one, in relation to the business world. In some areas, voluntary organizations provide a direct alternative to, and a kind of yardstick for, business organizations. Nonprofit hospitals and research organizations, for instance, operate in competition with close commercial counterparts. A number of nonprofit groups make it their business to keep a critical gaze on business, including labor union activity, as well. Potentially freer from the influence of powerful economic interests, nonprofit groups can act as detached overseers of the market place in ways that government agencies and legislators are often restrained from doing.

—Bringing the sectors together. Nonprofit organizations frequently serve to stimulate and coordinate activities in which government or business or both interact with voluntary groups to pursue public purposes. Organization for community development is one example of this synergistic role. Another is the practice by a group such as The Nature Conservancy of enlisting the help of industry in the form of low-interest loans to buy land for preservation and conservation purposes, land that may eventually be turned over to government ownership. The fact that voluntary organizations have neither commercial interests to pursue nor official status often makes them best suited to act as intermediary or coordinator in activities involving government and business.

—Giving aid abroad. In a time of heightened nationalistic sensitivities, especially where official American actions abroad are concerned, nonprofit organizations have been able to offer aid in situations where government help would be politically unacceptable. Workers for the American Friends Service Committee, for instance, were able to remain behind in Da Nang during the North Vietnamese takeover of that city and were able to help war victims there even though the United States government was considered hostile by the city's occupiers. As a Ford Foundation annual report observed a few years ago: ". . .Our welcome in sensitive areas often derives from the fact that we are not a government."

—Furthering active citizenship and altruism. While the previous categories deal mainly with the important roles nonprofit organizations serve for the society as a whole or for certain beneficiary segments of the society, one of the broadest and most important functions voluntary groups perform derives not so much from what they do for beneficiaries as what they do for participants. Voluntary groups serve as ready and accessible outlets for public-spirited initiative and activity—for philanthropy broadly defined. In a complex urbanized and suburbanized society, the individual acting alone can hope to make little impress on community or national problems, is often at a loss to find and help those who need help. Many government agencies have highly structured work arrangements and cannot or do not readily receive the assistance of public-spirited citizens. But those so minded can usually join or can help form a voluntary organization as an effective vehicle for altruistic action, and this possibility itself serves as a constant encouragement to altruism, to an active involvement in public causes, which is of the very essence in a healthy democratic society.

New Frontiers and an Ageless Rationale

These vital roles for voluntary organizations continue to serve and influence areas of society that have traditionally been the concern of the nonprofit sector. In addition, many new or greatly expanded concerns of voluntary activity have emerged in recent years as challenging new frontiers of the sector and of its particular capabilities. "Over the past 20 years," observes Pablo Eisenberg, head of the Center for Community Change, "hundreds if not thousands of new local organizations have been created to deal with issues such as ecology, consumer problems, economic and social self-determination, public-interest law, poverty and neighborhood revitalization...groups with different purposes and structures and, in some cases, constituencies." Indeed, a recent survey indicates that possibly as many as 40,000 environmental organizations alone have sprung up throughout the country, mostly in the last few years. And in a Commission study of philanthropy in five cities, one major conclusion is that "nonprofit, tax-exempt organizations continue to grow in each of the cities studied."

For all the absorptions by government and despite severe financial difficulties of many voluntary organizations...it would appear, in other words, that the impulse to associate is still very strong. Indeed, there are social currents in motion that should be adding fresh impetus and vitality to this ageless expression of man's community with man.

One current is the sense of alienation that modern men and women are widely viewed as experiencing in the face of giant, impersonal institutions of government and business. The generally smaller size and more perceptible humanity of voluntary groups—be they block associations, local chapters of the American Legion or women's rights organizations—would appear to offer at least a partial antidote to any contemporary malaise stemming from feelings of ineffectiveness or unidentity. As Richard W. Lyman, president of Stanford University, wrote recently in an essay entitled "In Defense of the Private Sector," "People everywhere are yearning for the chance to feel significant as individuals. They are yearning for institutions built on a human scale, and responsive to human needs and aspirations. Is this not precisely what we have believed in and worked for, long before it became so popular to do so?"

In addition to responding to an existential yearning, the voluntary sector should appeal more than ever today in terms of its bedrock grounding in the spirit and political philosophy of pluralism—in the idea that society benefits from having many different ways for striving to advance the common weal. The federal government's unavailing efforts to control the economy follow many frustrating social programs of the Great Society and both add to the evidence of our senses that in our increasingly complex society there is no one body, one governing structure, that holds the answers to society's problems, is equipped to find the answers by itself or could put them into effect if it did. In the wake of Watergate, moreover, we are probably less persuaded than ever to stake our destiny totally on the wisdom or beneficence of centralized authority. This sorry and sordid chapter in recent history has dramatically demonstrated the virtues of diffusion of power and decentralization of decision making in public affairs, and it has demonstrated the correlative virtues of a vigorous public-minded and independent sector. The sector ideally should not compete with government so much as complement it and help humanize it, however. Nor because of institutional inertia or self-protectiveness should it or parts of it stand in the way of proper extensions of government into areas where, because of the demands of scale or equity, the private sector simply cannot fill a collective want. The sector should not be at odds with government, in other words, so much as outside of it and in addition to it.

In furtherance of its own role of serving the public interest, government at the same time should actively encourage a large and vigorous voluntary sector that can help carry the burdens of public services. For to operate effectively, and humanely, government must take care not to overload its own mechanisms by attempting to bring every public purpose directly under its direction and control.

The late Walter Lippmann recognized this central importance to government, and to American society at large, of nongovernmental organization. American democracy, he wrote a number of years ago, "has worked, I am convinced, for two reasons. The first is that government in America has not, hitherto, been permitted to attempt to do too many things; its problems have been kept within the capacity of ordinary men. The second...is that outside the government and outside the party system, there have existed independent institutions and independent men..." His observation describes the ultimate rationale for a "third" sector in

American society, a rationale that applies as fully for today and tomorrow as it did for yesterday.

References

William D. Andrews, "Personal Deductions in an Ideal Income Tax," *Harvard Law Review*, Vol. 86, No. 2, December 1972.

Robert J. Blendon, *The Changing Role of Private Philanthropy in Health Affairs.**

Blair T. Bower, *The Role of Private Philanthropy in Relation to Environment—Pollution.**

Robert H. Bremner, *Private Philanthropy and Public Needs: An Historical Perspective.**

John J. Carson and Harry V. Hodson, eds., *Philanthropy in the '70's: An Anglo-American Discussion*, Council on Foundations, Inc., New York, 1973.

Earl F. Cheit and Theodore E. Lobman III, *Private Philanthropy and Higher Education.**

Coalition for the Public Good Thru Voluntary Initiative, *Statement Prepared for the Commission on Private Philanthropy and Public Needs.**

Wilbur J. Cohen, *Some Aspects of Evolving Social Policy in Relation to Private Philanthropy.**

Commission on Foundations and Private Philanthropy, *Foundations, Private Giving and Public Policy*, University of Chicago Press, Chicago, 1970.

Committee on the Law and Practice Relating to Charitable Trusts (Nathan Committee), *Report on Charitable Trusts*, Her Majesty's Stationery Office, London, 1952.

Council on Foundations, Inc., *Private Foundations and the 1969 Tax Reform Act.**

Fred R. Crawford, *Non-Economic Motivational Factors in Philanthropic Behavior.**

Pablo Eisenberg, "The Filer Commission: A Critical Perspective," in *The Grantsmanship Center News*, Vol. 2, No. 1, December, 1974–January, 1975.

Donald A. Erickson, *Philanthropy, Public Needs and Nonpublic Schools.**

Solomon Fabricant, "Philanthropy in the American Economy," *Foundation News*, Vol. X, No. 5. September–October, 1969.

Caryl P. Haskins, *The Role of Private Philanthropy and Public Support of Science in the United States.**

Hans H. Jenny, *Philanthropy in Higher Education.**

Janet Koch, *The Role of Philanthropy in the Environmental Field—Preservation of Natural Lands and Historic Properties.**

Robert L. Lamborn, Cary Potter, Al H. Senske, *The Nonpublic School and Private Philanthropy.**

Richard W. Lyman, "In Defense of the Private Sector," *Daedalus*, Winter, 1975.

William G. McLoughlin, "Changing Patterns of Protestant Philanthropy 1607–1969," in *The Religious Situation*, Beacon Press, Boston, 1969.

National Center for Voluntary Action, *A Report on Voluntary Activities and Leadership Opinion.**

Robert A. Nisbet, *Community and Power*, Oxford University Press, New York, 1962.

David Owen, *English Philanthropy, 1660–1960*, Harvard University Press, Cambridge, 1964.

Gabriel G. Rudney, *Scope of the Private Voluntary Charitable Sector, 1974.**

John F. Shannon and L. Richard Gabler, *The Exemption of Religious, Educational and Charitable Institutions from Property Taxation.**

David Horton Smith and Burt R. Baldwin, "Voluntary Association and Volunteering in the United States," in *Voluntary Action Research 1974*, D.C. Heath and Company, Boston, 1975.

Lawrence M. Stone, *The Charitable Foundation: Its Governance.**

T. Nicolaus Tideman, *Employment and Earnings in the Non-Profit Charitable Sector.**

United States Senate, Report of Proceedings, Subcommittee on Foundations, Committee on Finance, *The Role of Foundations Today and the Effect of the Tax Reform Act of 1969 Upon Foundations*, October 1 and 2, 1973.

United States Senate, Report of Proceedings, Subcommittee on Foundations, Committee on Finance, *Impact of Current*

* Denotes reports and studies undertaken for the Commission.

Economic Crisis on Funds and Recipients of Foundation Money, November 25, 1974.

Joseph L. Vigilante and Ruth Kantrow, *The Voluntary Social Agency Experiments, Innovates, Demonstrates, and Influences Public Social Policy: The Community Service Society of New York 1930–1970.**

Burton A. Weisbrod, *The Size of the Voluntary Nonprofit Sector: Concepts and Measures.**

Burton A. Weisbrod, "Toward A Theory of the Voluntary Non-Profit Sector in a Three-Sector Economy," in *Altruism, Morality and Economic Theory*, Edmund S. Phelps, Ed., Russell Sage Foundation, New York, 1975.

Laurens Williams and Donald V. Moorehead, *An Analysis of the Federal Tax Distinctions Between Public and Private Charitable Organizations.**

Ellen Winston, *Some Aspects of Private Philanthropy in Relation to Social Welfare.**

Adam Yarmolinsky, *The Tax Legislative Process and the Appropriations Process.**

Adam Yarmolinsky, *Philanthropic Activity in International Affairs.**

Paul N. Ylvisaker and Jane H. Mavity, *The Role of Private Philanthropy in Public Affairs.**

ARTICLE 7 ⎯⎯⎯⎯⎯⎯⎯⎯
Unfair Competition by Nonprofit Organizations with Small Business: An Issue for the 1980s
U.S. Small Business Administration

I. Introduction

Increasingly, tax-exempt nonprofit organizations are engaging in commercial activities in competition with for-profit small firms that pay Federal, state and local taxes for the privilege

SOURCE: *Nonprofit Organizations and Unfair Competition*, 1983, U.S. Small Business Administration, Washington, D.C.

of doing business. The phenomenon has caused growing concern in recent years as cutbacks in Federal grants and heightened competition for private giving have led more nonprofits to look to for-profit activities as a source of dependable operating revenue.[1] Competition between nonprofits and for-profits is occurring in traditional service industries such as merchandise sales, health care and travel. It is also occurring in newer fields such as laboratory testing, audio-visual services, engineering consulting and data processing.[2]

The issue of competition by nonprofits with small business is part of the much larger problem of government competition with the private sector.[3] To the extent that the Federal government subsidizes nonprofit organization activity through the corporate income tax exemption in the Internal Revenue Code, nonprofit activity represents a form of indirect government competition with the private sector. This can be distinguished from direct government competition with the private sector, in which the government supplies to itself commercial goods and services which are available from the private sector.

Although the "unfair competition" issue has received some attention in the past,[4] it is now emerging as a major policy question for the 1980s. In order to better define the issue, we must move away from anecdotal complaints of unfair competition and establish a framework for analyzing the policy questions raised. To that end, Section II of this paper will discuss economic and policy aspects of the nonprofits competition issue. What are the rationales for granting nonprofits tax-exempt status and are they still valid? What is the level of commercial activity by nonprofits in various industries? What is the economic effect of the tax exemption and other factors on competition between nonprofit and for-profit firms?. . .

II. Policy and Economic Aspects of Competition Between Nonprofit and For-Profit Enterprise

A. Policy Aspects

Nonprofit organizations have been exempt from the Federal corporate income tax for as long as that tax has existed. Yet the rationale for the exemption is unclear. This may have been an acceptable state of affairs when the nonprofit sector was chiefly composed of charity organizations such as the American Red Cross and the Salvation Army. But it is not adequate today when an increasing number of nonprofits are "operating" or "commercial" nonprofits—organizations such as nonprofit hospitals, day care centers, nursing homes, research institutes and publication houses that receive few donations and charge prices for the goods or services that they produce.

1. The "Public Goods" Rationale

The most common rationale offered for exempting nonprofits from taxation is that they provide services such as health care, education and basic research that for some reason would not be supplied in the absence of a tax subsidy by competitive for-profit firms.[5] This "public goods" rationale suggests that nonprofits should be granted tax exemption for providing services that would otherwise have to be provided by the government.

The "public goods" rationale may be valid in relation to nonprofit charities, such as the Salvation Army and CARE, that render aid to the poor and distressed. But it hardly seems to justify the tax exemption for many nonprofit hospitals, nursing homes and day care centers operating today. These organizations render little or no charitable services, and in fact seem to target their services at those who can pay. If nonprofit hospitals and vocational schools are granted tax-exempt status in order to encourage them to provide these services, why are for-profit hospitals and vocational schools, of which there are thousands, not granted a similar exemption? Furthermore, the fact that nonprofits are increasingly competing with for-profit firms in a wide range of activities is evidence that many nonprofits are not providing "public goods" which private competitive firms will not otherwise produce.

2. The "Quality Assurance" Rationale

The second major justification for exempting nonprofits from taxation is the so-called "quality assurance" or "fiduciary duty" rationale.[6] This theory posits that nonprofits provide services, such as health care and education, where consumers are ill-equipped to judge the quality of services offered before the purchase is made. Having these services performed by tax-exempt nonprofits assures the public of quality and protection in situations where for-profit firms might charge excessive prices for inferior service.

This rationale has superficial appeal in the case where a person is selecting, for example, an appropriate nursing home for an aging parent. But, in fact, there is no empirical evidence that nonprofits provide higher quality services than for-profits engaged in similar activities.

Furthermore, there are large numbers of commercial nonprofits today performing activities such as analytical testing, computer software production, research services and consulting services. In these areas, the purchasers of the services are sophisticated and hardly need the "protection" of nonprofit providers in order to avoid unsuitable for-profit sellers. Also, granting nonprofits a subsidy through the tax exemption is at best an inefficient way to assure quality services. It would seem a much more effective—and fairer—course to impose tough disclosure requirements and other regulations on *all* providers of services in areas where we feel the public needs special protection (e.g., health care, vocational education). In fact, given the extent of Federal and state regulation of medical care, and the availability of private litigation to reach instances of malpractice, an adequate quality assurance system may already exist in the health care industry.

3. Conclusion

The traditional rationales for exempting nonprofits from Federal income taxation do not withstand close scrutiny, particularly as applied to the modern-day "commercial" nonprofits that offer goods and services in direct competition with for-profit firms. Much of the current confusion that surrounds application of the criteria for granting tax-exempt status to a nonprofit organization can be traced to the lack of a clear understanding of the rationale for the exemption. It is time for a critical reappraisal of the principles that supposedly justify the special tax treatment that nonprofits receive.

Conclusion [of this governmental position paper]

The increasing phenomenon of nonprofit organizations engaged in commercial activities in competition with for-profit small businesses cannot be ignored. The traditional justifications for granting nonprofits tax-exempt status have been stretched beyond recognition by this development. Policymakers in the Congress and in the Executive Branch must undertake a thorough evaluation of the changing role of the nonprofit in our society and economy. Appropriate revisions in Federal statutes and regulations governing nonprofits are necessary to reflect the existence of the commercial nonprofit sector, and to remedy the unfair competition now imposed on for-profit small businesses.

Notes

1. See, for example, Schmitt, "Survival of Nonprofits May Depend on Their Entrepreneurial Savvy," *Washington Post*, July 27, 1983.

2. See Section III of this paper for a more detailed description of the types of nonprofits competition occurring in these industries today.

3. See the U.S. Small Business Administration, *Government Competition: A Threat to Small Business* (1980). This was the report of the SBA Advocacy Task Group on Government Competition with Small Business.

4. See *Hearings on Government Competition with Small Business*, before the Subcommittee on Advocacy and the Future of Small Business of the Senate Committee on Small Business, 97th Congress, First Session (1981). See also the *Hearing on Government Competition with Small Business*, before the Subcommittee on Monetary and Fiscal Policy of the Joint Economic Committee, 97th Congress, First Session (1981).

5. Statement of Professor Burton A. Weisbrod, Economics Department, University of Wisconsin at Madison, before the Symposium on Nonprofits Competition with Small Business, July 27, 1983. See also Weisbrod, *The Voluntary Nonprofit Sector* (Lexington Books, 1977).

6. Statement of Professor Henry Hansmann, Yale Law School, before the Symposium on Nonprofits Competition with Small Business, July 27, 1983. See also Hansmann, "The Rationale for Exempting Nonprofit Organizations from Corporate Income Taxation," reprinted as "Why Are Nonprofit Organizations Exempted from Corporate Income Taxation," in Michelle White, ed., *The Interaction of the Public, Private and Nonprofit Sectors* (Washington, D.C.: Urban Institute, 1981).

ARTICLE 8
Unfair Competition and Corporate Income Taxation*
Susan Rose-Ackerman†

"If something is not done. . . , the macaroni monopoly will be in the hands of the universities."[1]

When a group of wealthy graduates donated the Mueller Macaroni Company to the New York University (N.Y.U.) Law School in 1948, the university persuaded a court to give Mueller's profits tax-exempt status because N.Y.U. was a nonprofit entity.[2] Two years later, Congress amended the Internal Revenue Code to narrow this exemption: Henceforth, only the "related" business ventures of nonprofits would be tax exempt.[3]

Very little money has been collected under this provision.[4] Instead, it has channeled the "active" investments of nonprofits into "related" areas. Universities, for example, are no longer in the pasta business, but they continue to sell

* Research support for this paper was provided by Yale University's Program on Nonprofit Organizations. I wish to thank Bruce Ackerman, Boris Bittker, George Cooper, Henry Hansmann, and John Simon for helpful comments.
† A.B. 1964, Wellesley College; Ph.D. 1970, Yale University. Professor of Law and Political Economy, Columbia University.

housing and meals, perform contract research and testing, and operate publishing houses.[5] Of course, the meaning of "related" is not obvious and the Internal Revenue Service (IRS) and the courts have experienced predictable difficulties settling on a definition.[6] The unresolved issue of the law's coverage will be of growing concern to nonprofits since current cuts in marginal tax rates and in government subsidies will undoubtedly induce many nonprofit firms to consider profitmaking activities as a way to raise funds.[7] As nonprofits try to enter new fields, such as genetic engineering and cooperative research relationships with private firms,[8] Congress and the IRS will have to decide whether to facilitate or impede these activities, placing new strains on a generation-old policy.[9]

The particular problem of competition from nonprofits raises a more general issue. A variety of tax-favored entities compete with for-profit firms in a broad range of industries.[10] When, if ever, will "unfair" competition by tax-favored firms be a legitimate problem for public policy? Congress's response to complaints of unfair competition has been inconsistent at best. The Internal Revenue Code has all but eliminated the tax advantage of mutual and cooperative banks and insurance companies,[11] but agricultural cooperatives enjoy a relatively favorable tax status.[12] Utilities operated by state and local governments are exempt from the corporate income tax, while private regulated companies are not.[13]

Instead of ad hoc responses to particular claims of unfair competition, we need a framework for analyzing the policy questions that arise whenever a tax-favored firm competes with firms that pay the corporate income tax. Two different claims, both based on the notion of "horizontal equity"[14] are frequently confused in the policy debate.[15] The first approach compares firms within the *same* industry and asserts that it is unfair for the tax system to favor one competitor over another.[16] The second approach compares for-profits across different industries—those with and those without tax-favored firms. Here it is said to be "unfair" for some firms to compete with tax-favored organizations when for-profit corporations in other industries compete only with taxable firms.

The first approach to horizontal equity makes the claim, for example, that N.Y.U. should pay taxes on its Mueller pasta business simply because the Ronzoni Company pays taxes on its macaroni profits. This view assumes that the fairness of tax policy should be assessed comparing the income statements of the competing companies. But it is obvious that the ultimate impact of N.Y.U.'s pasta activities was not felt by the Ronzoni Company but by the human beings associated with it as investors, workers, and consumers. Sophisticated students of tax policy routinely incorporate this point in their assessments of fairness. Rather than speaking of fairness to corporate entities, they have pierced the organizational veil to consider the interests of human beings.[17] Under this "person-oriented" perspective, the first fairness claim collapses. The different tax treatment of competing organizational forms does not imply that Ronzoni and N.Y.U. would charge different prices for their macaroni or pay different wages to their workers. It implies only that N.Y.U. would keep a larger share of Mueller's profits than would Ronzoni's owners. Once we look beyond the organization, this difference does not seem to violate principles of horizontal equity: Why must a fair tax code treat students and scholars who are the beneficiaries of Mueller's profits as if they were "equal to" Ronzoni's investors?

The second approach to horizontal equity gives a more meaningful interpretation to the complaints of Ronzoni's investors and will be used in the analysis that follows. Under this view, Ronzoni investors would argue that the relevant horizontal comparison is with investors in industries which do not face competition from tax-favored firms. After all, at an earlier point in time, owners of shares in pasta-making companies could have chosen to invest in other businesses instead. In the absence of a tax on unrelated business activities, N.Y.U.'s entry into the pasta business would mean that investors who at one time were similarly situated are now earning different returns. This, at least, raises the possibility of a claim of horizontal inequity: If pasta investors *are* harmed, why should they be called on to bear a greater share than others of the social costs of tax favoritism to nonprofits?

Legally trained commentators have avoided this normative question by doing some inadequate positive economics. They have argued that firms that compete with nonprofits are not generally worse off than those that compete only with for-profits.[18] If this is true, the unfairness issue simply does not arise. I will demonstrate that previous analysts have dismissed the issue of "unfair" competition too quickly. While I agree that nonprofits are no more likely to engage in predatory pricing than for-profits,[19] I will show that for-profit investors may be injured even when predation does not occur. For-profit investors' claims of injury are neither obviously correct nor patently false. Their validity depends both on one's definition of fairness and on a set of factual issues including the market structure of the industry in question, the information available to firms before they enter, the costs of leaving the industry, and the efficiency of capital markets. Both the firms that complain of injury and the legal scholars who minimize the problem of unfair competition have over-simplified the issue and missed critically important features of the problem.

The economic analysis in Part I proceeds in three stages. First, I discuss competition between taxable and tax-exempt firms in a competitive economy where entrants correctly foresee the presence of tax-exempt competitors. Next, I drop the assumption of perfect foresight and show how for-profit firms will be affected by the tax and organizational status of nonprofits in the case of unanticipated competition. To conclude Part I, I assume that the economy is imperfectly competitive, so that nonprofits compete with for-profits in an oligopolistic setting. After specifying in Part I the market conditions under which for-profit investors may be harmed, Part II turns to the normative question. I suggest that the distinctions made in the positive economic analysis will enlighten, if not fully resolve, the problems of identifying "unfair competition." The analysis demonstrates that the present tax on nonprofits' "unrelated" business income is exactly the wrong way to deal with the problem, generating more "unfairness" than it has prevented. While an economically sophisticated definition of unfairness is possible, its application involves subtle empirical issues—so subtle that they may be beyond the administrative capacities of the IRS.

As a consequence, outright repeal of the tax on unrelated business activities seems like the best policy response.

I. The Importance of Market Structure

The policy debate has tended to view "unfair competition" in black-and-white terms. Either "unfairness" is the inevitable result of nonprofit entry, as for-profit firms and their congressional allies claim, or it almost never happens—as legal scholars assert.[20] If, however, we try to locate the debate within a framework emphasizing market structure and imperfect information, the claims made on both sides seem overly broad.

For-profit firms advance two arguments to justify protection against nonprofit competition. First, they claim that nonprofits will cut prices below the prices that taxable firms could charge. Economically oriented legal commentators have generally dismissed the price cutting claim by arguing that if price cutting were profitable, for-profit competitors would do it too.[21] But this argument ignores the possibility that nonprofits can affect market prices without resorting to overtly predatory behavior. Even in a competitive market where firms are too small to affect market prices individually, the entry of nonprofits could lower prices by shifting the overall industry supply curve. Nonprofits may be willing to enter an industry even when marginal for-profit firms are just breaking even. If for-profits cannot easily exit, supply will be larger, returns will be smaller, and price will be lower than in an industry without nonprofit firms. And in an oligopolistic industry, where individual firms *can* affect price levels, equilibrium prices might be lower when one of the major competitors is tax-exempt even though no one ever sets prices below cost.[22]

Second, for-profits argue that nonprofits will grow more quickly than for-profits and be less vulnerable to bankruptcy because they accumulate earnings faster.[23] While these claims have been accepted by most legal scholars,[24] their importance depends critically on the efficiency of capital markets. The more efficiently the capital market operates, the less important are retained earnings. If, however, lenders have difficulty evaluating a firm's investments, the firm may prefer to exploit internal sources of funds, and firms with high levels of retained earnings have an advantage.[25]

To assess the validity of the price cutting and retained earnings arguments, and thereby move from critique to contribution, requires a more systematic treatment that models the important market structures separately. To focus on the links among tax status, capital structure, and profitability, I will stylize the differences between firms in an extreme way. There are only two types of firms: for-profit corporations subject to the corporate income tax and nonprofit, tax-exempt corporations that can issue no equity and must raise capital through borrowing or gifts.[26] Nonprofit firms engage in tax-exempt business activity to provide funds to subsidize their primary activities. Therefore they want to maximize expected profits. I shall also assume that nonprofit firms are, on the average, as efficient as for-profits. Firms need not be identical, but any differences in costs or productivity are not systematically related to organizational form. The production of services by nonprofits is not complicated by ideological commitments or ineffective management.[27] Only tax and capital structure differences are important.

A. Anticipated Competition from Nonprofits

If an industry were perfectly competitive with easy entry and exit of firms, complaints of "unfair competition" would always be invalid. A for-profit firm that was losing money in competition with a nonprofit would simply leave that industry and earn the competitive rate of return elsewhere.[28]

But in many situations, human and physical capital are not fungible, and exit is therefore costly.[29] Even when exit is difficult, however, there is no reason to assume automatically that for-profit firms are suffering from "unfair" competition from nonprofits. In particular, whenever for-profits could reasonably have expected nonprofit competition at the time of their initial commitment to the industry, they would have included that fact in their calculations of expected returns and made their decision to invest accordingly. They would not have invested unless they

expected to do at least as well there as in alternative investments.[30] Therefore, in the case of anticipated competition, no claims of unfairness can be substantiated even if exit is difficult. This argument is independent of any particular model of nonprofit behavior. So long as the entry and subsequent behavior of nonprofits were anticipated, taxable firms could have no grounds for complaint.

The real world, however, frequently does not conform to the stringent conditions imposed here. The next section examines the fairness claims that might arise if exit is costly and if competition from nonprofits is unanticipated.

B. Unanticipated Competition

Competitive returns represent the opportunity cost of money and time invested in the firm. If entrepreneurs and investors had chosen not to establish a particular firm, they could have invested elsewhere at competitive rates. If a firm earns less than this competitive return and if exit is costly, the owners will suffer losses relative to what they could have earned elsewhere. Thus, one can pose the issue of unanticipated competition in the following way: Suppose that investors, when they decide to enter an industry, anticipate that all competitors will be for-profit firms. When many of the competitors turn out to be nonprofits, under what conditions should we expect the investors to earn "subcompetitive" returns?

In the absence of conscious predatory behavior, the only way nonprofits can affect for-profits is through "excessive" entry. That is, because of the tax treatment of nonprofits and the costs of exit, the industry has more firms, earning lower gross returns, than the for-profit investors expected ex ante. To show how "excessive" entry can occur, suppose that nonprofit entrepreneurial activity is concentrated in a single industry and that the nonprofit sector is small relative to the economy as a whole. Therefore, the sector's investment decisions have no noticeable effect on overall market rates of return. I shall also make the realistic assumption that, despite the tax avoidance potential of 100% debt financing, profit-maximizing taxable firms will have capital structures that mix debt and equity.[31]

Given these assumptions, we can derive the formal conditions under which nonprofit entry can depress for-profit returns below competitive levels.[32] Basically, "excessive" entry occurs when nonprofits have excess cash to invest and the return they can obtain by lending their money on the bond market is lower than the rate of return on active, entrepreneurial investments.[33] This will often be the case under my assumptions if the corporate tax rate exceeds the tax rate on individual income and if capital gains taxes are low. Nonprofits will continue to enter until their presence drives down industry returns to the point where marginal nonprofits are indifferent between passive and active investments. When that happens, marginal for-profits will want to leave the industry because they will be earning "subcompetitive" returns that are less than the market return on riskless assets. Because of the costs of exit, those firms will earn less than market returns whether they stay in business, go bankrupt, or sell out.[34]

The importance of this conclusion depends, first, on the concentration of nonprofit investments in particular industries; second, on the number of marginal for-profit firms in any industry earning only competitive returns; and third, on the assumption that nonprofits have excess cash available for investment. If the productive activities of nonprofits are broadly diffused, there will be little impact on profits anywhere in the economy. In fact, if tax-exempt firms have no special efficiency advantages in any industry, one would expect them to seek to maximize returns by establishing firms in a broad range of industries, thus earning close to a competitive return in each one. Since nonprofits control only a small proportion of the economy's resources,[35] one would not expect them to be able to push returns down much below ordinary competitive rates if their funds were evenly spread across the economy. Further, if most for-profit firms are more than marginally profitable, few firms will want to exit from industries which nonprofits enter, although all will earn somewhat less than they did before the entry of nonprofits.

Finally, if the nonprofits must borrow funds from banks or other lenders, the cost of capital may be too high to make active entrepreneurship worthwhile, even if the corporate tax rate exceeds the individual rate. Nonprofits might, for example, be charged rates that exceed competitive returns because lenders have difficulty monitoring the nonprofits' behavior.[36] Nonprofit managers must then decide whether to use a combination of gifts and loans to start new businesses, taking into account that nonprofits cannot enjoy the tax advantages of debt that accrue to for-profits. The smaller the pool of internal funds available to the nonprofit, the higher the rate of interest charged, and the larger the efficient scale in the industry, the less likely it is that active nonprofit entry will occur. Indeed, if the cost of borrowing is high enough, entry may only occur if the nonprofit is more efficient than existing marginal for-profits.[37] But in that case, if some for-profits were eventually driven out of business, there would be a net efficiency gain.[38]

Of course, there is no reason to believe that a nonprofit's capital structure disadvantages just match its tax advantages. Efficient for-profits may suffer losses if the entry of nonprofits is concentrated in their industry, or efficient nonprofits may fail to enter because they are unable to obtain adequate and affordable capital. If, as I have assumed, efficiency is not systematically associated with organizational form, then the form that is most favored by the tax system and the capital market in a particular situation would be able to exploit whatever opportunities arise. It is therefore possible that some efficient for-profit entrepreneurs and investors will earn subnormal returns if nonprofit entry is concentrated in a few industries. The extent of loss cannot categorically be affirmed or denied; it is an empirical issue to be resolved on a case-by-case basis.

C. Oligopoly

The impact of tax-exempt firms on their taxable competitors can be quite different if an industry is oligopolistic rather than competitive.[39] I shall show that the claims of for-profit firms to suffer "harm" may well be valid in an oligopoly with a fixed number of firms.

1. Effect of nonprofit status on output.

In an oligopolistic market, a firm's tax status may affect its marginal choices, and a tax-exempt firm may have a higher output and a larger effect on market price than a tax-paying firm.[40] To see how this can happen, consider a simple duopoly model in which a for-profit firm A, faces a single competitor B, which may be either a tax-exempt nonprofit financed by gifts and debt or a taxable for-profit. Assume, first, that there is no risk of bankruptcy and that lenders require the same minimum rate of return on both bonds and stocks.[41] Lenders require for-profit firms to maintain a ratio of debt to total capital below a specified level, and all firms purchase debt at a fixed rate that is independent of the debt-equity ratio and the level of private giving to nonprofits.[42]

Whatever its tax status, firm B produces the quantity that maximizes profits by equating the marginal revenue gain from an increase in output (after tax for the for-profit firm) with the sum of the marginal increases in operating costs and capital costs from the same increase in output (again, after tax for the for-profit firm). Firm B's profit-maximizing output will depend on its tax status if the tax affects its marginal decisions. This is true under the current system which taxes "accounting" rather than "economic" profits. That is, the tax is levied only on the return to equity, not on capital costs that take the form of interest on debt.[43] So long as some of its marginal capital cost is raised through stock issues, then, it costs the for-profit more to expand production than it does a comparable nonprofit. At the level of output that maximizes net profits for the

for-profit, marginal revenues would exceed marginal costs for the nonprofit. Therefore, as long as marginal revenue falls with increases in output and marginal operating and capital costs increase or remain constant, the nonprofit will choose a higher level of output than the similarly situated for-profit.[44]

2. Impact on for-profit competitors.

We are now ready to ask how the for-profit firm, A, is affected by the organizational and tax status of its competitor, B. Suppose, for concreteness, that both firms behave as Cournot oligopolists.[45] That is, each one maximizes profits assuming that the output of its rival remains constant. We can then draw reaction functions[46] Ψ_A and Ψ_B that show how firms A and B, respectively, will respond to the output choices of the other firm. Thus Ψ_A shows the profit-maximizing output chosen by A, given its belief about B's output choice.

Figure 1 illustrates a possible set of reaction functions where q_A is A's output and q_B is B's output. They have been drawn as straight lines, but all we really know is that they are downward sloping.[47] We established above that, *ceteris paribus*, B produces more when it is tax-exempt than when it is taxable. Thus, the reaction function of the tax-exempt firm, q_B^1, is everywhere above that of the taxable firm, q_B^2,

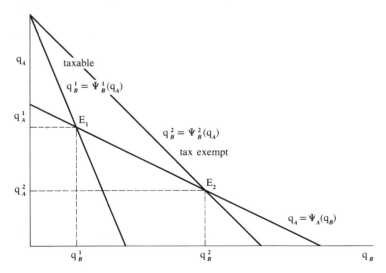

FIGURE 1

except when $q_B = 0$. Since, under the Cournot model, the reaction function for A is unaffected by B's tax and organizational status, the equilibrium level of q_B is higher and that of q_A is lower when B is tax-exempt. A is unambiguously worse off when its competitor is a tax-exempt nonprofit.

3. Importance of bankruptcy risk.

But this simple model overstates the injury that a nonprofit can impose on a for-profit. To proceed further, we should take account of the possibility of bankruptcy and default. In general, the interest rate lenders can charge is not fixed for all borrowers. Lenders charge highly leveraged firms higher rates to compensate for their increased risks of bankruptcy.[48] Unless nonprofits are very well endowed or have superior access to donations, they must finance themselves with debt. The risk of bankruptcy may therefore be lower for for-profits since they are partially financed by equity investments. This may make for-profit firms more effective competitors because they have superior access to capital funds. The advantages of the for-profit's capital structure and the risk-sharing feature of the corporate income tax[49] may outweigh the for-profit's tax disadvantages. As a consequence, the nonprofit may produce less output than a for-profit because the nonprofit is either rationed in the capital market,[50] or charged high rates by lenders. A may now *prefer* to face a nonprofit competitor.[51]

When bankruptcy is possible, firm managers and shareholders will be concerned not only with expected return but also with risk. In a duopoly or oligopoly, management would therefore be concerned both with its own *absolute* level of resources and with its vulnerability to bankruptcy *relative* to other firms in the industry: *Ceteris paribus*, a firm's risk of bankruptcy is negatively related to its competitors' risks. To see this, one need only recognize that if demand is unexpectedly low, everyone faces a heightened risk of bankruptcy, but a firm's risk is lower if there are other firms that are more marginal than it is. Marginal firms, with the smallest cushion of past profits, will exit first, thus pushing up prices and improving market conditions for those that remain.

In this regard, for-profits frequently claim that nonprofits are less likely to go bankrupt than for-profits. Since exit normally implies a loss of

wealth and outside sources of capital are not always available to tide a firm over bad years, retained earnings can be an important factor in a firm's survival. Because of their exemption from the corporate income tax, nonprofits are believed to accumulate more earnings in good years to cover losses in subsequent years. If this claim is correct, the relative immunity of nonprofits makes their for-profit competitors relatively *more* vulnerable to bankruptcy. The truth of this claim, however, depends on the availability of loss carryovers in the tax law. If there is full carryover, a firm is never taxed unless it actually earns profits over time. Thus, whether the nonprofit firm has an advantage in the bankruptcy context turns on the existence and completeness of loss carryovers, not on the corporate tax exemption alone. In fact, although loss carryover provisions are not complete, they are quite generous—losses generally can be carried back three years and forward fifteen years.[52] When profits oscillate from positive to negative as time passes, a taxable firm is treated almost like a tax-exempt firm on any gains which are balanced by losses in other years. For-profits will only be disadvantaged when they have a run of losses that lasts more than eighteen years with major losses in the middle of the period—more than three years after the last profit in the past and more than fifteen years before the first profit in future.[53] In short, nonprofits' lower risk of bankruptcy has been over-emphasized by their for-profit competitors. Current tax law treats the two organizational forms almost identically.

In conclusion, a for-profit oligopolist would prefer to compete with another for-profit whenever nonprofits have no special difficulties obtaining capital and corporate loss carryover provisions are incomplete. But the for-profit will prefer a nonprofit competitor whenever nonprofits have difficulty raising capital, and are therefore small and ineffective competitors.[54] Once again, while "harm" is possible, its extent depends upon a set of factual conditions determined by the details of the tax law and the operation of the capital market.

II. "Unfair Competition" and Economic Analysis

I have isolated two very different market structures under which for-profit investors may suffer from the presence of nonprofit competition. Each situation requires a different policy analysis. One complaint of unfair competition is easy to dismiss; the other forces us to confront some hard questions of economic justice.

The claims of unfair competition raised by oligopolists should not be taken seriously. American antitrust and regulatory policy makes it clear that there is no public commitment to the maintenance of profits resulting from economic concentration. If successful antitrust litigation forces a cartel to disband, or an oligopolist to divest an acquisition, private investors cannot obtain compensation for their loss of monopoly profits.[55] Similarly, firms should not be entitled to special protection when the production decisions of nonprofits lower their oligopoly returns.

A harder case arises when investors are deprived of competitive returns by the unanticipated entry of nonprofits. It is true that investors in a capitalist economy do not imagine they are guaranteed a competitive return by the government: Tastes may change, competitors may develop new technology, and so forth. But when competitive losses can be traced to particular government actions, the state has a special responsibility to justify its conduct.[56] Thus, the fifth amendment requires compensation if the government confiscates private property.[57] Of course, nothing so extreme is in question here. Rather than seizing firm assets, the government is "merely" manipulating the business environment to the advantage of nonprofit firms. Furthermore, it will never be entirely clear how much of the investor's losses are due to the tax-exempt status of some competitors and how much is due to other causes. On the level of constitutional theory, it is not clear what difference the "indirect" character of the government's taking ought to make in assessing the firms' right to compensation.[58] Whatever the theory, however, the case law plainly suggests that contemporary courts would refuse to extend the fifth amendment to cover tax-related claims of "unfair competition."[59]

Courts, however, are not the only institutions concerned with unfair governmental manipulation of the business environment. As the current tax law indicates, Congress itself has chosen to restrict nonprofits in the name of fairness. But the tax on "unrelated" business income is exactly the wrong way to respond to the problem. The nonprofit sector is, after all, rather small relative to the economy as a whole.[60] If the sector's productive business investments were spread across the economy, they would be unlikely to have much competitive impact.[61] But the tax on "unrelated" business income prevents such dispersion. Tax-exempt firms must now concentrate their profitable endeavors in those few lines of business judged to be "related." For example, the growth of gift shops and vacation tours operated or sponsored by nonprofit organizations may be, in part, a response to the conditions of the tax law.[62] Such concentration in a few areas makes it much more likely that the business activities of nonprofits will impose losses on competitive for-profit firms. Of course, these losses were only unanticipated by firms that were in the industry at the time of the substantial entry of nonprofits. But since the IRS and the courts continue to modify the definition of "unrelated," the statute probably continues to impose new windfall gains and losses on competing for-profit corporations as well as on nonprofits that rely on superseded rulings.[63]

It appears, then, that the tax on unrelated business activity creates more unfairness than it can possibly prevent. It should therefore be repealed. It is less clear what, if anything, should be put in its place. If the IRS is to pinpoint instances of "unfair" competition, it would have to carry out an economic analysis that hinges on difficult issues of market structure. Nonprofits might be given the right to enter *any* business subject to a finding by the IRS that further entry is likely to depress for-profit returns below competitive levels. Regulations explicating this standard would emphasize three factors—the prevailing rate of return in the industry, the speed and volume of nonprofit entry, and the costs of exit for for-profit firms. As similar inquiries in antitrust and public utility regulation suggest, this will often require the use of a great deal of discretion.[64] Nevertheless, the principles are clear: First, firms earning supercompetitive profits have no right to protection from "unfair" competition.[65] It is only when this first principle is satisfied that a second issue should be reached. Here, the IRS would determine whether nonprofits are entering at a rate that could have a substantial impact on for-profit returns. Finally, the IRS would have to be convinced that the exit costs of for-profits will be substantial. Once again, the use of discretion is inevitable—but the existence of very specialized human and physical capital would be the focus of concern.

A successful showing of unfair competition would be rare under these guidelines. Indeed, the process seems so cumbersome, and the gains in fairness so elusive, that a simple repeal of the present tax on unrelated income seems the better alternative. By permitting nonprofits to enter any profitmaking industry, repeal will reduce the pressure on for-profit firms in areas that are "related" to the primary activities of nonprofits. While this new freedom may increase the overall level of nonprofit entrepreneurial activity,[66] the diffusion of this activity throughout the economy reduces the chance that investors in a particular industry will suffer substantial unanticipated losses from nonprofit entry.[67]

Notes

1. *Revenue Revision of 1950: Hearings Before the House Committee on Ways and Means*, 81st Cong., 2d Sess. 579–80 (1950) (remarks of Rep. Dingell), *quoted in* Note, *The Macaroni Monopoly: The Developing Concept of Unrelated Business Income of Exempt Organizations*, 81 HARV. L. REV. 1280, 1281 n.10 (1968) [hereinafter cited as Note, *The Macaroni Monopoly*].

2. *See* C.F. Mueller Co. *v.* Commissioner, 190 F.2d 120 (3rd Cir. 1951); Note, *The Macaroni Monopoly, supra* note 1, at 1281. N.Y.U. also owned a leather company, a piston ring factory, and a chinaware manufacturing operation. Other colleges and universities owned enterprises manufacturing automobile parts, cotton gins, and food products, and operated an airport, a street railway, a hydroelectric plant, and a radio station. *See* Kaplan, *Intercollegiate Athletics and the Unrelated Business Income Tax*, 80 COLUM. L. REV. 1430, 1432 (1980).

3. Revenue Act of 1950, Pub. L. No. 81–814, §§ 301, 331, 64 Stat. 906, 947–53, 957–59 (codified at 26 U.S.C. §§ 502–514 (1976)). Several commentators have reviewed this law. *See* Bittker & Rahdert, *The Exemption of Nonprofit Organizations from Federal Income Taxation*, 85 YALE L.J. 299 (1976); Cooper, *Trends in the Taxation of Unrelated Business Activity*, 29 INST. ON FED. TAX'N 1999 (1971); Kaplan, *supra* note

2; Note, *Colleges, Charities and the Revenue Act of 1950*, 60 YALE L.J. 851 (1951) [hereinafter cited as Note, *Colleges, Charities, and the Revenue Act of 1950*]. For a discussion of changes made in the treatment of nonprofit firms by the 1969 and 1976 tax law revisions, see Bittker & Rahdert, *supra,* at 316–30; Kaplan, *supra* note 2, at 1431.

4. *See* Webster, *Effect of Business Activities on Exempt Organizations*, 43 TAXES 777 (1965). In the last six fiscal years the total tax collected was less than .05% of corporate income tax collections. Total fiscal year collections were $24,970,000 in 1977, $27,470,000 in 1978, $24,970,000 in 1979, $27,920,000 in 1980, and $34,310,000 in 1981. Internal Revenue Service, Data on Taxes Collected on Form 990T (unpublished IRS staff calculation).

5. Bromberg, *University Audits by IRS*, PHILANTHROPY MONTHLY, Feb. 1980, at 18 (newsletter).

6. Some of this confusion arises because the law seeks to tax "unrelated" business activity, *see* I.R.C. § 513(a) (1976), even though the legislative history speaks of "unfair" competition. *See* Kaplan, *supra* note 2, at 1433–44. *See also* Treas. Reg. § 1.513–1(b), T.D. 7392, 1976–1 C.B. 162, 168–69. Mansfield, *Some Aspects of Taxation of Business Income of Exempt Organizations*, in 3 STAFF OF HOUSE COMM. ON WAYS & MEANS, 86TH CONG., 1ST SESS., TAX REVISION COMPENDIUM 2067 (House Comm. on Ways & Means Comm. Print 1959) [hereinafter cited as TAX REVISION COMPENDIUM]; Webster, *supra* note 4. For discussion and commentary on these exercises in definition, see Cooper, *supra* note 3; Grant, *Taxation of Exempt Charitable Organizations Engaging in Business Activities*, 4 U.C.L.A. L. REV. 352 (1957); Greenbaum, *Business Dealings by Charities*, 14 INST. ON FED. TAX'N. 127 (1956); Webster, *supra* note 4.

7. The cuts will reduce tax incentives for individuals to donate money by decreasing the value of the charitable deduction on the margin. This may well outweigh the "income effect" of the tax cut, i.e., taxpayers have more money to spend and may contribute some of this excess to charity. At the same time, government spending cuts will reduce nondonative sources of income for nonprofits and decrease publicly

funded alternatives to private largesse. The Economic Recovery Tax Act of 1981 attempts to compensate for its disincentives to donate by means of an "above-the-line" charitable deduction for taxpayers who do not itemize their deductions. Economic Recovery Tax Act of 1981, § 121, I.R.C. § 170 (West Supp. 1982).

8. *See, e.g.*, N. BRODSKY, H. KAUFMAN & J. TOOKER, UNIVERSITY/ INDUSTRY COOPERATION (1980); Reinhold, *Government Scrutinizes Link Between Genetics Industry and Universities*, N.Y. Times, June 16, 1981, at 16, col. 1; *Industry's Role in Academia*, N.Y. Times, July 22, 1981, at D1, col. 3. *But see* note 66 *infra*.

At present, "all income derived from research for federal or state governments and, in the case of a college, university or hospital, all income derived from research performed for any person" is tax-exempt under I.R.C. §§ 512(b) (7)–(8). *See* Myers, *Unrelated Business Income: A Suddenly Explosive Issue*, in N.Y. PRACTIC- ING LAW INSTITUTE, SEVENTH BIEN- NIAL CONFERENCE: TAX PLANNING FOR FOUNDATIONS, TAX-EXEMPT STATUS AND CHARITABLE CONTRIBUTIONS 223 (1978).

9. I address only one of the public policies that differentiate between firms on the basis of organizational form. For example, nonprofits obtain lower postal rates, exemption from property taxes, and favorable treatment on government contracts. *See* U.S. SMALL BUSINESS ADMINISTRATION, GOVERN- MENT COMPETITION: A THREAT TO SMALL BUSINESS 74–79 (1980) (report of the advocacy task group on government competition with small business).

10. Recent data from the Census Bureau's 1977 Census of Service Industries indicate the extent to which taxable and tax-exempt firms coexist in various service industries. *See* U.S. DEP'T OF COMMERCE, BUREAU OF THE CENSUS, 1977 CENSUS OF SERVICE IN- DUSTRIES: OTHER SERVICE INDUSTRIES 53–1–2, 53–1–3 (1981) (Geographic Area Series, No. SC77–A–53, pt. 1 (1981)) (Table 1, Summary Statistics for the United States: 1977) (survey- ing the major service industries where competi- tion occurs, but omitting competition between subsidiary organizations, such as university book stores or cafeterias, and for-profit firms).

11. In the savings and loan and insurance industries, Congress has responded to complaints of "unfair" competition by equalizing the tax treatment of mutual and for-profit companies. *See* Klein, *Income Taxation and Legal Entities*, 20 U.C.L.A. L. REV. 13, 60 (1972).

12. The actual income tax laws facing cooperatives are complicated, but the basic implication of their special treatment is that they face lower tax rates on earnings than corpora- tions. For a summary of the law, *see* M. ABRAHAMSEN, COOPERATIVE BUSINESS ENTERPRISE 225–41 (1976). Cooperatives' lower tax liabilities arise mainly because the bulk of patronage dividends paid to members are not taxable to the cooperative. Agricultural cooper- atives also have access to low-cost loans from special banks and from members' contributions. They are, however, unable to raise capital through public issues of common stock.

13. *See* Ely, *Federal Taxation of Income of States and Political Subdivisions*, in 3 TAX REVISION COMPENDIUM, *supra* note 6, at 2091; Gilpin, *Business Income of Exempt Organ- izations—Tax Equalization—Electric Utility Service Organizations*, in 3 TAX REVISION COMPENDIUM, *supra* note 6, at 2077.

14. Horizontal equity is the principle that taxes should be equal for entities in equal posi- tions. *See* A. ATKINSON & J. STIGLITZ, LECTURES ON PUBLIC ECONOMICS 353–56 (1980).

15. A third claim should be kept separate because it deals with efficiency, not fairness. Thus when for-profits are harmed as a result of the superior efficiency of tax-favored firms, the claim that the *tax* law gives the successful firms their competitive advantage is obviously unjustified. Rather than restrict this form of "unfair competition," the entry of efficient non- profits ought to be encouraged. For an analysis of this claim, *see* Hansmann, *The Rationale for Exempting Nonprofit Organizations from Corporate Income Taxation*, 91 YALE L.J. 54 (1981). In such markets as daycare, hospitals, and education, for-profits may only be able to sur- vive if they differentiate their product from that provided by nonprofits.

16. Klein, *supra* note 11, at 58 ("if the tax system favors one competitor over another without good reason, the unfavored competitor can properly claim injustice").

17. *See, e.g.*, A. ATKINSON & J. STIGLITZ, *supra* note 14, at 160–226; Warren, *The Relation and Integration of Individual and Corporate Income Taxes*, 94 HARV. L. REV. 717 (1981).

18. *See* Note, *Preventing the Operation of Untaxed Business by Tax-Exempt Organizations*, 32 U. CHI. L. REV. 581, 591–92 (1965) [hereinafter cited as Note, *Preventing Untaxed Business*]. *See also*, Klein *supra* note 11, at 61–68; Note, *The Macaroni Monopoly, supra* note 1, at 1281 n.11; Note, *Colleges, Charities and the Revenue Act of 1950, supra* note 3, at 876.

19. Kaplan, *supra* note 2, at 1465–66; Klein, *supra* note 11, at 65–66; Note, *Colleges, Charities and the Revenue Act of 1950, supra* note 3, at 876. In an oligopolistic market prices may be lower if one of the competitors is nonprofit. *See* notes 45–54 *infra* and accompanying text. This price is not predatory in the usual sense of a seller who "cuts price below the level of its rivals' costs and perhaps also its own costs for protracted periods, until the rivals either close down operations altogether or sell out on favorable terms." F. SCHERER, INDUSTRIAL MARKET STRUCTURE AND ECONOMIC PERFORMANCE 335 (2d ed. 1980).

20. For a summary of the arguments on both sides, see 1 TAX REVISION COMPENDIUM, *supra* note 6, at 3. The most extended discussion by a legal scholar is in Klein, *supra* note 11. *See also* Bittker & Rahdert, *supra* note 3; Kaplan, *supra* note 2; Note, *The Macaroni Monopoly, supra* note 1; Note, *Colleges, Charities and the Revenue Act of 1950, supra* note 3.

Spiro discusses several recent cases where for-profits claimed to suffer from "unfair" competition because of nonprofits' favorable tax status. *See* T. Spiro, "Unfair Competition" Between Taxable and Tax-Exempt Organizations: Three Case Studies (Supervised Analytic Writing, Yale University 1979). He looks at an unsuccessful travel industry challenge to the travel activities of the American Jewish Congress and other tax-exempt organizations, Am. Soc'y of Travel Agents v. Blumenthal, 566 F.2d 145 (D.C. Cir. 1977), *cert. denied*, 435 U.S. 947 (1978). After losing in the courts, the travel industry attempted to influence IRS revenue rulings directly. A recent ruling was more favorable to the industry. *See* Rev. Rul. 78–43, 1978–1 C.B. 164 (stating that the University of North Carolina

Alumni Association's travel income was "unrelated," and hence taxable).

Spiro's second case involves the office products industry, where "sheltered workshops" for the handicapped compete with for-profit firms. The for-profits' trade association, the Office Products Manufacturing Association (OPMA), claimed unfair competition, but a Treasury Revenue Ruling upheld the tax exemption of sheltered workshops. *See* Treas. Reg. § 1.513–1(d)(4)(ii) (1967). Unlike the travel agents, OPMA has brought no court challenges and has concentrated on the important nontax advantages of sheltered workshops. *See* T. Spiro, *supra*.

A third example involves a court challenge brought by a taxable, commercial laboratory against a nonprofit corporation that promotes "manufactures, and the mechanic and useful arts." Structure Probe, Inc. v. Franklin Inst., 450 F. Supp. 1272 (E.D. Pa. 1978), *aff'd*, 595 F.2d 1214 (3d Cir. 1979). Structure Probe alleged that the Franklin Institute violated the Sherman Act, 15 U.S.C. § 2 (1976), in its sale of scanning electron microscope (SEM) services. The suit also claimed that the Institute's sale of SEM services violated its nonprofit charter. The court rejected both claims. 450 F. Supp. at 1288, 1290.

21. *See* Kaplan, *supra* note 2, at 1466; Klein, *supra* note 11, at 65–66; Note, *Colleges, Charities and the Revenue Act of 1950, supra* note 3, at 876.

22. Price theory demonstrates that marginal firms will be earning a competitive rate of return on their investment. *See* note 28 *infra* and accompanying text. Readers unfamiliar with basic price theory should consult a basic microeconomics text such as J. HIRSHLEIFER, PRICE THEORY AND APPLICATIONS (2d ed. 1980).

23. *See* H.R. REP. NO. 2319, 81st Cong., 2d Sess. 579–80 (1950) ("The tax-free status of these. . .organizations enables them to use their profits tax-free to expand operations, while their competitors can expand *only* with profits remaining after taxes."); Klein, *supra* note 11, at 255. There is a strong implication that firms do not have access to outside financing. *See generally* U.S. SMALL BUSINESS ADMINISTRATION, *supra* note 9.

24. *See, e.g.*, Kaplan, *supra* note 2, at 1466. One student commentator argues that a tax-exempt business can accumulate a larger surplus

than a taxable business, which may help it to weather lean years and to expand. *See* Note, *Colleges, Charities and the Revenue Act of 1950, supra* note 3, at 876. Another argues that

> the fast accumulation of capital made possible by tax-free profits is an advantage in any field. Where the market is expanding, the exempt enterprise will have a greater surplus to invest in production and distribution facilities, and, in anticipation of higher net profits, can compete more effectively for supplies, capital assets, and outside financing. Even in an industry with inelastic demand the untaxed business will be able to invest in improvements at a faster rate than its competitors.

Note, *The Macaroni Monopoly, supra* note 1, at 1282. *But see* Klein, *supra* note 11, at 66–67 (denying the special importance of retained earnings); Note, *Preventing Untaxed Business, supra* note 18, at 592 (same).

25. I assume here that profit-maximizing organizations will invest in the activities expected to yield the highest return. With perfect information and identical risk preferences, banks and firms would rank investment opportunities in the same way. Firms would be indifferent between borrowing from a bank or using their own funds, and borrowers could obtain funds either from banks or from firms lacking profitable investments within their own company. Asymmetric information changes this result. Banks and other lenders may have trouble monitoring a firm's use of investment funds. Therefore, they will charge an interest rate that takes account of this risk, and they may ration credit to the firm. In that case, retained earnings will be a cheaper source of funds for a firm than bank debt even taking into account "opportunity cost"—the return which the funds could earn if invested outside the firm.

26. Although I do not explicitly discuss the idiosyncrasies of cooperatives, mutuals, or government corporations, much of the basic analysis can be applied to these organizations with a suitable modification of the assumptions concerning tax status and capital constraints.

27. I make this assumption not because it is necessarily realistic, but because it permits me to focus on the difference in tax treatment. Bittker

and Rahdert suggest that "the business practices of charity-owned enterprises [may be] characterized more by caution than boldness." Bittker & Rahdert, *supra* note 3, at 320. Their claim is, however, an empirical assertion that has not been supported by systematic investigation. *See* D. Young, If Not For-Profit, For What? A Behaviorial Theory of the Non-Profit Sector Based on Entrepreneurship (1981) (unpublished manuscript, Yale University Program on Non-Profit Organizations) (case studies of nonprofit entrepreneurship).

28. In equilibrium in a competitive industry marginal firms earn zero "economic" profits and positive accounting profits. Their accounting profits include both a return to the equity capital invested in the firm, reflecting the opportunity cost of that capital, and the value of the entrepreneurs' time. Economic profits are only positive when a firm's return exceeds what owners could earn by withdrawing their money and time and investing them elsewhere in the competitive economy. On the distinction between economic and accounting profits, *see* J. HIRSHLEIFER, *supra* note 22, at 265. Bankruptcy costs would be small since they include only the administrative costs of going through the procedure. *See* Warner, *Bankruptcy Costs, Absolute Priority and the Pricing of Risky Debt Claims*, 4 J. FIN. ECON. 239 (1977) (estimates of the relatively small administrative costs of railroad bankruptcies).

29. Capital is malleable before it is put in place, but once embodied in equipment it cannot be changed easily. A firm has many choices before it has embraced a particular investment strategy. After the plant and machinery are purchased, the firm's choices are limited by the resale market for specialized capital. *See* R. ALLEN, MACRO-ECONOMIC THEORY: A MATHEMATICAL TREATMENT 256 (1967).

30. If all such competition were anticipated by for-profit investors, then the ratio of taxable to tax-exempt capital in the economy as a whole might affect overall rates of return, but taxable firms in *direct* competition with tax-exempt firms would be at no special disadvantage.

Harberger argues that in a competitive economy, a tax on corporate profits will, in the long run, lower overall returns to capital irrespective of where the capital is invested. Harberger, *The Incidence of the Corporation Income Tax*, 70 J. POL. ECON. 215 (1962). *See* McLure,

General Equilibrium Incidence Analysis: The Harberger model after ten years, 4 J. PUB. ECON. 125 (1975), for an assessment of Harberger's contribution and a summary and critique of the research spawned by Harberger's original article.

In contrast to Harberger, Stiglitz contends that in the absence of bankruptcy risks the corporate profits tax can be viewed as a lump-sum tax on corporations so long as the personal tax rate on bond interest exceeds the corporate rate. *See* Stiglitz, *Taxation, Corporation Financial Policy and the Cost of Capital*, 2 J. PUB. ECON. 1 (1973). This result depends on features of the tax law Harberger does not consider—that is, "on the interest deductibility provisions and on the fact that capital gains are taxed only upon realization." *Id.* at 33. If interest payments are not deductible, and if depreciation allowances equal true depreciation, then the tax is distortionary and capital flows from the taxed to the untaxed sector. King notes that "[t]his is similar to the conclusions of Harberger's (1962) model except that in our case equilibrium is determined by marginal and not average rates of return." King, *Taxation, Corporate Financial Policy, and the Cost of Capital: A Comment*, 4 J. PUB. ECON. 271, 276 (1975). Stiglitz pulls together and extends the discussion by viewing the tax in turn as "a tax on capital in the corporate sector, a tax on entrepreneurship in the corporate sector, a tax on pure profits in the corporate sector, and a tax on risk taking." Stiglitz, *The Corporation Tax*, 5 J. PUB. ECON. 303, 303 (1976).

31. Taxable firms can deduct interest paid on debt, but all returns to equity are taxed. Given this fact, for-profit firms might avoid taxes on profits by relying entirely on bonds to raise capital. If firms were 100% debt financed, the corporate income tax would be a tax on the pure or "economic" profits of inframarginal firms. *See* note 28 *supra*. The tax would not affect any firm's marginal choices, and hence firms would not care about the tax status of their competitors. In a competitive world, the marginal firms earn no excess "economic" profits, and hence the tax treatment of profits would be irrelevant. For-profit firms would be indifferent to the tax status of their competitors, and no issue of "unfair" competition would arise.

Despite these tax incentives, for-profits do not rely solely on debt for their capital requirements. There appear to be several reasons for this, one of which is the IRS's disfavor for 100% debt financing. *See* B. BITTKER & L. STONE, FEDERAL INCOME TAXATION 783–785 (5th ed. 1980). In addition, the more highly leveraged a firm is, the more likely are lenders to require higher rates on loans. These higher rates reflect the practical difficulties of monitoring managers and the increased likelihood of bankruptcy as the ratio of loans to equity increases. Therefore, a for-profit firm faces a cost of capital that depends on its capital structure and may well prefer a mixture of debt and equity in spite of the tax advantages of debt.

Modigliani and Miller initiated the current literature on firm capital structure. *See* Modigliani & Miller, *The Cost of Capital, Corporation Finance and the Theory of Investment*, 48 AM. ECON. REV. 261 (1958) (arguing that in a competitive world, with perfect capital markets, no taxes and no risk of bankruptcy, the capital structure of a firm has no effect on its value). Their article was followed by numerous attempts to develop alternative models, including models stressing monitoring and agency costs. *See e.g.*, Stiglitz, *Some Aspects of the Pure Theory of Corporate Finance: Bankruptcies and Takeovers*, 3 BELL J. ECON. & MGMT. SCI. 458 (1972); Jensen & Meckling, *Theory of the Firm, Managerial Behavior, Agency Costs and Ownership Structure*, 3 J. FIN. ECON. 305 (1976); Myers, *Determinants of Corporate Borrowing*, 5 J. FIN. ECON. 147 (1977); Ross, *The Determination of Financial Structure: The Incentive-Signalling Approach*, 8 BELL J. ECON. 23 (1977).

Miller, however, argues both that bankruptcy costs and agency costs are small and that the tax advantages of debt have been overrated. Miller, *Debt and Taxes*, 32 J. FIN. 261, 263–64 (1977). He further argues that equity investments are beneficial to high bracket taxpayers since capital gains are taxed at a lower rate than bond interest payments, and that this fact will be reflected in the market returns to bonds and stocks. *Id.* at 266–68. Thus, the tax laws will determine the debt-equity ratio for the economy as a whole, but there is no optimum ratio for any individual firm. *Id.* at 269. This result, of course, depends upon the assumption of insignificant bankruptcy and agency costs so that lenders are indifferent to the debt-equity ratios of individual firms.

32. Suppose that individual investors all have the same preferences toward risk, and that capital markets are competitive with market rates set so that individual investors are indifferent between bonds and stocks. To characterize this fact, suppose that there is a riskless asset which earns an after-tax rate of return of v and that all risky assets have nominal or expected returns set so that they are equivalent to a certainty of v. To avoid unnecessary complications, assume that firms issue no dividends, that the personal income tax rate on bond interest is s, that capital gains are untaxed, and that the corporate tax rate is t. This means that the nominal rate on bonds is r where $r = v/(1-s)$ and that the gross profit rate is w where $w = v/(1-t)$.

Suppose, further, that a nonprofit has some excess cash to invest. Since its interest earnings are tax-exempt, the nonprofit can earn the equivalent of r if it invests in the bonds of other firms. If it operates a tax-exempt business itself, it will earn w so long as the nonprofit believes that it will be just as efficient as the marginal for-profit.

Thus, in this simple case, it will establish a new business if w is greater than r, that is, if t exceeds s. When this condition holds, the nonprofit obtains tax benefits from either type of investment, but the benefits are greater for productive or "active" investments. If there are many nonprofits in this same situation, they will enter the industry until the marginal nonprofit earns r from its productive investment. At that point, many for-profit firms may want to leave the industry. Any firm that earned a pretax return of w before the entry of nonprofits is now earning r, which is less than w when t is greater than s.

33. If nonprofits were taxed on all productive "business" activities but not on passive investments, then in equilibrium nonprofits would compare the rate of return on active investments with the rate for a hypothetical risk-free investment. If we assume that they can earn no more than the marginal for-profit in an active investment, then nonprofits would only invest in bonds since they would still be tax-exempt. (I assume throughout that nonprofits are such a small force in the bond market that the rate of return is unaffected by their choice.)

Students of public finance may wonder how this rather large change in behavior can be consistent with Stiglitz's claim that, under certain conditions, the corporate income tax does not affect investment choices. See A. ATKINSON & J. STIGLITZ, *supra* note 14, at 142–46; Stiglitz, *supra* note 30, at 32. Stiglitz considers a case with no bankruptcy risks, where marginal investments are financed by borrowing, interest payments are deductible, and true economic depreciation is deducted to compute tax liability. Then, the firm's marginal investment decisions will remain unchanged whether or not it is subject to the corporate income tax. Furthermore, if the depreciation allowance exceeds economic depreciation, the tax system may actually encourage investment. This result, however, refers only to the *marginal* behavior of existing firms. Stiglitz assumes competitive markets and does not deal explicitly with entry and exit. Thus, while the marginal choices of nonprofits may well be unaffected, they will seek to make a discontinuous change and exit from the industry if their profits become taxable.

34. In the case discussed in text, the nonprofits' impact on for-profits turns on the asymmetric tax treatment of bonds and stocks, not on the nonprofits' tax advantages per se. Suppose, for example, that nonprofits faced the same tax rate on both bonds and stock. Then they would also favor direct investment over bond purchase so long as t is greater than s for other investors. See note 32, *supra*.

35. See Hansmann, *The Role of Nonprofit Enterprise*, 89 YALE L.J. 835, 835 n.1 (1980) (estimating that the nonprofit sector accounted for about 2.8% of national income in 1974).

36. This could happen if lenders believe that nonprofit organizations are particularly untrustworthy users of investment funds. Lenders might prefer to lend to entrepreneurs with some direct ownership interest in the enterprise who will benefit financially if returns are high. See Jenson & Meckling, *supra* note 31. Compare this supposition about the relative untrustworthiness of nonprofits as borrowers with the argument that nonprofits may be seen as more trustworthy than for-profits by donors and consumers. See Hansmann, *supra* note 35.

37. Tax disadvantaged firms, *see* note 34 *supra*, would be unable to borrow at all unless they were markedly more efficient than ordinary for-profit firms.

38. If as Hansmann, *supra* note 15, supposes, nonprofit firms are inefficiently capital constrained because of their inability to raise equity capital, then the likelihood that their for-profit competitors will earn subnormal returns is low so long as the two organizational forms are equally efficient.

39. The authors in Note, *Preventing Untaxed Business, supra* note 18, never go beyond competitive assumptions. Klein, *supra* note 11, at 61–66, uses an oligopoly model in which firms do not behave strategically. An oligopoly model is also implicit in Note, *Colleges, Charities, and the Revenue Act of 1950, supra* note 3, at 876, while competitive assumptions are implicit in Note, *The Macaroni Monopoly, supra* note 1, at 1281.

40. These issues did not arise in Part I–B because the firms were in a competitive industry. No individual firm could affect the performance of the industry by its choice of output level or price. In an oligopolistic industry this is no longer true. The essence of an oligopolistic industry is the close link between the behavior of one firm and the performance of another.

41. I thus abstract from differences in the tax treatment of these individual investments as well as from the relative riskiness of different types of investments.

42. I later consider the risks of bankruptcy and default. *See* text accompanying notes 48–53 *infra*.

43. To an economist, one of the costs of doing business is to provide a "normal" rate of return to invested capital, equal to what could be earned in alternative investments. "Economic" profits are measured as the excess of revenues over these and other costs. *See* note 28 *supra*.

44. If the corporate tax were levied on "economic" profits, firm *B*'s tax status and capital structure would be irrelevant, and firm *A* would be indifferent to the tax status of its competitor. It may look with envy at the higher profits of the tax-exempt firm, but these profits have no effect on its *own* performance.

To see this, suppose that firm *B* acts like a Cournot oligopolist. In other words, *B* maximizes profits holding the quantity *A* produces constant. *See* J. HENDERSON & R. QUANDT, MICROECONOMIC THEORY: A MATHEMATICAL APPROACH 222–31 (1971).

Let *B*'s profits, Π_B, be

$$\Pi_B = [p(q)q_B - c(q_B)](1-t) \qquad (1)$$

where p $\quad$ = price,

$\quad q_A$ $\quad$ = quantity produced by A,

$\quad q_B$ $\quad$ = quantity produced by B,

$\quad q$ $\quad$ = $q_A + q_B$,

$\quad c(q_B)$ = total cost of producing q_B,

$\quad t$ $\quad$ = corporate tax rate.

Then, if the second order conditions hold, *B*'s profits are maximized at:

$$\frac{d\Pi}{dq_B} = (1-t) [p'(q) q_B + p-c'(q_B)] = 0 \quad (2)$$

In a Cournot model, $p'(q) = \dfrac{dp}{dq_B}$ since firm *B* takes *A*'s output as given. Clearly, the level of q_B that solves (2) does not depend upon *B*'s tax rate. Firm *A* does not care about the tax status of its competitor. *See* Klein, *supra* note 11, at 63 (presenting a simple preliminary model); Note, *Preventing Untaxed Business, supra* note 18, at 591–92.

In contrast, when the tax is levied on "accounting" profits, a firm's tax status can affect its behavior. Then in long-run steady state equilibrium, "economic" profits are:

$$\Pi_B = (1-t) [p(q) q_B - \hat{c}(q_B) - rB(q_B)]$$
$$- rE(q_B), \qquad (3)$$

where $\hat{c}(q_B)$ = operating costs,

$\quad r$ $\quad$ = interest rate,

$\quad B(q_B)$ = dollar value of capital raised by sales of bonds,

$\quad E(q_B)$ = dollar value of other capital from equity or gifts.

Let $K(q_B)$ = dollar value of capital, let β equal the ratio of debt to total capital required by those who lend to for-profits, and let gifts equal some fixed dollar amount, $\overline{G}$. (I do not analyze the general strategic question of the trade-off between debt financing and the generation of private donations.) We can now ask how a competitor will act if, on the one hand, it is a for-profit with $t>0$, $\beta<1$, $B(q_B) = \beta K(q_B)$ and $E(q_B) = (1-\beta)K(q_B)$, or, on the other hand, a nonprofit with $B(q_B) = K(q_B) - \overline{G}$, and $E(q_B) = \overline{G}$. Capital raised through gifts has the same opportunity cost as equity capital since it can be invested at rate r. Thus, for the taxable for-profit firm:

$$\Pi_B^1 = (1-t) [p(q) q_B - \hat{c}(q_B) - r\beta K(q_B)] - r(1-\beta)K(q_B). \qquad (4)$$

For the nonprofit:

$$\Pi_B^2 = p(q) q_B - \hat{c}(q_B) - rK(q_B). \qquad (5)$$

Maximizing Π_B^1 and Π_B^2 with respect to q_B, and assuming the second order conditions hold, yields for the for-profit;

$$0 = (1-t) [p'(q) q_B + p - \hat{c}'(q_B) - \beta rK'(q_B)] - r(1-\beta) K'(q_B), \qquad (6)$$

and for the nonprofit;

$$0 = p'(q) q_B + p - \hat{c}'(q_B) - rK'(q_B). \qquad (7)$$

In the short run, if capital is fixed so $K'(q_B) = 0$, both types of competitors make the same profit maximizing output choices. If, instead, capital can be varied, the nonprofit will produce more output. To see this, suppose that each firm produces the same output. But then $-t (p'q_B + p - \hat{c}'(q_B) - \beta rK'(q_B))$ would have to equal zero. Substituting from (7), this implies that $-t(1-\beta) rK'(q_B) = 0$. But this is impossible so long as the marginal product of capital is positive. Thus, in general, when (7) is solved for q_B so that the nonprofit is maximizing net returns, the for-profit has marginal after-tax costs that exceed marginal revenues. So long as marginal costs increase (or remain constant) with q, and marginal revenues fall, the level of output chosen by the nonprofit is too large for the for-profit. Therefore, firm A is better off if its competitor is a for-profit firm.

The basic idea of this modeling exercise is that nonprofits set marginal revenue (MR) equal to marginal variable cost (MVC) plus marginal capital cost (MKC), while for-profits set $(1-t)$MR equal to $(1-t)$MVC + $(1-\beta t)$MKC. Since $\beta < 1$, $(1-t)$ is smaller than $(1-\beta t)$. Thus MR$-$MVC is larger than MKC at the taxable firm's profit-maximizing output.

45. *See* J. HENDERSON & R. QUANDT, *supra* note 44, at 222–28.

46. *See id.* at 226 (explaining reaction functions).

47. The lines slope downward because firm A maximizes profits at a lower level of output

the higher the output of firm B, and vice versa. *See id.* at 222–28.

48. The risk is higher because more of the firm's debt takes the form of fixed rate securities that must be repaid so long as any excess over operating costs is available. With equity investment, a firm's owners and managers have more freedom to decide how much income to pay out in dividends and how much to retain for investment and as a hedge against losses.

49. *See* Gordon, Taxation of Corporate Capital Income: Tax Revenue v. Tax Distortions (1981) (unpublished manuscript, Bell Laboratories) (stressing the risk-spreading benefits of the corporate income tax); Stiglitz, *The Corporation Tax*, 5 J. PUB. ECON. 303, 307–08 (1976) (same).

50. *See* D. JAFFEE, CREDIT RATIONING AND THE COMMERCIAL LOAN MARKET (1971) (attempting to explain why lenders may ration credit rather than raising interest rates); Jaffee & Russell, *Imperfect Information, Uncertainty, and Credit Rationing*, 90 Q. J. ECON. 651 (1976) (same).

51. In Figure 1, the positions of q_B^1 and q_B^2 would be reversed.

52. I.R.C. § 172(b) (West Supp. 1982).

53. In an inflationary world, loss carryforwards are less valuable than loss carrybacks unless they are somehow indexed to take account of price changes.

In addition to the loss carryover provisions, the Economic Recovery Tax Act of 1981 provides another benefit to loss-making corporations. The "safe harbor lease" provision of the Act allows them to sell their unused investment tax credits by engaging in sale-leaseback arrangements with business organizations in high marginal tax brackets. *See* Economic Recovery Tax Act of 1981, § 201(a), I.R.C. § 168(f)(8) (West Supp. 1982). Tax-exempt nonprofits are not eligible to participate since the law requires that both sides of the transaction be eligible to receive the investment tax credit. The only exception is for mass transportation vehicles, *id.*, a clause designed to benefit cities with large mass transit systems.

54. However, in many areas where competition is most brisk, nonprofits cannot be viewed as capital constrained. A fairly common pattern is competition between nonprofits that are "subsidiaries" of large, wealthy tax-exempt organizations such as universities, museums, or churches,

and for-profit firms that are small corporations with little or no access to national capital markets. This pattern is common in research and residential care for the retarded or mentally ill.

These cases stand in contrast to nursing homes, hospitals and publishing houses, where for-profits are frequently organized into chains or are part of larger corporations. Organized child day care services with a mix of chains, small independent for-profits and nonprofits, and nonprofits affiliated with churches and universities are intermediate cases. *See* C. COELEN, F. GLANTZ & D. CALORE, DAY CARE CENTERS IN THE U.S. 3, 83 (1979). Therefore, the for-profit firms that are most likely to complain about "unfair" competition will be those that both face the affiliates of well-endowed institutions and are themselves rationed in the capital market. In fact, this does seem to be the case. The major cases in this area involve travel agents and a testing laboratory. *See* Kaplan, *supra* note 2; T. Spiro, *supra* note 20.

55. The Sherman Act and the Clayton Act both seek to penalize firms which monopolize industries. Instead of compensation, violators may be subject to fines and triple damages awards. *See* F. SCHERER, *supra* note 19, at 494–495.

The debate in antitrust policy over controlling market structure versus controlling behavior suggests that an active policy to reduce monopoly profits wherever they occur would be controversial. This debate does not imply, however, a public commitment to preserving monopoly returns.

56. *See* B. ACKERMAN, PRIVATE PROPERTY AND THE CONSTITUTION 145–50 (1977); L. TRIBE, AMERICAN CONSTITUTIONAL LAW 456–65 (1978); Michelman, *Property, Utility and Fairness: Comments on the Ethical Foundations of 'Just Compensation' Law*, 80 HARV. L. REV. 1165 (1967).

Graetz, *Legal Transitions: The Case of Retroactivity in Income Tax Revision*, 126 U. PA. L. REV. 47 (1977), discusses the issue in the context of changes in the income tax law, but he fails to note the relationship between losses caused by tax law changes and unconstitutional takings of property. Instead he assumes "that any tax law changes considered here do not amount to 'takings'." *Id.* at 64 n.54. He then goes on to present a range of arguments for and against

grandfathering. Although "firm conclusions are difficult," he wishes to make the tax law "flexible" and argues that "[p]eople should make investments with the expectation that political policies may change." *Id.* at 87. On the similarities between taxation and takings, *see* Ackerman, *Four Questions for Legal Theory*, in NOMOS XXII, PROPERTY 351, 362 (J. Pennock & J. Chapman eds. 1980).

57. U.S. CONST. amend. V. *See also* B. ACKERMAN, *supra* note 56, at 116–118, 133–35; L. TRIBE, *supra* note 56, at 459–63; Michelman, *supra* note 56.

58. Michelman argues that a utilitarian policymaker would require compensation to be paid only if the public measure "can easily be seen to have practically deprived the claimant of some distinctly perceived, sharply crystallized, investment-backed expectation." Michelman, *supra* note 56, at 1233. For a broader view of the takings clause, *see* B. ACKERMAN, *supra* note 56.

59. *See* Alco Parking Corp. v. City of Pittsburgh, 417 U.S. 369 (1974) (tax designed to harm competitive position of for-profit firms does not constitute a taking).

60. *See* note 35 *supra*.

61. *See* Klein, *supra* note 11, at 63–64 n.212. If a nonprofit should obtain control of a large firm in some industry, it would be likely to do no more than limit monopoly profits in that industry.

62. T. Spiro, *supra* note 20, details the legal challenges of for-profit providers in these industries.

63. *See* Cooper, *supra* note 3; Greenbaum, *supra* note 6; Kaplan, *supra* note 2; Webster, *supra* note 4. For example, the IRS currently appears to be tightening the definition of "unrelated" at least with respect to universities. *See* Bromberg, *supra* note 5.

64. In Smyth v. Ames, 169 U.S. 466 (1898), the Supreme Court held that a public utility is entitled to a fair return on the value of its investment. It refused, however, to indicate precisely the economic meaning of its standard, saying "[h]ow such compensation may be ascertained, and what are the necessary elements in such an inquiry, will always be an embarassing question." *Id.* at 546. This standard was replaced in the 1940s by a standard that asked whether "the total effect of the rate order [is] unjust and unreasonable."

Federal Power Comm'n v. Hope Natural Gas Co., 320 U.S. 591, 602 (1944). Tribe notes that this is a test which "only the most egregiously confiscatory rate structure would have difficulty meeting." L. TRIBE, *supra* note 56, at 461 n.3 (1978).

65. This is the implication of the antitrust laws and of rate of return regulation for public utilities. *See* F. SCHERER, *supra* note 19, at 475–94; note 55 *supra*.

66. The increase will be larger if nonprofits are permitted to borrow to finance these investments. Currently, nonprofits can invest in real estate without paying taxes on their earnings, but they are not permitted to borrow to finance these investments. *See* Bittker & Rahdert, *supra* note 3, at 322–25. If, in fact, tax-exempt firms took advantage of their favorable tax position to engage in arbitrage so that a major share of the economy's investment funds passed through their organizations, then the hands-off policy recommended in the text would have to be re-examined. However, since lenders do not lend at favorable rates to highly leveraged firms, such arbitrage is unlikely given the limited resources available to tax-exempt firms from private donations.

67. Current changes in the depreciation allowances permitted for tax purposes, *see* Economic Recovery Tax Act of 1981, § 201, I.R.C. § 168 (West Supp. 1982), will reduce the taxes of most corporations. This tax reduction will work against any expansion of nonprofit investments in competitive markets by reducing the tax advantages of debt. It is no longer so likely that nonprofits will find that productive investments will dominate the purchase of bonds for purely tax reasons.

ARTICLE 9 ────────────────
Nonprofit Organizations
The Lost Opportunity
Lester M. Salamon

With the same energy that Franklin Roosevelt sought government solutions to problems, we will

SOURCE: From Palmer and Sawhill's THE REAGAN RECORD, Copyright © 1984 by The Urban Institute. Reprinted by permission of Ballinger Publishing Company.

seek private solutions. The challenge before us is to find ways once again to unleash the independent spirit of the people and their communities.... Voluntarism is an essential part of our plan to give the government back to the people.

—*Ronald Reagan, October 1981*

In few areas did the Reagan administration enter office with a clearer sense of purpose than in its commitment to voluntarism and private action as a way to respond to national needs. Yet in few areas were its concrete achievements more difficult to discern. Committed to a new approach to public problems stressing private initiative instead of public action, the administration never managed to convert that commitment into a serious program of action. In the process, it lost an important opportunity that existed in 1980 to develop an improved partnership between government and voluntary organizations as an alternative to purely governmental solutions to social problems.

The story of the Reagan administration's performance in the area of private-sector initiative and voluntary action is not only important in its own right, however. It is also important for what it can tell us about how the administration performed where its goals were not simply to cut spending, but to launch a program of genuine policy change. To tell the story, this chapter first examines the nature of the opportunity facing the administration, then reviews the administration's response, and finally analyzes the available evidence on the impact of the administration's policies on private voluntary agencies.

The Opportunity

The unusual opportunity that confronted the Reagan administration in 1981 to improve the relationship between government and voluntary institutions in American life and chart a new course for dealing with the nation's social problems arose from a number of developments over the previous decade: first, widespread dissatisfaction over the perceived ineffectiveness of government programs; second, growing strains that had surfaced in relations between government and nonprofit institutions; third, increasing concerns about a decline in charitable giving; and fourth, the convergence of a useful body of knowledge to guide a major reorientation of policy along lines that the new administration would have found congenial. To put the administration's performance in context, it is useful to explore the nature of this opportunity and the background against which the administration's actions and inactions took place.

Background: The Nonprofit Sector. A useful starting point is the private, nonprofit or charitable sector, since this is the set of organizations most likely to take on the functions that government would no longer perform or perform a different way. More a legal construct than a coherent entity, the nonprofit sector formally includes the 850,000-odd entities listed on the Internal Revenue Service's Exempt Organizations Master File, plus numerous religious organizations and informal groups. These organizations are as diverse as mutual insurance companies and child care centers, college fraternities and major hospitals, art galleries and political parties, religious congregations and nursing homes. What these organizations have in common is that they are private in structure yet not profit seeking. What is more, they perform functions judged to be publicly relevant or socially desirable, on the basis of which they are exempted from federal income taxation. Twenty-six different subsections of the Internal Revenue Code are required to spell out the types of organizations that qualify for tax exemption on this basis.

To make sense of this sector, it is useful to distinguish four major types of organizations: first, those that serve primarily their own members, such as professional associations and social and recreational clubs; second, those that serve essentially sacramental religious functions, such as churches, synagogues, mosques, and other religious congregations; third, those that serve a public or charitable purpose, but do so chiefly by channeling funds to other nonprofits, such as private foundations and United Way organizations; and fourth, those that serve primarily a public or charitable purpose, direct their efforts to a broader public than only the immediate members of the organization, and provide actual services in such areas as health care, education, the arts, and others.

Of these four types of nonprofit organizations, the last is of principal concern here as it provides the clearest expression of the public purpose concept that is the ultimate rationale for tax-exempt status.* Included are hospitals, health clinics, private universities, adoption agencies, nursing homes, day-care centers, neighborhood development organizations, private elementary and secondary schools, museums, art galleries, and symphonies. Also relevant are the funding organizations, but their activities can be examined through the income they provide to the service organizations.

Private organizations of this sort have roots deep in American history. As Alexis de Tocqueville observed in the 1830s:

> Americans of all ages, all stations of life, and all types of disposition are forever forming associations. . .to give fetes, found seminaries, build churches, distribute books and send missionaries to the antipodes. . . . In every case, at the head of any new undertaking, where in France you would find the government or in England some territorial magnate, in the United States you are sure to find an association.[1]

Despite the important social, economic, and political changes that have taken place since de Tocqueville wrote, voluntary organizations continue to play a vital role in American society. Although gauging the scope of that role with any precision is difficult given the available data, some rough measure can be obtained by combining data from a variety of official and

---

* The trade and social organizations are less relevant for our purposes because their services are restricted to members, and are thus not properly charitable or educational in purpose. Reflecting this, contributions to them are not tax deductible though the organizations themselves are tax-exempt. Sacramental religious organizations are also less relevant because, although they provide some services, this is not their primary purpose. Along with churches and funding organizations, this fourth group corresponds closely to what the Internal Revenue Code classifies as Section 501(c)(3) organizations, those serving charitable, educational, scientific, and related purposes. In addition to being tax exempt themselves, 501(c)(3) organizations are also eligible to receive tax-deductible contributions.

unofficial sources. † Based on Internal Revenue Service data, for example, we estimate that the charitable-service component of the nonprofit sector contains approximately 375,000 formally constituted entities.* This means that there are almost five times as many nonprofit service organizations as there are special districts and units of general government in the country, and about half as many incorporated nonprofit service organizations as there are for-profit corporations in the service sector of the economy.

Drawing on a combination of government data from the Internal Revenue Service, Census Bureau, and Bureau of Labor Statistics, combined with individual subsector surveys, we estimate that this set of charitable-service nonprofit

---

† All tax-exempt organizations except churches are required to file for tax-exempt status from the Internal Revenue Service (IRS) and to submit an annual information form, but many never do. In addition, the IRS system for classifying organizations makes it difficult to sort out the organizations that fall within the charitable-service component of the sector or to differentiate types of organizations within this component. The Census Bureau conducted a 1977 survey of exempt organizations, but the data are both out of date and imperfectly representative, since the bureau relied heavily on IRS data to generate its survey list.
* This figure represents the number of 501(c)(3) organizations recorded on the IRS Exempt Organizations Master File, after deleting religious congregations and funding organizations.

organizations had expenditures in 1980 of $114 billion and employed just over 4.6 million people. To put it another way, these organizations account for about 5 percent of the gross domestic product and about a quarter of the service employment in the nation. In some fields, nonprofits account for an even larger share of total employment— 48 percent in higher education, over 50 percent in social services, close to 60 percent in hospitals. As reflected in figure 8.1, well over half of all nonprofit expenditures and employment is concentrated in the health area, primarily in hospitals. Educational organizations account for another 20 percent of both expenditures and employment, with the remaining 20 percent split among an assortment of social service, civic, and cultural institutions that together constitute more than 80 percent of the organizations in the sector.

This nonprofit charitable-service sector is both large and in a continual process of change: a recent survey we conducted of some 3,400 such organizations, exclusive of hospitals and higher educational institutions, revealed that over 60 percent had been created since 1960. † This continued vitality of the nonprofit sector has somewhat confounded conservative critics of the American version of the welfare state, who have

---

†For details on this survey, see Michael F. Gutowski and Lester M. Salamon, *The Invisible Sector,* forthcoming.

EXPENDITURES ($114.2 billion)

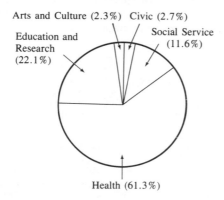

Arts and Culture (2.3%)   Civic (2.7%)

Education and Research (22.1%)   Social Service (11.6%)

Health (61.3%)

EMPLOYMENT (4.646 million employees)

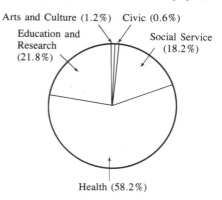

Arts and Culture (1.2%)   Civic (0.6%)

Education and Research (21.8%)   Social Service (18.2%)

Health (58.2%)

FIGURE 8.1   The Scope of the Nonprofit Sector, 1980.

SOURCE: Expenditure data from Lester M. Salamon and Alan J. Abramson, *The Federal Budget and the Nonprofit Sector* (Washington, D.C.: The Urban Institute Press, 1982), p. 15: employment estimates based on Bureau of Labor Statistics and Census Bureau data.

viewed the expansion of state power as inherently antagonistic to the voluntary sector.[2] How, then, can we explain this apparent vitality? What is the function of this set of organizations and how can we account for its durability?

There is, as yet, no generally accepted theory that can satisfactorily answer these questions and explain the workings of the nonprofit sector. But there are five strands of thought that bear on the question. One stresses simple historical accident, the fact that communities came into existence in America before government emerged. Lacking government institutions to handle their collective needs, Americans turned to voluntary associations, which were thus an established form when governments took shape and remained a significant presence even as government expanded.

A second school of thought focuses on the limitations of both the market and political institutions in providing the levels and types of collective goods and services that various groups within our pluralistic society consider appropriate. The limitations of the market are easy to see: the particular goods and services offered by the nonprofit sector are usually ones which the beneficiaries themselves could not afford and which require some form of collective action to be produced. But as a provider of "collective goods," the government, too, is limited by the need to generate sufficient political support for action, and by the need to make services available uniformly throughout a political jurisdiction. By contrast, nonprofit institutions provide a mechanism for producing "collective goods" considered necessary by one segment of the community even in the absence of full majority support. What is more, the nonprofit sector offers a way to target benefits more precisely, to escape the rigidities of large government bureaucracies, and to offer more personal ties to recipients. The more diverse the community, therefore, or the more entrenched the hostility to government involvement, the more extensive is nonprofit activity likely to be.[3]

A slightly different rationale for the nonprofit sector derives from what has been termed "contract failure," the fact that some goods or services either are so complex or are purchased under such conditions that consumers are unable to evaluate them effectively.[4] This is the case, for example, wherever the individual or organization footing the bill is not the one receiving the service—as is the case with welfare services or care for the aged. Nonprofit organizations have appeal in such cases because, compared with their for-profit counterparts, they presumably have fewer incentives to abuse the trust that consumers necessarily place in them.

Yet another rationale for nonprofit activity arises less from its presumed advantages in producing particular goods and services than from its presumed broader impact on the character of American society. Private, nonprofit organizations are important from this perspective because of the contribution they make to pluralism and liberty, to the preservation of multiple centers of thought and action, and thus to the potential for experimentation and for expression of multiple points of view.[5]

A final explanation of the durability of nonprofit organizations in the United States—and the explanation that has most relevance here—has to do with the relationships that have been forged between nonprofit organizations and government. Overlooked by many theorists of the "alternative-to-government" view of the private sector[6] is the peculiar way in which governments have been carrying out their responsibilities in the United States. In particular, the tremendous growth of government during recent decades has involved less the expansion of direct service delivery than the provision of funds to support the delivery of services by others. Governments at all levels have turned increasingly to a wide assortment of third parties to help them respond to public needs. The result is a pervasive pattern of "third-party government" that effectively blurs the distinctions between public and private sectors.[7]

In some areas, this creation or use of nonprofits has been dictated by substantive programmatic considerations, such as the desire to create a community-controlled mechanism for providing services and developing leadership in the War on Poverty. In other cases, the use of nonprofits is motivated by considerations of convenience or efficiency, by the fact that nonprofits are already active in a field and able to carry out the functions government wants performed without the need to establish new government delivery systems. Finally, the funneling of public resources into the private sector is often an incidental consequence of the government's decision to preserve choice of service providers for beneficiaries of particular programs (e.g., Medicare). Whatever the specific form, the cooperation between governments at all levels and nonprofit institutions has become extensive: our estimates indicate that by 1980 federal support alone amounted to approximately $40 billion—35 percent of the total revenues of nonprofit charitable-service organizations (table 8.1). By comparison, private charitable contributions to these same organizations from individuals, foundations, and corporations, totaled approximately $22 billion.*

The relationships that have developed between government and nonprofit institutions make it possible to set priorities and generate resources through a democratic political process, while still leaving the actual delivery of services in the hands of private organizations operating on a smaller scale than government agencies. But these relationships also have a number of problems, stemming in important part from the ad hoc fashion in which the relationships have been forged, with little attention to the careful demarcation of responsibilities. Concerned about accountability in the expenditure of public funds, governments often impose procedures that are administratively burdensome and threatening to the independence and informal character of nonprofits. Payment delays, underfunding of overhead costs, and other such problems further strain the relationships. Finally, considerable

sensitivity can arise over who actually determines organizational purposes—the voluntary boards nominally in control or the government program managers who provide the funds.

Although these concerns have a long history in government-nonprofit relations, they intensified greatly in the 1960s and 1970s as the scope of government involvement in fields of traditional nonprofit action increased. Concerns also began to grow about the viability of the philanthropic base of the nonprofit sector. For one thing, political pressures were building to curb perceived abuses of the tax exemption accorded to charitable contributions, particularly as they applied to private foundations. At the same time, the growth of charitable giving was not keeping pace with the growth of overall personal income. Between 1969 and 1979, for example, private giving as a share of gross national product declined from 2.1 percent to 1.8 percent.[8] One reason for this has been continual liberalization of the "standard deduction," and expansion of the number of taxpayers who take the standard deduction to over 70 percent of the total. This is important because taxpayers who itemize their tax deductions, and can therefore claim a deduction for charitable contributions, tend to give more to charity than comparable taxpayers who do not itemize. The increasing use of the standard deduction may thus have dampened the growth of giving.

---

* Of the remaining 45 percent of nonprofit income, approximately 5 to 10 percent came from other levels of government. The remainder came from a combination of fees and charges and earned income.

The 1970s: Development of Voluntary-Sector Agenda. Confronted by these challenges and prompted by the passage of the 1969 Tax Reform Act containing significant restrictions on

TABLE 8.1 Nonprofit Revenues from Federal Programs, 1980

Type of Organization	Federal Support (in $ billions)	Total Expenditures (in $ billions)	Federal Support as Share of Total (percentage)
Social service	7.3	13.2	58
Civic	2.3	3.2	72
Education and research	5.6	25.2	22
Health care	24.9	70.0	36
Arts and culture	0.3	2.6	12
TOTAL	40.4	114.2	35

SOURCE: Lester M. Salamon and Alan J. Abramson, *The Federal Budget and the Nonprofit Sector* (Washington, D.C.: The Urban Institute Press, 1982).

private foundations, the nonprofit community began to organize a response. The first and most important element of this response was the formation in 1973 of a private, blue-ribbon Commission on Private Philanthropy and Public Needs chaired by John Filer, chairman of Aetna Life and Casualty Company. The Filer Commission undertook a detailed inquiry into the health and characteristics of the nation's nonprofit sector, focusing particularly on the declining base of charitable support and the growing role of government. While acknowledging the dangers that the growth of government posed to the autonomy and character of the nonprofit sector, the commission in its 1975 report urged not that public support be constrained, but that private assistance be encouraged and expanded. Accordingly, the Filer Commission called for the establishment of a permanent national commission on the nonprofit sector, the expansion of corporate philanthropy, and a series of tax changes designed to encourage charitable giving.[9]

While the Filer Commission focused on nonprofit funding, a second effort, housed at the Washington-based American Enterprise Institute for Public Policy Research (AEI), sought to redefine the role of voluntary organizations and other so-called mediating structures such as neighborhood, church, and family within the modern welfare state. Rejecting ultra-conservative hostility to government involvement in serving community needs, this "mediating structures" project developed a way to square the conservative preference for voluntary institutions with existing government-guaranteed protections for those in need. It did so by proposing a much more explicit partnership between government, voluntary organizations, and other mediating institutions, under which government would strive at a minimum to avoid harming such institutions in its policies and seek "wherever possible" to "utilize mediating structures for the realization of social purposes." Thus, for example, proposals were advanced to underwrite the activities of tenant associations in managing inner-city housing, to encourage home-based care for the aged, and to rely on existing community institutions to handle foster care. As the leaders of this project summarized the thinking behind such proposals, "We suggest that the modern welfare state is here to stay, indeed that it ought to expand the benefits it provides—but

that *alternative mechanisms are possible to provide welfare-state services."*[10]

Unfortunately, the proponents of this "mediating structures" paradigm took too little account of the extent to which existing government program structures already used mediating institutions for the realization of social purposes, emphasizing instead the ways in which government harmed such institutions. Nevertheless, by virtue of its explicit acceptance of federal welfare responsibilities and its commitment "not to revoke the New Deal but to pursue its vision in ways more compatible with democratic governance," the AEI project offered a bridge between the conservative and liberal traditions and a program of action around which a conservative president might muster liberal support.

The process of developing a private-sector agenda begun by the Filer Commission and the "mediating structures project" benefited also from two developments occurring toward the end of the decade. The first was the formation in 1979 of a major new national association, Independent Sector, intended to represent all segments of the philanthropic community—funders as well as service organizations—in national policy deliberations and to foster greater awareness of and appreciation for the role of the "third sector."* Potentially, Independent Sector provided a vehicle for mobilizing support behind voluntary action of the sort that the AEI "mediating structures" project had developed. At about the same time, the conservative Heritage Foundation produced its own analysis of the status of philanthropy in America and reached many of the same conclusions as the Filer Commission. The result was to give a conservative stamp of approval to a program of action originally formulated by a moderate-liberal coalition of business, foundation, and voluntary-agency leaders.[11]

By the time the Reagan administration took office in early 1981, therefore, the pieces were in place—both analytically and politically—for a significant redirection of national policy that could place greater reliance on voluntary organizations, rationalize government's relationships with them, and foster a more sensible partnership between government and philanthropic

---

* This association now represents close to 500 foundations, associations of voluntary organizations (e.g., the YMCA, The Salvation Army, Catholic Charities), and corporate giving programs.

institutions in carrying out public purposes. A consensus had tentatively formed around four key elements of the redirection: first, increased financial support for programs that rely on "mediating institutions" to carry out public purposes; second, tax changes to encourage private charitable giving;† third, a set of management reforms to ease the burdens that existing federal programs often imposed on nonprofit providers; and fourth, increased use of challenge grants and similar devices to encourage organizations to supplement public support with private resources.

To be sure, these strands of thought had yet to coalesce into a coherent program of action. Also, voluntarism still provoked a degree of cynicism among liberals, while conservatives frequently had trouble squaring their fondness for the concept of voluntary organization with their hostility to some of the more activist neighborhood groups that had formed in the 1960s. Nevertheless, the sense of shared concern was striking, insofar as it spanned a considerable range of ideological and political persuasions, and even social and economic positions. Some of the thinking was reflected in the policy initiatives of the Carter administration—particularly in its urban policy, emphasizing as it did the need for a "new partnership" between public and private institutions. However, most of the ideas had hardly been tapped in any serious way. They were thus available for adoption by a new administration, particularly one committed to what the 1980 Republican platform termed the restoration of "the American spirit of voluntary service and cooperation, of private and community initiative."

The Reagan Response

Against this backdrop, the Reagan administration's handling of the nonprofit sector constitutes

a significant lost opportunity. Instead of forging a new coalition in support of a positive program of cooperation between government and the voluntary sector, the administration relied primarily on exhortation and on the expected success of its economic program to suffuse the country with voluntaristic spirit. The problem, however, was that the administration's tax and budget actions had serious negative implications —apparently never clearly thought out—for the overall health of the nonprofit sector. Insofar as the administration acted at all with specific regard for this sector, the actions—chiefly establishment of a task force—must be judged tepid at best and wrong-headed at worst. Meanwhile, the administration pushed a set of administrative changes widely perceived as threatening to the nonprofit sector. Thus, the lost opportunity is at least in part attributable to the simple fact that the administration's real priorities clearly lay elsewhere, in the major program of spending cuts, tax reductions, and defense buildup. But the situation is also in part attributable to an unwillingness to face up to the complex realities that characterized existing government-nonprofit relations, exacerbated by the hostility of a few individuals in the administration to particular types of organizations. To see this, it is useful to examine briefly the three major kinds of actions the administration took that touched most directly on the voluntary sector: spending and tax action, the formation of a Presidential Task Force, and changes that occurred or were proposed in the administration of some of the government's relations with the nonprofit sector.

Spending and Tax Cuts. Although the primary motivation for the combination of spending and tax cuts embarked on in 1981 was clearly economic, the cuts came to be defended as well for the contribution they could make to the restoration of voluntarism and private action. This defense was rooted in the conservative theories mentioned earlier, which regard the growth of government as seriously jeopardizing the position of the voluntary sector by robbing it of its "functional relevance." From here it was an easy step to the conclusion that the best way to revitalize the voluntary sector was simply to get government out of the way. In this sense, spending and tax cuts would create a new

† These included provisions to soften the "pay-out" requirements facing foundations, to liberalize the treatment of charitable contributions of appreciated property, and to permit taxpayers who take the standard deduction to claim "above the line" deductions for charitable contributions. The pay-out requirement in the 1969 tax act stipulated that private foundations must pay out in grants either the full value of their earnings or 5 percent of their assets, whichever was higher.

opportunity for the resurgence of the voluntary sector.

The scale of the opportunity to be thus created for the philanthropic sector was quite substantial, however. In the initial budget proposed for the period FY 1982 to FY 1985, the administration would have cut federal spending in program areas in which nonprofits are active by the equivalent of $115 billion in real terms below what would have been spent had FY 1980 spending levels simply been maintained. The bulk of the cuts would have come in the fields of social services, employment and training, and housing and community development, where we projected that overall federal spending would have declined by 57 percent in real terms between FY 1980 and FY 1985.[12]

By reducing government service provision, these spending cuts promised to increase demand for the services of nonprofit organizations. Never acknowledged, however, was that they would simultaneously reduce the revenues these organizations had available to meet even the pre-existing level of demand. In particular, we estimate that by FY 1985, after adjusting for inflation, the administration's proposed reductions in federal spending would reduce the federal support to nonprofit social service organizations by 64 percent below what it was in FY 1980. For community development organizations the drop would be 65 percent, and for education and research organizations, 35 percent.[13] In addition, some of the programs most clearly oriented toward stimulating private, nonprofit action—such as the community action program, neighborhood "self-help" housing, and some of the demonstration programs under the Comprehensive Employment and Training Act—were targeted for the sharpest cuts. Under the circumstances, the administration's protestations of support for nonprofit organizations and public-private partnership came to have an exceedingly hollow ring to leaders within the philanthropic community, and the potential support within this community for the administration's efforts began to slip quickly away.

The other prong of the administration's economic recovery program—the tax cuts—also had a hidden hook for the voluntary sector. An extensive body of research has found that, among taxpayers who itemize their deductions, higher tax rates are associated with a greater willingness to give to charity and lower tax rates with reduced propensities to give.[14] Because charitable contributions are tax deductible, the real "cost" of giving is the difference between what the taxpayer gives and what the taxpayer would have owed the government in the absence of the gift. For someone in the 70 percent tax bracket, for example, the net cost of giving a dollar to charity is only thirty cents, whereas for someone in the 40 percent tax bracket, the cost is sixty cents. In other words, as tax rates fall, the real cost of giving rises, and ample evidence attests that this real cost rise discourages giving.

Preoccupied as it was with the macroeconomic consequences of its tax-reduction proposals, the Reagan administration gave scant attention to these potential negative impacts on charitable giving. What is more, it opposed the proposals advanced by the philanthropic community to offset some of the potentially harmful effects by instituting an above-the-line charitable deduction for nonitemizers and liberalizing the foundation pay-out requirement—both proposals advanced by the Filer Commission and supported by Independent Sector and a broad coalition of voluntary groups. Although both measures passed over administration objections, the above-the-line charitable deduction passed only in watered-down form, with a phase-in provision, a cap, and a termination date. As a result, even after taking account of the increased income the tax act would leave private individuals, we estimated that the 1981 tax act would reduce individual charitable giving approximately $10 billion over the 1981–1984 period below what would have existed under prior law.[15]

Task Force on Private Sector Initiatives

Recognizing somewhat belatedly that a menu of spending and tax cuts hardly added up to a positive program for encouraging nonprofit action, the Reagan administration moved in late 1981 to create a Presidential Task Force on Private Sector Initiatives to "promote private sector leadership and responsibility for solving public needs, and to recommend ways of fostering greater public-private partnerships."[16] Chaired by Armco Steel President William

Verity, this task force was to bring together several dozen private-sector leaders to work closely with administration officials in developing an action program. As the president put it at the end of his speech announcing the formation of the task force: "I'm not standing here passing this off to you as solely your task, and the government will wash its hands of it. We intend a partnership in which we'll be working as hard as we can with you to bring this about."

Translating this promise into action, however, turned out to be far more difficult than was initially supposed. Despite the president's apparent personal commitment to the concept, "private-sector initiatives" never caught on as a serious policy effort. Although a special White House Office for Private Sector Initiatives was established, it was more a part of the White House public relations operation than a part of its policy operation, and was at any rate divorced from the budget decision making going on in the Office of Management and Budget (OMB) and the Treasury. Nor did the task force itself ever really jell as a shaper of policy; instead, it functioned the way the White House Office did, as an outreach effort to the press, outside groups, and local officials. If the leadership either of the task force or the White House Office ever seriously addressed the theoretical and policy issues formulated by the Filer Commission, AEI, the Heritage Foundation, and Independent Sector, there is little evidence of it in the actions taken.* The major activity involved amassing a data bank of innovative private-sector initiatives and organizing counterparts to the president's task force in local communities across the country.[17] Although these efforts usefully publicized the concepts of voluntarism and private action to solve public problems, and therefore buttressed the administration's effort to change public thinking about the role of government and involve private-sector leaders in public problem solving, the tangible effects were fairly limited. *Newsweek* was thus exaggerating only in part when it pointed to the delivery of 5,000 copies of Pat Boone's record "Lend a Hand" to

radio stations across the country as one of the most substantive accomplishments of the effort.[18]

Administrative Changes

Contributing further to the administration's lack of credibility as the supporter of an effective program of voluntarism and public-private partnership were a number of administrative actions that served to erode further its relations with the voluntary community. The first was the administration's decision to eliminate the government's principal vehicle for promoting community-based voluntary organization, the Community Services Administration (formerly the Office of Economic Opportunity). The second was to appoint as the head of ACTION, the government's voluntary action agency, a particularly ardent conservative who early on began an effort to stop funds from going to liberal, activist organizations. Simultaneously, as part of its budget program, the administration sought to eliminate or significantly scale back the postal subsidy for nonprofit organizations, which would have seriously hampered their direct mail fundraising efforts.

Even more significant for the voluntary sector were two further administrative developments. The first was an effort to restrict access to the federal government's annual work-place charitable drive—the Combined Federal Campaign (CFC). The largest work-place charitable solicitation in the nation, the CFC functioned from its inception in 1957 through the mid-1970s as a mechanism for raising funds for a small number of large charities, such as United Way, the Red Cross, and the American Lung Association. In the 1970s, however, a variety of independent charities, many of them minority run or advocacy oriented (such as the Black United Fund and Planned Parenthood), managed to secure access to the CFC, and thus challenged the dominance of the established charities. With United Way support, the Reagan administration moved to reverse this trend, developing a draft executive order that would bar from the CFC any charity that provided abortion or abortion counseling, or that engaged in lobbying or litigation on public policy issues. Leaked to the press in late 1981, this draft executive order sparked

_____

* Indeed, the task force leadership pointedly rejected an offer from the American Enterprise Institute to develop a more explicit program of action built around the "mediating structures" paradigm.

a prolonged battle between the Office of Personnel Management (which supervises the CFC) and a broad coalition of independent charitable organizations. This struggle led ultimately to issuance of a slightly revised presidential executive order in February 1983, which a U.S. District Court then declared unconstitutional. In the process, the administration added considerably to the apprehensions of the more liberal elements of the voluntary community.

Even more widespread apprehensions were created by yet another administrative move: an effort launched by the counsel of the Office of Management and Budget to rewrite the accounting principles applicable to voluntary organizations as well as to many other contractors with government. Concerned that public funds were going to support advocacy activity, OMB proposed to revise its Circular A-122, which sets guidelines for organizations that receive government support. Under the proposed revised rules, organizations that engage in "political advocacy" would have to isolate all funds and resources used for this purpose from those used to fulfill their government contracts, if the government contract represented as much as 5 percent of their budget. An organization that engaged in "political advocacy" might therefore have had to maintain separate offices and administrative structures—one for the government contract work and one for the advocacy activity. Not surprisingly, the reaction from the philanthropic community was exceedingly hostile and the administration once again found itself in the middle of an intense battle with many of the organizations that might naturally have been its allies.

Not content simply to ignore the AEI "mediating structures" agenda, the administration thus seemed determined to violate the AEI's basic principle that "public policy should cease and desist from damaging mediating structures." Whether this was conscious policy or simply the working out of the uncoordinated preferences of individual administration appointees, the cumulative effect on the voluntary sector was unmistakably chilling. As Brian O'Connell, president of the broad-based Independent Sector, pointed out in testimony before a subcommittee of the House Government Operations Committee in early 1983, the administration's combination of rhetorical support for voluntarism and budget

policies hostile to the charitable sector had made many leaders of voluntary organizations "skeptical, if not cynical, about the president's interest." "Against this uneasy backdrop," O'Connell continued, the administrative changes proposed by the administration, particularly the proposed change in the rules governing political advocacy, "have changed the skepticism and cynicism to bewilderment and hostility."[19]

The Impact

Aside from the question of whether the Reagan administration failed to take actions that might have capitalized effectively on the opportunity that seemed to exist to improve the federal government's relations with the voluntary sector and to develop a new approach to coping with domestic problems, it is important to analyze the actual impact of the actions the administration did take. It is necessary to ask, in other words, not simply whether the Reagan program failed to help nonprofits but also whether it did them real damage. For this purpose, we draw on two principal bodies of data: first, an analysis of the implications for nonprofit organizations of the actual changes in federal spending approved by Congress and the president for the period between FY 1980 and FY 1984; and second, a major survey we conducted of nonprofit, human service, and arts agencies in late 1982 and early 1983 to determine how government budget cuts were affecting nonprofit agencies and how the agencies were responding.

Federal Budget Changes

In FY 1980, the federal government spent $148.3 billion on programs in fields where nonprofit organizations are active.* This figure represented slightly more than one-fourth of all federal expenditures and one-third of all nondefense

---

* "Programs in fields where nonprofits are active" includes all programs for which changes in the funding levels are judged to have direct implications either for the demand for nonprofit services or for the revenues of nonprofit organizations. For a fuller discussion, see Salamon and Abramson, *The Federal Budget and the Nonprofit Sector*, pp. 22–25.

expenditures. About 35 percent of these expenditures went for health services; about 25 percent for needs-tested income assistance; about 20 percent for "social welfare" (including social services, employment and training, and community development); about 15 percent for education; and the remaining 5 percent for international assistance, arts and culture, and conservation.

As a result of the Omnibus Budget and Reconciliation Act of 1981, the level of federal spending on these programs declined in real terms by about 5 percent between FY 1980 and FY 1982 after adjusting for inflation. Excluding Medicare and Medicaid, which continued to grow, the drop was a much larger 13 percent. Following these significant reductions in FY 1982, however, Congress generally resisted the further sharp cuts in these program areas

proposed by the administration for FY 1983 and FY 1984. At the same time, health care finance programs continued to grow. The result is that, by FY 1984, total federal spending on programs of relevance to nonprofit organizations was down 3 percent below FY 1980 levels with health included, and by 15 percent with health excluded (table 8.2). In short, although less extreme than the administration originally proposed, a significant reduction occurred in federal support in a variety of program areas (particularly social welfare, education, and the environment) likely to affect the demand for nonprofit services.

The reductions just outlined had implications for nonprofit revenues, not just for service demands. In particular, if we assume that the share of each program's resources going to nonprofits in FY 1984 was roughly equivalent to the

TABLE 8.2 Changes in Federal Spending in Fields Where Nonprofit Organizations Are Active, FY 1984 vs. FY 1980 *(in constant 1980 dollars)*

| | Outlays (1980 $ billions) | | Percentage Change |
Program Area	FY 1980	FY 1984ª	FY 1984 vs. FY 1980
Social welfare	28.5	18.6	−35
Social services	7.3	5.7	−22
Employment and training	10.3	4.1	−60
Community development	10.8	8.8	−19
Education and research	22.0	17.1	−22
Elementary, secondary	7.0	5.4	−23
Higher	10.4	6.9	−34
Research	4.7	4.8	+2
Health	53.0	63.2	+19
Medicare, Medicaid	49.1	60.0	+22
Health services	4.0	3.1	−23
Income assistance	36.4	37.2	+6
International aid	6.9	7.3	+4
Arts and culture	0.6	0.5	−17
Environmental	0.7	0.4	−43
TOTAL	148.3	144.2	−3
TOTAL excluding Medicare, Medicaid	99.2	84.2	−15

a. In FY 1980 dollars.
SOURCE: Author's calculations based on federal government data from Office of Management and Budget and Congressional Budget Office documents. Figures for FY 1984 are estimates reflecting congressional actions on the FY 1984 budget. Actual FY 1984 spending may differ as a result of changes in economic conditions, different spending rates, and supplemental appropriations.

share they received in FY 1980, then the federal budget changes enacted as of the start of 1984 translate into overall reductions in nonprofit support from the federal government of between 1 and 2 percent in FY 1982 and FY 1983, and an actual increase of 3 percent in FY 1984, as noted in table 8.3. However, these figures are somewhat misleading because they largely reflect the impact of the continued growth of Medicare, and to a lesser extent Medicaid, reimbursements to hospitals. With health care excluded, the value of federal support to the remaining types of nonprofit organizations dropped an estimated 27 percent between FY 1980 and FY 1984.

Impact on Nonprofits

Whether these reductions in federal spending actually show up in the balance sheets of nonprofit organizations cannot be determined from topdown budget analysis alone. Too many other factors can intervene along the way. For example, state and local governments may have decided to offset or intensify federal cuts through their own funding decisions; local delays may have occurred in putting the cuts into effect because of ongoing contractual arrangements; the *share* of program

resources going to support nonprofit service delivery rather than delivery by state or local government agencies may have changed. To gain a clear view of actual impacts, we conducted a major survey of nonprofit charitable service organizations, exclusive of hospitals and higher educational institutions, in sixteen localities across the country. The localities were selected to provide a reasonable cross section of the nation in terms of region, size, economic circumstance, urban and rural character, and philanthropic tradition.[20]

The first conclusion that emerges from this survey confirms our earlier finding that government plays a substantial role in the financing of nonprofit activities in this country. Sixty-two percent of the organizations responding to our survey reported receiving some government support in 1981, and government accounted for a significant 41.1 percent of their total revenues.* This makes government the largest single source of revenues for these organizations, with the other two major sources—fees and service charges (28 percent) and private giving (20 percent)—far behind.

* Because agencies frequently do not know which level of government is the actual source of the government funds they receive, the figures reported here are for all levels of government.

TABLE 8.3 Estimated Changes in Nonprofit Revenues from the Federal Government, FY 1980 vs. FY 1984, by Type of Organization

Type of Organization	Outlays (1980 $ billions)		Percentage Change
	FY 1980	FY 1984[a]	FY 1984 vs. FY 1980
Social services	6.5	4.2	−35
Civic	2.3	1.8	−22
Education and research	5.5	4.6	−16
Health	24.9	30.2	+21
Foreign aid	0.8	0.6	−25
Arts and culture	0.4	0.2	−50
TOTAL	40.3	41.6	+3
TOTAL excluding Medicare, Medicaid	16.7	12.2	−27

a. In FY 1980 dollars.
SOURCE: Author's calculations based in part on federal government data from Office of Management and Budget and Congressional Budget Office documents. Data for FY 1984 are estimates based on congressional action in the FY 1984 budget as of the beginning of the fiscal year.

The extent of reliance on government varied widely, however, among different types of agencies. In particular, mental health, legal services, and housing and community development organizations all received more than 60 percent of their total income from government in 1981, contrasted with 15 percent for arts and cultural agencies. But even among the types of agencies in which the government share of total support is smallest, the proportion of agencies receiving some government assistance was substantial. In fact, except for education (chiefly private elementary and secondary education), well over half of all the nonprofits we surveyed in every field received some government support. Government budget decisions are thus very relevant to a sizable

segment of the nonprofit community, even though the impacts of the decisions vary markedly.

Between 1981 and 1982, the organizations we surveyed reported a 6.3 percent reduction in their government support (table 8.4). Among some types of agencies, however, the loss of government support was even larger: 29 percent for legal services organizations, 16 percent for housing and community development organizations, 13 percent for employment and training agencies, and 9 percent for social service organizations. By contrast, government cutbacks were far less pronounced among institutional/residential care, health, mental health, and arts and culture agencies. In fact, the institutional/residential care institutions registered an overall

TABLE 8.4   Real Changes in Nonprofit Revenues and in Support from Government by Type, Age, and Size of Agency, 1981–1982

Type of Agency	Percentage Change in Government Support	Percentage Change in Total Agency Expenditures
By Primary Service Area:		
Legal services/advocacy	−28.8	−15.5
Housing/community development	−15.6	+1.9
Employment/training	−12.7	−6.3
Social services	−8.8	−4.0
Multiple purpose	−8.1	−1.7
Education/research	−7.3	+0.6
Culture/arts/recreation	−1.3	+5.7
Health care services	−1.3	+3.3
Mental health	−0.1	+6.5
Institutional/residential care	+4.1	+4.4
By Age (year formed):		
Pre-1930	−2.6	+1.9
1930–1960	+1.3	+2.3
1961–1970	−12.7	−4.5
1971–present	−6.7	+1.5
By Size (expenditures):		
Small (under $100,000)	−1.8	+9.7
Medium ($100,000 to $1 million)	−4.9	+2.7
Large (over $1 million)	−6.7	−0.4
ALL AGENCIES	−6.3	+0.5

NOTE: In comparing the columns the reader should bear in mind that since government funds accounted on average for about 40 percent of total revenue for these organizations, a 6.2 percent reduction in government support will translate into only a 2.4 percent reduction in total agency income.
SOURCE: Michael Gutowski and Lester M. Salamon, *The Invisible Sector.*

increase in the value of their government support, reflecting in all likelihood the continued
growth of the federal Medicaid program. When
this information is combined with the data on
changes in government funding by agency age
(in the same table), it is clear that the reductions
in government support were most marked among
agencies created in the 1960s. In other words,
it was the "Great Society" agencies that seem
to have suffered most under the Reagan administration. These impacts are all the more notable
in view of the fact that the survey was carried
out in late 1982, before the full results of the
federal budget changes had shown up.*

The evidence, outlined above, of the impact
of government budget cuts on nonprofit agencies
tells only part of the story of the consequences
of this administration's policies toward the
nonprofit sector. To understand the rest of it, we
need to see what happened to the nongovernment
sources of income for these agencies, since one
of the central tenets of the administration's
Economic Recovery Program was that some or

* The survey results also compare 1982 agency receipts
to 1981 levels rather than the 1980 levels used as a
baseline for the earlier budget discussion.

all of the loss of government support could be
made up through private charitable contributions.

On the surface, the evidence of overall
change in nonprofit expenditures seems to support this optimistic expectation (table 8.4). In
particular, although the real value of total government support to these organizations declined by
about 6 percent between 1981 and 1982, overall
organization expenditures increased by 0.5 percent, even after adjusting for inflation. Real
increases occurred in several of the nongovernment sources of support, particularly direct
individual giving, fees and charges, foundations,
and corporations, all of which grew by more
than 5 percent even after adjusting for inflation.
Given the economic downturn that had begun
when our survey was conducted, this was a
notable achievement.

Examination of the absolute dollar amounts
in table 8.5, however, makes it clear that the real
explanation of the capacity of the nonprofit sector to close the funding gap left by federal budget
cuts was not the increases that occurred in private
charitable contributions. Rather, the major part
of the explanation was the increase that occurred
in income from fees and service charges. Almost
60 percent of the income that enabled the average

TABLE 8.5 Changes in Revenue for the Average Nonprofit Agency, 1981–1982, by Source

Source	Income from Source, FY 1981 (in 1981 dollars)	Change in Income from Source, 1981–1982	
		Amount (in 1981 dollars)	Percentage
Government	295,665	–18,530	–6.3
Corporations	21,639	+1,261	+5.8
Foundations	24,253	+1,262	+5.2
United Way	38,165	+712	+1.9
Religious and other federated funders	19,317	+703	+3.6
Direct individual giving	42,747	+3,387	+7.9
Fees, charges	200,001	+13,251	+6.6
Endowment, investments	32,097	+1,323	+4.1
Other	40,134	+891	+2.2
Unallocated	3,595	–599	NA
TOTAL	717,613	+3,661	+0.5

NA = not applicable.
SOURCE: Gutowski and Salamon, *The Invisible Sector.*

agency to close the gap left by federal budget cuts and achieve a modest 0.5 percent overall real gain came from such fees, and another 6 percent came from endowment and investment income. Thus, earned income, which comprised 55 percent of the nongovernmental income of these agencies in 1981, made up 65 percent of the increase in revenues for the average agency between 1981 and 1982. Private giving from all sources, which comprised 45 percent of the nongovernmental income of these agencies in 1981, accounted for only 35 percent of the increase. In other words, the philanthropic share of agency income actually declined.[21]

Reflecting this situation, not all types of agencies were able to make up for the government cuts. In general, agencies that focus chiefly on the poor and that have the least access to fee income did the worst (as is apparent from table 8.6). Thus, legal services, employment and training, social services, and multiple service agencies all had above-average reductions in government support and below-average increases in fees and charges. These agencies were also at the high end of the scale in terms of reliance on government support to start with. Although such agencies did manage to increase their private charitable support, the increases were not sufficient to recoup losses in government support. For these types of agencies, therefore, the expectations of the Economic Recovery Program clearly did not work: far from allowing these agencies the support needed to expand their services to fill the gaps left by government cutbacks, the available philanthropic support did not even allow the agencies to maintain prior levels of activity.

A quite different picture emerged for the six types of organizations that posted real increases in expenditures between 1981 and 1982 (mental health, arts and culture, institutional care, health and housing). Typically, these organizations either experienced relatively modest reductions in government support, or relied on government support less than average, or both; they also had access to above-average increases in fees and charges. The one exception is the housing and community development organizations, which started the period with extremely high reliance on government support, experienced sharp reductions in that support, but were nevertheless able to generate alternative sources of support from virtually all other sources. In the process,

we hypothesize, they probably somewhat altered their program mix, turning to fee-generating activities such as provision of day-care services and the like.

The picture that emerges from this analysis of changes in the funding base of the nonprofit, charitable-service sector thus casts doubt on both the doomsayers and the Pollyannas. Because the federal cuts were less severe than originally proposed, because not all agencies were equally dependent on government support to start with, and because many agencies managed to increase fees and charges significantly, some types of agencies—particularly those in health-related areas and arts and culture—managed to achieve real growth in expenditures between 1981 and 1982, and to move the average for the organizations examined here slightly into the black. At the same time, however, agencies in fields where the government cutbacks were most noticeable and where access to additional fee income is limited, ended up worse off despite some real increases in private philanthropic support. Finally, although the charitable-service sector as a whole managed to hold its own between 1981 and 1982, it was not in a position to expand its services to fill in for the much larger reduction of direct government services in these fields.

Conclusion

The Reagan administration entered office with a significant opportunity to redefine the way services are delivered in the American version of the modern welfare state and to forge a new model of partnership between government agencies and voluntary groups. Both the political and intellectual roots of such a reorientation of policy had been laid in the 1970s, and a coalition of leaders in the philanthropic and nonprofit communities was eager to push this agenda along. Instead of seizing this opportunity, however, the administration was content to rely mostly on rhetoric, while putting uncritical faith in the workings of its economic program to revitalize the nonprofit sector. In the process, the administration exposed this sector to a period of considerable fiscal strain. Faced with reduced government support —and unable to cover costs from private charity—those agencies in a position to do so

TABLE 8.6 Changes in Real (Inflation-adjusted) Support for Selected Types of Nonprofit Organizations, 1981–1982, by Source (*percentages*)

Type of Agency	Government	Corporations	Foundations	United Way	Religious and Other Federated Funders	Direct Individual Giving	Fees, Charges	Endowment/ Investments	Other	TOTAL
Legal services	−29	+11	+3	+5	+5	+4	+19	−12	−7	−16
Employment/training	−13	+9	−29	−9	+5	+18	+1	−11	+5	−6
Social services	−9	+1	−2	+4	+3	+4	+4	−3	−6	−4
Multipurpose	−8	+25	−3	+1	+3	+7	+4	+14	−10	−2
Education/research	−7	+2	+14	−3	+7	+7	+3	−1	+5	+1
Housing, community development	−16	+19	+7	−5	+3	+50	+45	+37	+4	+2
Health care	−1	+2	+2	0	−12	−2	+7	+16	0	+3
Institutional/residential care	+4	−4	+34	+4	+11	+23	+5	+9	0	+4
Arts, culture	−1	+3	+8	+4	−2	+11	+9	+3	+5	+6
Mental health	0	+16	−6	−2	+49	−20	+29	+2	+130	+7
ALL AGENCIES	−6	+6	+5	+2	+4	+8	+7	+4	+2	+1

SOURCE: Gutowski and Salamon, *The Invisible Sector.*

turned increasingly to their commercial activities, expanding their reliance on fees and charges. Agencies not in a position to pursue this course found themselves unable to sustain even prior levels of activity, let alone expand enough to meet new demands created by government retrenchment. By emphasizing the importance of private sector initiatives and voluntary action, the Reagan administration has put the philanthropic sector on the agenda of American politics in a forceful way. But by pursuing a serious assault on a broad range of domestic programs that help to sustain the sector financially, without accompanying this with a positive program of action, the administration may have set back its own private-sector agenda for some time to come and discredited voluntarism further as a serious policy alternative.

Acknowledgments

This chapter draws heavily on the results of The Urban Institute's Nonprofit Sector Project, a national effort to examine the scope and structure of the private, nonprofit sector in this country and the impact on this set of organizations of recent changes in public policy. The Nonprofit Sector Project is supported by more than thirty corporations, community foundations, and national foundations from all parts of the country. The author wishes to express his gratitude to all these supporters, as well as to the other members of the Nonprofit Sector Project staff who made important contributions to developing the data reported here: Alan Abramson, Leah Goldman, Michael Gutowski, Paul Lippert, Anita MacIntosh, James Musselwhite, Harriett Page, and Lauren Saunders.

Notes

1. Alexis de Tocqueville, *Democracy in America*.

2. See for example, Robert A. Nisbet, *Community and Power*, 2d edition (New York: Oxford University Press, 1962), pp. 98, 109, 268.

3. This line of thought is developed most clearly in Burton Weisbrod, *The Voluntary Nonprofit Sector* (Lexington, Mass.: Lexington Books, 1978), pp. 1–15.

4. Henry Hansmann, "The Role of Nonprofit Enterprise," *Yale Law Journal*, vol. 89, no. 5 (April 1980), pp. 835–901.

5. This view of government is articulated in the Commission on Private Philanthropy and Public Needs, *Giving in America* (Washington, D.C.: Government Printing Office, 1975). See also Nisbet, *Community and Power*; and Brian O'Connell, ed., *America's Voluntary Spirit: A Book of Readings* (New York: The Foundation Center, 1983).

6. This alternative-to-government view has been developed most forcefully in the writings of Robert Nisbet, who views "the momentous conflicts of jurisdiction between the political state and the social associations lying intermediate to it and the individual" as "the most fateful . . . of all the conflicts in history." See his *Community and Power*, p. 268.

7. For a fuller explanation of this concept of third-party government, see Lester M. Salamon, "Rethinking Public Management: Third-Party Government and the Changing Forms of Government Action," *Public Policy*, vol. 29, no. 3 (Summer 1981), pp. 255–257; Lester M. Salamon, "Block Grants and the Rise of Third-Party Government: The Challenge to Public Management," testimony before the Joint Economic Committee, U.S. Congress, July 15, 1981.

8. Estimates from *Giving, U.S.A., 1982 Annual Report* (New York: American Association of Fund Raising Counsel, Inc., 1981), p. 32.

9. *Giving in America: Toward a Stronger Voluntary Sector*, Report of the Commission on Private Philanthropy and Public Needs (Washington, D.C.: Government Printing Office, 1975).

10. Peter L. Berger and Richard John Neuhaus, *To Empower People: The Role of Mediating Structures in Public Policy* (Washington, D.C.: American Enterprise Institute for Public Policy Research, 1977), p. 1. See also Robert Woodson, *A Summons to Life* (Washington, D.C.: American Enterprise Institute for Public Policy Research, 1981); John Egan, John Carr, Andrew Mott, and John Roos, *Housing and Public Policy: A Role for Mediating Structures* (Cambridge, Mass.: Ballinger Publishing Company, 1981).

11. Stuart Butler, *Philanthropy in America: The Need for Action* (Washington, D.C.: The Heritage Foundation and the Institute for Research on the Economics of Taxation, 1980).

12. Lester M. Salamon and Alan J. Abramson, *The Federal Budget and the Nonprofit Sector* (Washington, D.C.: The Urban Institute Press, 1982), p. 26.

13. Ibid., p. 51.

14. See, for example, Michael K. Taussig, "Economic Aspects of the Personal Income Tax Treatment of Charitable Contributions," *National Tax Journal*, vol. 20, no. 1 (March 1967), pp. 1–19; Robert A. Schwartz, "Personal Philanthropic Contributions," *Journal of Political Economy*, vol. 78, no. 6 (November-December 1970), pp. 1264–1291; Martin Feldstein, "The Income and Charitable Contributions: Part I— Aggregate and Distribution Effects," *National Tax Journal*, vol. 28, no. 1 (March 1975), pp. 81–100; James N. Morgan, Richard F. Dye, and Judith H. Hybels, "Results from Two National Surveys of Philanthropic Activity," in Commission on Private Philanthropy and Public Needs, *Research Papers*, vol. 1 (Washington, D.C.: Department of the Treasury, 1977), pp. 157–323; and Charles T. Clotfelter and C. Eugene Steuerle, "Charitable Contributions," in Henry Aaron and Joseph Pechman, eds., *How Taxes Affect Economic Behavior* (Washington, D.C.: The Brookings Institution, 1981), pp. 403–466.

15. For a more detailed analysis of the likely impact of the 1981 Tax Act on private individual giving, see Charles Clotfelter and Lester M. Salamon, "The Impact of the 1981 Tax Act on Individual Charitable Giving," *National Tax Journal*, vol. 35, no. 2 (June 1982), pp. 171-187.

16. "Remarks of President Ronald Reagan at the Annual Meeting of the National Alliance of Business," *Public Papers of the President of the United States: Ronald Reagan, 1981* (Washington, D.C.: Government Printing Office, 1982), p. 885.

17. For further details on this task force and its operations, see Renee Berger, "Private Sector Initiatives in the Reagan Era: New Actors Rework an Old Theme," in Lester M. Salamon and Michael Lund, eds., *The Reagan Presidency and the Governing of America* (Washington, D.C.: The Urban Institute Press, 1984).

18. "The Hard-Luck Christmas of '82: With 12 Million Unemployed and 2 Million Homeless, Private Charity Cannot Make Up for Federal Cutbacks," *Newsweek*, December 27, 1982.

19. Testimony of Brian O'Connell before the Subcommittee on Legislation and National Security of the Government Operations Committee of the United States House of Representatives, March 1, 1983.

20. In particular, one large metropolitan area, one medium-size metropolitan area, one small metropolitan area, and one rural county were selected in each of the four major Census regions. In most of these sites, the full population of nonprofit service organizations other than hospitals and higher education institutions was identified and surveyed by mail. In the larger communities (New York, Chicago, San Francisco, Pittsburgh, and the Twin Cities) random samples of organizations were used. Altogether, 6,868 valid organizations were surveyed, of which 3,411—or 49.7 percent—responded. For a fuller discussion of the results of this survey and of the methodology employed, see Michael Gutowski and Lester M. Salamon, *The Invisible Sector.*

21. This conclusion finds support as well in the data on national patterns of private giving as of 1983, which were recently released by the American Association of Fund-Raising Counsel. According to these data, nonreligious private giving increased from $26 billion to $33.9 billion between 1980 and 1983. After adjusting for inflation, this represents a real increase of $2.05 billion, or 8 percent. Of this total, almost half represents contributions to hospitals and other health providers, leaving an increase of $1.07 billion for all other nonreligious organizations. By comparison, between FY 1980 and FY 1983 we estimate that federal government support for these same types of nonprofits declined by $4.2 billion. In other words, with these data, it appears that private giving made up for about one-fourth of the projected government cuts experienced by nonprofit service organizations outside of hospitals. Although some portion of the increased religious giving that occurred during this period may also have found its way to these organizations, the overall picture from the national giving estimates still seems highly consistent with our more detailed survey results. See, *Giving USA:*

1983 (New York: American Association of Fund-Raising Counsel, 1984).

ARTICLE 10
100 Years of Tax Policy Changes Affecting Charitable Organizations
Gary N. Scrivner

Introduction

Charitable organizations have allowed themselves to be defined in large part by reference to their status as organizations exempt from taxation under specific provisions of the Internal Revenue Code including Sections 501, 521, 526, 527 and 528.[1] One commentator observed the various categories of exempt organizations are not ". . .the result of any planned legislative scheme . . .(but were) enacted over a period of eighty years by a variety of legislators for a variety of reasons. . ."[2] There appear to have been three basic reasons why these charitable entities were considered to be entitled to tax exemption: "heritage," "morality" (public policy), and "special interest" legislation. This same commentator concluded: "While it is clear, in retrospect, that many of the exemption provisions have long outlived their historic justification, it is also clear in contemporary application that many of them continue to play a very crucial role in the law of tax exempt organizations. . . ."[3]

Let's thus try to explain how heritage, morality, and special interests help to form and affect changes in the very nature of charitable organizations. The Tariff Act of 1894 was the first major piece of tax legislation enacted by Congress that specified the entities subject to taxation.[4] Prior to this, exemption existed merely by virtue of statutory commission. The Tariff Act of 1894, however, imposed a flat two percent tax on corporate income, forcing Congress to face the task of defining the appropriate subjects of tax exemption. Section 32 of The Tariff Act of 1894 provided for exemption for nonprofit charitable, religious, and educational organizations, fraternal beneficiary societies, certain mutual savings banks, and mutual insurance companies.[5] In addition, the income tax

charitable contribution deduction originated in the 1894 statute.

A year later though, the 1894 act was declared unconstitutional thereby relegating exempt organizations to the pre-1894 statutory ommission state of affairs.[6] Focusing only on charitable organizations as described in the present Internal Revenue Code Section 501(c)(3), the 1894 act stated: "Nothing herein contained shall apply to. . .corporations, companies or associations organized and conducted solely for charitable, religious or educational purposes."[7] This is not inconsistent with the older English common law concept of philanthropic, nor those concepts of almost any earlier civilization or religion. This illustrates the heritage reasoning for charitable organizations mentioned above. Our early legislators were not setting any precedent by exempting religious or charitable organizations.

With respect to the morality or public policy grounds upon which organizations are granted exemption, this is a derivative of the concept that they perform functions that, in the organization's absence, government would have to perform. Therefore, government should be willing to forgo tax revenues for the public services rendered. The Supreme Court has observed: "The State has an affirmative policy that considers these groups as beneficial and stabilizing influences in community life and finds this classification (exemption) useful, desirable and in the public interest."[8] Even as early as 1924, the Court noted: "Evidently the exemption is made in recognition of the benefit which the public derives from corporate activities of the class named, and is intended to aid them when not conducted for private gain."[9] In addition, in a frequently cited case from 1877, the Supreme Court stated: "A charitable use, where neither law nor public policy forbids may be applied to almost anything that tends to promote the well-doing and well-being of social man."[10]

The third consideration underlying the concept of exemption, that is special interests, may be illustrated by examining some of the categories under Section 501, other than Section 501(c)(3), such as Section 501(c)(5) labor, agricultural, or horticultural organizations, Section 501(c)(6) business leagues, chambers of commerce, or trade associations, Section 501(c)(9) employee beneficiary societies, or Section (c)(19) veteran's organizations. Each of these types of entities (and numerous others), are granted exemptions generally because of the political power these special interest groups represent or the legislature's feeling these groups (veterans particularly) should be rewarded for past services to the country.

Revenue Act of 1913, to 1950

Although the 1894 act succumbed to constitutional challenge, the Sixteenth Amendment to the Constitution was ratified and the Revenue Act of 1913 was passed containing measures comparable to the 1894 act and permanently establishing tax exemption for certain organizations.[11] At least one commentator has indicated Congress believed these organizations should not be taxed and found that proposition sufficiently obvious as to not warrant extensive explanation.[12] This argument is supported by the fact that the Committee Reports for the 1913 act contain no explanation for the inclusion of these provisions. To tax these entities would be to disavow a part of our nation's heritage. Alexis de Tocqueville commented on this heritage in his masterpiece *Democracy in America* first published in 1830:

> Americans of all ages, all conditions, and all dispositions constantly form associations. They have not only commercial and manufacturing companies, in which all take part, but associations of a thousand other kinds, religious, moral, serious, futile, general or restricted, enormous or diminutive. The Americans make associations to give entertainments, to found seminarys, to build inns, to construct churches, to diffuse books, to send missionaries to the antipods; in this manner they found hospitals, prisons and schools. If it is proposed to inculcate truth or to foster some feeling by encouragement of a great example, they form a society. Wherever at the head of some new undertaking you see the government in France, or a man of rank in England, in the United States you will be sure to find an association. . . . [13]

This comment was of course made some eighty years prior to the enactment of the Revenue Act of 1913. This heritage was discussed

further by John Stewart Mill in *On Liberty*, published in 1859: "With individuals in voluntary associations. . .there are varied experiments and endless diversity of experience. What the State can usefully do is to make itself a central depository, and active circulator and difusor, of the experience resulting from many trials. Its business is to enable each experimentalist to benefit by the experiments of others; instead of tolerating no experiments but its own."[14]

Exemption from taxation for certain types of not-for-profit organizations is a principle larger than the Internal Revenue Code. Citizens combatting problems and reaching solutions on a collective basis, in associations, is inherent in the very nature of American societal structure. Thus, the Revenue Act of 1913 did little to change the nature or existence of not-for-profit organizations, it merely served to define those organizations for the purpose of administrative convenience in the collection of an income tax.

One major difference in the 1913 act and the 1894 act is that the statute in 1913 contained a reference to *scientific purposes*—an apparent byproduct of the Industrial Age. In addition, the prohibition concerning the inurement of net income to private persons was added by the 1913 Act.[15] Subsequent revenue acts continued expansion of the various charitable categories. The Revenue Act of 1918 added the prevention of cruelty to children and animals and in 1921, community chest funds, foundations, and literary groups were also made tax exempt. Arguably this would not have been necessary had the term "charitable" been used in the English common law sense. One commentator has noted that had Congress intended to rely on the common law definition of charity, there would have been no need to add to the statutory law at all as was done in 1913.[16]

The prior exemption requirements were generally carried forward to the Revenue Act of 1934 at which time the rule that "no substantial part of the activities of an exempt organization can involve the carrying on of propaganda or attempting to influence legislation. . ." was added.[17]

The Revenue Acts of 1936, 1938, and 1939 did little to affect the rules for exempt organizations, with two exceptions. The Revenue Act of 1936 made the charitable contribution deduction available to regular corporations.[18] In addition, the Revenue Act of 1938 stated: "The exemption from taxation of money or property devoted to charitable and other purposes is based upon the theory that the government is compensated for the loss of revenue by its relief from the financial burden which would otherwise have to be met by appropriations from public funds and by the benefits resulting from the promotion of the general welfare."[19]

The Revenue Act of 1950

The *feeder organization rules* were added to the law in 1950 as a legislative mandate against the *destination of income theory*. This theory viewed the use of an organization's income for charitable purposes to be of a greater consequence than the source of its funds. The principle problem with the destination of income theory was that it allowed exempt organizations to undercut for-profit business which, of course, must take taxes into account in pricing their goods and services. The House Ways and Means Committee Report accompanying the Revenue Act of 1950 concluded the feeder organization provision was intended to "deny exemption of a trade or business organization . . . (I)t appears clear to your committee that such an organization is not itself carrying out an exempt purpose. Moreover, it obviously is in direct competition with other taxable businesses . . ."[20]

The Senate Finance Committee Report accompanying the corresponding Senate version of the bill states that the provision applies "to organizations operated for the primary purpose of carrying on a trade or business for profit, as for example, a feeder corporation whose business is the manufacture of automobiles for the ultimate profit of an educational institution."[21] This provision focused primarily on the deprivation of tax exempt status to organizations whose primary purpose was a commercial one. In addition to the feeder organization rules, the unrelated business income tax rules[22] were added in response to perceived unfair competition by nonprofits. The primary objective of the unrelated business income tax was to eliminate this source of unfair competition by placing those unrelated activities on the same tax basis as the private business endeavors with which they had

to compete. The House Ways and Means Committee Report on the Revenue Act of 1950 further observed:

> The problem at which tax on unrelated business income is directed here is that of unfair competition. The tax free status of . . . (exempt) organizations enables them to use their profits tax free to expand operations, while their competitors can expand only with the profits remaining after taxes. Also, a number of examples have arisen where these organizations have, in effect, used their tax exemption to buy an ordinary business. That is, they have acquired the business with no investment on their part and paid for it in installments out of subsequent earnings—a procedure which usually could not be followed if the business were taxable.[23]

The Senate Finance Committee further observed in 1950 that the unrelated income tax was to apply to "so much of . . . [an organization's] income as rises from active business enterprises which are unrelated to the exempt purposes of the organization."[24] The taxation of unrelated income was seen as a more effective sanction in the long run for authentic enforcement of the requirements for tax exempt status than the denial of exempt status. Only if a substantial portion of an organization's income is from unrelated sources is an organization to be denied tax exemption.[25]

The Internal Revenue Code of 1954

A major restructuring of the Code occurred in 1954,[26] much like the one in 1939, resulting in a complete renumbering of all the sections of the Code to the system we continue to use to this day. When we talk of a Section 501(c)(3) organization we are referring to the number assigned by the 1954 act. Thus, the 1954 Code has had a great deal to do with how we defined exempt organizations over the past 30 years, how they were formed, and how the rules have been enforced. The act also added some new rules to the exemption statute: The listing of organizations was expanded to include organizations formed for the purpose of "testing for public safety," and Section 501(c)(3) organizations were expressly forbidden to "participate in, or intervene in (including the publishing or distributing of statements), any political campaign on behalf of any candidate for public office."[27]

Remarkably, these added restrictions had little influence on the growth of the nonprofit sector during the 1950s. It wasn't until 1959 that the Treasury Department issued many of the regulations explaining the provisions of the 1950 act and 1954 Code affecting exempt organizations.[28] At the time, these regulations were considered to expand vastly the definition of the term *charitable* and approached closely the common law definition.[29] This definition has become the law on the subject.[30]

> The term 'charitable' is used in Section 501(c)(3) in its generally accepted legal sense and is, therefore, not to be construed as limited by the separate enumeration in (that section) of other tax exempt purposes which may fall within the broad outlines of charity as developed by judicial decisions. Such term includes: relief of the poor and distressed or of the underprivileged; advancement of religion; advancement of education or science; erection or maintenance of public buildings, monuments or works; lessening of the burdens of Government; and promotion of social welfare by organizations designed to accomplish any of the above purposes, or (i) to lessen neighborhood tensions; (ii) to eliminate prejudice and discrimination; (iii) to defend human and civil rights secured by law; or (iv) to combat community deterioration and juvenile delinquency.[31]

New exemption categories were added in 1968 for "cooperative hospital service organizations" and "cooperative service organizations of operating educational organizations."[32] The beginnings of a distinction between private foundations and public charities first appeared in 1964 with the introduction of distinct percentage limitation differences based on 30 percent of adjusted gross income for gifts to public charities versus 20 percent for gifts to private foundations.[33] While no other significant tax legislation affecting charitable organizations was passed in 1969, the sector remained under scrutiny during this period, most notably private charitable grantmaking foundations. Extensive congressional studies were conducted throughout the 1960s because it was thought these organizations were being used to further private rather than public interests.[34]

The Tax Reform Act of 1969

Prior to the 1969 act, Code Section 503 provided the basic standards of conduct for charitable organizations. The Tax Reform Act of 1969, however, repealed Section 503 and brought into law the most extensive and burdensome changes in tax policy affecting charitable organizations since the code was first enacted.[35] A series of restrictions, prohibitions, new filing and reporting requirements, and excise taxes were added affecting charitable entities, particularly private foundations.[36] In fact, private foundations—as distinguished from public charities—were first clearly defined by the act.[37]

Generally, a *public charity* is one which, in connection with accomplishing its exempt purpose, receives a substantial amount of its annual support or revenue from the general public, or supports another charitable organization that does. A private foundation does not.[38] The restrictions on private foundations include limitations on transactions between the foundation and related parties, prohibitions against risky investments, lobbying, and political action, and limitations on who the foundation may support. Some commentators have intimated that the 1969 act resulted in the demise of hundreds of foundations.[39] Despite the changes, however, private foundations appear to have flourished. Some 22,000 private grantmaking foundations now exist, owning assets in excess of $41 billion and making annual grants of over $3 billion.[40] The perceived abuses that led to the enactment of the restrictions contained in the act, whether or not they existed in fact, are believed to have been eliminated.[41]

The Tax Reform Act of 1969 also redefined the percentage limitations for deductions of charitable contributions, providing higher (50 percent) limits for gifts of cash; first enumerated many of the limits for noncash contributions; and restricted the deduction of gifts in trust.[42] In fact, the entire tax law surrounding charitable contributions and tax exemption have been inextricably linked since the 1969 act.[43]

One court described these various sanctions as follows: "The language of the...Act, its legislative history, the graduated levels of the sanctions imposed, and the almost confiscatory level of the exactions assessed convince us that the exactions in question were intended to curb the described conduct through pecuniary punishment."[44] The Joint Committee explanation of the act goes on extensively in its listing of the restrictions and limitations. It should be required reading for foundation executives, officers, directors, managers, and trustees.[45]

The Tax Reform Act of 1976

The late 1970s and early 1980s were prolific tax act times, many of which have had significant impacts on charitable organizations. The Tax Reform Act of 1976 specifically added to the list of charitable entities, organizations fostering "national or international sports competition (but only if no part of its activities involve the provision of athletic facilities or equipment)..." and added the *safe harbor rules* on permissible legislative activities [Section 501(h)] mentioned briefly above.[46] The rules were to prevent "subjective and selective enforcement."[47]

The act exempted small hospitals from the UBTI rules for income from certain services provided to other small hospitals.[48] For example, the Senate bill would have exempted income from laundry services. This provision was subsequently deleted, and substantial litigation has resulted because of its omission from the statute.[49]

The 1976 act also contained a number of special interest provisions related to exempt organizations other than charitable organizations, including an expanded definition of the term *agricultural* for Section 501(c)(5) organizations and an exclusion from the UBTI rules for certain income received by retirement homes.[50] The adoption of Code Section 528 as part of the 1976 act clarified the tax treatment of homeowner's associations. The act also added a new category of tax exempt organizations, commonly referred to as *qualified group legal services plans*.[51] Finally, the act contained a number of other minor changes affecting charitable organizations.

The Revenue Act of 1978

Although the 1978 act had fewer changes to the rules affecting charitable organizations than the 1969 and 1976 acts, the changes were rather significant.[52] For instance, Congress believed that the 4 percent excise tax on private foundations was far in excess of the resources needed to administer the law of tax exempt organizations.[53] Thus, the tax was reduced from 4 percent to 2 percent for taxable years beginning after September 30, 1977. However, Congress remained concerned that the IRS devote adequate resources to auditing charitable and other exempt organizations which the excise tax on private foundations pays for.[54] The IRS was directed to report to Congress on the extent of its audit activities involving exempt organizations. The IRS was to notify Congress of "any administrative problems...experienced in the course of enforcement of the Internal Revenue laws with respect to exempt organizations."[55] The Revenue Act of 1978 also added a provision allowing bingo game income realized by most exempt organizations to be exempt from the UBTI rules.[56]

During the late 1970s and early 1980s, a number of pieces of legislation were introduced that could have had significant impacts on the structure and viability of the nonprofit sector. One of the bills that was not passed (the Tax Restructuring Act of 1979) would have eliminated charitable contribution deductions for 84 percent of the taxpaying public.[57] This provision, as first proposed in 1977 by President Carter, would have narrowed the constituency for the contribution, implying it was a mere tax shelter for the wealthy.[58] This, of course, has been shown to be an incorrect assumption. Charitable giving is pervasive among all income levels with charitable giving proportionately higher at lower income levels.[59]

The Economic Recovery Tax Act of 1981

President Reagan signed the Economic Recovery Tax Act of 1981 into law on August 13, 1981, and for the first time individuals could avail themselves of the so-called above the line charitable contribution deduction.[60] The term *above the line* means the charitable contribution deduction is taken against gross income to arrive at adjusted gross income—not from adjusted gross income as an itemized deduction under the general rules. This treatment allows taxpayers to take charitable contribution deductions even if they don't itemize deductions.[61] This addition to the law appeared to be a major shift in tax policy affecting charitable organizations and was viewed by the nonprofit sector and Congress as important to the future viability of the sector.

> It (the new legislation) would . . . restore a bit more independence and vitality to the voluntary sector. It will add a bit to the ability of ordinary working men and women to determine how and on what some of his or her money is spent. It will in some small measure retard the process that has been described as a slow but steady conquest of the private sector by the public. Accompanying a mounting wariness toward government, there is a widening appreciation by the American people that the unique and vital role played by private, nonprofit organizations in our nation's economy. . . this appreciation. . .constitutes the fundamental rationale for this legislation. . . first introduced in the 95th Congress. Moreover, it is familiar to every American as the basic principle of Federalism: that the National Government should assume only those responsibilities that cannot satisfactorily be carried out by the states, the localities, and by the myriad private structures and organizations, both formal and informal, that comprise the American society.[62]

But, the government giveth and the government taketh away. Shortly after the passage of this favorable tax legislation, came a number of President Reagan's budget cuts which are thought to have resulted in a loss of revenue of $110.4 billion to the nonprofit sector during the years 1981 through 1984.[63]

A number of other important changes occurred, including one relating to annual income distribution requirements for private foundations. Prior to the 1981 act, foundations were required to distribute the greater of their adjusted net income from investments or their so-called minimum investment return (generally defined as 5 percent of the fair market of the foundation's investment assets). This "greater of" requirement was eliminated by the act, thus allowing foundations to distribute only their minimum investment return regardless of net income. Any income in excess of 5 percent may be accumulated by the foundation.[64] Some authors have suggested that this change actually resulted in reduced distributions to charity, [65] but the overall result appears to have been favorable by allowing foundations to perpetuate their existence for future charitable needs.

Another change important to charity, particularly for scientific and educational organizations, was the addition of a tax credit for increasing research and experimentation activities. The act contained a 25 percent tax credit for increasing expenditures for research and experimentation in a trade or business. Since much of this type of research is contracted out by private businesses to charitable scientific and educational organizations, it became an important and greatly enlarged source of revenue. It appears that companies entered into research they may not have undertaken without the added incentive of a tax credit.[66] A number of other provisions directly or indirectly benefited charitable organizations, not the least of which was a reduction in corporate tax rates which coincidentally reduced the tax rates imposed on unrelated business taxable income.

Tax Equity and Fiscal Responsibility Act of 1982

As was previously mentioned, the Tax Reform Act of 1976 added to the list of exempt organizations those that foster national or international sports competition, but only if no part of their activities involve the provision of athletic facilities or equipment. TEFRA lifted the restriction on the provision of athletic facilities or equipment for certain sports organizations.[67] It is conjectured that the change was made to facilitate the improvement of the U.S. Olympic Committee's training facility in Colorado Springs in preparation for the 1984 Los Angeles Olympics. Although this act was intended to simplify and restructure the tax Code, this was really the only direct change of any significance affecting charitable organizations.[68]

The Deficit Reduction Act of 1984

The Deficit Reduction Act of 1984 was one of the most comprehensive and complex revisions ever attempted of our tax system. While many of its provisions were aimed at cracking down on what Congress believed were tax-abusive transactions, the news for exempt organizations was generally favorable. The act is in fact, two acts in one: The first part (Division A) is aimed at tax reform, and the second part (Division B) is for spending reduction.[69]

The act made a number of very favorable changes to the tax rules affecting private foundations in an attempt to mitigate some of the more negative results flowing from the 1969 Tax Reform Act's restrictions. These changes included: Increasing the limit on deductibility of contributions to private foundations for certain gifts and allowing a five year carryforward period for excess contributions where none previously existed;[70] exempting certain "operating" foundations (such as museums) from the 2 percent excise tax on net investment income; liberalizing the definition of persons who are related to a foundation; reducing the 2 percent excise tax to 1 percent if the foundation makes additional charitable distributions; limiting the amount of administrative expenses a foundation may claim; and, giving the IRS discretionary authority to abate certain excise taxes imposed by the 1969 act.[71]

The act changes reporting and disclosure requirements for exempt organizations and individuals with respect to deductions for charitable contributions requiring appraisals and reports for noncash gifts above a certain amount and penalties for overvaluation.[72] Other changes include the tax exempt leasing provisions which virtually eliminated the sale-leaseback as a form of financing for exempt organizations, changes to the UBTI rules, and exemption for certain child care organizations.[73]

The liberalization expressed through these provisions indicates a favorable shift in policy reflective of the president's emphasis on self sufficiency and voluntarism. However, large budget deficits tended to mollify the effect of the policy changes.

Tax Reform Act of 1986

As a result of continued pressure to address the burgeoning deficit, President Reagan's tax proposals to the Congress for fairness, growth, and simplicity were submitted to Congress on May 29, 1985. Most of these proposals found their way into the Tax Reform Act of 1986. (The 1954 Code was renamed the 1986 Code.) Some recommendations were expected to have significant adverse effects on charity. For instance, *The Chronicle of Higher Education* estimated that charitable contributions would decrease by at least 17 percent if the president's proposals were adopted.[74] While there was disagreement about the effect a reduction in marginal tax rates would have on charitable contributions,[75] it is now apparent that the simplification efforts resulted in fewer people itemizing deductions and, for that reason, reduced charitable deductions could have resulted.

Other changes that directly or indirectly affect charitable organizations include the elimination of trusts as income shifting devices, repeal of the deduction for charitable contributions for those who do not itemize, subjecting other itemized deductions to limitation or outright elimination, repeal of income averaging and research credits, and an add-back of all itemized deductions for alternative minimum tax purposes.[76]

The 1986 changes in tax policy reflect a new emphasis in public policy, mirroring public discontent with the dinosaur of a tax code that existed. The Code's complexity and perceived inequity, despite the implicit fairness of graduated tax rates, have resulted in frustration, anger, and, in some cases, revolt. A simplified filing procedure, coupled with elimination of tax breaks for the wealthy, should ultimately result in increased revenue. It is common sense that if something is easy to comply with, more people will comply. Unfortunately the 1986 act did little to accomplish these goals. In fact, the act was the longest and most complex piece of tax legislation ever considered and increased the frustration and confusion of the general public.

The 1987 Act and Beyond

One of the primary movements of the 1980s for tax exempt organizations has been the increased emphasis on self-sufficiency precipitated by declines in traditional funding sources and continued increases in demand for services. The Urban Institute's Nonprofit Sector Project estimated that federal support for the nonprofit sector declined by more than $110.4 billion between 1980 and 1984.[77] Yet the sector continues to experience exceptional growth. For example, between 1977 and 1982, total expenditures for the sector grew some 86 percent from $114 billion to $213 billion, and total assets (excluding religious organizations) grew 145 percent from $134 billion in 1975 to about $328 billion in 1983.[78]

Much of this growth has been financed through commercial ventures and other nontraditional sources of income. For example, there has been a dramatic increase in the use of taxable subsidiary corporations to assist in the management of for-profit enterprises and to protect the favored tax status of nonprofit organizations. The Internal Revenue Service issued some 593 private letter rulings to charitable organizations authorizing multi-entity structures between 1977 and 1986. In the prior decade, only eight such rulings were issued.[79] The presumed increase in income-producing commercial activities is supported by source of income data provided by the Treasury Department. For example, although contributions increased from $.6 billion in 1946 to $31.3 billion in 1978, contributions as a percent of total revenue decreased from 17 percent to 13 percent during that period—while other revenue (such as business receipts, interest, dividends, rents, royalties, and other income) grew from 57 percent in 1946 to 75 percent in 1978.[80]

With the increased commercial activity by nonprofit organizations has come increased scrutiny by business, Congress, and especially the Internal Revenue Service. In 1983, taxable businesses formed the Business Coalition for Fair Competition. Sponsored in large part by the U.S. Small Business Administration, the Business Coalition expressed its concern over competition from tax exempt entities through a 1984 SBA report, *Unfair Competition by Nonprofit Organizations with Small Business*.[81] Competition was also on the agenda of the August 1986 White House Conference on Small Business and was the subject of a special report by the Government Accounting Office to the Joint Committee on Taxation of the U.S. Congress.[82] In 1987, hearings on commercial activities of nonprofit organizations began before the House Ways and Means Committee and included testimony by the Deputy Assistant Secretary of the Treasury for Tax Policy who offered recommendations and suggestions for further legislative debate.[83]

Much of the debate is over the unrelated business income tax (UBIT) statutes and their ability to eliminate or control unfair competition. The Revenue Act of 1987 originally contained a number of provisions that would have extended the scope of the UBIT, but the provisions did not make it into the final Bill. However, debate over various proposals continues in the House Ways and Means Committee. In a March 25, 1988, memorandum from Oversight Subcommittee Chairman J. J. Pickle (D.-Tex), recommendations for revision of the *substantially related test* of the statute, along with numerous other proposals, were presented to the full Committee.[84]

There had been no comprehensive evaluation of the tax rules affecting exempt organizations since 1969 (at least not until the 1984 report).[85] While the 1970s and early 1980s were prolific tax act times, changes made to the exemption and unrelated business income sections in 1976, 1978, 1981, 1982, 1984, 1986, and 1987 tax acts were minor and did not affect the basic exemption requirements or UBIT rules. However, the question of so-called unfair competition has become one of the most hotly contested tax questions of the 1980s. For-profit businesses argue that nonprofits have a competitive advantage.[86] Nonprofits argue that for-profit business has encroached upon traditional nonprofit activities (such as health care, child care, health, and fitness facilities). The ends justify the means.[87]

The Possibility of Future Actions

The 1984 SBA report contained a number of suggested alternatives for dealing with the issue of intersector competition including:

1. A complete federal prohibition on all unrelated activities;
2. Higher tax rates for unrelated activities;
3. Fundamental changes to the definition of UBIT;
4. A percentage limit on permissible unrelated activities; and

5. A repeal of some or all statutory exceptions to the UBIT. [88]

In the March 25, 1988, memorandum from House Ways and Means Oversight Subcommittee Chairman Pickle (D.-Tex), many of these options were incorporated into suggestions for changes to the UBIT. Specific recommendations included restricting the use of taxable subsidiaries and joint ventures to avoid loss of exemption; elimination of various exceptions and exclusions to the UBIT; and application of the UBIT to specific commercial activities of nonprofits such as gift shop/bookstore sales, sales of medical equipment and devices, income from health and fitness programs, travel and tour services, food sales, certain veterinary services, hotel facility income, and advertising income.[89] One of the most controversial proposals is the redefinition of unrelated business income, including modification or elimination of the substantially related test. Substitution of an *inherently commercial test* would extend the UBIT to certain activities considered per se unrelated, such as the sale of goods and services.

The Oversight Subcommittee also considered a *directly related test* to replace the substantially related test. Under this approach, only income from directly related activities would escape. An April 15, 1988, letter from Assistant Treasury Secretary Chapoton to Pickle argued that a directly related test would "wreak administrative havoc among exempt organizations and, possibly, within the Internal Revenue Service." [90] The assistant secretary pointed out that such a basic change in the structure of the tax could have an adverse affect on legitimate activities and would require a complete "reexamination of all activities currently considered to be substantially related." [91] Chapoton reminded the subcommittee that although the definition of *substantially related* is murky at best, the distinction between existing law and *directly related* is "not at all clear." [92] Chapoton was not the only one who opposed the proposed options. The outcry against the proposal was enormous, with over 300 letters received from tax exempt and other groups.[93] Similarly, Chapoton dismissed the *inherently commercial* concept as unclear and requiring a total review of exempt organization activity.

In June 1987, IRS Commissioner Lawrence Gibbs, told the subcommittee he did not want a piecemeal approach to amending the statutes. And, in testimony to the subcommittee on May 9, 1988, Chapoton made it clear that the Treasury Department does not want a major overhaul of the UBIT statutes. Chapoton's sharpest criticisms were reserved for fundamental changes to the substantially related test. Perhaps these comments and other testimony positively influenced the subcommittee, as Chairman Pickle made a point of indicating the subcommittee and Treasury are "moving in tandem on the UBIT issue." [94]

Although the substantiality test of the UBIT statute may have been too loosely interpreted by the courts and the IRS, it appears to be the most acceptable legal model that gives the courts sufficient flexibility to enforce public policy. It appears to be consistent with current legal theory in that it is up to the courts to evaluate individual facts and circumstances in making decisions about the nature, scope, and motivation of each activity.

At least for the time being, Congress may be in argreement with this approach. On June 4, 1988, the Oversight Subcommittee backed away abruptly from any fundamental change to the substantially related test of the statute. [95] But, I predict this is the area where exempt organizations are most likely to experience significant future policy change.

Conclusion

This paper has examined the myriad changes in tax policy over the past one hundred years, trying to focus on the reasons why changes have occurred (more than on what the changes were). We have seen how the three bases—tradition, public policy, and special interests—have all played a part in shaping tax policy and, ultimately, the very nature of nonprofit organizations.

Notes

1. Title 26, United States Code, also referred to as *the Code*.
2. McGovern, J. (1976). The exemption provisions of subchapter F. *Tax Lawyer, 29,* 523.
3. Ibid.
4. 28 Stat. 556.
5. Ibid.
6. *Pollock v. Farmers' Loan and Trust Co.,* 157 U.S. 428 (1895).
7. Op. cit., No. 4.

8. *Walz v. Tax Commission*, 397 U.S. 664, 673 (1970).

9. *Trinidad v. Sagrada Orden de Predicadores*, 263 U.S. 578, 581 (1924).

10. *Ould v. Washington Hospital for Foundlings*, 95 U.S. 303 (1877).

11. 38 Stat. 166.

12. Hopkins, B. (1983). *The Law of Tax-Exempt Organizations*. New York: Ronald Press.

13. Tocqueville, A. de (1830). *Democracy in America*. New York: Doubleday Press.

14. Mill, J. S. (1859). *On Liberty*. Indianapolis: Hackett.

15. Op. cit., No. 12.

16. Hopkins, Op. cit.

17. 48 Stat. 700.

18. 49 Stat. 1674. See also: McAdam, T. (1985). *Doing Well by Doing Good: The First Complete Guide to Careers in the Nonprofit Sector*. New Haven: Yale University Press.

19. House Report 1438, 61st Congress, 1st Session (1909).

20. House Report 2319, 81st Congress, 2nd Session (1950).

21. Senate Report 2375, 81st Congress, 2nd Session (1950).

22. The term *unrelated business taxable income* is defined in the Internal Revenue Code (Sections 511–514) generally as any "trade or business, regularly carried on which is not substantially related" to the organization's exempt purpose. This is a highly technical area of tax law. Further description and analysis of what constitutes an unrelated trade or business is believed to be beyond the scope of this paper. However, the reader is referred to: Scrivner, G. and Callaghan, C. (1980). A path to self-sufficiency. *Philanthropy Monthly*, September, 1980.

23. Op. cit., No. 20.

24. Op. cit., No. 21.

25. Op. cit., No. 24.

26. 68A Stat. 163 (Chapter 736).

27. Ibid.

28. Code of Federal Regulations, Title 26, Part I.

29. Hopkins, Op. cit.

30. While regulations generally do not have the force of law, subsequent rulings and court decisions have upheld the regulation, and congress has had the opportunity. Yet, it has refrained from adopting a statutory definition.

31. Regulation Section 1.501(c)(3)–1(d)(2).

32. Revenue and Expenditure Control Act of 1968, 82 Stat. 269 (Act Title I, Section 109).

33. Ibid.

34. See Rep. W. Patman, "Tax-exempt Foundations and Charitable Trusts: Their Impact on Our Economy," *Chairman's Report to (House) Select Committee on Small Business*, 87th Congress, 1st Session (1962); *Treasury Department Report on Private Foundations*, Committee on Finance, U.S. Senate, 89th Congress, 1st Session (1965); Fremont-Smith, M. (1965), *Foundations and Government*, Report of an international conference of charitable foundations and similar institutions held at Ditchley Park, 18th-21st of November, 1966. Also, Revenue Ruling 67-149. 67-1 C.B. 133.

35. Public Law 91–172.

36. Specific enumeration of these complex provisions is beyond the scope of this paper. The reader is referred to: Lashbrooke, E. (1984). *Tax-exempt Organizations*. Englewood Cliffs, N.J.: Prentice-Hall.

37. Hopkins, Op. cit.

38. See Code Sections 4911, 4940–4947.

39. American Association of Fund Raising Council (1982), *Giving USA*. New York: The Association.

40. Odendahl, T. (1985). *Private Foundation Formation, Growth and Termination: A Report on Work in Progress*. New Haven: Yale University Press.

41. Hopkins, Op. cit.

42. Op. cit.

43. Golden, W. (1970). Charitable giving in the 1970s: The impact of the 1969 act. *Taxes, 48*, 787.

44. *In re. Unified Control Systems, Inc.*, 586 F. 2d 1036 (5th Cir., 1978). Also see *Farrell v. U.S.*, 80-1 USTC 9833 (E.D. Ark. 1980).

45. Joint Committee on Internal Revenue Taxation, *General Explanation of Tax Reform Act of 1969*, 91st Congress, 2nd Session (1970).

46. Public Law 94-455.

47. Senate Report No. 94-938, 94th Congress, 2nd Session (1976).

48. Code Section 513(e).

49. Amendment No. 315, 122 Congressional Record 25915 (1976) and *HCSC Laundry v. U.S.*, 624 F 2d 428 (3rd Cir., 1980); *Metropolitan Detroit Area Hospital Services, Inc. v. U.S.*, 634 f. 2d 330 (6th Cir., 1980); and

Community Hospital Services, Inc. v. U.S., 47 AFTA2d 81-999 (6th Cir., 1981), etc.

50. Section 501(g) and Pre-1976 Section 512(b)(14).

51. Section 501(c)(20).

52. Public Law 95-600, and House Report 95-842, 95th Congress, 2nd Session (1978).

53. Ibid.

54. Ibid.

55. Ibid.

56. Section 513(f)(2)(A).

57. Hopkins, Op. cit.

58. House Report 5665, 96th Congress, 1st Session (1979).

59. Hodgkinson, V. & Weitzman, M. (1984). *Dimensions of the Independent Sector: A Statistical Profile*. Washington, D.C.: Independent Sector.

60. Public Law 97-34.

61. Section 170(1).

62. Senator P. Moynihan, 127 Congressional Record S7962 (July 20, 1981).

63. Salamon, L. & Abramson, A. "The Federal Government and the Non Profit Sector: Implications of the Reagan Budget Proposals," Urban Institute, May, 1981, reproduced at 127 *Congressional Record* S7964 (July 20, 1981). See also Eisenberg, P. (1982). Federal budget cuts and future challenges. *Corporate philanthropy*. Washington, D.C.: Council on Foundations.

64. Section 823, Economic Recovery Tax Act.

65. Hopkins, Op. cit.

66. Section 44(f).

67. Section 501(j), Section 286 Tax Equity and Fiscal Responsibility Act.

68. Ibid.

69. No author. (1984). *A Complete Guide to the Tax Reform Act of 1984: Includes all Tax Revisions of the Deficit Reduction Act of 1984: As Presented to the President*. Englewood Cliffs, N.J.: Prentice-Hall.

70. 1984 TRA Section 301 (a).

71. 1984 TRA Section 302-306. See also Act Sections 307-310 and 312-314.

72. 1984 TRA Section 155 and 156.

73. 1984 TRA Section 31 and 32, 311, 731.

74. Palmer, S. (1985). Charities charge gifts would drop 17 percent under Reagan tax plan. *Chronicles of Higher Education, Vol. XXX, No. 16*.

75. Clotfelter, C. (1985). Tax reform proposals and charitable giving in 1985. *Prepared for Public Policy and Its Impact on Giving and Volunteering Panel*; and Davie, B. (1985). Tax rate changes and charitable contributions. *Tax Notes*, March 11.

76. *Explanation for the President's Tax Proposals to Congress for Fairness, Growth, and Simplicity*. Research Institute of America, May 1985.

77. Salamon, L. & Abramson, A. "The Federal Government and the Nonprofit Sector: Implications of the Reagan Budget Proposals," Urban Institute, May, 1981, reproduced at 127 *Congressional Record* S7964, (July 20, 1981).

78. Hodgkinson, V. & Weitzman, M. (1986). *Dimensions of the Independent Sector: A Statistical Profile (2nd ed.)*. Washington, D.C.: Independent Sector.

79. McGovern, J. J. (1988). The use of taxable subsidiary corporations by public charities —A tax policy issue for 1988. *Tax Notes*, March 7, 1128.

80. *Tax Policy: Competition Between Taxable Businesses and Tax-exempt Organizations*, Briefing Report to the Joint Committee on Taxation, U.S. Congress, Government Accounting Office, Washington, D.C., GAO/GGO-87-40B, February 1987, p. 18.

81. U.S. Small Business Administration, Washington, D.C. (3rd ed.), 1984.

82. Government Accounting Office, Op. cit.

83. McGovern, Op. cit., p. 1129.

84. *Tax Notes Microfiche Database*, Arlington, Doc. 88-3070, April 4, 1988.

85. Small Business Administration, Op. cit.

86. For example, Nonprofits drop the 'Non'. *New York Times*, Business Section, November 24, 1985, p. 1; and Cry of 'Unfair competition' evokes mixed response. *Washington Post*, Washington Business Section, August 15, 1986, p. 15.

87. For example, Wellford, H. (1985). *The Myth of Unfair Competition by Nonprofit Organizations*, New York: Commissioned by Family Service of America and The National Assembly of National Voluntary Health and Social Welfare Organizations. Also, Taylor, S. (1988). Taxing public charities out of business: A solution in search of a problem. *Tax Notes*, May 9, 1988, 753–758.

88. Small Business Administration, Op. cit.

89. *Tax Notes Microfiche Database*, Op. cit.

90. Jones, P. (1988). Treasury objects to fundamental changes in UBIT. *Tax Notes*, May 2, 1988, 548.

91. Ibid.

92. Ibid.

93. Jones, P., Treasury advocates UBIT fine tuning; But UBIT overhaul not needed. *Tax Notes*, May 16, 1988, 791–793.

94. Jones, P. Op. cit., Note 26, p. 791.

95. Jones, P. (1988). Ways and means oversight committee given list of UBIT proposals. *Tax Notes*, June 27, 1988, 1498–1499.

CHAPTER THREE
Planning and Policy Formulation

Introduction

Nonprofit organizations require strategic planning, a mission, values, and culture to provide a stabilizing sense of identity or purpose. They need such overarching "maps" for selecting goals, objectives, and programs that can show the way to effective goal attainment with rational expenditures of limited resources. Organizations in the nonprofit sector—as well as the government and for-profit environments surrounding them—are undergoing a period of fundamental change (Mitroff, 1987; Morgan, 1988). This is a time of unparalleled opportunity and danger. Societal changes throughout the world are redefining national and community priorities in the United States, thus affecting organizational missions. Without a clear sense of identity and a strategic plan, nonprofit organizations flounder in a sea of competing sorrows, always at the whim of whatever well-articulated hard luck story motivates action.

Strategic planning and policy formulation are to a nonprofit organization as triage is to a hospital emergency room: They are the means for sorting through things so that a course of rational action can be selected from among the many possible alternatives. A nonprofit organization that lacks a sense of identity and direction and is without current interpretations of its fundamental organization, program mission, and purpose, is akin to a hospital staff that treats the first patients that come through the emergency department door rather than people who are experiencing the most life-threatening conditions. Just as protocol is necessary for a hospital staff to make sound resource allocation decisions, protocol is equally necessary for a nonprofit organization's decision makers striving to meet unlimited community needs within the limits of resource and marketplace realities.

Resource allocation decisions are one side of the decision protocol; resource development and fundraising are the other. All too frequently nonprofit organizations do their own type of programmatic ambulance chasing. Lacking program identity and purpose, they respond to a request for proposal announcement not because the program fits their mission, but because they have a need to chase dollars to support current operations.

Strategic planning and policy formulation are the methods—the tools and processes—people use to decide and then to act upon such fundamental identity issues as: who and what our organization is and is not; how our organization fits into and attempts to shape its particular environment; how we cope with changes in environmental influences (and in turn how we influence our environment); what we value, and what business (or line of endeavor) we are in. Strategic planning and policy formulation set parameters, or limits, within which day-to-day decisions will be made. They help the board of directors and the staff bring order out of confusion.

The very process of creating an organizational mission and strategy enables a board of directors and staff to conceptualize the environment and the NPO's place in it. It helps to build a common set of shared assumptions, language, and information. When an organization's identity, mission, and strategy are widely accepted, the result is a more consistent and less conflict ridden decision-making process, and more productive communications with internal and external constituencies. A viable strategic plan establishes the parameters for political and program debates within the context of the NPO's human, managerial, and fiscal resource capacities.

138

The terms *strategic planning* and *policy formulation* have been used as though they were interchangeable. Indeed, in the sense that we use them here, there are many similarities, but there also are some important differences. Strategic planning and policy formulation are similar in that they both involve selecting from among many competing goals and objectives (and, often, the competing goals and objectives are all very desirable). They are both processes for deciding on changes in organizational mission, purpose, identity, and goals as well as the resources and strategies to enact identity and pursue goals. Both also involve decisions that change the character or direction of an organization. Strategic planning and policy formulation both deal with fundamental organizational identity, purpose, and basic overarching strategies for trying to achieve the purpose.

Digman (1986, p. 27) describes four levels of strategy roles that require planning: the societal role, corporate role, business unit role, and functional/operating role. Here we address three of Digman's strategy roles. For example, a human service delivery organization might ask itself:

- Are we truly in the business of helping people who are not able to care for themselves? Or, in fact,
- Are we in the business of developing the capabilities of our members by providing them with opportunities to help people who are not able to care for themselves (*societal role*)? Or,
- Are we in the business of strengthening our city by helping to establish and support other groups and organizations that help people who cannot care for themselves (*corporate role*)? Or,
- Are we in the business of providing ongoing support to parents and other close relatives of people who are not able to care for themselves, so the relatives can "keep going" (*functional/operating role*)?

Strategic planning and policy formulation are also similar in that they both emphasize external and internal environment scanning. Choosing among purposes and strategies requires collecting and using information about the external environment as well as about internal strengths, weaknesses, and preferences of important constituency groups. For example, George Steiner (1979), one of the most widely known authors on strategic planning, incorporates expectations of major outside interests and expectations of major inside interests as important elements in his strategic planning model. Steiner emphasizes that outside and inside interests, or "stakeholders" (Mitroff, 1983), affect and are affected by identity, purpose, and strategy decisions. James D. Thompson (1967) was one of the first students of organizations to suggest that organizations are constantly gathering information, a process he calls *environmental scanning*. To a large extent environmental scanning, or *reading the environment* (Morgan, 1988), is what strategic planning and policy formulation are about (Bozeman, 1987). It occurs when a board of directors interprets the environment in which its organization's mission is implemented; considers ways to refine, refocus and increase influence, and at the same time maintain current production and service delivery. It is through the process of environmental scanning that nonprofits develop new solutions and suggest changes in existing methods. Innovation provides for social experimentation, thus adding to the justification for policy amendment and change and, more globally, to one of the primary justifications for the existence of the nonprofit sector itself.

The basic difference between strategic planning and policy formulation depends upon how quantitatively one approaches strategic planning. The more one sees strategic planning as a series of quantitative analyses that extensively utilize econometrics, operations research, heuristic models, applied statistics, and other quantitative decision techniques and approaches, the more important the differences are. These differences are not simply methodological. Policy formulation emphasizes the importance of dealing with differences among competing values that must be reconciled before an organization can implement strategies. Some advocates of strategic planning think likewise, but certainly not all of them.

The more quantitative the orientation of a strategic planner, the less likely it is that these types of value differences will be incorporated into the strategic planning/policy formulation processes. Quantitative planning and decision processes are not designed to deal with conflicting noncommensurate values. Values conflicts typically are resolved through political means rather than rational analysis, and political means do not fit well into quantitative models. Quantitative methods are not designed to take into account irrational behavior and human idiosyncrasy. Quantitatively oriented strategic planners often assume agreement about values—at least about values beyond economy and efficiency—when they are considering alternatives, and then proceed with their analyses.

Consider again the sample strategic questions about purpose and identity we posed a few paragraphs earlier. The example presented four potentially competing organizational roles or purposes (lines of endeavor). Whichever prevails will make a marked impact on the organization's decisions about how to allocate its resources and the type of programs it will offer. Quantitative analyses of costs and benefits may help the board and staff to make informed choices among competing programmatic resource allocation alternatives, but they will not resolve the moral decision about the nature of the organization's "business."

Quantitative strategic planning methods are invaluable for helping for-profit organizations cope with these types of decision dilemmas. For example, market opportunity and production costs can be compared against each other for profit implications. Although it is popular these days to argue that for-profit companies do not focus solely on "the bottom line"—and they do not to the total exclusion of all other motives and values—the profit and loss statement remains the final scorecard of for-profit ventures.

Nonprofit organizations must be cautious in their reliance on quantitative planning methods for yet another reason: They are expected to meet external needs and, equally important, to do things in ways that are preferred (valued) by important internal constituencies. If not, people withdraw or act politically to redefine organizational purpose. Economy, efficiency, or profit is, at best, only half of the strategic decision weighting. Politics and values are essential ingredients of the policy formulation processes. On the other hand, the more a nonprofit organization is willing to let money issues determine its purposes (the pursuit of profits or the avoidance of losses as its primary determinant of corporate identity) the more adequately quantitative-type strategic planning processes will suffice for it.

In public and private sector organizations, policy analyses usually are conducted by staff (not line) employees or consultants as a preparatory stage in a strategic planning process. By role, policy analysts are not decision makers and are not expected to participate in the strategic planning process beyond the analysis of policy. However, in the nonprofit sector, where most organizations are small and few have extensive staff structures, the task of policy analysis often is carried out by the decision makers themselves and often with only limited amounts of "sophisticated" information available to them. When decision makers with incomplete factual information both conduct the preparatory analyses and take responsibility for conducting strategic planning, it is imperative that the normative decision criteria used— the value preferences that are "plugged into" the strategic planning models—are brought out, illuminated, and consciously acknowledged.

The differences between strategic planning and policy formulation are thus mostly questions of emphasis, responsibility, separation of roles, and elucidation of value sets. These two macro-strategy formulation processes have the same targets: They focus on the same overarching levels of organizational identity, mission, and purpose. They differ mostly about how much one can assume as givens about an organizational identity when making resource allocation decisions. They also differ, although mostly in degree, about the usefulness of quantitative methods for making decisions that involve value differences.

Strategic planning requires the coming together of a group of significant stakeholders to define identity, purpose, philosophy, and strategy. Although consensus is infrequent among such groups of people who represent divergent perspectives of the organization, the planning and policy formulation functions usually result in a sharper sense of organizational purpose. Usually, this is positive for the organization and its members. Sometimes, however, consensus only develops when losers in the contest to define organizational identity simply withdraw from participation.

The first article reprinted here is Siri Espy's "Corporate Identity and Directions" from her 1986 book, *Handbook of Strategic Planning for Nonprofit Organizations*. Espy contends that strategic planning begins with organizational identity and direction. Indeed, corporate values and philosophy are transmitted, imparted, and perpetuated through the process of defining organization mission and purpose. Espy also reminds us that planning is circular. A clearer identity results from strategic planning and is an essential prerequisite for beginning to plan. A nonprofit organization must understand its own particular stakeholders, environment, corporate identity, program targets or markets, and goals—programmatic and financial. From Espy's standpoint, an up-to-date policy plan is as critical to the operations as are current copies of the articles of incorporation and bylaws. "Corporate Identity and Directions" provides a very straightforward overview of some tried-and-true qualitative strategic planning methods (such as Strengths, Weaknesses, Opportunities, and Threats [SWOT] Analysis; and environmental scanning).

The second article, "Planning and Management in Nonprofit Organizations," by John O. Alexander, also emphasizes the importance of nonprofits engaging in effective, practical, identity/purpose-based strategic planning. Alexander views planning as a concern "with the future impact of present decisions; it is the process through which the leadership influences the future rather than being its victim." He explains the major steps in strategic planning, who should be involved, the responsibilities of the executive director, and the importance of communicating planning about planning progress and process throughout the organization. Strategic planning is the set of activities that analyzes for whom an organization exists (market or constituency?), where it fits in the broader environmental context, who it exists for, and why. Alexander's piece provides an uncomplicated, perhaps even elemental, reminder to nonprofit managers of the need to plan, the basic planning steps, and that planning is possible in nonprofit organizations.

According to John Bryson, evolving nonprofit organization self-awareness defines the function of strategy as extending the "mission to form a bridge between an organization (or community) and its environment." In "Formulating Strategies to Manage the Issues" (the third article reprinted in this chapter), Bryson differentiates grand organizational strategy from planning unit strategy, program or service strategy, and functional strategy. "Strategy may be thought of as a pattern of purposes, policies, programs, actions, decisions, or resource allocations that define what an organization is, what it does, and why it does it." Bryson emphasizes strategic planning as "strategic thinking and acting, not necessarily the preparation of a strategic plan." A number of benefits and a five-part strategic planning developmental process are reviewed.

Taken as a whole, the articles that comprise this chapter acknowledge the importance of strategic planning and policy formulation as vital organizational functions. The processes and the results of macro-level planning tend to bring members of a nonprofit organization's important internal and external constituency groups to the same page, reading the same words at the same time from the same book. However, you will see that all of the articles arrived at this conclusion by different routes and with different emphases.

References

Alexander, J. O. (1980). Planning and management in nonprofit organizations. In T. D. Connors, (Ed.), *The nonprofit organization handbook* (Chapter 2). New York: McGraw-Hill.

Andrews, K. (1980). *The concept of corporate strategy* (rev. ed.). Homewood, IL: Irwin.

Anthony, R. N. (March–April 1964). Framework for analysis in management planning. *Management Services*, 18–24.

Bozeman, B. (1987). *All organizations are public: Bridging public and private organizational theories*. San Francisco: Jossey-Bass.

Brandt, S. G. (1982). *Strategic planning in emerging companies*. Reading, MA: Addison-Wesley.

Bryson, J. M. (1988). *Strategic planning for public and nonprofit organizations*. San Francisco: Jossey-Bass.

Digman, L. A. (1986). *Strategic management*. Plano, TX: Business Publications, Inc.

Dror, Y. (September 1967). Policy analysts: A new professional role in government service. *Public Administration Review*, 27, 197–203.

Espy, S. N. (1986). *Handbook of strategic planning for nonprofit organizations*. New York: Praeger.

Glueck, W. F. (1980). *Business policy and strategic management* (3rd ed.). New York: McGraw-Hill.

Henry, N. (1980). *Public administration and public affairs*. Englewood Cliffs, NJ: Prentice-Hall, 212.

Mitroff, I. (1983). *Stakeholders of the organization mind*. San Francisco: Jossey-Bass.

Mitroff, I. (1987). *Business not as usual*. San Francisco: Jossey-Bass.

Morgan, G. (1988). *Riding the waves of change*. San Francisco: Jossey-Bass.

Quinn, J. B. (Fall 1977). Strategic goals: Process and politics. *Sloan Management Review*, 19(1), 21.

Schendel, D., &, Hofer, C. W. (Eds.). (1979). *Strategic management: A new view of business policy and planning*. Boston: Little, Brown.

Steiner, G. A. (1979). *Strategic planning: What every manager must know*. New York: The Free Press.

Thompson, A. A., & Strickland, A. J. III. (1980). *Strategy formulation and implementation*. Plano, TX: Business Publications, Inc.

Thompson, J. D. (1967). *Organizations in action*. New York: McGraw-Hill.

ARTICLE 11 ————————————
Corporate Identity and Directions
Siri N. Espy

At some point in the life-cycle of virtually every organization, its ability to succeed in spite of itself runs out.

Richard Brien

Defining the nature and purpose of your organization is a basic task in the planning process, and one that may prove to be more difficult than it sounds. Without clear knowledge of your present whereabouts, it is difficult to progress to setting goals for your organization. As you begin the planning process, a number of identified issues unique to your organization will be explored. However, there are also some fundamental issues that warrant exploration and clarification in any organization. One of the basics, marketing issues, will be explored in Chapter 5 [not included here], and must be kept in mind when dealing with other planning issues. Other fundamental issues of corporate identity and organizational definition must be addressed early in the planning process.

Fundamental Organizational Issues

A first step in determining your destination is to get a firm fix on your present location. Planning a trip to Denver will be a very different task depending on whether you are starting out from Boulder or Bangor. Taking a good look at your present position and corporate identity will provide information that is fundamental to taking the next step. Although you work in the organization and perhaps spend most of your waking hours within its walls, it is easy to glide along without ever examining some of the most basic issues of all.

What Business Are We In?

The immediate answer to a simple question such as this is, "Of course, we are in the business of:

- Providing housing to the homeless, OR
- Offering education to adults, OR
- Sheltering abused women, OR
- Helping families reduce debt and budget resources."

However, on closer examination, these answers are probably oversimplifications and fail to give your organization credit for all the many tasks and ancillary services that are involved in your overall operation. Stop and think about what you actually do. An agency for the homeless might also provide meals, access to clothing, counseling, recreation, information on employment, and referrals to other agencies for medical care. This list differs greatly from the simple statement, "We provide housing to the homeless," and it more fully describes what your organization actually does. It also more clearly accounts for where resources are spent, and may help to pinpoint areas where needs exist.

By taking a close, careful look at what business you are actually in, you can begin both to enumerate and eventually to summarize the various aspects of the service you provide. You may find that your organization is creeping into areas of service that were never formally planned for or approved. You may also find that less time and resources are being allocated for what was once your primary service. These shifts in service delivery are normal and healthy for any organization as long as they are recognized and dealt with in a productive manner. By acknowledging that your business may not be what it was or what you thought it to be, you begin to open the door to a careful exploration of your needs and options.

Shifts in the definition of your business are inevitable and the need for redefinition does not mean that your organization has failed. Trends in the provision of health care toward outpatient services, the move toward deinstitutionalization and mainstreaming, the legalization of abortion, and the shortage of adoptable babies are all examples of forces which over the years have driven many nonprofit organizations to redefine what business they are in. In the day-to-day climate of putting out fires and survival, some of these changes can be assimilated into various parts of the organization without their importance and impact being fully recognized. The exploration and definition of what business you are in will help you better define and get in touch with the realities around you.

Once you have detailed the nuts and bolts of your organization, your next task is to capture its essence. Summarizing a variety of services is not an easy task, yet it is important to identify the central concept or concepts around which your agency is organized and attempt to define your services accordingly.

Look at the difference between the following two statements:

"We are in the business of providing services to abused children."

"Our organization provides group, individual, and family counseling to abused children and their families. We assist with referrals to public assistance, legal aid, mental health, medical care, and other needed services. We work closely with the local children's services agency to provide for foster care or temporary shelter where needed. We provide volunteers to assist stressed or high-risk parents in coping with their children. Our goal is to support and educate families to eliminate abusive patterns and foster healthy interactions."

Certainly, the second statement gives the reader a much clearer idea of the organization's business than does the first. This clarification is important for a number of reasons:

- Knowing where you are and stating it clearly will help you to proceed effectively with your plan.
- A clear statement of purpose is important for fund raising. Most potential donors would be "grabbed" more by the second statement, and feel that their money was supporting a worthy cause.
- It is difficult to sell or market your services without a clear definition of what they are. For public consumption, you must have clearly defined statements about your services.
- Potential consumers of your service need to know exactly what you do and how your

services might differ from those other agencies. In order to ensure access to appropriate persons, you need to clearly state whom you can help and how.

- Your staff needs a unifying concept of the organization's business and activities. It is important to know in what sort of wheel you are a cog.

As you proceed, it will be important to have a good working definition of your business that is broad enough to include all that you currently are. However, be prepared to see that definition change and expand as you move along with the planning process.

What Will Happen If We Stay in Exactly the Same Business?

In order to look at where you are to go next, it is beneficial to look at the consequences of doing nothing. What will be your organization's fate if you decide to stay exactly where you are for the next five years? Even without a crystal ball, it is possible to make some projections based on your knowledge of trends in your field. Looking back on the past five or ten years, you can probably identify trends or factors that contributed to the redefinition of your organization's business. Perhaps the growing numbers of single-parent families, an economic downturn in your service area, or an epidemic of drug abuse in the schools have significantly altered the nature of what you do or the means by which you provide your services.

Take a look at the givens in the external environment and then try to project their consequences, using any statistics, information, or "expert testimony" you may be able to gather. If your area is hard-hit by unemployment and loss of health-care benefits, the consequences of staying in a business exclusively dependent on third-party reimbursement could be disastrous. If the number of single mothers is a growing phenomenon and your father-daughter program is a major part of your organization, you could find yourself in a serious situation. By taking a look at some of your services in light of these trends, you can begin to see the need for a serious examination of your organization, its mission, and its future.

Try to identify service areas or programs that are high-risk over the next few years. This does not automatically target them for extinction; with some creative alterations or changes in market these very services can help you to come out on top. However, without identifying potential problems you could find yourself standing still and being passed by other agencies who had the foresight to be innovative and future oriented.

What Business Would We Like to Be In?

After you have carefully scrutinized your present position and areas where change is likely to be desirable, you can proceed to some creative thinking on your destination. Chances are that you and your staff already engage in periodic daydreaming about the future. Perhaps you can identify a number of new and exciting components that might be added to your program or new directions you've thought of taking. Generally these are probably dismissed or placed on an overloaded "back burner," where they disintegrate over time.

At this point in the planning process, you can take those dreams off the shelf and give them some thought. Reality will eventually catch up with you, but the advantage of dreaming is that sometimes strategies will emerge to help those dreams come true. As a general rule, it is probably best to start out by looking at businesses related to your present services and programs. For example, a combination veterinary clinic and center for the rehabilitation of heroin addicts might have a few problems in defining and marketing its services. But there are many creative ways to redefine your business in terms that will help to build a better future.

Several examples exist of nonprofit organizations that decided to broaden the business they were in and profited by their foresight. One is the community college; rather than defining their business as providing a two-year education to high school graduates, they defined their business more comprehensively, allowing for the proliferation of adult education and informal courses, which now are a primary market and source of revenue for many community colleges. Another example of the redefinition of a business is evolving within the health-care field. Rather than

retaining a narrow definition of providing in-patient care to the sick, many hospitals have stated that they are in the business of providing health care or even "wellness services." In doing so, they have broadened their markets and sources of revenue and have kept up with changing times.

By deciding what business you would like to be in, you are opening the door for your organization's growth. This does not mean that you are committed to moving in that direction tomorrow, but rather moves you closer to a long-range strategy or blueprint for growth. Perhaps there are intermediate steps or other areas to be explored along the way, but taking a hard look at what you would eventually like to do brings it a step closer to reality.

The SWOT Analysis

The SWOT analysis sounds as though it should be useful in extermination, and indeed if used properly it should enable you to exterminate some ignorance and myths about your organization. This technique calls for the examination of your organization's *strengths, weaknesses, opportunities,* and *threats.* It is a means of exploring both your internal and external environments and coming to some conclusions about your options and issues.

The SWOT analysis can be used either as a brainstorming technique, where the group convenes and shares ideas freely, or as a written exercise to be done individually, or both. This is an exercise in which the group process can be helpful, as one idea will often lead to another. The use of a blackboard or large sheets of brown paper hung on the wall will help the group to track the process and might stimulate new ideas. Unfortunately, it is not magic in itself, but merely a tool to gather information to be channeled into the planning process.

The first step in the SWOT analysis is to identify your organization's *strengths.* Think about all aspects of the organization. Perhaps your staff is a particular strength, or your program for retarded children. Again, attempt to be as specific as possible. What is it about your staff that makes them an organizational strength? Are they especially compassionate, hardworking, well trained, or well known in the community? What is beneficial about your program for retarded children? Is it a good program clinically, from a public relations standpoint, or does it have some unique feature? By specifically identifying your areas of strength, you begin to pinpoint possible building blocks for your organization. A reputable staff might be used to provide training at a later date, and a successful program for retarded children could spawn a counterpart for retarded adults. As in any business, it is important for a nonprofit agency to know its strengths and use them to every possible advantage. Strengths can take a number of forms:

- The organization is well managed.
- The cost-containment program has led to an excess of revenue over expenses.
- We have the largest program for adoption services in the state.
- We have an excellent speakers' bureau which has provided fantastic PR and increased referrals.
- Our physical facility is attractive.
- We have an active and growing force of volunteer workers.

Identification of strengths such as these will also serve to provide a good opportunity for giving credit where credit is due and increasing your confidence; you have done something right, and can do it again!

The identification of organizational *weaknesses* proceeds in much the same manner as the identification of strengths, and in fact can be done concurrently with the analysis of strengths; often the exploration of one will elicit ideas about the other. In defining your weaknesses, there are again a number of perspectives to be examined. Generally, your staff's perceptions of weaknesses will generate some interesting ideas. This process, however, has the potential to become threatening. While your staff is unlikely to object to hearing their programs or departments identified as strengths, identifying some aspect of the organization as a weakness can offend the person or persons who feel an ownership of the issue. It helps, again, to be as specific as possible about the nature of the weakness and avoid blanket condemnations of any part of the organization. Keeping the discussion as objective as possible should help to minimize the

number of offended parties. However, the life of the organization should come first, and avoiding unpleasantries could have serious consequences when major problems remain unsolved. Weaknesses might look like this:

- We are in a tight spot financially and are limited in what we can attempt as a result.
- Our public image has been tarnished by the recent arrest of a staff member.
- We lack adequate psychiatric coverage.
- Our organization is not well known outside the small town in which we are based.
- We have had a high staff turnover, which has led to instability.
- Our organization has had difficulties responding to change.

When you have developed a list of weaknesses, scrutinize them carefully. These areas may warrant some time and attention as you proceed with your plan. Weaknesses can be minor and easily correctable, or they can require major revamping and pose a serious threat to the future of your organization. By identifying and exploring areas of weakness, you can develop plans for eliminating or working around them.

Opportunities can exist in many areas. You may already have a handle on what your organization could or should be doing in the future. Opportunities can take many forms:

- Grant money has become available to fund certain types of programs.
- A new trend or phenomenon such as cocaine addiction or eating disorders provides logical opportunities for expansion.
- The local community has a shortage of family practice physicians and may be ripe for a clinic.
- Your organization is located near an expanding, prosperous area that could be a good target for new services.
- A local agency has expressed interest in working jointly with you on the development of an innovative program.
- A rental property is available at a reasonable rate in an area you've targeted for expansion.

Identifying your opportunities allows you to plan for their becoming realities. Some of these opportunities may need to be watched over time, and others may warrant a closer look and can be assigned to a project team for a study of their feasibility. Others may not be worth any further attention, and can be dismissed. Here, the arts of planning and management prevail. Your staff's perspectives and input can prove exceedingly valuable as you proceed.

Threats are generally external, although occasionally there may be a situation within your organization that poses a threat. If you suspect embezzlement of funds, that is certainly a threat from within, but it is not a long-range planning issue! Most threats relate to circumstances that may prove harmful to your organization in the near or distant future. They might include:

- A new organization is opening across the street that is targeting your clients as its customers.
- A proposed cutback of the federal funds on which several of your programs depend.
- The changing demographics of your area indicate that there will no longer be many young people to utilize your recreation program within five years.
- The declining economy in your county has resulted in a 25 percent reduction in donations over the last two years.
- Proposed accreditation regulations will mean more paperwork and less direct service time for your staff.
- A pro-life group is picketing your women's health service and intimidating your clients.

Threats such as these can hold major consequences to your organization if they are not addressed. Attempting to anticipate threats can help you to prepare for them, and can help you to budget for changes in funding or utilization of services. Planning for eventual threats can also help you to fight back—to explore new sources of grant money or other revenue, to change your target population, or to move to a new location. Ignoring threats is a dangerous business; hopefully we can learn to shoot, retreat, or regroup before we see the whites of their eyes!

Do not expect or attempt consensus as you carry out the SWOT analysis. It is a sign of a good process if a number of different ideas are generated. It should also not be surprising if the participants in the analysis do not agree. Each person comes to the planning process with a unique viewpoint based on his or her position in the organization, length of service, personality, and outlook on life. Two staff members might see the same aspect of your organization very differently; one as a strength, and the other as a weakness. This disagreement might reflect different perspectives, and it may also mirror reality; there are times when an organization's biggest strength is also its major weakness. For example, a very popular educational program for underprivileged children is losing money on a daily basis. Educational specialists and the controller might label this program as a strength and a weakness, respectively, and both would be correct. Eliciting this kind of information as concretely as possible can prove valuable, although it may be uncomfortable and produce raised eyebrows at the time.

The completion of the SWOT analysis is one rather comprehensive tool for examining your organization both in terms of its internal structure and operations and its position in the overall environment. Issues discovered at this stage can become fodder for planning groups, or can be earmarked for exploration at a later date; clearly it is impossible to do an exhaustive review of every issue relevant to the organization. Hopefully, the concept of analyzing your strengths, weaknesses, opportunities, and threats will become an ongoing part of your planning and management activities. Such a list is never static and is subject to rapid and frequent change.

Environmental Scanning

Environmental scanning describes the process of looking at the world around you. As in the identification of threats and opportunities, it is geared to the analysis of external data. There are a number of factors that affect your operation, and identifying them can be a helpful step in planning your response to circumstances that help to control your destiny. Environmental scanning probably already occurs informally on an ongoing basis within your organization. On a formal basis, it can be beneficial to look carefully at factors that have an impact on the following areas:

Economic. The realities of funding, the economic condition and climate of your area, and reimbursement issues all fall into this category. The economic realities cannot be ignored in the development of a strategic plan.

Legal or regulatory. Changes in laws or the regulations applying to society or nonprofits can have a major impact. Changes in the Medicare system, accreditation standards, drunk driving laws, and child abuse reporting regulations can have a major impact on an organization's operations, potential markets, and funding.

Political. The political environment can be influenced by nonprofit agencies and their constituencies; lobbying efforts can be successful, and the development of an awareness of the workings and events of the political system can help an organization to be aware of changes that are on the way.

Technological or medical. The development of new drugs to treat mental illness, advancements in equipment for the disabled, and new diagnostic procedures are examples of changes in technology that can impact nonprofits. Keeping abreast of new developments can allow your organization to be at the forefront of new ideas, and can help you to provide the best, most up-to-date service to your clients.

Social. An awareness of social realities is essential to nonprofit, people-oriented businesses. Higher divorce rates, more open acknowledgement of homosexuality, two-career families, and latchkey children are only a few of the trends that will have an affect on many nonprofit organizations. These social phenomena will govern to some extent how you operate, what services are needed, and who your market might be.

Demographic. A knowledge of who is out there will help you to gear your services accordingly and better define your market. Getting a handle on the demographics of your clientele and the general population in your area can yield some interesting information concerning your appeal and reputation. Demographics also help you to determine a possible demand for services, and can pinpoint promising locations for expansion.

Competitive. Identifying and compiling data on your competitors is a vital part of strategic planning, and will be explored in some depth in the marketing chapter. Knowing who your competitors are is a first step in increasing your market share.

Environmental scanning is a means whereby your organization can systematically examine and compile data on a number of factors that will be significant to you now and in the future. Again, centralizing information on these factors can help you to understand and investigate the realities that will play a major role in the development of your strategic plan.

Identifying the Givens

In any organization, there are a number of elements that are not open to change. To minimize wheel-spinning and to understand the implications of these realities, you will need to identify what they are. Since strategic planning involves looking at fundamental issues, it is important to know how fundamental your analysis can be.

Givens might exist because of limits imposed on the organization externally or by the choice of those who set the policies and philosophy by which the organization lives. For example, an agency that is part of the state human resources department is limited in terms of its funding and corporate control; it would have a difficult time becoming an independent agency and ignoring state wage scales and guidelines. Likewise, hospitals must abide by detailed operating standards in order to be accredited and receive third-party reimbursement. Some of the givens do limit our creativity, but can also challenge it. Knowing that there is little control over factors important to your operation can be frustrating, but if this is an issue in your organization, it may help to explore what those limits actually are and whether you have any flexibility within the framework of that reality.

Some of the givens are imposed by the organization and are fundamental to that agency's identity. An osteopathic hospital has a clearly defined operating philosophy and employs osteopathic physicians. An alcoholism program may be based on the Alcoholics Anonymous model of recovery and espouse total abstinence from mind-altering drugs. A women's health clinic that provides family planning services may choose to assume a pro-choice position on the issue of abortion. These are all very fundamental issues for these organizations; any shift in these philosophies would radically alter the structure and mission of the organization. There are times when such shifts are warranted; perhaps some of your fundamental assumptions are now open to question due to changes within the organization or in the external environment. By defining these givens, you define your identity and areas that are basic to the organization's existence.

Sacred Cows

Nearly every organization keeps a few sacred cows hidden away somewhere. Their size and number vary, but their impact is almost always felt. Clues to the presence of sacred cows can include statements such as:

- "But we've always done it this way!"
- "Joe has worked here for twenty years and has always run our men's group on Wednesday nights."
- "I know that program is losing money and has been poorly utilized, but the director is invested in it."
- "How could we possibly add a class for slow learners? Our staff is not qualified and we always fill these slots from within."

The common thread in these statements is an irrational entrenchment in the past and maintaining the status quo. Many organizations avoid boat-rocking at all costs, allowing sacred cows to thrive at the expense of the greater good. Identifying sacred cows is risky because of their status, and may take a fair amount of courage. Asking gentle but pointed questions about these assumptions may help to flush out irrational or outdated assumptions and subject them to closer scrutiny. Suggesting that a closer look be taken may initially be viewed as an act of heresy, but it may yield to a productive discussion. Even if the conclusion is to allow the sacred cow a long and happy life, recognizing this limitation is useful knowledge as you proceed with your plan.

Corporate Identity Issues

Once you have analyzed, scrutinized, and itemized, the next step is to summarize. What have you learned about your organization, about who you are and what you do? The development of specific, written statements of corporate identity help to define your organization to your staff,

stakeholders, donors, and the public who will hopefully be aware of your existence.

The Mission Statement

Every nonprofit should have a mission—a reason for being and doing what you do. The mission statement is a way of capsulizing in understandable form the reasons why your organization exists. While you may have several volumes of technical, indecipherable policy and procedure manuals, the mission statement captures the essence or unifying concept of the organization.

Having a mission statement is important in differentiating your organization from all the others, and can serve as a cornerstone for your corporate planning. It is important to reexamine your mission statement if you already have one, or to develop one if you do not.

Looking back at your statements regarding the businesses you are in and would like to be in is a good starting point for the development of your corporate mission. Try to develop a mission statement that both describes what you do and allows room for anticipated growth and movement if possible. All your activities should fall within the realm of your statement. If your mission is to provide volunteer management assistance to small businesses, how do you explain your program for assisting the elderly with income tax returns? A good mission statement will encompass your services and programs in a way that is broad enough to be inclusive but narrow enough to be meaningful. "We help people" might cover most nonprofits, but gives us no information to distinguish one from another, and fails to help us know if we should go to this agency for financial assistance or the amputation of a hangnail.

A good mission statement should not exceed the limits of the human memory. If your staff cannot repeat it with a little prompting, it is probably too long or complicated. Mission statements will hopefully have an element of zinginess, and may be useful for marketing, fund raising, or creating public awareness. The development of a solid mission statement is an exercise in creativity and might be fodder for a brainstorming session or a contest.

Knowing what your mission is can help you to clearly articulate what your programs consist of and to respond to questions about your organization. The ability to say, "Smalltown Clinic is an organization dedicated to the prevention and treatment of stress-related illnesses in a drug-free environment" allows you to succinctly explain and easily understand what you are in business to do. It's a great deal different from saying, "Well, we help people with nervous conditions feel better."

Corporate Values and Philosophy

Why do you do what you do the way you do it? This complicated question might have a number of complicated answers, which hopefully will relate in most cases to your corporate philosophy. Smalltown Clinic does not prescribe valium for stress-related illnesses, because of a fundamental belief that drugs do not resolve stressors in the best way possible. It is not because they lack physicians to prescribe the drug, because valium is expensive, or because the nearest pharmacy is several miles away. The decision is made for reasons of corporate values and philosophy.

Having a well-defined, written philosophy statement provides backing to the mission statement. It explains the reasons behind the mission statement and defines the fundamental beliefs of the organization. A nurse who believes that valium is a wonder drug in dealing with stress and a patient who is looking for a prescription would not be happy at Smalltown Clinic. This clearly stated philosophy will save both parties time and aggravation if they read and believe it, and endeavor to either find an organization that will better suit their needs or decide to be flexible enough to give the drug-free approach a try.

Hopefully your philosophy will serve as a unifying force for your staff and stakeholders. It also gives a clear message to the outside world about your commitment to what you do. Within the for-profit world, McDonald's has been recognized for their brief, repeatable statement of corporate values: Q.S.C.V.—Quality, Service, Cleanliness and Value. This simple statement provides the basis for corporate priorities and actions, and can serve as a powerful public relations tool as well.

While your philosophy may lack the simple appeal of the hamburger world, you can try to communicate as clearly as possible what is important to you. This philosophy, once developed, deserves a prominent place in your organization —in hiring and orienting staff, in promotional literature, and perhaps even in your reception area.

Corporate Charter or Bylaws

The examination of corporate documents such as the corporate charter and bylaws can be complex and require the assistance of legal counsel. Yet, they may do a great deal to define who you are. As your organization grows and evolves, a review of such documents may warrant attention. At times, these documents may require some revision and updating to reflect reality. While there may not be immediate serious consequences of being at odds with organizational bylaws, in the long run you can avoid problems if the documents are clear and not open to question. As you explore issues of corporate identity, bylaws may need reexamination or updating to keep up with the direction in which you are moving.

The Organizational Chart

Hopefully your organizational chart reflects your actual corporate structure and how your corporate structure works. If so, your task may be greatly simplified. This is an area that can cause confusion over roles, responsibilities, and relationships if it is not well defined. A related issue to be addressed is the examination of possible changes in the organizational structure as the agency follows the course that is being charted.

The subject of organizational structure is a book in itself, but several fundamental questions will need to be addressed:

- Does the present structure work?
- Are modifications needed, and if so, what form might they take?
- Do reporting relationships and departmental organization make sense?
- Where will we place new services or altered existing ones?

A poorly designed organization, like the dinosaur, could be doomed to extinction. If one department encompasses too many functions or no one is really in charge of a key area, your plans and goals may be at high risk for failure. Examination of overloads, roadblocks, and poorly designed departments can serve as the basis for significant improvement. Growing organizations, like poorly remodeled houses, can be the victims of unplanned growth, with functions added randomly, based on who has the time or is unassertive enough to assume the function. Within several years, an unwieldy structure can be the result.

Serious consideration should be given to the placement of new or evolving services within the organization. Examining your structure in terms of function, work flow, and compatibility of purpose can help you to assimilate change more smoothly. Perhaps your new service warrants another level of management, or it might be a possibility for absorption into a similar department or division. Decisions such as these can make a major impact on the eventual operation of the service.

It should be noted that it is nearly impossible to have a completely objective discussion of organizational chart issues. We all know that the Director of Adult Services is our friend Mary, and the Supervisor of the Northern Center is Joe, whom we've never cared for. Likewise, we know where we fit in and how changes might impact us. Nevertheless, as managers we are called on to deal with difficult issues and to do the best we can.

Identification of Stakeholders

In your organizational life, as in your personal life, it is important to know who cares about you. If you have been effective in carrying forth your mission, there should be a number of people who would be affected to varying degrees if you closed shop tomorrow. Identifying these persons will help you to know both who you serve and who you can count on for funding, backing, and positive word of mouth. As mentioned earlier, a demographic analysis of your clientele is a fundamental step in the strategic planning process. Looking at this data is a logical starting point for the identification of your stakeholders, but

they will undoubtedly extend beyond those you physically serve.

Stockholders in a for-profit corporation are those who are financially invested in the corporation. They will prosper through its success, and decline as a result of its failures. Stakeholders in the nonprofit sector are similar in that they are invested in your success. Naturally, the individuals who come to you for your services and programs have a stake in your survival. If they avail themselves of your services voluntarily, they would be likely to feel your loss and might be subject to the inconvenience of finding a substitute elsewhere. Stakeholders, however, include those with other forms of interest in your organization, as well.

Many families who have lost a loved one to cancer feel an investment in the success of organizations involved in cancer treatment and research. These individuals may never have come into direct contact with the organization, but might know that it provided support and information to a relative, or feel a personal commitment to the discovery of a cure for cancer. The families of patients in psychiatric treatment may develop a real investment in the work of the hospital. Women who have undergone mastectomies are often excellent volunteers in agencies that assist in coping with survival after surgery. All of these persons can be identified as sources of support for the agency's programs, whether in terms of contributions of time, money, or a positive public image.

Identifying and exploring your stakeholders can be a big boost to your success. Forming auxiliaries, advisory boards, or volunteer associations has proven helpful to many organizations in carrying out new programs, maintaining services, and raising the funds needed for operations. Knowing who cares can be a valuable asset for nonprofit organizations, many of which do not charge a fixed fee to cover the cost of their services and must count on concerned citizens for their survival. Incorporating the benefits of stakeholders into your strategic plan can help you achieve the results you are seeking.

Goal Development

As you begin to clarify some of the issues your organization is dealing with, these issues must be translated into statements of organizational goals and objectives. These goals should be made on the corporate level as well as the departmental level. While many organizations complete goals and objectives on an annual basis, it is important to understand both goals and objectives and where they fit into the planning process.

Goals are statements that describe broad, abstract intents, states, or conditions. They define the desired destination or outcome the organization is attempting to achieve. The following are examples of goals:

- We want to be the best-known hospital in our region within the next five years.
- Our goal is to cut our operating costs by 10 percent without affecting the quality of our services.
- Within three years, we want to increase the utilization of our early childhood program by 25 percent.

A clearly written goal will be specific and include time frames when possible. Just to state that your goal is to improve your services is not very informative; it would be better to state what services you will strive to improve and in what way.

An *objective* is a statement that describes specific, desired outcomes or results, and may address the actual actions or mechanisms for achieving those outcomes. Objectives are plans that are geared toward reaching identified goals. For example, a hospital whose goal is to become the best known in the region might state the following objectives:

- Increase name recognition in the next county by scheduling at least one speaker per month in that area.
- Sponsor a health fair at a local mall to familiarize the public with our programs and services.
- Develop an innovative, homelike birthing center to attract publicity and positive word of mouth from patients.

The assumption is that the achievement of these objectives will bring the hospital a step closer to the actualization of its goal of becoming better known. A clear objective will explain what you plan to do, why, and how. Specific action items may need to be added in order to clarify steps

in achieving each objective, and it is important to include time frames for implementation and persons responsible for the implementation of each item. A well-written objective will be measurable; it will be easy to determine whether it has been achieved.

Clear statements of goals and objectives are important in the planning process, as they serve as vehicles for the articulation and eventually the tracking of planned courses of action.

The Superordinate Goal

A superordinate goal is a statement of the institution's primary or overriding goal. It can be somewhat general in order to encompass a number of smaller goals, but again must be specific enough so that it is meaningful. This statement can become a rallying cry for your staff, and a focal point for your activities. In developing a superordinate goal, think about the primary outcome or outcomes you hoped to achieve when you committed yourself to the development of a strategic plan. Take a look at your analysis of what business you are in and what business you want to be in; examine carefully the goals you have set to date. Any statement of goals at this point should be considered preliminary and tentative, subject to final review as the plan is developed and committed to paper.

The importance of a superordinate goal may vary from organization to organization, but having a unifying concept for your strategic and long-range plans can help to clarify your intentions and directions. The superordinate goal will deserve a prominent place in your planning document when it is developed. While each organization's superordinate goal may have a different flavor, examples might sound like this:

- To develop a regional reputation for providing residential treatment and education services to autistic children.
- To provide high-quality educational materials, training, and consultation on home safety on a national scale.
- To serve the unemployed in Home County by providing counseling, training in job-seeking skills and resume writing, and information on local job opportunities.

These superordinate goals do not necessarily describe the organization's present situation; rather, they describe the condition or state the organization hopes to achieve as a result of its planning. The agency for the unemployed mentioned above might currently have a staff of two running groups on a weekly basis to support the unemployed in Home County. However, their superordinate goal statement summarizes their intentions to develop a training program and job information bank. The details of their proposed course of action in attaining these goals would be included in their plan, developed by task forces who are digging for information and determining how the agency might best implement these plans on a practical level. The superordinate goal statement clarifies and reminds you of where you want to go.

Corporate Goals

In any but the smallest organization, there will be a need to develop goals on the corporate level, which will encompass the organization as a whole, and the departmental or divisional level, which will cover smaller functional units and support the corporate goals.

The corporate goals should be related to the achievement of the superordinate goal, and should state the priorities for the entire organization for the period covered by the plan. In the example above, corporate goals might include:

- Increase counseling efforts for the unemployed to include group, individual, and family support.
- Develop and implement a training program on resume writing and job search skills.
- Form a network of local businesses to gain information on the availability of employment opportunities.

In this case, these may be the primary goals for the organization as a whole over the next five years. To be complete, the goals would be complemented by the development of specific objectives detailing how, when, and by whom those goals are to be achieved. The goals may then be delegated to the departmental level if this is appropriate in terms of the organizational structure. If there are separate education and counseling divisions, for example, they will be

responsible for the development of their respective programs.

Goals on the corporate level should set the tone for departmental goals. They should relate to the organization's mission and the furthering of its overall progress. It is on this level that reorganization, restructuring, or redefinition of the organization should occur, and issues such as these should definitely appear on the list of corporate goals. Realistically, some of these goals will remain the primary responsibility of the chief executive officer, and some will be delegated to other managers or staff.

The development of coporate goals will be greatly simplified if you have done your homework on other fundamental issues of corporate identity and structure. They will reflect these findings and conclusions, and will form a vital part of your plan for the future.

Departmental or Divisional Goals

The development of departmental goals must be related to overall corporate goals and the organization's superordinate goals. In an organization that has made a decision to phase out its program for the parents of Down's syndrome children, departmental goals should not include the hiring of an additional counselor for this purpose. The coordination of departmental with corporate goals is a real benefit of developing a systematic and well-orchestrated plan; it is important that all parts of the organization pull in the same direction.

Once overall corporate goals and directions have been developed, departmental goals should not be difficult. If a corporate goal is to develop an educational program on job-seeking skills, then the education department's goals should include plans for implementing this service, and should include detailed information on actions needed and time frames for their accomplishment. This tie-in forms a clear audit trail so that the organization can track all the components of its plan and determine their status. It also helps to avoid a sudden realization several years down the road that someone was supposed to develop a new program. In the heat of battle, it is easy to lose sight of your goals and plans for their attainment.

Departmental goals might not always relate directly to corporate goals. In the planning process, the group might come across a more effective way to provide services or a possibility of streamlining the department's operations. These discoveries are important to recognize and note; while they may not tie directly to the corporate directions, they may improve the overall functioning of the agency and therefore deserve a place in the department's goals over the next several years.

Departmental goals, however, should always be reviewed at the corporate level to determine their compatibility with the overall course of action; if implementation of the goal will cost $20,000 at a time when the corporate goal is cost-containment, further discussion and exploration may be warranted.

At the department as well as the corporate level, strategy and goal-setting are important. Especially in a large organization where departments may enjoy a degree of autonomy, it is helpful to have a framework for actions and decisions, and to chart a course for the department over a multi-year period. The development of departmental goals can help managers to manage more efficiently, to develop guidelines for operations, and to measure their performance in supporting the efforts of the organization as a whole.

Financial Goals and Plans

Depending on the needs of the organization, financial planning will assume varying degrees of importance. The picture will be different in a small agency struggling for survival than in a well-established organization with a large endowment. In either case, the development of financial plans and the consideration of financial realities will play an important part in the development of the strategic plan.

An organization for which financial issues are paramount may decide to make this area a major focus of the planning process. A task force might be formed of the financial officer, development director, and several department managers who explore financial problems and develop long-term strategy for increasing the flow of funds into the agency and wisely spending the funds available. This task might include an examination of the capability of the organization's stakeholders to increase support and the feasibility of adding new programs and services that might be revenue-producing. The development of a financial plan might extend several years into the future, and in any case must be an ongoing effort.

Financial realities must be considered in all other planning; whether a separate financial plan is developed, a hard look must be taken at the financial feasibility of proposed services, programs, and alterations in the organization's course. These must be based on as much hard data as can be mustered, including figures on past performance, revenue, and expense, and projections on future funding sources. Even a well thought-out, much-needed service can be destined for failure if financial planning is not carried out as an integral part of its development.

Depending on the sophistication of the organization's staff, outside assistance might be needed for financial planning. This is an area where the importance of good information and knowledge cannot be underestimated. The development of an accurate forecast of the financial picture is fundamental to the success of the plan. Changes in the economic picture, funding, and the impact of inflation are the subject of endless speculation by high-level experts, and can be difficult for a small organization to project. However, a thorough exploration of the past, present, and possible future scenarios must be undertaken in the development of a workable plan.

Fund-Raising Goals and Plans

An important part of the development of a strategic plan is an examination of the organization's ability to fund its projects and programs. As part of the formulation of a long-range funding strategy, fund-raising issues will play an important role.

Nonprofit organizations almost invariably rely on donations from outside sources to fund or subsidize their programs and services. The flow of this funding, however, is generally not under the direct control of the organization, and is subject to conditions of the economy, regulatory changes, and the whims of donors. Building a stable base of donors is an essential part of nonprofit management, and one that requires long-term commitment. Whether development efforts are low-key volunteer activities or the domain of fund-raising professionals in your organization, the integration of fund-raising issues into the strategic plan is vital.

Identification of stakeholders, addressed earlier, is a good tool for identifying potential donors. Also, you may need to do some homework to learn about foundations and corporations in your area with which you may not already be familiar. Find out what sorts of interests they express and what projects they have funded in the past. Familiarize yourself with key personnel within those organizations, and look for contact points through your staff, board of directors, and committed stakeholders. By learning more about potential donors, you can secure valuable input into your planning process. This can assist you in determining whether there is a potential for a startup grant for a new service, or in discovering what programs are fundable, and molding your plans to fit that reality.

A long-term fund-raising strategy might consist of the development of an annual or regular appeal, giving programs for designated services, and the establishment of a centralized source of information within your organization on local foundations. By learning to tap these sources, you may greatly expand your prospects for success.

Setting clear-cut goals in the area of development is also possible and desirable within the framework of the long-range plan. While you will undoubtedly take whatever donations you can get, it helps to begin placing some realistic expectations on those donations based on past history, available figures from similar organizations, and the expectations you have for the success of your new approaches. Goal-setting is a good way of measuring the success of your plans, and will help you to project your needs over a multi-year period. Donations totaling $50,000 can be a measure of success or failure, depending on your needs, goals, and the amount of time and money required to raise them.

The development of a strategic plan can also assist you in knowing the direction your agency will take, which will significantly aid your ability to appeal for funding. Having a clear direction can help you convince potential donors of the importance of their part in your efforts, and can help to give them a better idea of what they are funding. While appealing to the emotions of donors is an undeniable factor in giving, the presence of a well thought-out plan to deal with little children or homeless adults will place your appeal on more solid ground.

ARTICLE 12

Planning and Management in Nonprofit Organizations

John O. Alexander

Planning! Why Bother?

Planning for the nonprofit organization is the activity over which the excellent executive and volunteer agonizes most and lesser executives and volunteers take most pains to avoid. Simply to sit down and do nothing but plan, addressing yourself to the future and the resources of your organization, may be one of the most difficult jobs that any responsible executive will have. Yet unless planning is done well, the organization for whom the executive is responsible may look forward to nothing more than being cast about by the winds of circumstance and fortune like a gum wrapper at a crosswalk. Every activity we perform today has some impact on the future. Is it not sensible, therefore, to influence the future by the activities one performs today?

The Nature of Planning

Planning can be best defined as the rational determination of where you are, where you want to go, how you are going to get there, and how you will know when you have arrived. It is the process through which objectives are established and resources are allocated. Planning is concerned with the future impact of present decisions, it is the process through which the leadership influences the future rather than being its victim.

Planning is oriented to results rather than self-perpetuation. It is the front end for decision making when the organization budgets, determines

SOURCE: "Planning and Management in Nonprofit Organizations" by J. O. Alexander. In T. D. Connors (Ed.), *The Nonprofit Organization Handbook*. Copyright © 1980 by McGraw-Hill Book Company. Reprinted by permission.

policy, raises funds, looks for constituent support, establishes the executive directors' evaluation and compensation, accepts performance objectives for staff, evaluates its own impact within the framework of its mission, or attempts to solicit grants for its further operation.

Society's toleration of institutions is waning. Public and private monies are drying up for organizations that have been judged altruistic but impotent. Organizational Darwinism is continuing to build; those NPOs that have not planned and managed their operations as effectively as needed will either wither or regress to becoming "clubs" that may serve the interpersonal needs and social satisfaction of a closed group, but drift largely out of contact with the real social and personal needs they should address.

Getting Started in Planning

It is a common perception in all organizations that when times are good you don't have to plan and when times are bad, you are too busy overcoming crisis situations to plan. The work ethic of our society has tended to inspire the picture of an organizational executive in frenzied activity rather than professional contemplation.

The first step in an organization's planning process is to develop the mental attitude that unless you are spending at least 20 percent of your time in planning, you are probably operating under a disadvantage that is jeopardous to the organization. Further, the executive *must* involve the board of trustees and the staff in the process of planning and achieving organizational change. Any plan conjured up in a vacuum has poor prospects for achievement.

The Crisis of Expectations

The beginning of a planning process is many times motivated by a crisis of expectations. When expectations and performance are at variance, one knows that planning and communication betweeen the major inside and outside forces that impact an organization's performance has been left to chance.

Impacting the nonprofit organization and its expectations are the eight major forces shown in Figure 3.1.

The constituents or beneficiaries of the organization's existence
Government and regulatory agencies
Members
The board of trustees
The chief executive and key staff
Other staff and support services
Volunteers
Funding sources

Steps to Organizing the Planning Process

The rigor of planning for the planning session is one that cannot be overemphasized. Who is involved in the process, its location, the method of communication, the environment for planning, the information necessary to continue planning, and the expectation of the first planning experience all must be strategized by the prime mover of the nonprofit organization. This *cannot* be delegated. Planning is the prime responsibility of the organization leader and should be handled personally by that individual except for the clerical tasks of arranging for meeting materials and room accouterments. There are four major steps in preparing for the process of organizational planning.

Selecting the Planning Team

A planning team represents a group of individuals of not more than twelve and seldom less than eight persons representing the interests of the board of trustees, the executive, and key staff members. Most typically, the planning team comprises the executive committee of the board, the executive director, and those individuals reporting directly to that executive director. The absence of any one of those three components jeopardizes the reality and output of the planning process itself. Each of the planning team members must have the capability and desire of making a unique contribution to the base of information and the reality of output in the planning process.

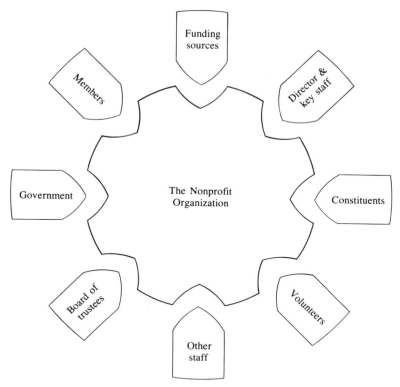

FIGURE 3.1 Expectation impact forces.

The Planning Director Assignment

The three common truths of all meetings are the following:

> The person who writes the meeting agenda controls the discussion *content*.
> The person who directs or leads the meeting controls the *process*.
> The individual who writes the minutes controls the *results*.

It is the unusual executive director, staff member, or executive committee member who can lead an internal planning process with credibility. If at all possible, it is of primary importance to assign the leadership and recording of the planning process to an individual from *outside* the organization itself. Preferably, this should be a professional organization consultant, experienced academician, or seasoned volunteer

from industry or a related field who can take a position as a neutral party with responsibility for process but not for decision making.

As the process progresses, the planning director will write the result of each segment of the process on succeeding flip chart sheets and tape them to the wall for group reference. Special arrangements should be made to copy verbatim the information on these flip chart sheets into typed form either as the process progresses or immediately after its conclusion. All participants must receive copies of these documents, and agreement must be reached beforehand concerning their confidentiality.

The Planning Environment

It is preferable to obtain space for your planning session away from day-to-day normal operations. No planning session should last less than one complete day, with two to three days being most desirable.

The facility should be residential in nature, not requiring participants to commute during the planning activities. This allows participants to spend their informal hours together as well as during the formal planning process itself. It reduces the interpersonal barriers and any initial "freeze" that is normally present at the beginning of a planning process, whether masked or not.

Allow for breaks in the morning and afternoon and at least one hour for lunch together in a separate room. Evening sessions may be scheduled, but not for longer than two hours and after a minimal one-and-one-half to two-hour dinner break. Naturally, when evening sessions are scheduled, a cocktail hour would be inappropriate until after the evening session is over.

The room itself should be windowless or curtained with lots of wall space. Entry should be from the rear of the room. Ideally, the table at which individuals sit should be round or elliptical. If this arrangement is not available, oval, rectangular, U-shaped, or square table setups are acceptable. One must take great pains to avoid a room setup similar to a classroom or a long narrow table that restricts one's eye contact with other members of the team. Trustees, executives, and staff should be seated at random, not as opposing groups.

The equipment for a planning session need not be expensive. Although a blackboard or chalk is acceptable, it is not desirable. Far better are two standing flip charts (newsprint) which can be used to log results that are later affixed to the wall with masking tape. Several colors of felt-tipped markers should be available for use on the flip charts.

Each individual in the process should be provided with an 8½ by 11 note pad or loose-leaf sheets and a folio in which to place notes taken at the session. It is always best to have a supply of spare pens or pencils for those whose writing implements break or run out during the course of the process. Standing place cards should be set in front of each person for those in the group not familiar with other names and functions.

The executive director is responsible to see that key data are brought to the planning session for reference as the process moves forward. This key data, drawn generally from the past three complete years of existence, should comprise the following at minimum:

Report on history and resources
Analysis of the external environment
Organization constitution, by-laws, policies, and purpose
Records relating to attendance, participation, income, and expense for special events or ongoing services
Organization structure and assignments
Membership records by year
Treasurer's reports
Other special information describing funding
Meeting minutes
News releases

. . . prior to holding the session, the expectations of the process must be communicated to all persons concerned.

Communication and Expectations

The fact that planning is taking place should not be shrouded in mystery to those who are not a part of the planning team. Further, the very fact that a planning session has been scheduled should be communicated to members, constituents, volunteers, funding sources, and other individuals and organizations that touch your NPO. In this communication their prior input should be encouraged even though their direct participation in the process is not possible. This reduces the potential for holding the process in a vacuum as well as providing input for those involved in the decision making. Some organizations may even see fit to send questionnaires to key individuals and organizations soliciting their input on particular questions or areas that would be important to the conduct of the process.

On the other hand, it would be dangerous to build unwarranted fears or expectations on the part of those who are not participating in the process. As one communicates to individuals outside the planning group, the following realistic expectations may be conveyed as general information:

That the organization will examine its mission, purpose, and performance against its perceived mission

That the group will review its service to those who depend on the nonprofit organization

That the planning process will attempt to isolate key areas for future budgeting and organizational attention

That the goals set during this planning session will be both short term and long term, and that the NPO will require the assistance and cooperation of many people to help carry them out

This communication may form the basis of a news release, an informational mailing, or be a part of a questionnaire designed to gather information and attitudes prior to the holding of the process. Naturally, the date for the planning process should be far enough in advance so that reasonable accommodations can be obtained and the necessary information and communication go forth well prior to the event.

In most voluntary organizations, the planning process is best held in casual dress over a weekend, usually starting Friday night and ending Sunday at noon. Unfortunately, it is not advisable to invite spouses. Certainly past attitudes, religious convictions, and traditions will play a part in making a decision in this area.

Conducting the Planning Process: Asking Yourself the Tough Questions

Good planning, whether at General Motors or your local school PTA, must ask itself the same tough questions that the planning process comprises. The team planning process, however, is segmented between work that must be done by the executive director and staff, by the team composed of the board executive committee plus the executive director and staff, as well as inputs required from other staff levels, volunteers, members, and those served. Key portions of the planning process as it progresses must be approved by the full board of trustees and the membership when applicable.

Nonprofit organization planning is divided into six major steps as follows:

I. Preparation by the executive director and key staff members
   A. How have we existed?—History and resources
   B. Where do we exist?—External environment
II. Team planning by executive committee, director, and key staff members
   A. For whom do we exist?—Market or constituency
   B. Who are we?—Mission or purpose
   C. Where is the future taking us?— Assumptions
   D. What helps or deters our effectiveness?—Strengths and weaknesses
   E. What are the things that we must do well?—Key result areas and indicators
   F. How do we want to exist?— Organization objectives
   G. What next approaches should we use?—Strategies
III. Approvals and feedback by full board of trustees
   A. Presentation of:
      1. Mission statement
      2. Key result areas and indicators
      3. Objectives
   B. Review and approval for dissemination of those items
IV. Action planning and accountability assignments by executive director and key staff members
   A. How do we make the approved objectives and strategies work?— Action plans
   B. Who will be the prime workers?— Assigning responsibilities
V. Resource allocation by executive committee, director, and key staff members
      How do we apportion our people and funds?—Budget and organization
VI. Final approval by full board and/or membership is required of budget and organization plans

Figure 3.2 [not shown here] represents a matrix of those groups and individuals impacting and participating in the planning process. The pages that follow explain in greater depth the questions to be answered and the work to be done in the NPO planning process.

I. Preparation by Executive Director and Staff

A. How Have We Existed?—History and Resources Prior to convening the planning team, the executive director and staff must assemble the data necessary to gain perspective about the performance and the momentum of the organization. The executive director will assemble a report that will reflect the NPO's record of the numbers of individuals touched by the organization and funding patterns. This report should form an assessment of where the organization presently is so that realistic objectives can be set later in the process. A narrative portion to this report should be developed that outlines individual projects, achievements, nonachievements, and the executive director's opinion of where the organization is going should the present structure and philosophy be left in place.

B. Where Do We Exist?—External Environment It is axiomatic to state that organizations are more likely to change as the result of outside pressure than internal initiative. Indeed, it is this very outside pressure that causes a nonprofit organization to exist in the first place. The executive director and staff must develop an analysis (updated frequently) of those forces that impact the nonprofit organization both positively and negatively. This includes government, other organizations offering competing or parallel services, unmet demands for member or constituent services, parent organization restrictions or demands, and any other influences that affect the behavior of the NPO.

II. The Team Planning Process Comprising the Executive Committee, Director, and Key Staff Members

The steps that follow are those that are to be achieved in the planning environment described earlier in this publication. Figure 3.2 [not shown here] depicts the extent of participation by the various individuals and groups affecting the nonprofit organization.

Prior to beginning this team planning process, the executive director will have provided the board executive committee with the information on history, resources, and external environment. This information will be used as a planning base for the team planning process.

A. For Whom Do We Exist?—Market or Constituency The first question to address to the team responsible for planning the future of a nonprofit organization is "who would miss us if we were gone—or had never existed?" The answer to this question from the planning team will be a guideline for the mission statement that follows this step and will act as a description of the market for the nonprofit organization's services. Answers and discussions concerning this question should reveal the major groups and needs served by that organization and for whom future planning must be targeted. Special emphasis should be made by the planning director to discuss the changes and the nature of this market in the past compared to today's realities. At the end of this discussion, there should be ouptut from the group listing the various markets served and the services provided to each of these markets.

B. Who Are We?—Mission or Purpose With the planning team having received input and conducted discussion on the history, resources, external environment, and market definition of the nonprofit organization, the organization mission or purpose is the next step in the process. The mission statement will most frequently be a paragraph of no more than twenty-five or thirty words representing the broadest and most comprehensive description of what the organization intends to perform. Descriptors of a mission statement include the following:

A statement as to what business the organization is in and wants to be in in the future; the reason it exists.

The statement is result oriented and not activity oriented; it is realistic and not a wish.

It is not what an organization can do but the *reason* for doing it.

It is the "excelsior" for which an organization exists although its techniques for making this happen may vary by circumstance.

It is outward or client oriented as opposed to inward or organizationally bound.

It is the essence and the *sine qua non* of organizational activity—the last purpose to be abandoned.

The establishment of a mission statement will provide boundaries around the organization's planning. It provides a focus to the planning activity to follow. By directing resources into agreed channels of results, defusion of effort can be minimized. The prime purpose of the mission statement is as a communication device to unify the concept of the organization for the board, staff, and constituents. It is a statement that could be published in a newspaper so that the entire community could understand and grasp the nature of the organization. It is directed toward service and not self-indulgence; it is your reason for existence.

C. Where Is the Future Taking Us?—Assumptions

Assumptions should be addressed toward the future impact of the nonprofit organization's market, competition, government, cultural and demographic changes, economic impacts, sociological movements, and adjustments to the value systems of those who provide to or are serviced by the nonprofit organization. As objectives are carried out, one must constantly reflect against assumptions that form the base of the objective. As conditions that affect assumptions change, the organization must be responsive to changes in the objectives it has made when initial assumptions prove off target. Continuous control and monitoring of assumptions by the nonprofit organization is essential to maintain relevance of services, staffing, and resource allocation.

Planning is not a one-time exercise. It is based on a continual review of assumptions against reality, of anticipated forces versus actual trends. As reality and that which is anticipated appear to be at variance, adjustments to the plan will be in order.

D. What Helps or Deters Our Effectiveness?—Strengths and Weaknesses

The rigor of listing the strengths and weaknesses of a nonprofit organization permits the planning group to isolate not only the factors that have caused the success of the organization, but those ongoing problem areas to which it must address itself in its planning. Typically, the planning group will find it easier to isolate weaknesses than to enumerate strengths. It is these weaknesses or deterrents that inhibit the effectiveness of the organization's move-

ment and therefore are foremost on the minds of those who are members of the planning team.

It is recommended that an instrument be distributed in which the members of the planning team are able to indicate, in free form, the five most important weaknesses and strengths of the organization. It is desirable that the planning director develop a system to quantify the magnitude of these strengths and weaknesses as perceived by the group. For example, the director may suggest that the group assume that five strengths and weaknesses represent 100 percent of all of the strengths and weaknesses of the organization. They therefore are to assign values by percent against each strength and weakness, so that when added together they will equal 100 percent in each category.

It is further recommended that this survey be anonymous to encourage candor not possible in group interaction. The nonbiased outsider as planning director is a tremendous advantage in collecting and calculating the results of this poll while maintaining anonymity of input.

Most organizations have found when establishing perceived strengths and weaknesses that the strengths become input data to planning whereas weaknesses are problem areas to be attacked. In other words, there is far more to be gained in the short run in diminishing or eliminating weaknesses than attempting to build on specific strengths. The former is a "win–win" situation, whereas the latter could be "win–lose." In the planning process to follow, these weaknesses will be addressed in the development of objectives to overcome factors inhibiting the effectiveness of the organization.

E. What Are the Things We Must Do Well?—Key Result Areas

Key result areas are the single most important ingredient toward developing organizational plans and objectives. They can best be characterized as those areas of organizational activity in which continued failure would either jeopardize the organization itself or the job of the key administrators. Typically, these key result areas would fall into the following classification and indicators depending on the nature of the nonprofit organization (see table, p. 162).

Some of the key result areas and their indicators will apply to any nonprofit organization. It is unlikely indeed that all would apply

Key Result Area	*Indicators*
Constituent service	Attendance
	Inquiries
	Cases handled
	Requests for information
	Requests for service
	Documented complaints
	Number of meetings, events, or services performed
	Different or new geographic participation
	Different types of services by participation
Volunteer, member, and board participation	Number of volunteers active
	Number of voluntary days/hours
	Percent of increase/decrease of voluntary participation
	Type of voluntary participants
	Percent increase/decrease of members
	Member dropouts
	New members inducted
	Members on active committees and working groups
	Number and types of services to members
	Member turnover rates
	Participation of board members on active committees and service functions
	Number of board meetings
	Number of board resignations
	Board attendance at meetings
Staff performance	Staff grievances
	Staff turnover
	Ratio staff to administration
	Ratio staff to clients or individuals served
	Ratio staff to total income/expense
	Staff absenteeism
	Resignations versus terminations
Financial management	Cost per unit of client service
	Cost for membership fulfillment
	Cost for repair and building custodial services
	Cost ratio of staff to administration
	Cost ratio of services by type
	Grants received
	Cost of grants administration
	Membership dues paid
	Amount of delinquent membership dues
	Grant funds received
	Ratio staff to income
	Total income
	Expense for consumable items
	Expense for equipment
	Expense for building, purchase or lease

Key Result Area	Indicators
The legislative effectiveness	Number of contacts with legislative leaders Amount of favorable versus unfavorable legislation Appearances before legislative groups to testify Legislation influenced
Public and media relations	Press releases: published versus issued Favorable versus unfavorable press coverage Newsletter/bulletins issued to general membership or constituents

to any single organization. The listing above indicates the manner in which one classifies key result areas and indicators necessary to determine success or failure in planning and in performance. Many larger organizations will declare a recess prior to going into objective setting. As you can imagine, the data necessary to determine past performance in the above areas and indicators may not be at the fingertips of the planning team. It becomes the team's decision, therefore, whether to go back to research the data of key result indicators or to select those for which data are available and use them as a planning base.

It must be emphasized that no clear-cut objective can be set from the above indicators unless past data are available to determine what the baseline momentum is of the nonprofit organization. Combined with weaknesses to be overcome, key result areas and their indicators are the base for objective setting.

F. How Do We Want to Exist?—Organizational Objectives With the completion of describing the organization key result areas and their indicators as well as weakness areas to be attacked, objective setting is the next major function in the planning process. Objectives can best be described as stated levels of performance or effectiveness desired by an organization. Objectives may be ongoing or with specific dates based on a point in time. The most effective objectives should be measurable. Qualitative objectives should be included, since the purpose of objectives is not only to measure growth and effectiveness but also to communicate priorities. It must be remembered that:

> Objectives in themselves are an end and not a means to achievement.

> They state what you want, not what you are going to do.

> They must be realistic enough to be implemented within the organization's resources.

> They should show "stretch," that is, achievement that probably would not have been possible with a "business-as-usual" approach to operating the nonprofit organization.

> The best objectives are those in which achievement is quantifiable within a period of time.

There will be ongoing objectives that will relate to continuous activities within the nonprofit organization. Without objectives, however, an organization is unable to communicate its priorities from the board to the staff and the community effectively. The statement of clear-cut organizational objectives based on key result areas may many times spell the difference between receiving or losing community support and funding.

The nonprofit organization should strive to develop between five and ten key objectives as a result of the first planning process. As planning becomes a "lifestyle" within the organization and problem solving and crisis solutions become less frenetic, then additional key objectives can be developed during future planning updates. The recommendation in objective setting is to start modestly but attempt to achieve all the objectives set out for the organization.

G. What Next Approaches Should We Use?—Strategies The setting of strategies is an exercise in which an organization asks itself *what it is going to do* to reach objectives as opposed to *how it is going to do it*. Once objectives are set, strategies are determined for attaining those objectives. As Figure 3.3 indicates, strategies are the ingredients that fill the gap between the NPO's objectives and where simple momentum would take it if it did nothing more than carried on business as usual.

As strategies are determined, an accompanying cost/benefit analysis must take place to validate the strategy within the constrictions of the organizational resources. Strategies therefore become the way in which objectives can be reached with consideration of cost/benefit but without enumeration of the action steps necessary to make them come true.

III. Board of Directors Approval

At this point, three important results of the team planning process have surfaced that will affect the course of the organization over the coming years:

The mission statement
Key result areas indicators
Organizational objectives

Before work begins on the implementation of strategies, formal board approval is necessary to be certain that the planning process and its outcomes have the support of the board of trustees. It is possible that the board may wish to input or adjust the mission statement, add to key result areas, or revise objectives. At the conclusion of this session, the board is to approve the distribution of the mission statement, key result areas, and objectives to the organization's staff, volunteers, members, and constituents so that adequate time is permitted for feedback by these groups. At the option of the board, this communication may request input or ideas for the action plan to be conducted by the executive director and the key staff members of the NPO. Regardless of whether input is requested, it is essential that the organization communicate these areas to those individuals affected most by the NPO's impact.

IV. Development of Action Plans and Accountabilities by the Executive Director and Staff

A. How Would We Make These Approaches Work?—Action Plans Action

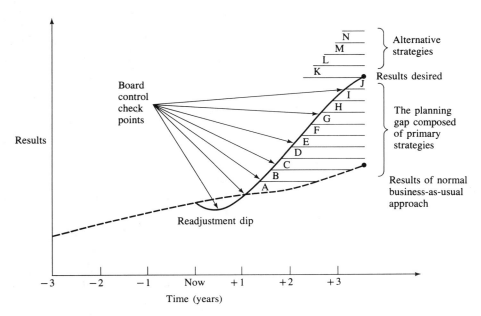

FIGURE 3.3 Filling the planning gap.

planning represents an outline of the key steps or actions that must be taken to implement strategies or strategic programs. Action plans should include a due date for each major step and the person responsible for implementation. Action plans provide a controlling mechanism that will indicate that strategies are being followed through and provide the means of controlling the achievement of the overall plan.

The executive director and staff should prepare a set of action plans for each strategy to be implemented. Procedurally, objectives should be Roman numbered, strategies alphabetized, and action plans Arabic numbered under each strategy. There are a number of formats available for converting objectives into action plans. The simplest of all possible forms is merely to indicate at the top of a sheet of paper the objective to be accomplished over the strategy to be implemented. Below that appears a listing of the action steps, dates, and accountabilities necessary to implement the strategy. This is duplicated for each objective and each strategy of the organization.

B. Who Will Be the Prime Movers?— Assigning Responsibilities The action plan itself indicates the responsibilities for programs and action steps. Many times, however, organizations that follow through on the planning process realize that in order to achieve what the team has decided upon, some reorganization must take place and jobs occasionally restructured to address themselves to meeting the objectives of the organization, as opposed to job descriptions that may have been written during another era. Moreover, as an accountability device, it would be well for the nonprofit organization to use the objectives of the planning process as an evaluative mechanism for its entire staff, including the executive director.

V. Reconvening of the Planning Team Consisting of the Executive Committee, Director, and Key Staff

How Do We Apportion Our People and Funds?—Budget and Organization Prior to presenting the organization's plan and budget to the board of directors and membership, the planning team is reconvened to assign funds and resources to the action plan approved, prior to bringing them before the full board of directors and membership. Activities taking place within the team planning process are as follows:

A review of the action plans and responsibilities developed by the executive director and staff.

The weeding out by priority of action plans that would appear to be less effective in the utilization of the organization's resources.

The associated expense is applied to action plans that have been approved by the planning team.

The necessary reorganization assignment or refinement of position descriptions is reviewed and approved by the team prior to executive board review.

It must be kept in mind that a budget is not a plan, nor is a plan a budget. The budget is a mechanism by which a plan is implemented.

It is at this point that the board executive committee has given direction to the executive staff to carry out the action plans and associated expense that have been developed in a participative environment. These directions and allocation must now have final board and/or membership approval.

VI. Final Approval

At the conclusion of the planning process, the full board must naturally approve the allocation of funds, and implementation of action plans to meet the objective that it had previously reviewed and approved in step III of this planning sequence. The executive committee and the NPO director at this point should be fully qualified to field questions from either board members or the membership regarding the implementation of the process. There will be no reason to feel defensive or naive; the documentation, background, and considered direction of the organization has now been set.

Evaluation of the Staff and Control of the Plan

The cascading benefits from a planning process include the entire spectrum of personnel evaluation activities so necessary to maintaining communication as well as motivation of the staff from top to bottom. Using the assumption that the objectives of the organization and the objectives of its chief executive officer are in parallel or indeed synonymous, one has already developed an evaluation mechanism for the executive director through implementation of the plans and objectives that has been established. Justification of staff should be based on need to meet the objectives decided upon in the planning process. Evaluation of staff should be based on achievement of objectives and not the activities listed in a job description or, lacking such job descriptions, the assumptions on the nature of the job which may be in conflict between the person doing it and those evaluating performance.

Summary

The above represents the preparation and process of planning for the nonprofit organization. If at all possible, these arrangements and this process should be maintained by the organization to get the kind of results it needs to operate more effectively in the future while reducing the "mysticism" of the planning process.

This chapter is designed to provide a procedure for nonprofit organizations to use in presenting their own planning process. Every organization has its own characteristics and personality. The fact remains that the organization that plans is the organization that will survive and grow in the coming years. It is no longer a question of whether to plan, but how well your plans should be structured. Whether the nonprofit organization is a church, a trade or professional association, a labor union, service organization, social action group, political party, or any organization that measures its success not in dollars but in impact, then implementing the best of the planning discipline will help that organization make its mark on society, not out of a need for self-perpetuation but out of a desire to achieve something that would not have been possible otherwise.

ARTICLE 13 _____
Formulating Strategies to Manage the Issues
John M. Bryson

Every innovation is a failure in the middle.
Rosabeth Moss Kanter

The art of progress is to preserve order amid change, and change amid order.
Alfred North Whitehead

Changes in degree lead to changes in kind.
Karl Marx

Strategy may be thought of as a pattern of purposes, policies, programs, actions, decisions, or resource allocations that define what an organization is, what it does, and why it does it. Strategy therefore is the extension of mission to form a bridge between an organization (or community) and its environment. Strategies typically are developed to deal with strategic issues, that is, they outline the organization's response to fundamental policy choices. (If the goal approach to strategic issues is taken, strategies will be developed to achieve the goals; or, if the vision of success approach is taken, strategies will be developed to achieve the vision.)

This definition of strategy is purposely very broad. It is important to recognize patterns across organizational policies, decisions, resource allocations, and actions large and small. General strategies will fail if specific steps to implement them are absent. Further, strategies are prone to failure if an organization has no consistency among what it says, what it pays for, and what it does. The definition of strategy offered here calls attention to the importance of this consistency.

Rosabeth Kanter observes that "every innovation is a failure in the middle" (1983). They are failures in the middle because they *must* be. By definition, they have never been tried before (at least by the organization), and success can be determined only after they are implemented. The broad definition of strategy is used to help assure that strategic changes (a kind of innovation), while they may be failures initially, are successes in the end.

Also, according to this definition every organization already *has* a strategy; that is, for every organization there is already some sort of pattern across its purposes, policies, programs, actions, decisions, or resource allocations. The pattern just may not be a very good one. It may need to be refined or sharpened or changed altogether for it to be an effective bridge from the organization to its environment.

Strategies also can vary by level and time frame. Four basic levels include:

1. Grand strategy for the organization as a whole.
2. Strategic public planning unit (SPPU) or strategic nonprofit planning unit (SNPPU) strategies. Note, however, that if the organization as a whole and the SPPU or SNPPU are synonymous, the first two categories will be the same; if not, SPPUs or SNPPUs may be divisions, departments, or units of larger organizations.
3. Program or service strategies.
4. Functional (such as financial, staffing, facilities, and procurement) strategies.

Strategies also may be long-term or fairly short-term.

Strategies are different from tactics. Tactics are the short-term, adaptive actions and reactions used to accomplish limited objectives. Strategies provide the "continuing basis for ordering these adaptations toward more broadly conceived purposes" (Quinn, 1980, p. 9).

Purpose

An example of a strategy statement for an organization is presented in Exhibit 8. The organization is the Amherst H. Wilder Foundation of St. Paul, Minnesota, a large nonprofit operating foundation active in health and welfare. In 1984 the foundation had an endowment and assets worth more than $170 million, spent more than $5 million of trust income, employed 950 people, and served more than 38,000 people (Bryson, King, Roering, and Van de Ven, 1986). The strategy statement outlines the grand strategy for the foundation during 1982–1986, but also includes aspects of program, service, and functional strategies. The statement is short and to the point. It is easily communicated and

---

EXHIBIT 8 Wilder Foundation 1982–1986 Strategy Statement.

As a board and staff, for the next five years the Foundation will:

1. *Continue as an operating, direct service, health and welfare agency,* 90% in the greater St. Paul metropolitan area with minor emphasis on support services such as: consultation, training, and community-wide cooperative approaches.
2. *Provide direct services for primary areas:* (1) outpatient and residential psychiatric services to children; (2) residential and home services to elderly; (3) correction services to children and adults; (4) administration of housing.

   In addition, special emphasis will be placed on training, education, consultation, and research through Wilder Forest, Office of Research and Statistics, and Management Support Services to other agencies.
3. *Within direct services for primary area:*
   a. direct service to members of low- and moderate-income families;
   b. a gradual change to working with groups in comparison to one-to-one relationships;
   c. direct service to a large range of persons: clients, members, participants, residents, attendees;
   d. increased use of volunteers;
   e. programs funded through: (1) leveraging income ($3 of outside funds for $1 of trust income) to increase impact, and (2) investing in comparison to direct use (grants) of trust income;
   f. cooperation with other organizations.
4. *General policies will include:* annual funding of liabilities, balancing budgets, and perpetuity of trust.

SOURCE: Reprinted by permission of the publisher from "Strategic Management at the Amherst H. Wilder Foundation," by J. M. Bryson, P. J. King, W. D. Roering, and A. H. Van de Ven, *Journal of Management Case Studies,* 1986, *2*, 118–138. Copyright © 1986 by Elsevier Science Publishing Co., Inc.

understood. And it provides guidance for decision making and action at higher levels within the organization.

Unfortunately, very few governments, public agencies, or nonprofit organizations have such a clear strategy statement, whether explicit or implicit. As a result, there is usually little more than an odd assortment of policies to guide decision making and action in pursuit of organizational purposes. In the absence of such direction, the sum of the organization's parts can be expected to add up to something less than a whole.

The purpose of the strategy development step therefore is to create a set of strategies that effectively link the organization and its constituent parts to the external environment. Typically these strategies will be developed in response to strategic issues, but they also may be developed to achieve goals or a vision of success. . . .

Desired Outcomes and Benefits

Several desired planning outcomes may come from this step. First are various strategy statements. The organization might seek a grand strategy for itself. It also might want SPPU or SNPPU, program or service, and function strategy statements for its constituent parts. A complete set of these statements is probably warranted if the organization has chosen the vision of success approach; the set would be necessary to clarify strategies for achieving the vision. On the other hand, the organization may have more limited aims. If it has chosen the direct approach it may simply want a statement of how it will deal with each issue. Or if it has chosen the goal approach, it may want statements that clarify how it will achieve each goal.

Second, the organization may or may not wish to have a formal strategic plan at the end of this step. Remember that what is important about strategic planning is strategic thinking and acting, not necessarily preparation of a strategic plan.

The plan, if it is developed, probably would include the organization's mission statement; mandates to be met; SWOT analysis (at least as an appendix); strategic issues, or goals, or vision of success; and strategies (grand, SPPU or SNPPU, program or service, or functional),

including guidance for implementation. Possible contents of a strategic plan will be discussed later in this chapter.

Third, at the conclusion of this step, planners may seek formal agreement to push ahead. If a strategic plan has been prepared, this agreement may include formal adoption of the plan. Formal agreement may not be necessary, but it usually enhances legitimacy of strategic actions and provides an occasion for communicating widely the intent and content of such actions.

Finally, as is true throughout the process, actions should be taken when they are identified and become useful or necessary. Otherwise, important opportunities may be lost or threats may not be countered in time. It is also important to ease the transition from an old reality, whatever that may have been, to the new reality embodied in the emerging strategies. If the transition can be broken down into a small number of manageable steps it will be easier to accomplish than if it requires a major leap.

Ten benefits of the strategy development step can be identified.

1. A fairly clear picture will emerge—from grand conception to detailed implementation—of how the organization can meet its mandates, fulfill its mission, and deal effectively with the situation it faces. This picture provides the measure of clarity about where an organization is going, how it will get there, and why, that is an important part of most successful change efforts (Dalton, 1970; Kanter, 1983). A new reality cannot be fully realized until it is named and understood (May, 1969).

2. This new picture should have emerged from a consideration of a broad range of alternative strategies, which in itself should enhance organizational creativity and overcome the usual tendency of organizations to engage in simplistic, truncated, and narrow searches for solutions to their problems.

3. If actions are taken as they become identified and useful to achieve the new reality, that new reality will emerge in fact, not just in conception. If the strategic planning exercise has not become "real" for team members and key decision makers, it certainly will become real now (Boal and Bryson, 1987).

4. Early implementation of at least parts of major strategies will facilitate organizational learning. The organization will be able to find out quickly whether its strategies are likely to be effective, and they can be revised or corrected before being fully implemented.

5. Emotional bonding to the new reality can occur as it emerges gradually through early and ongoing implementation efforts. To return to the story metaphor, no drama can reach an effective and satisfying conclusion without a catharsis phase in which the audience is allowed time to break its emotional bonds with an old reality so that it can forge new bonds to the new reality. This bonding process is likely to fail if the gap between old and new realities is too large and not bridged in a series of "acts" and "scenes" (Hostager and Bryson, 1986; Quinn, 1980).

6. Heightened morale among strategic planning team members, key decision makers, and other organizational members should result from task accomplishment and early successes in the resolution of important issues. If the organization is pursuing an important mission and dealing with the fundamental questions it faces, it can expect involvement and excitement from key actors (Selznick, 1957).

7. Further strategic planning team development (and indeed broader organizational development) should result from the continued discipline of addressing fundamental questions constructively (Eadie and Steinbacher, 1985). Improved communication and understanding among team (and organizational) members should occur. Strategic thinking and acting are likely to become a habit.

8. If key internal and external stakeholder interests have been addressed successfully as part of the strategic planning process, a coalition is likely to emerge that is large enough and strong enough to agree on organizational strategies and to pursue their implementation. If a formal strategic plan is prepared, there is likely to be a coalition large enough and strong enough to adopt it, implement it, and use it as an ongoing basis for decision making.

9. Organizational members will have the permission they need to move ahead with implementation of strategies. Those who wish to preserve the status quo will find themselves fighting a rearguard action as the organization mobilizes to implement adopted strategies.

10. If all these benefits are achieved, the organization will have achieved progress in an effective and artful way. Following Alfred North Whitehead, the organization will have preserved order amid change, and change amid order. It will have built new and more effective bridges from itself to its environment, and from its past to its future. And people will be able to cross those bridges relatively easily and painlessly.

A Five-Part Process

I favor use of a five-part strategy development process, in which planners answer five questions about each strategic issue. (The approach is adapted slightly from one developed by the Institute of Cultural Affairs.) The questions themselves would be changed somewhat depending on whether the strategic issues, goal, or vision of success approach is used. The questions are:

1. What are the practical alternatives, "dreams," or "visions" we might pursue to address this strategic issue, achieve this goal, or realize this scenario?
2. What are the barriers to the realization of these alternatives, dreams, or visions?
3. What major proposals might we pursue to achieve these alternatives, dreams, or visions directly, or to overcome the barriers to their realization?
4. What major actions with existing staff must be taken within the next year to implement the major proposals?
5. What specific steps must be taken within the next six months to implement the major proposals and who is responsible?

The process begins conventionally by asking strategic planning team members to imagine grand alternatives to deal with the specific issue. Then comes an unconventional step—enumerating barriers to realization of the alternatives, instead of developing major proposals to achieve the alternatives directly. The listing of barriers at this point helps ensure that implementation difficulties are dealt with directly rather than haphazardly.

The next step asks for major proposals either to achieve the alternatives directly, or else indirectly through overcoming the barriers. Many organizations find that they must spend considerable time overcoming barriers before they can get on with achieving an alternative. For example, Central City found it had to spend time and resources modernizing its personnel system before it could seriously consider major proposals aimed directly at achieving its preferred alternatives for service delivery, economic development, and financial management. Other organizations may be able to move directly to achieve their preferred alternatives.

The answer to the fourth question will essentially be a one- to two-year work program to implement the major proposals. Note that the work will be done by existing staff within existing job descriptions. This question begins to elicit the specificity necessary for successful strategy implementation. The question also conveys the notion that any journey must begin where one is. For example, if full-blown implementation of the strategy will require more staff and resources, this question will ask strategists to be clear about what can be done, using existing staff and resources, to get *more* staff and resources. The question also begins to force people to "put their money where their mouths are." As the precise shape and content of strategy implementation emerges, it will become quite clear who is willing to go ahead and who is not.

The final question asks strategists to be even more specific about what must be done and who must do it. The implications of strategy implementation for organizational members will become quite real at the conclusion of this step. The specificity of actions and assignment of responsibilities to particular individuals are requisites of successful strategy implementation (Dalton, 1970). In addition, such specificity often will determine *exactly* what people are willing to live with and what they are not.

I have found that a strategic planning team can use the snow card process to answer each question. The technique allows for great creativity and at the same time facilitates development of organization-specific categories to hold the individual ideas. The categories that emerge will identify, in order, practical alternatives, barriers, major proposals, major actions, and specific steps. Suburban City, for example, developed its strategies to deal with its strategic issues using the five-part process and the snow card technique. . . .

Using this five-step process in conjunction with the snow card technique has several advantages. First, it keeps people from jumping immediately to solutions, a typical failing of problem-solving groups (Johnson and Johnson, 1987). Second, it keeps people from overevaluating ideas; it keeps idea creation and evaluation in a reasonable balance. Third, it forces people to build a bridge from where they are to where they would like to be. Fourth, it forces people to deal with implementation difficulties directly.

Finally, a particular advantage of the technique is that a great deal of unnecessary conflict is avoided simply because items proposed in answer to one question will drop out if no one suggests a way to handle them in the next step. For example, instead of struggling over the advantages and disadvantages of some major proposal to realize an alternative, the process simply asks the group what has to happen in the next year or two with existing staff within existing job descriptions to implement the proposal. If no one can think of reasonable responses, then an unnecessary struggle never happens. Of course, the group needs to make sure answers in previous steps are linked to answers in subsequent steps to keep some proposals from dropping from sight unintentionally.

It may not be necessary to answer all the questions; some groups find that they can collapse the last three into two or even one question. The important point is that the specifics of implementation must be clarified as much as necessary to allow effective evaluation of options and to provide detailed guidance for implementation. Recall that a strategy has been defined as a *pattern* of purposes, policies, decisions, actions, or resource allocations that effectively link the organization to its environment. The purpose of the questions, whether all five or only three are used, is to get the organization to clarify exactly what the pattern has to be and who has to do what if the link is to be truly effective.

Some organizations (and communities), particularly larger ones, find it effective to have their strategic planning team answer the first two questions using the snow card technique and then delegate to task forces, committees, or individuals the task of developing answers to the last three questions. These answers are then brought back for review and perhaps decisions by the team. Alternatively, the entire task of developing answers to all five questions may be turned over to a division, department, task force, committee, or individual who then reports back.

Yet another alternative is to use the two-cycle strategic planning process. . . . In the first cycle, divisions, departments, or smaller units are asked to identify strategic issues (or goals, or scenarios) and to prepare strategies, using the five-part process, within a framework established at the top. The strategies are then reviewed by cross-divisional or departmental strategic planning coordinating committees, including perhaps a cabinet. Once the cabinet, or in some cases a governing board, agrees to specific strategies, detailed operating plans may be developed. These plans would involve a detailed elaboration of answers to the last two questions.

Once answers have been developed to deal with a specific strategic issue (or goal or scenario), the strategic planning team is in a position to make judgments about what strategies actually should be pursued. . . . In particular, the team needs to ask:

1. What is really reasonable?
2. Where can we combine proposals, actions, specific steps?
3. Do any proposals, actions, or specific steps contradict each other, and if so what should we do about them?
4. What are we really willing to commit ourselves to over the next year?
5. What are the specific next steps that we *will* pursue in the next six months?

The process also helps with ongoing strategy implementation. Once specific strategies have been adopted and are in the process of implementation, the organization should work its way back up the original set of five questions on a regular basis. Every six months the last question should be addressed again. Every year or two the fourth question should be asked again. Every two or three years the third question should be asked. And every three to five years, the first two questions should be addressed again.

Strategic Plans

Strategic plans can vary a great deal in form and content. The simplest form of strategic plan may be nothing more than an unwritten agreement in the minds of key decision makers about the organization's mission and what it should do, given its circumstances. This is the most common form of strategic plan and clearly reflects a basic premise of this book—that strategic thinking and acting are what count, not strategic plans in and of themselves.

But coordinated action among a variety of organizational actors over time usually requires some kind of formal plan so that people can keep track of what they should do and why (Van de Ven, 1976a, 1976b). For one thing, people forget, and the plan can help remind them of what has been decided. The plan also provides a baseline for judging strategic performance. It also serves a more overtly political purpose: it usually amounts to a "treaty" among key actors, factions, and coalitions. Finally, the plan (perhaps not in all its details) can serve as a communications and public relations document for internal and external audiences.

The simplest form of written strategic plan, perfectly acceptable although somewhat crude, would consist of the final versions of several of the worksheets includ[ing] . . .

Mission statement
Mandates statement
SWOT analysis
Strategic issues (or a set of goals, or a scenario outlining the ideal future)
Strategies—practical alternatives, "dreams," or "visions"; barriers; major proposals; major actions; and specific steps
Vision of success, if one has been prepared

Most organizations will prefer, however, to use the final versions of the worksheets as background material for a written strategic plan. The worksheets might be attached as appendices. If this approach is taken, a table of contents might include the following headings (Barry, 1986):

Mission statement
Mandates statement
Grand strategy statement
Subunit (SPPU or SNPPU) strategy statements (if applicable)
Functional strategy statements
Program, service, or product plans, including strategy statements, goals, and target markets

Staffing plans, including full-time, part-time, and volunteers needed

Financial plans, including operating budgets for each year of the plan, plus any necessary capital budgets or fundraising plans

Implementation plans, including work programs

The mission and strategy statements in effect should constitute an executive summary of the plan. The plan itself need not—and should not—be overly long. If it is, it will be put aside or forgotten by key staff. However, a number of other sections may be included in the plan if necessary (Barry, 1986):

1. A statement of needs, problems, or goals to be addressed.
2. A vision of success, or picture of what the organization (or community) would look like if it fulfilled its mission and achieved its full potential.
3. The organization's structure, either current, proposed, or both.
4. Governance procedures (current, proposed, or both).
5. Key organizational policies (current, proposed, or both).
6. Relationships with key stakeholders (current, proposed, or both).
7. Assumptions on which the plan is based.
8. Marketing plans.
9. Facilities plans.
10. Contingency plans to be pursued if circumstances change.
11. Any other sections deemed to be important.

The task of preparing a first draft of the strategic plan usually should be assigned to a key staff person. Once the draft is prepared, key decision makers, including the strategic planning team, the governing board, and possibly several external stakeholders, should review it. Several modifications are likely to be suggested by various stakeholders, and if modifications improve the plan, they should be accepted. After a final review by key decision makers, the revised plan will be ready for formal adoption. The planning team then will be ready to move on to implementation, although many implementing actions may have occurred already as they have become obvious and necessary over the course of the planning process.

Process Guidelines

The following guidelines should be kept in mind as a strategic planning team formulates effective strategies to link the organization with its environment.

1. Remember that strategic thinking and acting are more important than any particular approach to strategy formulation or the development of a formal strategic plan. The particular way strategies are formulated is less important than how good they are and how well they are implemented. Similarly, whether or not a formal strategic plan is prepared is less important than the effective formulation and implementation of strategies.

2. Members of the strategic planning team may wish to review Resource Section D, "Advanced Concepts for Strategy Formulation and Implementation," at the end of [the original text]. It is very important that a variety of creative, even radical, options be considered during the strategy formulation process. The broader the range of alternative strategies the team considers, the more likely they will find effective strategies. Constant awareness of the variety of options available will help assure that a diverse set of possible strategies are considered before final choices are made.

Another way of making this point is to argue that an organization should *not* engage in strategic planning unless it is willing to consider alternatives quite different from "business as usual." If the organization is only interested in minor variations on existing themes, then it is wasting its time on strategic planning. It might just as well engage in traditional incremental decision making, or "muddling through" (Lindblom, 1959).

3. Incremental decision making, however, can be very effective if it is tied to a strategic sense of direction. Incrementalism uninformed by a strategic sense of direction is simply "muddling through," but when guided by a sense of mission, small decisions can accumulate over time into major changes. Quinn (1980) argues that most strategic changes in large corporations are in fact small changes that are guided by, and result in, a sense of strategic purpose. Karl Marx is perhaps the progenitor of this line of thought with his observation that changes in degree lead to changes in kind.

In effect there are two polar opposite strategies: big wins and small wins (Weick, 1984). The strategic planning process outlined in this book, because it highlights what is fundamental, may tempt organizations always to go for the "big win." But the big-win strategy may be a mistake. While big-win moves should be considered, the organization also should consider how a whole series of small wins might add up to big wins over time, with less risk and greater ease of implementation.

Consider what may seem to be an unusual example (Weick, 1984): the performance of the Pittsburgh Steelers in their first 115 games under head coach Chuck Knox. Through 1980 the Steelers gained a reputation of near invincibility and went on to win the Super Bowl several times. Their record—eighty-eight wins and twenty-seven losses—is particularly interesting if it is compared to opponents' records. Against opponents who won more than half of their games, the Steelers won twenty-nine and lost twenty-six, or slightly more than half (53 percent). But against opponents with less than .500 records, the Steelers won an astounding fifty-nine against one defeat, for a winning percentage of 98 percent.

So the Steelers gained their reputation for sheer power by winning all the easy ones. The lesson is that you can achieve great things not only through the big win (although big wins clearly can help) but also—perhaps necessarily—through a sequence of small wins. In other words, you may not be in a position to achieve big wins, or the big wins might not even count for much, if they are not built on a series of small wins.

4. Effective strategy formulation can be top down or bottom up. The organizations that are best at strategic planning indeed seem to combine these two approaches into an effective strategic planning system (Lorange and Vancil, 1977). Usually some sort of overall strategic guidance is given at the top, but detailed strategy formulation and implementation typically occur deeper in the organization. Detailed strategies and their implementation may then be reviewed at the top for consistency across strategies and with organizational purposes. Hennepin County, Minnesota (Eckhert, Korbelik, Delmont, and Pflaum, 1988) and the 3M Corporation (Tita and Allio, 1984), for example, have such systems.

5. Planners should select a preferred approach: should strategies be formulated in response to strategic issues, to achieve goals, or to realize a vision of success? Most organizations probably will choose the strategic issues approach, at least at first. The goals or vision of success approaches are more suitable for smaller, single-function, or hierarchically organized organizations, or organizations that have engaged in strategic planning for some time, and more useful for nonprofit organizations than governments or public agencies. It is important to repeat a point made in the previous chapter: the three approaches are interrelated. For example, an organization can start with the strategic issues approach and then develop goals based on its strategies. Goals, in other words, represent desired states in relation to specific strategies. Mission, goals, and strategies then can be used as the basis for developing a vision of success. Alternatively, an organization may go through several cycles of strategic planning using the direct or goals approaches before it decides to develop a vision of success, if indeed it ever chooses to do so. Or an organization may start with the ideal scenario approach and expand the scenario into a vision of success after it completes the strategy development step.

No matter which approach is chosen, the five-part process outlined in this chapter provides an effective way to formulate strategies, particularly if the snow card technique is employed in each step. The questions will change only slightly depending on approach. The strategic planning team may wish to assign different questions to different groups or individuals. If, for example, the team wishes to identify major alternatives and barriers to their achievement, it might ask task forces to develop major proposals and work programs to achieve the alternatives or to overcome the barriers. Hennepin County, Minnesota, used more than thirty different task forces to develop strategies to deal with strategic issues (Eckhert, Korbelik, Delmont, and Pflaum, 1988).

6. Strategies should be described in enough detail to permit reasonable judgments about their efficacy and to provide reasonable guidance for implementation. Hennepin County (1983) provides a useful example. The planning team asked the various task forces to describe proposed strategic alternatives with regard to:

Principal components or features

Intended results or outcomes

Timetable for implementation

Organizations and persons responsible for implementation

Resources required (staff, facilities, equipment, training)

Costs (startup, annual operating, capital)

Estimated savings over present approaches

Flexibility or adaptability of strategy

Effects on other organizations, departments, or persons

Rule, policy, or statutory changes required

Effects outside the county

Other important features

7. Alternative strategies should be evaluated against agreed-upon criteria prior to selection of specific strategies to be implemented. Those involved in strategy formulation probably should know in advance what criteria will be used to judge alternatives. Again, Hennepin County provides an interesting example. The cabinet of top administrative officials use the following set of criteria to evaluate strategies before adopting any or referring any to the county board for adoption (P. Eckhert, personal communication, 1986):

Acceptability to key decision makers, stakeholders, and opinion leaders

Acceptance by the general public

Technical feasibility

Consistency with mission, values, and philosophy

Relevance to the issue

Cost and financing

Long-term impact

Staff requirements

Cost-effectiveness

Flexibility or adaptability

Timing

Client or user impact

Coordination or integration with other programs and activities

Facility requirements

Training requirements

Other appropriate criteria

8. The organization should consider developing a formal strategic plan. Such a plan may not be necessary, but as the size and complexity of the organization grow, a formal, written strategic plan is likely to be increasingly useful. The strategic planning team should first agree on major categories and on general length so that the actual preparer has some guidance. Indeed, a general agreement on the form of the strategic plan probably should be reached during the negotiation of the initial agreement (Step 1), so that key decision makers have some general sense of what the effort is likely to produce and surprises are minimized.

It is conceivable, of course, that preparation and publication of a formal strategic plan would be unwise politically. Incompatible objectives or warring external stakeholders, for example, might make it difficult to prepare a "rational" and publicly defensible plan. Key decision makers will have to decide whether a formal strategic plan should be prepared, given the circumstances the organization faces.

9. Even if a formal strategic plan is not prepared, the organization should consider preparing a set of interrelated strategy statements describing grand strategy; subunit (SPPU or SNPPU) strategies; program, service, or product strategies; and functional strategies. To the extent they are agreed upon, these statements will provide extremely useful guides for action by organizational members from top to bottom. Again, however, it may be politically difficult or dangerous to prepare and publicize such statements.

10. A normative process should be used to review strategy statements and formal strategic plans. Drafts typically should be reviewed by planning team members, other key decision makers, the governing board, and at least selected outside stakeholders. Review meetings themselves need to be structured so that the strengths of the statements or plan are recognized and modifications that would improve on those strengths are identified. Review sessions can be structured around the following agenda (Barry, 1986):

1. Overview of plan.
2. General discussion of plan and reactions to it.
3. Brainstormed list of plan strengths.
4. Brainstormed list of plan weaknesses.
5. Brainstormed list of modifications that would improve on strengths and minimize or overcome weaknesses.
6. Agreement on next steps to complete the plan.

11. It is very important to discuss and evaluate strategies in relation to key stakeholders.

Strategies that are unacceptable to key stakeholders probably will have to be rethought. Strategies that do not take stakeholders into consideration are almost certain to fail. Strategists should use techniques such as Nutt and Backoff's "Classifying the Stakeholder" matrix . . . to design winning coalitions for strategy adoption and implementation.

12. The organization should have budgets and budgeting procedures in place to capitalize on strategic planning and strategic plans. Hennepin County, Minnesota, for example, makes sure that monies tied to implementation of strategic plans are flagged so that they always receive special attention and treatment. They also are attempting to develop a special contingency fund to allow "bridge" funding, so that implementation of strategies can begin out of sequence with the normal budgeting process.

Most important, however, is the need to make sure strategic thinking precedes, rather than follows, budgeting. Unfortunately, the only strategic plans most organizations have are their budgets, and those budgets typically have been formulated without benefit of any strategic thought. Attention to mission, mandates, situational assessments, and strategic issues should precede development of budgets.

13. It is important to allow for a period of catharsis as the organization moves from one way of being in the world to another. Strong emotions or tensions are likely to build up as the organization moves to implement new strategies, particularly if these strategies involve fairly drastic changes. Indeed, the buildup of emotions and tensions may prevent successful implementation of the strategies. These emotions and tensions must be recognized and people must be allowed to vent and deal with them (Dalton, 1970; Hostager and Bryson, 1986). Such emotions and tensions must be a legitimate topic of discussion in strategic planning team meetings. Sessions that review draft statements can solicit modifications that will deal effectively with these emotional concerns.

14. The strategy formulation step is likely to proceed in a more iterative fashion than previous steps because of the need to find the best fit among elements of strategies and of different strategies and levels of strategy with one another. Strong process guidance and facilitation, along with pressure from key decision makers to proceed, probably will be necessary to reach

a successful conclusion to this step. Process champions, in other words, will be especially needed if this step is to result in effective strategies.

15. If the organization will not go on to develop a vision of success, some sense of closure to the strategic planning process must be provided at the end of the strategy formulation step. Formal adoption of a strategic plan can provide such a sense of closure. But with or without a strategic plan, some sort of ceremony and celebration probably is required to give participants the sense that the strategic planning effort is finished for the present and that the time for sustained implementation is at hand (Bryson, Van de Ven, and Roering, 1987).

16. Completion of the strategy development step is likely to be an important decision point. The decision will be whether to go ahead with strategies recommended by the strategic planning team. Actually, a number of decision points may result. Proposed strategies to deal with different strategic issues are likely to be presented to the appropriate decision-making bodies at different times. Thus, there would be an important decision point for each set of strategies developed to deal with each strategic issue.

Summary

This chapter has discussed strategy formulation. Strategies are defined as a *pattern* of purposes, policies, programs, actions, decisions, or resource allocations that defines what an organization is, what it does, and why it does it. Strategies can vary by level, function, and time frame; they are the way an organization (or community) relates to its environment.

A five-part process for developing strategies was outlined, and suggestions were offered for the preparation of formal strategic plans. It was again emphasized that strategic thinking and acting are important, not any particular approach to strategy formulation, or even preparation of a formal strategic plan.

References

Barry, B. W. *Strategic Planning Workbook for Nonprofit Organizations*, St. Paul, Minn.: Amherst H. Wilder Foundation, 1986.

Boal, K. B., and Bryson, J. M. "Charismatic Leadership: A Phenomenological and

Structural Approach." In J. G. Hunt, B. R. Balinga, H. P. Dachler, and C. A. Schriescheim (Eds.), *Emerging Leadership Vistas*. Elmsford, N. Y.: Pergamon Press, 1987.

Bryson, J. M., King, P. J., Roering, W. D., and Van de Ven, A. H. "Strategic Management at the Amherst H. Wilder Foundation." *Journal of Management Case Studies*, 1986.

Bryson, J. M., Van de Ven, A. H., and Roering, W. D., "Strategic Planning and the Revitalization of the Public Service." In R. Denhardt and E. Jennings (Eds.), *Toward a New Public Service*. Columbia, Mo.: Extension Publications, University of Missouri, 1987.

Dalton, G. W. "Influence and Organizational Change." In G. Dalton, P. Lawrence, and L. Greiner (Eds.), *Organization Change and Development*. Homewood, Ill.: Irwin, 1970.

Eadie, D. C., and Steinbacher, R. "Strategic Agenda Management: A Marriage of Organizational Development and Strategic Planning." *Public Administration Review*, 1985.

Eckhert, P., personal communication, 1986.

Eckhert, P., Korbelik, K., Delmont, T., and Pflaum, A. "Strategic Planning in Hennepin County, Minnesota: An Issues Management Approach." In J. M. Bryson and R. C. Einsweiler (Eds.), *Strategic Planning—Threats and Opportunities for Planners*. Chicago and Washington: The Planners Press of the American Planning Association, 1988.

Hennepin County, Minn. *Strategic Planning Manual*. Minneapolis: Office of Planning and Development, Hennepin County, 1983.

Hostager, T. J., and Bryson, J. M. "Poetics and Strategic Management." Discussion

paper no. 59. Minneapolis: University of Minnesota, Strategic Management Research Center, 1986.

Johnson, D. W., and Johnson, F. P. *Joining Together—Group Theory and Group Skills*. (3rd ed.) Englewood Cliffs, N. J.: Prentice-Hall, 1987.

Kanter, R. M. *The Changemasters*. New York: Simon & Schuster, 1983.

Lindblom, C. E. "The Science of Muddling Through." *Public Administration Review*, 1959.

Lorange, P., and Vancil, R. F. *Strategic Planning Systems*. Englewood Cliffs, N. J.: Prentice-Hall, 1977.

May, R. *Love and Will*. New York: Norton, 1969.

Nutt, P. C., and Backoff, R. W. "A Strategic Management Process for Public and Third-Sector Organizations." *Journal of the American Planning Association*, 1987.

Quinn, J. B. *Strategies for Change: Logical Incrementalism*. Homewood, Ill.: Irwin, 1980.

Selznick, P. *Leadership in Administration*. Berkeley and Los Angeles: University of California Press, 1957.

Tita, M. A., and Allio, R. J. "3M's Strategy System—Planning in an Innovative Organization." *Planning Review*, 1984 (September).

Van de Ven, A. H. "A Framework for Organization Assessment." *Academy of Management Review*, 1976a.

Van de Ven, A. H. "On the Nature, Formation, and Maintenance of Relations Among Organizations." *Academy of Management Review*, 1976b.

Weick, K. "Small Wins: Redefining the Scale of Social Problems." *American Psychologist*, 1984.

CHAPTER FOUR
Governance: The Roles and Functions of Boards of Directors

Introduction

Chapters One through Three explore the relationships between the nonprofit organization and its external environment. Chapter One looks at the world of nonprofit organizations and why they exist. Chapter Two asks how a nonprofit organization tries to fit into an environment that is largely dominated by government (and for-profit) organizations and funding sources. Chapter Three examines how nonprofit organizations attempt to anticipate, adapt to, and/or alter their environment to their advantage.

In Chapter Four we turn to an examination of the formal legal and functional roles and mechanisms by which nonprofit organizations are governed. Thus, Chapter Four addresses the formal linkages between the internal workings of a nonprofit organization and its external environment. Since these linkages are established in law, governance is about things related to the ultimate authority, accountability, and responsibility for a nonprofit organization; its organizational boundaries, purposes, people, resources, contracts, and actions as defined by state law, Internal Revenue Service codes and rules, and the organization's bylaws and charter (or, articles of incorporation or articles of association). Corporations (nonprofit and for-profit) are *artificial persons*, groups of people who obtain a legal identity and legal standing by incorporating or, in the case of some nonprofit organizations, by legally associating.

Nonprofit organizations become corporations when they incorporate under the statutes that are specific to nonprofit organizations in their state of incorporation. The statutes for incorporating as a nonprofit organization are somewhat similar to (yet differ from) the statutes for incorporating as a for-profit corporation. All states' statutes of nonprofit incorporation specify that the board of directors is the ultimate point of responsibility and accountability for the corporation. Some state statutes also define the specific responsibilities of boards. The courts also have been active in defining the basic responsibilities of boards. For example, in the now famous *Sibley Hospital Case*—officially, *Stern* v. *Lucy Webb Hayes National Training School* (381 F. Supp. 1003 [D. DC, 1974])—the Federal District Court for the District of Columbia held (among other things) that nonprofit corporation trustees are responsible for active supervision of management and for overseeing the financial management of the nonprofit organization.

By statute, a nonprofit organization's articles of incorporation and bylaws must specify the board composition, its responsibilities, and the rules and procedures under which the board of directors will govern the corporation. The legal objective is to ensure that the board of directors (or board of trustees) abides by applicable laws, sees that its activities are directed toward the purposes stated in its articles of incorporation, and protects the organization and its assets through oversight activities. In most instances, nonprofit corporation statutes deal with boards of directors as legal entities (once again, as artificial persons), not as individual people. When directors are acting in their capacity as members of a board, for the most part they are not people in the eyes of the law. They are part of a corporation board unless they individually violate provisions of law, bylaws, or articles. In recent years, however, courts have been more willing to hold individual board members coresponsible for the collective actions of boards of directors. Participation in such board matters requires a degree of candor and willingness to accept risks. Legal liability and risk are features of governance in all organizations. Nevertheless, it can be minimized. The *corporate veil* is the legal assumption that actions taken by a corporation are not the actions of its owners or directors, and that these owners cannot usually be held responsible for corporate actions. In a similar fashion, the nonprofit board of trustees is protected from undue personal liability when it is incorporated.

Governance is the function of oversight and administration that takes place when a group of people come together to legally incorporate under the laws of a state for a non-profit organizational purpose. Governance is "a general term referring to the collective actions of a board of directors or board of trustees in its governing of a tax-exempt organization (Ott & Shafritz, 1986, p. 172). It includes being a member of a board of directors exercising and expressing one's attitudes, beliefs, and value systems on matters pertaining to the organization. *Governance is governance,* not management; and many of the functions of governance are the same for the nonprofit sector as in the for-profit sector (Dayton, 1987).

A board of directors is essential for most organizations. While there are many other informal groups in and around nonprofit organizations—including many that possess substantial power—our interest in this chapter is the formal organization as designated by the articles and, if tax-exempt, by the Internal Revenue Service. Incorporation is necessary when the group decides to apply for federal or private foundation funds or otherwise to take advantage of a corporate legal identity. Incorporation is accomplished by the founding members filing bylaws and articles of incorporation with the appropriate governmental agencies, specifying the organization's governance structure, roles, and processes.

Nonprofit governance may sound like an unnecessary complication or a contradiction in terms to some observers. Nonprofit organizations are not really governed, are they? Charity is charity, and philanthropy is philanthropy. Why is governance necessary to give something away or to provide services that are not for the personal gain of those who are involved? Why then all the fuss over organization, management, and governance? Is it necessary? To be misinformed about charity and philanthropy in this limited context is not surprising or uncommon. America has always been considered a generous country. People give away money and resources all the time. What is there to know?

It is only in modern times that legal structures and formal rules have seriously affected the intent of people to help their neighbor. The complexity of our society, the force of law (particularly those involving Internal Revenue Service codes), and citizens' growing concerns about potential abuses, fraud, and violations of nonexplicit expectations (*implied social contracts*) between nonprofit organizations and their communities, have all combined to change the ground rules. A well-functioning, informed, and to an extent, influential board of directors is essential for long-term organizational survival. Nonprofits need access to the advice and services of lawyers, CPAs, bankers, physicians, other professionals, as well as leaders of community groups. Networks of information, interorganizational linkages, and knowledge come together through boards of directors (Middleton, 1987). NPOs need the benefit of free or near-free advice. For example, consider just the dramatic tax law changes in recent years. Many charitable tax deductions that were eligible in 1986 no longer are in 1989. Given the day-to-day energy necessary to administer a nonprofit, very few executive directors have the time to stay current on the tax specialization to the degree necessary, for instance, to direct a resource development campaign that targets estate planning for potential givers. Or, for example, consider the need for board members to have legal advice about a pending personnel action that could expose an ongoing pattern of theft that hadn't been detected because of weaknesses in the organization's financial control system.

Given the increasing complexity of society, the development of effective boards of directors is imperative, particularly for tax-exempt entities. Memorials, trusts, and individual donations all have been affected. Without rapid access to accurate information from an expert who is also a sympathetic board member, the nonprofit organization may be at considerable risk.

This information-gathering function is but one vital part of a larger responsibility and accountability role that needs to be filled by board members, linking the nonprofit with its world. Individual board members not only have clearly identified responsibilities as the organization's formal internal control and oversight mechanism; but they fill equally important—if not more important—boundary spanning roles, bridging the organization and segments of its environment. Thus, board members are information channels who buffer an organization from external pressures and attract external resources and information through their established networks of relationships.

Bureaucratic models of organization (Shafritz & Ott, 1987, Chapters One and Three) tend to assume that nonprofits are closed systems operating in stable environments with rigid procedures, clear hierarchies of authority, and specific focuses of activities. In contrast, Milofsky (1987) argues that neighborhood-based organizations (NBOs) may provide a better model of nonprofits for the future. An NBO is a variety of nonprofit organization, usually short-lived and with a single or limited number of purposes, that operates as a web of affiliation with a more flexible, fluid, and democratic structure. NBOs are more responsive to needs as they arise, more able to influence their environments through informal channels, and otherwise acknowledge the changing nature of their environments. NBOs and, in recent years, nonprofits in general, are being characterized as inseparable parts of a larger social system (their environments) rather than as entities themselves. Thus, if the boundary spanning role is taken seriously, the implications for board members are substantial. At least in concept, board members' responsibilities to the external environment may take priority over their responsibilities to the organization. Their role as trustee of the public interest may exceed their responsibilities as overseer of the nonprofit's program, staff, traditions, and history.

Four articles on governance are included in this chapter. The first two are about the mechanics of governance. The final two represent reflections on board participation: "crusty" advice from Alfred Stern, a former chairman of the board at Mount Sinai Medical Center in New York City; and philosophical reflections on morality and ethics of board participation by McGeorge Bundy of the Ford Foundation.

The chapter's first article is an original contribution by Michael Ostrowski on the changing needs and functions of governance in organizations at different stages of maturation. Ostrowski applies a life cycle model of organization proposed originally by Greiner (1972) to the changing needs and relationships between a board of directors and staff, depending on the life cycle stage of a nonprofit agency.

Terry McAdam and David Gies's 1985 article, "Managing Expectations: What Effective Board Members Ought to Expect from Nonprofit Organizations" reprinted here, deals with expectations as a key component of "the glue which holds a (nonprofit) organization together." When expectations are not explicitly developed and clearly communicated, effective relations between board and staff are not likely. The article prescribes the basic expectations an effective board member should have, especially regarding key organizational factors such as administrative and management information, fiscal information, and human resource management. Fifteen questions are suggested for use as governance guides by members of boards of directors. Using these questions can provide trustees and staff with one useful set of communication tools for establishing clear and effective communications about expectations.

Alfred Stern's article, "Instilling Activism in Trustees" (1980) takes a different and interesting approach to the roles and responsibilities of board directors and leadership. Stern's piece reflects his experience as the elected chairman and chief officer of a major hospital. Although Stern views his most important role as symbolic, he sees himself as being literally responsible for the hospital. He regularly occupied an office in order to increase his availability to communicate with all levels of staff. Involvement, commitment, and being a catalyst for change were Stern's primary objectives. Stern's article provides an interesting example of the diversity in perspectives and motivations of volunteer board members, the special talents they bring to management, and the structural challenges that exist in non-profits as a result of governance structures and the personalities of board members.

In contrast with Stern, McGeorge Bundy's 1975 monograph, *The Moral and Social Responsibilities of the Trustees of Foundations*, is written from the perspective of a staff person in charge of one of the largest foundations in North America. Bundy identifies the uniquely limited constituencies representing philanthropic accountability as government regulations, salaried staff, and representatives of the founding family. The obligation of the foundation is to make choices. Trustees have the responsibility to stay "informed, to advise, to warn, and to forbid."

These two concluding articles are interesting in their dissimilarities. Stern is a business-man who volunteered considerable time to a nonprofit board responsible for overall management of Mount Sinai Hospital, including resource development (fund-raising) activities. As chief officer and chair of the board, Stern intensely feels a sense of impor-tance and propriety. Bundy is an employee, though admittedly at a high level and presumably highly paid. Bundy is responsible to the foundation's board for resource allocation deci-sions. As such, Bundy's approach to governance roles is different. Stern is more symbolic; Bundy is more analytical, merging his interpretation of family values with the needs of the community.

Governance is the overseeing of organizational activity within a legal and ethical framework. It is far reaching; indeed, it is supreme in nonprofit organizations. Yet, the contrast between Stern and Bundy reemphasizes clearly the fundamental point that the func-tion of governance is always as seen through the eyes of the beholder. A board president may use different words than Stern, but that individual will usually be as ego-involved as Stern. Individuals in management positions, like Bundy, usually have rules of fair play foremost in mind: Who is responsible for what part of the action and how?

References

Barnard, C. I. (1939). *The functions of the executive*. Cambridge, MA: Harvard University Press.

Bundy, M. (March, 1975). Foundation trustees: Their moral and social respon-sibilities. In Ciba Foundation Sym-posium 30: *The future of philanthropic foundations*. Amsterdam & New York: Associated Scientific Publishers.

Connors, T. D. (1980). The board of direc-tors. In *The nonprofit organization hand-book* (Chapter 2). New York: McGraw-Hill.

Conrad, W. R, & Glenn, W. E. (1983). *The effective voluntary board of directors*. Athens, OH: Swallow Press.

Dayton, K. N. (1987). *Governance is governance*. Washington, DC: Independent Sector.

Greiner, L. E. (July–August, 1972). Evolution and revolution as organizations grow. *Harvard Business Review*, 41.

Herman, R. D., & Van Til, J. (Eds.). (1989). *Nonprofit boards of directors: Analyses and applications*. New Brunswick, NJ: Transaction Publications.

Houle, C. O. (1989). *Governing boards*. San Francisco: Jossey-Bass.

McAdam, T. W., & Gies, D. L. (October–December, 1985). Managing expectations: What effective board members ought to expect from nonprofit organizations. *Journal of Voluntary Action Research*, 14(4), 77–88.

McCurdy, H. (1977). *Public administration: A synthesis*. Reading, MA: Benjamin/Cummings.

Middleton, M. (1987). Nonprofit boards of directors: Beyond the governance function. In W. W. Powell (Ed.), *The nonprofit sector: A research handbook* (pp. 141–153). New Haven, CT: Yale University Press.

Milofsky, C. (1987). Neighborhood-based organizations: A market analogy. In W. W. Powell (Ed.), *The nonprofit sector: A research handbook* (pp. 277–295). New Haven, CT: Yale University Press.

O'Connell, B. (1976). *Effective leadership in voluntary organizations*. Chicago: Follet Publishing.

O'Connell, B. (1985). *The board member's book*. New York: The Foundation Center.

Ott, J. S., & Shafritz, J. M. (1986). *The Facts on File dictionary of nonprofit organization management*. New York: Facts on File.

Selznick, P. (1957). *Leadership in administration*. New York: Harper & Row.

Shafritz, J. M., & Ott, J. S. (1987). *Classics of organization theory* (2nd ed.). Pacific Grove, CA: Brooks/Cole.

Simon, H. A. (1947). *Administrative behavior*. New York: Macmillan.

Stern, A. R. (January–February, 1980). Instilling activism in trustees. *Harvard Business Review*. (pp. 24–32).

ARTICLE 14 ─────────────
Nonprofit Boards of Directors
Michael R. Ostrowski

Describing the role and purpose of nonprofit boards of directors is a monumental task. Some of the degree of difficulty stems from the diversity in types of nonprofit organizations including, for example, credit unions, cemetery corporations, social clubs, political action groups, as well as local YMCAs, Visiting Nurse Associations, and children's organizations. To make the task somewhat more manageable, this article focuses on boards of directors as they operate within the context of public charities, the types of nonprofit organizations that generally fall under the Internal Revenue Service Code Section 50l(C)(3). This narrowing and focusing on Section 50l(C)(3) organizations still leaves a wide spectrum of organizations from Harvard College to the local Little League Baseball Association. One of the unique structures these organizations have in common is a board of directors, although it may be called something else, such as board of trustees or governors.

There are several ways of approaching the role of the board of directors in nonprofit organizations. One of the most important is to understand the legal role of boards in nonprofit organizations. The laws, both statutes and case law, form the foundation for the purposes and roles of nonprofit boards.

This article can only talk about the nonprofit corporation and the responsibilities, liabilities, and roles of the board of directors in a general way because each state has its own laws or statutes regarding nonprofit corporations. There is a fairly broad range of variability from state to state in the kind of structure, responsibilities, and general legal approach taken in state statutes toward nonprofit corporations. The American Bar Association, in an attempt to provide direction to legislators, has drafted a model nonprofit corporations act (A.L.I.–A.B.A., 1964). The original model act was drafted in 1952, revised in 1964, and revised a second time in 1987. This model act serves as the guideline to states developing their own nonprofit corporation statutes. It has set the national tone for state law in this area.

State statutes fall into three rough categories: Those that wholly or partly follow the model nonprofit corporations act; those with separate nonprofit corporation statutes that depart substantially from the act; and those with single corporations acts, that is, an act that covers both profit and nonprofit corporations.

It is important for nonprofit managers to understand the nonprofit corporation act in their own states. If an organization has legal counsel it is worth asking for a consultation. Even a small nonprofit organization can get some direction from a board member who is an attorney. State statute really forms the foundation upon which the roles and responsibilities of board members are based and sets the legal parameters for the operation of nonprofit corporations.

Another set of laws that sets the foundation or parameters for the board of directors' responsibilities is the Internal Revenue Code and related rules. There are two excellent books in this area: *The Law of Tax Exempt Organizations*, by Hopkins (1980) and *Non-Profit Corporations, Organizations, and Associations*, by Oleck (1980). These two books should be on every nonprofit manager's bookshelf or Christmas list. They are reference works that make workable sense of the Internal Revenue Code as well as some of the broader parameters of federal and state law regarding nonprofit corporation boards.

A theme that emerges from an overview of nonprofit law is a somewhat higher standard of ethical behavior and oversight for board members of nonprofit corporations than for business entities. In business corporations, shareholders have a direct financial interest and the board represents that interest. Shareholders have an opportunity to remove board members through their proxy votes at annual meetings if there is some crisis or a significant failure on the part of that board. Having a "bottom line" in terms of profit and loss provides a very direct yard stick of board and management performance in the business community.

The nonprofit community does not have the same level of safeguards. Many nonprofit boards are not directly responsible to a membership that has control over the board, so they become a self-perpetuating body without accountability. There are no shares in nonprofit corporations and there definitely are no shareholders with any financial interest in nonprofit corporations to provide business entity-type accountability. Often nonprofit corporations are providing the kinds of community services that are not directly quantifiable in a "bottom line" sense. That is, the public cannot generally measure the impact of a recreation program or visiting nurse program or children's activity program in one direct tangible way as in a for-profit corporation. These two general issues have led the public and the nonprofit community as a whole to expect more from nonprofit corporate directors than is generally expected from business corporate directors, particularly in terms of objectivity and level of involvement.

Despite all of my disclaimers regarding the difficulty of generalizing about responsibilities of nonprofit board members, several categories of responsibilities seem to underlie a vast majority of the state statutes and federal codes relating to nonprofit boards. These general responsibilities are clearly articulated in the American Bar Association Model Nonprofit Act.

The first general responsibility all board members have is loyalty to the nonprofit corporation. Loyalty is best described as an obligation to act in the best interest of the organization. The duty of loyalty obligates board members to place their loyalty to the nonprofit corporation above any opportunity for personal gain (generally referred to in corporate law as the *doctrine of corporate opportunity*). An individual cannot use an investment opportunity available or suitable to the corporation for personal gain.

The second general responsibility involves business dealings with board members. All states take one of two approaches to business transactions between nonprofit corporations and their board members.

The most general approach (and the one taken in the Model Nonprofit Act) permits business dealings with corporate directors as long as there is full disclosure and a fair, open process in arriving at a contract with a board member. Whether a board member can in fact provide services or have a business relationship with the nonprofit is most often articulated in the bylaws. The second major approach a few states take and many nonprofits have incorporated in their bylaws, completely prohibits business dealings with board members. The audit standards for nonprofit organizations require auditors to disclose and footnote all business dealings with corporate directors. This sometimes has unexpected consequences. Recently I had a personal experience. Our attorney is an honorary member of our board of directors with no voting power. Our business relationship with him was footnoted in our audit. The insurance company that provides our directors and officers liability coverage excluded dealings with that board member from its coverage.

Nonprofit boards and managers need to weigh carefully the relative advantages and disadvantages of business dealings with board members. Sometimes board members offer services or products at a substantial discount, a practice that is to the advantage of the nonprofit. However, even if the process is open and well documented, there still may be an appearance of impropriety to the general public and therefore the nonprofit's public image is exposed to a risk. The public has come to expect a higher standard of responsibility and morality in using charitably contributed dollars, so even the appearance of impropriety is often highly risky.

A third general responsibility of board members is to apply the *duty of care standard*. This concept is articulated in the Model Nonprofit Corporations Act's general standard: Directors shall discharge their duties "with the care an ordinarily prudent person in a like position would exercise in similar circumstances." This duty does not guarantee that correct decisions will be made nor does it hold a director to any kind of unreasonable standard. The duty of care standard is meant to convey the responsibility of directors to act in a well-informed and reasonable way in the best interest of the organization. Directors have a duty to be well informed—to read the materials that are provided to board members and raise questions about the accuracy of reports if they do not seem to be fully disclosing. It also mandates a level of involvement with the organization that allows board members to make reasonable decisions. Although attendance at every meeting is not required, attendance at most committee meetings and board meetings is necessary to be fully informed and to adequately meet the duty of care standard. The duty of care standard is meant to engender a context of reasonableness to the duty of board members. Within this context, board members can rely on the reports and information provided by staff members—if they ask questions and truly attempt to understand the information provided. It also gives them a framework, a set of limits, for delegating authority to staff members, particularly the chief executive officer.

The fourth general duty of directors is to *manage funds in the best interest and in accordance with the purposes of the organization.* Several states have enacted more strict and specific statutory standards on management of nonprofit organization funds. Some states have adopted an excellent guideline developed by the American Bar Association called the *Uniform Management of Institutional Funds Act.* The act talks about the fiduciary responsibility in managing funds in business and nonprofit corporations. The management of funds is one of the more sensitive issues. Funds are entrusted by donors (or the public) to the charitable organization to carry out a tax-exempt charitable purpose with little oversight. The duty for oversight, particularly in the financial area, falls squarely on the shoulders of the board of directors. Directors should be clear about the state statutes regarding their responsibility for being fully familiar with monthly financial reports and annual audits that are done in the organization. Boards should have a finance or audit committee to oversee the report of the auditor including the all-important *management report* that speaks to the internal processes and safeguards in the financial system. All board members should feel confident that the financial statements are fully disclosing the organization's finances. Having directors with special expertise in financial areas can be important to a board since this is one of the areas of close scrutiny.

Directors should also pay attention to deadlines for filing tax forms and all other reporting requirements that are a part of contracts or operations that pose potential tax liabilities. Directors are personally responsible for submission of tax forms and are subject to penalties for late filings. Most states require nonprofit corporations to file an annual report with the secretary of state, the attorney general, or some subdivision thereof. Directors may have others prepare the reports but directors are, in the last analysis, responsible.

The final general area of board responsibility is to set the *general policies in employment practices* for the organization. Typically board members of larger staffed organizations are not directly involved in the hiring or firing of personnel. However, they are responsible for the development of personnel policies and for reviewing the implementation of those policies.

Almost any book on nonprofit organizations will include a list of roles, responsibilities, or qualities that a good board ought to have. I suggest reading several of these checklists of board responsibilities and qualities, and then developing a list of your own integrating the wisdom of a variety of sources. Very little research exists on the actual roles of boards of directors as they are carried out in nonprofit organizations (Middleton, 1987). Below is a list that I particularly like from a 1982 piece by John W. Nason, published by the Association of Governing Boards of Universities and Colleges. Nason's list includes twelve functions for boards of directors:

Twelve Functions for Boards of Directors
1. Appointing the chief staff officer.
2. Supporting the chief staff officer.
3. Monitoring the chief staff officer's performance.
4. Clarifying the institution's mission.
5. Approving the long-range plans.
6. Overseeing the program of the organization.
7. Ensuring financial solvency.
8. Preserving institutional independence.
9. Enhancing the public image.
10. Interpreting the community to the organization.
11. Serving as a court of appeal.
12. Assessing board performance.

Similar lists are in most books on nonprofit organizations or nonprofit boards. These lists are remarkably similar to lists for directors in for-profit business corporations. This is not surprising because, as I have demonstrated, nonprofit corporation law is an offshoot of corporate law.

The real limitation of lists of board member functions is that most such lists present a static view on nonprofit organizations. Typically, the view presented reflects the assumption that the board of directors sets organizational policy and provides oversight and planning input. The professional staff implements the policy and provides most of the raw data and information for board policy decisions. This basic assumption does not reflect the great diversity existing in the nonprofit community. Not all nonprofit organizations are fully mature, well-staffed organizations with business managers, executive directors, legal counsel, and support services. This is the configuration of many larger, long-standing organizations that tend to get most of the attention from authors and researchers. A large number of nonprofit organizations are at a much earlier stage in their organizational life cycle and therefore the board roles are different.

In addition to the board's role, the relationship of the board to staff, particularly to the chief executive officer, is often the victim of static organizational assumptions. The historical division of responsibility has the board responsible for establishing broad personnel, financial, and program policies. The staff takes leadership in implementing policies and providing the service. Conrad and Glenn (1983), in their book, *The Effective Voluntary Board of Directors*, acknowledge the ongoing tension between board and staff. They see this tension as a dynamic and constructive tension, and they prescribe a balance between board intrusion into implementation and staff intrusion into policy. They acknowledge that the balance is different for each organization based on its stage of development and historical traditions. That balance is, to a large degree, based on where it is in its organizational life cycle.

In talking about organizational life cycles I borrow heavily from a 1972 article by Larry E. Greiner, "Evolution and Revolution as Organizations Grow."* Greiner lays out a perspective of how businesses go through developmental phases, each characterized by a period of growth and stability ending in a crisis which then leads to the next phase. The balance of this essay reinterprets Greiner's basic concepts into the context of the nonprofit organization.

There are a number of keys to understanding the growth and development of an organization. The three most prominent are the age, size,

*SOURCE: Reprinted by permission of the *Harvard Business Review*. An exhibit from "Evolution and Revolution as Organizations Grow" by Larry E. Greiner (July/August 1972). Copyright © 1972 by the President and Fellows of Harvard College; all rights reserved.

and growth rate of the particular organization and its service industry. In Greiner's Table 1, the *age of the organization* is the horizontal axis, the *size of the organization* is the vertical axis, and the *growth rate of the industry* is the slope of the line. This model vastly oversimplifies what happens to real organizations in the real world since increased age does not always equal increased size. For example, it does not take into account major reorganizations or retrenchments due to funding cutbacks. Rather, the model is intended to provide an idea or picture of how organizations go through different phases paying attention to the role of the board and staff in each organizational phase.

Phase One

Nonprofits in Phase One are often begun by a group of volunteers or sometimes even by an entrepreneurial person interested in a particular issue or believing strongly that the community has a specific need that they might meet (Young, 1985). Our local Big Brothers/Big Sisters chapter was formed ten years ago by a group of a half dozen people truly concerned about children living in single-parent homes having less of an opportunity than those in two-parent homes. The national MADD (Mothers Against Drunk Driving) organization was formed by one person in response to the tragedy she experienced in her life when her child was killed by a drunk driver. Phase One is characterized by a great deal of creativity and a high level of energy often reaching zealousness. Many agencies begin as causes. Often, one individual serves as the spark plug or initiator of the organization. Initiators may be the founder or may be another person of unusual talent, energy, and charisma who takes on the cause. Organizations in this phase are the quintessential nonprofit voluntary organization, the type of organization most nonprofits started as. At this phase, the organization may be just an informal group or may be incorporated, but the volunteers are both the board and the staff.

In the Big Brothers/Big Sisters chapter I spoke of, the board members volunteer as big brothers and big sisters, recruit their friends as additional volunteers, and raise money by holding a half dozen special events throughout the year.

The board *is* the organization. There is no differentiation between a staff administrative role and board policy role. Included in this Phase One–type organization are those nonprofits that have only a few staff members. They are often organizations where a charismatic leader becomes the chief staff member. A children's health service in my town was founded by one pediatrician and her friends who began doing well-baby clinics. The clinic has evolved as an organization to the point where the pediatrician is now the chief executive officer and the clinic has a number of staff as well as a board of directors. She continues to be the founder and the cornerstone on which everything is built for that organization. This is typical of Phase One organizations that rely heavily on the talents and charisma of one person. There is often tremendous energy in this beginning phase of organization. It seems as though something new is being created, so it requires a good deal of grass roots energy. Even when there is staff, these types of organizations are characterized by collegial relationships, long hours, low pay, yet high degrees of professional and emotional reward from being a part of a cause and making a difference.

The crisis that ends Phase One often is a crisis of leadership. As small Phase One organizations grow, the board members realize they cannot do all the work. They must hire a staff person. All too often the charismatic leader begins to flounder when the organization must write grants, complete tax forms, keep books, have audits, buy insurance, do employee performance reviews, and all the thousands of technical tasks of running a nonprofit organization. So, as the organization proceeds toward Phase Two, the established leadership runs into trouble with the way the new organization is developing. Many small nonprofits go out of existence at this point, often appropriately so since they were founded in response to a specific community need and have accomplished their mission. Other organizations fail because the charismatic leader leaves, and the organization was so dependent on that central founder that it did not become institutionalized: It did not develop a strong identity as an organization separate from the charismatic leader.

The role of the board in these organizations is very hands on: They type, write checks, raise money, do walkathons, and utilize the experience of the individuals on the board. The attorneys on the board write the articles of incorporation and bylaws; the accountants do the books, the physicians do physical exams. The board is the organization. It is often difficult for a board to weather the transition from Phase One to Phase Two since its roles change dramatically. Many board members really enjoy being involved with every aspect of the organization in its service to the community and cannot step back into a policy role as administration becomes more complex (Ott, 1989).

Phase Two

Phase Two begins when a fledgling, charismatic, grassroots organization really moves to institutionalize and become organized in its business operations. A chief executive officer is hired and often several other staff members. Job descriptions and policy manuals are written, charts of accounts and accounting systems get developed, inventories are taken, and purchasing order systems are mandated. Budgeting becomes a key issue during this phase, and work standards are adopted. Communication becomes much more formal and impersonal as the hierarchy of titles and positions build.

Many nonprofit agencies are in Phase Two. They have been around for five or ten years or more and now are receiving grants from several funding sources, have contracts for provision of services through the state government, and may be receiving some federal money. They have regular annual audits, may be involved in more than one fiscal year, and have developed a level of complexity that requires professional management.

The role of the board during this phase usually is dominated by:

- Passing on new personnel policies,
- Being involved with choosing an accountant,
- Setting up audit review committees, and
- Paying general attention to the organization's growth.

As Phase Two heads toward its ending crisis, board members may feel that all they ever talk about is business, fund raising, job descriptions, and policies. They may have a nagging feeling of loss: They get no emotional satisfaction from seeing the impact of the nonprofit on clients. During this phase a much clearer differentiation evolves between what is policy and what is administration. During the initial parts of Phase Two, this may cause some serious difficulties with boards intruding into administrative areas and vice versa. Toward the end of Phase Two, the board may feel that it has become nothing more than a rubber stamp for administrators.

The Phase Two organizational crisis also typically is characterized by employee discontent and frustration with the centralization of authority and the development of what feels like bureaucratization. Long-term employees who have experienced the free-wheeling freedom of Phase One, with its high and heady job satisfaction, may be particularly uncomfortable with the growing business-like nature of the organization. Where did the clients go? Where are old values of caring? Staff discomfort may be exacerbated by an executive who over-controls and over-determines the directions and services of the organization.

Phase Three

Phase Three evolves from the successful decentralization of the organization. By this phase of development, the nonprofit typically has reached a size where there are several supervisors or program directors for the day-to-day supervision and budget planning for projects and programs. What needs to be done is to empower the employees: Allow them to recapture some of the energy of Phase One by, in a sense, making the Phase Three organization into a group of well coordinated Phase One organizations under one corporate identity. Communications with the top are often infrequent and accomplished by memo or brief visits. During this phase the board may diversify and decentralize as well. Some funding sources require advisory committees for certain projects, and there may be the involvement of one or two board members as volunteers in specific projects. For example, a local family service agency developed two federally funded projects, one providing services for senior citizens and the other relating to runaway teens. Each had its separate advisory committee. These advisory committees reported to the board yet each had a sense of autonomy and involvement with its particular project. During this phase there may also be merger and acquisitions with this larger organization picking up programs or agencies that were floundering.

The crisis of Phase Three occurs when management and/or the board begins to develop a sense that it is losing control. Autonomous programs, advisory boards, and acquisitions have become so self-directed—or so parochial—that they are not furthering the overall mission of the organization. This is a very difficult time for board members. Committees argue with one another; advisory committee chairpersons and the president of the board of directors clash frequently. Often, Phase Three conflicts center on the fact that funding may have to be curtailed in a project for which a board committee has developed a deep sense of ownership. They take it upon themselves to advocate for their project regardless of the context of the overall organization good. This phase also gives rise to yet another set of conflicts between administration and board. Advisory committees and subcommittees become invested in projects to the extent that they intrude into administrative areas. They want to hire their own staff or do a project in a way that has been the prerogative of professional staff.

Phase Four

Phase Four is a time of coordination. Top management centralizes, operates, and institutionalizes its management team. Coordination improves, fragmentation is reduced, and centralized decision making with the whole organization in mind becomes a more prominent theme.

For the board, there is a greater degree of integration of separate projects and advisory committees into the board as a whole. Orientations are much more structured. Often there are planning retreats for board members that focus on the total mission of the organization. The Phase Four crisis occurs when centralization creates red tape and dissatisfaction among staff and board. Often during this phase of organizational growth, functions such as data processing are centralized, accounting acquires a business manager who is very bottom line focused, and procedures become very weighty. Distance develops between management and the day-to-day line workers who deliver the services.

At the board level, the crisis also has to do with over-involvement in business operations, which often are the sole content of board meeting deliberations. Board members may feel that they are over-oriented or over-directed by staff. They feel disconnected from the services being provided by the organization and long for a return to a real involvement with the children, the elderly, or whomever is the service target.

Phase Five

The final phase is one of collaboration. The organization tries to overcome the red tape crisis by focusing on solving problems quickly through team action, combining staff task forces across programs and functional lines, and using mechanisms such as time-limited task forces and spontaneous conferences by key managers. This is the hallmark of the matrix-type organization. The nonprofit attempts to develop a culture of collaboration, collegiality, and cross system fertilization.

Board members feel a sense of balance between their responsibility to oversee the business operations and their involvement in the service policies of the organization. There are meaningful orientation and planning retreats that are not overprescribed by staff or the executive committee of the board. Typically at this phase, several staff members are consistently interactive with the board, and there is a broader range of input from staff to the board without attempts to circumvent top administration. Relationships between board and top administrators are flexible and comfortable. Responsibility is differentiated: The board focuses on organizational and program policy; the staff generally works on administration, management, and program implementation. There is, however, flexibility and comfort with some movement up, back, and across boundaries.

This developmental look at nonprofit charitable organizations is a realistic view of how they change and develop through time. Each of us who is associated with the nonprofit sector knows of examples of organizations in different phases. Because the growth rate of nonprofits in some communities is slow, it is not unusual to find many nonprofits in the first, second, and third phases of organizational development. The board roles are very different in each phase, and the types of member characteristics and the optimal mix of such characteristics are quite varied. In Phase One, active, involved, hard-working board members may be the nonprofit's most valuable commodity. In Phase Three, a well-connected, wealthy board member may be the most important addition to a board. The balance of responsibilities shift as organizations change and develop over time.

References

A.L.I.–A.B.A. Joint Committee on C.L.E. (1964). *Model Nonprofit Corporations Act, by Committee of Corporation Laws of the American Bar Association, Section of Corporations, Banking and Business Law.*

Conrad, William R. Jr., & Glenn, William E. (1983). *The effective voluntary board of directors.* Athens, OH: Swallow Press Books.

Hadden, Elaine M., & French, Blaire E. (1987). *Nonprofit organizations: Rights and responsibilities for members, directors and officers.* Wilmette, IL: Callaghan and Co.

Hopkins, Bruce E. (1980) *The law of tax exempt organizations* (4th ed.). New York: Wiley.

Greiner, Larry E. (July–August, 1972). Evolution and revolution as organizations grow, *Harvard Business Review*, 41: 35–45.

Middleton, Melissa (1987). Nonprofit boards of directors: Beyond the governance function. In W. W. Powell (Ed.), *The nonprofit sector: A research handbook* (pp. 141–153). New Haven, CT: Yale University Press.

Nason, John W. (1982). *The nature of trusteeship: The role and responsibilities of college and university boards.* Washington, DC: Association of Governing Boards of Universities and Colleges.

Oleck, Howard O. (1980). *Non-profit corporations, organizations, and associations*

(3rd ed.). Englewood Cliffs, NJ: Prentice-Hall.

Ott, J. S. (1989). *The organizational culture perspective.* Pacific Grove, CA: Brooks/Cole.

Young, Dennis R. (1985). Entrepreneurship and organizational change in the human services. In D. Young, *Casebook of management for nonprofit organizations.* New York: Haworth Press.

ARTICLE 15

Managing Expectations: What Effective Board Members Ought to Expect from Nonprofit Organizations

Terry W. McAdam and David L. Gies

This article discusses the widespread condition existing in many nonprofit organizations (NPOs) in which board members are not given and do not develop clear expectations of their roles and responsibilities (or the role of the staff in helping the board carry out its functions). The article identifies board members themselves as primarily responsible for this condition and suggests why clarity of expectation is important, yet sometimes difficult to achieve. Next, it discusses insuring against organization dysfunction. Then, the article presents a series of questions which can serve as useful board tools with illustrations of their application in clarifying board roles and responsibilities. The result of such application should be a strengthened NPO performance.

The authors conclude that a nonprofit organization board member will be both more constructive and more effective in helping guide the NPO in carrying out its mission by posing and reviewing the answers to these questions.

SOURCE: "Managing Expectations: What Effective Board Members Ought to Expect for Nonprofit Organizations," by T. W. McAdam and D. L. Gies, October–December. 1985, *Journal of Voluntary Action Research, Vol. 14, Number 4,* pp. 77–88. Copyright © 1985 by Journal of Voluntary Action Research. Reprinted by permission.

Moreover, the NPO's staff will be more efficient, effective, satisfied in their work, and clear about their roles and responsibilities in the process.

Why Clear Expectations Are Important

The nonprofit sector, though somewhat hidden from much of society's view (or at least not readily identifiable by many persons as a separate segment), represents approximately 5% of the Gross National Product and "one-third of the employment in the nation's rapidly growing service sector" according to Salamon and Abramson (1982: 222). These statistics demonstrate the magnitude and value of resources being coordinated and controlled by the nonprofit sector. The responsibility to be clear about board leadership and effective in the conduct of this leadership has never before been more critical. Clear expectations regarding the board's role is important because it represents a significant contribution to meeting the needs of American people.

Lack of clarity about mission, role, function and responsibility deprives the organization of one of the key elements of sound leadership—i.e., a knowledgeable, wise and purposeful board of directors. Current environmental conditions surrounding nonprofit organizations demand knowledgeable leadership by board members. President Reagan has advocated "giving the government back to the people through voluntarism" (1981). This approach of returning the provision of social goods to private nongovernmental programs will require greater capacity of voluntary boards to lead effectively. In the face of this new national emphasis on voluntary leadership, nonprofit organizations are demonstrating a mix of both strong and weak leadership.

Ineffective voluntary boards are the result of many factors, including limited communication and understanding of mission. Mission changes with environment. The environment is always changing. This situation of change (at varying rates) requires constant vigilance on the part of the Board of Directors, Chief Executive Officer, and staff in order to adjust the organization to its always-new environment. Lack of attention to the organization's environmental position causes unnecessary stress, resulting in organizational dysfunction.

Insuring Against the Risk of Organizational Dysfunction

State legislation and the Internal Revenue Service require a board of directors to incorporate and document the purpose of the organization before tax-exempt status can be granted. But there are disturbing trends in the insurance industry which support the notion that many voluntary boards may be facing an increasing risk of being judged to be dysfunctional. The authors recently investigated several of these trends for this paper. Today's trends reflect a shift of responsibility from the public sector to the nonprofit sector and an increase in legal actions against voluntary leadership. According to our national source there have been significant changes in the insurance industry's coverage of nonprofit board liability. Minimum annual premium increases for this type of insurance have been in the 25% to 40% range. Increases are expected to go much higher in the near term.

There have also been significant increases in the "writing" of such insurance policies over the past several years. "It is safe to say that writings increase yearly anywhere from 35% to 75% or higher." [1] At this rate the demand for board malpractice and/or liability insurance will more than triple in three years making 1988 a critical and possibly desperate period in which voluntary board membership may be inhibited due to personal financial exposure. Granted, there are to date few cases where individuals have suffered as a result of a litigation in the nonprofit sector. But the trends indicate insurance companies are providing for increased defense costs and further increases are anticipated. In 1984 there were 15 major insurance companies offering nonprofit organization liability coverage. Currently this number is down to five or fewer companies. Moreover, the subject of leadership risk and its relationship to the insurance industry deserves further study.

Despite such disturbing news many people continue to accept the responsibility to serve on boards and attempt to meet community needs. Individual motives for voluntary service are numerous. We asked people who risk service on a nonprofit board why they bother. Their responses are listed in rank order as follows:

• To influence the institutional practices of an organization which is providing a social good.
• To express a commitment to the community.
• To affect public policy.
• To achieve some personal recognition.

Another important reason is that people care very much. Brian O'Connell describes the personal meaning of volunteering in the context of community service, that "caring and service are giving and volunteering" (O'Connell, 1985: 3). Yet the caring doesn't always lead to effective institutional action. Often this is because the players are not clear about their roles and responsibilities—they need to clarify and manage well their expectations.

In the nonprofit organization, many board members lose their effectiveness as organizational actors. It is as if the economic conditions, organizational/management issues and solutions they confront in the for-profit or government sectors where they are employed are not transferred when these same people are analyzing nonprofit organization management issues. Administrative procedures and controls in a nonprofit organization are often different when compared to for-profit or government organizations. Perspectives are different because the motivation of volunteers and many times the staff are different. For example, board members in nonprofits are not paid for their contributions. Compare this voluntary action to shareholders in the for-profit sector in which individuals participate to enhance their financial positions. Nonprofit "shareholders" or volunteer board members participate in order to affect public policy or one of the other reasons listed earlier.

Not only are the dynamics and participatory incentives different between sectors in our society, the relatively lower level of resources, defined as senior staff time, available for managing the board of director relationships impairs nonprofit organizations (Conrad and Glenn, 1983: xv). More often than not, many members of nonprofit organization boards are uninformed and taken for granted. The Chief Executive Officer spends time with only one or two key figures and leaves the other voluntary members ignorant due to an inadequate management information system and process for disseminating and modifying the information to be provided.

Ignorance can be deadly! The thinking nonprofit organization board member must take initiative to ensure he/she understands what is going on. Nonprofit organizations can benefit significantly from new voices or consciences. The reader could become such a voice for constructive change and benefit significantly from increased accountability.

The next section offers a few questions/tools which might help clarify the board member's role and, thus, enable more effective institutional behavior to take place. Consider these questions as specific tools to help your nonprofit organization's staff to stay out in front of the organization's mission, resources, key problems and opportunities, remembering that it is the overall health and performance of the organization for which the board of directors has accepted both responsibility and liability.

What Are the Right Questions?

There are at least 15 questions a thinking board member should consider asking during the first year of service on a nonprofit organization's board. The timing of asking these questions, of course, depends on the size of the organization, the state of organizational development, and the level of sophistication and management capacity of the staff. Board members can also select from among this ideal list those questions which they believe will generate the most constructive activity for the organization. The questions are divided into three groupings: (1) administrative and management information, (2) fiscal information, and (3) human resource planning.

The balance of this article will review these three groups of questions providing selected situational examples of activities which lead to poor communication between the board of directors and administrative staff and describe actions and/or tools which can help clarify roles and authority, thus strengthening the management capacity of all parties.

Questions About Administrative Information

The first question is a strategic one, aimed at making sure board members are on the same wavelength with one another and the staff regarding the nonprofit organization's basic mission and purpose. This key question is: Are the mission and objectives of the organization specifically stated in writing?

- Are operational objectives connected to a comprehensible and clearly-stated mission statement? After attending a few meetings, can board members describe in brief and succinct terms what the organization is all about? Would most of them say pretty much the same thing? If not, are there any actions planned to forge the consensus necessary to release the organizational power that can stem from a unanimity of purpose?
- Were the objectives discussed and approved by the Board?
- Are objectives measurable at least to some degree? (Has anyone ever tried?)
- Are objectives reviewed annually?
- Do these objectives (and the mission upon which they rest) make sense to you as a lay person in today's environment?

Understanding these strategic mission/purpose questions is essential to successfully reaching the organizational goals. If confusion reigns, there can be many useful sign posts to be found in the mandates for the organization (if it were stimulated by government action) or by the minutes of the incorporators.

For example, handicapped consumers of rehabilitation services were empowered under the Rehabilitation Act, Title VII, Part B, to develop nonprofit organizations specifically for the purpose of providing independent living rehabilitation services. The nonprofit independent living rehabilitation system began in 1979 and in a very short period of time has grown into a major source of service delivery and advocacy power. This group of agencies came into their own effectively through clear conceptualization of today's environment and a concise review of program performance by informed board members. In many cases the board members were inexperienced in trusteeship and governance principles initially, but many were quick to ask the right questions and set forth an orderly process to answering those questions most relevant to helping the nonprofit organization achieve its goals.

The second administrative question focuses on board member responsibilities and accountability: Are there written policies regarding board member responsibilities and accountability? For example:

- Is there a board orientation meeting. . .or written background and briefing materials provided to new board members?
- Is overall board responsibility for the organization's business affairs under applicable state laws clear?
- Is there a stated attendance requirement for board meetings?
- Are committee and subcommittee structure, membership and responsibilities clearly spelled out?
- Does the board approve retention of outside auditors and legal counsel? Is the process for these actions clearly spelled out?
- Are the legal liabilities which board members may face discussed? What, if any, provisions are taken to reduce risk for board members and insure against remaining risks?
- Are fund-raising responsibilities made clear? Is there an explicit financial target for the board as a whole? As individuals? Are specific fund raising tools or training provided (e.g., sample letters, fund raising, training sessions and the like)?
- Is tenure of board terms with specific dates of expiration for each member specified in writing?
- Are the number of terms before retirement or temporary separation from board stated?

- Are nomination procedures in the hands of the board subcommittee? How is this subcommittee appointed? Do its members rotate?
- Is *individual* independence on the board encouraged and/or protected? The environment at board meetings should be supportive to minority opinions. All alternatives and opinions should be heard to avoid reaching a compromise at the least common denominator.

The Pacific Crest Outward Bound School (PCOBS) in Portland, Oregon has recently done a good job of outlining many of the items in this question group via a recently-developed "Board Book" which contains, *in writing*, the answers to a number of these questions. By sending a copy to all board members (especially new ones), a foundation is being laid upon which good individual board member practices can be built. A portion of the PCOBS Board book table of contents is attached as Appendix 1.

The third administrative question is: Are the levels of authority between board and staff and among staff (where appropriate) clear?

One of the best examples of a straightforward-approach to this question was executed by a YMCA based in a major Eastern city. They used a simple written chart which spelled out the action and then the organizational level which could authorize the action. Table 1 gives a partial illustration of the approach.

The fourth group of administrative questions is aimed at the efficacy of the organization's communication with the balance of its environment, the key question being: Does the organization

TABLE 1   Authorized Personnel Actions by Authority

Nature of Action	*Level in Organization*			
	Dept. Mgr.	**Div. Mgr.**	**CEO**	**Board**
Employ New Person	Up to $20K	Up to $30K	All over $30K	Approve Annual Personnel Budget
Increase Wage	All in dept.	All in div.	All	Approve Budget
Purchase of Services of Significant Capital Items	All up to $X	Up to $Y	Up to $Z	All over $Z

communicate effectively its purpose and methods to its appropriate constituencies?

- Do board members endorse and approve the basic elements and/or underpinnings of the organization's message? Said another way, has the board signed off on a basic communication strategy? Does anything about it exist (and been reviewed) in writing?
- Do board members ever participate meaningfully in delivering the message? Has the reader been briefed regarding how?
- Are there concrete measures taken periodically about communication effectiveness?
- Does the communication ever have a constructive influence on public policy? How?

A good example of boards communicating effectively with their constituencies can be found in the independent living rehabilitation movement. While legislative activity by staff members of nonprofit organizations receiving public funds is discouraged to some degree (within given guidelines), board members can constructively influence public policy. The positive political energy generated by the nonprofit sector is largely the result of board members effectively communicating important public issues to community leaders—if in fact, they themselves are not the recognized community leaders volunteering services on a board of directors. Fundamentally, constructive influence on public policy by the voluntary sector is critical to our democratic process.

The fifth group of administrative questions looks at basic organizational performance issues, starting with this key question: Does the board periodically reassess the agency's overall performance and its continued need to exist? For example:

- Does staff ever spend time with board members and vice-versa to get to know one another? This informal time provides a more useful and less threatening environment in which performance appraisal and constructive change can take place.
- Do board members ever meet clients of the agency? If not, why not?
- Is there a program to ensure board members visit the field (see the agency in action) periodically?

- Is it clear to the board what the direct benefits of the program are to the community? Are these written down and periodically reassessed by the board?
- Is there any self-evaluation process?

The Greater New York Fund (the United Way giving organization in New York City) has developed a very useful NPO self-assessment process including a written guide (1984).

An effective board member should also want to know the answer to the sixth administrative question: Does the board balance its (and perhaps the organization's) entrepreneurial zeal with adequate and concrete fiduciary responsibility?

Upon examining the continued need to exist, new ventures and problems to address are often discovered. During times of constricting budgets there is powerful temptation to diversify programming areas in search of revenue generating projects. This can be desirable, but thinking board members must balance their fiduciary obligations. Here are a few tools to help (more will also be outlined in the second section on fiscal questions):

- Do the organization's by-laws allow for programmatic diversification? Have members been given and studied carefully these by-laws?
- Is expansion into related or semi-related areas in the best interest of the organization's mission and current goals?
- Is the nonprofit organization moving into the profit sector, thereby using its nonprofit status to unfair advantage? A "little" encroachment may be useful...but you need to get the borders crisply drawn.

The U.S. Small Business Administration's publication "Unfair Competition by Nonprofit Organizations with Small Business: An Issue for the 1980's" (Small Business Administration, 1983) raises several interesting policy issues the reader may wish to help his/her board address. Board members should ask very pointed and to-be-concretely-answered questions about (1) the financial impact of new ventures, (2) the staff skills required, and (3) the impact of new ventures in the minds of the organization's various publics. Directors should weigh the anticipated "public good" and any projected impact on commercial activity very carefully and should ask the following question: Is there a vigorous administrative improvement effort under way? For example, has the board and/or staff looked at:

- Cost control (did the last budget review identify any particularly troublesome areas. . .and has staff reported on progress, in writing)?
- Cost reduction efforts (are they described to the board, and are results specified)?
- Adequate cost reimbursement from outside sources and/or fee schedules?
- Aggressive programs to secure new sources of income (what Directors are specifically involved in these activities, and are any Directors providing leadership in this regard)?
- Cost/program sharing with similar agencies?

For example, a group of summer camp owning NPOs located in and around New York City joined together several years ago to identify and implement joint cost saving activities such as pooled camper transportation, shared maintenance and shared specialty instructors. In addition they conducted joint inter-agency activities to increase each agency's earned and unearned income. Initially called the Camp Management Project, it now functions as the Association for Recreation Management.[2]

Finally, an effective board member should ensure he/she has the top line information needed upon which to make timely and sound decisions. Hence, this key question: Is the management information provided to board members timely and useful?

- Are most major problems identified and discussed before the "total crisis" stage?
- Do board members ever see written reports of agency progress vs. objectives?
- Do board members sign off on written major program plans before they are executed? (It is easier and cheaper to prevent mistakes than to correct them afterwards.)
- Do board members understand the basic sources and uses of the agency's financial and human resources? (See Appendix 2 for an illustrative list of top-line reports which may help structure discussions with senior staff executives.)
- Is it relatively easy for Directors to secure information from the staff when it is requested?

- Is the information presented to the board clear; and are quantitative reports understandable, reasonable to interpret and properly labeled, footnoted and sourced?

Questions About Fiscal Information

The first area for consideration regarding fiscal information is the NPO's communications with regulatory bodies, contributors and the public. The key question is: Do the nonprofit organization's financial statements accurately and completely state the agency's financial status? What assurances does the board have?

- Are all publicly required reports filed on time? Is there a written list of them and their due dates?
- Which reports should be shared with key donors? All donors? The general public? Other key constituencies?
- Is the FICA account really paid up?
- Is there an audit subcommittee?
- Are the staff and board bonded? Is the insurance at a sufficient level?
- If the agency operated at a deficit last year, how was the deficit financed? Has there been any discussion, substantively, about whether it was worth it?

The second area has to do with longer term questions, the key question being: Is there a long-term financial resource plan?

- What are the program and financial plans for the short, medium and long term? Did the board specifically approve a written plan?
- Has the board initiated any specific longer-range development programs? Has there ever been an objective review of the long-range mission of the organization? Did anyone from the board participate in any way (i.e., sign off on the work plan, participate in a staff briefing)?
- If concrete plans and/or programs exist, how is progress toward them reviewed and reported to the board?

Failure to plan in a longer time frame (as well as a shorter one) can result in both missed opportunities (e.g., not accommodating a large demographic shift such as an influx of a particular ethnic group with different service needs or tastes) or missing the opportunity to prevent a major problem (e.g., not recognizing a rapidly widening gap between fees charged/reimbursements received and costs).

Next, in the financial area, the effective board member should ask: Do the budgetary and actual expenditure procedures reflect fairly well the financial capacity of the agency to conduct its affairs? Is a budget developed, with management's assistance, even leadership, which reconciles realistically the organization's financial resources with its programs? What will prevent the agency from "running away" financially?

Finally, looking at financial control can also be very important. The key question: Is there a periodic board review of the key financial control mechanism by the finance or audit committee of the board?

- Does the finance committee also function as the audit committee? Are both sets of responsibilities clearly identified and executed?
- Is there a periodic review of the key financial control mechanisms? By whom?
- Is the board satisfied with activities being executed to safeguard the NPO's assets?

Note that this last review can be as simple as ensuring that two parties handle checks to a much more complex review of the adequacy of the organization's accounting and auditing practices.

Human Resource Management

One of the most valuable resources within the nonprofit sector are the people who work within the sector. Sound and sensitive human resource management is critical to effective organizational performance. And, it often is an area in which attention to it is forfeited for the immediate attention to some other crisis. In fact, problems with staff relationships and the management of personnel are one of the most litigated areas of nonprofit organization management, consuming considerable board time and concern. "Equal Opportunity Employment" and requirements for "Affirmative Employment" are issues nonprofits support, but NPOs are not immune from legal action of employees. The board must monitor the actions of the executive director and senior staff

in their management of personnel. The following question may stimulate some constructive dialogue between the board and management—a healthy and perhaps preventative interchange: Is there an adequate human resource development program for the agency staff?

- Is there an annual performance review for the executive director?
- Are his/her performance expectations spelled out clearly in writing in advance?
- Is the director's performance reviewed in writing by the chairman?
- Is there an adequate senior executive compensation plan...and is any of his/her compensation tied to clearly articulated performance standards?
- Has the executive director implemented sound personnel practices? Are these ever monitored by board members?
- Are there specific personnel training plans connected to the mission of the organization's objectives? For each person?
- Are written performance reviews conducted for all staff at least annually?
- Do written job descriptions exist?
- Has the board acted on compensation and expense guidelines?
- Are fringe benefits simply and fully explained in writing?
- Is the termination procedure clear?
- Is there a plan or at least periodic discussion regarding executive succession for all senior positions? Most good managers are known for having at least one replacement "in the wings."

Both the Ford Foundation and the New York Community Trust (New York City's Community Foundation) have made considerable progress in developing concrete tools in the human resource development area specifically applied to program officers in foundations. Personnel evaluation forms identify many of the key skills and behavior traits necessary to be a good foundation program person (copies are available by mail).

Second, you need to observe the answer to this question: Does the board recruit new members with fresh ideas and perspectives?

We all know organizations which become rigid and uncompromising, some nearly comatose, by the lack of fresh ideas brought in by new staff or board members. Probing "why" they come into this position may have a very constructive long-term impact on the board.

Finally, does the board member understand how the enterprise is organized? Specifically: Does the Board understand and approve of the NPO's overall organizational structure without becoming enmeshed in individual decisions on staffing or substructure?

This is difficult but important. It is important for thinking board members to be knowledgeable about internal staff relationships and the effect of past organizational structure decisions on program efficiency. Caring organizations generally reward past good individual performance with job security. Over time, the organizational patterns change and promotional decisions or decisions to keep someone who should have been terminated can be detrimental. Board members should be in tune with internal culture, history, and past decisions in order to provide for balance, equity and sound personnel management.

Conclusion

The articulation and answering of these basic questions is no guarantee to NPO effectiveness. But, the mere process of the query, like the Hawthorne effect, is likely to stimulate improved institutional behavior. Moreover, since a number of these questions are rooted in "reasonable" managerial/public administration theory, they should, unto themselves, strengthen the process. Finally, as board members, as in life, learning is essential to leadership. John F. Kennedy said it best: "Leadership and learning are indispensable to each other."

Appendix 1

Pacific Crest Outward Bound School: Selections from the Table of Contents

I.   Board of Trustees.
      A. Memo to New Board Members from Executive Director of the School.
      B. Board List (Names, Addresses, Telephone Numbers).
      C. Mailing List (Board and Staff).
      D. Telephone Listing (Board and Staff).

      E. Board by Class and Term.
II.   By-Laws and Mission Statement.
III. Board Responsibilities and Key Dates to Remember.
IV.   Committees.
      A. Committee Members.
      B. Description of Committee Functions.
      C. Development Fund-Raising Teams.
V.   History and Philosophy.
VI.   Statement of Key Operations Principles of the School.
VII. Frequently Asked Questions & Answers.
VIII. Administrative Staff Job Descriptions.
IX.   Budget.
X.   Summary of Financial Highlights.

Appendix 2

Sample Summary of Top-Line Board Reports

Report Name:	Suggested Frequency:
1. Trial balance sheet.	1. Semi-Annually.
2. Statement of income and expense.	2. Quarterly.
3. Budget variance report.	3. Quarterly.
4. Formal performance review of executive director.	4. Annually.
5. Fund-raising progress report.	5. Quarterly.
6. Programmatic performance vs. objectives.	6. Annually.
7. Minutes of board meetings.	7. After every meeting.
8. Follow-up reports on topics raised at board meetings.	8. Periodically.
9. Investment reports.	9. Annually.

Notes

1. Data describing current trends in the insurance industry were provided by one of the top five underwriters in the country. Because of the demand for this type of coverage, the underwriter

requested anonymity. While insurance companies are in the business of providing protection, our source did not want to encourage or bring attention to one particular product.

As nonprofit organizations and voluntary boards become more dominant, leadership risk factors, historical costs, and frequency or probability of litigation will be projected. As better NPO statistics are available, new supply will equal the sector's growing demand.

2. For further information, contact John Cimarosa, North River Company, 22 Oak Street, Westport, CT 06880 (212) 477-2244.

References

Conrad, William R., Jr. and William E. Glenn (1983). *The effective voluntary board of directors*. Athens, OH: Ohio University Press.

Greater New York Fund (1984). *Self-evaluation for human service agencies*. New York Fund (99 Park Avenue, 10016).

O'Connell, Brian (1985). *The board member's book*. New York: The Foundation Center.

Reagan, Ronald (1981). "Message to congress."

Salamon, Lester M. and Alan J. Abramson (1982). "The nonprofit sector." In John L. Palmer and Isabel V. Sawhill, (Eds.), *The Reagan Experiment*. Washington, DC: Urban Institute Press.

U.S. Small Business Administration (1983). *Unfair competition by nonprofit organizations with small business: an issue for the 1980's.*" Washington, DC: Small Business Administration.

ARTICLE 16 —————————————————
Instilling Activism in Trustees
Alfred R. Stern

Two years ago, when I was a candidate for chairman of the board of the Mount Sinai Medical

SOURCE: Reprinted by permission of the *Harvard Business Review*. "Instilling Activism in Trustees" by Alfred R. Stern (January/February 1980). Copyright © 1980 by the President and Fellows of Harvard College; all rights reserved.

Center in New York City, one of its trustees pulled me aside to confide: "I really don't think I'm in favor of your election as chairman. You haven't given Mount Sinai enough money."

For years, one of the principal criteria for appointment to many hospital and other volunteer boards was the amount of money personally given or raised. But today the responsibilities of the chairman and the board members have become too great for money to be the major criterion for board appointments.

In my campaign for the chairmanship, I offered my fellow trustees the following: I knew the institution reasonably well because of my position as development chairman, and I had the time to give to the job. There were a lot of good people being considered for the position of chairman, many of them more experienced in the Medical Center than I, but to carry out this complex job in addition to a full-time business position would have been extremely difficult.

I told my colleagues that to at least the early phase of my chairmanship I could devote half my time. I was at a point in my business career where this was possible, and I wanted to make a commitment to Mount Sinai.

The stewardship of our country's nonprofit organizations offers a great challenge to business executives. Semiprivate, semipublic institutions occupy a special place in our society, and their management demands a special kind of attention. Business people have an important role to play in guiding these not-for-profit enterprises, and that role is increasingly an activist one.

Hospitals in particular—given the economic realities of the day—need leadership and support from concerned people. If they are to be run effectively, three conditions need to be met:

1. Responsible leadership must be identified and encouraged.
2. Trustees and institutional executives alike must be educated to the demands being placed on them.
3. Future challenges must be analyzed and prepared for now.

My own experience permits me to speak out on the particular subject of hospital boards, but service to other types of nonprofit organizations involves similar demands—a point to which I shall return.

Encouraging Good Leadership

When I became chairman of the board at Mount Sinai, I followed an established precedent and became the chief executive officer as well.* Mount Sinai is unusual among hospitals in making its board chairman its CEO, and this double responsibility has convinced me of the need for firm leadership in health care institutions.

I brought with me three things I have come to consider invaluable—a background in business, the determination to be an activist chairman, and sufficient free time to carry through that determination. Spending 20 hours a week or more on my duties at Mount Sinai has been the rule rather than the exception.

I found it helpful, even necessary, to take an active interest in the workings of all of the 18 standing committees on which trustees serve. This involvement has been a primary factor in my own education and has underscored my belief that good leadership qualities are important at all levels of governance. Chairmanship of committees, no less than of boards themselves, demands such qualities.

My responsibilities have included the shaping and motivating of committees (with this requirement in mind) and the larger task of building a board from which committees might be drawn. Establishing a balanced and highly motivated board is perhaps the first task of effective leadership. This means sensitivity to the institution and its changing needs, to the evolving community it serves, and to the availability of candidates who can serve both the institution and the community through membership on the board.

In our case, this has meant an active search for qualified women and for minority candidates to represent the growing number of Hispanics the hospital now serves. We have also sought medical and academic professionals from the outside who can bring expertise and perspective to our sessions. As chairman, it is my responsibility to

* *Author's note:* Mount Sinai has three boards: the Hospital, the School of Medicine of the City University of New York, and the Medical Center, Inc. (the latter, although primarily a fund-raising organization, serves as the coordinating body for policymaking of the hospital and the school). I serve as chairman of all three boards.

tell prospective board members what is expected of them; if I did not brief them in advance, I would have no justification for complaining later should the trustees not fulfill their responsibilities.

'Crisis management':   Effective leadership means more than building a responsive and responsible board, and nowhere has the value of experience in business seemed so pertinent as in "crisis management." During my tenure at Mount Sinai, we have faced two situations that illustrate the role an involved board chairman can play in hospital management during crises. The first was a potential crisis in labor relations; the second was an actual crisis resulting from the collapse of a building fragment.

Not long ago we faced contract negotiations with our hospital workers. While a strike was not promised by the union, it was a distinct possibility, and I felt we should be prepared. We started planning about a year ahead for the eventuality of nonsettlement, examining our attitudes and developing a strategy. I was kept fully informed all along and took part in some of the meetings. As we sought to develop a coordinated point of view on the strike issue, I also met with the chairman of the board and the chief executive of each major teaching hospital in the city to discuss common labor problems.

At Mount Sinai, we have a trustee personnel and labor relations committee, and through it we urged our staff to plan for the operational problems attendant on a strike and to be thoroughly organized in advance.

We had a peculiar situation, unknown to traditional labor management, because the negotiations were largely out of our hands. We were not in the position of a private business deciding how much it can afford and how much it is willing to give. Our negotiations were actually in the hands of the state, where the money comes from—the hospital itself being in a deficit position. But even if the negotiations broke down and we had to take a strike, we were still responsible for providing adequate health care and in need of a timetable for possible cutbacks in service, based on crisis priorities.

Fortunately, no strike occurred; but preparing for such an eventuality well in advance is good management, whether in business or in nonprofit institutions.

Real crises, almost by definition, cannot be foreseen. One of the worst situations we faced happened a week after I was elected to my job at Mount Sinai. A seven-foot piece of a new building's outer shell came loose, tumbling down and spearing into the ground at two o'clock in the morning. We had to make a lot of decisions fast—getting the area cordoned off and contacting lawyers, builders, and so forth.

The first priority was to see that no further disintegration occurred so that there would be no threat to passersby. This meant checking with the company that had provided the steel—but their lawyers were insisting on silence. They needed protection in case of litigation, while we needed expert information to prevent a possible disaster.

Fortunately, one of our trustees happened to know the president of the company involved; we made arrangements to meet and talk with him, thus loosening the legal logjam. Effective management in this case meant personal diplomacy not only with a second party but also with our own lawyers, who were wary of the legal implications of such a meeting. Nevertheless, we had to act.

Such personal diplomacy is, of course, sometimes dismissed as cronyism, but having trustees who are widely acquainted with those in a position to offer aid can be genuinely valuable. In all circumstances—not just crisis situations—it behooves those who govern not-for-profit service institutions to develop as wide a network of contacts as possible. Only thus can the institution's clientele receive the best services.

Educating Oneself & Others

Effective leadership inevitably involves education, and this is as true in the nonprofit field as in any other area of national life. This process has meant educating myself as well as others. As CEO I am more directly involved in decision making than is the board chairman of a typical medical center. Therefore, I require more information and better communication with the corporate officers of Mount Sinai. This, in turn, has ultimately led to a better-informed board of trustees.

My direct link is with the Medical Center's president, who also serves as dean and president of the School of Medicine. We meet together

weekly for several hours, discussing matters of policy and future plans. Day-to-day operations are in the hands of an executive vice president, a senior vice president in charge of education and research, and a senior vice president in charge of clinical services.

This operations trio was set up after I had studied the Mount Sinai situation for six months and realized that the president's time was being consumed by operational details. Reorganization was in order, and I was able to work it out with both the hospital staff and the trustees from my strategic position in the middle.

As a businessman, I learned early the vital importance of apportioning time carefully and of delegating authority whenever possible. I have been able to help the president of Mount Sinai rethink his procedures along these lines so he could get out from under the piles of paperwork that had kept him from more important tasks. Individuals who have grown up in the academic-professional world can often profit from the experience of businessmen when it comes to good management—not only of money but of time and personnel resources.

My own education and that of the hospital and school administrative staff have been only part of the story. I spoke earlier of the mystique that has long kept trustees at arm's length from the actual ongoing activities of health care centers. Working to overcome this drawback is part of the genuinely activist approach I take.

Improving the trustees' level of awareness regarding hospital governance was one goal of a trustees conference we held recently. From Friday afternoon through late Saturday night, the trustees took part in an intensive series of sessions with members of the hospital staff and in seminars they themselves led. Several outside speakers added insightful thinking and discussion regarding the hospital's future.

We borrowed the idea for such a session from the corporate world, of course, and it served the purposes of our hospital board exceedingly well.

We made it a homegrown affair; trustees chaired each of the sessions, and the degree of participation was very high. We had 30 hours in which to get acquainted not only with each other but also with many hospital staff members the trustees would not normally have met. The sessions were free from any decision making, emphasizing instead the opportunity to learn from and get to know each other.

The most significant outcome of the meeting was the trustees' recognition of the government's changing role in the health care industry. In 1978, over 50% of the Mount Sinai Hospital's revenues and 60% of the School of Medicine's income came from government sources. With public funds come public regulation and scrutiny; Mount Sinai reports to no fewer than 160 local, county, state, and federal bodies.

To kick off the conference, we called on a bright young state official whose agency has the responsibility of approving all major acquisition, renovation, and construction programs for hospitals in the state. Following his excellent presentation on the inner workings of his agency, the trustees engaged him in a lively discussion about the impact the government was having on private philanthropy.

For example, many of the trustees, who had been long-term donors as well as active fund raisers for the institution, were astonished to learn that if private funds were donated to an institution with a specific philanthropic purpose in mind, then that philanthropic goal could not be carried out unless the state approved the project and issued a certificate of need. For the first time, many of our trustees recognized that the rules of the game had changed.

That opening presentation provided a framework for the following day's discussion on all aspects of Medical Center operations. It became clear that trustees would no longer ask, "How much money do you need to accomplish this program?" Rather, they would need to ask, "How do we work with the state and other levels of government to accomplish what we want?"

A similar conference, now scheduled to be held every few years, should prove most worthwhile in helping to demystify the hospital for the very trustees who are responsible for its survival.

A little knowledge, of course, can be a dangerous thing. And a good board chairman has to know how to keep trustees from trespassing on professional territory while seeing to their greater involvement in matters of legitimate concern. It is one of many balancing acts demanded of an activist chairman.

Educating trustees, like educating oneself, is a constant requirement. The demand for it increases steadily as the demands of changing times and circumstances impinge on the evolving role of third-sector institutions (e.g., hospitals, schools, museums, and related cultural and service organizations).

Thus part of my role as chairman of the board has been to balance present realities with those of the past, to balance a future of public service against a history of private service. This means being sensitive to the needs of a growing Hispanic and black clientele, for example, as well as to the Jewish community, which has so often rallied to the support of the hospital's facilities and resources. It is a situation shared, of course, with any number of hospitals that also began as religious-based care centers.

Analyzing Future Challenges

Administrators of nonprofit institutions must confront a multitude of future uncertainties, particularly in hospitals. When I first discussed the possibility of developing a long-range plan for the Medical Center, the president said, "How do we know what medical care is going to be like in the future?" Others said, "The health industry is too complex a business for planning and is full of too many unknowns." I had a tough job explaining to people that the number of unknowns in the health care field is no greater than in industry.

Long-range strategic planning is a relatively new development among health organizations. I thought it imperative that an institution in Mount Sinai's position undertake a major planning effort. The hospital, founded in the 1850s, is housed in a complex of several old buildings, some of which date back to the turn of the century. The school, less than ten years old, is housed in one of the newest and largest medical buildings in the country.

Combined, the hospital and school needed to assess what services they were going to offer—whether they were going to continue to maintain their current areas of specialty or shorten or expand their programs. Also, they needed to consider what people they expected to be serving. From its upper Fifth Avenue location on the edge of Harlem, the Mount Sinai Medical Center now serves several communities, but who will it serve in the future? We needed to know.

Once the decision was made to start a long-range planning effort, we needed to choose a planning committee of trustees who were willing to make a major commitment in time and energy to develop the plan. We were fortunate to have on our School of Medicine board an executive from a leading drug company that was heavily involved in long-range planning in the medical field.

In addition, we tapped a former dean of a prestigious medical school who had recently been appointed to the board. Others included an architect and a number of investment bankers. And we made certain to choose a group of trustees who represented the longtime tradition of Mount Sinai as well as those more recently appointed to the board.

The planning committee has met twice a month for the past year. Although I am an ex officio member of the committee, I have attended almost 100% of the planning meetings. I try not to participate too actively in the committee discussions because I do not want to interfere in the planning process. Nevertheless, I think it important to attend the meetings to show my commitment.

Shortly after the trustees' effort got under way, we began to recognize the need to involve our medical staff more actively in the planning process. Under the president's direction, an advisory group of senior representatives from the clinical area and basic sciences was formed to assess and analyze our current services and programs from a medical perspective. The group was charged with studying the kind of services Mount Sinai should offer in the future—what programs should be maintained, phased out, or developed.

Meetings of the president's advisory group were held separately from those of the trustee group. For the past year, each of the two groups worked on its own, and I served as the link between them. Although there were people on the trustee committee better versed in the planning process than I, the president and I decided I should be the link because the physicians knew me well.

The first responsibility of the trustee group was a study of key decisions and issues facing the Medical Center. Out of this work came a one-page mission statement outlining the direction in which the center should be going. This statement is being shared with the advisory group, and once agreement is reached between the two committees, it will be submitted to the board of trustees for ratification.

As far as we know, Mount Sinai has never had a statement of this kind in its 125-year history. The mission statement in and of itself is a major step in charting the course for the Medical Center's future.

Concluding Thoughts

In reviewing the role I developed as chairman over the past two years, I believe we have made headway toward two major goals within the Medical Center: (1) establishing a philosophy of change and (2) providing a catalyst for change.

Philosophy of change: Members of the medical and management staffs have become more cognizant of the planning process in all aspects of their work. We have made an effort to discuss planning and the need for it in all of the major forums of the Medical Center. We have kept the trustees' effort as visible as possible to show the significance that we place on our planning activities. I hope that the import of planning will begin to filter down to all levels of the organization.

In addition, I think we have been successful in reorienting trustees, administrators, and medical staff to the new ways of doing business in the health industry. The rules of the game have indeed changed. The quasi-public nature of a medical center requires that its board get to know its constituencies and make decisions which are in their best interest.

Thus, in the past year, we have set up a community board to advise the trustees on key patient care, education, and research decisions and on how they affect the various communities we serve. We continue opening up other channels to become sensitive to the needs of our constituents.

Catalyst for change: My job is to get a project started and then let other people do it. With the trustees, I encouraged the nominations committee to reach out for the finest talent available to fill openings on the board. The nominating chairman and I invested a considerable amount of time in meeting with candidates— giving them an opportunity to get to know us and the direction toward which we were heading.

Once elected, we made sure the new board members had a chance to actively participate on board committees. We gave them assignments in their fields of interest. It is not enough to get board members excited about what they are going to do; it is important to find out which roles work for them. This is a casting problem, and out of good casting come good performances.

When I first took office, I made it clear to staff in all areas of the Medical Center that I intended to be accessible to them. I started and still continue to make rounds in each department of the Medical Center. I have been to patient care areas, to research labs, and to student meetings. I cannot really say that any major changes have taken place as a result of my visits, but my availability has become known and the visits have been received favorably by all levels of employees.

When I started this job, I established an office in the Medical Center—a symbol of the fact that I was available to all employees. I developed an agreement with the president of the Medical Center that any staff member could come to visit me provided he or she had the supervisor's approval. I felt that my role was not to be judgmental or to make decisions. Rather, it was to get to know the workings of the Medical Center and to better understand the problems and issues it faces.

Perhaps as CEO of the Medical Center I have assumed greater responsibility than colleagues who are board chairmen in other nonprofit institutions. I am neither full time nor paid. Fundamentally, I do not run this medical institution and have no intention of doing so. And I think that any lay person who would take on such a role would be making a big mistake.

My CEO role does, however, have its advantages. I am more involved in the executive decisions made by the president and the executive vice president of the Medical Center. My perspective is different from the president's (who is physician oriented) or the executive vice president's (who is management oriented). They come to me one step earlier in the decision-making

process and keep me informed about the operations end.

The CEO role also gives board members greater assurance of involvement in the Medical Center, since one of their members is actively participating in the early developments of the decision-making process.

An activist role taken by the chairman of the board should influence and inspire its members to assume equally active roles. The agenda of a medical center's board is enormous —there are plenty of assignments for board members. However, the assignments must be clearly defined, the right people must be chosen to fill them, and results have to be visible to inspire trustees to continue on other projects.

The major risk a chairman runs in instilling activism in trustees is that they might cross the fine line and get involved in operating decisions. From time to time, the enthusiasm of certain board members has caused them to overstep their bounds and try to influence staff people in areas that should not be their concern. Discretion should be exercised to maintain staff morale and board enthusiasm.

A hospital trusteeship is a major public responsibility. It must be taken seriously. A trustee has a moral and social obligation to learn about the institution he or she serves and to maintain as active a role as possible in policymaking. At times, a trustee's role is frustrating, for hospital politics are far more intricate than a business executive could imagine. But the intellectual challenge is great, and the need for answers to the problems of health care delivery in this country involves us all.

ARTICLE 17 ————————————————

The Moral and Social Responsibilities of the Trustees of Foundations
McGeorge Bundy

Let me begin with two comments designed to explain and to limit the rather sweeping title of

SOURCE: Reproduced from Ciba Foundation Symposium No. 30 (The Future of Philanthropic Foundations) by permission of The Ciba Foundation, London (Publisher, Exerpta Medica/Elsevier/North-Holland, Amsterdam) 1975.

my remarks. First, that title is not of my making
—except insofar as I am responsible for having
accepted the suggestion of the organizer of this
symposium, Dr. Wolstenholme. I suppose he
assumed that at the least I would bring the
experience of having lived for eight years with
a lively and energetic group of trustees, and that
if there was a risk in comments of this sort from
a foundation president, the risk was mine alone.
And I suppose I accepted his suggestion mainly
because of the unexpected pleasure of having an
opportunity to talk about the duties of foundation trustees in a setting in which my own
employers cannot talk back. But I do want you
to know, at the start, that mine is at most an aux-
iliary responsibility for the sweeping and general
character of the topic.

My second preliminary point is that on the
simple ground of incompetence I must limit these
observations to the situation of foundation
trustees in the United States. The legal and social
setting of the private foundation differs widely
from one country to another, and I know just
enough about the work of European foundations
to know that it would be foolish for me to attempt
to generalize about the responsibilities of their
trustees on the basis of a primarily American
experience. The best I can hope is that these
remarks, in the measure that they relate effectively to the American situation, may be helpful
to those concerned with other institutions for
their value as a form of comparative sociology.
I shall be talking about the trustees of the
endowed private American foundation.

* * *

The board of trustees of the endowed private
foundation in the United States has a freedom,
authority and long-run accountability which are
unequalled elsewhere among American institutions. All other boards of trustees or directors
work in settings in which a number of other strong
constituencies have shaping roles in the life of the
institution. In the foundations I am considering,
there are only three such constituencies with
important powers: government, with its power to
regulate; salaried staff, with its power to recommend and to execute; and representatives of the
founding family, with powers that vary widely.

The power of government has been used in
a most limited way; the power of salaried staff

is entirely delegated. The senior programme
officers of foundations hold office at the pleasure
of the trustees. The tenure of the university professor, which protects both him and his subject
matter for his working life, is the exception, never
the rule, in a foundation. Trustees may choose
not to exercise their power over staff—but they
have it.

Governmental regulation is essentially negative in character, in that it tells trustees what they
may *not* do. It is true that there are a number
of positive requirements in the Tax Reform Act
of 1969, including a small but objectionable tax,
but in the main the new regulations are aimed
at ensuring that foundations are *not* used for
certain prohibited purposes. Their legitimate purposes are defined as educational, scientific and
charitable, but it turns out on close inspection
that this definition itself is negative. Foundations
are *not* for partisan politics, *not* for profit, *not*
for personal advantage, and *not* for lobbying.
Some of the regulations designed to achieve this
result are complex, and a few have restrictive
implications beyond their framers' intent, but in
the main trustees are free to spend their money
on whatever kinds of things can reasonably meet
these four negative tests. Under United States law
the fields of permitted charitable activity are
extraordinarily wide.

The third potentially limiting factor is more
varied—the desires of the donor and his family
or other spokesmen. Sometimes these desires
will be expressed in the terms of the foundation
charter or in those of a later gift or bequest. In
such cases the obligation of trustees is clear,
unless and until there arises a serious question
of the practicability of following the donor's
terms—and then the remedy is in court. But often
the situation is less clear. The charter may be
unrestrictive, and the trustees may include a mix
of family and nonfamily trustees. Both kinds of
trustees can then be quite uncertain about the
degree to which the foundation's charitable
activities should be defined by the past or present
interests of the founder or his family.

Both our law and our customs make it proper
for a board of trustees to decide this question in
any way it pleases, as long as its activities remain
truly charitable. It is not wrong, in law or in
morals, for a board of trustees to decide that
because the donor was interested in mediaeval

manuscripts 'his' foundation will be devoted to the charitable and educational acquisition of such manuscripts, and to nothing else. It is equally consistent with our law and our customs for a foundation dominated by one family to direct its charitable efforts in the directions that seem best to the present leaders of the family, even long after the founder is gone. Indeed, the board of trustees can properly be composed of family members alone. Moreover, since boards of trustees are usually self-perpetuating, it is within the rights and powers of a founding family to follow this course if it chooses.

What is essential is that the board must make a choice in this matter. The choice need not be flat or fixed, but it cannot be avoided. Moreover, when trustees do decide to let their actions be governed by family preferences not formally set forth in the instrument governing their trust, it is important for them to be explicit—with themselves and with the public—about what they are doing and why. It does not serve the good reputation of a foundation, or of foundations generally, for a board to support any particular family charitable interest without a quite explicit statement that this is what it is doing. (To emphasize that I am not opposed to such action in itself, let me remark that the largest single action of my own trustees, in recent years, was a set of grants which will in the end bring a total of $100 million to the Henry Ford Hospital in Detroit. The charitable case was persuasive, the family tie obvious, and the action explicitly connected to that tie in our announcement.) Where trouble can come, to trustees and to their institutions, is where those matters are fudged.

Let us assume a foundation, then, in which the choice about the role of the family's charitable interest is clear. Let us assume also that the family connection, if any, is such that it leaves the trustees with something more important to do than ratify family choices.

In this situation the permissive framework of the law and the absence of external or internal constituencies with strong vested rights combine to confer great freedom on foundation trustees. That freedom in turn creates an inescapable necessity for choice. The trustees of a new, or newly rich, foundation must make major initial choices, and while no institution is wholly exempt from the necessity that its past will partly define

its future, trustees of continuing foundations have an evident duty to review those choices and to reaffirm or change them.

The first critical choice is of programme areas. Even when the charter or other binding instruction defined a general area of interest—education, or the State of Texas, or health, or Christian character—there will be problems of programmatic choice that can hardly be avoided. It is possible, of course, to choose not to choose. A board of trustees with a commission to work in the field of education can simply sit back and see who turns up. The trouble is, however, that every educational mendicant in the country will then turn up. To defend themselves from inundation, the trustees will have to tell *someone* which requests they wish to take seriously, and the moment they do this they begin to define a programme.

I believe, therefore, that whether a board begins by an explicit attempt to define its work or by a 'simple' process of choosing the 'best' proposals it gets, it is in fact framing a programme. And I believe that one of its central responsibilities is to recognize that this is what it is doing and to articulate and explain its decisions as clearly as it can. I do not mean to suggest that a board should bind itself, against its own real purpose, by adopting extensive and restrictive regulations in pursuit of illusory clarity. A good board will usually want to support some exceptional actions precisely because of their exceptional value—and that is part of what a foundation's freedom is for. Moreover, we have good foundations, I think, whose principle of action is an intentional and determined eclecticism. It may be that a determined external student could find, in some of this deliberate eclecticism, patterns of behaviour which could give guidance as to what is and is not likely to be attractive to a particular foundation. But that possibility only underlines the desirability of self-awareness about one's programme priorities and candour in their exposition.

To me the necessity for programme choice is one of the three central moral and social responsibilities of trustees. The trustees may share this duty with advisers, and especially with any professional staff, but they cannot shed it. And in particular, I believe, they make a mistake when, in effect, they allow some existing pattern of charitable practice to set their priorities for them. This is the line of least resistance, in most cases, and for just this reason it is open to grave question. I must emphasize that I am not opposing support for causes or institutions with a great tradition behind them; it can often happen that exactly what the future needs is reinforcement of some ancient enterprise. What I *am* saying, however, is that the ground of judgement should be what the future needs, not what the past has been. Even if one's style of thought leads to an unshakable belief in the need to reinforce inherited strength (and it is a style of thought that I respect), there will be very grave problems of choice in selecting the institutions, or parts of institutions, that most need help. Let me pick my example from a field in which the Ford Foundation is not active. Nothing seems to me harder or more needed than a series of choices about the ways and means of connecting the limited but free funds of private philanthropy with the current first needs of the extraordinary set of men and institutions who made American science in the mid-twentieth century one of the glories of human history. I think one good starting point would be to say that one wanted to help preserve and reinforce the very best of what the past has given us. But that would be only a starting point. The argument about why, where and how would be long, and the choices would be hard. Surely both the argument and the choices would best be framed in terms of what the future demands, not what the past has been.

Let me note here that any board of trustees, in facing such hard choices, must take account of what others are and are not doing. For the large general-purpose American foundation the most important of these 'others' now is usually the Federal Government, and the question I have raised about science is one on which, not many years back, one might have looked with hope and confidence to Washington for leadership. It is, I think, a necessary responsibility of foundation trustees, precisely because their funds are both small and free, in comparison to those of the non-profit world as a whole, to make their programme choices with a sharp eye out for what others are and are not doing. This rule, drawn from the single field of science, becomes all the more important when a foundation has no other charge than to serve human welfare. Nothing is easier,

for example, than to point in 1974 to the re-emergence on a worldwide scale of the simple but central problem of human hunger. But it is not at all easy to make the best possible choice as to what a private foundation can do about that problem.

At exactly this point the prudent trustees of a general-purpose foundation are likely to look around for some professional advice. And so we come to the second of the central responsibilities of trustees: their responsibility for the quality of those upon whom they rely for counsel. The central and most important example here, and the one with which I happen to have direct experience, is the relation between trustees and any full-time staff.

First and most obviously, the trustees are responsible for choosing the chief executive officer. Here my own position may make me less than a perfect judge of what trustees should and should not do. But I can assert three broad principles: first, trustees should never keep a chief executive officer beyond the point at which they are persuaded that they can do better with someone else; second, trustees, even of very large, complex and professionalized foundations, should not delegate, even to the most trusted of presidents, their final responsibility for programme choice; and third, even when—as they often should—they delegate wide direction in execution and give great weight to professional recommendations, trustees should make the fullest possible use, both formally and informally, of the power of constitutional monarchs elsewhere: to be informed, to advise, to warn—and I would add the quite different power to forbid. A good president and a good board of trustees should in the nature of things have occasional strong differences, and the president should not be allowed to win them all. I am happy to say that by this standard the Ford Foundation is very well run.

But the decisive requirement between board and staff is not that they should sometimes differ. It is rather that they should learn to trust and use each other. There are many patterns for such a relationship, and no single one deserves to be a universal model. But when they work, they have certain common elements—openness, mutual respect and trust, restraint in second-guessing at the level of detailed choice, the rigorous avoidance of pressure on behalf of friends or against enemies, and a habit of closing ranks when a hard decision has been made.

In a large foundation these relations cannot all be funnelled through the single office of the president. Trustees and professionals will need more sustained and serious access to each other than a single senior officer can provide. Let us remember that by definition they are trying to do something very difficult indeed: to use limited amounts of money in the best possible way on an issue important to the future of the race. Whether that issue be as large as hunger or as 'small' as mediaeval manuscripts, the best way is unlikely to be the simplest. So there is no substitute for a sustained and serious exchange of information and judgement between responsible professionals and responsible trustees. If this exchange is constricted to what can be said back and forth by a single executive, however well-meaning and accomplished, there will soon be unhealthy consequences.

One special and difficult responsibility of trustees toward staff is to prevent ossification of either personnel or programme. Presidents, programme officers and programmes may not have tenure, but they do acquire status, and it is important that trustees should guard against any hardening of such status beyond their power or desire to intervene. While there is no sovereign virtue in frequent change for its own sake, since much of the best of foundation work has been effective only after persistent and sustained effort, still it is true that if a foundation board becomes the prisoner of its commitment to a particular staff and programmes, it loses a part of the very freedom which, because it is so rare, is its most precious characteristic. Even the best and strongest of boards must take special precautions on this front. They are part-time people coping with full-time people, after all, and the need for such precautions is only increased when the staff is able and strong. The trustees must keep their own eyes, and the staff's eyes, steadily on what is best for the future, so they must be on guard against those who think they already know—a precaution, one may add in passing, which is as necessary in the making of new appointments as in the assessment of long-time associates.

The third and final general responsibility of foundation trustees is to ensure that the foundation's activities are fully and fairly explained to appropriate public authorities and to the interested public. This may or may not be a job for trustees themselves, or even for any one foundation acting alone, but it is a job they must insist on getting done. Failure on this front has been common in the past—and in my own direct experience presidents have been more at fault than trustees. But the uphill battle for reasonable legislation in 1969 and the very great improvements we have seen since then are evidence of the importance which attaches to this task. Where freedom and authority are great, society will always demand accountability sooner or later. The best way to meet this demand, which can be presented in unpredictable ways and at unexpected times, is to meet it constantly, energetically, and in advance. Moreover, the responsibility extends back from mere explanation into a duty to examine how far any particular programme may contain within it seeds for misunderstanding. The freedom which the government has granted to foundations will endure only as long as it remains acceptable to the public opinion of a democracy.

* * *

There are many more things one could say about the responsibilities of trustees. There is the whole field of financial trusteeship, worth a lecture in itself, and there is the legal and moral duty to be sure that the foundation does in fact conform to the law, in letter and in spirit. But I would close with a different and ultimate requirement—the requirement of moral courage. It is not morally easy to make choices that respect the future against the past and the present. It is not morally easy to assert one's obligation of final judgement against a determined and skillful staff. It is not morally easy to defend choices that may not be immediately popular. It is usually very hard indeed to do what is right instead of what merely pleases the powerful. But this is what foundation trustees are for. Where they fall short of this standard, they fall short of doing all they could in positions of extraordinary opportunity. Where they meet it—and I am proud to know dozens who do—they render a great and undervalued public service, and no one is more in their debt than those who work for them.

CHAPTER FIVE

Managing Nonprofit Organizations

Introduction

All organizations require managing. But is managing in the nonprofit sector sufficiently different from managing in public and private sector organizations to be a separate subject? Obviously, we think it is, but the answer is not totally clear. Some aspects of nonprofit organization management are unique, while others overlap and coincide with private and public sector organization management. Wherein lie the unique aspects?

Note how our *Introduction* and the four prior chapters have tried to show how nonprofit organizations (and thus their management functions) are affected by their unique contexts, philosophies, governance structures, value systems, and the legal ground rules under which they operate. For example, the nonprofit organization, like most public sector organizations, has multiple and often conflicting objectives and constituencies to satisfy. Most nonprofits are service-providing organizations, frequently delivering services that originate from a legislative mandate (such as, private preschools that provide an array of human services for infants from birth through age five who have or are at risk of developing mental or physical disabilities). In these instances, the nonprofit service-providing organization often works through a contractual relationship with a public agency and is at least indirectly accountable to the general public as well as to its board of directors and membership. In instances where services originate from a local concern not mandated by legislation, there still are accountability expectations to the constituency group as well as to the board of directors.

Just as nonprofit organizations vary in structure and culture according to their functions, they also vary by their primary sources of income. Some nonprofit organizations derive most of their financial support from private sources (for example, private foundations, corporate foundations, corporate gifts, and contracts for services); others from the general public (for example, community fund-raising drives and subscription campaigns); others from members (such as fraternal and professional membership organizations); others from the public sector (through grants, contracts, and subsidies); and yet others from combinations of these sources. All of these influences affect the nature of the nonprofit organization, its management needs, and the type of manager who will succeed in it.

Thus, there is enough that is unique about managing in the third sector to warrant focusing attention on it. As well, almost anyone who has managed a nonprofit organization or served on a board of directors knows there are differences in how and what such a manager does. The nature and rationale for the differences often are not immediately evident, but the existence of differences is indisputable. One very important reason why the management of a nonprofit organization differs is its grants economy-based existence rather than an exchange economy-based existence (Boulding, 1981). Often, the nonprofit manager is responsible for resources that do not directly yield tangible results or measurable outcomes. Managing in nonprofit organizations, by its very nature, tends to be more subjective than managing organizations based in an exchange economy.

Limiting the number of subtopics and articles for inclusion in this chapter was difficult. Because there are numerous articles in the literature of nonprofit organization management on such subjects as accounting, financial management, responsibilities of chief executive officers, supervising employees and delegating, and program evaluation, we decided to exclude these topics from the chapter. On the other hand, we believe that some vitally important topics have not received enough attention, such as the systems of ethics and values required to be an effective manager in this sector. And, in some cases, we simply were not satisfied with the current literature; for example, the literature on computing and information systems for management decision making, and—most glaringly—the management of change in nonprofit organizations. Thus, the chapter readings emphasize these topics. Some excellent pieces exist, and we have included a chapter from Anthony and Herzlinger's (1975) pioneering book on management control in nonprofit organizations.[1] Further, we are very pleased that three scholar–practitioners agreed to write original contributions to fill important voids in the recent literature of nonprofit organization management: institutional ethics (Hank Rubin, Roosevelt University), computing/management information and control systems (E. Samuel Overman, University of Colorado at Denver), and the management of change (Jacquelyn Wolf, University of Toronto).

Rubin's article wrestles with the complex issue raised by McGeorge Bundy in the concluding article in Chapter Four; the development and implementation of systems of ethics and the accompanying systems of accountability. This topic is of vital concern to those who would manage nonprofit organizations and to those who accept responsibility for people who manage nonprofit organizations. Rubin proposes a model for differentiating the ethical dimensions of the private for-profit, public, and nonprofit sectors, and then examines the unique ethical conditions of the nonprofit sector.

Rubin carefully sets the stage: "Organizations don't act, people do. Organizations don't misbehave, people do." Within nonprofit institutions, then, there are administrators who not only are expected to act ethically but also to establish climates—to act as "the fibers that transfer and weave legal and normative ethics into the fabrics of their institutions" —in order to ensure ethical behavior on the part of others ("technicians") who work in them. The roles people fill in nonprofit organizations (administrative and technical) and the societal contexts that give rise to standards of ethics (legal and normative) are the elements of Rubin's two-by-two matrix for differentiating the ethical conditions in the three economic sectors. The article concludes that application of the model is complicated in the public and nonprofit sectors. Although human actions are directed toward attainment of missions in all three sectors, "it is only in the nonprofit sector that missions are so narrow, diverse, and unintegrated as to preclude (or render exceedingly difficult) their aggregation and, thereby, to preclude the defining of a context of uniform normative ethics for the whole sector."

Anthony and Young's 1988 chapter (see Note 1), "Characteristics of Nonprofit Organizations" reprinted here, describes ten characteristics of nonprofit organizations that "affect the management control process in those (nonprofit service) organizations." Anthony and Young quickly make it clear that for them, *affect* means "reduce the effectiveness of." The confounding characteristics are (p. 54):

1. The absence of a *profit* measure.
2. Different *tax and legal* considerations.
3. A tendency to be *service organizations*.
4. Greater *constraints* on goals and strategies.
5. Less dependence on clients for *financial support*.
6. The dominance of *professionals*.
7. Differences in *governance*.

8. Differences in *senior management*.
9. Importance of *political influences*.
10. A *tradition* of inadequate management controls.

Anthony and Young group the factors into two classes: *technical* (involving the lack of profit motive and problems of measuring outputs), and *behavioral* (all of the other characteristics listed). The technical characteristics (problems) "are inherent in the fact that the organization is a nonprofit." In contrast, "the significance of these behavioral characteristics is twofold: (1) most of the behavioral factors that impede good management control can be overcome by proper understanding and education; (2) unless these other problems *are* overcome, the improvements in the technical area are likely to have little real impact on the management control process."

In this chapter's second original article, E. Samuel Overman examines the uses, misuses, and underuse of computers and information technology in the nonprofit sector. Overman provides an overview of the typical reasons why managers in nonprofit organizations implement information and computing systems: to reduce uncertainty, improve communication and control, and have information as a resource. The article then develops a taxonomy of the stages of computer reform and the management assumptions that accompany each. The most interesting aspects of Overman's article, however, are the findings of his study on computer usage in twenty-three nonprofit mental health centers. The study concludes that relatively low levels of computer usage, primarily for unsophisticated management purposes, are the norm. Overman suggests that computing needs to receive a higher priority emphasis from management if it is to develop beyond its current levels.

Jacquelyn Wolf's original contribution, "Managing Change in Nonprofit Organizations," brings this chapter on managing to a close with an examination of perhaps the most complex and certainly a most important nonprofit management function, currently and for the foreseeable future. Intelligent management of change is an extraordinarily difficult endeavor in any organization. According to Wolf, nonprofit organizations are no exception and, in addition, they possess unique characteristics that make the change task appear to be perhaps even more difficult than in for-profit and public organizations. It should come as no surprise that these characteristics are liberally described in Chapters One through Four and include, for example:

• Breadth of purpose,
• Complex environmental interfaces,
• Diverse staff and volunteer interests, and
• Structures that must satisfy the often-competing demands of multiple organizational cultures and subcultures.

Following an overview of what has been learned about organizational change over the past three decades, Wolf uses recent research findings about *transformative change* processes (Kilmann & Covin, 1988) to elucidate practical "truisms" "for the nonprofit manager who wants to implement major change in an organization." These truisms reflect Wolf's image of organizational change as an ongoing, untidy, complex, reiterative, circular process, rather than a neat, linear, problem-solving model. Planning for change needs to reflect the recurring barriers to organizational change: fear of loss of control, needless uncertainty (that is, avoidable, in contrast to inevitable, uncertainty during change), and *real* threats to some people; threats, for example, to a diminution of their personal value to the nonprofit organization, or to the demise of cherished programs. Wolf concludes: "Vision, commitment, maturity, sensitivity, inclusiveness, and an action orientation—these qualities and skills more than entrepreneurial wizardry or dazzling political panache, are required by the successful nonprofit manager in the turbulent environment of the last decade of this millennium."

Note

1. R. N. Anthony & R. E. Herzlinger wrote the first edition of *Management Control in Nonprofit Organizations* in 1975, which is listed in the references. The fourth edition (1988) is by Anthony and Young.

References

American Institute of Certified Public Accountants. (1979). Statement of position 78-10: Accounting principles and reporting practices for certain nonprofit organizations. New York: AICPA.

Anthony, R. N., & Herzlinger, R. E. (1975). *Management control in nonprofit organizations.* Homewood, IL: Irwin. (See Chapter Note [1]).

Boulding, K. E. (1974). Technology and the integrative system. In L. D. Singell (Ed.), *Kenneth E. Boulding collected papers: Volume four: Toward a general social science.* Boulder, CO: Colorado Associated University Press.

Boulding, K. E. (1981). *A preface to grants economics: The economy of love and fear.* New York: Praeger.

Bryce, H. J. (1987). *Financial and strategic management for nonprofit organizations.* Englewood Cliffs, NJ: Prentice-Hall.

Callaghan, C., & Connors, T. D. (1982). *Financial management for nonprofit organizations.* New York: American Management Association.

Cleveland, H. (1985). *The knowledge executive: Leadership in an information society.* New York: Dutton.

Connors, T. D. (Ed.). (1980). *The nonprofit organization handbook.* New York: McGraw-Hill.

Dayton, K. N. (September, 1987). *Governance is governance.* Washington, DC: INDEPENDENT SECTOR Occasional Paper.

Drucker, P. F. (Fall, 1973). Managing the public service institution. *The Public Interest, 33.*

Drucker, P. F. (September 8, 1988). The nonprofits' quiet revolution. *Wall Street Journal.*

Herzlinger, R. (January–February, 1977). Why data systems in nonprofit organizations fail. *Harvard Business Review,* 81–86.

Hopkins, B. R. (1980). *The law of tax exempt organizations* (4th ed.). New York: Wiley.

Institute for Voluntary Organizations. (1983). *Designs for creative management* (rev. ed.). Chicago: Institute for Voluntary Organizations.

Kanter, R. M. (1983). *The change masters.* New York: Simon and Schuster.

Kilmann, R. H., & Covin, T. J. (1988). *Corporate transformation: Revitalizing organizations for a competitive world.* San Francisco: Jossey-Bass.

March, J. G., & Olsen, J. P. (1976). *Ambiguity and choice in organizations.* Bergen, Norway: Universitetsforlaget.

Martin, J., & Overman, S. E. (Summer, 1988). Management and cognitive hierarchies: What is the role of management information systems? *Public Productivity Review, XI* (4).

Payton, R. L. (August, 1984). Philanthropy as a vocation. In R. L. Payton, *Major challenges to philanthropy: A discussion paper for Independent Sector.* Washington, DC: The Independent Sector.

Ramanthan, K. V. (1982). *Management control in nonprofit organizations.* New York: Wiley.

Weber, M. (1922). Politics as a vocation. In H. H. Gerth & C. W. Mills (Eds.), *Max Weber: Essays in sociology.* Oxford, UK: Oxford University Press.

Wholey, J. S., Abramson, M. A., & Bellavita, C. (1985). *Performance and credibility.* Lexington, MA: Lexington Books.

Wolf, T. (1984). *The nonprofit organization: An operating manual.* Englewood Cliffs, NJ: Prentice-Hall.

Yankelovich, D. (1981). *New rules.* New York: Random House.

ARTICLE 18 ───────────────
Dimensions of Institutional Ethics: A Framework for Interpreting the Ethical Context of the Nonprofit Sector
Hank Rubin

What constitutes "ethical" conduct within non-profit organizations? Is it something more than the absence of illegality? Is it something less than pure and simple altruism? When our treasurer absconds with the nonprofit's funds, we know that that's unethical. When our board closes its eyes to weak management, sloppy books, and legitimate creditors' pleas, we have a sense, too, that that's somehow unethical.

There are inescapable ironies inherent in the examination of ethics within the nonprofit sector: this sector, after all, is predicated upon altruism and altruism, like ethics, is an ultimate good. Certainly, *people* work within this sector and people are capable of doing bad things. But the people who are drawn to working within this sector are presumably drawn by the urge to act out their altruism and, therefore, should generally be linked by bonds of shared goodness. The incidents of bad action, therefore, should be comparatively minimal in this sector and can be attributed to only three phenomena: the presence of people drawn to the sector by nonaltruistic motives, the acquiescence of deluded altruists to self-serving temptations, and the presumption of some in the sector that unethical means may be justified by altruistic ends.

The irony is that ethics *is* a significant issue in this sector. While unethical behavior in the nonprofit sector is empirically less felonious than it is in the other two sectors,[1] it is—in its own way—no less pervasive. In this sector, because we expect more good, we accept less bad; and the standards which we employ are much more sensitive to deviation. Our observations of unethical behavior in this sector principally cluster under "nonfeasance" and "malfeasance" by board and staff members. This behavior plays itself out through nonaction (e.g., nonpayment of taxes, board members' inattention to staff management problems, failure to scrutinize financial statements) and purposeful action (ranging from theft of property or funds to sloppy and extravagant purchasing practices to discriminatory refusal to serve categories of clientele to purportedly innocent misrepresentations in funding proposals of credentials, fiscal status, or quality of program operations).

The purpose of this chapter is to help advance the study of nonprofit organizations by proposing a philosophically sound model for differentiating the ethical dimensions of each of the three sectors (business, government, and nonprofit) and by discussing the unique ethical conditions of the nonprofit sector.

The Dimensions of Ethics

"Legal" and "Normative"

Ethics, like goodness and beauty, are concepts defined by rather arbitrary standards. Clarity of what is ethical, what is good, and what is beautiful exists only among groups of people who have agreed upon consistent standards. In society, such agreement takes the form of cultural norms, traditions, and laws. Laws are hard and fast; violations are relatively unambiguous. Norms and traditions (while sometimes written into law) are more vague and transient and exist only as long as informal consensus maintains them. These are the *societal contexts* that define the ethics of any sector—formal laws and informal normative expectations. When a person steals, a law is broken. When a person exaggerates the service capability of an organization in order to impress a prospective donor, a normative expectation is violated. We will refer to these contexts as "legal ethics" and "normative ethics" respectively.[2]

With certain obvious and irrelevant exceptions (irrelevant for this discussion), legal ethics apply across all three sectors. Civil and criminal laws are relatively constant and their enforcement (for better or for worse) is reasonably predictable. Legal ethics for all three sectors are affected by these laws at the federal, state, and municipal levels and, when they differ, differ principally on the matter of money: where it comes from, who it goes to, and how it is reported.[3]

On the other hand, normative ethics—what society accepts as ethical behavior in keeping with relevant norms and traditions—vary sector by sector. This is true because norms and traditions are simply vehicles by which a society moves forward and, since the three sectors entail manifestly distinctive cultures driving toward definitionally different ends, these vehicles are somewhat different for each of the three sectors. This tells us that, in order to define the normative ethics of any sector, we must have a clear sense of the destination, or purpose, of the sector. The private sector has set its course on *profit* and aims to get there by the most efficient route possible; that was easy. Government's general destination is the enforcement of laws via the bumpy route of equity and some degree of financial accountability.[4] The nonprofit sector, however, has no generic sector-wide destination. It follows the broad path of voluntarism and philanthropy toward the countless individual missions of the organizations that comprise the sector.

A word or two about "effectiveness." Effectiveness is most aptly viewed as a label applied to individuals and organizations that progress toward predetermined organizational destinations (missions) while complying with the laws and conforming to normative behavioral expectations. Effectiveness is strategic behavior measured by cultural and sector-specific values. What may be viewed as effective behavior in one culture and in one sector may not be viewed the same way in another. Furthermore, effectiveness has nothing to do with the social acceptability of an organization's mission, only with the manner in which individuals and organizations progress toward it. While effectiveness entails a relationship with legal ethics, it is fundamentally a normative ethic insofar as its priority is culturally defined.[5]

"Administrative" and "Technical"

Standards of legal and normative ethics prescribe the behavior of *people within organizations.* Organizations don't act, people do. Organizations don't misbehave, people do. Therefore, societies design laws and normative expectations in order to encourage socially productive action and to discourage misbehavior by people. Within institutions, there are two *categories of individuals* who convey and are constrained by society's legal and normative ethics—administrators and technicians.[6] For the sake of this analysis: administrators are those with planning, management, and supervisory responsibilities; technicians are professionals who practice a trade and/or exercise the technical skills necessary to deliver the goods or services produced by the institution.

We expect our administrators not only to act ethically but to establish climates that ensure legal and normative ethical behavior throughout their institutions. Presumptively, they are guarantors and weather vanes of ethical conduct. Their managerial practices and ethos are the fibers that transfer and weave legal and normative ethics into the fabrics of their institutions.

Managerial practices and ethos share a common core of similarity across the three sectors but vary in many of the specifics of their application. Compliance with the standards of legal ethics is, of course, the baseline expectation of administrators in all three sectors; beyond that, however, administrative roles are less consistent. While bookkeeping, information management, market relations, staff supervision, and more are expected of administrators in each sector (the common core), specifics in the application and administration of each of these vary (to greater and lesser degrees) sector to sector. Staffing and supervisory models vary between the sectors as do models of revenue generation, volunteer utilization, and the processes by which policy making is influenced. Even the units of analysis used to evaluate effectiveness and efficiency are different for the three sectors (i.e., dollars, laws, and people). Finally, to the extent that technological capabilities and limitations vary across the sectors, so too must the supervisory and facilitative practices and ethos of the administrators. In short, while legal responsibilities of administrators are clear and somewhat consistent, *modus operandi* are relatively inconsistent;[7] moreover, normative expectations of administrative responsibilities and behavior are even less consistent.

The ethical conduct of technicians is prescribed not only by the general legal and normative standards that affect their sector and by the sector-specific and institution-specific standards imposed by their administrators, but by formal codes and procedural expectations established within their professions (normative ethics) and by laws that apply specifically to their professions (legal ethics) as well. Electrical engineers, social workers, and fund raisers all operate within the added ethical constraint of what we call "professionalism." The ethical expectations and constraints of "professionalism" apply irrespective of which sector the technician operates within.[8] And compliance with the codes, expectations, and laws of professionalism is a *sine qua non* of the ethical atmosphere of any institution. Finally, to the extent that any technicians participate in the processes of planning, managing, and supervision then they too directly weave their legal and normative ethics into their institutions as do their administrators.

The Proposed Model

We now have the elements of a simple two-by-two matrix which enables us to differentiate the ethical conditions of each of the three sectors. Across the horizontal axis are the *societal contexts* that give rise to standards of ethics—legal and normative. On the vertical axis are listed the categories of individuals within institutions who effectuate, transmit, and are constrained by society's ethical standards—administrative and technical.

With a great deal of work, the four boxes of this matrix can be filled in; converting this from a theoretical model to an applied model for comparing the three sectors.[9] For the matrices developed for each sector, this would entail:

Legal Ethics—an exhaustive list of all federal, state, and municipal laws and regulations affecting all legally incorporated institutions within all three sectors,[10] a comparable list of laws and regulations with specific implications for the sector; a comparable list of laws, regulations, and professional codes of conduct affecting

each administrative and technical position within the sector.

Normative Ethics—an empirically valid list of (cultural) expectations and constraints held in the common consciousness of the public relative to all legally incorporated institutions within all three sectors;[11] a comparable list derived from relevant publics or constituencies relative to the sector; and a comparable list derived from relevant constituencies within and outside the professions relative to *each* administrative and technical position within the sector.

Administrative—a comprehensive list of all administrative positions within the sector (so that universal, sector-specific, and profession-specific regulatory conditions and normative expectations may be developed for each position).

Technical—a comprehensive list of all technical positions within the sector (so that universal, sector-specific, and profession-specific regulatory conditions and normative expectations may be developed for each position).

Ethics and Accountability Within the Nonprofit Sector

Legal ethics define baseline expectations for both civility and professional conduct and join with normative ethics to provide the context for the development of standards of professional "accountability." Ethics, by defining acceptable behavior, enables accountability.

Accountability and ethics are inextricably bound: boards of directors are accountable for professional legalities of all board and staff

A Model for Defining the Ethical Dimensions of Each Sector

	LEGAL ETHICS	NORMATIVE ETHICS
ADMINISTRATIVE "Practices and Ethos"		
TECHNICAL "Professionalism"		

members operating within their institutions just as administrators and technicians are accountable for the normative standards of institutional progress toward prescribed destinations (read "purpose" or "mission") and for the paths they travel to get there (see the discussion regarding the definition of normative ethics above).

Generically, the leadership of for-profit corporations are held accountable for achieving profit and efficiency through behavior that conforms to the legal and normative ethical context of the sector. Government officials, in general, are held accountable for enforcing designated laws through behavior that conforms to the ethical context of their sector and subsectors. And nonprofit administrators and board members are held accountable for the attainment of the disparate missions of their organizations within the attendant ethical context of their sector as a whole and of their (type of) organizations in particular.

The complexity of the issue of accountability within the nonprofit sector lies in the juncture of two characteristics:

1. The nonuniformity of the purposes—and, therefore, of the normative ethics—of the organizations that comprise the sector, and
2. The higher standards of normative ethics that society imposes on this sector because we expect more good and accept less bad from its participants.

Both of these characteristics reside to some degree in government as well. The purposes of the FBI and the City Department of Streets and Sanitation certainly appear quite different. And we do expect to be able to hold our elected and appointed government officials to the highest standards of ethical accountability. But at least four things differentiate the government from the nonprofit sector on these characteristics as well:

1. Despite the apparent nonuniformity of missions of various government agencies, the originating sources of their missions are relatively uniform—their respective legislatures. Through prescribed electoral and lobbying procedures, the public can and does directly influence the legislative and regulatory mandates of governmental agencies. In contrast, there is no real accountability controlling the self-selected missions of nonprofit organizations[12] and neither

the individual organizations nor the entire nonprofit sector is held accountable to the general public in this same way. In other words, the missions ("destinations") of all government agencies are fully defined by an integrated body of laws (and regulations that have the force of law) whereas the missions of organizations comprising the nonprofit sector are not integrated but are freestanding and independently developed. As a result: (1) the missions of individual governmental organizations are paramount ethical considerations because they exist in order to advance the mission(s) of the government as a whole, whereas (2) in the nonprofit sector virtually all legal missions are acceptable (relative to standards of general public accountability) and the issue of ethics principally rears its head on the question of "effectiveness." [13]

2. Government organizations tend to be much more complex and comprehensive in their scope relative to their missions than do nonprofit organizations (nonprofit organizations tend to be much more limited in terms of both the scale and constituency of their missions). The sociology of complex organizations suggests that this factor alone is a sufficient predictor of markedly different cultures and climates within each sector.

3. Not only is the governmental sector more porous to general public accountability relative to its missions and practices, but the players in government (elected and appointed officials) are also more directly accountable to the general public. Elected officials can be voted out of office and appointed officials can be subject to lobbying campaigns for removal or reassignment. While the leadership of nonprofit organizations must be sensitive to public opinion regarding personnel, no *formal* mechanisms exist for this kind of public accountability in the nonprofit sector.

4. Finally, the governmental sector is in a perpetual climb back from its fall from grace: The nonprofit sector has yet to fall. Sadly but pervasively, the general public regards government officials as unaccustomed and unresponsive to normative ethics; petty and grand corruption is perceived as commonplace and cynicism too often characterizes public perception of government ethics. The nonprofit sector —in the no-man's land between the Ivan Boeskys and the Richard Nixons—has not been rocked by the types of scandals that deplete the public's

confidence.[14] The nonprofit sector, on its own, bears the public scrutiny once reserved for Caesar's wife, and this has profound impact upon the ethical expectations of the sector.[15]

As a result of all of this, the model developed above becomes complicated in its application to these two sectors, but in different ways. The government sector, both by law and by relevant constituency, is best understood as a composite of subsectors (e.g., military, judiciary, regulatory, transportation, education, health provision, etc.) and requires, therefore, a completed matrix for each subsector. The nonprofit sector—while idealized as a relatively innocent whole—is best understood as a collection of scattered, private (i.e., not accountable to the general public), and narrowly focused independent organizations that (for purposes of our analysis) are too limited to cluster into comparable subsectors and too diverse to be treated as a whole. This logic leads to the conclusion that, while our model applies generically to the private sector (probably involving just one matrix[16]) and requires separate matrices for each subsector of the government sector, its application in the nonprofit sector will theoretically require either one matrix for each organization or one for each of a relatively large number of small and carefully defined subsectors.

In all three sectors, human action in institutions is directed toward attainment of missions. It is only in the nonprofit sector that missions are so narrow, diverse, and unintegrated as to preclude (or render exceedingly difficult) their aggregation and, thereby, to preclude the defining of a context of uniform normative ethics for the whole sector or for significantly aggregative subsectors. Within the nonprofit sector, therefore, the mission of each organization becomes the definitional fulcrum of its normative ethics.

Notes

1. While data are not maintained on crime rates across the three sectors, this comparison is deduced from statistics on felony convictions (between 1980 and 1986) contained in statistical sourcebooks published by the FBI, the Justice Department, the Treasury Department, the U.S. Postal Inspection Service, and the Administrative Office of the United States Courts. Deductively, the nonprofit sector falls into the statistical category of "other" which is defined as those who are not employed in: government-funded entities, the military, government, or private businesses. Granted, this is a rough hewn statistic, but the disparity between the sectors is large enough to be at least suggestive. Approximate number of felony convictions (1980–1986) of people employed by: government 103,500; military (all branches) 266,000; for-profit entities 389,000; and other 19,500.

2. Some have advised this author that society has little to do with defining ethics and that, rather, their definition comes from a higher source. The concept of a universal ethic is the foundation of religion. This concept maintains that certain behaviors are inherently good or bad irrespective of pervasive and practical societal standards. Lord knows that the author does not intend to ignore this perspective. Rather, religious ethics are treated here as a significant definitional component of the ethnic cultures (groups) that comprise society. As such, religious ethics emerge as legal ethics and normative ethics in direct proportion to the political potency and social influence of the ethnic culture that maintains them.

3. A body of laws that may be construed as a functional subset of criminal law are those that demand effectiveness (and efficiency) on the part of individuals legally responsible for administrative leadership in each of the sectors. These laws are not designed in order to differentiate the three sectors but, nonetheless, do tend to be different for each sector.

4. The mission of government is certainly more complex than this but, nonetheless, unarguably revolves around the making and enforcement of laws. The important point here is the (simplified) consistency of missions *within* the government sector. This point is further discussed in the section on "Ethics and Accountability."

5. We normatively expect more efficiency than effectiveness from private corporations and more effectiveness than efficiency from government. (For years, it was presumed that society could afford to permit inefficiency and ineffectiveness within the nonprofit sector.) Certain cultures place a high value on quick and commanding progress toward goals while others

prefer patient social organizing in preparation for any progress or institutional change.

6. We are leaving out four smaller categories of institutional players: policy makers, clericals, consultants/contractors, and manual laborers. Policy makers (lawmakers in the government sector and board members in the private and nonprofit sectors) are a special category which demands a whole separate analysis vis-a-vis ethical conduct. While each of the other three categories warrants it as well, these are not examined here because they would significantly complicate this analysis without appreciably adding to it. Analysis of ethical considerations regarding clerical and contractual participants in the nonprofit sector is needed. For clerical support this is especially true as their MIS functions give them ever-greater access to —and control of—institutional data. For contractual participants this analysis becomes increasingly important as the size and demand for this subsector grows.

7. The story is told of a group of major corporate and nonprofit leaders who joined together in Chicago in the 1960's to form a coalition called Educon so as to tackle some of the city's public education problems. Despite mutually good will, the coalition fell apart because the decision-making processes inherent to the two sectors proved to be so different, so alien and frustrating to "the opposite parties," as to become a source of incompatibility.

8. Certain professions are more concentrated in one sector than in the others (e.g., many more social workers operate within the nonprofit sector than in the private or government sectors) and, therefore, may disproportionately influence the definition of normative ethics and some of the legal ethics in their weighted sector.

9. Similarly, this model can be used within an individual institution in order to define the organization's unique ethical environment.

10. While this list of trans-sectoral laws would not help us to differentiate the ethical dimensions of the three sectors, it would help us to develop comprehensive definitions of the dimensions of each sector.

11. The same note as the preceding applies here.

12. Although specified government agencies may act in an exclusionary fashion to prevent groups that are organized around certain types of missions from acquiring legal nonprofit status.

13. Please see the discussion on "effectiveness" above.

14. Although Jim and Tammy Bakker's corruption of donors' faithful contributions has sent governmental tax officials scurrying to tighten regulations affecting all tax-exempt organizations, in the public's eye this appears to be a problem limited to the evangelical religious subsector of the entire nonprofit sector.

15. Consider that a nonprofit arts organization that produces "bad" art might be considered (normatively) unethical; whereas a comparable government organization would simply be held accountable for meeting relevant legal mandates and a for-profit organization would be held accountable simply for making profit.

16. Although a practical case may be made to differentiate between the ethical context of small "ma and pa" companies versus large complex bureaucratic companies.

ARTICLE 19 _____

Characteristics of Nonprofit Organizations
Robert N. Anthony and David W. Young

Although the precise line between for-profit and nonprofit organizations is fuzzy, the following definition is adequate for the purpose of this book: *A nonprofit organization is an organization whose goal is something other than earning a profit for its owners. Usually its goal is to provide services.* This definition corresponds approximately to that in most state statutes.[1]

The definition also emphasizes a basic distinction between the two types of organizations. This distinction is the cause of many management control problems that are peculiar to nonprofit organizations. In a for-profit company, decisions made by management are intended to increase (or at least maintain) profits, and success is measured, to a significant degree,

SOURCE: From *Management Control in Nonprofit Organizations,* 4th Edition, by R. N. Anthony and D. W. Young. Copyright © 1988 by Richard D. Irwin, Homewood, Illinois. Reprinted by permission.

by the amount of profits that these organizations earn. (This is not to say that profit is their only objective, or that their success can be measured entirely in terms of profitability; that would be, of course, an overly simplistic view of most businesses.) By contrast, in nonprofit organizations, decisions made by management are intended to result in providing the best possible service with the available resources; success is measured primarily by how much service the organizations provide and by how well these services are rendered. More basically the success of a nonprofit organization should be measured by how much it contributes to the public well-being.

Since *service* is a more vague, less measurable concept than *profit*, it is more difficult to measure performance in a nonprofit organization. It is also more difficult to make clear-cut choices among alternative courses of action in such an organization because in most nonprofit organizations the relationship between costs and benefits, and even the amount of benefits, are difficult to measure. Despite these difficulties, an organization must be controlled. Its management must do what it can to assure that resources are used efficiently and effectively. Thus, the central problem is to find out what management control

policies and practices are useful, despite the limitations.

Sharpening the Distinction

Our distinction is not black and white. A for-profit company must render services that its customers find adequate if it is to earn a profit, whereas a nonprofit organization must receive funds from operating revenues or other sources that are at least equal to its expenses if it is to continue to render services. The distinction, then, is based not on the need for funds, per se, but on the predominant attitude toward the purposes for which these funds are used.

Nor does the distinction relate solely to the types of services provided. Some hospitals, medical clinics, schools, even religious organizations are set up explicitly as for-profit organizations, even though the services they provide often are thought of as being provided by nonprofit organizations. For example, the following table shows the distribution in three classes of short-term general hospital entities and beds in 1984 (as compiled by the American Hospital Association):

	Entities		Beds	
	Number	Percent	Number	Percent
Government	2,003	32.5	315,000	27.8
Nongovernment, nonprofit	3,366	54.7	717,000	63.3
Proprietary	786	12.8	100,000	8.9
Total	6,155	100.0	1,132,000	100.0

In addition to the proprietary (i.e., for-profit) hospitals, an increasing number of nonprofit hospitals are being managed by for-profit companies.

Nature of the Nonprofit Sector

Any categorization of nonprofit organizations themselves is certain to have gray areas.

Nevertheless, for purposes of the discussion that follows in this chapter, as well as the references, examples, and cases we use in the remainder of the book, the categories shown in Exhibit 2.1 will serve as a useful frame of reference. As this exhibit indicates, an important distinction is between governmental and private nonprofit organizations. Within the governmental category, the division among federal, state, and local entities provides a useful organizing

EXHIBIT 2.1 Categories of Nonprofit Organizations

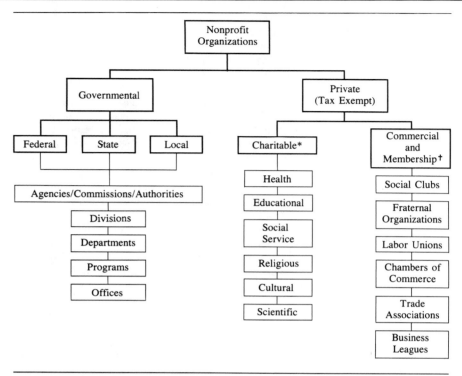

* Donor contributions are tax deductible.
† Donor contributions are not tax deductible.

scheme; any of these entities can have agencies, commissions, authorities, and the like, which can be further subdivided into divisions, departments, programs, offices, and so forth, although not necessarily in the hierarchy shown in the exhibit.

Within the private (i.e., tax-exempt) category, an important distinction is between charitable organizations, for which donor contributions are tax deductible, and commercial and membership organizations, whose donor contributions ordinarily are not tax deductible. The former category includes organizations such as health, educational, and social service; in the latter are entities such as social clubs, fraternal organizations, and labor unions.

Diversity of Demands on Managers

As Exhibit 2.1 suggests, the term *nonprofit sector* can refer to a quite heterogeneous set of entities,

with diverse activities, clientele, technological resources, and funding sources. Because of these differences, and many others, any discussion of management control in nonprofit organizations must be viewed as a highly contingent one; that is, a management control system that works for one nonprofit organization quite likely will not work for another. Nevertheless, there are certain management control principles that are applicable to almost all nonprofit organizations, and certain issues that all nonprofit managers invariably confront as they attempt to improve the effectiveness and efficiency of their organizations. It is these that are the focus of this book.

Size and Composition of the Nonprofit Sector

Exhibit 2.2 gives some idea of the magnitude of the class of organizations on which this book focuses. The figures are not exact because the

EXHIBIT 2.2   Number of Nonagricultural Employees in Nonprofit Organizations

	Number of Employees (millions)		Percent Change 1975–1985
	1975	1985	
Federal government	2.7	2.9	7.4
State government	3.2	3.8	18.8
Local government	8.8	9.7	10.2
Health services:			
Nursing, personal care facilities	0.8	1.2	50.0
Hospitals	2.3	3.0	30.4
Education	1.0	1.3	30.0
Social services	0.7	1.3	85.7
Membership organizations	1.5	1.5	0
Total nonprofit	21.0	24.7	17.6
Total nonagricultural	76.9	97.6	26.9
Nonprofit as percent of total	27.3	25.3	

SOURCE: U.S. Department of Commerce, *Statistical Abstract of the United States* (Washington, D.C.: Government Printing Office, 1987).

census categories do not quite conform to the definition of nonprofit that is used here. They are, however, satisfactory as a basis for some general impressions. As can be seen, nonprofit organizations employ about 25 percent of the nation's nonagricultural work force. As this exhibit indicates, local governments are by far the largest employers, with hospitals the largest nongovernmental employers (although the figures for this category may be somewhat overstated, since there was no way of eliminating for-profit organizations).

The Internal Revenue Service estimated in 1982 that there were 1.2 million nonprofit organizations. The federal government is by far the largest *single* nonprofit organization. Its

immensity is difficult to comprehend. In 1984 it owned 727 million acres of land and 438,000 buildings (occupying 2.7 billion square feet). The 1988 federal budget was $1.24 trillion, of which the Department of Health and Human Services (DHHS) had the largest share, $450 billion, followed in magnitude by the Department of Defense with $298 billion. The largest department in terms of employees is the Department of Defense, which in 1987 had 1.1 million civilian employees. The Department of Health and Human Services had 140,000 employees in 1987.

Spending for nongovernmental nonprofit organizations has not grown particularly fast. As Exhibit 2.3 indicates, when operating expenditures are converted into constant (1972)

EXHIBIT 2.3   Operating Expenditures of Nonprofit Organizations (excluding government)

	1980	1985	Percent Change
Current expenditures (billions)	$143.1	$238.7	66.8%
Constant (1972) dollars (billions)	76.9	88.0	14.4
Per capita (in 1972 dollars)	338.00	369.00	9.2

SOURCE: V. A. Hodgkinson and M. S. Weitzman, *Dimensions of the Independent Sector: A Statistical Profile*, 2nd ed. (Washington, D.C.: Independent Sector, 1986).

dollars, they changed by only about 14 percent between 1980 and 1985, and by less than 10 percent on a per capita basis.

Many nonprofits make extensive use of volunteer labor, such that Exhibit 2.2, which looks at only *paid* employees, understates the amount of effort expended on behalf of these organizations' clientele. As Exhibit 2.4 shows, religious organizations make the most use of volunteers, but almost all other nonprofits use this relatively free resource as well. (Unfortunately, since these totals come from different sources, and are for a different year, it is difficult to reconcile them to those in Exhibit 2.2.)

In general, it is quite difficult to find good information on the magnitude and activities of nonprofit organizations. In an effort to improve the quality of this information, the Ford Foundation made several grants during the past five years or so. A number of publications have emerged from these activities, some of which are listed in the references at the end of the chapter.

Summary of Characteristics

In the remainder of this chapter we discuss certain characteristics of nonprofit organizations that affect the management control process in such organizations. These characteristics are arranged under the following headings:

1. The absence of a *profit* measure.
2. Different *tax and legal* considerations.
3. A tendency to be *service organizations*.
4. Greater *constraints* on goals and strategies.
5. Less dependence on clients for *financial support*.
6. The dominance of *professionals*.
7. Differences in *governance*.
8. Differences in *senior management*.
9. Importance of *political influences*.
10. A *tradition* of inadequate management controls.

Of these, the first characteristic is the most important, and since it affects all nonprofit organizations, it will be discussed at some length. Each of the others affects many, but not all, nonprofit organizations, and the effects vary. They therefore are tendencies, rather than pervasive characteristics. Furthermore, again with the exception of the first, these characteristics are not unique to nonprofit organizations.

The Profit Measure

All organizations use resources to produce goods and services, that is, they use inputs to produce

EXHIBIT 2.4 Paid Employees and Volunteers in Nonprofit Organizations, 1984

	Number of Paid Employees (000s)	Number of Volunteers (000s)	Total Employees	Volunteers as Percent of Total
Health services	3,116	524	3,640	14.4%
Education/research	1,484	372	1,856	20.0
Religious	646	2,204	2,850	77.3
Social service	972	1,071	2,043	52.4
Civic, social, fraternal	328	367	695	52.8
Membership, sports, recreational	111	351	462	76.0
Arts and culture	98	154	252	61.1
Foundations	18	—	18	0
Legal services	15	—	15	0
Total	6,788	5,043	11,831	42.6

SOURCE: V. A. Hodgkinson and M. S. Weitzman, *Dimensions of the Independent Sector: A Statistical Profile*, 2nd ed. (Washington, D.C.: Independent Sector, 1986).

outputs. An organization's *effectiveness* is measured by the extent to which its outputs accomplish its goals, and its *efficiency* is measured by the relationship between inputs and outputs. In a for-profit organization the amount of profit provides an overall measure of both effectiveness and efficiency. The absence of a single, satisfactory, overall measure of performance that is comparable to the profit measure is the most serious problem inhibiting the development of effective management control systems in nonprofit organizations. In order to appreciate the significance of this statement, we need to consider the usefulness and the limitations of the profit measure in for-profit organizations.

Usefulness of the Profit Measure

The profit measure has the following advantages: (1) it provides a single criterion that can be used in evaluating proposed courses of action; (2) it permits a quantitative analysis of those proposals in which benefits can be directly compared with costs; (3) it provides a single, broad measure of performance; (4) it permits decentralization; and (5) it facilitates comparisons of performance among entities that are performing dissimilar functions. Each of these points is discussed below and contrasted with the situation in a nonprofit organization.

1. Single Criterion. In a for-profit business, profit provides a way of focusing the considerations involved in choosing among proposed alternative courses of action. The analyst and the decision maker can address such questions as: Is the proposal likely to produce a satisfactory level of profits, or is it not? Is Alternative A likely to add more to profits than Alternative B?

The decision maker's analysis is not so simple and straightforward as the above might imply, however. Even in a for-profit organization, objectives other than profit usually must be taken into account, and many proposals cannot be analyzed in terms of their effect on profits. Nevertheless, these qualifications do not invalidate the general point: profit provides a focus for decision making.

In a nonprofit organization, there often is no clear-cut objective function that can be used in analyzing proposed alternative courses of action. The management team of a nonprofit organization often will not agree on the relative importance of various objectives. Thus, in a municipality, all members of the management team may agree that the addition of a new pumper will add to the effectiveness of the fire department, but there may be disagreement on the importance of an expenditure to increase the effectiveness of the fire department as compared to a comparable expenditure on parks, or streets, or welfare.

2. Quantitative Analysis. The easiest type of proposal to analyze is one in which the estimated cost can be compared directly with the estimated benefits. Such an analysis is possible when the objective is profitability: profit is the difference between expense and revenue, and revenue is equated to benefits.

For most important decisions in a nonprofit organization, there is no accurate way of estimating the relationship between inputs and outputs; that is, there is no way of judging what effect the expenditure of X dollars will have on achieving the goals of the organization. Would the addition of another professor increase the value of the education which a college provides by an amount that exceeds the cost of that individual? How much should be spent on a program to retrain unemployed persons? Issues of this type are difficult to analyze in quantitative terms because there is no good way of estimating the benefits of a given increment of spending.

3. Performance Measurement. Profitability provides a measure that incorporates within it a great many separate aspects of performance. The best manager is not the one who generates the most sales volume, considered by itself; or the one who uses labor most efficiently; or the one who uses material most efficiently; or the one who has the best control of overhead; or the one who makes the best use of capital. Rather, the best manager is the one who does best, on balance, on the combination of all these separate activities. Profitability incorporates these separate elements. The key consideration is not the details of the operating statement; rather it is the "bottom line." This measure is valuable both to the managers themselves and to those who judge their performance. It provides managers with a current, frequent, easily understood signal as to how well they are doing, and it provides others with an objective basis for judging the managers' performance.

Since the principal goal of a nonprofit organization should be to render service, and since the amount and quality of service rendered cannot be measured numerically, performance with respect to goals is difficult and sometimes impossible to measure. The success of an educational institution depends more on the ability and diligence of its faculty than on such measurable characteristics as the number of courses offered or the ratio of faculty to students, for example.

Although financial performance should be at most a secondary goal, its importance is sometimes overemphasized. This can happen when managers with experience in for-profit companies become involved in nonprofit organizations. Accustomed to the primacy of profits, they frequently find it difficult to adjust to their new environment.

4. Decentralization. Because for-profit organizations have a well-understood goal and because the performance of many individual managers can be measured in terms of their contribution toward that goal, top management can safely delegate many decisions to lower levels in the organization.

If an organization has multiple goals and no good way of measuring performance in attaining these goals, it cannot delegate important decisions to lower level managers. For this reason, in government organizations many problems must be resolved in Washington or in state capitals rather than in regional or local offices. The paperwork and related procedures involved in sending problems to senior management and in transmitting the decisions on these problems back to the field can be quite elaborate, and give rise to part of the criticism that is levied against bureaucracy. Such criticism is often unwarranted because, in the absence of something corresponding to the profit measure, there is no feasible way of decentralizing.

5. Comparison of Unlike Units. The profit measure permits a comparison of the performance of heterogeneous operations that is not possible with any other measure. The performance of a department store can be compared with the performance of a paper mill in terms of the single criterion, which was the more profitable? Profitability therefore not only provides a way of combining heterogeneous elements of performance within a company; it also provides a way of making valid comparisons among organizations that have the same goal, the goal of profitability, even though the size, technology, products, and markets of these companies are quite different from one another.

In nonprofit organizations, organizational units can be compared with one another only if they have similar functions. One fire department can be compared with other fire departments and one general hospital with other general hospitals, but there is no way of comparing the effectiveness of a fire department with the effectiveness of a hospital.

Tax and Legal Considerations

Most nonprofit organizations benefit from certain provisions of tax legislation. The general nature of these benefits is summarized below. Some of the legal implications of *nonprofit* also are described briefly, particularly with respect to the generation and distribution of an excess of revenues over expenses, and with regard to the development of for-profit subsidiaries. This information should be taken only as a broadbrush approach and not as a substitute for a legal or tax opinion.

Tax Considerations

Nonprofit organizations ordinarily are exempt from income, property, or sales taxes. Individuals or entities who provide funds to these organizations may be exempt from paying taxes on the interest income of bonds they purchase, and the contributions and gifts they make may be tax deductible. We will discuss each item separately.

Income Taxes.   Most nonprofit organizations are exempt from paying federal, state, and municipal income taxes on the income that is related to their nonprofit status. (They do report their revenues and expenses to the Internal Revenue Service on Form 990.) If they generate income from *unrelated business activities,* that is, activities that are unrelated to their nonprofit charter, they pay tax on this income. The line between unrelated activities and tax-exempt activities frequently is not clear, however. For example, in most instances, a YMCA does not pay income taxes on the income from its gymnasium and swimming pool, even though it competes directly with for-profit physical fitness centers who offer services using these types of facilities. If, on the other hand, the YMCA shifts its mission too radically, its tax-exempt status may be called into question.

A nonprofit organization can lose its tax-exempt status if it engages in substantial lobbying activities, if it participates in political campaigns, or if a "substantial part" of its income results from activities that are unrelated to its charter.

There are essentially two ways in which a nonprofit organization can conduct for-profit activities while still preserving its general tax-exempt status: it can pursue a venture which is either (1) *related* to its tax-exempt purpose or (2) unrelated but *insubstantial.* If the organization's for-profit activity falls into the first class, it will preserve its tax-exempt status and pay no federal income taxes. If the activity falls into the second class, the organization will pay "unrelated business" income taxes on the portion of its activity that is unrelated, but will maintain its general tax-exempt status. In all cases, if a nonprofit's tax-exempt status is to be preserved, the net income from nonincidental activities must not inure to the benefit of private individuals.

Property Taxes and Sales Taxes. Government, charitable, religious, scientific, and educational organizations are exempt from local property taxes. In many states and municipalities, they are also exempt from sales taxes on the goods and services that they sell. In addition, they may be exempt from social security contributions and enjoy reduced postal rates. In comparing the costs of a nonprofit organization with those of a for-profit one in the same industry, the costs of the former are inherently lower in this respect. However, it should be noted

that some nonprofit organizations—particularly universities—make "contributions in lieu of taxes" to their local municipalities.

Tax-Exempt Bonds. As of 1987, interest income received by a holder of bonds issued by states and municipalities is not taxed by the federal government or by the state in which the issuer is located. Some states issue bonds whose proceeds are used by nonprofit hospitals and educational institutions, and the income on these bonds usually is tax exempt also. Because bondholders do not pay taxes, they are willing to accept a lower interest rate on a nonprofit's bonds than on a similar grade bond whose interest is taxable income. As will be seen in Chapter 9 [not reprinted here], this difference affects the analysis of proposals for acquiring new capital assets.

Contributions. Individuals and corporations who make contributions to charitable organizations can itemize and deduct these contributions in calculating their taxable income, although the lower income tax rates under the Tax Reform Act of 1986 reduce the tax advantage of these contributions. The organizations that qualify for these deductions are spelled out in detail in Sections 170 and 501(c)(3) of the Internal Revenue Code. (For this reason, charitable organizations frequently are termed "501(c)(3) organizations.") As Exhibit 2.1 indicates, they include entities established for religious, charitable, health, scientific, literary, and educational purposes; nonprofit veterans' groups, cemeteries, and day-care centers also are included. (States, municipalities, and fraternal organizations *are* included in this group if the contributions they receive are designated for the above purposes.)

Legal Considerations

There are two legal issues that are of great concern to most nonprofit managers: (1) ownership of the entity and (2) generation and distribution of a profit or surplus, that is, an excess of revenues over expenses.

Ownership of the Entity. A for-profit organization is owned by its shareholders, who expect to receive dividends as a return on the equity capital that they furnish. By contrast, non-profits cannot obtain equity capital from outside investors; instead, their equity capital must be *donated*. Moreover, a nonprofit organization cannot distribute assets or income to, or otherwise operate for the benefit of, any individual. (Indeed, trustees usually serve without monetary compensation.) There is nothing comparable to stock options, which constitute an important incentive in many for-profit organizations.

When a nonprofit organization is dissolved or converted to a for-profit status, the entity's value is transferred to another nonprofit organization or to the state or municipality in which it operates, never to private individuals. In the case of a conversion, the determination of the amount of value is a central concern of the state agency charged with regulating nonprofit organizations. This is because the entity's real value may be greater than the difference between its recorded assets and liabilities, and, when this is the case, the determination of the appropriate amount becomes a matter of judgment.[2]

Surplus Generation and Distribution. Legally, a nonprofit organization is allowed to earn an excess of revenues over expenses; this is its principal means of accumulating the equity capital that may be needed for (*a*) expansion, (*b*) the replacement of fixed assets, or (*c*) as a buffer in the case of temporary hard times. In general, it is prohibited from paying out any of its accumulated excesses of revenue over expenses in the form of cash dividends.

In accordance with a 1983 Internal Revenue Service decision (*Revenue Procedure 83-36*), a nonprofit organization can establish a profit-sharing plan under certain conditions without affecting its tax-exempt status. In making this determination, the IRS decided that profit-sharing plans could have a favorable effect on employees' performance, and thus could further an organization's charitable purposes.[3] The regulation prohibits a nonprofit organization from adding a portion of a surplus to its managers' salaries *after the fact*; that is, there must be a profit-sharing plan in place prior to any sort of distribution of the excess.[4]

For-Profit Activities

Under certain circumstances, nonprofit organizations can create for-profit subsidiaries, and they are permitted to pay out dividends. For example, a nonprofit research laboratory may have a subsidiary that holds patents developed by its employees; it gives these employees ownership shares in the subsidiary, and thereby rewards them with a share of license fees for patents they have developed.

If an incorporated nonprofit engages in a for-profit activity, it has the option of carrying out that activity within its own corporate structure or reorganizing in such a way that the activity is carried out in a separate but wholly owned subsidiary. The key advantage of a distinct corporate entity is that it does not jeopardize the tax-exempt status of the parent organization nor put the parent's assets at risk.[5]

Service Organizations

Most nonprofit organizations are service organizations. A company that manufactures and sells tangible goods has certain advantages, from a control standpoint, that a service organization does not have.

Goods can be stored in inventory, awaiting a customer order. Services cannot be stored. If the facilities and personnel that are available to provide a service today are not used today, the potential revenue from that capability is lost forever.

Service organizations tend to be labor intensive, requiring relatively little capital per unit of output; it is more difficult to control the work of a labor-intensive organization than that of an operation whose work flow is paced or dominated by machinery.

It is easy to keep track of the quantity of tangible goods, both during the production process and when the goods are sold, but it is not so easy to measure the quantity of many services. We can measure the number of patients that a physician treats in a day, for example, and even classify these visits by type of complaint, but this is by no means equivalent to measuring the amount of service the physician provides to each of these patients.

The quality of tangible goods can be inspected, and in most cases the inspection can be performed before goods are released to the customer. If the goods are defective, there is physical evidence of the nature of the defect. The quality of a service cannot be inspected in advance. At best, it can be inspected during the time that the service is being rendered to the client. Judgments as to the adequacy of the quality of most services are subjective, however, since for the most part, measuring instruments and objective quality standards do not exist.

Constraints on Goals and Strategies

Within wide limits, a for-profit organization can decide on the industry or industries within which it is going to do business, it can choose any of a number of different ways of competing in its industry, and it can change these strategies if management decides that a change is desirable. Most nonprofit organizations have much less freedom of choice, and they tend to change their strategies slowly, if at all. A university adds or closes a professional school less frequently than a large corporation adds or divests an operating division. A municipality is expected to provide certain services for its residents: education, public safety, welfare, and so on. It can make decisions about the amount of these services, but in general it cannot decide to discontinue them.

Furthermore, many nonprofit organizations must provide services as directed by an outside agency, rather than as decided by their own management or governing board. Private social service organizations must conform to state or municipal guidelines. Many hospitals must obtain a *certificate of need* in order to engage in large-scale capital projects. Organizations receiving support from the government must conform to the terms of the contract or grant. Moreover, the charter of many nonprofit organizations specifies in fairly explicit terms the types of services that can be provided.

Finally, federal and state legislatures not only limit total permitted spending and specify the amounts for certain programs, but they frequently dictate the amount that can be spent

for certain cost objects, such as travel. Similarly, many donors to nonprofit organizations restrict the purposes for which funds they contribute can be spent. In all instances, the management control system must assure that the limitations and restrictions are adhered to.

Diversification through New Ventures

Despite the various constraints they face, many nonprofit organizations have grown and diversified considerably during the past several years, including, as mentioned above, the formation of for-profit subsidiaries. In general, the process of deciding on a new venture is a complex one, involving a variety of legal, strategic, and managerial concerns. We discuss these concerns in a generic way in Chapter 8 [not reprinted here], under the topic of programming.[6]

Competitive Implications. In many instances, starting a new venture has helped a nonprofit organization to subsidize activities that otherwise might not have been financially feasible. This is a strategy that has become increasingly important to nonprofit organizations during the 1980s with the substantial reductions in federal assistance.

For some nonprofits, the production of new goods and services has put them in direct competition with for-profit organizations, particularly small ones. One survey reported that the issue of unfair competition from nonprofit organizations placed third among the top concerns of business people attending the White House Conference on Small Business in the summer of 1986. The Small Business Administration addressed this issue in a booklet entitled *Unfair Competition by NonProfit Organizations with Small Business: An Issue for the "80's."* The booklet argues that, since nonprofit organizations pay no taxes, they can compete unfairly with many small businesses.

Example. The Downtown Los Angeles YMCA operates a 110,000 square-foot facility that includes a large pool, indoor running track, and six racquetball and handball courts. Owners of the private Los Angeles

Athletic Club claim that the Y's nonprofit status allows it to charge $390 a year for membership, as contrasted with the Athletic Club's $960.[7]

Example. In July 1983 Planned Parenthood began offering its own trademarked brand of condoms, and by May 1984 had sold over 1 million. It then began to develop its own line of over-the-counter contraceptives.[8]

Example. MacNeal Hospital, near Chicago, entered into a joint venture with Damon Corp., a diversified biotechnology company in Massachusetts, to conduct blood and urine tests, as well as cell and tissue studies. Damon splits its profits from commercial medical testing with MacNeal, and MacNeal saved an estimated $750,000 in purchasing costs because of the greater scale of operations at its testing lab.[9]

The Business Coalition for Fair Competition, a group that has been formed to resist competition from nonprofits, has made an effort to address the financial consequences of the competition issue. It points out that nonprofit revenue rose from $114.6 billion in 1975 to $314.4 billion in 1983, and that 76 percent of the 1983 revenue was derived from sales of goods and services. It is, of course, not clear whether the growth came from: (1) expanded sales of goods and services that do not compete with small businesses (e.g., hospital care), (2) expanded sales of goods and services that already were competing with small businesses (e.g., Girl Scout cookies), or (3) sales of goods and services that are relatively new to the nonprofit arena (e.g., tanning salons at a YMCA).

The movement of nonprofits into new activities has been counterbalanced in some instances by a movement of for-profit firms into activities that traditionally have been nonprofit. This is particularly true in the health care field, where considerable debate has raged over the merits of such a shift, particularly with respect to its impact on the cost of health care.[10]

Source of Financial Support

A for-profit company obtains its financial resources from sales of its goods and services.

If the flow of these revenues is inadequate, the company does not survive. Thus, the market dictates the limits within which the management of a for-profit company can operate. A company cannot (or, at least, should not) make a product that the market does not want, and it cannot sell its products unless their selling prices are in line with what the market is willing to pay.

Some nonprofit organizations also obtain all, or substantially all, their financial resources from sales revenues. This is the case with most community hospitals (as contrasted with teaching hospitals), with private schools and colleges that depend entirely on tuition from students, and with research organizations whose resources come from contracts for specific research projects. Such organizations may be called *client-supported organizations*. They are subject to the forces of the marketplace in much the same way as are for-profit organizations in the same industry: proprietary hospitals, colleges, and for-profit research organizations.

Other nonprofit organizations receive a significant amount of financial support from sources other than revenues from services rendered. These may be called *public-supported organizations*. In these organizations there is no direct connection between the services received and the resources provided. Individuals receive essentially the same services from a governmental unit whether they pay high taxes or low taxes. Unrestricted grants by a government or by a foundation are not made because of services provided to the grantor. Appropriations made by a state legislature to a university, a hospital, or other organization are not related directly to the services received by the taxpayers from these organizations.

Contrast Between Client-Supported and Public-Supported Organizations

In almost all instances, client-supported organizations want more customers, since more customers imply more revenues, and more revenues imply greater success. In public-supported organizations there is no such relationship between the number of clients and the success of the organization. If the amount of its available resources is fixed by appropriations (as in the case of government agencies) or by income from endowment or annual giving (as is the case with many educational, religious, and charitable organizations), additional clients may place a strain on resources. In a for-profit, or a client-supported nonprofit organization, therefore, the new client is an opportunity to be vigorously pursued. In some public-supported organizations, the new client may be only a burden, to be accepted with misgivings.

This negative attitude toward clients gives rise to complaints about the poor service and surly attitude of bureaucrats. Clients of client-supported organizations tend to hear "please" and "thank you" more often than clients of public-supported organizations.

In some public-supported organizations, the contrast with the motivations associated with market forces is even stronger. A welfare organization should be motivated to decrease its clientele, rather than add to it; that is, it should seek ways of rehabilitating clients, thus removing them from the welfare roles. The Small Business Administration should work to change high-risk businesses into low-risk businesses which will no longer need the special services that the SBA provides. The idea that an organization should deliberately set out to reduce its clientele is foreign to the thinking of for-profit managers.

Competition provides a powerful incentive to use resources wisely. If a firm in a competitive industry permits its costs to get out of control, its product line to become obsolete, or its quality to decrease, its profits will decline. A public-supported organization has no such automatic danger signal.

As a substitute for the market mechanism for allocating resources, managers of public-supported organizations compete with one another for available resources. The physics department, the English department, and the library, all try to get as large a slice as possible of the college budget pie. In responding to these requests, senior management tries to judge what services clients should have, or what is best in the public interest, rather than what the market wants. In the public interest, Amtrak provides railroad service to areas where it is not economically warranted; similarly, the U.S. Postal Service maintains rural post offices.

Just as the success of a client-supported organization depends on its ability to satisfy clients, so the success of a public-supported organization depends on its ability to satisfy those who provide resources. Thus, a state university maintains close contact with the state legislature, and a private university may place somewhat more emphasis on athletics than the faculty thinks is warranted in order to satisfy contributors to the alumni fund. Furthermore, acceptance of support from the public carries with it a responsibility for accounting to the public, frequently to a greater degree than exists in a for-profit organization.

Professionals

In many nonprofit organizations, the important people are professionals (physicians, scientists, combat commanders, teachers, pilots, artists, ministers). Professionals often have motivations that are inconsistent with good resource utilization, and their success as perceived by their professional colleagues reflects these motivations. Some implications of this are given below.

Professionals are motivated by dual standards: those of their organizations and those of their professional colleagues. The former are related to organizational objectives; the latter may be inconsistent with organizational objectives. The rewards for achieving organizational objectives may be less potent than those for achieving professional objectives.

Many professionals, by nature, prefer to work independently. Examples are academicians, researchers, and physicians. Because the essence of management is getting things done through people, professionals with such a temperament are not naturally suited to the role of managers. For this and other reasons, managers in professional organizations are less likely to come up through the ranks than is the case in for-profit organizations.

Although the leadership job in a responsibility center of a nonprofit organization may require more management skills than professional skills, tradition often requires that the manager of such a unit be a professional. Many military support units are managed by military officers, even though a civilian might be a better qualified manager. Traditionally, the head of a research organization was a scientist; the president of a university, a professor; the head of a hospital, a physician. This tradition seems to be diminishing, however.

In a professional organization, the *professional quality* of the people is of primary importance and other considerations are secondary. In a professional organization, promotion is geared to the criteria established by the profession rather than those of the organization, per se, and thus may not place much emphasis on efficiency and effectiveness of the organization as a whole. These criteria do not always accurately reflect the individual's worth to the organization. Moreover, professionals tend to need a longer time to prove their worth than managers in for-profit organizations.

Professional education does not usually include education in management and quite naturally stresses the importance of the profession rather than of management. For this and other reasons, professionals tend to underestimate the importance of the management function. Bluntly, they tend to look down on managers. The following quotation from Lewis Thomas, a physician, illustrates the typical attitude:

> A university, as has been said so many times that there is risk of losing the meaning, is a community of scholars. When its affairs are going well, when its students are acquiring some comprehension of the culture and its faculty are contributing new knowledge to their special fields, and when visiting scholars are streaming in and out of its gates, it runs itself, rather like a large organism. The function of the administration is solely to see that the funds are adequate for its purposes and not overspent, that the air is right, that the grounds are tidy—and then to stay out of its way.[11]

Financial incentives tend to be less effective with professional people either because they consider their current compensation to be adequate or because their primary satisfaction comes from their work. In Thoreau's words, the professional "marches to the beat of a different drummer."

Professionals tend to give inadequate weight to the financial implication of their decisions. Many physicians, for example, feel that no limit should be placed on the amount spent to save a human life, although in a world of limited resources such an attitude is unrealistic.

Governance

Although the statement that shareholders control a corporation is an oversimplification, shareholders do have the ultimate authority. They may exercise this authority only in times of crisis, but it nevertheless is there. The movement of stock prices is an immediate and influential indication of what shareholders think of their management. In for-profit organizations, policy and management responsibilities are vested in the board of directors, which derives its power from the shareholders. In turn, the board delegates power to the president, who serves at the board's pleasure, acts as the board's agent in the administration of the organization, and who is replaced if there are serious differences of interest or opinion.

Governing Boards in Nonprofit Organizations

In many nonprofit organizations the corresponding line of responsibility is often not clear. There are no shareholders, members of the governing body are seldom paid for their services, and they may be chosen for political or financial reasons rather than for their ability to exercise sound judgment about the organization's activities. The governing body frequently is insufficiently informed about major issues facing the organization, and its decisions therefore are not always optimal. Thus, governing boards tend to be less influential in nonprofit organizations than in for-profit ones.

The governing board of a nonprofit organization, as an absolute minimum, has the responsibility to act when the organization is in trouble. Since there is no profit measure to provide an obvious warning, the personal appraisal by board members of the health of the organization is much more important in a nonprofit organization than in a for-profit business corporation. In order to have a sound basis for such an appraisal, board members need to spend a considerable amount of time learning what is going on in the organization, and they need to have enough expertise to understand the significance of what they learn.

Many governing boards do an inadequate job of this. There is not even a general recognition that this is the board's responsibility. In universities, for example, a widely quoted maxim is that "The function of a Board is to hire a president and then back him, period."[12] In hospitals, boards frequently are dominated by physicians who are qualified to oversee the quality of care but who may neither have the expertise, nor the willingness to check up on the effectiveness and efficiency of hospital management. In government organizations at all levels, auditors check on compliance with the statutory rules on spending, but there are few oversight agencies that pay attention to how well management performs its functions. Although legislative committees look for headline-making sins, many committees do not have the staff or the inclination to arrive at an informed judgment on management performance.

Government Organizations

In government organizations, external influences tend to come from a number of sources, leading to a diffusion of power. Some of the reasons for this are given below.

In state and federal governments there is a division of authority among executive, legislative, and judicial branches. Consequently, there are often conflicting judgments about objectives and the means of attaining them. In a for-profit company the board of directors and chief executive officer usually have similar objectives.

There may also be a vertical division of authority among levels of government (federal, state, and local), each responsible for facets of the same problem. For example, the federal government finances major and many minor highways, and local governments construct and maintain other highways.

Agencies, or units within agencies, may have their own special-interest clienteles (e.g., Maritime Administration and shipping interests) with political power that is stronger than that of the chief executive of the agency.

Senior-management authority may be divided, particularly in those states where the expenditure authority is vested in committees of independently elected officials, and in local governments administered by commissions whose members each administer a particular segment of the organization (e.g., streets or

health). Elected officials, such as the attorney general, the treasurer, the secretary of state, or the director of education, may manage their organizations fairly independently. The mayor of Los Angeles has much narrower responsibility than does the mayor of New York because the county organization in California is responsible for many services that are performed by the city organization in New York.

The bureaucracy is often insulated from senior management by virtue of job security and rules, and career civil servants may know that they will outlast the term of office of the elected or appointed chief executive. If pet projects cannot be sold to the current boss, their sponsors may bide their time and hope to sell them to the next one. Conversely, if they dislike a new policy, they may be able to drag their heels long enough so that a new management will take over and possibly rescind the policy.

This fragmentation of authority complicates management control. A particularly significant consequence is that the public administrator comes to depend upon political power to influence those who cannot be directly controlled. Consequently, managers must manage their political credit as well as their financial credit; they must measure the political cost and benefit of alternative choices, as well as the financial cost and benefit. On the other hand, as the U.S. Constitution states, there are some strong compensating advantages to divided authority, with each branch serving as a check on the activities of the others.

Senior Management

Most organizations have a chief executive officer, or CEO. In a very few organizations, authority is divided between two persons, or among a small senior-management group, but these are exceptions to the rule and usually are not successful. In most business organizations there is no doubt that the chief executive officer has responsibility for everything. On that person's desk, as was on President Truman's, there is at least figuratively the sign, "The Buck Stops Here."

In some nonprofit organizations the chief executive officer does not have such overall responsibility. The secretary of state typically has responsibility for foreign policy, but not for what

is called the *administration* of the State Department. (Administration, as used here, seems to
mean the operation of the support functions of
the State Department, rather than a term that is
synonymous with management, which is the
usual context.)

Presidents of universities may say that they
are the leaders of a "community of scholars,"
and that they should not soil their hands by
becoming involved in other aspects of university
management, particularly the business aspects
(although this attitude is much less prevalent
today than it was a generation ago). The minister
of a church may feel that it is inappropriate to
become involved in temporal matters. Hospitals
typically have two lines of authority: administrative and medical, and it generally is difficult
for the CEO to become involved in management
of the medical staff. That responsibility rests with
the medical director.

In some organizations, senior-management
responsibility is divided between two persons.
The Number One person is "Mr. (or Ms.)
Outside," responsible for overall policy formulation and for relations with the outside world; the
Number Two person is "Mr. (or Ms.) Inside,"
responsible for operations. This is the essential
idea of the British parliamentary system; the
Number One person is appointed by the party
in power, and the Number Two person, the
permanent undersecretary, is responsible for
carrying out policies for whatever party is in
power. Such a division of responsibility exists
to a certain extent in U.S. government agencies,
but in general it is not as well accepted or as
widespread here as in the United Kingdom. A
two-headed organization can be effective if, but
only if, there is a close relationship between the
two persons, and a clear understanding that
Number One will not overrule Number Two in
disputes relating to operations.

Political Influences

Many nonprofit organizations are political; that
is, they are responsible to the electorate or to a
legislative body that presumably represents the
electorate. Some of the consequences of this
status are discussed below.

Necessity for Reelection

In government organization, decisions result
from multiple, often conflicting, pressures. In
part, these political pressures are inevitable—
and up to a point desirable—substitutes for the
forces of the marketplace. Elected officials
cannot function if they are not reelected. In order
to be reelected, they must, at least up to a point,
advocate the perceived needs of their constituents, even though satisfying these needs may
not be in the best interests of the larger body that
they are supposed to represent. Moreover, in
order to gain support for programs that are
important to them, elected officials may support
certain of their colleagues' programs, even
though they personally do not favor them. This
"logrolling" phenomenon is also present in
for-profit organizations, but to a lesser extent.

Public Visibility

In a democratic society the press and public feel
that they have a right to know everything there
is to know about a government organization. In
the federal government and some state governments, this feeling is recognized by "freedom of
information" statutes, but the channels for distributing this information are not always
unbiased. Although some media stories that
describe mismanagement are fully justified,
others tend to be exaggerated, or to give inadequate recognition to the fact that mistakes are
inevitable in any organization. In order to reduce
the opportunities for unfavorable media stories,
government managers take steps to reduce the
amount of sensitive, controversial information
that flows through the formal management control system. This lessens the usefulness of the
system. The number of problems to which formal
analytical techniques are applied is thereby
reduced because such techniques result in reports
that may be open to public inspection.

Multiple External Pressures

The electoral process, with institutionalized
public review through news media and opposing political parties, results in a wider variety

of pressures on managers of public organizations than on managers of private organizations, whether nonprofit or for-profit. There is more controversy about the decisions of elected public officials than those of business managers. In the absence of profit as a clear-cut measure of performance, these pressures may be erratic and illogical, or influenced by momentary fads. Frequently, these pressures tend to induce an emphasis on short-term goals, and on program decisions that are not based on careful analysis. Stockholders demand satisfactory earnings, whereas the public and governing bodies of nonprofit organizations tend to exert less pressure for good resource utilization.

Legislative Restrictions

Government organizations must operate within statutes enacted by the legislative branch, which are much more restrictive than the charter and bylaws of corporations, and which often prescribe detailed practices. In many instances it is relatively difficult to change these statutes.

Management Turnover

In some public organizations senior management tends to change rapidly because of administration changes, political shifts, military orders, and managers who only dabble in government jobs. Each change requires a learning lead time, and many of them result in changes in priorities. This rapid turnover results in short-run plans and programs which produce quickly visible results, rather than substantive longer-range programs.

Civil Service

There is a widespread belief that Civil Service regulations are essentially different from personnel regulations in some large companies. The best case in support of this view of the inhibiting effects of Civil Service can be made in certain state and municipal governments. In many such organizations, Civil Service laws effectively inhibit the use of both the carrot and the stick. A Civil Service syndrome develops as a result of

the tacit caveat signaled by the system structure: "You need not produce success; you merely need to avoid making major mistakes." This attitude is a major barrier to improving organizational effectiveness.

On the other hand, Civil Service regulations in many government organizations may be no more dysfunctional than are union regulations and norms in for-profit organizations. When one considers the restrictive and inefficient union rules regarding work assignments, such as the number of engineers and other personnel aboard trains, or the division between electricians and plumbers on a joint repair job, it appears that at least in some situations the Civil Service environment may be quite comparable. One difference is that union rules mostly affect those near the bottom of the organization, whereas Civil Service rules affect managers as well.

Tradition

In the 19th century, accounting was primarily *fiduciary* in nature; that is, its purpose was to keep track of the funds that were entrusted to an organization so as to ensure that they were spent honestly. In the 20th century, accounting in business organizations has assumed much broader functions. It furnishes useful information about the business both to interested outside parties and to management. Nonprofit organizations have been slow to adopt 20th-century accounting and management control concepts and practices.

The Accrual Concept

A simple but fundamental idea of modern accounting is the accrual concept, and particularly the emphasis on expense measurement. Other new techniques would not be possible without it. Essentially, the expense focus means that accounting should measure the cost of *resources consumed*, as contrasted with *resources purchased* (which is the obligation concept) or with *liabilities incurred* (which is the expenditure concept) or with *checks drawn* (which is the cash concept). Many federal government agencies and many state and local governments continue to emphasize the obligation concept, many other nonprofit organizations focus on the expenditure concept, and some still account on a cash basis. With the notable exception of hospitals, relatively few nonprofit organizations focus on the measurement of expenses. We discuss these issues in greater detail in Chapter 3 [not reprinted here].

Barriers to Progress

Since a nonprofit organization lacks the semi-automatic control that is provided by the profit mechanism, it needs a good management control system even more than a business does. Why have many such organizations, particularly government organizations, lagged behind? For government, there seem to be three principal explanations. First, for many years, there was a prevalent attitude to the effect that the differences between government and business were such that government could not use the management control techniques developed by business. Articles to this effect written by eminent authorities appeared in the 1950s, and this attitude continues to be implicit in some texts on government accounting. Second, the Congress, and particularly the House Committee on Appropriations, having become thoroughly accustomed to a certain budget format, is reluctant to shift to a new format. Because of the importance of the budget, this affects the whole management control system. A similar problem exists in many states. In part the reluctance is based on simple inertia, but it also reflects a suspicion—generally unwarranted—that the change is an attempt by the executive branch to put something over on the legislative branch. Third, many career officials appreciate the fact that a good management control system is two-edged: it provides new information for management, but it also provides new information for outside agencies—the Office of Management and Budget and the Congress. Sometimes, these officials are not anxious that outside agencies have access to the new and better information. In this regard, it is important to note that the second reason is based on the premise that the proposed formats provide poorer information, while the third reason is based on the premise that they provide better information; both cannot be correct.

Conclusion

The characteristics of nonprofit organizations described in this chapter can be grouped into two classes, one technical and the other behavioral.

The first class consists of matters described under the heading the profit measure; that is, the difficulty of measuring outputs and the relationships between inputs and outputs. The important observation that can be made about this class is that the problems described therein are inherent in the fact that the organization is nonprofit. Great improvements in output measurement are indeed possible, and the problem is so important that a considerable effort to make such improvements is worthwhile; but it must be recognized at the outset that the resulting system will never provide as good a basis for planning or for measuring performance as exists in for-profit organizations.

The second class consists of all the other topics. The significance of these behavioral characteristics is twofold: (1) most of the behavioral factors that impede good management control can be overcome by proper understanding and education; and (2) unless these other problems *are* overcome, the improvements in the technical area are likely to have little real impact on the management control process.

Appendix

Differences Among Nonprofit Organizations

The description in this chapter is intended to apply to nonprofit organizations in general; but, as emphasized at the beginning, the characteristics enumerated do not fit all such organizations equally well. In this appendix, we attempt to relate the broader description to each of the principal nonprofit industries. These are, of course, broad-brush generalizations to which many exceptions can be found in individual organizations.

Health Care Organizations

Hospitals, nursing homes, health maintenance organizations, clinics, and similar health care organizations closely resemble for-profit organizations. Indeed, were it not for the difference in objectives—service rather than profit—their management control problems would be similar to those of their for-profit counterparts. There are few differences between a voluntary hospital and a proprietary hospital. These organizations do have fewer competitive pressures than the typical business; most of their revenue is received from third parties (Blue Cross, insurance companies, and the government) rather than directly from clients; they are dominated by professionals; and they have no clear-cut line of responsibility to a defined group of owners. Spurred on by public concern about the rising cost of health care and by the necessity for justifying their fees on the basis of a plausible measurement of cost, and led by the American Hospital Association, the Hospital Financial Management Association, and the Congress of Hospital Administrators, many hospitals have made dramatic improvements in their cost accounting systems in recent years. Fewer, however, have improved their management control systems.

Educational Organizations

Private colleges and universities whose tuition approximates the cost of education also resemble their for-profit counterparts. To the extent that they are supported by contributions and endowment earnings, however, the relationship between tuition revenues and the cost of services is less close. As is the case with hospitals, they are dominated by professionals, and their governing boards tend to be relatively uninfluential. They are subject to strong competitive pressures, and these pressures are increasing because of the decline in student population that is inevitable in the remainder of this century. In recent years, under the leadership of the National Association of College and University Business Officers, many of them have made substantial improvements in their management control systems.

State colleges and universities are supported primarily by appropriations from state legislatures. Although these appropriations may be based on a formula that takes into account the number of students or the number of credit hours, they are not the same as fees charged to clients because the individual student (or parent) ordinarily does not make the decision that the education received is worth the amount charged. In other respects, they are similar to private

colleges and universities. In recent years, the legislative oversight bodies of some states have paid much attention to the financial management of their colleges and universities, and this has led to great improvements in their management control systems.

Public elementary and secondary schools generally use an accounting system developed under the auspices of the U.S. Office of Education, which is urged as a condition of federal support. Although revised in the late 1970s, it continues to be an inadequate system, and management control is hampered by its inadequacies. A few communities have developed excellent systems on their own initiative.

Membership Organizations

Membership organizations are those whose purpose is to render service to their members. They include religious organizations, labor unions, trade associations, professional associations, fraternal organizations, social and country clubs, cemetery societies, and political organizations. To the extent that they are supported by dues from the membership, fluctuations in the amount of such dues is an indication of the perceived value of services rendered by the organization, even though there is rarely a direct connection between an individual's dues and the services received by that individual. Many are dominated by professionals and have weak governing boards. Certain membership organizations, such as religious organizations and certain labor organizations, face strong competitive pressures; others, such as professional associations, have no effective competition.

Until recently, many religious organizations have had notoriously weak management control systems. In recent years, however, several denominations have developed good systems and have encouraged their use at local levels. Religious organizations have a particularly difficult problem in deciding on the programs to be undertaken and in measuring the value of services rendered. ("Souls saved per pew hour preached" is not a feasible measurement!)

Human Service and Arts Organizations

Human service organizations include family and child service agencies, the Red Cross, scouting and similar youth organizations, and various other charitable organizations. Arts organizations include museums, public broadcasting stations, symphony orchestras, theaters, and ballet companies.

With some notable exceptions, these organizations rely heavily on public support, either from the government or from contributions by individuals, companies, and foundations. Their revenues therefore do not directly measure the value of services provided to clients. Some are dominated by professionals; others are not. Those who provide support tend to exercise an increasing amount of influence over the financial affairs of these organizations.

In recent years, considerable improvements have been made in the management control systems of these organizations, primarily because of the influence of such organizations as the United Way of America and professional associations of museums and broadcasting stations, but significant opportunities for further improvement remain.

The Federal Government

Except for certain businesslike activities, such as the U.S. Postal Service, the federal government does not receive fees from clients. Its goals are multiple and fuzzy, and the value of its services is especially difficult to measure.

Governments are subject to external power influences and political influences more than is the case with other nonprofit organizations. These forces make its management control problem especially difficult. Furthermore, many federal agencies are unique (there is only one State Department), so there is no basis for comparing performance with other units. Some improvements have occurred in recent years, but, as illustrated by the fact that accrual accounting is still not fully implemented, much remains to be done.

State and Local Governments

Collectively, state and local governments are by far the largest category of nonprofit organizations. They are subject to a variety of external power influences and to political influences, and therefore have a difficult management control problem.

Generally, their revenues are not directly related to services provided to clients. Although

the person whose house is on fire is a client in one sense, the main function of the fire department is to protect the whole community. Proposals for specific programs are often political in nature and not subject to economic analysis. The objectives of these organizations are difficult to define in ways that permit measurement of their attainment. (What is adequate fire protection or police protection?)

Although management control in state and local government units is inherently difficult, good systems likewise are especially necessary. Such systems currently do not now exist in most governmental units, although there are a few notable exceptions. Development of adequate systems has been greatly hampered by the forces of tradition. Many government units keep their accounts solely on a cash receipts and disbursements basis, a practice that has been obsolete since the 19th century. Forces now at work, including public dissatisfaction because of recent revelations of poor management and pressures of the federal government in implementing the revenue-sharing program, seem likely to lead to improvements in the relatively near future.

Suggested Additional Readings

Anthony, Robert N. *Financial Accounting in Nonbusiness Organizations.* Stamford, Conn.: Financial Accounting Standards Board, 1978.

Clark, Robert C. "Does the Nonprofit Form Fit the Hospital Industry?" *Harvard Law Review,* May 1980, pp. 1417–89.

Powell, Walter W., ed. *The Nonprofit Sector: A Research Handbook.* New Haven, Conn.: Yale University Press, forthcoming.

Ramanathan, Kavasseri V. *Management Control in Nonprofit Organizations.* New York: Wiley, 1982.

Rudney, Gabriel. *A Quantitative Profile of the Nonprofit Sector.* PONPO Working Paper No. 40, Yale University Program on Non-Profit Organizations, November 1981.

———, and Murray Weitzman. *Significance of Employment and Earnings in the Philanthropic Sector, 1972–1982.* PONPO Working Paper No. 77 and ISPS Working Paper No. 2077, Yale University Program on Non-Profit Organizations, November 1983.

Notes

1. Some people prefer the term *not-for-profit* on the grounds that a business enterprise with a net loss is literally a *nonprofit* organization. *Black's Law Dictionary, Kohler's Dictionary for Accountants, Webster's Third New International Dictionary, Funk and Wagnalls Dictionary,* and *American Heritage Dictionary* do not list "not-for-profit," however. Practice varies widely among states and is not uniform for the statutes of a given state. In federal statutes, the usual term is *nonprofit.* In income tax regulations, *not-for-profit* refers to a corporation that is operated as a hobby of the owners.

2. For a discussion of this point, see David W. Young, "Ownership Conversions in Health Care Organizations: Who Should Benefit?", *Journal of Health Politics, Policy, and Law* 10, no. 4 (Winter 1986). See also Kenneth C. Dunn, Geoffrey B. Shields, and Joanne B. Stern, "The Dynamics of Leveraged Buy-Outs, Conversions, and Corporate Reorganizations of Not-for-Profit Health Care Institutions," *Topics in Health Care Financing,* Spring 1986.

3. For a discussion of some of the issues involved in establishing such a plan, see Charlotte P. Armstrong and Rylee Routh, "Profit-Sharing Choice for Non-profit Organizations," *Pension World,* April 1984. For a broader discussion of compensation in nonprofit organizations (principally trade and professional associations, however), see Towers, Perrin, Forster & Crosby, "Not-for-Profit Compensation," *Public Relations Journal,* May 1984. For a more general discussion of employee job satisfaction and rewards in nonprofit organizations, see Philip H. Mirvis and Edward J. Hackett, "Work and Work Force Characteristics in the Nonprofit Sector," *Monthly Labor Review,* April 1983.

4. For an expanded discussion of this point, see Mark V. Pauly, "Nonprofit Firms in Medical Markets," *AEA [American Economic Association] Papers and Proceedings,* May 1987.

5. The Spring 1986 issue of *Topics in Health Care Financing* has several articles devoted to the theme of corporate reorganization of nonprofit hospitals.

6. For a good description of some of the issues associated with for-profit ventures, see Edward Skloot, "Should Not-for-Profits Go into Business?", *Harvard Business Review,* January–February 1983. See also Herrington J. Bryce, *Financial and Strategic Management for Nonprofit Organizations* (Englewood Cliffs, N.J.: Prentice-Hall, 1986).

7. "Putting on the Ritz at the Y," *Time,* July 21, 1986.

8. "New Profits for Nonprofits," *INC,* May 1984.

9. Udayan Gupta, "Hospitals Enlist Profit-Minded Partners for Ventures to Generate New Business," *The Wall Street Journal,* January 23, 1987.

10. See, for example, A. S. Relman, "The New Medical-Industrial Complex," *New England Journal of Medicine,* 303 (1980), pp. 963–70; Carson W. Bays, "Why Most Hospitals Are Nonprofit," *Journal of Policy Analysis and Management* 2, no. 3 (1983); and Steven C. Renn et al., "The Effects of Ownership and System Affiliation on the Economic Performance of Hospitals," *Inquiry* 22 (Fall 1985).

11. Lewis Thomas, *The Youngest Science: Notes of a Medicine-Watcher* (New York: Bantam Books, 1983).

12. Perhaps because the academic environment nourishes writing, more has been written about college and university trustees than about other types of governing boards. Publications of the Association of Governing Boards of Colleges and Universities, One Dupont Circle, Washington, D.C., contain much material about the governance of colleges and universities. The classic book is still Beardsley Ruml and Donald M. Morrison, *Memo to a College Trustee* (New York: McGraw-Hill, 1959).

ARTICLE 20 ──────────────

Computing in Nonprofit Organizations

E. Samuel Overman

The much anticipated use and expected impact of computing and information technology in nonprofit organizations has become an inextricable part of the familiar rhetoric of management reform. Over a decade ago Regina Herzlinger in *Harvard Business Review* chastised nonprofit organizations for bad management because they did not pay attention to the details of information and control systems in their agencies (Herzlinger, 1977). Today, this situation is believed to have changed, or has it? In this essay we question what is the use, misuse, or underuse of computers and information technology in the nonprofit sector? What are the special obstacles to effective computing in the nonprofit sector?

There is an irresistible urge to compare the use of computers and information technology with other reform efforts to improve nonprofit organization performance. Historically, if nonprofit managers wished to reform their organizations it was usually accomplished through structural reorganizations, changes in personnel, or some combination of both. Today, changes in the management systems and the computers which drive them are at least one alternative to classic management reform. New management information systems in finance and accounting, client and case management, or even office automation provide an alternative to the modern nonprofit manager for improving organizational effectiveness.

But, like every management reform, computers and information technology have their costs and benefits for nonprofit organizations. Specifically, computers have been shown to alter the planning, management, and control balance in an organization. Computers may, for example, make a nonprofit organization more effective in controlling scarce resources, or it might make them more strategic in acquiring new resources. The discrepancy between the actual and expected function of computing in nonprofit organizations, and between the levels of management computers are intended to serve has yet to be seriously examined.

Computers and information technology have also been shown to have their own natural trajectory, or stages of development, within an organization, nonprofit or otherwise. Computer use naturally proceeds from more rudimentary and experimental applications to sophisticated and comprehensive decision support systems or artificial intelligence. To better understand the obstacles to computing in nonprofit organizations it is necessary to examine the relationship between the stages of computing on one side, and the functions of computing or the planning–management–control balance on the other.

Despite the rhetoric and hyperbole surrounding the use, misuse, and underuse of computers and information technology in the public and private sectors, there is reason to suspect that we may have underestimated the centrality of using computers and information technology for management reform in nonprofit organizations.

The Functions of Information and Computing

The key assumption for management has always been that computing would provide a tool for systematically relating data and information to organizational goals and objectives. This has always been the function of computing in organizations, albeit somewhat tenuous. When managers spend thousands of dollars on computers and information systems that fail to accomplish the tasks they were designed to do, we have reason to doubt either the effectiveness of the computer technology or management's purpose and use of the information.

In providing information for organizational effectiveness several important theoretical developments stand out. First, information was originally seen as a way to *reduce uncertainty* and slow the process of organizational entropy (Shanon, 1974). This theoretical assumption has led in most instances, regardless of sector, to the insatiable desire for greater quantities of information, and eventually for more reliable, more timely and less costly information. The use of information for decision making is largely guided by the belief that more and better information will improve decision making by reducing uncertainty, and thereby improve the likelihood of increasing organizational effectiveness.

The second development in information theory came via the field of cybernetics, the science of *communication and control*. In the cybernetic vision information was to be used for control of natural and human systems. In cybernetics information drives the system. The classic example being the thermostat collecting and using information to control and regulate the temperature of the home (Ashby, 1956). It was soon realized that information systems, computerized or not, could control human behavior in organizations be they budget and accounting systems or performance appraisal systems (Lawler and Rhode, 1976).

The third and most recent development in information theory has been to view *information as a resource* in society and organizations. The list of popular books that address this theme of information resource management is already large and rapidly growing. Most are positive (e.g., Marchand and Horton, 1986), and a few are more critical (e.g., Roszak, 1986) about the information revolution. In this view information is a resource not just for control but for power, strategy, and ultimately competitive advantage in the post-industrial environment. But information is unlike the land, labor, and capital resources of classical economics. Information expands as it is used and is therefore not scarce; information is compressible and transportable at great speeds; and information is not exchanged but shared and is difficult to own (Cleveland, 1985).

Information is also only part of larger cognitive and management hierarchies. The cognitive hierarchy states that information is derived from data when it is organized, and produces knowledge when it is given a context and purpose. This knowledge can in turn be used wisely or not so wisely. The management or organizational hierarchy is generally accepted to be on three levels: control or operational, tactical or managerial, and strategic or planning levels. It is the mix and more so the match between these cognitive and management hierarchies that produces successful management information systems (Martin and Overman, 1988).

The important point within this notion of information as a resource in an organization is that, like people and money, it too needs to be managed. There are questions not only of effectiveness and efficiency but of access, security, and privacy that need continual attention. There are certain levels of the organization at which certain types of information are more appropriate. Clearly the function of computing is to provide information in the planning, management, and operational processes of the organization, but how has computer technology itself altered the balance of power among these levels

of management activity and the type of information produced?

The Stages of Computer Reform

The association of information with computer technology is truly synergistic. This powerful combination of computers and information has produced a whole new vocabulary and list of acronyms into the management lexicon. This new vocabulary is a result of the explosive growth and tremendous technological innovation within the computer industry.

The first commercially available computer produced in the United States is generally acknowledged to be the Universal Automatic Computer (UNIVAC I). Containing over 5,000 vacuum tubes, it was the first computer to use stored programs. It reached notoriety when on loan to CBS News for the 1952 elections it predicted a landslide victory for Eisenhower from a sample of just 7%. Network and election experts refused to believe it's accuracy, but the UNIVAC eventually came within 1% of predicting the electoral vote. Of the seven original UNIVAC I machines made, three were bought by the Census Bureau (Roszak, 1986).

The nature of early computing was number crunching and massive data processing through what are called transaction processing systems or *data base management systems* (DBMS). Early computers were difficult to operate and maintain and were the province of computer scientists working long hours in cool basement rooms. Keeping track of vast quantities of data on such organizational matters as payroll and inventory was what they were good at doing, but outside of some scientific and engineering uses, not much else. Computers could help control the operational functioning of an organization.

The next generations of computers replaced vacuum tubes (first generation) with transistors (second generation) and now integrated circuits (third generation) (Flamm, 1988). Concommitantly, computers were able to take on increasingly more sophisticated tasks within the organizations, such as budgeting and project management. Other factors contributed to the increasing relevance of computing in the organization. Decreasing costs, relative to labor and other capital resources, distributed computers out of the basement and into the office. New procedural, symbolic and natural languages, and software have been developed which make the hardware both more accessible and versatile. Finally, a new class of computer literates, the users, developed within the organization who could develop and implement various *management information systems* (MIS).

MIS has become the standard-bearer of organizational computing, but it is not a terminal stage as many are prone to believe. The incessant demand for greater and more sophisticated applications of computer technology to organizational needs already has, or eventually will reach every manager's desktop. Through *decision support systems* computing is expected to bring large quantities of relatively unstructured information not just to experts and trained users, but to complete the iron triangle, it will be readily accessible and easily interpretable to top level managers as well (Overman and Simanton, 1986). Networked systems with seemingly unlimited communications environments in which managers can make interactive inquiries to support their decisions and plans is already commonplace in some organizations. This is not to say that large-scale DBMS and big computers crunching numbers in brightly lit, cool basements have disappeared, nor has or will MIS, still a dream to many organizations, wither on the vine. It is readily apparent, however, that there are stages to the growth and development of computers and information technology in all organizations, government, private, and nonprofit. Furthermore, these stages are associated with how information is used or not used within these organizations. Table 1 combines all the elements discussed thus far and provides a framework for looking at computing in nonprofit organizations.

Nonprofit Computing

What is the state of computing and information management in nonprofit organizations? What are the uses of and obstacles to computing in nonprofit organizations? These are not easy questions for several reasons. First, the nonprofit sector is itself very diverse, ranging from classic service or educational and voluntary organizations to foundations, churches, and even special interest groups. Second, there is not yet a single way to capture information on nonprofits as there is with national, state, and local governments or with private industry groups. These factors should not deter us from our efforts to understand computing in nonprofit organizations, but it does require a more cautious and qualified approach. Thus, most of the findings and conclusions in this paper are based on a study of twenty-three nonprofit mental health centers.

The Use of Computing in Nonprofit Organizations

The first question about level of use is how many nonprofit organizations use computers and for what purpose? Of the twenty-three nonprofit organizations studied, twenty use computers to produce data, and of these only thirteen have systems sophisticated enough to produce integrated reports based on information provided by

TABLE 1 Some Basic Differences Between Computer Orientations

Characteristic	Control	Management	Strategic
Type of system	DBMS	MIS	DSS
Purpose of system	data	information	knowledge
Processing	centralized	distributed	networked
Input/Output	batch/printouts	interactive/reports	interactive/inquiries
Analyst	programmer	user	manager
Applications	payroll inventory	budgeting program	decision planning

the computer. The other seven nonprofit organizations are computerized, but only at a very basic level of data production. About two-thirds, or fifteen, of the twenty-three can generate reports required by the state directly from computer programs, the remainder do it manually. Thus, while one could conclude that most nonprofit organizations are computerized, it is probably the case that this computerization in nearly one-half is little more than rudimentary data processing.

In addition, there is a narrow range of what data is collected, but a very wide range of how this data is collected and stored. In this sample, information is collected on clients (i.e., demographic), services to them, costs of these services (i.e., billing), and the providers of these services (i.e., personnel). In only a handful of instances are these separate types of information capable of being integrated whereby a report could be generated, for example, on types of services by types of providers and the cost of these services. Between the nonprofit organizations there is a wide disparity, however, in how these data on clients, costs, services, and providers are collected and computerized. Suffice it to say that the lack of common definitions, similar to diagnostic related groups, are totally absent, which leads each center to develop its own data categories and definitions.

Overall, the pattern suggested by the nonprofit service organizations studied here is that the predominant type of system is the basic data base management system, and only in the most sophisticated instances are there signs of creating true management information systems. Many of the computerized applications amount to little more than inventories of clients, services, and providers constituting basic data processing.

A second concern in nonprofit computer use is to determine how processing is accomplished. In the computerized nonprofit organizations studied here most maintained centralized processing capabilities. Seven of the computerized centers contract out their computing services to a private computer service bureau that operates a relatively large mainframe computer. Those with in-house computing capabilities rely primarily on a single mini-computer. Some printouts were seen but most of the computerized centers are, as mentioned, producing standardized reports either for the state or other regulatory agencies.

Overall, the pattern suggested here is that only a handful of the larger nonprofit organizations with a high enough volume of service can afford the luxury of doing their own computing. There is a very definite economy of scale to computing in nonprofit organizations, where many are too small to justify the expenses of acquisition and maintenance, and instead rely on contracts with external firms who in turn rely on larger economies of scale and centralized computing services. When computing is accomplished by the nonprofit organization it is generally centralized, and only rarely do we run across the computer on every desk being used for something other than word processing.

Third, who are the people involved in nonprofit computing? Of the twenty-three nonprofit organizations studied here, twelve had their own unique customized systems designed and operated for the most part by their own personnel, two actually shared a system and personnel between them, six more relied on private firms for their expertise in software development, and the remaining three were not, as already pointed out, computerized at all. Clearly, most nonprofit computing is still in the hands of data processing experts, internal or external to the organization, and only rarely are well-informed users involved in computing. Many within the organization eschew the use of computing, which may be a function of the client-centered attitudes and social work backgrounds of most nonprofit personnel in this instance. There is the rare instance where a case worker or therapist from within the organization has taken great interest, whether by desire or order, in computing and developed highly useful, though highly unique, applications for their agency. The executive directors and managers generally showed indifference to this study which belies a level of involvement in information management by nonprofit managers, supporting Herzlinger's claim that the failure of data systems in nonprofit organizations is due to lack of managerial emphasis and attention (Herzlinger, 1977). When management did get involved it was more out of concern over financial accountability, not computing services.

In summary, computing in nonprofit organizations, and certainly those studied here, appears to be very much at the first stage of DBMS with a primary orientation toward production and control. Even the most sophisticated organizations operate at basic levels of MIS, though it would always be possible to find the highly sophisticated computerized nonprofit organization. The next question we naturally ask is why is it that nonprofit computing appears to exist at such basic levels? Asked another way, what are the obstacles to effective computer use in nonprofit organizations?

Obstacles to Computing in Nonprofit Organizations

There are several factors influencing the use of computing in nonprofit organizations that may be unique to the nonprofit sector. First, the economics of nonprofits is certainly a factor in at least one way already discussed, that is, the small size of many nonprofit organizations and the required economies of scale for effective computing. But more broadly, the diversity of nonprofit funding requiring different accountability procedures may have an even greater impact on nonprofit computing. Frequently in nonprofit organizations there is a separation of the provider of the service from the financing of that service. For example, the state accounted for 42% and private insurers 32% of the nonprofit organizations' income in this study. Dependence on grants, gifts, and other foundations further complicates the financial accountability structures faced by many nonprofit organizations. The separation of provider from funding leads to greater accountability demands on the nonprofit organization, but often without the financial means being made available to assure this accountability. In other words, accountability structures and particularly computerized accountability is considered as administrative overhead. Most funding organizations would rather see their money spent on direct service provision. Generally, computing is a very low priority among nonprofit managers and nonprofit boards. If computing in the nonprofit organization is to improve, then the better funded nonprofit associations, like the Independent Sector or the Council of Foundations, will need to invest

in both the study and development of computing in their organizational members.

The politics of the nonprofit sector also presents significant obstacles to computing. Like the small private business, and unlike the typical government organizations, the nonprofit organization is most often an independent entity. Though there may exist nonprofit support services for technical assistance or professional associations for particular groups of nonprofit workers, most nonprofits exist in a very competitive environment. Contrary perhaps to popular belief, nonprofit organizations do compete and generally do not share. This is certainly true in this sample of nonprofit mental health centers. Nonprofit organizations compete for both resources and a market niche, which in turn leads to a tremendous level of diversity within the nonprofit sector. Insofar as it affects computing, this diversity is of at least two types, procedural and technical, or both how they accomplish their tasks and the technology (not just computing) used to accomplish their tasks. If there is one thing that is hard for the computer industry to adapt to it is just such procedural and technical diversity. Effective and economical computing depends on a level of standardization and commonality that is currently absent in most of the nonprofit sector. In order to reverse this situation nonprofit organizations will need to enter into greater resource sharing and cooperative ventures than heretofore attempted.

Finally, something must be said, as diplomatically as possible, about the people who go into nonprofit organizations and their general lack of computing expertise. Certainly there are a great many extremely sophisticated systems developers and computer users in nonprofit organizations. But in combination with the economic and political factors mentioned above, computing is slow to develop within the nonprofit sector at least partially because of the "missing link" between the computer and the organization, that is the people who make both work. As with most service oriented professions, interpersonal and social skills dominate technical skills in both educational preparation and in-service training. If nonprofit computing is to advance, particularly in the service realm, then certainly more attention will need to be given to staff development.

Certainly some or all of these obstacles may change in the future, but right now they pose significant problems for computing in nonprofit organizations. Computing may be slow to develop in the nonprofit sector, but there is no reason to believe it cannot succeed.

Conclusions

This study of computing in nonprofit organizations has found that relatively low levels of computer use exist. Most computing in nonprofits is based on simple database management systems, and information is generally used for the purpose of organizational control. The development of computing in the nonprofit sector is generally hampered by economic, political, and human resource factors. If computing is to develop in the nonprofit sector it will need to become a higher priority.

References

Ashby, W. Ross. (1956). *An introduction to cybernetics*. London: Chapman & Hall.

Cleveland, Harlan. (1985). *The knowledge executive: Leadership in an information society*. New York: Dutton.

Davis, Gordon B., & Olson, Margrethe H. (1985). *Management information systems* (2nd ed.). New York: McGraw-Hill.

Flamm, Kenneth. (1988). *Creating the computer*. Washington, DC: The Brookings Institute.

Herzlinger, Regina. (January–February 1977). Why data systems in nonprofit organizations fail. *Harvard Business Review*, 81–86.

Lawler, Edward E., & Rhode, John G. (1976). *Information and control in organizations*. Pacific Palisades, CA: Goodyear.

Machlup, Fritz, & Mansfield, Una [Eds.]. (1983). *The study of information*. New York: Wiley.

Marchand, Donald, & Horton, Forest. (1986). *Infotrends: profiting from your information resources*. New York: Wiley.

Martin, John, & Overman, E. Sam. (Summer 1988). Management and cognitive hierarchies: What is the role of management

information systems? *Public Productivity Review*. XI, no. 4.

Overman, E. Samuel, & Simanton, Don. (November 1986). Iron triangles and issue network of information policy. *Public Administration Review, 46*, special issue, pp. 584–589.

Roszak, Theodore. (1986). *The cult of information*. New York: Pantheon.

Shanon, Claude E. (1974). A mathematical theory of communication. In David Slepian (Ed.), *Key papers in the development of information theory*. New York: The Institute of Electrical and Electronics Engineers, Inc., pp. 5–18.

ARTICLE 21 _____
Managing Change in Nonprofit Organizations
Jacquelyn Wolf

Joan Califano, the new executive director of the local child and family service agency, was brought into the position from another city following the retirement of her predecessor, who had founded the agency eighteen years previously. The former executive director was highly regarded among professionals in the field, and the staff are extremely proud of the agency and loyal to the traditions he established. Joan also admired the former leader but feels there is a need for some new program directions. She particularly wants to provide improved services for troubled adolescents in the city's growing Hispanic community, but when she talks about the need and her vision with the senior staff team, they raise endless objections about resource constraints and other program priorities. But she senses their objections are to her, and to any change in the agency. . . .

The nursing staff of Kincare Home Nursing Services has always shared shifts equally, on a rotation basis. During the past year, the community has been experiencing a worsening shortage of nurses while demands for services, such as those provided by Kincare, have increased. Executive Director Jim Cunningham researched the problem and found many R.N.s live in the city but are not working in the field because their family commitments make shift work difficult. In response to an exploratory ad he placed in the local paper, fifteen well-qualified applicants have applied for part-time positions with fixed hours. This would solve the agency's staff shortage, but present staff are outraged that in the future some nurses will have fixed hours while others must continue to rotate shifts. Jim has offered premium pay to those on shifts, but it hasn't had the hoped-for calming effect. . . .

The Midtown Symphony is an orchestra that during its twenty-five years has built a growing audience and community support. Never too adventurous, it has relied on a classical, popular repertoire. Two years ago, its new conductor—a young maestro with good critical credentials—began to urge the board to broaden its horizons. After a year of careful planning and discussion, the board agreed two of the symphony's six annual concerts should be modern, "new music" works, and subscribers were prepared through newsletters and articles in program brochures. Ticket sales were strong but by the close of the season, many season subscribers had indicated that they didn't like the new direction and would not be back. Following several heated sessions, the board voted to continue the new policy hoping patrons could be educated over time. But nearly a quarter of the board resigned because of this issue in the month that followed the affirmation. Annual donations are down 15 percent and the corporate sponsors who underwrote the modern concerts are showing reluctance to renew support for this year's contemporary selections. . . .

These three situations will sound all too familiar—and may evoke some cynical chuckles —for experienced managers and policy volunteers in nonprofit organizations. It is one of fate's cruel ironies that the nonprofit sector, which takes justifiable pride in its philosophy of responsiveness to expressed community need, finds itself equally as perplexed and frustrated as its public and private counterparts when implementing change at the organizational and individual level. In fact, in both programs and administration, it sometimes seems as if organizational change is more difficult to effect in voluntary organizations. A number of unique characteristics contribute to this heightened perception of change difficulty for the nonprofit organization.

Change in Nonprofit Organizations Has Unique Characteristics

Its Nonprofit Nature

The culture associated with nonprofits is one of high integrity, an altruistic mission, and strongly felt values about the contribution the particular organization makes to the individual and the community. Most nonprofits produce services, and public and client reactions to the organization often are based on evaluations of personal experiences with the process of planning and delivery. The policies, programs, and organizational environment for clients, staff, and volunteers are as—or more—important to the individuals as are the goals or end results of those services.

Its Breadth of Purpose

Those who draft mission statements for nonprofits generally do not flinch at the enormity of the proposed task. Frequently, such statements will be sweeping (e.g., "to improve the quality of life for Jefferson County's developmentally disabled," or "to provide a broad range of community-based alternative arrangements for troubled youth in Massachusetts"). This gives the board considerable scope in the design of program activity, but such breadth is not helpful when the organization must inevitably define its service parameters. Private enterprise finds its parameters by judging alternatives against profitability and wealth-generation criteria. Public sector organizations face more complexity in design and service delivery but can fall back upon statutory and regulatory definitions of boundaries. Nonprofits must somehow define the highest priority needs for Jefferson County's developmentally disabled, or the troubled youth of Massachusetts, without going beyond what the community desires and expects from this trust relationship.

Its Demanding Environment

During the 1980s, new variables have been added to the environment of nonprofits. Demand for services has increased, while donative resources have not kept pace. Operating grants are in decline, while contract and project funding mechanisms have increased. The sector is more professionalized, and funders expect administrative efficiency and demonstrated entrepreneurial spirit. On the other hand, funders and the public get nervous if the nonprofit is *too* businesslike and is perceived to be competing effectively with business, especially for government contracts. No wonder nonprofits seem to have such difficulty implementing change: They must show hard-hitting business capacity, accompanied by compassionate concern and advocacy for the needy!

Its Volunteer–Staff Mix

Volunteers, so critical to governance (and often to service delivery) of nonprofits, have different needs from their involvement with the organization than do paid staff. The challenge is to retain the definition of mission, shaping of values, and determination of policies within the volunteer contributions to the organization, and to integrate this with the contributions of staff who are increasingly professional, competent, and have the benefit of a larger overview and information base than most volunteers.

Its Increasingly Mixed Structure

A growing number of nonprofits derive income from revenue-generating activities. In larger enterprises, this can result in two conflicting cultures within the same organization: The traditional culture of an altruistic charity, dedicated to providing services and advocacy for the less advantaged; and an entrepreneurial, marketing-oriented culture in the portion of the organization that sells services or goods (often in competition with proprietary providers) to a more upscale clientele. Implementing program or administrative changes which will satisfy both cultures is an extremely difficult task.

These differences do not lessen the need for the nonprofit manager, paid or volunteer, to better understand how change takes place among individuals and groups in organizations, and what strategies appear to have been successful for others. As in any learning enterprise, it seems appropriate to begin with a review of what we know about change as a process—and what we don't.

What Do We Know About the Change Process in Organizations?

Among the dictionary definitions of change are "to substitute; to exchange; to make different or alter." While these definitions suggest some disturbance to the current state of affairs, they pass no judgment as to whether the anticipated action is trivial or profound, or whether it has positive or negative consequences for those involved. Value-free descriptions of change, however, have no reality outside dictionaries, texts, and learned journals. Change is hard for both individuals and organizations. It consumes enormous energy and often requires heavy investment of scarce resources. In short, mostly we don't do it unless we have to, but in recent years the operating environment of all organizations—including nonprofits—has been so turbulent managers have been becoming more concerned about how to make change efforts less chaotic and more effective.

Not surprisingly, just about the time organizations were most in need of new learnings about change, researchers began to devote more attention to it. Until the early 1970s, research on change in organizations was a subset of the organization development (OD) literature. Friedlander and Brown (1974), in their review of the OD literature to that date, summarized the empirical knowledge about technostructural (e.g., job design) and human process (e.g., interventions, group development) methods for effecting change. While OD methods may improve morale and make people feel better about the organization, they concluded "there is little evidence. . .that organizational processes actually change or that performance or effectiveness is increased" (p. 334). The Friedlander and Brown survey indicates that most early research was focused on change within the organization, rather than on the organization's interface with its environment. White and Mitchell (1976), in a similar review, add that attitudinal or behavioral change experiments seem to focus on individuals or immediate subgroups, rather than on organizational direction and strategy.

After 1974, the pace of reflection and research picks up. Argyris and Schön framed new theoretical questions in *Organizational*

Learning (1978) and Schaller (1978) drew from Kurt Lewin's philosophical roots to build a model for managing change which begins with an "outsider" identifying for group members the discrepancy between their current situation and the ideal, and ends with recommendations for "freezing the change" (institutionalizing the new set of conditions). Goodman and Kurke (1982) updated previous reviews and found five major themes in the planned organizational change literature since 1977.

Goodman and Kurke's Findings About Organization Change

The focus on intervention methods and strategies has persisted. Katz and Kahn (1978), in their classic work on organizations, discussed change in terms of alternative methods at individual, group, and organizational levels of analysis. In terms of effectiveness of these methods, the strongest literature has concerned job redesign, indicating general satisfaction, growth satisfaction, and internal motivation from job changes, but less firm results on absenteeism and performance.

More attention has been given to the introduction of large-scale multiple system interventions. Quality of Working Life (QWL) experiments, a feature of the late 1970s and early 1980s, appeared to have positive effects on work attitudes, lower absenteeism, positive effects of safety, and some mixed results on productivity; but at the price of increased stress for middle managers and supervisors, and with unresolved problems of managing individual differences and maintaining these interventions over time.

More attention has been paid to developing technology for assessing planned organizational change. Researchers have conceived models of assessment, developed more standardized measures to assess organizational instrumentation, begun to use more complicated time series designs (rather than single observations after the experimental change), and moved toward more sophisticated use of analytical and statistical procedures.

Researchers have increasingly begun to document failures of planned organizational change. Attention has been focused on better theory development and on the problems of maintaining a change once it has been initially implemented.

The level of theorizing about organizational change has increased dramatically. The tradition of using general frameworks, begun with Lewin (1951), continued but more specific propositions also began to emerge: For example, respecting change in the context of union management relations (Kochan and Dyer, 1976), whether change efforts in economic (versus non-economic) organizations will be more successful, or whether internal or external change agents are most effective (Dunn and Swierczek, 1977).

Apart from these five major trends in the literature on *planned* organizational change, Goodman and Kurke also found three general trends in the literature relating to *adaptive* change (modifying the organization to fit its environment). Two of these adaptive change themes focus on the impact of the external environment on the organization, but from quite different perspectives:

• Research with a population ecology perspective hypothesized that the survival of organizations depends not on managerial choices and reactions to the environment, but on other aspects of how the general organization functions and processes. Therefore, to understand change, they argue, study the differences in environment among successfully adaptive organizations, and examine the slow changes in structures, processes, and competencies over successive generations of changes in successful organizations. (Aldrich, 1979; Hannan and Freeman, 1977; McKelvey, 1982.)

• Researchers who focus on organizations interfacing with environments argue that managers' choices about how to interact with their environments are the most important explanation for change. (Hall, 1980; Pfeffer and Salancik, 1978; Snow and Hrebiniak, 1980).

The final theme that Goodman and Kurke examine with respect to adaptive change focuses on innovation within organizations. This literature includes the study of personality attributes of people who are or are not innovative, and examination of methods for measuring perceptions of innovation or its different phases. (Hedberg, Nystrom, and Starbuck, 1976; March and Olsen, 1976; Weick, 1977; Zald and Berger, 1978).

After their exhaustive search of the literature of change for empirical findings managers could clutch to their breasts, Goodman and Kurke concluded: "There is no neatly drawn theory of change...nor is it clear that such a theory could be constructed in the near future" (1982, p. 1). A frustrating summary, and one that leads the practicing manager to ask, "Why don't we know? After all, people have been making changes, as individuals and in groups, since the beginning of civilization!" The trouble with that quite reasonable query lies in the word "people." When studying the behavior of human beings, unfortunately, we must rely on their own testimony, and we are placed in the position of studying our own species—a less than objective prospect in some philosophical and research circles. In describing the human experience, our perceptions and perspectives (and the widely differing variables and interactive effects which occur) make precision and comparability almost impossible.

Does that sound like bad news? Here's the good news: Lack of comparable empirical findings doesn't mean that we know nothing about how change takes place or how to manage that process more effectively. At least since Ecclesiasticus, writers have opined on change, and their views add to our own intuitive personal and career experience. One of the interesting developments in the organizational change literature during the mid- and late-1980s is the approach taken by more qualitatively oriented researchers. Moving beyond the generalized prescriptive frameworks of the OD theorists of the 1950s and 1960s, they have begun to gather this collective, intuitive human experience about various elements of the change process in order to classify it and draw conclusions for action.

Kilmann and Covin's Findings About Corporate Transformation

Illustrative of this approach is the work of Kilmann and Covin (1988) in *Corporate Transformation*.

The book was the product of an interactive learning process, which included a major conference, between academics and practitioners of organizational change. The strength of this approach lends some credibility to the key themes that recur throughout *Corporate Transformation*, representing areas of agreement and disagreement regarding what organizational transformation (i.e., major, revolutionary change) is and should be.

One important consensus developed at the conference was that organizational transformation is qualitatively different from organization development. OD typically is applied to individual parts of the organization, with little awareness or involvement by senior management, and relies on focused techniques such as team building. Transformation must be conducted quite differently, Kilmann and Covin conclude, in summarizing the ten areas of agreement identified at the conference:

1. Transformational change is often a "no other choice" adaptation to a very different external environment, while OD historically was more often spurred by an interest in experimenting with new management methods rather than a concern for survival.

2. Formulating a new vision fundamentally different than the present state, may be the most important part of the transformation process.

3. Both executives and organizational members must be convinced the old ways aren't working anymore, and that a new organization can be created to replace the current inadequate one.

4. Changing job descriptions, rules, regulations, and policies is not enough to ensure a different way of functioning. Major efforts must focus on behavior changes which will involve some pain for everyone, including senior management.

5. Change must focus on the entire organization or system. However, different departments or units of the organization will absorb the change in different degrees and timeframes.

6. Organizational transformation should be led by line management, preferably by senior management, in order to ensure the necessary resources and commitment will be available.

7. Organizational transformation is "ongoing, endless, and forever" (Kilmann and Covin,

1988, p. 6), in contrast to the well-defined timeframes of OD or more traditional improvement efforts, such as management by objectives or quality circles.

8. Top management must lead the effort, but outside experts should be used to facilitate at least some parts of the process.

9. What is known about organizational transformation is rapidly changing since few large scale, organization-wide transformations are complete. "Actually, any organization that plans to wait for the methods for transformation to be proven effective is probably writing its own epitaph" (Kilmann and Covin, 1988, p. 7).

10. There are many different methods and approaches in transforming an organization, but all have the common goal to increase the flow of information across all levels of the hierarchy and across all organizational units.

While the experts and participants at this conference agreed on these major themes, they disagreed on a number of other issues, and these disagreements are important for the practicing manager who hopes to achieve an organizational turnaround:

- Is it enough for top management to make sure that everyone else will be transformed, or do they need to ensure that they themselves will be transformed along with everyone else?
- Most popular examples of organizational transformation have a dynamic person in charge. Must that person be the chief executive, or can a senior manager, if more charismatic, lead the charge?
- Should transformation start at the top or from the bottom?
- Which aspects of change are fundamental: reward systems, strategy and structure modifications, documenting new mission statements, etc?
- Can a separation be made between the participating member and the organization, in terms of the effects of change?
- Most transformation efforts seem to be *reactive* to outside changes, which have caught the organization by surprise and threatened its survival. Can top management be taught to be proactive and to learn to anticipate environmental changes?

- If transformation is to be led by line and senior managers, what is the appropriate role for staff personnel and human resource departments?

Moving Toward Action

What does all the above mean for the nonprofit manager who wants to implement major change in an organization? The following truisms emerge from the above discussion of the literature and underlie effective change planning:

- Organizational change is a process, not an event. It is difficult to pinpoint when it begins—with vague "readiness" or coherent intent—and it is integrated over a lengthy period of time, ranging from an optimistic eighteen months or so to three years and more.
- Change is a people-centered process. It may involve physical alterations in site, technology, and structure but the manager's concern ultimately will be with the involvement, commitment, resistance, and acceptance by those involved as stakeholders. In the case of the nonprofit organization, the people-centered orientation must consider impacts on board members, service volunteers, clients and donors, as well as on employees.
- Someone very senior in the organization must have a vision of what life will be like after the change effort is undertaken. The vision need not be developed with a lot of detail—that can happen as the planning process goes along—but it should be conceptualized in terms of key characteristics and with respect to how the future will differ from the present organizational position.
- A planning framework is desirable, but don't expect to dot the i's and cross the t's. It won't be possible to anticipate all the steps and potential outcomes: Indeed, to try to do so would preclude adequate participation by those whom the changes will affect.
- Beware of emulating too closely the success of others. Effective change efforts are highly contextual. What worked at a children's aid society in Kansas City may not work at the ballet, or even at a children's aid society in St. Louis. When studying the successes of others, try to focus on why those involved felt it went

well in terms of process and participation, rather than focusing on specific outcomes of their change process.

• Persuasion and participation are far stronger tools than brute force in implementing change. More force produces more resistance.

Accepting these truisms for the moment, is there any common theme that seems to run through the successful change efforts cited by the literature and from experience? The most common theme appears to be the need for effective communication throughout the organization right from the beginning (Hirschhorn, 1983; Margulies and Wallace, 1973; Odiorne, 1981). Those affected want to know and understand the reasons why the change is being undertaken, and this frequently takes more than one attempt at explanation. Those who identify closely with the organization— particularly staff, board members, and volunteers —are more likely to be on board if they receive a lot of information very early. It is frustrating and demoralizing to be among the last to know,

particularly if you feel you are (or should be) an insider! The timing of information disclosure, and careful determination of the circulation list for memoranda and verbal announcements should be a priority consideration with a nonprofit organization, which depends more than most others upon the continued good will of a wide variety of stakeholders (Mitroff, 1983). In addition, as the change process proceeds, it will be important to encourage and listen to feedback from those same stakeholders, to give credit broadly for good ideas, and to provide ongoing explanations as to why some suggestions are not used.

A Framework for Planning

Many scholars and practitioners have developed models for planning a major change process, most of which vary only moderately in sequencing and emphasis. Almost all of these follow fairly closely the classic problem-solving formula.

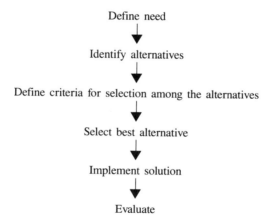

This basic model makes considerable intuitive sense: Major change is usually motivated by the desire to solve a problem by seeking a new direction. The classical model, however, is too neat for real life. It assumes a logical linear followthrough from need to solution, which most managers will not recognize from their experience. The messiness of two-steps-forward-one-step-back, nonrational learning is truer to organizational life.

The model presented in Figure 1 incorporates many features of earlier work, particularly

that of Kirkpatrick (1985), Lippitt (1981), and Kanter (1983), but it attempts to overcome some of the linearity of those models.

The outside circle divides the process into stages. Two stages, *diagnosis* and *participation*, cover the broadest territory. In this case, life follows art: These two stages are the most energy and resource intensive. Diagnosis is often thought of as a preliminary activity, but it is also important in assessing probable reactions to tentative plans, and is required again when evaluating outcomes to determine the need for fine tuning

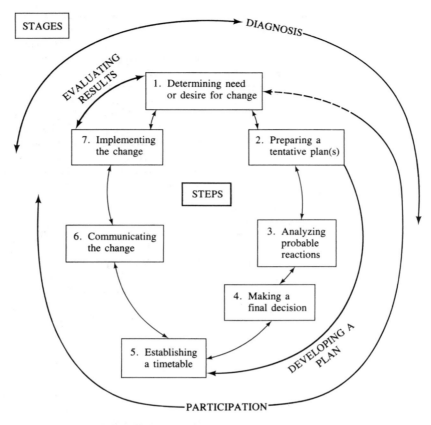

FIGURE 1. A Manager's Model for Change

or further shifts in direction. Participation permeates all the intermediate steps of the process; many would argue that it should begin when need is being determined. The other two stages, *developing a plan* and *evaluating the results*, are important but tend to be less messy and complex —and more subject to the use of established planning and evaluation tools—than diagnostic or participative models.

The inner circle sets out a number of planning steps, which follow clockwise as in the classical model. But note the double-headed arrows: They signal that new information may be discovered at any stage that requires the manager to return to a previous stage to adapt and modify. One of the limitations of this diagram is that it only indicates one-step movement (in the interest of not confusing the reader too

much). In a real organization change effort, while forward movements seldom may skip a step, backward movements may be more than one step if new data or events indicate the need for more significant restructuring of the change plan. This will become clearer as we develop the elements of the model in more detail.

Diagnosis

Apart from the need for high levels of participation in the change plan, this may be the most important change element for the manager. Unless the manager has a very broad database for scanning the organization's internal and external environments, it is all too easy to design a nifty solution for the wrong problem. Before suggesting some components of such a database, it is necessary to offer two definitional disclaimers. First, *data* usually conjures up a vision of reports, surveys, and statistics. These may be necessary; they certainly are not sufficient. In addition, the manager must develop an effective, informal network for gathering intuitive information about the environment; impressions gathered from topics of interest in the media, from informal social conversations at community gatherings, and from key informants in the stakeholder community. Much of this information will not be quantifiable, but it is valid and is particularly helpful in sorting the important "hard" statistics in survey data from the more trivial figures.

Second, this diagnostic, data-gathering period is not entirely reflective. That is, no one expects—nor is it appropriate for—the manager to delay action until all necessary information has been collected. Successful managers combine data collection and diagnosis with action, with each informing the other (Isenberg, 1984). As new information comes in and affects activity being undertaken, this may change the nature of the problem or of the proposed solution.

The object of the diagnostic activity is to determine what the real problem is, rather than attempting to find solutions to issues that turn out to be symptoms. The diagnostic process also helps the manager learn where the change efforts need to be focused, since most solutions will be implemented in nonprofit organizations without the total resources that might be desirable.

As a beginning point, the manager needs to become systematically aware of all of the forces that operate on the organization. This is particularly true for nonprofit organizations, which are mandated to operate as community trusts. They have special and privileged tax status, their board members have fiduciary responsibilities on behalf of the community, and most are dependent to some extent on donated time or dollars. Among the categories of data the manager will want to acquire for on-going decision making are the following.

An understanding of organizational context. What is the mission and purpose of the organization? Within what geographical parameters does it operate? What are the

socioeconomic and cultural indicators of the communities in which it works? What regulations and laws constrain it? Who are its competitors? With what organizations does it normally cooperate or form coalitions? Who are its clients and what are their service characteristics? From what community pools does it draw its board members, service volunteers, and most of its donations? What is its public and private funding environment?

Knowledge of its organizational culture. What are the norms (unwritten expectations of behavior) that staff and volunteers seem to operate within? What have been the historic styles of management; more autocratic or more participatory? Is the style of the organization formal or informal in terms of how people dress, address one another, use language, run meetings, or observe time and schedules? Is information shared freely among many levels of the organization, or is it treated as "bargaining chips" of power? What are the organizational rituals around the announcement and observance of promotions, retirements, and firings? What lessons do the organization's "war stories" communicate when they are repeated to new staff or retold at informal gatherings? (See Blake and Mouton, 1982; Deal and Kennedy, 1982; Kilmann, 1984; Ott, 1989; Schein, 1985).

Understanding functional tasks performed within the organization. What jobs are performed by employees or volunteers? Are many of these jobs routinized, with little variety or creativity? Or are they highly variable, with a requirement for independent and mature judgment? Do most jobs require that everything was done yesterday, or are time horizons more leisurely? How interdependent are employees among themselves and with volunteers? What are the ongoing training and professional development requirements in order to maintain quality service and fulfill legal obligations?

Knowing the people who make the organization run. What are the sets of skills and knowledges that employees and volunteers must have before they can perform the functional tasks of the organization? What values of human service delivery do the organization's people have or does the organization try to inculcate? What are the learning styles of key staff and volunteers? What assumptions do they make about the organization or the nature of the service it delivers? What interests and professional or political biases are part of the long-term goals of the staff and volunteers?

Understanding the organization's formal structure. What structure does the organization chart show? Is it largely flat, or are there several layers of hierarchy? What are the control systems around decision making and use of resources? What are the policies on recruitment, selection, rewards, and advancement? How are reporting relationships determined?

Understanding space and technological resources. What is the physical setting(s) of the organization? What square footage, number and size of rooms, and possible configurations are available in the event of a change in direction or program? What files, records, and statistical data are kept and in what form? What means of communication are available to staff among themselves and with others outside the organization (e.g., electronic mail, fax, etc.)? In what ways do the physical settings and the technological resources affect the ability of the organization to adapt to changing environments?

As noted earlier, the most important aspect of a good diagnostic database is improved capacity to identify basic problems requiring change and improved ability to prioritize when resources are limited. But there are other advantages to having a good diagnostic database. It helps the manager to assess individual and group willingness and capacity for change. It also allows the manager to assess his or her own motivation and resources to initiate and sustain change. Remember the lengthy time required to integrate major change into the organization? Are you ready to invest between eighteen and thirty-six months in a change effort if your diagnosis indicates it may be inappropriate or futile without preliminary foundations being laid?

Good diagnosis also allows the manager to determine progressive change objectives during the planning period, and to determine whether outside consultants would be useful or necessary.

Finally, it enables the manager to make timing decisions. Is the organization ready for a major program change? Should this be preceded by reorganization? Will it take longer than expected because of some environmental factors identified?

Developing a Plan

This stage of change planning is largely a pencil-and-paper exercise. The manager (in consultation with a few key stakeholders) should assess how many steps or stages will be involved in the change, and who needs to be involved at each point, as well as how that is to happen. Will additional data need to be researched? Are extra resources—financial or human—going to be required temporarily or permanently? There are a number of planning texts, manuals and workbooks available to the nonprofit manager that provide suggestions, forms, and processes for this stage of change planning (Bryce, 1987; Connors, 1980; Espy, 1986; Hardy, 1972; O'Connell, 1976).

Participation

This most critical part of the change process involves two overarching considerations. First, what will be the strategies for involving and motivating others? The manager will need the advice of key staff and board members to determine this, and it may not be as easy as it sounds—especially if staff or volunteers are embittered, cynical, or apathetic as a result of previous organization performance. Often, some "teachable moment" must be captured in the organization's lifecycle to rejuvenate energies, such as the process of appointing a new executive director or implementing a major new program.

Second, what extra training or skills will staff and volunteers require to effectively perform in the changed conditions? The knowledge gained during diagnosis with respect to skill levels and learning styles of organizational members will be useful here, as will the analysis of functional tasks within the organization.

Overcoming Resistance to Change

Finally, the manager will need to forecast the biggest fears and problems that staff and volunteers will have as the change unfolds, and how these can be dealt with. Rosabeth Moss Kanter (1985) identifies several common reasons why resistance to change is encountered in organizations. Some of the more important resisters are discussed below, with a few suggested remedies.

Loss of Control

When someone cries: "But we've always done it this way at North Road Baptist!", their concern may not be simply preservation of tradition and routine. They may feel the change is being done *to* them; the situation makes them feel powerless. Such reactions are especially common when the change seems planned by only a very few people, and information is held closely and presented as a *fait accompli* to the larger group. When this happens, the ways of the past—and picayune rules of procedure—assume great importance.

The solution, logically enough, is large doses of widespread involvement in the change planning. Board members, staff, and service volunteers all need to find points of input for their energies in order that the final effort is owned by everyone. One way to accomplish this is through breaking the change effort into discrete tasks and assigning them to committees and task forces. Altier (1986) provides a number of useful guidelines to managers who wish to use task forces effectively. They can be particularly suitable to nonprofit organizational environments because they enable so many functional and organizational stakeholders to have a role.

Altier cautions that each task force needs to be directly linked to the decision-making structure of the organization by having a key executive as a member of it, providing proper leadership. The task force should have a well-defined and time-limited task, so that it knows what it is to do and when its work is done. Its terms of reference should spell out: What is expected is a well-conceived course of action, not just nonspecific recommendations.

Insofar as possible within the organization's governing structure, the task force should be given the power to resolve issues or make limited decisions without being subject to many subsequent reviews. Neither staff nor volunteers will believe the organization is serious about using their input in the change process if an in-group

on the board or in the executive offices has the power to ignore or significantly change any work they do.

Apart from carefully written terms of reference, the most important aspect of establishing task forces is determining membership. Who among staff and volunteers are most knowledgeable about this particular aspect of the situation? Who cares the most about it and who may bring a unique point of view to the discussion? The task force should include people who are knowledgeable but also people who have influence in the various constituencies they represent so that the decision reached can be sold to others. Members should *want* to be there: "They should be excited about the opportunity and consider it a compliment to have been asked to participate (and they also should consider it a necessary, but short-lived imposition on their time" (Altier, 1986, p. 71).

Altier suggests six or eight people are an ideal task force size—small enough to make certain that every member has an important role, but large enough to avoid excessive caution. However, if more people are necessary to bring all the perspectives together, do it and just be prepared for the increased time that will be required in the analysis. The task force should get started as soon as the need is identified and, if specific data are needed to come to a conclusion, task force members should identify those needs specifically as they proceed.

One knotty problem in establishing task forces when the political environment is sensitive is choosing the leader. If the leader is too powerful, members may not want to express their opinions fully or consider a wide range of options. If the leader has no formal authority in the organization, others who are more powerful may dominate the meetings. If the leader represents one constituency over another, members may suspect there is a hidden agenda in that person's appointment. Leaders may be chosen either from inside or outside the organization and, for nonprofits, this is an ideal opportunity to involve new volunteers or consultants who are willing to provide a specific amount of time to a single task (but aren't yet ready to take the plunge to serve on the board). The first consideration must be that the leader has expertise in handling groups. Management consultants and employees of major corporate training departments are good places to look for volunteer task force leaders.

In terms of output, the task force should be asked to keep it short and sweet. A few pages should be enough, outlining its conclusions, the key reasons underlying these, and the recommended course of action.

To be effective as part of a larger change effort, the work of each committee or task force must be coordinated and seen to be leading to the common goal. This requires a coordinating body, which includes senior staff and volunteers and leaders of each of the task forces to establish a peer environment that heightens a sense of accountability to the common task. Each task force needs to know when its conclusions are needed and which other groups are depending upon this work to be completed by the established deadline.

An overall *critical path*, setting out all of the tasks that must be completed and the independent–dependent relationships and task sequencing, can be very helpful to all stakeholders. When the Canadian province of Manitoba decided to reorganize its child and family services in the early 1980s, the plan involved dissolving one large nonprofit agency and replacing it with six others to be governed by community boards and mandated (for the first time) to deliver preventive as well as remedial services. The changeover was to occur during an eighteen-month period. Nearly 300 individuals were serving on planning task forces and committees; collateral agencies (law enforcement, schools, public health) were to be involved; and more than 1,000 staff (belonging to three unions) were to be deployed in the new system. The provincial government subcontracted with a nonprofit agency, the Social Planning Council of Winnipeg, to oversee and coordinate this massive process. Approximately 500 key tasks were identified in the change planning process, and these were entered into a computerized critical path planning program. Workshops were held with all committees and employees involved in the changeover, including interested community groups, to explain the critical path process and how it worked and could be adjusted. Throughout the eighteen months, the plan was updated on a monthly basis, and the critical path

method—at first criticized as being inappropriate for a human-service environment—became very popular with the system's stakeholders. Everyone could see the total project and all its components. Everyone knew when certain tasks were to be done and by whom. When a task group seemed to be falling behind in its work, others called them into accountability by pointing out that they could not complete the next tasks without this input. Union representatives were able to spot places where they should have input or make a contribution, or where potential problems might arise if they were not resolved at an early stage.

In short, those affected by the change felt involved in the process and knew they had not lost control. This fear of loss of control may be even more critical in the nonprofit sector than in others because individuals are not only vested in their careers, but usually are extremely committed to the values of the organization and to the clientele it serves.

The planning structure described above is complex, often cumbersome for those who must coordinate it, highly energy-intensive and, on the face of it, very time-consuming at the front end of the process. But, the Manitoba system changeover was completed on schedule, with no labor disruptions or grievances, no service disruptions to the clientele, and with the election of six new boards of agencies plus development of bylaws and training programs for those boards. (See Sale and Wolf, 1985, for fuller discussion of this case.)

Excessive Uncertainty

Any major change will involve a greater or lesser degree of uncertainty for organizational participants. Assuming there is a well-defined goal or vision for the future, none of us can be completely sure what will happen tomorrow, let alone next year. This lack of certainty is natural and, far from being totally negative, can provide extra motivation to make positive results happen. However, in major organizational change there can be a false level of uncertainty: Information that is known is not widely enough shared. This type of uncertainty can be combatted by using some of the techniques described above: Breaking the larger change effort into smaller steps, drawing connecting lines between sequential and independent-dependent steps, and involving many participants on committees and task forces.

Still more uncertainty can be dispelled through a well thought out information and communication program during the changeover. Special newsletters, regularly scheduled briefing sessions at staff and board meetings, occasional informal and "brown-bag" question-and-answer sessions with senior staff and board members, and similar techniques can all be used to keep people informed of progress. Failure to pay close attention to the need for communication can cause people to make mistakes, to take inappropriate actions or decisions that make the planning process more inflexible, and can encourage widespread disaffection or dispute. This is true for changes of all kinds, but particularly for those that include some negative components, such as when the organization is cutting back or retrenching.

A first sign that the information program needs boosting is an epidemic of rumors. Rumors are not only diversionary and destructive but also can result in much more management time and energy being devoted to correcting the misinformed environment they produce. Hirschhorn (1983) writes that rumors have at least four purposes: to structure and reduce anxiety; to make sense of limited or fragmented information; to organize a strategic posture; and to signal status or power.

If stakeholders are unable to relate their fears about the future to a specific set of events or decisions, rumor or conjecture allows them to focus on specific alternatives and decision makers. Oddly enough, this may reduce anxiety "because people can now mobilize to fight a specific enemy rather than a vague fear" (p. 50). Rumors can structure individuals' sense of panic, so they have a sense of options open to them in terms of resistance or other alternatives. Rumors also give people an excuse to talk with one another about their fears, and sharing creates a collective bonding.

Rumors that seek to make sense of the situation are designed to fill in critical gaps. Management may have told stakeholders part of the story, but it's a part that in isolation does not make sense. The rumor that emerges will provide logical threads tying together seemingly unconnected bits of information in order to provide a credible explanation of events.

The two other sources of rumors that Hirschhorn identifies are not as well-intended. Staff or board members may use rumors as a tactic to create coalitions, organize resistance, or to achieve some purpose unrelated to current events but rooted in past hostile situations or relationships. Or, some staff or board members may simply develop and repeat rumors to show that they have status and power: "I'm an insider and, with respect to this rumor, you're an outsider" (1983, p. 52).

No one can prevent rumors but there are effective strategies for managing them. Some of Hirschhorn's suggestions for managing those that arise from excessive uncertainty are:

- Specify target dates when decisions will be made;
- Clarify sets of decision alternatives under different scenarios so participants will know how the organization can respond to different events;
- Create a timeline that relates the change planning process within the organization to other important deadlines outside the organization, such as deliberations by legislative committees, deadlines of foundations or government agencies, etc.;
- Encourage worst-case thinking so that people can bring their greatest fears into the light of full discussion; and
- Reach decisions which are viable across a range of possible events.

Real Threats

In many major changes, there will be real losers; individuals whose status will be changed in ways they do not find positive, or the organization itself may experience reverses that make it less powerful and not as attractive to staff and volunteers as it previously was. In both these situations, it is always best to let those affected know as soon as possible. Putting off the bad news creates extra stress and anxiety, and prevents people from making choices that will allow them to get on with their lives. It can be a relief to know the worst, rather than continuing with a black cloud of uncertainty over one's head.

Above all, management should not pretend that no one will be hurt if, indeed, they may be. People will quite rightly be outraged if a negative surprise is sprung on them at the last minute. They will feel they have been lied to, and that senior management did not trust them with information that was critical to their own life planning. Obviously, when only a few individuals will be adversely affected, these persons should be identified early in the process and private conversations should be held with them to identify the situation and outline alternatives. Wherever possible, the organization should be supportive of actions that will make the negative change as positive as possible. For example, if some employees are to be laid off, they can be given advance notice and provided with office and clerical support to begin their job search right away. Counseling and other supports can be made available by the organization, as well.

If an entire office or program is being closed down, individual conversations should be preceded by an announcement and informal discussion session with the entire group, so that everyone receives the bad news at the same time. The manager should be prepared to discuss a wide range of alternatives at that meeting. Will employees have jobs made available to them in other offices or programs? Have all sources of interim or ongoing funding been explored? How much time remains before funding runs out? What kind of termination package and services will the organization offer? What rules of procedure or priority will govern any reassignment choices?

Not Valuing Past Contributions

The need and desire for a major change is often presented by a relatively new manager. The new broom may need to sweep clean, but if the manager needs to continue working with the same staff, a feather-duster approach may be more effective than vigorous use of steel wool. There is no need for the new manager to denigrate preceding organizational actions and programs as either idiotic or antediluvian. Most of the people will have been an active part of that past: They put their hearts and souls into accomplishing its goals. More appropriately, the new manager can cite those things that were of value in past programs, and what they contributed to

the needs of that time. Now, however, environmental conditions both inside and outside the organization call for a different approach. Just as staff and volunteers worked effectively to accomplish previous program goals and strategies, the manager is certain they will have the strength and flexibility to adapt to what the organization needs now.

Concerns About Future Competence

Both staff and volunteers may resist a new proposal if they fear they do not have skills or competencies to function effectively in the changed environment. These fears can be overcome by, first, strong assurances by the manager and the board that individuals will be supported in undertaking training programs to upgrade skills where required. Second, this is an ideal opportunity to utilize a committee or task force approach to identify new job tasks in the changed environment and to specify the competencies and training programs that will be required. Staff members also will need to be assured that they will have a "break-in" period to practice newly acquired skills and become comfortable with these—and that stupid questions will be cheerfully entertained by senior management during this period.

Past Resentments

Every organization has at least one, possibly more, staff or board member who is bitter, cynical, and feels the organization has always done him or her wrong. Any new suggestion for change is treated as an opportunity to once again recite the litany of unresolved grievances. In some cases, careful listening by the manager may result in an option emerging that deals with some of these past feelings of bitterness and reenergizes the individual. If the manager inherited the problem and was not part of the past grievance, it sometimes is sufficient to give the individual a chance to air the grievance and then to say: "You're right, Joe, there seems to have been some injustice in the past but there is nothing I can do to right that. How can we get on with making the future better for us and the organization?" This acknowledges the person's feelings of injustice or rejection, but puts responsibility squarely with them to become part of the new solution.

Realistically, however, the bitterness may be so ingrained that neither of these more happy scenarios will result. If retirement or dismissal are not imminent options, the time-honored bureaucratic strategies of lateral shuffling or gradual isolation may be the only alternatives.

There are many more reasons for resisting change than the ones just discussed, but these represent some of the most common and pervasive resisters. If a major change is contemplated in an organization, rest assured at least one and possibly all of the above will bubble up during the change process. The important thing to remember is that there are remedial strategies for almost all resistance. What is required is careful analysis of the opposition to the new change, a willingness to listen and involve participants in decisions, and flexibility about adjusting both the process and the timing of the planned change.

From the "people participation" perspective, there is one other important factor to consider during this phase of change planning. People who have wholeheartedly given themselves to the development of the past will grieve its death. If a cohesive work group must be reassigned, if a long-term program must be closed down, if a physical office location must be moved—all of these are situations where grief must be dealt with, even if participants are looking forward to future changes.

The manager must legitimize the grieving process so that it is not seen as disloyalty to the change plans. One way to do this is to hold a wake. The author was once the founding executive director of a management support organization for nonprofit agencies, sponsored by a university and a community foundation, and advised by an active community board. After a five-year demonstration project, it seemed appropriate for a variety of reasons to close Project Manage and to incorporate many of its activities into more established community organizations. However, "Manage" (as it came to be known) had been extremely successful and had utilized large numbers of volunteers, many of whom had strong emotional attachments to the project and did not want to see it closed. After working through all the appropriate quasi-legal processes and communicating the closure to its constituents, "Manage" held a wake, complete with fiddle music, Irish whiskey, food, and eulogies. A casket borrowed from the drama department held its publications, black balloons and funeral candles decorated the room. Arriving mourners were issued black armbands. Representatives of advisory groups each had a chance to talk about their group's role and commitment to the project and its values. Hysterically funny and morbidly embarrassing incidents in the project's history were recounted, and everyone patted each other on the back for a job well done. The event received wide and positive media coverage but, more important, those who had made Project Manage a success were able to let it die a graceful death, to be reincarnated (in part) in other places and other ways. Enthusiasm for the new was able to succeed affection for the old.

Evaluating the Results

The final stage in the change model is evaluation of the results. After all is said and done, after everyone has invested enormous energy and resources into turning the organization toward a new direction, what has changed? Does the organization provide more or better service? Is the clientele better off, unaffected, or less well served than before? What are the specific positive effects on the clients, staff, board members, other agencies, volunteers, and the community at large? What are the negative effects of the change (almost always there are some even if on balance the change is positive)? What adjustments can the organization make at this point to improve the outcome still further?

There are a variety of formal and informal mechanisms for assessing results, and a wide range of texts and manuals available to the nonprofit manager who wishes to learn more about these (Anthony and Herzlinger, 1975; Hatry, 1973; Wholey, et al 1986). Suffice it to say in this space that in a nonprofit organization process the evaluation should be as collective as the diagnostic and participation aspects of change planning. Just as all the organization's stakeholders are interested in being involved in affecting the change of direction, so they will want to be involved in assessing the outcomes.

Is it all worth it? The answer will be highly contextual. In some cases, change will be forced on the organization because of external conditions; in other cases, individual managers will drive the organization toward their internal visions. The choices made by some organizations to change will lead them in new and fruitful directions, allowing them to more effectively fulfill their mandate of service to the community. The choices of others will result in their decline or demise, which may be appropriate or not. What is certain is that change—like death and taxes—is unavoidable. The perceptive and astute manager will marshal experience and skills gained in all parts of his or her life to increase the range of choices and the quality of decision making to meet the demands of a changing world. Vision, commitment, maturity, sensitivity, inclusiveness, and an action orientation—these qualities and skills more than entrepreneurial wizardry or dazzling political panache, are required by the successful nonprofit manager in the turbulent environment of the last decade of this millennium.

References

Aldrich, H. E. (1979). *Organizations and environments.* Englewood Cliffs, NJ: Prentice-Hall.

Altier, W. J. (1986). Task forces—An effective management tool. *Sloan Management Review, 27*(3): 69–76.

Anthony, R. N., & Herzlinger, R. (1975). *Management control in nonprofit organizations.* Homewood, IL: Irwin.

Argyris, C., & Schön, D. A. (1978). *Organizational learning: A theory of action perspective.* Reading, MA: Addison-Wesley.

Blake, R., & Mouton, J. S. (1982). *Productivity: The human side.* New York: Amacom.

Bryce, H. J. (1987). *Financial and strategic management for nonprofit organizations.* Englewood Cliffs, NJ: Prentice-Hall.

Connors, T. D. (Ed.). (1980). *The Nonprofit Organization Handbook.* New York: McGraw-Hill.

Deal, T. E., & Kennedy, A. A. (1982). *Corporate cultures: Rites and rituals of corporate life.* Reading, MA: Addison-Wesley.

Dunn, W. N., & Swierczek, F. W. (1977). Planned organizational change: Toward grounded theory. *Journal of Applied Behavioral Science, 13*(2): 135–157.

Espy, S. N. (1986). *Handbook of strategic planning for nonprofit organizations.* New York: Praeger.

Friedlander, F., & Brown, L. D. (1974). Organization development. *Annual Review of Psychology, 25:* 313–341.

Goodman, P. S., & Kurke, L. B. (1982). Studies of change in organizations: A status report. In Paul S. Goodman (Ed.), *Change in organizations.* San Francisco: Jossey-Bass.

Hall, W. (1980). Survival strategies in a hostile environment. *Harvard Business Review, 58:* 75–85.

Hannan, M. T., & Freeman, J. (1977). The population ecology of organizations. *American Journal of Sociology, 82:* 929–965.

Hardy, J. M. (1972). *Corporate planning for nonprofit organizations.* New York: YMCA.

Hatry, H. (1973). Practical program evaluation for state and local government officials. Washington, DC: The Urban Institute.

Hedberg, B. L., Nystrom, P. C., & Starbuck, W. H. (1976). Camping on seesaws: Prescription for a self-designing organization. *Administrative Science Quarterly, 21:* 41–65.

Hirschhorn, L. (1983). Managing Rumors. In L. Hirschhorn (Ed.), *Cutting back.* San Francisco: Jossey-Bass.

Isenberg, D. (1984). How senior managers think. *Harvard Business Review, 62*(4): 81–90.

Kanter, R. M. (1983). *The change masters.* New York: Simon and Schuster.

Kanter, R. M. (1985). Managing the human side of change. *American Management Association Management Review, 4:* 52–56.

Katz, D., & Kahn, R. L. (1978). *The social psychology of organizations (2nd ed.).* New York: Wiley.

Kilmann, R. H. (1984). *Beyond the quick fix: Managing five tracks to organizational success.* San Francisco: Jossey-Bass.

Kilmann, R. H., & Covin, T. J. (1988). *Corporate transformation: Revitalizing organizations for a competitive world.* San Francisco: Jossey-Bass.

Kirkpatrick, D. L. (1985). *How to manage change effectively.* San Francisco: Jossey-Bass.

Kochan, T. A., & Dyer, L. (1976). A model of organizational change in the context of union-management relations. *Journal of Applied Behavioral Science, 12:* 59–78.

Lewin, K. (1951). *Field theory in social science.* D. Cartwright (Ed.). New York: Harper & Row.

Lippitt, R. (1981). *Making organizations humane and productive.* New York: Wiley.

March, J. G., & Olsen, J. P. (1976). *Ambiguity and choice in organizations.* Bergen, Norway: Universitetsforlaget.

Margulies, N., & Wallace, J. (1973). *Organization change: Techniques and application.* Glenview, IL: Scott, Foresman.

McKelvey, W. (1982) *Organizational systematics: Taxonomy, evolution, classification.* Berkeley: University of California Press.

Mitroff, J. (1983). *Stakeholders of the organization mind.* San Francisco: Jossey-Bass.

O'Connell, B. (1976). *Effective leadership in voluntary organizations.* New York: Association Press.

Odiorne, G. (1981). *The change resisters.* Englewood Cliffs, NJ: Prentice-Hall.

Ott, J. S. (1989). *The organizational culture perspective.* Pacific Grove, CA: Brooks/Cole.

Pfeffer, J., & Salancik, G. R. (1978). *The external control of organizations: A resource dependence perspective.* New York: Harper & Row.

Sale, E. T., & Wolf, J. T. (1985). Using network analysis in human service planning: Fitting the pieces together. *Business Quarterly, 50*(3): 30–35.

Schaller, L. (1978). *The change agent.* Nashville, TN: Abingdon Press.

Schein, E. H. (1985). How culture forms, develops, and changes. In R. H. Kilmann, M. J. Saxton, & R. Serpa (Eds.), *Gaining control of the corporate culture.* San Francisco: Jossey-Bass.

Snow, C. C., & Hrebiniak, L. G. (1980). Strategy, distinctive competence, and organizational performance. *Administrative Science Quarterly, 25:* 317–336.

Weick, K. E. (1977). Organization design: Organizations as self-designing systems. *Organizational Dynamics, 6:* 31–46.

Wholey, J. S., Abramson, M., & Bellavita, C. (1986). *Performance and credibility: Developing excellence in public and nonprofit organizations.* Lexington, MA: Lexington Books.

White, S. E., & Mitchell, T. R. (1976). Organization development: A review of research content and research design. *Academy of Management Review, 1*(2): 57–73.

Zald, M., & Berger, M. (1978). Social movements in organizations: Coup d'etat, insurgency and mass movements. *American Journal of Sociology, 83:* 823–861.

Entrepreneurship and Promotional Management

Introduction

Marketing, entrepreneurship, and promotional management are relatively new areas of interest in the nonprofit sector. The first published argument that nonprofit organizations should engage in marketing even though they face somewhat unique circumstances (that we have been able to locate) is in Philip Kotler and Sidney Levy's (1969) article, "Broadening the Concept of Marketing." The first textbook on the subject, also by Kotler, was not published until 1975. Although some nonprofits have engaged in business enterprise-type activities at least since the turn of this century,[1] only scattered attention was paid to such income-generating activities prior to 1980. Since 1980, most nonprofit organizations have increased the size, breadth, and form of their income generating functions. Many of the causes are identified in earlier articles in this collection.[2] Skloot (1987, pp. 380–381) cites four major reasons:

1. Double-digit inflation in the late 1970s greatly increased the expenditures of nonprofit organizations; new revenues were needed, and traditional fund-raising approaches clearly would not suffice.

2. When the Reagan administration reduced federal domestic spending in functional areas where nonprofits had long been active—most notably in the delivery of human services—nonprofit organizations had to seek out new sources of income.

3. The Reagan administration philosophically favored turning over services to private sector organizations and, in essence, encouraged nonprofit organizations to adopt commercial, entrepreneurial-type, income-generating strategies.

4. With government funding on the decline, competition for corporate and foundation grants increased without commensurate increases in philanthropic funds.

Although the true impacts of the 1986 tax reform act on charitable giving are not yet known, the higher cost of donations (see Scrivner in Chapter Two) may decrease traditional contributions and thus provide a fifth reason for increasingly aggressive income-generating activities by organizations in the nonprofit sector.

This chapter focuses on nonprofit organizations' entrepreneurial-type business ventures and their marketing of goods and services. Philip Kotler (1982) defines an entrepreneurial organization as "one with a high motivation and capability to identify new opportunities and convert them into successful business" (p. 113). Dennis Young (1981) espouses a similar view but is slightly more inclusive. According to Young, entrepreneurs "found new organizations, develop and implement new programs and methods, organize and expand new services, and redirect the activities of faltering organizations" (p. 136). Kotler seems to limit entrepreneurship to new business ventures, whereas Young appears also to permit inclusion of other innovative activities. We agree with both of them that opportunism—creating and capitalizing on chances to make money, "sell" ideas, or meet emergent needs—is at the core of entrepreneurship.

Entrepreneurship is a frame of mind, a willingness to create and to be receptive to opportunities, an orientation toward risk-taking ventures. Business enterprise activity has been the focus of nonprofit entrepreneurial thinking in the 1980s. However, nonprofit organizations can also be entrepreneurial in their approaches to funds from historically productive sources. They cannot allow the current interest in entrepreneurship to allow them to forget their traditional revenue-generating activities. The tried-and-true revenue generators continue to be extremely important sources of funds. Most nonprofit organizations are experienced in obtaining money from at least one of them, and nonprofit managers need to be good at getting money from them. But perhaps most importantly, business ventures are not the best solutions to all nonprofits' needs for additional revenue. They "can be dangerous. They can compromise the organization's charitable mission, disrupt operations, raise thorny legal issues, and cause substantial financial harm" (Skloot, 1987, p. 381).

In addition to the articles on entrepreneurship and marketing, this chapter concludes with two time-tested, revenue-generating nonprofit functions: grassroots community fundraising and grantsmanship.

First, however, Benson Shapiro's 1973 *Harvard Business Review* article, "Marketing for Nonprofit Organizations," reports on one of the very earliest field research studies on marketing in private nonprofit organizations (nonprofit organizations that are not government supported). Shapiro seeks to demonstrate the importance of management having an *exchange process orientation* (an orientation that the organization should offer something of value in exchange for needed resources) in the marketing function of nonprofit organizations. There are three core marketing tasks of the nonprofit manager: resource attraction, resource allocation, and persuasion. He describes the use of communication, distribution, pricing, and product in the performance of these tasks.

In his 1982 book, *Marketing for Nonprofit Organizations*, Philip Kotler identifies three levels of nonprofit organization entrepreneurship:

• *The Responsive Organization*; "one that makes every effort to sense, serve, and satisfy the needs and wants of its clients and publics within the constraints of its budget" (p. 33).

• *The Adaptive Organization*; an organization that "operates systems for monitoring and interpreting important environmental changes and shows a readiness to revise its mission, objectives, strategies, organization, and systems to be maximally aligned with its opportunities" (p. 76).

• *The Entrepreneurial Organization*; one with "high motivation and capability to identify new opportunities and convert them into successful businesses" (p. 113).

In "The Responsive Organization: Meeting Consumer Needs," which we have included in this chapter, Kotler describes responsive organizations as ones "that stand out from their competitors in the consumer's mind" because they are able to "imbue their employees with a spirit of service to the customers." Kotler describes the important steps in implementing a responsive nonprofit organization strategy: Develop a clear sense of organizational mission; create an exchange process orientation; identify important publics; establish an organizational image that communicates the mission and orientation to the publics; and focus on creating customer satisfaction.

Dennis Young has been the most prolific and, in our opinion, the most sensitive observer of nonprofit entrepreneurship during the turbulent 1980s. Young's contribution to this volume,

"Entrepreneurship and Organizational Change in the Human Services," consists of excerpts from the introduction to his 1985 *Casebook of Management for Nonprofit Organizations*. Young's underlying theme is "the understanding of how and why organizations undertake change and how changes in programs and organizational structure can be effectively developed and administered" (p. 1). Effective management of a nonprofit organization requires leadership that can foresee the need to change directions and "to lead an organization through constructive adaptations in advance of debilitating crises" (p. 5).

Young proposes four general perspectives on how and why change occurs:

1. Changes often occur when (and because) an organization is solving important internal problems;
2. Changes happen because entrepreneurs are present to exploit opportunities;
3. Organizational changes usually "reflect trends and long-term developments in the social, economic, and technological environment"; and
4. Change typically follows the culmination of an important new idea.

Although Young cautions nonprofit managers not to seek ready-made approaches to entrepreneurship, he presents several "common principles and lessons that seem to underlie success" for nonprofit enterprise ventures.

The articles by Shapiro, Kotler, and Young thus set the stage for our two articles about specific aspects of entrepreneurship: business enterprise-type activities and obtaining foundation grants.

The broad cutbacks in government funding for human services during the 1980s forced many nonprofits to provide a broader range of services to more people, often with fewer direct financial resources (see Chapter Two). In "Enterprise in the Nonprofit Sector," (which is reprinted in this chapter), James Crimmins and Mary Kiel (1983) report on the findings of their survey that show that nonprofit organizations, faced with staff layoffs and program reductions, have used "enterprise to diversify their funding bases, expand their programs, and stay afloat while other sources of support are vanishing." The survey also provides an historical perspective on entrepreneurial enterprises in nonprofits. The authors provide empirical evidence of some reasons for nonprofit enterprise successes, including, for example, attitude, business savvy, and degree of compatibility with the organizational mission.

Crimmins and Kiel underscore the importance of cooperation and development of an attitude of working toward common goals among the service-providing and the entrepreneurial personnel in a nonprofit organization. The survey found that the successful nonprofit enterprise seems to flourish in two disparate settings: "Among the asset-lean, grass roots nonprofits struggling to survive, or in the larger, asset-rich organizations that have the leeway to take risks and develop enterprise programs." Most importantly, however, enterprise is important to nonprofits, and it needs to grow, "but under careful conditions and with the proper context. The bottom line is the institution's mission, and enterprise is just another means to that end."

The chapter's final selection, "How to Qualify for a Foundation Grant: A Sophisticated Primer," by Theodore and Randall Kauss, offers advice and examples from their personal experiences as veteran grantsmen, and from Ted Kauss as a grantsmaker. The authors' practical suggestions for increasing success with grants are grouped into three categories: *Basics* (preparing to write a grant request), *Bolts and Nuts* (developing a grant proposal), and *Believers/Achievers* (making a formal presentation and following up on a proposal whether or not it is funded).

Kauss and Kauss conclude with twelve summary tips to serve as guides in qualifying for a foundation grant and satisfying the donor.

Notes

1. For example, the Metropolitan Museum of Art in New York City opened its first official sales store in 1908.

2. See the Introduction to Chapter Two and the articles in that chapter by Salamon and Scrivner.

References

Alexander, J., & Brooks, D. C. (1986). New dimensions in board-CEO relations. *Trustee, 39*(6), 24–27.

Coddington, D. C., & Moore, K. D. (1987). *Market-driven strategies in health care.* San Francisco: Jossey-Bass.

Cooper, P. D. (Ed.). (1985). *Health care marketing: Issues and trends.* Rockville, MD: Aspen.

Crimmins, J. C., & Kiel, M. (1983). Introduction. In J. C. Crimmins & M. Kiel, *Enterprise in the nonprofit sector* (pp. 14–32). Washington, DC: Partners for Livable Places and, New York: The Rockefeller Brothers Fund.

Fine, S. (1981). *The marketing of ideas and social issues.* Columbus, OH: Grid.

Flanagan, J. (1982). How to do it. In J. Flanagan, *The grass roots fundraising book* (2d ed.). Chicago: The Swallow Press.

Fox, K. F. A., & Kotler, P. (Fall 1980). The marketing of social causes: The first ten years. *The Journal of Marketing,* 24–33.

Gaedeke, R. M. (1977). *Marketing in private and public nonprofit organizations: Perspectives and illustrations.* Santa Monica, CA: Goodyear.

Grennon, J., & Barsky, R. (1980). Case studies in nursing home entrepreneurship. (PONPO working paper.) New Haven, CT: Yale University, Institute for Social and Policy Studies.

Kotler, P. (August 1978). Educational packagers: A modest proposal. *Futurist,* 239–242.

Kotler, P. (1982). The responsive organization: Meeting consumer needs. In P. Kotler, *Marketing for nonprofit organizations* (2d ed.). (pp. 32–74). Englewood Cliffs, NJ: Prentice-Hall.

Kotler, P., & Levy, S. J. (January 1969). Broadening the concept of marketing. *Journal of Marketing,* 10–15.

Lachner, B. J. (Fall 1977). Marketing—an emerging management challenge. *Health Care Management Review,* p. 27.

Lovelock, C. H. (1984). *Services marketing.* Englewood Cliffs, NJ: Prentice-Hall.

Lovelock, C. H., & Weinberg, C. B. (Eds.). *Readings in public and nonprofit marketing.* Palo Alto, CA: Scientific Press.

Moskowitz, J. (1989). Increasing government support for nonprofits: Is it worth the cost? In V. A. Hodgkinson & R. W. Lyman (Eds.), *The future of the non-profit sector.* San Francisco: Jossey-Bass.

Shapiro, B. P. (September–October 1973). Marketing for nonprofit organizations. *Harvard Business Review,* 123–132.

Skloot, E. (1987). Enterprise and commerce in nonprofit organizations. In W. W. Powell (Ed.), *The nonprofit sector: A research handbook* (pp. 380–393). New Haven, CT: Yale University Press.

Weinberg, C. B. (1980). Marketing mix decision rules for nonprofit organizations. In J. Sheth (Ed.), *Research in marketing* (pp. 191–234). Greenwich, CT: JAI Press.

Williams, H. S. (July–August, 1980). Entrepreneurs in the non-profit world. *In Business.*

Young, D. R. (1981). Entrepreneurship and the behavior of nonprofit organizations: Elements of a theory. In M. White (Ed.), *Nonprofit firms in a three-sector economy* (pp. 135–162). Washington, DC: The Urban Institute.

Young, D. R. (1983). Entrepreneurship. In D. R. Young, *If not for profit, for what?* (pp. 21–41). Lexington, MA: Lexington Books.

Young, D. R. (1985). Entrepreneurship and organizational change in the human services. In D. R. Young, *Casebook of management for nonprofit organizations* (pp. 1–21). New York: The Haworth Press.

ARTICLE 22 ─────────
Marketing for Nonprofit Organizations
Benson P. Shapiro

For years, certain successful marketing techniques that were once considered to belong almost exclusively to profit-motivated business enterprises have been used advantageously by alert managers in private nonprofit organizations. However, many other managers of nonprofit organizations have failed to recognize that marketing is as intrinsic to the nonprofit sector as it is to the business community.

There are four key business concepts that provide the basis for marketing thought and action in the nonprofit environment. Consider:

1. The *self-interest* aspect of the transaction or exchange, in which both the buyer and the seller believe they are receiving greater value than they are giving up.
2. The *marketing task*, which stresses the importance of satisfying customer needs.
3. The *marketing mix*, the elements of which are the tools that marketers use, such as advertising and public relations, channels of distribution, pricing, and product policies.
4. The idea of *distinctive competence*, in which the company concentrates on what it does best because doing so maximizes profits.

These four marketing concepts are closely related. Self-interest forces the consumer to search out the best way to fulfill his needs and the company to search out the most efficient way to satisfy the consumer. Thus the marketing task is based on the idea of a transaction. The marketing mix merely enumerates the tools the marketer has for satisfying the consumer. And distinctive competence makes sense because any company, with its limited competence and resources, can most

Author's Note: I wish to thank the Marketing Science Institute and the Division of Research of the Harvard Business School for their support of the study from which this article is drawn.

profitably serve only those consumer needs which it can most efficiently serve.

In this article, I shall show how the last three of these business concepts apply to marketing in private nonprofit organizations and provide examples of their successful application (I shall not bother discussing the concept of self-interest; it can be taken for granted).

The Marketing Task

As we have just seen, the marketing task in the business sector is based on the idea that good company management leads to satisfied consumers which, in turn, leads to company profitability. This works because the company has but one primary constituency to which it provides products and from which it receives funds. The typical private nonprofit organization, however, operates in a more complex manner. It has two constituencies: clients to whom it provides goods and/or services, and donors from whom it receives resources.

Thus the profit-motivated company has one marketing function—namely, to facilitate a direct two-way exchange—which simultaneously includes both resource allocation (providing goods and services) and resource attraction (obtaining revenue). By contrast, the nonprofit organization must approach these two tasks separately because they involve separate constituencies.

This dichotomization gives the nonprofit organization flexibility. The approach it uses for clients need not be the same as the one it uses for donors, provided the managers of the "nonprofit" believe that this is both ethical and effective. Along with flexibility, however, the nonprofit's dual constituency makes the marketing task more complex, since there are two different functions to perform and two different "consumers" to satisfy. If the organization is to be successful, it must satisfy both parties.

It is relatively easy to measure marketing success in the business community. One can look at a company's profit growth or profitability relative to that of competitors, or at sales growth or sales volume relative to that of competitors. Although consumer satisfaction with a product or service, or with some particular aspect of a product or service, can also be measured in other ways, sales volume and profits are the key criteria in the final analysis.

The success measurement of the nonprofit organization's resource attraction is analogous: if the donors contribute, they are satisfied; if they do not, they are not. This measure is not, however, a valid measure of the success of the total organization. While the profit-motivated company is judged to be successful when it accomplishes its primary objective (i.e., making money), the nonprofit organization which receives large donations can be considered successful in attracting contributions but not necessarily in satisfying its clients. Father Flanagan's Boys Town, for example, appears to be considerably better at fund raising than at child raising.[1] The overall success of the nonprofit organization can be measured only in terms of the attainment of goals related to client satisfaction.

To complicate the nonprofit's situation further, activities which lead to the satisfaction of client needs may meet with the disapproval of the donor. This is especially likely to occur in an organization which is changing its objectives. The United Methodist Church, to illustrate, found that many of its members (donors who provide much of its financial support) were not pleased by its growing interest in helping blacks who were not parishioners.

For nonprofit organizations whose donors and clients are identical—such as country clubs or consumer cooperatives—the classic measure of business success, financial viability, is also a valid measure of overall success.

Let us now look more closely at the nature of the marketing task in the nonprofit organization. Specifically, how it is derived from resource attraction, resource allocation, and persuasion.

Resource Attraction

Some private nonprofit organizations, such as The Ford Foundation and The Rockefeller Foundation, raise operating funds by investing the contributions made by their family sponsors. Thus such organizations are in the enviable position of not having to seek contributions.

Most nonprofits, however, must find contributors. Some organizations do this on their own; others join forces. Joint fund-raising organizations can be based on geography (e.g., United Fund and Community Chest) or on some other common tie (e.g., the United Negro College Fund). Resource attraction is often carried out by professional fund raisers, and it is typically the nonprofit organization's most sophisticated marketing function.

While those who give to nonprofit organizations are inevitably getting something in return, the quid pro quo varies considerably. As Philip Kotler noted: "Many give to community chests to relieve a sense of guilt because of their elevated state compared to the needy. Many give to medical charities to relieve a sense of fear that they may be struck by a disease whose cure has not yet been found. Some give to feel pride." [2] Undoubtedly, others give to "insure a place in Heaven," to show the extent of their financial resources, or in response to personal pressure.[3]

Resource attraction typically takes one of two approaches, advertising or personal selling. Generally, the advertising campaign is used when an organization is attempting to generate many relatively small contributions from a large number of potential donors; personal selling, to obtain larger contributions from a more limited but highly identifiable group of potential donors. If the organization has broad appeal and can attract enough volunteers, it can use a personal selling approach to a mass campaign, such as the Mothers' March on Polio and the annual Halloween UNICEF drive.

Personal selling to potential large donors is often thought to be most effective when the solicitor can make a direct exchange with the donor. The exchange need not be explicit. For example, retailers may be particularly successful in soliciting donations from suppliers, because the suppliers are pleased to be able to win goodwill in an ethical manner. The flattery involved in being solicited by a prominent member of the community is another inducement, often sufficient to prompt a large donation.

Resource attraction is a highly sophisticated marketing task which includes all the basic elements of business-oriented marketing. The first assignment is a dual one of segmenting the donor "market" into homogeneous groups and of determining which appeal or "product" position will be most effective for that segment. Different segments are amenable to different approaches.

For example, a state university might appeal to alumni on the basis of their loyalty and emotional attachment, to parents of students on pride in their children, to individuals on state pride and lower taxes, and to businesses on the basis that the university improves the economy of the state and produces well-trained employees.

Once the different approaches are developed, nonprofits must take care to ensure that the appeals are congruent but can be kept separate. The emphasis is consistently on providing the donor with a reason for giving and on making it easy for him or her to give.

An important aspect of resource attraction is the determination of the amount to be raised from fees for goods and services. In this way, clients may actually be donors. For example, most universities raise part of their money from tuition and other student fees. Hospitals charge most of their patients for services rendered. But some nonprofit organizations expect their clients to pay nothing. Typically, such organizations either cater to the needs of the poverty stricken or they provide relatively small services, often advisory (e.g., Travelers Aid).

Resource attraction is more than just fund raising. In addition, it includes obtaining volunteer labor, services, and goods such as raw materials. Goodwill Industries' appeals for repairable merchandise are resource attraction.

Resource Allocation

In the nonprofit organization, resource allocation is somewhat analogous to product policy in the business company. In a company, the key product-policy question is: "What business are we in?" The answer defines the products to be offered and the consumers to be served. Often, it even determines the communications and distribution policy. Similarly, the nonprofit organization must determine its basic function or mission.[4] It must decide who its clients are and what it will provide them. This task is obviously much easier for the single-purpose organization than for the multimission organization. The United Fund of Greater New York, for example, provides funds to 425 community agencies and thus has a very long and complex "product line."

Nondonor Persuasion

Only a comparatively few nonprofit organizations involve themselves in the third marketing function—that is, persuading people to do something which the organization desires but which makes no direct contribution to the organization itself. Examples include antilitter campaigns, voter-registration campaigns, and health campaigns encouraging people to have themselves examined for various diseases.

For some organizations, persuasion is the central task. The Student Vote campaign, for example, was organized solely to get young people to register after the minimum voting age was changed from 21 to 18. Campaigns of this type are distinguished from resource attraction in that they do not ask the individual to interact with the organization. The individual contributes to the achievement of the goal of the organization by changing his or her attitude and behavior, not by contributing funds or by accepting goods or services as a client.

The Marketing Mix

In this section, I shall discuss each major element of the marketing mix—communications program, distribution channels, pricing, and product policy —with reference to the three functions of nonprofit marketing: resource attraction, resource allocation, and persuasion.

Communications Program

This element of the marketing mix, which includes advertising and personal selling is relevant to both resource attraction and persuasion. Persuasion is, in fact, solely a communications function.

Advertising activities: Fund raising depends heavily on advertising, which is generally intended to produce relatively small donations from a large number of donors. Some organizations utilize general mass media for advertising because their managers believe that they can effectively appeal to many different types of people. The United Fund in Boston, for example, received contributions from 400,000 donors in its 1971–1972 campaign, largely through persuasive mass media advertising. Obviously, this was a very effective means of reaching large numbers of people with a relatively complex message concerning the community needs to which the United Fund addresses itself.

Other organizations use a more focused approach, with the conviction that their appeals are most attractive to a particular segment of the donor population. Colleges and universities have traditionally emphasized the alumni in fund raising and have relied on direct mail and advertising in their magazines. The alumni magazine, in fact, serves two important fund-raising purposes: (1) it helps create a positive attitude toward the institution and toward the idea of "belonging" among active alumni supporters, and (2) it delivers the actual appeal.

Furthermore, ethnic related charities often use media which appeal to the particular ethnic group. The United Jewish Philanthropies in Boston, for example, depends heavily on the newspaper *The Jewish Advocate* for both editorial support and advertising space.

Previous donors are another important market segment on which advertising can focus. CARE uses direct mail advertising to past givers and appears to keep detailed records of the results. Past contributors are obviously a good potential pool because they are aware of the organization and have, or did at one time have, reason to support it. Political campaign organizers are becoming increasingly aware that a list of past donors is a valuable asset and are spending substantial sums to generate such lists.

Still other organizations have taken a third approach to segmenting the "market" of potential donors. They use mass media in an attempt to reach segments of the population that are able to give more than average. The United Negro College Fund, for example, has advertised in *Business Week*, undoubtedly because its readers are both wealthier and better educated than the average citizen. The organization probably reasoned that better-educated people are more anxious than others to support education.

Whatever the approach to the market, the nonprofit's advertising message is generally designed to provide the potential donor with a reason to give. In essence, the organization exchanges its product for the donor's money.

Usually, the persuasion function in the nonprofit organization is also based on advertising, which sometimes is tied in with fund raising. Probably the best known campaign of this nature is the American Cancer Society's "Fight Cancer With a Check-Up and a Check" approach.

Conservation and ecology groups have been quite active communicators in alerting the public to the problems they perceive and in obtaining active support for their causes. Some of these campaigns have stressed the importance of non-monetary contributions (e.g., the Smokey the Bear program against forest fires).

Advertising is also used with respect to resource allocation—that is, in communicating with potential clients of the organization.[5] Sometimes the communication is a by-product of fund-raising activities. One organization which provided training for blind people found that its fund-raising campaign also informed blind people of its services.

More often, however, the communications program is especially designed to attract clients. Museums, symphonies, and other cultural organizations put a great deal of effort into attracting audiences. In cases like these, the cost structure of the organization makes such efforts worthwhile. Most of the costs are fixed—that is, they do not vary with the number of clients. Thus, if a symphony attracts one additional spectator to a performance, the price of the ticket is almost all added "profit" because the cost of servicing the spectator is very little; the orchestra and the hall cost just as much without the additional spectator.

Alcoholism and drug rehabilitation centers find it especially difficult to attract the clients whom they are designed to serve. In fact, the communication decision sometimes becomes a crucial resource allocation issue: How much to spend communicating to prospective clients and how much to spend serving clients? The previously mentioned training organization for the blind, for example, found that is has to devote a substantial portion of its efforts to attracting clients.

Personal selling: This important means of communication, used primarily in fund raising, is most effective when the audience is small and the message complex. Often, the message is especially tailored for a particular listener, such as when large donations are sought from a few people. One United Fund, for example, raises over 10% of its funds from 850 large individual contributors, who represent less than 1% of the total number of contributors. Nearly 30% of its contributions are made by another 1,500 company contributors. Since fund-raising drives usually produce such a pattern, the personal selling approach is justified. The size of the gift is worth the cost of the sales call.

Some fund-raising drives rely on mass personal selling campaigns. Although the sales people are volunteers, with little or no training, the approach often succeeds because (a) it ensures that the population is informed of the drive, and (b) it uses person-to-person contact to encourage the potential donor to give.

The mass personal selling campaign is really a two-step proposition: attracting the volunteer salesmen and sales managers, and the actual fund raising. Obtaining the volunteers is often a mixture of advertising and personal selling; recruitment efforts focus on people who have participated before.

Fund raising itself can also be looked on as a two-stage operation: getting donors to make an initial contribution, and then attempting periodically to raise that contribution. Once the donor has made an identifiable contribution (i.e., one which can be traced back to him), he can be approached by special direct mail and personal selling campaigns. (Before the initial contribution, it is often so difficult to identify good prospects that expensive, focused direct mail and personal selling campaigns are not warranted.)

Personal selling can also be a means of attracting clients. It is particularly useful when a would-be client has indicated some interest in an organization but is unsure of what action to take. Outreach programs designed to inform potential clients about birth control methods are used in many clinics. Drug and alcoholic rehabilitation centers often use ex-addicts and alcoholics to explain their experiences to potential clients. Alcoholics Anonymous, for example, has made extensive use of this approach. Many neighborhood health clinics have outreach programs in which professional and nonprofessional community personnel spread the clinic's message to the surrounding area.[6]

Religious organizations often use missionaries and evangelists to explain their points of view. In the industrialized countries, the professional evangelism of organizations such as the Billy Graham Crusade and the Campus Crusade for Christ are prime examples. Other religious organizations, such as the Mormons and the Jehovah Witnesses, use volunteer "salesmen" who sometimes are well-trained but who "sell" for only a limited time.

Many colleges endeavor to attract top students using recruiting teams, which are usually combinations of full-time administrators and part-time alumni salesmen.[7] These recruitment programs sometimes focus on special types of potential clients (e.g., outstanding athletes).

Distribution Channels

All nonprofit organizations must be concerned with communications, but relatively few of them deal with channels of distribution. For those which do, life's growing complexity—particularly in sprawling metropolitan areas—has increased the importance of their choice of distribution channels.

In profit-motivated companies, channels of distribution perform two primary functions: they provide location utility and information. The retailer or wholesaler distribution channel is valuable to the manufacturer both because it provides a place to sell the product and also because it transmits information about it. In addition, the channel often offers ancillary services, such as credit and post-sales service.

In the nonprofit environment, the importance of distribution channels is location, which is relevant to resource attraction in three ways:

1. Location can make donation easier. Some fund-raising drives place collection tins in high-traffic locations, such as stores and movie theaters. Location performs the same function

in mass personal selling campaigns. The donation is either collected directly or by means of
a preaddressed envelope, relieving the donor of
some work. The ubiquitous Salvation Army
collectors who solicit funds between Thanksgiving and Christmas are a particularly conspicuous example of location policy easing the
donor's job.

2. Location can provide a base for local
fund raising and operations. It is easier to get
volunteers to work near their homes rather than
far away.

3. Location can provide credibility and
show the organization's interest in an area, both
of which facilitate fund raising. When the local
businessman asks why he should give to the
organization, the fund raiser can respond, "We
have a convenient clinic (or campus or museum)
right here where your family and employees can
use it."

More important, however, is the role of location
in resource allocation. The location becomes a
part of the product. In Michigan, students who
live too far from Ann Arbor to attend classes on
the University of Michigan's main campus can
attend classes on its Flint or Dearborn campuses.

Location is especially crucial to potential
clients who live in ethnic neighborhoods and who
fear the outside world. Often, transportation and
language barriers aggravate the problem.
Crusades for immunization against various
diseases and distribution of birth control information have both, on occasion, been impeded
by poor location.

Pricing Considerations

In a profit-motivated company, pricing links
resource allocation to resource attraction. The
company charges a price which exceeds its costs
for goods and services. Thus by attracting more
funds than it spends, it creates a profit and financial viability.

As noted earlier, many nonprofit organizations also charge fees for their services. In some,
such as consumer cooperatives, the fees equal
the costs and the organization operates at the
break-even point; it does not have to generate
additional funds from nonclient donors.

There are several reasons why other nonprofit organizations might want to move toward
"self-sufficiency" through a single constituency
system in which client fees are the sole source
of financial support. First, it simplifies the marketing function because the organization deals
with only one constituency. Second, if management satisfies the clients (through judicious resource allocation), it can expect financial viability.
In other words, the financial fate of the organization rests on its actual ability to meet client needs,
not on its ability to convince donors that it meets
client needs. Third is the apparent "justice" of
a system in which the users are also the payers.

Many nonprofit organizations recognize the
attractiveness of moving toward a single-constituency system. Some nonprofit organizations,
however, cannot charge sufficient fees for their
services. This is particularly true of welfare and
charitable organizations whose primary purpose
is to help those without the ability to pay.

Once a nonprofit organization becomes a
self-sufficient, single-constituency operation, it
is a close analogue of the profit-oriented company. Therefore, traditional business concepts
and techniques can be applied to its marketing
needs. However, a nonprofit organization whose
charter or mission prohibits a client-supported
system must operate with two constituencies—
donors and clients—and this presents two pricing considerations.

One consideration is monetary. As we have
seen, symphonies and museums have admission
fees, hospitals charge for services, and universities charge tuition.

But the price can also be nonmonetary. Thus
it can include many things more personal than
money, such as time, effort, love, power, prestige,
pride, friendship, and the like. Alcoholics
Anonymous, for example, charges a very high
price—commitment not to drink and public
admission of one's problem. The Third Nail, a
drug rehabilitation center, expects its clients to
abstain from drugs and to contribute time and
effort toward the maintenance of the center.

One reason for the intangible part of the
price is the thought that commitment makes a
more willing client. The higher the price,
presumably, the more value the client places on
the services he receives and the harder he works
to take advantage of those services.

All clients are not necessarily charged the same price; at the symphony, seat locations are priced differently. Sometimes different categories of clients (e.g., students, the elderly) are charged lower fees. Volume discounts may be offered. Health clinics often charge a patient less proportionately for extensive care than for a minor service.

It is difficult to provide equity in pricing, however, because the value provided to the non-profit organization by the donor (price) or to the client by the organization (product) varies among individuals. Even if the same price is asked for all, it is never as easy for some people to give or pay as for others.

Some members of Alcoholics Anonymous undoubtedly find it easier than others to announce their problems publicly. This type of inequity is also found in monetary prices: money is dearer to some people than to others, both because of the person's resources and because of his or her subjective attitude toward money.

Donors are charged differing prices of many types. In the purely monetary transaction, contributors give different amounts; thus they are paying different prices. Donors also provide time and effort in varying amounts, as workers, managers, or trustees. For both donors and clients, a minimum price may be set or implied; membership fees are a typical means of establishing a minimum price.

Product Policy

This element is at the very core of business marketing. It determines the products which a company offers and, implicitly, the consumers to whom it will offer them.

A nonprofit organization must have two sets of product policies, one for donors and the other for clients. The definition of product is probably more important in the nonprofit environment than in the business sector because the nonprofit's product is more elusive than just goods and services. Broadly defined, the organization's product includes intangibles such as personal satisfaction, pride, a feeling of belonging, and a "warm feeling inside." [8]

The complexity of product policy varies from one organization to the next. Some nonprofit's have a relatively simple policy because their charter or mission is limited. Certain organizations specialize in providing warm lunches for the elderly or toys for poor children at Christmas. If resources are limited, a crucial decision is the trade-off among the quality of the product, number of clients served, and quantity of the product. Still, the decision is relatively simple and well-defined.

Product policy is more complex in an organization with a tightly focused mission but with many ways of accomplishing that mission. Health organizations provide good examples. The Cancer Society, for one, has a number of ways of fighting this disease, such as research, treatment, informing the public, working with government regulating agencies, and so forth. Furthermore, the Cancer Society must assign priorities among the various types of cancer and among various regions of the country. It can emphasize prevention, detection, or treatment.

Probably the most complex product policies are those of umbrella-type organizations, such as the United Fund and large foundations. The United Fund of Greater New York, as cited earlier, provides support for over 425 services, ranging from the Boy Scouts and Girl Scouts to hospitals and health organizations. The needs of their various clients must be carefully balanced.

It is clear that product-policy decisions are resource-allocation decisions. The organization has a limited amount of resources to allocate to various activities. It is difficult, and often impossible, to assess the actual benefits of current products; it is even more difficult to assess the benefits of prospective products. The problem of assessing benefits is further aggravated when different groups of clients are involved.

Product policy is also related to resource attraction. But the donor's benefits are elusive; therefore, they are often difficult to sell. In recognition of this fact, some organizations have attempted to lower the price to the donor through various techniques, such as tax benefits, and to increase the value of their products.

Many nonprofit organizations believe that it is important to supplement their intangible products with more concrete goods, even if with only token or symbolic gifts. Thus a minimum donation to CARE gets a Mother's Day greeting sent to people of the donor's choice. The donors undoubtedly realize that the minimum contribution necessary to obtain the gift substantially exceeds its actual monetary value. Nevertheless, the concrete nature of the gift makes the transaction more attractive. Even a certificate of giving can make a transaction concrete.

A more complex product-policy approach involves double sets of donors. In such a system, the organization solicits one set of donors (sometimes individuals and sometimes businesses) for donations of goods or services which it then sells (often by auction) to another set of donors.

Distinctive Competence

The private business sector of the U.S. economy operates on a competitive basis. That is, companies compete with one another for the consumer's support, and those whose efforts are successful are rewarded with a strong sales performance and financial viability. The competitive system may not work quite so smoothly and sharply in actuality as it does in theory, but it is generally self-correcting: companies prosper when they meet consumer needs successfully; they fail when they do not.

This self-correcting mechanism is not found in the nonprofit sector for two reasons. *First*, many of the needs served by nonprofits are so great that clients cannot choose between "competing" organizations; they have to settle for what they can get. Whereas competition is greatest in any business environment where supply exceeds demand, in the nonprofit sector demand often exceeds supply. Clients have little choice and all organizations can survive. *Second*, the financial viability of the organization depends on resource attraction rather than on resource allocation; thus poor servicing of clients does not ensure financial doom.

The imbalance between supply and demand may be temporary, but the discontinuity between resource allocation and financial viability is built into the system's structure.

The situation might be corrected by creating a quasi-market in which the clients control the financial viability of the organization. Several ideas have been advanced for creating markets in certain nonprofit industries, particularly in those which receive large amounts of government funds, such as education and housing. One proposal that has been discussed at length is to give parents chits with which to pay for their children's education at any of a variety of private educational institutions.

Competition forces a profit-motivated company to do what it does best, and to do it efficiently. If the structure of nonprofit markets cannot be altered to allow for the introduction of competition, the benefits of competition might instead be realized through changes in the organization's attitude toward itself and toward other organizations which provide the same or similar services.

Much could be accomplished through interorganizational cooperation, especially in education and health care. If jealousies could be put aside, individual organizations could voluntarily restrict their activities to providing the services they are best able to provide. They would band together for those tasks which are more efficiently performed through joint effort than through individual action.

Many nonprofit organizations are beginning to evaluate their roles in terms of the consumers they serve, the products they offer, and their own distinctive competence—those things that they do better than anyone else. Thus there may be an opportunity to use cooperation for the same purpose as competition.

Concluding Note

In this article, I have sought to demonstrate that there is a definite marketing function in private nonprofit organizations, and that the managers of such organizations should attempt to improve their understanding of the exchange process and their ability to define their product. Realistic marketing analysis and planning can enable private organizations to substantially improve their operations.

I have purposely omitted from my discussion any mention of government nonprofit organizations up to this point. That is because private and government nonprofit organizations differ from one another in the nature of the donor's responsibility: taxpayers are required to contribute the funds needed by government organizations; donations to private organizations are usually voluntary.

The difference becomes blurred when private organizations are partially financed by government funds (e.g., the college and university building programs financed by the federal government) or when government organizations are partially financed by voluntary contributions (e.g., state universities and the Smithsonian Institution).

Notes

1. "Boys Town Bonanza," *Time*, April 10, 1972, p. 17.

2. *Marketing Management: Analysis, Planning, and Control* (Englewood Cliffs, New Jersey, Prentice Hall, 1972), p. 875.

3. See Steven E. Diamond, "Multiple Sclerosis Society: Fund Raising Strategy" (Boston, Division of Research, Harvard Business School, 1970), No. 9-571-020; see also Sidney J. Levy, "Humanized Appeals in Fund Raising," *Public Relations Journal*, July 1960.

4. See Seymour Tilles, "Strategies for Allocating Funds," HBR January–February 1966, p. 72; see also L. Richard Meeth, "Innovative Admissions Practices for the Liberal Arts College," *Journal of Higher Education*, October 1970, p. 535.

5. For a good analysis of client communication, see Gerald Zaltman and Ilan Vertinsky, "Health Service Marketing: A Suggested Model," *Journal of Marketing*, July 1971, p. 19.

6. Ibid., p. 27.

7. For a description of a proposed program, see L. Richard Meeth, op. cit., pp. 537–538.

8. For an outstanding description of the nature of a product in a political campaign see Joe McGinnis, *The Selling of the President 1968* (New York, Trident Press, 1969).

ARTICLE 23 ────────────

The Responsive Organization: Meeting Consumer Needs

Philip Kotler

SOURCE: Philip Kotler, MARKETING FOR NON PROFIT ORGANIZATIONS, 2e, © 1982, pp. 33–72. Reprinted by permission of Prentice Hall, Inc., Englewood Cliffs, New Jersey.

The Northminster Presbyterian Church of Evanston, Illinois, is an example of a highly responsive organization. We define a responsive organization as follows:

A **responsive organization** is one that makes every effort to sense, serve, and satisfy the needs and wants of its clients and publics within the constraints of its budget.

The result is that the people who come in contact with these organizations report high personal satisfaction. "This is the best church I ever belonged to." "My college was terrific—the professors really taught well and cared about the students." "I think this hospital is fine—the nurses are cheerful, the food good, and the room clean." These consumers become the best advertisement for that institution. Their goodwill and favorable word-of-mouth reaches other ears and makes it easy for the organization to attract and serve more people. The organization is effective because it is responsive.

Responsive organizations stand out from their competitors in the consumer mind. Recently a major bank interested in improving its service level sought to identify and interview those companies that had an outstanding reputation for service. The candidates included Delta Airlines, Marriott Hotels, Disney, Inc., and McDonald's. Each of these service organizations managed to imbue their employees with a spirit of service to the customers. For example, employees at Disney go out of their way to answer visitors' questions, pick up litter, smile, and be friendly. Disney, Inc., continuously interviews visitors to find out what they thought of the park, food, rides, employee attitudes, and so on. Based on these responses, they constantly try to improve their guests' experiences at the park.

Unfortunately, most organizations are not highly responsive. They fall into one of three groups. The first group would like to be more responsive but lack the resources or power over employees. The organization's budget may be insufficient to hire, train, and motivate good employees, and to monitor their performance. Or management may lack the power to require employees to give good service, as when the employees are unionized or under civil service and cannot be disciplined or fired for being insensitive to customers. One inner-city high school principal complained that his problem was not poor students but poor teachers, many of whom were "burned out" in the classroom and uncooperative but who could not be removed.

It's about time somebody exposed Northminster for what it really is.

You may be shocked at what's been going on in the church these days.

Oh, you're probably familiar with what the church is. It's that grey stone and stained glass building on the corner. It's crowded on Sunday mornings. And it's that place you haven't been for awhile because you've been busy. Busy growing up. Busy getting married. Busy having children.

Well, we've been busy too.

A shocking list of activities.
We're far more involved with your family, with Evanston and with the world than you might imagine.

For example, if you have children in this area in the Boy Scouts, Cubs, Campfire Girls or Brownies, there's a good possibility that they're already meeting here.

And if you have children 7th grade through high school, maybe they should be meeting here.

Bragging is not our style. But there's a lot going on. And if you'll spend the few minutes it takes to complete this page, you may discover that your family will enjoy sharing ours.

Families seen laughing out loud.
To recapture some of the warmth and friendship of having relatives close by, we join together for brunches, pot lucks, picnics and nights at the YMCA.

For the family there are campouts at Stronghold, Wisconsin, weekends at Saugatuck, Michigan and father daughter/son dinners.

It's not fundamental religion, just fundamental.

TV turned off, tube goes blank.
Some evenings and weekends we get together for intellectual explorations. There're parenting workshops for parents of teens, a role playing workshop for developing interpersonal relationships, a theater group just for the fun of it, CPR training, an aldermanic forum for the neighborhood, and experts from other fields to stimulate ideas and conversation.

Neighborhood not the same.
A portion of our time and effort and income go into help for the community.

We support neighborhood houses, the Presbyterian home, Lake View Academy and Evanston Open Pantry. We've had special days for the blood drive and Evanston Hospital.

And we operate Helpline—an emergency hotline and help service. (One of its benefits is finding transportation for the elderly.)

Not satisfied to stay home.
Part of our income goes to help people elsewhere.

Northminster supports the Coptic Evangelical Organization in Egypt. We provide a service center for young people on the northside of Chicago, and send funds to the Ludhiana (India) Christian Medical College.

Along the way we send help to the Cambodian Relief fund, the Asian Immigration service center and the hunger fund.

About 22% of our yearly income is distributed as gifts of support. That's around $60,000.

Scandalous activities.
Not all of the time we spend together is serious.

There are bridge nights, bowling leagues, film festivals, square dancing and even a cheese tasting party. They're simple diversions with old friends and new ones.

Children seen, heard.
It's never been easy to be a teenager, and this generation is no exception.

But even pre-teens need more support than ever before, to avoid drugs, alcohol and still have the contact of a supportive group.

We've developed a program for them called *Sidedoor*. It compliments our very successful *Tuxis* group of high school age people.

Sidedoor is open to any 7th or 8th grader in the community. It's a 6 day a week open door program with activities, like ice skating, bowling, hiking, rap sessions, films, or simply dinner with friends.

For younger children there's the Christian Day School and in the summer a Vacation Church School.

Other activities investigated.
For young adults we're planning singles nights at the church.

For older adults there are Dinners for Eight, a loosely organized plan for entertaining at home. It was called Gourmet Dinners until someone pointed out that ordering pizza couldn't really be classed as gourmet.

There's a new adult activity group being formed for daytime meetings to coincide with Day School hours.

After Sunday services during the summer there are casual coffee and lemonade get-togethers on the church lawn.

And there's a traditional Northminster Sunday Picnic started by a parade to a nearby park.

There are ice cream socials, dinners with other churches, a rummage sale, and a book and bake sale.

One Sunday the young people of the church take over and conduct the service.

Northminster not a country club.
A large part of what the church has to offer isn't as easy to put into a category and list as what we've shown above.

But it's important.

It's the quiet peace the church can provide.

It's the strength and vigor it can impart.

It's the opportunity to ask and explore the questions you have no answers to.

And, it's the chance to work out answers with the support of others in the real world.

What are you doing Sunday?
We would like you to come and share in our activities. The fun and the prayer, the outward and inward activities we share.

Sunday services for Easter will be 8:30 and 10:00 A.M.

Northminster is on Central Park Avenue just south of Central Street in northwest Evanston.

Come and join us.

NORTHMINSTER PRESBYTERIAN CHURCH

Dr. Robert A. Chesnut, Pastor

2515 Central Park
Evanston, IL 60201
869-9210

SOURCE: An ad appearing in the *Evanston Review*, April 3, 1980, p. 77.

Lacking funds and/or power over employees keeps these organizations from improving their responsiveness.

A second group of organizations are unresponsive simply because they prefer to concentrate on other things than customer satisfaction. Thus, many museums are more interested in collecting antiquarian material than in making this material relevant or interesting to museumgoers. The U.S. Employment Service may be more interested in the number of people they process per hour than in how much help each one really receives. When these organizations are mandated to exist or are without competition, they usually behave bureaucratically toward their clients.

Finally, there are always a few organizations which intentionally act unresponsively to the publics they are supposed to serve. A local newspaper recently exposed a public aid food stamp office that chose to be inaccessible in order to minimize the public's use of its service:

> There is no sign on the building indicating that the food stamp office is inside. . .there also was no sign anywhere in the building directing applicants to the basement, no sign on the door leading to the stairs, and no sign on the door to the office itself. The only indication that a food stamp office is located in the building is a small, handwritten sign on the door at the top of the stairs. Adding to the inconvenience, the food stamp office was closed from March 10 to April 8.[1]

We are going to assume that most organizations want to be more, rather than less, responsive to their clienteles and publics. The concept of a responsive organization makes the following assumptions:

1. Each organization has a *mission*.
2. To perform its mission, the organization needs to attract resources through *exchange*.
3. The organization will undertake exchanges with a large number of *publics*.
4. The publics will respond to the organization in terms of their *image* of the organization.
5. The organization can take concrete steps to improve the *satisfaction* it creates for various publics.

Each of the italicized concepts serves as an important tool for understanding and improving organizational responsiveness.

Mission

Every organization starts with a mission. In fact, an organization can be defined as a *human collectivity that is structured to perform a specific mission through the use of largely rational means.* Its specific mission is usually clear at the beginning. Thus, the original mission of the Northminster Presbyterian Church was to deepen religious faith among believers through offering religious training and worship. Over time, this church added further services to meet other needs of its members, until it is no longer easy to distinguish between the church's core mission and its peripheral missions. Is the church basically a religious center, a social center, or a mental health center? The church's growing responsiveness to other needs is changing its character and its membership composition.

Each organization that wants to be responsive must answer two questions: *responsive to whom and to what?* An organization cannot serve everyone and every need. If it tried to serve everyone, it would serve no one very well. From time to time, each organization must reexamine its mission.

Years ago, Peter Drucker pointed out that organizations need to answer the following questions: *What is our business? Who is the customer? What is value to the customer? What will our business be? What should our business be?*[2] Although the first question "What is our business?" is simple sounding, it is really the most profound question an organization can ask. A church should not define its business by listing the particular services it offers. It should identify the underlying need that it is trying to serve. The church might decide that it is in the "feeling good" business, that is, helping people feel better about themselves and the world. Or it might decide that it is in the "hope" business, that is, helping people feel that they will eventually experience joy and fulfillment, either in this life or in the next. Ultimately, a church has to decide what its mission is so as not to lose

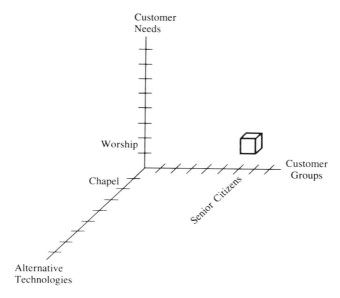

A. A Highly Focused Church

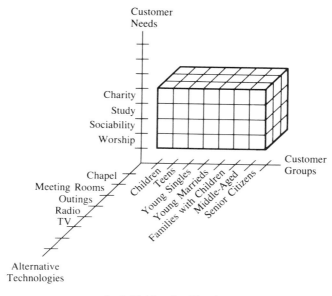

B. A Multiservice Church

FIGURE 2.1 The Mission Scope of Two Churches

sight and confuse it with a lot of intermediate goals and services that it might provide.

Clarifying the organization's mission is a soul-searching and time-consuming process. Different members will have different views of what the organization is about and should be about. One organization held numerous meetings over a two-year period before membership consensus developed on the real mission of the organization.

A helpful approach to defining mission is to establish the organization's scope along three dimensions. The first is *consumer groups*, namely, *who* is to be served and satisfied. The second is *consumer needs*, namely, *what* is to be satisfied. The third is *technologies*, namely, *how* consumer needs are to be satisfied.[3] For example, consider a church that serves mainly senior citizens who only want a simple worship service every Sunday. This church's mission scope is represented by the small cube in Figure 2.1A. Now consider the mission of Northminster Presbyterian Church, which is approximately that shown in Figure 2.1B. This church serves almost all age groups and meets at least four strong needs and provides services through the chapel, meeting rooms, classes, and outings.

Still other churches will have a different mission scope. A campus church will serve primarily students of a particular religious faith and meet a wide variety of needs (for belief, sociability, counseling, and so on) within the four walls of a religious house. On the other hand, Robert Schuller's church, Garden Grove Community Church (Garden Grove, Calif.) meets a wide variety of needs of 7,000 members and serves them through such modern technologies as radio, television, and cassettes, in addition to its $16 million "Crystal Cathedral."[4]

An organization should strive for a mission that is *feasible, motivating,* and *distinctive.* In terms of being feasible, the organization should avoid a "mission impossible." Pastor Robert Schuller wants his church to grow from 7,000 members to 25,000 members and may discover this to be infeasible. His followers must believe in the feasibility of this goal if they are to lend their support. An institution should always reach high, but not so high as to produce incredulity in its publics.

The mission should also be motivating. Those working for the organization should feel they are worthwhile members of a worthwhile organization. A church whose mission includes "helping the poor" is likely to inspire more support than one whose mission is "meeting the social, cultural, and athletic needs of its current members." The mission should be something that enriches people's lives.

A mission works better when it is distinctive. If all churches resembled each other, there would be little basis for pride in one's particular church. People take pride in belonging to an institution that "does it differently" or "does it better." By cultivating a distinctive mission and personality, an organization stands out more and attracts a more loyal group of members.

Exchange

To carry on its mission, the organization needs resources. It must be able to attract and maintain members, money, materials, staff, facilities, and equipment. If these resources became unavailable, the organization would cease to exist. Every organization is *resource-dependent.*

Methods of Obtaining Needed Resources

How can an organization obtain needed resources? There are four possible ways:

1. The organization can attempt to develop the resources through *self-production.* The members of the organization would build their own facilities and find their own materials.

2. The organization can attempt to use *force* to obtain the resources. The organization can threaten the resource owners or resort to theft.

3. The organization can *beg* for the needed resources and play on the sympathy of resource owners. This tactic tends to decline in effectiveness after a while.

4. The organization can offer something of value to resource owners in *exchange* for the needed resources. As long as an organization continues to produce value in the minds of resource owners, it is likely to attract the needed resources and survive.

The discipline of marketing is based on the last solution to the problem of resource dependency, that is, exchange. In modern society, most organizations acquire their resources through engaging in mutually beneficial exchanges with others. Organizations offer satisfactions (goods, services, or benefits) to markets and receive needed resources (goods, services, money, time, energy) in return.

Conditions Underlying Exchange

Formally speaking, exchange assumes four conditions:

1. *There are at least two parties*. In the simplest exchange situation, there are two parties. If one party is more actively seeking an exchange than the other, we call the first party a *marketer* and the second party a *prospect*. A marketer is someone seeking a resource from someone else and willing to offer something of value in exchange. The marketer can be a seller or a buyer. [5] When both parties are actively seeking an exchange, they are both called *marketers*, and the situation is one of *bilateral marketing*.

2. *Each can offer something that the other perceives to be of value*. If one of the parties has nothing that is valued by the other party, exchange will not take place. Each party should consider what things might be of value to the other party. Three categories of things tend to have value. The first is *physical goods*. A good is any tangible object—food, clothing, furniture, and so on—that is capable of satisfying a human want. The second is *services*. A service is any act that another person might perform that is capable of satisfying a human want. Services are usually characterized by an expenditure of time, energy, and/or skill. The third category is *money*. Money is a generalized store of value that can be used to obtain goods or services.

3. *Each is capable of communication and delivery*. For exchange to take place, the two parties must be capable of communicating with each other. They must be able to describe what is being offered, and when, where, and how it will be exchanged. Each party must state or imply certain warranties about the expected performance of the exchanged objects. In addition to communicating, each party must be capable

of finding means to deliver the things of value to each other.

4. *Each is free to accept or reject the offer*. Exchange assumes that both parties are engaging in voluntary behavior. There is no coercion. For this reason, every trade is normally assumed to leave both parties better off. Presumably each ended up with more value than he or she started with, since they entered the exchange freely.

Exchange is best understood as a process rather than as an event. Two parties can be said to be engaged in exchange if they are anywhere in the process of moving toward an exchange of things of value. The exchange process, when successful, is marked by an event called a *transaction*. Transactions are the basic unit of *exchange*. A transaction takes place at a time and place and with specified amounts and conditions. Thus, when a minister agrees to accept a new church position, a transaction takes place. Every organization engages in countless numbers of transactions with other parties—clients, employees, suppliers, distributors. Transactions themselves are a subset of a larger number of events called *interactions* which make up the exchange process. Transactions are those interactions that involve the formal trading of values.

Some Familiar Exchange Situations

Whenever two social units are engaged in exchange, it is useful to develop a diagram or map showing what is actually or potentially being exchanged between the two parties. Figure 2.2 presents five familiar exchange situations.

The first (Figure 2.2A) describes the classic commercial transaction. There are two parties designated respectively as *buyer* and *seller*. The seller offers things of value to the buyer in the form of goods and/or services. The buyer offers money in exchange. It is important to note that the designations "buyer" and "seller" are somewhat arbitrary, for we might also say that the party with money is offering to "sell" his money for goods. In fact, if both parties were exchanging goods, a condition known as *barter*, we could not easily distinguish the buyer from the seller. In this case, both could be called *traders*. In any event, two parties partake in a commercial transaction

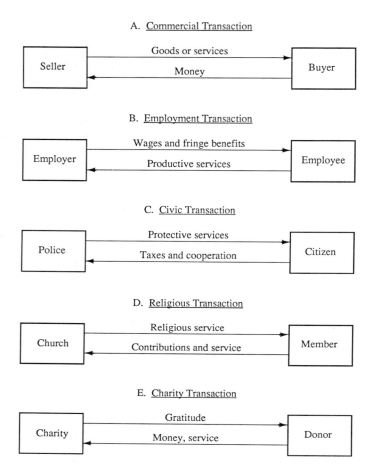

FIGURE 2.2 Familiar Examples of Exchange

because each expects to be better off after the exchange. The buyer expects more satisfaction from the goods than from other uses to which money can be put; and the seller has obtained a desired profit through the sale.

Another basic economic exchange is that between the employer and the employee (Figure 2.2B). The employee offers productive services (made up of time, energy, and skill) to the employer; in exchange, the employee receives wage and fringe benefits. There is also an overlay of psychological exchanges (not shown) in this relationship, such as fear, respect, loyalty, and so on.

A third type of exchange occurs between a local police department and the local citizens (Figure 2.2C). The local police department offers the citizens protective services; in exchange, the citizens provide taxes and cooperation. There is a question of how voluntary this transaction is, but we shall assume for the present that a social contract is voluntarily entered into between the police and the citizens.

A fourth exchange occurs between a church and its members (Figure 2.2D). The church offers its members religious services and experiences; in exchange, the members offer the church contributions and support.

A fifth exchange occurs between a charity and donors (Figure 2.2E). The charity offers the donor a sense of good conscience or well-being return for the donor's time, money, or other donations.

Analyzing Exchange Flows

The preceding diagrams show only the basic resources being exchanged by the two parties. A marketer interested in actualizing a potential transaction needs to make a more complete analysis of what the other party wants and what might be offered in return. We will illustrate this in the case of an employment transaction.

Suppose a hospital in a small town needs to attract a staff physician to replace one who has just retired. The hospital chief-of-staff makes some inquiries among physicians, medical school professors, and local medical society executives, and collects the names of a dozen prospects. Their resumes are screened by a hospital committee which establishes criteria of what it wants in a prospective physician. These wants can be represented in the following abstract way,

which says that X wants W from Y. In the concrete case, this is expanded to read:

Wants

1. competence
2. high admitting rate
3. cooperativeness
4. cost consciousness

That is, the hospital is looking for a physician who is competent, can bring a lot of patients to the hospital, is cooperative in committee work, and conscious of costs to patients and the hospital. The hospital will usually attach different weights to these wants.

Suppose the hospital search committee finds one physician who is highly attractive on these criteria. The physician has a private practice in a large city and is rumored to be looking for a small town practice. The chief-of-staff contacts the physician to gather information on this physician's wants. He establishes that the physician's wants are as follows:

Wants

1. competent colleagues and staff
2. improved income
3. good facilities and equipment
4. good living area

That is, the physician is seeking competent colleagues and staff, an improved income, good facilities and equipment, and a good part of the country to live in. It would be helpful to know the respective weights that the physician puts on these wants.

The hospital has to consider whether it can really make a good "case" to attract this physician. If the hospital is located in an unattractive area and its facilities are poor, there is little or no *exchange potential*. The hospital would have to offer the physician a substantially higher income to compensate for its deficiencies. On the other hand, the hospital's potential resources may match well the physician's needs and thus create a basis for a transaction.

In the latter case, the hospital will invite the physician for an interview. The staff will show its enthusiasm and the strong points about the hospital. If they like the visiting physician, the chief-of-staff will make an offer:

That is, X offers O to Y. In more concrete terms, the offer might be:

Offer

1. $60,000 salary
2. four-week vacation
3. secretarial service
4. one new piece of equipment worth $20,000

The physician might like the offer but suggest certain additions or modifications:

Counteroffer

1. $65,000 salary
2. five-week vacation
3. secretarial service
4. two new pieces of equipment worth $30,000

In turn, the chief-of-staff might make another counteroffer. This process of trying to find mutually agreeable terms is called *negotiation*. Negotiation either ends in mutually acceptable terms of exchange or a decision not to transact.

We have examined the exchange process as if it involved only two parties. But additional parties might be involved before an agreement can be struck. The chief-of-staff needs the board

of trustees' approval on the offer terms. The physician needs his or her spouse's approval and willingness to relocate to the small town. Thus, the buyer and seller might not act as two persons but as two organizations with each involving some participants.

We can illustrate a multiparty exchange process by introducing a physician's wife and her wishes into the picture. This is shown in Figure 2.3. The wife wants the hospital to help her find a job in her profession, hopes to find friendly physicians and wives at the hospital, hopes for a good income and home, and a good area for raising children. She wants her husband to be happy and to have enough time to give to the family. At the same time, the hospital hopes the wife will support her husband's work and participate in community affairs. Finally, the husband wants his wife to be supportive and happy in the new situation. Clearly, the hospital, as marketer, must take these various needs into consideration in formulating an offer to attract the physician.

When marketers are anxious to consummate a transaction, they may be tempted to exaggerate

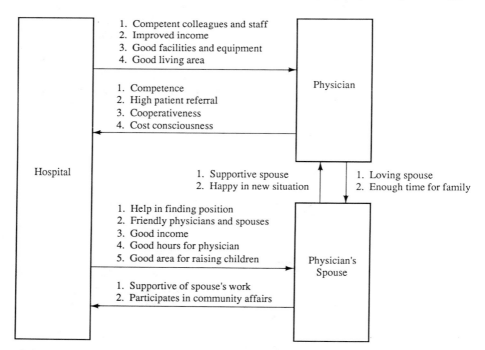

FIGURE 2.3 Three-Party Exchange Map Showing Want Vectors

the actual benefits of the product being offered. Thus, the chief-of-staff might be tempted to overstate the competence of the staff or understate the amount of expected committee work. He may succeed in attracting the physician but the physician will be turned into an unhappy customer. The physician will be dissatisfied because of the difference between his *expectations* and the hospital's *performance*. As an unhappy customer, he can be expected either to complain a lot, talk badly about the hospital to others, or quit, leaving the hospital with the task of finding another physician. The best transactions are those that deliver the expected values to the respective parties.

A Model of the Determinants of Exchange

Bagozzi has formulated a comprehensive model of the major determinants affecting exchange. The model is summarized in Figure 2.4. We will apply it to the hospital's problem of attracting the new physician to its staff.

First, we consider the two primary social actors involved in the exchange, namely, the chief-of-staff (source) and the prospective physician (receiver). The chief-of-staff and the prospective physician will engage in actions, communications, and information to influence each other. The chief-of-staff's influence will be a function of several personal qualities, namely, attraction, similarity to the physician, expertise, prestige, trustworthiness, and status. The prospective physician's perception of these qualities will be influenced by his self-confidence, self-esteem, sex, race, religion, social class, intelligence, and personality. The physician's ultimate decision will additionally be influenced by situational variables, such as the availability of alternative sources of satisfaction (other hospitals and career opportunities), the opinion of other parties (spouse, children, friends, and other colleagues), physical and psychological variables (time pressure for making a decision, number of issues that have to be considered, pleasantness of the surroundings, type of communication setting), and legal or normative variables (his contract with his present hospital and any normative concerns that might be triggered off by the thought of leaving his community).

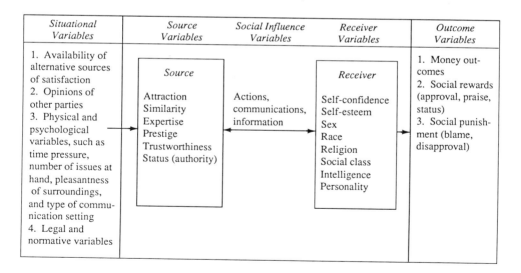

Situational Variables	Source Variables	Social Influence Variables	Receiver Variables	Outcome Variables
1. Availability of alternative sources of satisfaction 2. Opinions of other parties 3. Physical and psychological variables, such as time pressure, number of issues at hand, pleasantness of surroundings, and type of communication setting 4. Legal and normative variables	**Source** Attraction Similarity Expertise Prestige Trustworthiness Status (authority)	Actions, communications, information	**Receiver** Self-confidence Self-esteem Sex Race Religion Social class Intelligence Personality	1. Money outcomes 2. Social rewards (approval, praise, status) 3. Social punishment (blame, disapproval)

FIGURE 2.4 A Model of the Determinants of Exchange

SOURCE: Diagram adapted by the author from prose text in Richard P. Bagozzi, "Marketing as Exchange: A Theory of Transactions in the Marketplace," *American Behavioral Scientist*, March–April 1978, pp. 535–56.

The physician will also be influenced by his picture of the contrasting outcomes associated with his staying versus leaving his present hospital. Three kinds of outcomes can be envisioned. First, his money income will be influenced by the outcome. Second, he will experience different social rewards in the form of approval, praise, and status. Third, he might also experience some social punishment such as disapproval or blame.

Thus, a large number of factors will influence the exchange process involving a hospital and a prospective physician. The direction of influence of most of these factors is pretty clear, although their relative importance varies with each situation. This model is presented not as an elegant predictive theory of how an exchange situation will be resolved, but as a comprehensive view of the factors that the marketer will want to analyze in preparing a marketing plan.

Theories Predicting Exchange Outcomes

At the same time, there are some simple theories predicting how exchange situations will be resolved. Three of these theories will be briefly reviewed: economic theory, equity theory, and power theory.

Economic theory. Economists have spent the most time studying the conditions under which a transaction takes place. The basic concept in their analysis is that of *self-interest*. Individuals and organizations, when faced with two or more choices, will always favor the choice that will maximize their long-run self-interest. Put another way, people and organizations are *utility maximizers*. This interpretation of human behavior is rooted in a psychological theory that people basically respond to pleasure and pain in their activities and are able to calculate and sum the pleasure and pain consequences of different decisions.

Whether a transaction will be consummated between two social actors depends on the expected benefit-cost consequences for each actor. Economic theory holds that each actor will form an estimate of the expected personal net gain of engaging in the transaction. The expected personal net gain *(G)* is the difference between the total benefits *(B)* and the total cost *(C)* as seen

by the actor. In the case of actor i, the personal expected net gain is represented by:[6]

$$G_i = B_i - C_i$$

Whether the physician and hospital will consummate the transaction can now be predicted by this theory. There are three possible outcomes.

1. If both actors expect that their net gain will be negative, then no transaction will take place, for both actors will be worse off.
2. If both actors expect that the net gain will be positive, the transaction is likely to take place, because both will be better off. The only qualification here is that one or both actors might visualize still another transaction which will make him (them) even better off.
3. Finally, if one actor will be better off and the other worse off, a transaction will not take place unless the "better off" actor finds a way to compensate the "worse off" actor so that both will be better off. The "better off" actor can decide to accept a lower gain, just enough to leave the "worse off" actor with a slight positive gain.

We have examined the conditions under which two actors are likely to consummate a transaction. Economic theory would also like to predict the terms of exchange, but here it is less successful, at least in the case of a two-party transaction. Thus, in the case of the physician considering joining the new hospital, he may be willing to affiliate as long as the salary is at least $62,000 and his other conditions are met. The hospital might be willing to offer him as much as $67,000 as long as he is willing to meet its conditions. In other words, the physician expects a positive net gain at any salary greater than $62,000 and the hospital expects a positive net gain at any salary less than $67,000. Economists can predict that the physician will join the hospital and that the final salary figure will be somewhere between $62,000 and $67,000. However, they are not able to predict the specific figure. They see this as an issue that will be settled on other grounds, such as equity or power considerations.

Equity theory. One way for two parties to reach a "transaction price" within a negotiating range is to bring in considerations of equity. The two parties may be motivated to seek a price that they jointly consider to be "fair." For example, the chief-of-staff may propose that the physician's salary should have an equitable relation to the salary of another physician already on the staff. The other physician has the same background and skills, but has been in practice for one year longer than the prospective physician. He is earning $66,000. The chief-of-staff says that salaries usually rise $2,000 a year. He therefore offers the prospective physician $64,000, which is $2,000 less (or one year of salary less) than the earnings of the other physician, and bases this on equity considerations.

In general, equity theory holds that the two parties will seek to arrive at a "price" that appeals to their sense of fairness. Suppose the hospital is interviewing two candidates, Y and Z, for the position. In considering the salary to offer each, the chief-of-staff may be guided by his picture of the relative value each would contribute to the hospital. Equity theory would lead him to offer salaries that would satisfy the following relationship:

$$\frac{\text{Salary } Y}{\text{Salary } Z} = \frac{\text{Value of } Y}{\text{Value of } Z}$$

Thus, if candidate Y is considered to offer twice as much value to the hospital as candidate Z, the hospital can offer Y twice as much salary and feel that this is equitable. Of course, people might have other views of what constitutes equity.[7]

Power theory. Power theory takes a different view about how the two parties will arrive at a mutually agreed upon transaction price within a negotiating range. It sees each as driven to obtain the maximum possible gain, and as willing to exploit the power possessed to achieve it. If the prospective physician has more bargaining power than the hospital, the final price will be closer to the hospital's maximum of $67,000. If the hospital has more bargaining power, the final price will be closer to the physician's minimum of $62,000.

This leaves the question of what determines the amount of power each party has in the situation. X's power relative to Y is a function of (1) how much X needs some resource that Y has, and (2) how available is this resource from some alternative party.[8] In concrete terms, we can say that physician Y possesses considerable power if (1) hospital X badly needs to add a physician to its staff, and (2) there are few other qualified physicians who are available. In this case, the physician is in a seller's market and possesses considerable power to command the salary he wants.

In general, a transaction will take place when both parties gain. The transaction price will fall in a range between the minimum price that the seller will accept and the maximum price that the buyer will offer. Where the price settles will depend on equity and power considerations.

The reason that we examined exchange theory in detail is because it is central to being a responsive organization. To be responsive requires analyzing the other party's needs and wants and determining how far the organization can go toward satisfying them. An organization that is oblivious to or indifferent to the needs of the other party cannot, by definition, be responsive.

Publics

In every organization's life there are several publics, and the organization has to manage responsive relations with most or all of them. We define a public in the following way:

> A **public** is a distinct group of people and/or organizations that has an actual or a potential interest and/or impact on an organization.

It is fairly easy to identify the key publics that surround a particular organization. Consider a university. Figure 2.5 shows sixteen major publics with which a university deals. The publics include groups within the university and outside the university.

Not all publics are equally active or important to an organization. Publics come about because the organization's activities and policies can draw support or criticism from outside groups. A *welcome public* is a public that likes the organization and whose support the organization welcomes. A *sought public* is a public whose support the organization wants but which is currently indifferent or negative toward that organization. An *unwelcome public* is a public that is negatively disposed toward the organization and that is trying to impose constraints, pressures, or controls on the organization.

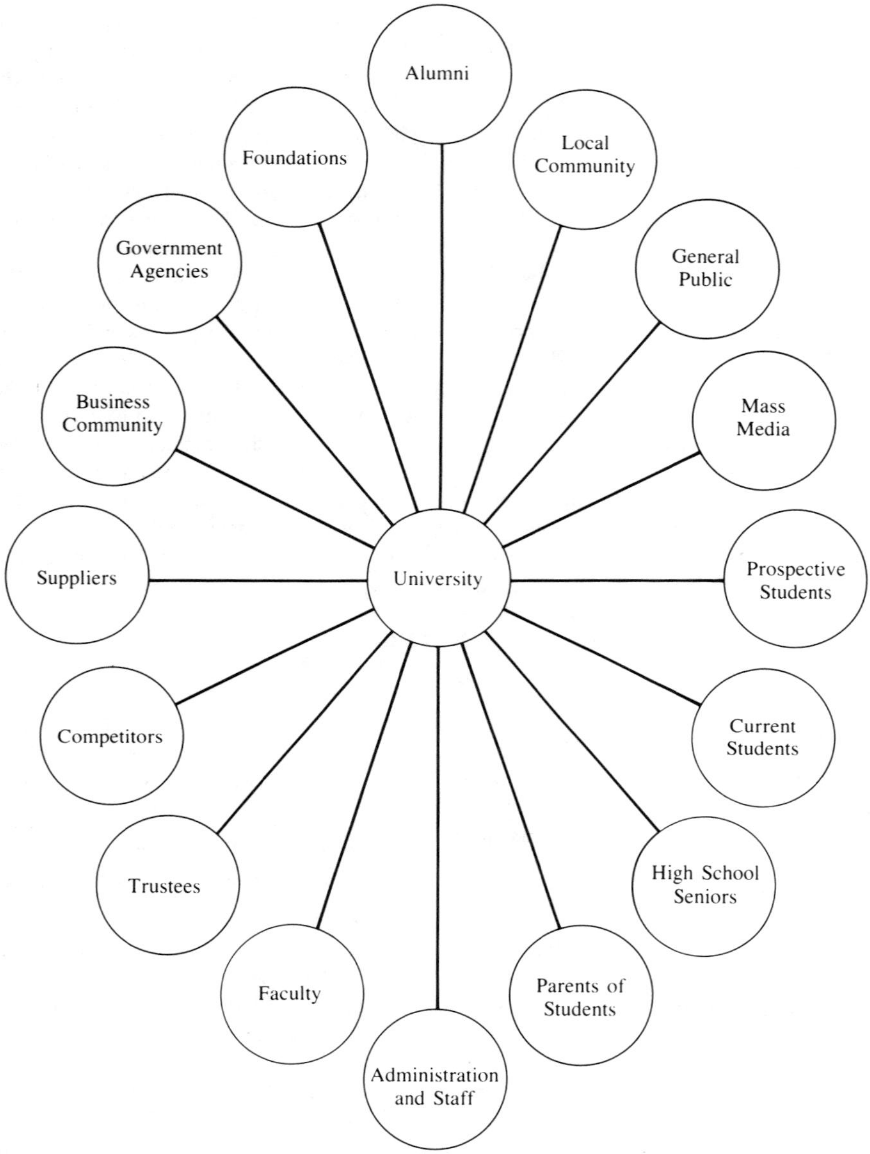

FIGURE 2.5 The University and Its Publics

Publics can also be classified by their functional relation to the organization. Figure 2.6 presents such a classification. An organization is viewed as a resource-conversion machine in which certain *input publics* supply resources that are converted by *internal publics* into useful goods and services that are carried by *intermediary publics* to designated *consuming publics*. Here we will look at the various publics more closely.

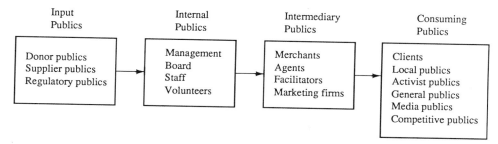

FIGURE 2.6   The Main Publics of an Organization

Input Publics

Input publics mainly supply original resources and constraints to the organization, and as such consist of donors, suppliers, and regulatory publics.

Donors.   Donors are those publics who make gifts of money and other assets to the organization. Thus a university's donors consist of alumni, friends of the university, foundations, corporations, and government organizations. Each university runs a development office consisting of a staff of professional fundraisers. This staff develops a philosophy of fundraising and specific proposals that might excite possible donors. It tries to match its financial needs with the appropriate donor groups. It tries to build value in the eyes of its donors so that they can feel pride and other satisfactions from their association with the institution.

Suppliers.   Suppliers are those organizations that sell needed goods and services to the focal organization. Nonprofit organizations often try to obtain price concessions or even free donations of goods and services but don't often succeed. In recent times, supply shortages and the rapidly rising cost of supplies have made skillful supply planning and purchasing more important than ever.

Regulatory organizations.   The third input public consists of regulatory organizations that impose rules of conduct. The regulatory publics of a university include federal, state, and local government agencies, trade unions, and various academic accreditation associations. The

focal organization must keep in close contact with these regulatory organizations and be ready to argue against regulations that will harm their ability to create value for their clients.

Internal Publics

The various inputs are managed by the organization's internal publics to accomplish the organization's mission. The internal publics consist of up to four groups: *management, a board of directors, staff,* and *volunteers.* (Public agencies are an exception and normally lack a board of directors and volunteers.)

Management.   Every organization has a management group that is responsible for running the organization. The top officer is called the president or chief administrator. Reporting to the president are high-level managers who are organized by functions, products, markets, and/or geographical areas. Thus, reporting to a college president are deans taking care of functions (e.g., business manager), products (e.g., dean of engineering school), and markets (e.g., dean of students).

Board of directors.   The president and the management team may be responsible to a board of directors (also called a board of trustees or overseers). The board's job is to oversee the organization and to make sure that it is operating efficiently to reach its objectives. Among the board's more important responsibilities are the following:

1. The board selects or approves the chief officer of the organization.

2. The board participates in setting or approving long-range strategy for the organization.
3. The board develops or approves policies for the conduct of organizational affairs.
4. The board develops or approves compensation levels and salaries of higher management.
5. The board participates in fundraising.
6. The board considers major issues that have come before the organization.
7. The board adds members who are influential and can provide further contacts with other influentials.
8. The board legitimizes the organization in the eyes of others.
9. The board provides specialized skills and advice, as would come from lawyers and businessmen.

Clearly the board is an important part of the organization, and in some organizations the most important part. Because of this, board members must be carefully selected. Most organizations seek "high-prestige" members, some seek "ordinary citizen" members, and others go after a mixture. A new small private college in Kentucky, for example, asked a wealthy and influential civic leader to head its new board. This person in turn attracted other prestigious individuals. The board then added members with certain skills, such as a lawyer, accountant, banker, and politician. Finally, one of the most prominent professors at the school was added to the board.

Board selection is very challenging. There is often a tradeoff between getting prestigious members on the board (who may miss a number of meetings and not be able to do much work) and working members on the board. Too many boards are window dressing and private clubs that do not get involved in what is really happening. Some managements want it this way, so that the board does not interfere with their plans and schemes.

Other managements want a more active board than the one they have. The board is too conservative and not willing to change with the times. Or it is not willing to work hard. Here management may have to take some drastic steps, such as asking certain members to drop out or setting up attendance rules and dropping those members who miss a certain number of meetings. The main way to create a working board is to hold frequent meetings, establish attendance rules, form working committees that must deliver reports, and, in general, establish the idea that work is expected.

Some boards are so involved in the organization that they are a major force in driving the organization to its best performance. They make demands on management to produce plans and results. They are a "whip" to the management group. Other boards are a drag on the organization. They are too conservative, and do not change with the times. They remember the organization as working a certain way and do not let it change with the times. Here is where management groups must market change to the board, get them "out of the dark ages." And this may require a marketing plan.[9]

Staff. The staff consists of the various employees who work on a paid basis. This would include middle management, secretaries, workmen, telephone operators, and so on. The staff would also include the skilled practitioners who deliver the organization's services to its consumers, such as the hospital's nurses, the college's professors, the police department's police officers, and the social agency's social workers.

Management faces the normal problems of building an effective staff: defining job positions and responsibilities, recruiting qualified people, training them, motivating them, compensating them, and evaluating them. We discussed earlier all the "marketing" work that one hospital took to recruit one physician, and now this example has to be multiplied by the number of new people an organization hires each year. Employee training is another critical task with significant marketing implications. Those employees who come in contact with consumers must be trained in a "customer service" orientation. A college whose professors are cold or indifferent to the students is much more likely to have falling enrollment than a college with student-oriented professors.

Motivating the staff takes careful planning. The staff wants several things from the organization: adequate salaries, fair treatment, respect and recognition, and the feeling of working for a worthwhile enterprise. Management must create these benefits if it expects to get in return solid work, high morale, and continuous support.

Employees are a "market" to which management must creatively communicate and relate.

Volunteers. Many nonprofit organizations —churches, charities, hospitals—use volunteers as an important part of their operations. The volunteers perform work which usually requires less skill, and this helps to keep down the costs of running the organization. On the other hand, volunteers are less controllable and often less productive. They may not show up for meetings, resist doing certain tasks, and tend to be slow in getting their work done on time. Some organizations claim to be able to accomplish more by increasing the size of the paid staff and reducing the number of volunteers.

At the same time, a better answer might be for the organization to improve its skill in managing and motivating the volunteers. Volunteers are sensitive to small slights, like not receiving recognition for a job well done, or being pushed hard. They feel that they are giving their time free and want to be appreciated and respected.

The competent volunteer staff manager will be skilled in attracting good and reliable volunteers and in motivating and rewarding them. A marketing approach means understanding the volunteers' needs and meeting them in a way which draws their support and hard work. The volunteer staff manager is likely to sponsor social functions for volunteers, confer awards for many years of service, and arrange a number of other benefits that will recognize their contributions.[10]

Intermediary Publics

The focal organization enlists other organizations, called marketing intermediaries, to assist in promoting and distributing its goods and services to the final consumers. For example, a college may decide to offer off-campus educational services to consumers who cannot avail themselves of courses offered on campus. The college may work with four different marketing intermediaries to distribute and promote its educational services and products. They are described below.

Merchants. Merchants are organizations —such as wholesalers and retailers—that buy, take title to, and resell merchandise. Suppose the college makes an arrangement with a local bookstore to carry and sell certain textbooks, where the bookstore cannot return the unsold books. The bookstore is performing a merchant role in the distribution system used by the college.

Agents. Agent middlemen are organizations—such as manufacturer's representatives, agents, and brokers—that are hired by producers to find and/or sell to buyers without ever taking possession of the merchandise. Suppose the college signs a contract with a person who agrees to recruit new students for the college. This person is acting as an agent for the college. The college would have to negotiate the terms on which the agent would be remunerated for services.

Facilitators. Facilitators are organizations —such as transportation companies, real estate firms, and media firms—that assist in the distribution of products, services, and messages, but do not take title to or negotiate purchases. Thus, the college will use the telephone company and the post office to send messages and materials to prospective students. These facilitators are paid a normal rate for their transportation, communication, and storage services.

Marketing firms. Marketing firms are organizations—such as advertising agencies, marketing research firms, and marketing consulting firms—that assist in identifying and promoting the focal organization's products and services to the right markets. The college will hire the services of these marketing firms to investigate, develop, and promote new educational services. The focal organization has to select these firms wisely and negotiate terms which are mutually rewarding.

Consuming Publics

Various groups consume the output of an organization. They are described below.

Clients. Customers represent an organization's primary public, its *raison d'être*. Drucker insists that the only valid definition of a business is to create a customer.[11] He would hold that hospitals exist to serve patients, colleges to serve students, opera companies to serve opera lovers, and social agencies to serve the needy.

Various names are used interchangeably to describe customers, such as consumers, clients, buyers, and constituents. The appropriate term is elusive in some cases. Consider a state penitentiary. The prisoners are clearly the penitentiary's consumers. A psychiatrist in the prison will have certain prisoners as clients. The prisoners are not buyers in the sense of paying money for the service; instead, the citizens are the buyers and they are buying protection from criminal elements through their taxes. The citizens are also the prison's constituents in that the prison exists to serve their interests. We might conclude that the citizens are the prison's primary customers.

What this illustrates is that an organization can have a multiple set of customers, and one of its jobs is to distinguish these customer groups and their relative importance. Consider this issue in relation to a state college. Who is the state college's primary customer? Is it the *students* because they consume the product? Is it the students' *parents*, who expect the college to transmit knowledge and ambition to their sons and daughters? Is it *employers*, who expect the college to produce people with marketable skills? Is it *taxpayers*, who expect the college to produce educated individuals? Or is it the college's *alumni*, who expect their alma mater to do notable things to give them pride?

Clearly, a college must take the interest of all of these "customer" groups into account in formulating its services and policies. At times, the college will aim to increase its service to one group more than to another. If the students complain about poor lectures and unavailable professors, then the administration will have to focus its energy on improving service to the students. This may require putting pressure on the professors to be more responsive to students. At other times, professors may complain that their teaching load is too heavy to get any research done, and the administration may seek additional money from alumni to finance lighter teaching loads. Most of the time the administration is busy balancing and reconciling the interests of diverse customer groups rather than favoring one group all the time at the expense of the other groups.

Local publics. Every organization is physically located in one or more areas and comes in contact with local publics such as neighborhood residents and community organizations. These groups may take an active or passive interest in the activities of the organization. Thus, the residents surrounding a hospital usually get concerned about ambulance sirens, parking congestion, and other things that go with living near a hospital.

Organizations usually appoint a community relations officer whose job is to keep close to the community, attend meetings, answer questions, and make contributions to worthwhile causes. Responsive organizations do not wait for local issues to erupt. They make investments in their community to help it run well and to acquire a bank of goodwill.

Activist publics. Organizations are increasingly being petitioned by consumer groups, environmental groups, minority organizations, and other public interest groups for certain concessions or support. Hospitals, for example, have had to deal with demands by environmental groups to install more pollution control equipment and engage in better waste handling methods.

Organizations would be foolish to attack or ignore demands of activist publics. Responsive organizations can do two things. First, they can train their management to include social criteria in their decision making to strike a better balance between the needs of the clients, citizens, and the organization itself. Second, they can assign a staff person to stay in touch with these groups and to communicate more effectively the organization's goals, activities, and intentions.

General public. An organization is also concerned with the attitude of the general public toward its activities and policies. The general public does not act in an organized way toward the organization, as activist groups do. But the members of the general public carry around images of the organization which affect their patronage and legislative support. The organization needs to monitor how it is seen by the public, and to take concrete steps to improve its public image where it is weak.

Media publics. Media publics include media companies that carry news, features, and editorial opinion: specifically, newspapers, magazines, and radio and television stations. Organizations are acutely sensitive to the role played by the press in affecting their capacity to achieve their marketing objectives. Organizations normally would like more and better press coverage than they get. Getting more and better coverage calls for understanding what the press is really interested in. The effective press relations manager knows most of the editors in the major media and systematically cultivates a mutually beneficial relation with them. The manager offers interesting news items, informational material, and quick access to top management. In return, the media editors are likely to give the organization more and better coverage.

Competitive publics. In carrying out its task of producing and delivering services to a target market, the nonprofit organization will typically face competition. Many nonprofit organizations deny the existence of competition, feeling that this is more characteristic of business firms. Thus, hospitals until recently did not like to think of other hospitals as competitors, and the YMCA does not like to think of other social agencies as competitors. They would rather think of all their sister organizations as providing needed services and not competing. Yet the reality of competition is driven home when one

hospital starts attracting many doctors and patients from another hospital, or a local YMCA starts losing members to local racquetball clubs and gymnasiums.

An organization must be sensitive to the competitive environment in which it operates. The competitive environment does not consist only of similar organizations or services but also of more basic things. An organization can face up to four major types of competitors in trying to serve its target market. They are:

1. *Desire competitors*: other immediate desires that the consumer might want to satisfy.
2. *Generic competitors*: other basic ways in which the consumer can satisfy a particular desire.
3. *Service form competitors*: other service forms that can satisfy the consumer's particular desire.
4. *Enterprise competitors*: other enterprises offering the same service form that can satisfy the consumer's particular desire.

We will illustrate these four types of competitors in relation to a small ivy-league college. Consider a high school senior deciding what to do after graduation. Suppose her decision process follows the path shown in Figure 2.7. The student realizes that she has several competing desires (*desire competitors*): getting an education, getting

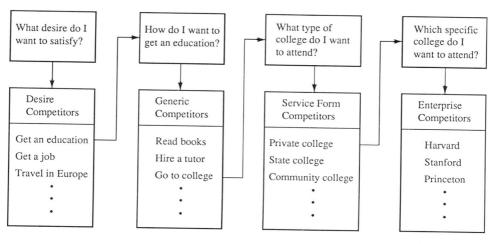

FIGURE 2.7 Types of Competitors Facing a Private College

a job, traveling to Europe, and so on. Suppose she favors getting an education. She then considers the best way to do this (*generic competitors*): read books, hire a tutor, go to college, and so on. She decides in favor of going to college. Then she considers what type of college (*service form competitors*): private college, state college, or community college. She favors a private college. This leads her to consider which private colleges to apply to (*enterprise competitors*): Harvard, Stanford, Princeton, and so on. Thus, this private college faces at least four types of competitors in attempting to attract this student.

Relation Between a Public and a Market

Having demonstrated that every organization is surrounded by a multitude of publics, we can now pose the question: What is the relation between a public and a market? The term "market" has a different origin than the term "public" and yet has several affinities with it.

From the point of view of an organization, a market is a *potential arena for the trading of resources*. For an organization to operate, it must acquire resources through trading other resources. In each case, it must offer something to the market to receive in return the resources it seeks. For this reason, we define a market as follows:

> A **market** is a distinct group of people and/or organizations that have resources which they want to exchange, or might conceivably be willing to exchange, for distinct benefits.

We can now see the affinities between a market and a public. A *public* is any group that has an actual or potential interest or impact on an organization. If the organization wishes to attract certain resources from that public through offering a set of benefits in exchange, then the organization is taking a *marketing viewpoint* toward that public. Once the organization starts thinking in terms of trading values with that public, it is viewing the public as a market. It is engaged in trying to determine the best marketing approach to that public.

Image

Responsive organizations have a strong interest in how their publics see the organization and its products and services. For it is the organization's image, not necessarily its reality, that people respond to. Publics holding a negative image of an organization will avoid or disparage the organization, while those holding a positive image will be drawn to it. The same organization will be viewed as responsive by some groups and unresponsive by other groups. Therefore, the organization has a vital interest in learning about its "images" in the marketplace and making sure that these images facilitate rather than impede the delivery of satisfaction.

An organization does not acquire a favorable image simply through public relations planning. Its image is a function of its *deeds* and its *communications*. Good deeds without good words, or good words without good deeds, are not enough. A strong favorable image comes about when the organization creates real satisfaction for its clients and lets others know about this.

Managers want to know the following things about image:

1. What is an image?
2. How can it be measured?
3. What determines the image?
4. How can an image be changed?
5. What is the relation between the person's image of an object and his/her behavior toward the object?

Definition of Image

The term "image" came into popular use in the 1950s. It is currently used in a variety of contexts: organization image, corporate image, national image, brand image, public image, self-image, and so on. Its wide use has tended to blur its meanings. Our definition of image is:

> An **image** is the sum of beliefs, ideas, and impressions that a person has of an object.

This definition enables us to distinguish an image from similar sounding concepts such as *beliefs, attitudes,* and *stereotypes.*

An image is more than a simple belief. The belief that the American Medical Association (AMA) is more interested in serving doctors than serving society would be only one element in a large image that might be held about the AMA. An image is a whole set of beliefs about an object.

On the other hand, people's images of an object do not necessarily reveal their attitudes toward that object. Two persons may hold the same image of the AMA and yet have different attitudes toward it. An attitude is a disposition toward an object that includes cognitive, affective, and behavioral components.

How does an image differ from a stereotype? A stereotype suggests a widely held image that is highly distorted and simplistic and that carries a favorable or unfavorable attitude toward the object. An image, on the other hand, is a more personal perception of an object that can vary greatly from person to person.

Image Measurement

Many methods have been proposed for measuring images. We will describe a two-step approach: first, measuring how familiar and favorable the organization's image is, and second, measuring the organization's image along major relevant dimensions.

Familiarity–favorability measurement. The first step is to establish, for each public being studied, how familiar they are with the organization and how favorable they feel toward it. To establish familiarity, respondents are asked to check one of the following:

If most of the respondents check the first two or three categories, then the organization has a serious image problem.

To illustrate these scales, suppose the residents of an area are asked to rate four local hospitals, A, B, C, and D. Their responses are averaged and the results displayed in Figure 2.8. Hospital A has the strongest image: Most people know it and like it. Hospital B is less familiar to most people but those who know it like it. Hospital C is negatively viewed by the people who know it but fortunately not too many people know it. Hospital D is in the weakest position: It is seen as a poor hospital and everyone knows it.

Clearly, each hospital faces a different task. Hospital A must work at maintaining its good reputation and high community awareness. Hospital B must bring itself to the attention of more people since those who know it find it to be a good hospital. Hospital C needs to find out why people dislike the hospital and take steps to mend its ways, while keeping a low profile. Hospital D would be well advised to lower its profile (avoid news), mend its ways, and when it is a better hospital, it can start seeking public attention again.

Semantic differential. Each hospital needs to go further and research the content of its image. One of the most popular tools for this is the semantic differential.[12] It involves the following steps:

1. *Developing a set of relevant dimensions.* The researcher first asks people to identify the

Never heard of	Heard of	Know a little bit	Know a fair amount	Know very well

The results indicate the public's awareness of the organization. If most of the respondents place the organization in the first two or three categories, then the organization has an awareness problem.

Those respondents who have some familiarity with the organization are then asked to describe how favorable they feel toward it by checking one of the following:

dimensions they would use in thinking about the object. People could be asked: "What things do you think of when you consider a hospital?" If someone suggests "quality of medical care," this would be turned into a bipolar adjective scale— say, "inferior medical care" at one end and "superior medical care" at the other. This could be rendered as a five- or seven-point scale. A

Very unfavorable	Somewhat unfavorable	Indifferent	Somewhat favorable	Very favorable

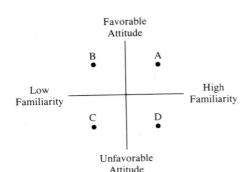

FIGURE 2.8 Familiarity–Favorability Analysis

set of additional relevant dimensions for a hospital are shown in Figure 2.9.

2. *Reducing the set of relevant dimensions.* The number of dimensions should be kept small so as to avoid respondent fatigue in having to rate *n* organizations on *m* scales. Osgood and his co-workers feel that there are essentially three types of scales:

- evaluation scales (good–bad qualities)
- potency scales (strong–weak qualities)
- activity scales (active–passive qualities)

Using these scales as a guide, or performing a factor analysis, the researcher can remove redundant scales that fail to add much information.

3. *Administering the instrument to a sample of respondents.* The respondents are asked to rate one organization at a time. The bipolar adjectives should be arranged so as not to load all of the poor adjectives on one side.

4. *Averaging the results.* Figure 2.9 shows the results of averaging the respondents' pictures of hospitals A, B, and C. Each hospital's image is represented by a vertical "line of means" that summarizes how the average respondent sees that institution. Thus Hospital A is seen as a large, modern, friendly, and superior hospital. Hospital C, on the other hand, is seen as a small, dated, impersonal, and inferior hospital.

5. *Checking on the image variance.* Since each image profile is a line of means, it does not reveal how variable the image actually is. If there were 100 respondents, did they all see Hospital B, for example, exactly as shown, or was there considerable variation? In the first case, we would say that the image is highly *specific*, and in the second case that the image is highly *diffused*. An institution may or may not want a very specific image. Some organizations prefer a diffused image so that different groups can project their needs into this organization. The organization will want to analyze whether a variable image is really the result of different subgroups rating the organization with each subgroup having a highly specific image.

The semantic differential is a flexible image-measuring tool that can provide the following useful information.

1. *The organization can discover how a particular public views the organization and its major competitors.* It can learn its image

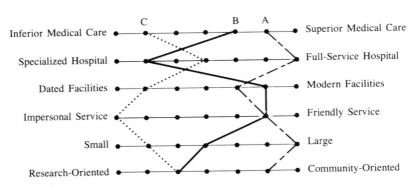

FIGURE 2.9 Images of Three Hospitals (Semantic Differential)

strengths and weaknesses along with those of the competitors and take remedial steps that are warranted.

2. *The organization can discover how different publics and market segments view the organization.* One can imagine that the image profiles in Figure 2.9 represent the images of one organization held by three different publics. The organization would then consider taking steps to improve its image among those publics who view the organization most unfavorably.

3. *The organization can monitor changes in its image over time.* By repeating the image study periodically, the organization can detect any significant image slippage or improvement. Image slippage signals that the organization is doing something wrong. Image improvement, on the other hand, verifies that the organization is performing better as a result of some steps it has taken.

Image Causation

What determines the image that a person holds of an object? A theory of image determinants would help the organization understand the factors that have caused its present image, and understand how to produce a change.

There are two opposite theories of image formation. One holds that image is largely *object-determined*—that is, persons are simply perceiving the reality of the object. If a hospital is located next to a lake and surrounded by beautiful trees, then it is going to strike people as a beautiful hospital. A few individuals might describe it as ugly but this would be dismissed as the peculiarity of certain individuals or their lack of real experience with the object. The object-determined view of images assumes that (1) people tend to have first-hand experience with objects; (2) people get reliable sensory data from the object; and (3) people tend to process the sensory data in a similar way in spite of having different backgrounds and personalities. These assumptions in turn imply that organizations cannot easily create false images of themselves.

The other school holds that images are largely *person-determined*. Those holding this view argue that (1) people have different degrees of contact with the object; (2) people placed in

front of the object will selectively perceive different aspects of the object; (3) people have individual ways of processing sensory data leading to selective distortion. For these reasons, it is held that people are likely to hold quite different images of the object. That is, there is a weak relation between the image and the actual object.

The truth lies somewhere in between—that is, an image is influenced both by the objective characteristics of the object and the subjective characteristics of the perceiver. We might expect people to hold rather similar images of a given object mainly under the following conditions: when the object is simple rather than complex; when it is frequently and directly experienced; and when it is fairly stable in its real characteristics over time. Conversely, people may hold quite different images of an object if it is complex, infrequently experienced, and changing through time. People have quite different images of a particular hospital because it is complex, infrequently experienced in direct contact, and changes through time.

Image Modification

The leaders of an organization are often surprised and disturbed by the measured image. Thus the chief administrator of Hospital C (see Figure 2.9) might be upset that the public sees the hospital as dated, impersonal, and of low quality. Management's immediate reaction is to disbelieve the results by complaining that the sample is too small or unrepresentative. But if the results can be defended as reliable, management must consider what it ought to do about this image problem.

The first step is for management to develop a picture of the *desired image* that they want to have in the general public's mind, in contrast to the *current image*. Suppose the management of Hospital C wants an image closer to that of Hospital A. Hospital C would like the public to have a more favorable view of the quality of its medical care, facilities, friendliness, and so on. It is not aiming for perfection because the hospital recognizes its limitations. The desired image must be feasible in terms of the organization's present reality and resources.

The second step is for management to decide which image gaps it wants to work on initially. Is it more desirable to improve the hospital's image of friendliness (through staff training programs, etc.) or the look of its facilities (through renovation)? Each image dimension should be separately reviewed in terms of the following questions:

1. What contribution to the organization's overall favorable image would be made by closing that particular image gap to the extent shown?
2. What strategy (combination of real changes and communication changes) would be used to close the particular image gap?
3. What would be the cost of closing that image gap?
4. How long would it take to close that image gap?

For example, management might decide that it would be more impactful, swifter, and less costly to improve the hospital's image of friendliness than to improve the physical facilities of the hospital. An overall image modification plan would involve planning the sequence of steps through which the organization would go to transform its current image into its desired image.

An organization seeking to change its image must have great patience. Images tend to be "sticky" and last long after the reality of the organization has changed. Thus, the quality of medical care might have deteriorated at a major hospital and yet it continues to be highly regarded in the public mind. Image persistence is explained by the fact that once people have a certain image of an object, they tend to be selective perceivers of further data. Their perceptions are oriented toward seeing what they expect to see. It will take highly disconfirming stimuli to raise doubts and open them to new information. Thus an image enjoys a life of its own for a while, especially when people are not likely to have new first-hand experiences with the changed object.

The Relation Between Image and Behavior

The reason why organizations are interested in image measurement and modification is because of the great influence they feel an image has on the behavior of people. They assume that there is a close relationship between the public's image of the organization and their behavior toward it.

The organization feels that it can obtain better public response by acquiring a better image.

Unfortunately, the connection between image and behavior is not as close as many organizations believe. Images are only one component of attitudes. Two people may view a hospital as large and have opposite attitudes toward a large hospital. Furthermore, the connection between attitudes and behavior is also tenuous. A person might prefer a large hospital to a small one, and yet end up in the small one because it is closer to home or the doctor recommended it.

Nevertheless, one should not dismiss image measurement and planning simply because images are hard to change and their effects on behavior are unclear. Quite the contrary. Measuring an object's image is a very useful step in understanding what is happening to the object and to point to some possible desirable changes in its image. Furthermore, though the connection between image and behavior is not strong, it does exist. The connection should neither be overrated nor underrated. The organization should attempt to make an investment in developing the best image it can for the advantages this might bring.

Satisfaction

A responsive organization is one that makes every effort to sense, serve, and satisfy the needs and wants of its focal clients and publics. Each organization must determine how responsive it wants to be and the appropriate systems for measuring and improving its satisfaction creating ability.

Levels of Organizational Responsiveness

Organizations fall into four levels of organizational responsiveness. They are shown in Table 2.1 and described in the following paragraphs.

The unresponsive organization. An unresponsive organization is at one extreme. Its main characteristics are:

1. It does not encourage inquiries, complaints, suggestions, or opinions from its customers.

TABLE 2.1 Four Levels of Consumer-Responsive Organizations

	Unresponsive	Casually Responsive	Highly Responsive	Fully Responsive
Complaint system	No	Yes	Yes	Yes
Surveys of satisfaction	No	Yes	Yes	Yes
Surveys of needs and preferences	No	No	Yes	Yes
Customer-oriented personnel	No	No	Yes	Yes
Empowered customers	No	No	No	Yes

2. It does not measure current customer satisfaction or needs.
3. It does not train its staff to be customer-minded.

The unresponsive organization is typically characterized by a bureaucratic mentality. Bureaucracy is the tendency of organizations to routinize their operations, replace personal judgment with impersonal policies, specialize the job of every employee, create a rigid hierarchy of command, and convert the organization into an efficient machine.[13] Bureaucrats are not concerned with innovation, with problems outside their specific authority, with qualifying human factors. They will serve people as long as their problems fall within the limits of their jurisdiction. People's problems are defined in terms of how the bureaucratic organization is set up rather than having the organization set up to respond to people's problems. Questions of structure dominate questions of substance; means dominate ends.

This kind of organization either assumes that it knows what its publics need or that their needs do not matter. It sees no reason to consult with its consumers. Many hospitals were bureaucratically operated in the 1960s when they had far more patient demand than beds. Consider the following:

Why is it necessary to awaken a patient a couple of hours before breakfast to wash his face?. . .Why does it sometimes take many minutes for a nurse to answer the patient's light?. . .We've all seen nurses standing in the hallway talking and ignoring call lights. . . . Too many hospitals are drab.[14]

Whether the physician, the house staff member or the nurse, the waiter, X-ray or emergency room, or the admitting clerk who is rude, the maid who bumps the bed while cleaning, the parking lot attendant who is less than helpful when the lot is full, the cafeteria that turns away visitors, the pharmacy that has limited hours for outpatients—all of this suggests that hospitals operate for their own convenience and not that of the patient, his family, and friends.[15]

Such an unresponsive organization brings about a host of undesirable consequences. The products and services are usually poor or irrelevant. Citizens or customers become frustrated and dissatisfied. Their dissatisfaction leads to rebellion, withdrawal, or apathy, and may ultimately doom the organization.

The casually responsive organization. The casually responsive organization differs from the unresponsive organization in two ways:

1. It encourages customers to submit inquiries, complaints, suggestions, and opinions.
2. It makes periodic studies of consumer satisfaction.

When American universities began to experience a decline in student applications in the early seventies, they began to pay more attention to their students and publics. College administrators who formerly were largely oriented toward problems of hiring faculty, scheduling classes, and running efficient administrative services—the earmarks of the bureaucratic mentality—now began to listen more to the students. They left their doors open, made occasional surprise appearances in the student lounge, encouraged suggestions from students, and created faculty-student committees. These steps moved the university into being casually responsive.

The result is to create a better feeling in the organization's customers. It is the first step in building a partnership between the served and the serving. Whether or not the increased customer satisfaction continues depends on whether the organization merely makes a show of listening or actually undertakes to do something about what it hears. It may merely offer a semblance of openness and interest without intending to use the results in any way. It sooner or later becomes apparent to the consumers that this is a public relations ploy. It can lead to greater strain because of rising consumer expectations than when the organization was completely unresponsive. If their voices fall on deaf ears, they resent the organization and may try to force it into greater responsiveness.

The highly responsive organization. A highly responsive organization differs from a casually responsive organization in two additional ways:

1. It not only surveys current consumer satisfaction but also researches unmet consumer needs and preferences to discover ways to improve its service.
2. It selects and trains its people to be customer-minded.

Many nonprofit organizations fall short of being highly responsive. Universities rarely take formal surveys of their students' real needs and desires, nor do they incentivize and train their faculty to be student-minded. Recently a small liberal arts college recognized this failing, and it developed the following philosophy to guide its professors:

The students are:
- the most important people on the campus; without them there would be no need for the institution
- not cold enrollment statistics, but flesh-and-blood human beings with feelings and emotions like our own
- not dependent on us; rather, we are dependent on them

- not an interruption of our work, but the purpose of it; we are not doing them a favor by serving them—they are doing us a favor by giving us the opportunity to do so

If this could be successfully implemented, the college would have moved a long way into being highly responsive.

The fully responsive organization. The highly responsive organization is free to accept or reject complaints and suggestions from its consumers, based on what it thinks is important and what it is willing to do. The public proposes and the organization disposes. A fully responsive organization overcomes the "we–they" distinction by accepting its customers as voting members. Its characteristics are:

1. It encourages the consumers to participate actively in the affairs of the organization.
2. It responds to the wishes of the organization's consumers as expressed through the ballot box or their representatives.

Among examples of fully responsive organization, at least in principle, are local town democracies, churches, trade unions, and democratic nation-states. The organization is seen as existing for and serving the interests of the citizen–members. There is no question of the organization going off on its own course to pursue goals that are not in the interest of its members. The organization shows an extreme interest in measuring the will of the members and responding to their wishes and needs.

When these principles are fulfilled, the expectation is that the citizen–members will be highly involved, enthusiastic, and satisfied. Recently, a Canadian university was searching for ways to build a more active alumni association. Just sending out newsletters about the school did not build up alumni pride or interest. It developed the idea of conferring membership status on its alumni, with certain privileges and voting rights on certain issues. Suddenly, the alumni became alive with interest in the school. This gesture proved very meaningful to the alumni, who had hitherto felt that the university was simply using them for their money.

The Concept of Satisfaction

Since responsive organizations aim to create satisfaction, it is necessary to define the term "satisfaction." Our definition is:

> **Satisfaction** is a state felt by a person who has experienced a *performance* (or outcome) that has fulfilled his or her *expectations*.

Thus, satisfaction is a function of the relative levels of expectation and perceived performance. A person will experience one of three states of satisfaction. If the performance exceeds the person's expectations, the person is *highly satisfied*. If the performance matches the expectations, the person is *satisfied*. If the performance falls short of the expectations, the person is *dissatisfied*.

In the last case, the amount of dissatisfaction depends upon the consumer's method of handling the gap between expectations and performance. Some consumers try to *minimize* the felt dissonance by seeing more performance than there really is or thinking that they set their expectations too high. Other consumers will exaggerate the perceived performance gap because of their disappointment.[16] They are more prone to reduce or end their contacts with the organization.

Thus to understand satisfaction, we must understand how people form their expectations. Expectations are formed on the basis of people's past experience with the same or similar situations, the statements made by friends and other associates, and the statements made by the supplying organization. Thus, the supplying organization influences satisfaction not only through its performance but also through the expectations it creates. If it overclaims, it is likely to create subsequent dissatisfaction; and if it underclaims, it might create high satisfaction. The safest course for the organization is to plan to deliver a certain level of performance and communicate this level to its consumers.

Measuring Satisfaction

Consumer satisfaction, in spite of its central importance, is difficult to measure. Organizations use various methods to make an inference about how much consumer satisfaction they are creating. The major methods are described below.

Sales-related methods. Many organizations feel that the extent of consumer satisfaction created by their activities is revealed by such objective measures as their *sales growth, market share*, and/or *repeat purchase ratio*. If these measures are rising, management draws the conclusion that the organization is satisfying its customers. Thus, if the Lyric Opera Company sells all of its seats and next year has a 100 percent subscription renewal rate, it must be satisfying its patrons. If a college manages to attract more students each year in a declining market, it must be satisfying its students.

These indirect measures are important but hardly sufficient. In situations of no competition or excess demand, these measures may be high and yet not reflect actual satisfaction, because consumers have no alternatives. In other situations, sales can remain strong for a while even after satisfaction has started to decline because dissatisfied patrons might transact with an organization a little longer out of inertia.

Complaint and suggestion systems. A responsive organization will make it easy for its clients to complain if they are disappointed in some way with the service they have received. Management will want complaints to surface up on the theory that clients who are not given an opportunity to complain might reduce their business with the organization, bad-mouth it, or abandon it completely. Not collecting complaints represents a loss of valuable information which the organization could have used to improve its service.

How can complaints be facilitated? The organization can set up systems that make it easy for dissatisfied customers (or satisfied customers) to express their feelings to the organization. Several devices can be used in this connection. For example, a hospital could place *suggestion boxes* in the corridors. It could supply exiting patients with a *comment card* which can be easily checked off (see Figure 2.10). It can establish a *patient advocate or ombudsman system* to hear patient grievances and seek remedies.[17] It can establish a *nurse grievance committee* to review nurse complaints.

An organization should try to identify the major categories of complaints. Thus a hospital might count the number of complaints about food,

You are a VERY IMPORTANT PERSON!

Will you let us know how we did?

We strive to provide the best possible hospital care to the patients who come to us. Please take a couple of minutes to complete this questionnaire; there is space on the back for additional comments, which will help us improve our service and continue Memorial's tradition of excellent patient care.

When completed drop it in the mail. It is addressed and the postage is paid.

Thank you for your valuable assistance.

Robert M. Magnuson

Robert M. Magnuson
President

Your room number _____

From _____ To _____

Male _____ Female _____

Your name, if you wish:

_____

A. Your admission: Yes No

   Were you courteously
   received and processed
   by the admitting
   office?   __ __

   Were you admitted to the
   hospital from the
   Emergency Department?   __ __

B. Your room:

   Was it ready for you?   __ __

   Was it attractive?   __ __

   Was it kept clean during
   your stay?   __ __

                       Yes No

   Was the proper
   temperature
   maintained?   __ __

   Were lighting and
   ventilation facilities
   adequate?   __ __

   Was your room quiet
   enough for you to rest?   __ __

C. Your meals:

   Was the food well-
   prepared and appetizing,
   considering your diet?   __ __

   Were you satisfied with
   the portions?   __ __

   Did hot food arrive hot
   at your bedside?   __ __

   Was your food served
   attractively?   __ __

   Overall, were you pleased
   with the food service
   during your stay?   __ __

D. Nursing service:

   In your opinion were
   the nurses skilled in the
   performance of their
   duties?   __ __

   Were they attentive to
   your needs and did they
   explain reasons for
   medications, treatments,
   and diagnostic
   procedures?   __ __

   Was your call for
   assistance answered with
   reasonable promptness?   __ __

E. Were you satisfied with
   the services given by:

   X-ray technicians?   __ __

   Laboratory technicians?   __ __

   Housekeeping
   personnel?   __ __

                       Yes No

   Nursing assistants,
   orderlies, and other
   nursing personnel?   __ __

   Volunteers?   __ __

   Telephone operators?   __ __

   Admitting clerks?   __ __

   Other personnel?   __ __

F. Were you informed about
   tests and treatments
   ordered by your
   physician?   __ __

G. Was your schedule
   arranged so that you could
   get enough rest?   __ __

H. Personal:

   Were your visitors
   courteously received?   __ __

   Were visiting hours
   satisfactory?   __ __

   Were services such as
   delivery of mail,
   flowers, and
   packages satisfactory?   __ __

I. Business office:

   Was the cashier courteous
   and helpful?   __ __

J. Overall, are you satisfied with
   your care at Memorial
   Hospital?   __ __

K. Overall, are you satisfied
   with the information given
   you about your health,
   your treatments, and
   follow-up care?   __ __

L. Would you recommend
   our Hospital to family
   members, friends and
   neighbors?   __ __

FIGURE 2.10 A Hospital Comment Card

nursing care, and room cleanliness and focus its corrective actions on those categories showing a high frequency, high seriousness, and high remediability.

A good complaint management system will provide much valuable information for improving the organization's performance. At the same time, a complaint system tends to understate the amount of real dissatisfaction felt by customers. The reasons are:

1. Many people who are disappointed may choose not to complain, either feeling too angry or feeling that complaining would do no good. One study found that only 34 percent of a group of dissatisfied people said they would complain.
2. Some people overcomplain (the chronic complainers) and this introduces a bias into the data.

Some critics have argued that complaint systems do more harm than good. By giving people an opportunity—indeed, an incentive—to complain, people are more likely to feel dissatisfied. Instead of ignoring their disappointment, they are asked to spell it out, and they are also led to expect redress. If the latter is not forthcoming, they will be more dissatisfied. Although this might happen, it is our view that the value of the information gathered by soliciting complaints far exceeds the cost of possibly overstimulating dissatisfaction.

Consumer panels. Some organizations set up a consumer panel to keep informed of consumer satisfaction. A consumer panel consists of a small group of customers who have been selected to make up a panel that will be sampled from time to time about its feelings toward the organization or any of its services. Thus, a hospital may set up a doctor panel that would be sampled periodically for its reactions or suggestions. A university may set up a student panel that would be sampled periodically for its reactions to current services.

Consumer panel members may volunteer or they may be paid for their time. Some provision is usually made to rotate membership on the panel to get fresh views from new people. The panel is typically a source of valuable information to the organization. At the same time, the information may not be completely trustworthy. The panel's representativeness can be called into question. People who do not like to be members of panels are not represented. Those who join the panel may be more loyal to the organization and thus less likely to see its faults.

Consumer satisfaction surveys. Many organizations supplement the preceding devices with direct periodic surveys of consumer satisfaction. They send questionnaires or make telephone calls to a random sample of past users to find out how much they like the service and what they might dislike about the service. In this way, they avoid the possible biases of complaints systems, on the one hand, and consumer panels, on the other.

Consumer satisfaction can be measured in a number of ways, three of which will be described here. We will illustrate them in a university setting.

Directly reported satisfaction. A university can distribute a questionnaire to a representative sample of students, asking them to state their felt satisfaction with the university as a whole and with specific components. The questionnaire would be distributed on a periodic basis either in person, in the mail, or through a telephone survey.

The questionnaire would contain questions of the following form:

Indicate how satisfied you are on the following scale:

Here five intervals are used, although some scales use only three intervals and others as many as eleven. The numbers assigned to the intervals are arbitrary, except that each succeeding number is higher than the previous one. There is no implication that these are unit distances. When the results are in, a histogram can be prepared showing the percentage of students who fall into each group. Of course, students within any group—such as the highly dissatisfied group—may have really quite different intensities of dissatisfaction ranging from mild feelings of disappointment with the university to intense feelings of anger. Unfortunately, there is no way to make interpersonal comparisons of utility and we can only rely on the self-reported feelings of the respondents.

If the histogram is highly skewed to the left, then the university is in deep trouble. If the histogram is bell-shaped, then it has the usual number of dissatisfied, indifferent, and satisfied students. If the histogram is highly skewed to the right, the university can be very satisfied that it is a responsive organization meeting its goal of delivering high satisfaction to the majority of its consumers. It is necessary to repeat this survey at regular intervals to spot any significant changes in the distribution. Furthermore, the respondents should check similar scales for the significant components of the university, such as its academic program, extracurricular program, housing, and the like. It would help to know how the various components of satisfaction relate to overall satisfaction.

Derived dissatisfaction. The second method of satisfaction measurement is based on the premise that a person's satisfaction is influenced by the perceived state of the object and his expectation. He is asked two questions about each component of the university; for example:

By finding the need deficiency score for each component of the university's product, the administration will have a good diagnostic tool to understand current student moods and to make necessary changes. By repeating this survey at regular intervals, the university can detect new need deficiencies as they arise and take timely steps to remedy them.

Importance/performance ratings. Another satisfaction-measuring device is to ask consumers to rate several services provided by the organization in terms of (1) the importance of each service, and (2) how well the organization performs each

---

The quality of the academic program:
a. How much is there now?

(min)	1	2	3	4	5	6	7	(max)

b. How much should there be?

(min)	1	2	3	4	5	6	7	(max)

Suppose he circles 2 for part a and 5 for part b. We can then derive a "need deficiency" score by subtracting the answer for part a from part b, here 3. The greater the need deficiency score, the greater his degree of dissatisfaction (or the smaller his degree of satisfaction).

This method provides more useful information than the previous method. By averaging the scores of all the respondents to part a, the researcher learns the average perceived level of that attribute of the object. The dispersion around the average shows how much agreement there is. If all students see the academic program of the university at approximately 2 on a 7-point scale, this means the program is pretty bad. If students hold widely differing perceptions of the program's actual quality, this will require further analysis of why the perceptions differ so much and what individual or group factors it might be related to.

It is also useful to average the scores of all the respondents to part b. This will reveal the average student's view of how much quality is expected in the academic program. The measure of dispersion will show how much spread there is in student opinion about the desirable level of quality.

service. Figure 2.11A shows how fourteen services of a college were rated by students. The importance of a service was rated on a four-point scale of "extremely important," "important," "slightly important," and "not important." The college's performance was rated on a four-point scale of "excellent," "good," "fair," and "poor." For example, the first service, "academic program," received a mean importance rating of 3.83 and a mean performance rating of 2.63, indicating that students felt it was highly important, although not being performed that well. The ratings of all fourteen services are displayed in Figure 2.11B. The figure is divided into four sections. Quadrant A shows important services that are not being offered at the desired performance levels. The college should concentrate on improving these services. Quadrant B shows important services that the college is performing well; its job is to maintain the high performance. Quadrant C shows minor services that are being delivered in a mediocre way, but which do not need any attention since they are not very important. Quadrant D shows a minor service that is being performed in an excellent manner, a case of possible "overkill." This rating of services according to their perceived importance and

Service	Service Description	Mean importance rating[a]	Mean performance rating[b]
1	Academic program	3.83	2.63
2	Housing quality	3.63	2.73
3	Food quality	3.60	3.15
4	Athletic facilities	3.56	3.00
5	Social activities	3.41	3.05
6	Faculty availability	3.41	3.29
7	" "	3.38	3.03
8	" "	3.37	3.11
9	" "	3.29	2.00
10	" "	3.27	3.02
11	" "	2.52	2.25
12	" "	2.43	2.49
13	" "	2.37	2.35
14	" "	2.05	3.33

[a]Ratings obtained from a four-point scale of "extremely important," "important," "slightly important," and "not important."

[b]Ratings obtained from a four-point scale of "excellent," "good," "fair," and "poor." A "no basis for judgment" category was also provided.

A.

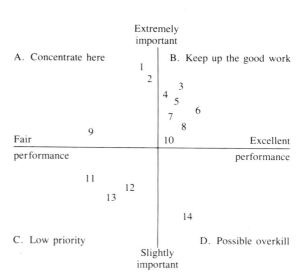

B.

FIGURE 2.11 Importance and Performance Ratings for Several College Services

performance provides the college with guidelines as to where it should concentrate its efforts.

Relation Between Consumer Satisfaction and Other Goals of the Organization

Many people believe that the marketing concept calls upon an organization to *maximize* the satisfaction of its consumers. This, however, is not realistic and it would be better to interpret the marketing concept as saying that the organization should strive to create a high level of satisfaction in its consumers, though not necessarily the maximum level. The reasons for this are explained below.

First, consumer satisfaction can always be increased by accepting additional cost. Thus a university might hire better faculty and build better facilities and charge lower tuition to increase the satisfaction of its students. But obviously a university faces a cost constraint in trying to maximize the satisfaction of a particular public.

Second, the organization has to satisfy many publics. Increasing the satisfaction of one public might reduce the satisfaction available to another public. The organization owes each of its publics some specific level of satisfaction. Ultimately, the organization must operate on the philosophy that it is trying to satisfy the needs of different groups at levels that are acceptable to these groups within the constraint of its total resources. This is why the organization must systematically measure the levels of satisfaction expected by its different constituent publics and the current amounts they are, in fact, receiving.

The organization hopes to derive a number of benefits as a result of creating high satisfaction in its publics. First, the members of the organization will work with a better sense of purpose and pride. Second, the organization creates loyal publics and this reduces the costs of market turnover. Third, the loyal publics say good things to others about the organization and this attracts new consumers without requiring as much direct effort on the part of the organization.

Summary

A responsive organization is one that makes every effort to sense, serve, and satisfy the needs and wants of its clients and publics within the constraints of its budget. The concept of a responsive organization rests on the concepts of mission, exchange, publics, image, and satisfaction.

Every organization starts with a mission that answers: What is our business? Who is the customer? What is value to the customer? What will our business be? What should our business be? A helpful approach to defining mission is to identify which customer groups will be served, which of their needs will be addressed, and which technologies will be used to satisfy these needs. A mission works best when it is feasible, motivating, and distinctive.

To carry out its mission, an organization needs resources. An organization can attract resources through self-production, force, begging, or exchange. Marketing is based on the last solution and assumes that there are at least two parties; each can offer something of value to the other; each is capable of communication and delivery; and each is free to accept or reject the offer. Exchanges take place when both parties expect to be better off after a transaction. The terms of the transaction will be influenced by economic, equity, and power considerations.

Organizations carry on exchanges with several publics. A public is a distinct group of people and/or organizations that has an actual or potential interest and/or impact on an organization. Publics can be classified as input publics (donors, suppliers, regulatory publics), internal publics (management, board, staff, volunteers), intermediary publics (merchants, agents, facilitators, marketing firms), and consuming publics (clients, local publics, activist publics, general public, media publics, and competitive publics). When the organization seeks some response from a public, we call it a market. A market is a distinct group of people and/or organizations that has resources which they want to exchange, or might conceivably be willing to exchange, for distinct benefits.

Responsive organizations are interested in their image because it is their image that people respond to. An organization's image is the sum of beliefs, ideas, and impressions that a person or group has of an object. Images can be measured by scaling techniques. Organizations can try to modify undesirable aspects of their image through changing their behavior and their communications.

The acid test of an organization's responsiveness is the satisfaction it creates. Organizations range from those which are unresponsive and casually responsive to those which are highly responsive and fully responsive. The more responsive organizations make use of complaint systems, surveys of satisfaction, surveys of needs and preferences, customer-oriented personnel, and empowered customers. Responsive organizations create more satisfaction for their publics. Satisfaction is a state felt by a person or group that has experienced organizational performance that has matched expectations.

Notes

1. Bill Grady, "This Food Stamp Office is Hiding," *Chicago Tribune*, May 22, 1980.

2. See Peter F. Drucker, *Management: Tasks, Responsibilities, Practices* (New York: Harper & Row, 1973), Chapter 7.

3. See Derek F. Abell, *Defining the Business: The Starting Point of Strategic Planning* (Englewood Cliffs, N.J.: Prentice-Hall, 1980), Chapter 2, esp. p. 17.

4. See C. Peter Wagner, *Your Church Can Grow* (Glendale, Calif.: G/L Publications, 1976), pp. 52–53. See also "Religion Inc.: 'Possibility Thinking' and Shrewd Marketing Pay Off for a Preacher," *Wall Street Journal*, August 26, 1976, p. 1.

5. See Philip Kotler and Sidney J. Levy, "Buying Is Marketing, Too," *Journal of Marketing*, January 1973, pp. 54–59.

6. Alternatively, the actor may judge the potential gain as the rate B_i/C_i—in other words, as a rate of return on investment.

7. For additional reading, see John W. Huppertz, Sidney J. Arenson, and Richard H. Evans, "An Application of Equity Theory to Buyer–Seller Exchange Situations," *Journal of Marketing Research*, May 1978, pp. 250–60.

8. See Richard M. Emerson, "Power-Dependence Relations," *American Sociological Review*, February 1962, pp. 32–33.

9. For an interesting discussion of hospital boards, see Alfred R. Stern, "Instilling Activism in Trustees," *Harvard Business Review*, January–February 1980, pp. 24ff.

10. See David L. Sills, *The Volunteers—Means and Ends in a National Organization* (Glencoe, Ill.: Free Press, 1957). Also note that

the National Center for Voluntary Action, 1785 Massachusetts Avenue, N.W., Washington, D.C. 20036, researches, runs seminars, and disseminates up-to-date techniques for managing volunteers.

11. Drucker, *Management*, p. 61.

12. C. E. Osgood, G. J. Suci, and P. H. Tannenbaum, *The Measurement of Meaning* (Urbana: University of Illinois Press, 1957). Other image-measuring tools exist, such as *object-sorting* (see W. A. Scott, "A Structure of Natural Cognitions," *Journal of Personality and Social Psychology*, Vol. 12, No. 4, 1969, pp. 261–78), *multidimensional scaling* (see Paul E. Green and Vithala R. Rao, *Applied Multidimensional Scaling*, New York: Holt, Rinehart and Winston, Inc., 1972), and *item lists* (see John W. Riley, Jr., ed., *The Corporation and Its Public*, New York: John Wiley & Sons, Inc., 1963, pp. 51–62).

13. See Anthony Downs, *Inside Bureaucracy* (Boston: Little, Brown, 1967).

14. Quoted from a speech given by Frank Sinclair at a public relations conference of hospital administrators.

15. Bernard J. Lachner, "Marketing—An Emerging Management Challenge," *Health Care Management Review*, Fall 1977, p. 27.

16. See Ralph E. Anderson, "Consumer Dissatisfaction: The Effect of Discomfirmed Expectancy on Perceived Product Performance," *Journal of Marketing Research*, February 1973, pp. 38–44.

17. See "Medical Ombudsmen: More Hospitals Move to Improve Service Through 'Advocates' Who Help Patients," *Wall Street Journal*, Friday, August 27, 1976.

ARTICLE 24 _____

Entrepreneurship and Organizational Change in the Human Services
Dennis R. Young

With few exceptions modern economists have paid scant attention in their conceptual work to

SOURCE: *Casebook of Management for Nonprofit Organizations*, by D. R. Young. Copyright © 1985 by Haworth Press, New York. Reprinted by permission.

entrepreneurship.[1] Conventional microeconomic theory is static, monolithic, and strictly structural in nature, concerned with the interaction of aggregate demand and supply functions (based on simple stereotypes of consumers and firms) and providing minimal insight into the range and variety of behavior of individual consumers or producers. In this same style, the theory views the interaction of supply and demand as an impersonal, automatic equilibrating process and is not concerned with the individuals and dynamic processes through which demanders and suppliers are brought together into new and changing markets. This structural bias of theory—particularly the inattention to market-making behavior—precludes most economists from seriously studying entrepreneurship and leaves the concept of entrepreneurship somewhat ambiguous and unclear.

In everyday usage the term *entrepreneurship* is associated with the organizing and managing of risky economic ventures for profit.[2] Scholars who have wrestled with the concept differ with this definition, and with each other, in terms of its emphasis on risk and profit, its lack of focus on innovation, and its failure to distinguish the entrepreneurial function from that of the manager, the capitalist or financeer, or the inventor. As Hoselitz indicates: "A study of economists' opinions on entrepreneurship leads to strange and sometimes contradictory results. Some writers have identified entrepreneurship with the function of uncertainty-bearing, others with the coordination of productive resources, others with the introduction of innovations, and still others with the provision of capital." [3]

Two questions arise concerning the definition of *entrepreneurship*. First, on what basis can this term be used in non-profit-making parts of the economy? (Clearly this practice is at odds with common usage.) Second, what specifically does entrepreneurship comprise? A precise idea of what is involved in entrepreneurship is needed in order to analyze its implications. Joseph Schumpeter, in his analysis of economic development, gives the classic definition of *entrepreneur*. [4] Schumpeter defines the entrepreneur as the individual who implements "new combinations of means of production." There are five possible types of these new combinations: (1) the introduction of a new economic good; (2) the

introduction of a new method of production; (3) the opening of a new market; (4) the conquest of a new source of raw materials of half-manufactured goods; and (5) the carrying out of the new organization of an industry, such as the creation or breaking up of a monopoly.

Schumpeter clearly focuses on implementation of change and innovation, as do other writers. For example, Angel, who studied development of the sun-belt cities of the United States, calls entrepreneurs "innovative capitalists." [5] Matthew Josephson, who wrote on nineteenth-century industrial development, defines the entrepreneur as "one who feels the turn of the current before others." [6] Collins and Moore, who studied individuals who undertook new business enterprises, define entrepreneurship as "the catalytic agent in society which sets into motion new enterprises, new combinations of production and exchange." [7]

Although the focus on innovation narrows the definition of entrepreneur from the broader concept of manager ascribed to by Marshall, the role of innovation in entrepreneurship can be overemphasized.[8] As Schumpeter indicates, *entrepreneur* is not synonomous with *inventor* or *idea generator*, for new ideas must be implemented to effect new combinations. Nor is the focus on innovation restricted to originality. Although Angel asserts that entrepreneurs differ from nonentrepreneurs because the latter "seek only to accumulate capital by mimicking established business methods...", [9] Schumpeter's definition would include mimicking behavior if it took place in a new context, for example, existing services to a new consumer group.

Entrepreneurship is usually associated with risk taking. As noted by Collins and Moore, "In the popular conception...the independent entrepreneur is a risk-taker—a man who braves uncertainty, who strikes out on his own, and who—through native wit, devotion to duty, and singleness of purpose—somehow creates business and industrial activity where none existed before." [10] Schumpeter's definition, however, quite purposefully contains no explicit reference to risk. Schumpeter's point is to separate the role of entrepreneur from that of capitalist and to indicate that entrepreneurs may undertake no special financial risk in developing new enterprise, as it is others' capital that they are employing:

The entrepreneur is never the risk bearer. ...The one who gives credit comes to grief if the undertaking fails. For although any property possessed by the entrepreneur may be liable, yet such possession of wealth is not essential, even though advantageous. But even if the entrepreneur finances himself out of former profits, or if he contributes the means of production belonging to his...business, the risk falls on him as capitalist or as possessor of goods, not as entrepreneur. Risk-taking is in no case an element of the entrepreneurial function. Even though he may risk his reputation, the direct economic responsibility of failure never falls on him.[11]

Although financial risk bearing can thus be conceptually separated from entrepreneurship, it is clear why risk is correlated with this function. First, entrepreneurs do often invest their own capital and, indeed, may be required to, in order to give other investors confidence in their commitment. (This situation does not, however, exist in the government and nonprofit sectors or in the context of entrepreneurship by large corporations, where entrepreneurs need not assume fiscal liabilities.) Also, as acknowledged by Schumpeter, risk may be other than financial. The outcomes of entrepreneurial activity are inherently less predictable than other forms of employment, yet entrepreneurs often put their reputations and careers on the line, in public view, with such ventures. Entrepreneuring may be safer than race-car driving, but it is more risky than the typical white-collar job. Furthermore, the inclination to take personal risks helps determine the boldness and innovativeness of ventures undertaken, for there seems an inevitable association between the degree of proposed change and the probability of failure.

Perhaps of the greatest interest here is the apparent connection of entrepreneurship to profit making. Cole, for example, defines entrepreneurship as "The purposeful activity...of an individual or group of associated individuals, undertaken to initiate, maintain, or aggrandize a *profit-oriented business* unit for the production or distribution of economic goods and services." [12] Despite the specific reference to the profit-making sector in this and other definitions and the

specifically market-oriented context in which Schumpeter's discussion is posed, entrepreneurship is described basically as an organizing and promoting activity, which may be paid for by wages or other means, and which can, indeed must, take place in all economic sectors—profit oriented or not. Schumpeter's concept of implementing new combinations seems entirely applicable to the production of government, or nonprofit-sector services, although the motives and the specific forms and procedures for undertaking new ventures may differ.

Schumpeter's five types of entrepreneurial venture are based on an industry as the unit of analysis and involve changes in an industry's product, input, consumers, technology, or organizational structure. Entrepreneurs, however, operate not at the industry level, but at the level of the firm—the two levels being synonomous only in the case of a monopoly. From the viewpoint of the entrepreneur, then, it is desirable to classify ventures differently. Although they may be aware of this potential, entrepreneurs do not necessarily seek to change an industry; rather, they aim to implement a successful, firm-level enterprise, if only because the factors under their control, except in the case of a monopoly, operate at the level of the firm.

Collins and Moore describe a basic dichotomy in the form of entrepreneurial ventures— the distinction between setting up new organizations and developing ventures within the context of existing organizations.[13] These authors indicate that the motives of entrepreneurs and the implications of either choice may be quite different. This point will be elaborated later. For the present discussion the relevant consideration is whether the establishment of a new organization or a new program within an existing organization necessarily constitutes an instance of entrepreneurship. The answer depends on whether something new is being done and whether the firm-level action has industry-wide implications of the kind outlined by Schumpeter.

In the case of a new firm or organization, entrepreneurship almost always seems to be involved. New organizations are formed either to fill some empty niche in the industrial landscape—to offer a new product or serve a different set of consumers—or to substitute an improvement in the current regime—for example, use of a new techology, more economical input factors, or change of product quality. Furthermore, the introduction of new organizations inevitably alters the structure of the industry (Schumpeter's fifth criterion), if only slightly. Even where a new organization simply imitates the methods and services of another, some degree of innovation is likely to be involved, except perhaps in establishing franchise outlets, such as fast-food restaurants and automobile dealers.

The class of ventures that take place in the context of existing organizations requires closer inspection. In particular, what constitutes a new enterprise or program within a given corporate structure? Certainly a shift of personnel or the rearrangement or relabeling of boxes on an organization chart should not qualify as an entrepreneurial venture unless it signals a more fundamental change. Various types of changes do qualify, however, in the sense of leading to potentially substantive changes in the industry. Certain of these programmatic changes are obvious. If an organization adopts a new technology, provides a new service, or seeks a new consumer group, it is implementing a new combination and hence entrepreneuring. If an organization undertakes a major expansion (through internal growth or mergers) or diversification of its goods and services, even if these products are conventional, implications may abound for other firms and for the structure of the industry as a whole (for example, a shift from many small to a few large firms). Hence the venture would qualify as entrepreneurial.

Suppose that an organization radically shifts its services from one type to another. If the new service is novel in some sense, then the venture is clearly entrepreneurial, but even if the shift is from one conventional service to another, the venture may be indicative of change in the sense of an industry-wide shift from one source of demand, which is drying up (such as the demand for slide rules), to another, which is growing (for example, electronic calculators).

Another form of programmatic change that takes place in the context of existing organizations and that often indicates entrepreneurial activity is the revival of a failing organization. Organizations begin to fail for a variety of internal and environmental reasons. According to Hirschman's analysis of the processes of "exit

and voice" a certain level of oscillation of organizational deterioration and recuperation is to be expected.[14] Correction of routine problems or reduction of slack through enforcement of existing methods and procedures or the shifting of personnel does not constitute entrepreneurship. Often, however, organizational failures are endemic to an industry. As noted above, the demand for certain products or services may decline because of changes in tastes or technological developments; changes in government policies may affect industrial fortunes (witness the role of public-university systems in the decline of some private universities or the effect on railroads of government spending on highways); or industries may age, and their technologies, capital facilities, and personnel capabilities may become obsolete (for example, the domestic steel industry or the older industrial cities of the Northeast). In such cases, entrepreneurial initiatives may succeed in turning organizations around through technological renovations, product reorientation, or structural changes in corporate financing and decision making, and these turnarounds may signal basic changes at the industry level.

In short, several types of developments at the organization (firm) level are strong manifestations of entrepreneurial activity. The establishment of new organizations constitutes one class. The development of new programs in the context of existing organizations is another. Both types of development can include the introduction of new goods or services, service to new consumer groups, introduction of new technical methods or inputs, or innovations in corporate structure and financing. New programs within established organizations may also encompass major growth and expansion or product diversification or simplification. Finally, the turnaround of failing organizations may be indicative of changes in products, clientele, methods, inputs, or financial and organizational strategies, all indicative of entrepreneurship.

In all these cases, of course, entrepreneurship is a matter of degree. New organizations and major programmatic changes in existing organizations (including organizational turnarounds) together provide many interesting cases. In some instances, ventures will be observed at the leading edge of industry-wide change. In other cases, imitative or following behavior may be an equally accurate characterization. In all cases, there will be some originality and some imitation, some industry-wide implications and some implications peculiar to the individual firm. It becomes a matter of judgment as to what constitutes a legitimate case of entrepreneurship and what does not. Nonetheless, the qualitative character of entrepreneurship is clear, as is the notion that new organizations and internal programmatic developments of the kinds just discussed are relevant manifestations.

The inclusion of new organizations and internal programmatic developments helps make obvious the omnipresence of entrepreneurship across the various sectors of the economy. Although the incidence and distribution of these events differ among the public, nonprofit, and profit-making sectors, both new organizations and new program developments occur continually in all sectors. New governments occasionally form to replace old ones or to fill in new niches (metropolitan governments in some urban areas, new special districts or municipal incorporations, and so on). New government bureaus are formed with greater frequency, and program and policy changes are even more common. Failing governments also manage to extricate themselves from difficulty through major structural and programmatic shifts. Hundreds of nonprofit agencies are newly incorporated annually, and many new programs are established by the thousands of existing nonprofit organizations, associations, and federations. And struggling nonprofit universities, social-service agencies, fine-arts, and performing-arts organizations and the like often save themselves from financial failure through entrepreneurial initiative.

Such a litany is, of course, familiar for the profit-making sector, in which many new businesses start each year, new products and technologies are developed, major corporations undertake multiple initiatives internally, and many firms come back from the edge of bankruptcy.

Because this book is fundamentally concerned with the nonprofit sector, particular illustrations from that part of the economy are useful to provide a specific sense of the nature and variety of nonprofit entrepreneurship and to indicate that nonprofit entrepreneurship is indeed a real, significant, and widespread phenomenon.

This aim is most easily accomplished by reviewing a few fields of endeavor in which nonprofit activity is common.

The author's field studies in the broad field of child welfare focus on various manifestations of entrepreneurial venture. Several cases illustrate the founding of new nonprofits from scratch, and other cases describe new agencies that are spin-offs of parent organizations. One study reviews the formation of a new agency through the merger of two parent agencies. Another documents the experience of a social agency that radically changed its services (to juveniles) from one type (detention) to another (diagnostic). Still other cases illustrate the creation of new services by established agencies. A final set of studies describe dramatic turnarounds and growth of previously failing organizations.

Additional documentation of nonprofit entrepreneurial ventures in social services exists in the literature. For example, a collection of vignettes of over one hundred successful self-help projects in economically disadvantaged communities across the United States is presented in *Uplift*, under the auspices of the U.S. Jaycees Foundation.[15] The projects cover a number of functional areas, including local economic development, education, employment opportunity, housing, social services, health services, offender rehabilitation, and community organization. The vignettes report the efforts of local people—housewives, working people, clergy, handicapped people, social workers, minority-group leaders, exoffenders, reformed alcoholics —to organize new programs and establish nonprofit organizations dedicated to solving or servicing some of the problems in their local communities.

Other literature is more confined and focused on particular cases. In a study of foster-care agencies by Young and Finch, several cases of entrepreneurial activity are cited, including an agency that was converted from proprietary to nonprofit form, agencies that changed or grew rapidly over short periods of time, agencies that developed innovative programs for delinquent children, and newly established agencies.[16]

Other children's service ventures have received more notoriety. Reverend Bruce Ritter has often been cited for his path-breaking developments at Covenant House, a nonprofit child-care agency—notably for its Under 21 program, which services teenagers in the Times Square area of New York City who have run away from home and become involved in prostitution and pornography.[17] Other examples include Hope for Youth, a group home for abandoned or abused boys, established on Long Island in 1969 by Elizabeth Golding, a retired family court judge;[18] the Human Resources Center, an education and training institution for the physically handicapped, founded in 1953 by Henry Viscardi, himself crippled from birth;[19] and a home for boys in Guatemala, established in 1977 by John Wetterer, an American Vietnam veteran, with the support of the American Friends of Children, which he also founded.[20] Finally, a case of youth-oriented social-service entrepreneurship is described in detail by Goldenberg in *Build Me a Mountain*, which documents the formation and early operation of the Residential Youth Center in New Haven, Connecticut.[21] The venture, which entails entrepreneurship by Goldenberg and a few of his associates, was funded by the U.S. Department of Labor through New Haven's community action agency and administered in conjunction with the Psycho-Educational Clinic of Yale University.

Another interesting case, provided by Moore and Ziering, describes several entrepreneurial efforts to address the heroin-addiction problem in New York City in the mid 1960s.[22] Moore cites new programs organized within the city's Addiction Services Administration and Health and Hospitals Corporation as well as a venture based at the nonprofit Beth Israel Hospital. The latter was led by Vincent Dole, who developed the technique of methadone maintenance and organized and expanded a program within Beth Israel with public-sector (city) support.

The particular area of services to the elderly has witnessed a burgeoning of entrepreneurial activity over the last two decades. In the context of residential care, most of the action has been proprietary, but nonprofit activity also abounds.[23] Recent case studies of newly established nursing homes by Grennon and Barsky provide detailed examples of two nonprofit nursing-home ventures.[24] Other examples are referenced by Vladeck.[25] Nonresidential services to the elderly are dominated more heavily by nonprofits.

Fueled in part by provisions of the Older Americans Act, initiatives in this field have skyrocketed. Activities include congregate meeting facilities, food and homemaker programs, transportation, health, and a variety of other services designed to enable the elderly to live in the community rather than in nursing homes. An outstanding example of nonprofit entrepreneurial activity in this area is the Minneapolis Age and Opportunity Center, Inc. (MAO), organized by Daphne Krause in 1969.[26] The MAO is considered a pioneering venture, developed from scratch by a highly energetic and determined layperson, to provide a range of health, home-support, economic, and other assistance to elderly in need in the Minneapolis region.

The growth of emergency-relief organizations and other major charities is a prime manifestation of nonprofit entrepreneurship and is often in the public eye. Some international efforts, such as Oxfam, established in England almost forty years ago to provide relief from famine,[27] or the now-legendary work of Nobel laureate Mother Theresa of India,[28] which has included the establishment of some 158 branch houses in thirty-one countries, are examples. In the United States, organizations like the Red Cross and the Salvation Army have long histories of organizing emergency-relief programs of various kinds.

The fund-raising activity of emergency-relief and other types of charities—specialized, like the American Cancer Society, or generalized, such as the United Way—constitute a rather visible aspect of nonprofit entrepreneurship. Fund raising for charitable causes has come to represent a business in many minds, raising suspicions about the wisdom and efficiency, if not propriety, with which such funds are disbursed. Certainly, as noted by Rose-Ackerman and others, the behavior of United Funds in establishing payroll-deduction plans and consolidating the fund-raising functions of multiple charitable causes through unified fund drives represents entrepreneurship—a developing of new combinations for production, in Schumpeter's terms.[29] (It has also engendered some resistance and indignation, as many such ventures do.)[30]

United Way and other large charities are nonsectarian, but similar entrepreneurial behavior is found in the church-oriented charities as well. Merging of the fund-raising efforts of such organizations as the United Jewish Appeal and the Federation of Jewish Philanthropies in New York is one example. Fund raising is not the only direct aspect of entrepreneurship manifested by church-sponsored and other charities, however. Aside from funding various established nonprofit operating agencies, such charities become involved in setting up new corporations and administering direct-service programs in a variety of fields. For example, Catholic Charities of New York has been active in promoting local parishes to establish senior-citizen centers and in establishing certain innovative programs, such as hospices for the terminally ill.

Another interesting entrepreneurial tack taken by some charities, especially those which have funded causes addressed to problems that have ultimately been remedied or ameliorated, is diversification into new fields. The branching of the March of Dimes from polio research into the problem of birth defects and of charities for the blind into services for the multiply handicapped provide familiar examples. Still, new charities continue to be formed, often reflecting the personal concerns of founders. An example is the Committee to Combat Huntington's Disease, established by the widow of Woody Guthrie, the folksinger who died of that illness.[31]

Another entrepreneurial direction taken by some charities and churches is providing services through commercial-type ventures. For example, the Agency for the Blind as well as a number of churches have been directly involved in housing construction for the elderly and handicapped.[32] Fund raising through commercial-type activities—cake sales, benefit performances, raffles, auctions—has become an established practice for churches and other charities and is not confined to this part of the nonprofit sector. Many nonprofit organizations in a variety of fields have come to rely on commercial activities peripheral to their main purpose, such as sale of publications, property rental, gift shops, and insurance and travel programs, to generate revenues in support of service programs. Where such activity competes with private business, such nonprofit entrepreneurship has generated resentment and required scrutiny by the IRS.

Philanthropic foundations—large ones, such as Rockefeller, Mellon, Ford, and Carnegie, established through amassed family fortunes; those such as Johnson, Exxon, and Lilly, founded by large corporations; and many smaller ones—are an integral part of the world of nonprofit entrepreneurship. Foundations differ from charities—they have to give away money rather than collect it. In terms of entrepreneurial activity, however, there are similiarities. For example, there are efforts, such as the New York Community Trust, to consolidate small, individual foundation resources to permit the funding of larger and more meaningful projects and to allocate resources in a more systematic way. More important, in providing services foundations have been active in the design and support of new ventures over a wide spectrum of social causes and often become involved in individual projects and programs. Areas such as research, higher education, social and economic development, and health are replete with illustrations of integral foundation involvement. The 1972 study by Nielsen reviews a variety of such examples;[33] in his subsequent book, Nielsen cites Andrew Carnegie and John D. Rockefeller as the developers of the modern foundation as a vehicle of social change and credits the Ford Foundation with stimulating modern-day support for the arts.[34]

The field of higher education has produced several examples of nonprofit entrepreneurship since World War II. *Academic Transformation,* edited by Riesman and Stadtman, focuses on the crises of the 1960s and discusses such examples as the innovations of Antioch, changes in programs at the University of Pennsylvania and Princeton, and the growth of Stanford.[35] The latter is by now a legendary success story, documented recently in the alumni paper, encompassing the transformation of a scholastically limited and financially insecure university into one of the economically and educationally strongest in the country.[36] President Wallace Sterling, Provost Frederick Terman, and others are credited with such major coups as the development of the Stanford Industrial Park and Stanford Medical Center, which exploited the riches of the university's real estate and emerging new technologies to push Stanford to the forefront of technical and academic excellence.

More recently, the resurgence of New York University (NYU) parallels the Stanford experience somewhat in its revival aspects. Under the leadership of John Sawhill, and with a boost from sales of (and reinvestment of revenues from) certain key assets, NYU expanded and began new construction at a time (the 1970s) when higher education was generally perceived to be in difficult straits.[37] Latent assets (Stanford's land, NYU's ownership of the C.F. Mueller spaghetti company) help explain these successes, but such assets by no means ensured active engagement in entrepreneurship. An interesting case to watch will be Emory University, recently the recipient of $100 million from Robert W. Woodruff of Coca-Cola.[38]

A rather offbeat example of entrepreneurship in higher education is provided by Nova University in Florida, which has pioneered in such areas as computer-assisted instruction and off-campus programs.[39] Nova was saved from bankruptcy in 1970 by the New York Institute of Technology, whose president, Alexander Schure, became chancellor of Nova. The expansionism of the New York Institute of Technology and the maverick nature of Nova's programs have stirred some local resentment in Florida, particularly since Nova became the prospective recipient of certain charitable bequests. Schure, however, appears to have a keen idea of what his own entrepreneurship is all about, arguing that institutions need to identify and exploit marketing trends to survive.

As chapter 4 [not reprinted here] will show, entrepreneurship commonly arises from institutional adversity. Stanford, NYU, and Nova bear witness to this. Other cases include the absorption of the troubled Peabody College by Vanderbilt[40] and the takeover of Simon's Rock College by Bard College.[41] Another manifestation is the burgeoning of extension programs and the opening of out-of-state branches by many universities, in a "frantic search for students."[42] Even in the era of fiscal stringency and projected enrollment declines, adversity is not the only springboard for entrepreneurship in higher education. Tufts, for example, has opened a major veterinary school in anticipation of synergistic growth with other health-science units on the campus.[43] Professional education has witnessed a great deal of recent nonprofit

entrepreneurship, not only in the expansion of schools in such growing disciplines as law, medicine, and business, but also in the birth of a whole generation of interdisciplinary schools since the late 1960s, for example, the School of Organization and Management at Yale, the Kennedy School of Government at Harvard, and the School of Urban and Public Affairs at Carnegie-Mellon University. In a related development, universities and their faculties have seized on the opportunities for funded research by establishing a myriad of nonprofit research institutes, such as Stanford Research Institute, Yale's Institution for Social and Policy Studies, Columbia's Center for Policy Research, and Michigan's Institute for Social Research.[44]

Research institutes outside the university context are another prime manifestation of recent nonprofit entrepreneurship. Such organizations as the Urban Institute (under the leadership of William Gorham), the Vera Institute of Justice, and the Research Triangle Institute have emerged as major providers of research and policy studies in the 1960s and 1970s, while older institutes such as the Brookings Institution and RAND Corporation have grown and diversified significantly in this area.[45]

As reviewed by Nielsen, health care is another field in which nonprofit entrepreneurship has flourished in various forms.[46] Recently, organizational units centered on medical innovations—open-heart-surgery units, organ-transplant programs, and burn-treatment centers—have been started in nonprofit medical centers. An especially interesting development is the hospice conceived by Dame Cicely Saunders in England and recently implemented in a number of U.S. nonprofit settings, including the Good Samaritan Hospital in West Islip, New York and Mercy Hospital in Rockville Center, New York.[47] These hospices are designed to provide a comfortable, hospitable environment for the terminally ill.

The rising costs, increasing governmental support, and growing sophistication and specialization of health care have spurred a number of different types of nonprofit organizational ventures. Somers and Somers identified the trends toward more comprehensive medical institutions and systems of care.[48] The advent of Medicare and Medicaid have led public hospitals, such as those administered by New York City's Health and Hospitals Corporation to contract and local voluntary (nonprofit) hospitals to absorb the case loads and in some cases the administration of formerly public facilities.

More commonly, successful nonprofit hospitals, such as Long Island Jewish—Hillside Medical Center in New York, have expanded through merger, that is, by acquiring nearby proprietary facilities or other nonprofits with administrative problems.[49,50] One motivation for such merger activity is the fact that expansion-minded hospitals have faced resistance to new building programs from cost-conscious government officials who believe that there are already too many beds available.[51] Buying up existing capacities circumvents this resistance.

Cost considerations are also a prime factor in the development of prepaid medical care provided by health-maintenance organizations (HMOs). Pioneered by the Kaiser Hospitals in California (see Lehman),[52] HMOs have begun to develop more rapidly with the advent of federal-assistance grants. The new Community Health Plan of Suffolk, the expansion into hospital care by the Health Insurance Plan of Greater New York (HIP), and the Blue Cross HMO in New Hyde Park are recent examples of HMO activity.[53]

The area of law services and legal advocacy provides additional examples of recent nonprofit entrepreneurship, for example, by Ralph Nader in the public-interest law movement. This includes the formation of research institutes, such as the Center for the Study of Responsive Law, and the founding of public interest law firms, gathering momentum around 1970 with support of the Ford Foundation.[54]

The performing arts constitute another broad area of activity where nonprofit entrepreneurship has lately been much in evidence. As reviewed by Nielsen, the number of major opera companies, symphony orchestras, dance companies, and legitimate theaters more than doubled in the 1968–1978 period.[55] Netzer cites the establishment of regional and touring companies, such as the Baltimore Opera Company and Trinity Square Repertory in Providence as significant developments.[56]

Many other examples are cited in the press. The Performing Arts Foundation (PAF) Playhouse in Huntington, New York is one illustration in the field of dramatic performance.[57,58,59] Founded in 1966 by a high-school teacher with a large grant from the U.S. Office of Education, the theater was intended as a medium for arts education and as a community theater for presentation of revivals. By 1974, however, the theater was seriously in debt and threatened with closing. Under the leadership of its board president—folksinger Harry Chapin—and newly appointed director Jay Broad and with substantial help from private foundations, government, and major corporations, PAF was transformed from a local repertory theater into a regional, professional theater which presents primarily original works. Over the period 1975–1978, the budget tripled, subscriptions rose from 2,000 to 14,000, and a new half-million-dollar theater was constructed. Unfortunately, the theater experienced renewed difficulties and folded a few years later, following Mr. Chapin's untimely death.

Other recent examples of nonprofit enterprise in drama include the Arena Stage in Washington, D.C. and the New York Shakespeare Festival in Manhattan. The Oregon Shakespeare Festival reflects nonprofit entrepreneurship on a smaller but no-less-interesting scale.[60] Founded by Angus Bowmer in 1935, it began as a community celebration of the Fourth of July, in Ashland, Oregon, with performances by students and faculty of Southern Oregon State College. The festival now runs a dozen plays per season in three theaters and draws a quarter of a million people.

On Long Island, orchestral music provided an active entrepreneurial context in the late 1970s. Originally two orchestras consisting largely of part-time musicians—the Suffolk Symphony and the Long Island Symphony—served the two counties of Nassau and Suffolk. With impetus from Harry Chapin, a full-time professional orchestra—the Long Island Philharmonic—was formed to replace these two orchestras. The Long Island Symphony, composed of resident musicians, refused to go out of business, however. Disbanded by its board of directors, this orchestra has reorganized as a musicians' cooperative.[61]

Ventures like the Kennedy Center in Washington or the Lincoln Center in New York represent major milestones of interdisciplinary performing-arts enterprise. The Lincoln Center, begun in 1959 under the leadership of John D. Rockefeller, was conceived as an urban redevelopment project that would bring under one roof a "community of the arts."[62] The center has indeed been an ambitious undertaking, now housing the New York Philharmonic Orchestra, the Metropolitan Opera, the New York City Ballet, the Juilliard School of Music, a repertory company, a chamber-music hall, and a library-museum. The Kennedy Center in Washington was envisioned as a national center for the performing arts during the Eisenhower years, but was reconceived as a memorial to John F. Kennedy after 1963. It opened in 1971 and has been developed under the dynamic joint leadership of Roger L. Stevens, board president, and Martin Feinstein, its first executive director.[63,64] Stevens, a lifelong theater entrepreneur, and Feinstein, a trained musician and impresario, are generally recognized to have helped put Washington on the cultural map with top-flight dramatic theater, ballet, music extravaganzas, summer opera, and visiting world-renown opera companies.

Art museums have been one of the most dynamic areas of nonprofit activity in recent years. As Meyer notes:

> Since 1950 the United States has committed at least a half billion dollars to the construction of 10.2 million square feet of art museums and visual art centers, the equivalent footage of 13.6 Louvres.[65]

New museums continued to be founded, often to display art forms not previously provided special recognition. The International Center of Photography in New York City is a recent example, as was the Museum of Modern Art (MOMA) in an earlier era (1929).[66] The recent activity of a group in Los Angeles to found a modern-art facility is an additional illustration.[67]

New museums are often set up to display the private collections of rich men who donate their treasure to the public. The Hirschhorn Museum in Washington, D.C. and the Kimbell Art Museum in Fort Worth (under the leadership of Richard Brown) are important recent examples.[68] Meyer describes additional examples, including the Norton Simon Museum in Pasadena and the Brundage wing of the De Young Museum in San Francisco.[69] The Parrish Museum in Southampton, New York is an older and smaller illustration of the same phenomenon.[70]

Other museums are founded by historically minded entrepreneurs to preserve local treasure. The new art museum (1978) of the Museums at Stony Brook (New York) is devoted to works of the local, renowned nineteenth-century artist William S. Mount. Other museums, like Gallery North in Setauket, New York, which recently converted from proprietary to nonprofit status, are established to display the works of local, living artists.

Within the realm of long-established museums, entrepreneurial activity seems to have taken at least three different directions—the development of new functional subdivisions, the undertaking of commercial ventures to generate financial support, and the creation of popular new exhibitions. An example in the first category is the plan of the Los Angeles County Museum to construct a modern-art wing.[71]

The engagement in commercial sales in support of organizational purposes is a relatively common phenomenon among nonprofits, but some recent initiatives by museums have drawn particular notoriety. In real estate, for example, the Museum of Modern Art in New York has undertaken construction of a forty-four story condominium over a six-story museum building in an effort to generate revenues to offset its increasing operational expenses.[72,73]

The project caused substantial protest, with critics charging that a profit and loss orientation would force the museum to alter its artistic priorities. Other objections included loss of tax revenues to the city and architectural considerations. In a similar vein, museums have enormously increased their activity in the domain of retail sales—for example, memberships that include magazine subscriptions, gift shops, and sale of art reproductions. The larger museums, at least, appear to have learned the lesson taught by Olson, that public goods can be better provided if they are tied in with selective private goods.[74] Hence the receipt of fine magazines (unavailable on newsstands) like *The Smithsonian* or *Natural History* or discounts on reproductions of museum pieces increases general-membership support. The Metropolitan Museum of Art reportedly grossed over $16 million in 1978 in commercial revenues (not including memberships and admissions). Smithsonian gift shops drew $7 million, and many other examples can be cited.[75]

The growth in commercial-sales revenue is closely tied to the most spectacular recent museum innovation—the grand exhibition, or supershow, best exemplified by the Metropolitan Museum of Art during the dynamic tenure of Thomas Hoving, with its King Tut (Tutankhamen) tour of 1978.[76] This exhibit was followed at the Metropolitan by other blockbusters, including Pompeii 79, Alexander the Great, and Treasures of the Kremlin, and by such grand exhibitions as the Cezanne and Picasso shows at the Museum of Modern Art.[77] These large and spectacular shows, often based on foreign-loan collections, have generated considerable revenues for the museums, largely through sales of reproductions and boosted interest in memberships, but they have also generated considerable tension and controversy in the museum world. Seen as a lifeline to rescue museums from the ravages of inflation, the shows are also said to threaten some of the nonprofit museum's basic purposes, such as the discernment of new directions in the art world, art education and research, and other artistic concerns not subject to popular appeal.

As for entrepreneurs in the world of nonprofit museums, the recently deceased Richard Brown and the dynamic Thomas Hoving provide captivating, if very different, examples. Brown was a scholar, teacher, and connoisseur whose desire, according to a colleague, was to "realize an institution that was concerned with excellence, that would provide the finest of visual experiences for the viewer."[78] Hoving, on the other hand, is generally acknowledged to be the most dynamic executive to enter the museum world in many years. A flamboyant entrepreneur, Hoving was characterized by one observer as "A P.T. Barnum."[79] At the Metropolitan Museum of Art, Hoving is credited with securing large, expensive, new collections and controversial art objects, with initiating a major building program that cost more than $70 million and with planning spectacular exhibits like Tutankhamen. Meyer cites several other fascinating entrepreneurial characters in the museum world, including S. Dillon Ripley of the Smithsonian, Francis Henry Taylor of the Metropolitan Museum of Art in the 1940s and 1950s, and Sarah Newmeyer of the Museum of Modern Art, each of whom was responsible for major innovations in museum operations.[80]

In most of the fields reviewed, parallel instances of entrepreneurship can be cited for the profit-making and governmental sectors as well. Proprietary hospitals and nursing homes, government social-service programs, public-education and research initiatives, public museums, and proprietary theater are all rich with contemporary examples. Thus, precisely what factors influence the selection of sector for entrepreneurial activity is not simply a superficial matter of associating a given service with a given economic sector.

Nonprofit entrepreneurship is not restricted to the several areas discussed above. Other fields, such as publishing or recreation, provide further illustrations. Some of the most often-cited recent examples of nonprofit entrepreneurship are not easily distinguished from market-oriented commercial ventures. For instance, the new YMCA facility in Washington, D.C. has a sauna, whirlpool, steam room, large pool, and so on and caters to the upper-middle class, with membership fees to match.[81] The Educational Testing Service (ETS) is another nonprofit enmeshed in controversy for its recent market-making behavior.[82] Having grown into an $80 million business, ETS is offering a more diversified set of aptitude and job-placement services, some say at the expense of profit-oriented business competitors. Finally, a venture like Erhard Seminars Training (EST), founded in 1971 by Werner Erhard and boasting a $15 million operation by 1978, has grown on the unique chemistry of evangelism, salesmanship, and a keen eye on what the market will bear for people who can pay to improve themselves.[83]

Nonprofit entrepreneurship is thus a diverse and widespread phenomenon. Yet it has been argued that the nonprofit sector suffers from a lack of entrepreneurship and entrepreneurial talent.[84] In relative terms, this may be true, but there are no adequate measures. What is clear, however, is that entrepreneurship in the nonprofit sector, as elsewhere, represents the cutting edge of the sector's activity, and, as such, its study helps to reveal the driving forces and underlying character of its member organizations.

Of course, entrepreneurship is just one important phase of activity that takes place in an economic sector, and entrepreneurs are just one set of actors who help determine the general patterns of behavior. Certainly, as observed in chapter 9 [not reprinted here], the motivations, intentions, and circumstances that characterize entrepreneurship may be dissipated over time, as entrepreneurs leave their ventures to successors or as they themselves change or face new exigencies. Furthermore. . .organizations are not only established or grow or change for the better, as normally reflected in entrepreneurship, but they also pass through stages of relative equilibrium and sometimes stagnate or die. These latter aspects or organizational life are also important in establishing overall sector patterns and trends, although it seems plausible that the incidence of entrepreneurship, or lack of it, during periods of organizational uncertainty or stagnation may help account for ultimate survival or demise. Entrepreneurial leadership, or lack of it, can never fully explain why organizations prosper or decline or behave in particular ways. Labor-market trends that affect the cost and availability of particular types of personnel, such as volunteers and paraprofessionals, the cost of other inputs, the nature of societal demands for particular types of goods and services, the alteration of public policies, the demands of labor unions, and the availability of capital may all be beyond entrepreneurial control yet may largely account for global shifts among fields of activity and sectoral shifts within a given field. Still, it may be argued that the manner in which entrepreneurial talent responds or fails to respond to such general changes in context will be highly informative of the vitality and behavior peculiar to particular sectors.

Entrepreneurship is viewed here as an especially useful focal point for attempting to characterize a number of crucial aspects of organizational and sectoral behavior—for example, the extent to which growth, innovation, self-aggrandizing, quality-emphasizing, cost-inflating, socially responsive, market-dominating, or zealously missionary activity are exhibited, or not exhibited, by nonprofit organizations. The reasons for this view are twofold.

First, entrepreneurs are often founding fathers of their organizations, and leaders in their industries. As such, their values and personal motivations for venture will tend to shape in a significant way the organizations that they are establishing or changing. Second, enterprise is the means through which many forms of organizational behavior are exhibited. If an organization is growth oriented, it will grow through enterprising. If it is innovative, it will innovate through new ventures. If it is self-aggrandizing or aspires to market dominance, these goals will be sought largely through the implementation of new enterprise. If such characteristics are lacking, there will be a dearth of entrepreneurial activity.

Still, as noted previously, describing entrepreneurial motives or the nature of enterprising projects alone is insufficient for generalizing to overall patterns of organization behavior. The role of entrepreneurs and the incidence of venture must be placed into a wider perspective in order to discern where entrepreneurship is likely to take place, how it will vary from one context to another, and how it will be shaped and modified by environmental circumstances.

Notes

1. The so-called Austrian school of economics is an exception. See Israel M. Kirzner, *Perception, Opportunity and Profit* (Chicago: University of Chicago Press, 1979). See also Israel M. Kirzner, *Competition and Entrepreneurship* (Chicago: University of Chicago Press, 1973).

2. See *Webster's New World Dictionary of the American Language*, College Edition (World Publishing Company, 1968).

3. B.F. Hoselitz, "Entrepreneurship and Economic Growth," *American Journal of Economic Sociology* 12 (1952).

4. Joseph A. Schumpeter, *The Theory of Economic Development* (Cambridge: Harvard University Press, 1949).

5. William D. Angel, "To Make a City: Entrepreneurship on the Sunbelt Frontier," in *The Rise of the Sunbelt Cities*, eds. David C. Perry and Alfred J. Watkins, Urban Affairs Annual Reviews, vol. 14 (Beverly Hills: Sage Publications, 1977).

6. Matthew Josephson, *The Robber Barons* (New York: Harcourt, Brace and World, Inc., 1962).

7. Orvis Collins and David G. Moore, *The Organization Makers*, (New York: Appleton-Century-Crofts, 1970).

8. Alfred Marshall, *Economics of Industry* (London: Macmillan and Company, 1964).

9. Angel, "Entrepreneurship."

10. Collins and Moore, *Organization Makers*.

11. Schumpeter, *Economic Development*.

12. Authur H. Cole, *Business Enterprise in a Social Setting* (Cambridge: Harvard University Press, 1959).

13. Collins and Moore, *Organization Makers*.

14. Albert O. Hirschman, *Exit, Voice, and Loyalty* (Cambridge: Harvard University Press, 1970).

15. Washington Consulting Group Inc. for the U.S. Jaycees Foundation, *Uplift: What People Themselves Can Do* (Salt Lake City: Olympus Publishing Co., 1974).

16. Dennis R. Young and Stephen J. Finch, *Foster Care and Nonprofit Agencies* (Lexington, Mass.: Lexington Books, D.C. Heath and Company, 1977).

17. Cheryl McCall, "Father Ritter's Mission in Rescuing Runaway Youths from Times Square Sex Peddlers," *People*, November 13, 1978.

18. Aileen Jacobson, "Where Unwanted Boys Find a Family," *Newsday*, August 4, 1979.

19. Maureen Early, "Walking Tall," *Newsday*, November 16, 1978. Also, Henry Viscardi, *A Laughter in the Lonely Night* (New York: Paul S. Eriksson Inc. 1961).

20. Leonard Levitt, "Uncle John," *Newsday*, April 15, 1979.

21. I. Ira Goldenberg, *Build Me a Mountain* (Cambridge: MIT Press, 1971).

22. Mark Moore and Mark Ziering, "Methadone Maintenance," (Case study, Kennedy School of Government, Harvard University, 1976).

23. Bruce C. Vladeck, *Unloving Care* (New York: Basic Books, 1980). Burton Dunlop, *The Growth of Nursing Home Care* (Lexington Mass.: Lexington Books, D.C. Heath and Company, 1979).

24. Jacqueline Grennon and Robert Barsky, "Case Studies in Nursing Home Entrepreneurship," (PONPO working paper, Institution for Social and Policy Studies, Yale University, 1980).

25. Vladeck, *Unloving Care*.

26. U.S. Congress, House Select Committee on Aging, Subcommittee on Health and Long-Term Care, *Innovative Alternatives to Institutionalization*, July 8, 1965.

27. William Borders, "Oxfam Takes Only One Side—The Side of the Hungry," *New York Times*, November 4, 1979.

28. Michael T. Kaufman, "The World of Mother Theresa," *New York Times Magazine*, December 9, 1979.

29. Susan Rose-Ackerman, "United Charities: An Economic Analysis" Working paper 822. (Institution for Social and Policy Studies, Yale University, August 1979).

30. Timothy Saasta, "Accusing the Biggest Charity of Greed," *Newsday*, November 26, 1979.

31. Colman McCarthy, "Singing Out for Woody Guthrie," *Newsday*, November 14, 1978.

32. James Barron, "When Churches Get Into the Business of Housing," *New York Times*, May 13, 1979.

33. Waldemar A. Nielsen, *The Big Foundations* (Twentieth Century Fund, New York: Columbia University Press, 1972).

34. Waldemar A. Nielsen, *The Endangered Sector* (New York: Columbia University Press, 1979).

35. David Riesman and Verne A. Stadtman, eds., *Academic Transformation*, Carnegie Commission on Higher Education (New York: McGraw-Hill, 1973).

36. Donald Stokes, "The Sterling Touch: How Stanford Became a World Class University," *The Stanford Observer*, October 1979.

37. Edward B. Fiske, "N.Y.U., Bucking National Trend, Expands Its Classes and Faculty," *New York Times*, November 26, 1979.

38. Gene I. Maeroff, "Emory U. Seeks New Stature on a Gift and a Dream," *New York Times*, November 18, 1979.

39. Gene I. Maeroff, "Suits Draw Attention to Unorthodox Education Combine," *New York Times*, May 14, 1976.

40. Edward B. Fiske, "Peabody College Approves Merger with Vanderbilt, Ending a Debate," *New York Times*, March 20, 1979.

41. Gene I. Maeroff, "Bard College Taking Over Early-Entrance School," *New York Times*, February 4, 1979.

42. "Some Colleges are Bobbing Up Everywhere," *New York Times*, January 7, 1979.

43. Michael Knight, "Tufts Plans Major New Veterinary School," *New York Times*, April 17, 1979.

44. Edward W. Lehman and Anita M. Waters, "Control in Policy Research Institutes: Some Correlates," *Policy Analysis* (Spring 1979).

45. Paul Dickson, *Think Tanks* (New York: Atheneum, 1971). Also, Bruce L.R. Smith, *The Rand Corporation* (Cambridge: Harvard University Press, 1966).

46. Nielsen, *Endangered Sector*.

47. Linda Field, "Suffolk Hospital Plans Hospice Program," *Newsday*, November 16, 1978.

48. Herman M. Somers and Anne R. Somers, *Medicare and the Hospitals* (Washington, D.C.: Brookings Institution, 1967).

49. Lawrence C. Levy, "Purchase of Hospital Seen Close," *Newsday*, May 27, 1979.

50. Ronald Sullivan, "Roosevelt and St. Lukes Merge Into One Hospital," *New York Times*, October 10, 1979.

51. Lawrence C. Levy, "Glen Cove Hospital Seeks Takeover," *Newsday*, December 26, 1978.

52. Edward W. Lehman, *Coordinating Health Care* (Beverly Hills: Sage Publications, 1975).

53. Neill S. Rosenfeld, "Prepaid Health Plans Flourish on L.I.," *Newsday*, November 25, 1978.

54. Joel F. Handler, Betsy Ginsberg, and Authur Snow, "The Public Interest Law Industry," chapter 4 in *Public Interest Law*, eds. Burton Weisbrod, Joel F. Handler, and Neil Komesar (Berkeley: University of California Press, 1978).

55. Nielsen, *Endangered Sector*.

56. Dick Netzer, *The Subsidized Muse* (New York: Cambridge University Press, 1978).

57. C. Gerald Fraser, "PAF Playhouse 'Grows', " *New York Times*, December 27, 1978.

58. Alvin Klein, "For PAF, Troubles Follow Success," *Newsday*, October 29, 1979.

59. Barbara Delatiner, "A New Theatre Opens and PAF is the Star," *New York Times*, January 7, 1979.

60. Edith Evans Asbury, "Angus L. Bowmer, 74, Founder of Oregon Shakespeare Festival," *New York Times*, May 29, 1979.

61. Barbara Delatiner, "Regrouped L.I. Symphony to Settle in Long Beach," *New York Times*, August 19, 1979.

62. Irving Kolodin, "Lincoln Center at 20: Old Problems, New Initiatives," *Newsday*, May 13, 1979.

63. Tom Prideaux, "The Man Behind Kennedy Center," *Review*, April 1979.

64. Harold C. Schonberg, "A Shock from Kennedy Center," *New York Times*, September 30, 1979.

65. Karl E. Meyer, *The Art Museum* (New York: William Morrow and Co., 1979), p. 13.

66. Hilton Kramer, article on the Museum of Modern Art, *New York Times Magazine*, November 4, 1979.

67. Grace Glueck, "2 New Contemporary Art Museums Are Being Planned for Los Angeles," *New York Times*, October 25, 1979.

68. Grace Glueck, "Richard Fargo Brown Dead at 63: Led Ft. Worth's Kimbell Museum," *New York Times*, November 7, 1979.

69. Karl E. Meyer, *Art Museum*.

70. Amei Wallach, "A Museum Looking to Get Engaged," *Newsday*, July 1, 1979.

71. Glueck, "Contemporary Art Museums."

72. Paul Goldberger, "The New MOMA: Mixing Art with Real Estate," *New York Times Magazine*, November 4, 1979.

73. Grace Glueck, "Modern Museum Head Hopeful Despite Setback from Court," *New York Times*, August 1978.

74. Mancur Olson, *The Logic of Collective Action* (Cambridge: Harvard University Press, 1965).

75. Olivia Buehl, "Museums and the Art of Retail," *Flightime* (Allegheny Airlines, April 1979).

76. Grace Glueck, "The Tut Show Gives a Midas Touch to Almost Everyone but the Viewer," *New York Times*, December 24, 1978.

77. Hilton Kramer, "Has Success Spoiled American Museums?" *New York Times*, January 14, 1979.

78. Glueck, "Richard Fargo Brown."

79. Grace Glueck, "How Fares the Met Museum in the Post-Hoving Era?" *New York Times*, April 8, 1979.

80. Karl E. Meyer, *Art Museum*.

81. Karen De Witt, "Plush New 'Y' Built on Controversy," *New York Times*, April 21, 1979.

82. Edward B. Fiske, "Student Testing Unit's Expansion Leads to Debate," *New York Times*, November 14, 1979.

83. Dave G. Houser, "Is est It?," *Sky* (Delta Airlines, March 1979).

84. Harold S. Williams, "Entrepreneurs in the Non-Profit World," *In Business*, July–August, 1980.

ARTICLE 25
Enterprise in the Nonprofit Sector
James C. Crimmins and Mary Kiel

enterprise—something undertaken; a project, mission business, etc., especially one requiring boldness or perseverance.[1]

Faced with the prospect of staff layoffs and program reductions, many nonprofit organizations are beginning to look beyond traditional funding sources. Fund-raising drives still flourish, but they have been supplemented by other income-producing sources, such as summer workshops, real estate developments, barter arrangements, cable television programs, and specialized magazines. There is a sense of explosive activity in the sector as more and more nonprofits search for viable alternatives to government and foundation grants, corporate gifts and individual donations, and fees and admissions that have funded their operations for so long.

In this sampling of a small fraction of the 850,000 nonprofits in the United States, we learned how nonprofit organizations are using enterprise to diversify their funding bases, expand their programs, and stay afloat while other sources of support are vanishing. Sixty-nine percent of the organizations we surveyed have given birth to new enterprise within the past twelve years. Sixty percent generate some of their revenues from enterprise activities. Although in 1981 the increase in charitable giving outpaced the inflation rate for the first time in three years (charitable giving rose 12.3 percent, while inflation averaged 8.9 percent), donations from individuals, foundations, and corporations could not make up for recent cuts in government funding at the federal, state, and local levels. These cuts, combined with an increase in the number of nonprofit organizations, means that more groups than ever are competing for a smaller slice of the "giving" pie. As Edward J. Pfister, chairman of the Corporation for Public Broadcasting, puts it, "People used to tell us, 'By God, whatever else you do, don't make money,'.... But times have changed."[2]

SOURCE: Reprinted by permission of Partners for Livable Places, Washington, D.C.

The purpose of this overview is to provide a historical perspective and place the budget crisis and needs of the moment in perspective. It also gives us an opportunity to report on our interviews with leaders of the institutions that are dealing with enterprise problems and opportunities. Later in this chapter we will discuss what we found to be at the heart of what is possible and what is not: attitude.

Nonprofit Enterprise: A Contradiction in Terms?

To many, "enterprise in the nonprofit sector" may seem a contradiction in terms. Traditionally, nonprofits in America have helped those who cannot help themselves; contributed to society's cultural, educational, and spiritual development; and campaigned for reform. Their very name—nonprofit—has often set them apart from the rest of enterprising America.

Yet, "a nonprofit organization is, in essence, an organization that is barred from distributing its net earnings, if any, to individuals who exercise control over it, such as members, officers, directors, or trustees.... It should be noted that a *nonprofit organization is not barred from earning a profit* [emphasis added]."[3] Whereas enterprise income earned by a for-profit business is distributed to its owners, shareholders, and others, all enterprise income earned by a nonprofit organization is plowed back into the organization. Most nonprofit enterprise supplements monies the organization receives through "giving" —grants, donations, bequests. Our survey results indicate that enterprise rarely comprises the majority of an organization's total income; in fact, only 22 percent of the groups in our sample earned more than 10 percent of their income through enterprise activities.

Who We Surveyed and Why

Our study focused primarily on nonprofits that have tax-exempt status under Internal Revenue Code 501(c)(3), a category that automatically qualifies donors for charitable contribution deductions. The organizations we surveyed can be classified loosely as either "arts" or "human services" and include such nonprofits as botanical gardens, family service organizations, opera companies, universities, and rehabilitation centers. Each of the 130 organizations that completed a questionnaire provided information on its program, financial status (including a comparison of revenue sources between fiscal years 1976 and 1981), investments, and fund raising. The questionnaire included a checklist of possible enterprise activities, as well as in-depth questions on the specific enterprises in which the organization was involved. A discussion of the survey's methodology is included in the appendixes [not reprinted here].

Specifically, this report focuses on the following questions:

- What types of nonprofits are using enterprise?
- What types of enterprise are being developed?
- What are the successes and failures?
- What trends and patterns are worth noting?
- What are some of the most innovative forms of enterprise?
- What legal, organizational, managerial, financial, and community issues are involved?
- How can a nonprofit evaluate its assets with enterprise in mind?
- What recommendations and new ideas have evolved from this?

What the Data Show

Although our response rate was low, our results closely paralleled comparable data from other sources. To test our conclusions, we gathered information on thirteen of the types of organizations we surveyed, including associations for the blind, child welfare groups, museums, symphonies, theaters, and zoos and aquariums, from a variety of professional organizations around the country. Their data on enterprise income, where available, support our belief that our sample represents a larger universe of nonprofits. Table A-10 in the appendix [not reprinted here] provides more information.

Whether these organizations were new to the enterprise field or old hands, over 60 percent of the nonprofits in our sample generated some revenues from enterprise activity, and 69 percent of these enterprises have been started since 1970 (see table).

Years Enterprises Were Started

Years	Percentage of Sample
Before 1940	9
1940–1949	2
1950–1959	8
1960–1969	12
1970–present	69
	100

During the past five years, over 60 percent of the groups with enterprise revenues have experienced an increase in the amount that enterprise contributes to their total income. We found that the organizations whose enterprise revenues have grown experienced more growth in total revenues (over 200 percent) than did the overall sample (139 percent).

We discovered that few generalizations could be made about the types of nonprofit organizations that engage in enterprise activities. Of the 22 percent of the organizations in our sample that generate 10 percent or more of their total revenues from enterprise activities, there is no concentration of size, geographic area, or type (see following table).

We did find that very small organizations, those with annual budgets under $100,000, in general do not rely on enterprise revenues to any significant degree. Very large organizations, those with budgets over $10 million, all engage in some type of enterprise activity. We found that those organizations with the least motivation to pursue profit-making ventures were the so-called "chamber of commerce" groups—that is, medium-size nonprofits, whether museums, historical societies, libraries, or symphonies, that are closely tied to the traditions and values of their communities. These organizations tend to be an essential part of the community identity and seem secure in the knowledge that the community will support and take care of them. They therefore have less incentive to pursue independent enterprise activities.

More than one-third of our sample generates 80 percent or more of their total budgets through *unearned* income (grants, endowment income, etc.), and of this third, 60 percent have

Budget Size vs. Enterprise "Revenues"

1981 Budget Size ($000)	*Enterprise Revenues as a Percentage of Total Revenue*				
	0	*1–1.99*	*2–4.99*	*5–9.99*	*10 or more*
0–100	63	6	19	6	6
101–300	48	11	9	7	25
301–600	60	20	—	—	20
601–1,000	38	25	—	25	12
1,001–1,500	63	12	—	—	25
1,501–4,000	12	25	25	13	25
4,001–10,000	44	—	14	14	28
10,001 and above	—	17	51	16	16

no enterprise revenues at all. However, of those organizations that receive 25 percent or less of their income from unearned sources, one-half have no enterprise revenues, indicating a high level of fee or admissions income, but no separate enterprise activities (see following table).

The History of Nonprofit Enterprise

Although it grew out of causes and social concerns similar to those that molded the British and European philanthropic traditions, the funding of the American nonprofit sector has always been more complex than its continental counterparts. Professor John G. Simon of Yale University points out,

> Nonprofit organizations in our society undertake missions that are, in other countries, committed to business enterprises or to the state. Here, we importantly, if not

exclusively, rely on the third sector to cure us, to entertain us, to teach us, to study us, to preserve our culture, to defend our rights and the balance of nature, and, ultimately, to bury us. And we rely on private philanthropy—third sector financing—to support activities that other nations support with public funds.[4]

Although, for the purposes of this study, we have refined the definition of enterprise to include only ongoing business activities, nonprofits have pursued enterprising ways of earning revenues since the time of the Pilgrims. The first nonprofits developed at the grassroots level, often as offshoots of community or church groups. When such groups discovered that money that couldn't be earned by passing the collection plate could be raised at the church bazaar, nonprofit enterprise was born.

Early nonprofit enterprises developed from the assets and skills that such groups had at their

Unearned Income vs. Enterprise—Total Sample

UI/TR[a]	*Enterprise Revenues as a Percentage of Total Revenue*				
	0	*1–1.99*	*2–4.99*	*5–9.99*	*10 or more*
More than 80%	20	4	4	4	1
61–80%	6	3	5	1	6
41–60%	6	3	6	3	8
26–40%	—	3	3	2	6
25% or less	3	—	2	—	1
Total	35	13	20	10	22

a. Unearned income as a percentage of total revenue.

disposal. Volunteers were (and still are) one of the most important assets, and since many were women, much grassroots nonprofit enterprise reflected women's skills and interests: Women's auxiliaries have traditionally held bake sales and rummage sales and sold cookbooks and home crafts to support a variety of charitable and cultural causes. Over time, these enterprises have evolved into solid business ventures, such as thrift shops, bookstores, coffee shops, and gift shops that contribute varying levels of income to nonprofit organizations.

In general, nonprofit enterprises have tended to reflect not only the assets of these organizations, but also the needs of the clients and constituencies they serve. Goodwill Industries' thrift shops developed out of the organization's commitment to training the handicapped. Museum restaurants were originally set up as a service to patrons, volunteers, and staff. University bookstores provided an essential commodity for students and faculty. Even the Girl Scouts, whose councils earn approximately 41 percent of their annual income from cookie sales, value the cookie-selling experience for teaching scouts such skills as "learning to work well with others. . .handling money. . .developing the satisfaction of a job well done." [5]

In the beginning, since these enterprises were primarily service oriented, profits often were not emphasized. In fact, whether they made or lost money was sometimes difficult to document, since few nonprofits kept separate books for their program and enterprise activities. There was no need; such enterprises were small and regarded as ancillary to the purpose of most organizations.

"Related" and "Unrelated" Income

According to Susan Rose-Ackerman, associate professor of economics at Yale University, nonprofit enterprise in America developed slowly and without much furor until 1950, when a group of wealthy graduates donated the Mueller Macaroni Company to New York University (NYU) Law School. NYU claimed that since Mueller's profits were going to the university, a nonprofit organization, the profits were exempt from corporate income tax. Mueller's competitor, the Ronzoni Company, sued, arguing that the

exemption gave Mueller an unfair competitive advantage in the pasta market. "In response," writes Rose-Ackerman, "Congress amended the income tax code in 1950 to eliminate this exemption. Henceforth, nonprofits would be permitted to retain an exemption only on 'related' business ventures." [6]

The problem of defining "related" has been with the sector since. Both the courts and the IRS have had trouble with the specifics of the definition, which has resulted in a certain nervousness on the part of nonprofits interested in enterprise activities. The university bookstore now has to decide whether selling toothpaste is related or unrelated to the function of the university: Do clean teeth serve the purposes of higher learning? On a more complex level, do such potential nonprofit business ventures as a university's genetic engineering lab or a restaurant run by handicapped workers constitute related or unrelated income? Says Rose-Ackerman: "As nonprofits try to enter new fields. . .Congress and the IRS must decide whether to facilitate or impede these activities through the income tax laws."

"The Great Society"

By the mid-1960s, the entire nonprofit sector was expanding at a prodigious rate. "Much of the growth began with the Great Society programs of the Lyndon Johnson era, which were established in an attempt to help the nation cope with an increasingly complex social and technical society." [7]

One of the most entrepreneurial brainchildren of this period was the Community Development Corporation (CDC) program, designed to encourage small business development in economically disadvantaged areas. CDCs are nonprofit organizations originally supported by federal government funding and set up in low-income communities across the United States. They offer an array of development-oriented programs, which include operating business enterprises; assisting neighborhood entrepreneurs; and building, rehabilitating, and managing housing. Considered by some to be the "granddaddies of nonprofit enterprise," CDCs have stimulated business in many low-income areas, and the positive "fallout" of the CDC movement has filtered into the rest of the nonprofit sector as well. Nonetheless, the longevity of their experience with enterprise also highlights many of the problems and issues that arise. Their failures have been as noteworthy as their successes.

Enterprise Pioneers

The other important pioneers in the nonprofit enterprise movement were organizations that had difficulty attracting outside funding: Drug and alcohol rehabilitation centers; halfway houses for ex-convicts; and programs for the mentally, physically, or emotionally handicapped have had to turn to self-generated income from the outset. Rather than be subject to the vagaries of governmental or philanthropic support, many of these groups have been able simultaneously to serve the needs of their clientele and to generate necessary income. The key to success is one valuable asset: an available labor pool.

Nonprofits that offer therapeutic and rehabilitative assistance to their clientele have learned to combine such training with enterprise activity. Workers in such programs, called sheltered workshops, carve decorative wooden clocks in Florida; produce pickles, mustard, and ketchup in Rhode Island; raise feeder pigs in upstate New York; and operate a recycling center in Seattle. The type of enterprise developed in such workshops depends on the needs and abilities of the workers, the skills and expertise of staff members or available volunteers, and the needs of the market area.

One sheltered workshop that has managed to become almost totally self-supporting is Bancroft Products in Concord, New Hampshire. A vocational rehabilitation center for the physically, intellectually, and behaviorally handicapped, Bancroft's goal is to teach its clients marketable skills that will help them get jobs outside the organization. The center runs an electronics assembly business, and its long-term contracts with three major electronics companies supply a steady stream of income to the organization. They recently started a firewood business and are considering entering the injection molding field. Chip Rice, the executive vice-president and CEO, emphasizes the usefulness of looking to the for-profit sector for good enterprise examples and

says that "Nonprofits must constantly develop new enterprise streams. Managers can't afford to become complacent."

The 1970s—A Time of Expansion

By the late 1960s, those nonprofits that had more or less "backed into" enterprise, whether through offering workshops in lighting and set design to support a fledgling theater company or starting a furniture-making business to teach handicapped workers new skills, were beginning to take their businesses a bit more seriously. An air of professionalism crept into the sector, as organizations reexamined their enterprises, systemized their operations, and compared notes with other nonprofits. As nonprofits became aware of the income-producing assets at their disposal, they explored such previously ignored money sources as using facility downtime, licensing the institution's name, and tapping new markets for goods and services. Universities calculated the expense of dormitories and classrooms standing empty all summer and opened their doors for conferences, seminars, and conventions. Zoos studied traffic patterns and erected stands selling everything from hot dogs to balloons to elephant food.

With the increased funding opportunities of "The Great Society," programs began to expand, which led to a need for more income and also to new possibilities for income-generating activities. The entire nonprofit sector was experiencing a scale of enterprise that simply hadn't existed twenty or even ten years before. It was highly visible in the larger institutions, where previously small museum gift shops were growing and making profits on everything from reproductions to stationery to bath towels. The effect filtered down to the small- and medium-size nonprofits; suddenly, everyone wanted to get into the act.

Federal Funding: The $21.2 Billion Cutback

Perhaps not a moment too soon. The rapid expansion of nonprofit programs during the 1960s and 1970s was financed not only by newly formed enterprises, but also, in large part, by the government. "While no one is sure how much federal aid nonprofit groups received, it is clear they shared in the tremendous growth of federal outlays to state and local government, which mushroomed from $10.9 billion in 1965 to $49.8 billion in 1975 and $89.8 billion in 1980." [8] In 1981, however, Ronald Reagan slashed the federal budget, and the bottom fell out of nonprofit funding.

The Urban Institute in Washington, D.C., estimates that federal government budget cuts will cost the nonprofit sector approximately $25.5 billion through 1984. Lester M. Salamon, director of the public management program at the Urban Institute, says that private giving from all sources for nonreligious purposes would have to increase 144 percent over the next five years to make up for government cuts and to keep pace with inflation—a growth rate four times faster than that of the five-year period just ended.

Even though the tax law has been amended, doubling the proportion of tax-free gifts that businesses can make (from 5 to 10 percent of pretax profits), it has at the same time drastically lowered income taxes for many corporations and top-bracket taxpayers. According to Brian O'Connell, president of Independent Sector, a coalition of national voluntary and philanthropic groups, this effectively reduces incentives for large charitable contributions. Other changes in the law, those which allow taxpayers who don't itemize other deductions to deduct charitable contributions, will encourage giving among lower- and middle-income taxpayers but will not make up the loss.

Federal cuts have also put the pinch on state and local governments, thus limiting the "filtering down effect" and curtailing funds available at the local level.

The response to this grim news, for many organizations in the sector, is "to act entrepreneurially. . . . A growing number of charitable organizations. . . have realized that if they're going to make it at all in the 1980s, they're going to make it on their own. . . . Non-profits are either selling products closely tied to their charities, or at least implementing sound business techniques in running the organizations." [9]

Organizations with a history of giving-oriented funding are considering enterprise for the first time. They have begun to reevaluate their managerial practices and count their available assets. Gift shops, extra land, and skilled staff

members are considered with a newly entrepreneurial eye. Boards members are consulted for their business expertise. Employees are drafted from the for-profit sector. As traditional income sources become scarce, the nonprofit sector has begun to develop an entire spectrum of income-producing possibilities. Scott McBride, president of Marketing General, Inc., a for-profit Washington, D.C. consultant to nonprofits, says, "I don't think the public is ready to see them [nonprofits] putting out automobiles or manufacturing perfume. . . but it's difficult to envision what nonprofits *can't* do [emphasis added]." [10]

The Spectrum of Nonprofit Enterprise

Although nonprofit enterprise is as old as the nonprofit sector itself, in our survey we discovered that, until very recently, most nonprofit enterprises were somewhat casual in nature. They often started as services to patrons, clients, or constituencies and were not really expected to contribute substantial income to the organization. Such classic nonprofit businesses as museum gift shops, university bookstores, and junior league cookbooks were often started by volunteer workers and didn't necessarily even turn a profit.

But as additional goods and services became a part of these "casual" enterprises, many organizations began to see that they were sitting on a wealth of income-producing possibilities. The museum gift shop that sold postcards could also sell reproductions, posters, and tote bags. It could branch out into mail order, reaching a much larger clientele. It could sell the use of its name for consumer articles ranging from clothing to coffee pots. It could offer museum tours around the world and from there start a full-scale travel service.

Our survey found that nonprofit enterprise has developed across a wide spectrum, ranging, at the near end, from enterprises *closely related* to the organization's program (ticket sales, tuitions, admissions) to, at the far end, business endeavors basically *unrelated* to the organization's program (real estate development, investments in industry).

Based on the data we gathered, we have "filled in" this spectrum with eight different enterprise categories under which, we believe, almost every possible nonprofit enterprise can be placed. The following table outlines the categories and

The Spectrum of Nonprofit Enterprise

NEAR/related to program · FAR/from program

| Program | Convenience | | Selling the Name | | Downtime | Extensions that are | |
	Near	Far	Giving	Royalties		Related	Unrelated
Revenues	Enterprise activity related to the type of organization		Marketing the name or prestige of the organization to a wider public (licensing the name)		Income derived from the downtime use of an organization's assets	Offshoot of regular program or necessities of the organization	Business venture totally unrelated to any aspect of the program
Services specified in the organization's charter / Revenues earned from the program delivery (earned income)	closely related	more distantly related	patrons or supporters (quid pro quo giving); contributions oriented				

· EXAMPLES ·

Program	Revenues	Near	Far	Giving	Royalties	Downtime	Related	Unrelated
Museum: Contemporary art exhibit	Admission charge	Sells postcards/prints in shop	Cafeteria open to public after hours	Sells tote bags with name/logo of museum	Sells reproductions of pottery in collection	Rents out exhibit halls for parties	Sponsors tour of European museums	Sells air rights to condominium developer
University: Undergraduate and graduate degrees	Tuition	Bookstore; room and board (dorms and cafeterias)	Record department in bookstore	Sells football jerseys, bookcovers with name of school	Takes patent on drug developed in laboratory—royalties earned; software developed, sold	Sells computer downtime; corporations use dorms and classrooms for conferences	Athletic department runs summer clinics	Leases extra land to farmers; real estate development
Rehabilitation program: Job training and counseling to handicapped	Fee for services (client pays and/or government reimburses)	Sells special supplies; provides family counseling	Provides taxi service for handicapped—rides for a fee	Sells T-shirts with name of organization	Sells manual explaining how to replicate its program; consulting	Sells counselor downtime to corporations	Sells product produced by handicapped workers	Invests money in solar energy company
Orchestra: Symphonic performances	Ticket sales	Sells programs at performances	Sells drinks during intermission	Sells mugs, paperweights with orchestra name/logo	Produces records of performances; television performances	Rents out hall during downtime	Offers classes or workshops on music; offers music lessons	Runs record store

illustrates them with examples. It should be noted that none of the four examples represents a real institution—it is rare if not impossible to find any nonprofit that engages in all eight types of enterprise; rather, they are composites of organizations contacted during our study.

The table starts at the far left with those enterprises most closely related to the organization's program or purpose and ends on the far right with those most distantly related to the organization's program or purpose. The categories follow:

- **Program** describes what the organization actually does; that is, the services specified in the organization's charter. Examples run the gamut of nonprofits, from ballet companies to zoological societies to halfway houses for runaway teenagers.

- **Program revenues** are income earned directly from program activities themselves, such as admissions for performances, tuition for classes, fees for services.

- **Convenience** is any enterprise activity related to the purpose or character of the organization that runs it.

Near signifies those convenience-oriented enterprises that are more *closely related* to the character of the organization: a university selling books or renting dorm rooms; a museum renting tape recorders and cassettes for exhibit tours.

Far signifies those enterprises that are more *distantly related* to the purpose of the organization: a college bookstore selling toothpaste; a rehabilitation center providing a taxi service for handicapped clients.

- **Selling (e.g., licensing) the name** is marketing the name or prestige of the organization in order to realize a profit.

Giving is contributions oriented and concentrates on the patrons or supporters of the organization. Opera lovers buy the company calendar and tote bag; supporters of an ecological nonprofit buy stationery and T-shirts showing the logo of the organization.

Royalties reach a wider public and involve selling the good name or valuable assets of the nonprofit. A museum can sell reproductions of pieces in its collection; a botanical garden can license the use of its name on packets of flower seeds.

- **Downtime** represents income derived from the use of a nonprofit's assets when the organization is not using them. These can be physical assets, such as space that can be rented to other groups (concert halls, offices, conference rooms), or they can be human resources, such as skilled personnel that are "hired out" to other organizations or corporations (computer programmers, counselors).

- **Extensions that are related** to the organization take the convenience category one step further. This involves expanding an enterprise activity related to the organization beyond its immediate needs and clientele. Examples include a university opening the student laundry to the public or starting a computer software firm and a nature center expanding its hiking tours of the Alps into a travel service.

- **Extensions that are unrelated** to the function of the organization conclude the spectrum. These may evolve out of physical assets that the group can leverage into income or may be strictly business investments that have nothing to do with the organization's purpose. Examples include real estate development of unused land; investments in any type of business, ranging from oil wells to pizza parlors.

"Deep Pockets"

Although nonprofit organizations have virtually every possible form of income-producing activity at their disposal, our study found that actual participation tends to concentrate in the areas of the enterprise spectrum that are most closely related to nonprofit programs. The categories at the left of the spectrum— "Program Revenues," in both "Near" and "Far Convenience" enterprise—are the most heavily utilized parts of the nonprofit enterprise spectrum. This concentration in certain areas often evolves into what may be called "deep pocket" giving; that is, reaching deeper into the pockets of supporters by offering, in addition to ways of giving, new products and services they can buy.

For example, a supporter of the Dayton Museum of Natural History in Dayton, Ohio, can become a life member, pay an admission fee to the museum (on Sundays), and buy knickknacks at the museum store and jewelry and fossils at its natural history shop. He or she may also support the animal adoption program, paying from $10 to $275 to support one animal in the museum for one year, or the "rent a duck" program, in which a family pays $3.75 to raise a duckling for six weeks before the museum releases it back into the wild. Finally, if the supporter belongs to a local nonprofit group, he or she might arrange for this group to use the museum facilities for some program or event and then give an appropriate donation to the museum.

Most nonprofit enterprises are not businesses per se; they are protected "greenhouse" enterprises that provide a way for an institution to deliver products or services in return for donations. "Why not buy your Christmas cards from the museum?" If the institution's name or reputation was not attached to the tote bag, cookbook, or calendar, it might not sell as well, and certainly not for the same price. Goodwill can be translated into revenues. Real estate transactions can also benefit from the institutional name and presence.

This does not mean that such "greenhouse" enterprises aren't profitable, nor that they cannot grow and expand. But they do tend to be limited to the geographic area where their name elicits a positive, giving response. "Greenhouse" enterprises usually expand beyond their home area only when the institution itself has a larger reputation. Launching into an unknown and broader market can be disastrous, and there is some indication that without external support and/or guidance, such ventures should not be tried.

Easy In, Easy Out

Most nonprofit enterprises tend to be street-level, retail businesses, such as gift shops, bookstores, and restaurants. They are extremely attractive to most nonprofits because, in addition to being logical off-shoots of their services, they are also often another way nonprofits can encounter their publics. In addition, they are ideally suited to volunteer labor. Most of us have had experience with such operations from the other side of the counter. They are easy businesses to enter.

Unfortunately, they are also easy businesses to get out of. Although some nonprofits have such advantages as free building space or facility downtime, and are often sheltered from having

to create and promote traffic (some of it comes naturally with the institution), they still encounter all the problems of other retail businesses. Retail enterprises are labor intensive and demand careful supervision; the profit margins are small and breakage and pilferage costs are high. They require working capital, are difficult to make profitable, and often end up in the red in both the for-profit and nonprofit worlds. Boutiques, bookstores, and bistros top the national bankruptcy lists. In addition, in the nonprofit sector such businesses often begin in an ad hoc fashion as services to patrons and may not be managed carefully enough to generate income for the organization.

Keeping the Books

In our discussions with nonprofit entrepreneurs, we discovered that one of the most common problems in nonprofit business (and in much nonprofit enterprise across the spectrum) is a tendency toward a generous approach to cost accounting. Space, cost of capital employed, utilities, promotion, and other normal business expenses are usually not attached to the enterprises involved. The cost of goods sold is often the only cost accounted for. Many nonprofits do not keep separate books for their enterprises and their programs, with the result that it is difficult to know how much (if any) real income the enterprise is contributing to the organization. Costing out *all* expenses is a necessary part of determining what a nonprofit should or should *not* be doing with enterprise.

For example, if a university starts a computer programming service during its downtime, it should cost out such expenses as rent, lights, and heat to determine how much income the business is really producing. It is also important to look carefully at enterprises that are already successful: The university's computer programming business may make $1,500 per week; however, if the university rented out computer time on an hourly basis during off hours, it might make $4,500. Although the university is already operating a successful enterprise, another enterprise might be even *more* successful.

Nonprofits have a tendency to welcome *any* enterprise success and not to think, as do successful for-profit entrepreneurs, that something else might gain the organization more income. Could something else have yielded a greater return on the worry, sweat, and time invested? Recently, however, institutions have begun to reevaluate their enterprises and to apply stricter standards of judgment to their success. The problem is that it is tough to look "found money" in the eye.

Entrepreneurial Management

Successful enterprises in the nonprofit sector, as in the for-profit sector, depend on the skills of the people who run them. An openness to trying enterprise activities on the part of the board and staff members is essential to the success of any nonprofit business venture. If individuals involved in the organization believe that "making money is not the proper role for a nonprofit institution," then it is extremely difficult to start and carry through any type of income-producing program.

But a positive attitude toward enterprise is not enough to ensure its success. The organization's management must also have the business skills and experience necessary to run a profit-producing venture. Management issues touch almost every aspect of nonprofit enterprise—finance, personnel, and operations, as well as relations with the board, the clientele, and the community. If the organization's management, particularly the executive director, thinks entrepreneurially, the nonprofit is more likely to take advantage of the fullest range of enterprise choices. If not, the institution will probably follow more traditional paths of income generation.

The director of a nonprofit organization is perhaps the single most important influence on whether the institution engages in successful enterprise activities. An entrepreneurially oriented director will encourage new enterprise, reexamine those in which the organization is already engaged, and diversify the organization's funding base in as many ways as possible. He or she will look at what similar organizations have done and will seek help from those involved with the organization, whether staff, clients, patrons, or board members, as well as individuals and institutions in the for-profit sector that can assist the organization in the enterprise areas it is considering.

Utilizing an Organization's Assets

Successful nonprofit enterprise usually involves working with assets an organization already has at its disposal; the stories of entrepreneurs that have turned such assets into successful nonprofit businesses can be found in chapter 2 [not reprinted here]. But sometimes an institution can "earn" a great deal of income by successfully streamlining its existing operation.

Under the leadership of Crawford Lincoln, president, and L. Charles Kuhn, vice-president for business and finance, Old Sturbridge Village in Massachusetts has maximized the profit-producing potential of the institution's assets by bringing its entire operation to an impressive level of efficiency. The five photography labs that previously served the village have been condensed into one, the bookkeeping system has been computerized, and the purchasing for its retail shops has been centralized. In addition, a hydroelectric plant that will produce power for the site is being built on the property. This efficiency has paid off: In the past five years, the profit on the shops in the village has risen almost sevenfold.

Most nonprofit organizations have business managers whose skills lie in keeping the books and watching the bottom line. But in our interviews with nonprofits around the country, we found that there is a dearth of forward-thinking, entrepreneurial managers in the nonprofit sector. Where they *do* exist, they can be found running the most successful enterprises. Where they are lacking, directors and business managers with little entrepreneurial background, training, or inclination are either struggling to build and develop ventures or are turning their backs on income-producing possibilities available to the institution. In chapter 5 [not reprinted here], we discuss developing and integrating a position called "director of enterprise" into a nonprofit organization, as well as finding the proper person to fill this role.

Between the Lines

The board assumes an active role in the income-producing activities of many nonprofits. Here again, the attitude of board members can have a strong effect on whether a nonprofit gets involved in enterprise activities. If trustees adopt a cautious fiduciary attitude, they will tend to discourage enterprise. Knowing the myriad of possible business pitfalls, they may try to discourage "ill-equipped" and "untrained" institutions from entering the sector. A conservative board that would rather not deal with the concepts of "related" and "unrelated" income, let alone sit down and work out a game plan with the IRS, is unlikely to be interested in pursuing enterprise activities. Directors who are themselves unwilling to take the leap into the sector have been known to present IRS regulations and penalties—with the cooperation of their treasurers —to their boards in order to scare them away from any type of business involvement.

Yet a board whose members are entrepreneurially minded can do much to foster the growth of enterprise in a nonprofit organization. Individual members with strong business experience can expose a nonprofit to a variety of income-producing activities. The board can help guide an executive director with little enterprise experience toward and through ventures most suited to the institution. Trustees can provide much-needed contacts in the for-profit world for possible joint ventures, as well as guidance in such enterprise areas as real estate, downtime, and licensing.

For example, the board of directors for Bancroft Products, the sheltered workshop described earlier, is involved in all stages of the enterprise activities of the organization. Most of the trustees are from the private sector, and they have been instrumental in the successful development and running of Bancroft's electronics and firewood businesses. Now that Bancroft is considering the injection molding business, the board is evaluating the entire project, including the capital investment required. The board is also helping the director with the financial review of the entire organization. In this case, it is clear that the board has a great deal of confidence in the director's ability to manage these enterprises.

A Matter of Attitude

Reviewing all of our reporting, we have come away with an understanding that forward-thinking, enterprising individuals are the most

important motivators behind successful nonprofit enterprises. If such individuals are respected and supported by their institution, then enterprise works. If not, enterprise is likely to fail. Yet institutions that have entered into enterprise often treat their entrepreneurs as outsiders. The "earners" are separated from the "doers," a split that only works against what both groups are trying to accomplish. This situation can waste a great deal of energy, not to mention money. It is our hope that entrepreneurs will follow the path of fund raisers, who had to work to be accepted as a part of nonprofit organizations. It is the responsibility of both parties—old-line staff and new members—to see to it that enterprise and program staff work together, not at cross purposes, for the good of the entire organization.

The problem is that the sector in general has traditionally attracted people who are more interested in the program aspects of the organization than in the business side. Many people who work in nonprofits, often for less pay than they would make in the for-profit sector, do so because they believe in the mission or function of the organization they serve. They have chosen career paths linked to "service" and "culture" and seem unwilling or unable to mesh such goals with the reality of earning revenues.

Initially, therefore, directors and staff members, as well as trustees and volunteers, may resist any form of enterprise activity, fearing that it will somehow detract from the organization's main purpose. When, however, funds get so short that enterprise is the only alternative to cutting programs, staff, boards, clients, and patrons alike are usually persuaded that enterprise represents a worthy, and sometimes the only, alternative.

The Last Resort

Many of the organizations we surveyed turned to enterprise as a last resort—an approach to take when the funding was cut, the program expanded, the donations dropped. Successful nonprofit enterprises often seem to be those that have either been started under the pressure of need or have resulted from a plethora of assets at the nonprofit's disposal. In a lucky few instances, the two joined together; often, however, enterprise seems to flourish among the asset-lean, grassroots nonprofits struggling to survive, or in the larger, asset-rich organizations that have the leeway to take risks and develop enterprise programs.

Institutions that are less motivated by their circumstances or their communities to venture may see enterprise as incompatible with their purpose. Some know that their potential for enterprise is limited, or that their strengths lie in traditional fund raising or fees. Others are simply reluctant to rearrange their organizations or to upset the status quo. Still others are frightened by what they don't know and would prefer to leave profit-making to the for-profit sector.

But it is here that we would like to sound a cautionary note: Funding cutbacks are making enterprise important to even the comfortable "chamber of commerce" nonprofits, and smaller grassroots groups may see enterprise as the one thing that can save them. But it is not the answer for everyone. No matter how successful enterprise ventures may prove to be in the sector in the years to come, they will not be able to cure all of its financial ills. Some institutions will do spectacularly well—their ventures will flourish, they will branch out into other businesses, they may eventually become entirely self-supporting. Others will be able to keep from going under, or from operating with deficits, but will still rely on more traditional "giving" sources or fees and admissions for the bulk of their income. Still other nonprofits are probably inherently unsuited to any enterprise activity at all, because of the organization's structure, because of the type of work they do, or even because their fund-raising efforts are so successful that no additional funding is necessary. It is important for nonprofits to consider the particulars of their own organization—its strengths and weaknesses; its clientele, program, director, board, staff; and a myriad of other important factors—long before launching into any enterprise.

Too many nonprofits are looking for a formula—a grant request guideline for getting into enterprise. But there is none. Institutional assets and community needs should be combined into a formula that will work for the individual nonprofit. The most useful formula is often one that is compatible with the person in charge of making the enterprise happen. When the question is asked, "What enterprise should we choose?", the answer is simply *the one that works*.

The Bottom Line

The bottom line is that enterprise *is* making an incremental difference. It is not the magic answer. It works for those who make it work. But it needs help and guidance to be really effective. The rest of this report provides additional ways of looking at what is going on and what can be done.

Enterprise is still emerging, it is an adolescent—at least in the arc of its life cycle. It needs careful understanding so that it is not misread, mismanaged, or undone before it has a chance to reach its potential.

Perhaps the best way to judge the importance of enterprise in the nonprofit sector is by its absence. If it were *not* present, a great many institutions would be gone and others severely crippled. Enterprise is important; it matters and it needs to grow, but under careful conditions and within the proper context. The bottom line is the institution's mission, and enterprise is just another means to that end.

Notes

1. *The New American Webster Handy College Dictionary* (New York: New American Library, 1972), p. 159.

2. Jane Mayer, "Survival Tactics: Cuts in Federal Aid Lead Public TV to Try a Bit of Free Enterprise," *The Wall Street Journal*, March 10, 1982.

3. Henry B. Hansmann, "The Role of Nonprofit Enterprise," *The Yale Law Journal*, April 1980, p. 838.

4. John G. Simon, "Research on Philanthropy" (A talk at the 25th Anniversary Conference of the National Council on Philanthropy, Denver, Colorado, November 8, 1979).

5. Girl Scouts of America, "Girl Scout Cookie Backgrounder" (New York: Girl Scouts of America, n.d.).

6. Susan Rose-Ackerman, *Unfair Competition and Corporate Income Taxation*, Program on Non-Profit Organizations, Yale University, Working Paper 37, pp. 1–2.

7. Eugene H. Fram, "Changing Expectations for Third Sector Executives," *Human Resource Management*, Fall 1980, pp. 8–15.

8. Neal R. Peirce and Erin MacLellan, "Nonprofit Groups Are Trying to Learn How to

Cope with Federal Budget Cuts," *National Journal*, August 22, 1981.

9. Dave Lindorff, "Lending a Hand to the Poor," *Venture*, October 1981, pp. 86–92.

10. Dexter C. Hutchins, "The Nonprofit Alternative," *Venture*, April 1980, pp. 34–38.

ARTICLE 26 ─────────────
How to Qualify for a Foundation Grant: A Sophisticated Primer
Theodore R. Kauss and Randall J. Kauss

Background

Although qualifying for a grant from a private foundation obviously is not impossible (even though it may seem so at times), it certainly isn't easy. However, we wish to share with you some practical ideas, strategies, and techniques for nonprofit organizations (NPOs) to consider when approaching foundations for grant awards which could improve your chances for success.

It was determined that we wanted to direct our thoughts to a broad-based audience of grant seekers which could range from neophytes just getting started in fundraising to experienced development officers looking for a few new ideas or the reinforcement of their present practices. Thus, the subtitle, "A Sophisticated Primer." In the preparation of this piece, we gathered information from many sources including representatives of a variety of foundations, literature from the *Foundation News* and the Council on Foundations, Inc., and our own combined personal experiences spanning several decades as grantsmen and, one of us, for over ten years as a giver (foundation executive—a job made in Heaven). We're aware of possible pitfalls when following an eclectic approach based on policies and procedures of a modest sampling from a few of more than 20,000 private foundations, however, we're confident that our remarks are representative of those of many foundation officials.

To guide you in your quest for foundation grants, we suggest three B's; 1) Basics, 2) Bolts (and Nuts), and 3) Believers/Achievers. The *Basics* will get you ready for the preparation of the grant request, the *Bolts* will help you in the

development of your proposal, and *Believers/ Achievers* will enhance all phases of your project, especially the formal presentation and next steps.

At the risk of sounding like T.V.'s Lt. Columbo, "there's one more little thing" before getting on with this subject. Private foundations are required to give away each year as grants an amount equal to 5% of their corpus. Thus, don't be hesitant about asking foundation officials to consider your requests. After all, those of us who have the special opportunity to be paid for giving away someone else's money cannot justify our professional existence unless large numbers of fundraisers seek our assistance.

Basics

You should be able to state the mission of your organization succinctly. A line or two will do. Some foundation representatives have short attention spans, so don't risk losing them before you reach your important points. If your purpose is not on paper or has not been reduced to its least common denominator, remedy the situation immediately. Involve your board chairman, chief executive officer, board members, co-workers, program participants, and other supporters. Once this step has been completed, determine what the long-range plan (three to five years) should be for your nonprofit organization. Identify your needs and priorities. At least an in-house feasibility study is in order. Most NPOs have a membership which includes talented financial, management, and legal advisors who may offer their services without a fee. Expert input can be invaluable (and inexpensive). However, don't overlook the possibility of hiring a consultant or contracting with an appropriate firm to conduct the feasibility study and to assist you with planning and developing your formal written proposal for consideration by a foundation.

Ripple Effect

Make sure that the project you identify in your proposal as the primary or critical one for your program is one with a far-reaching impact. Most foundation representatives like to see the *ripple effect*. Your pebble in the pond should cause large waves. However, if you are seeking help just to keep afloat, you should be getting a sinking feeling, and with justification. Bailouts are not attractive to donors.

Just as most debates are won in the library, most successful grant proposals are generated through research and study. Your homework will include finding out whatever you can about potential funders. Your best sources include *The Foundation Directory,* several publications from the Grantsmanship Center (for example, the *Foundation News*), and directories of state and local foundations. If you should decide to purchase these, they are available at prices ranging from a few dollars to close to $100. But you can find most of them in your neighborhood library at no charge. Use them to identify the foundations that consider grants to projects or organizations with a mission the same as or similar to yours. Focus your efforts on these potential funders; especially those situated in or near your community. Although projects with only local impact have been funded by national foundations, your best chances generally rest with local foundations or local regional offices of major corporate giving programs.

The Initial Contact

When you have zeroed in on the foundation that appears to be a potential sponsor for your project, make contact with one of its representatives. A letter requesting a copy of the most recent annual report, guidelines, and deadlines for grant proposals is appropriate. When they respond, you will have the specifics you need to develop your formal proposal.

Bolts and Nuts

The Preliminary Call

After the initial contact has provided the information that enables you to become familiar with the foundation's purposes and procedures, call for an appointment to meet with one of the program officers to have a preliminary discussion. Of course, if their guidelines state that they don't want personal contacts, abide by these directives. However, many foundations do welcome your

visit if you've done your homework. By the way, don't go with a long wishlist—just discuss your first priority (you might slip in a second idea if the listener seems receptive). Since this visit is prior to submitting your formal request, make sure that you listen closely for clues to help make your proposal more attractive and competitive. Often, you will strengthen your case if a key member of your constituency accompanies you. Volunteers who are committed to your programs can catch the attention and interest of foundation officials who can easily become distracted (or even cynical) when only those who are paid for working with a project make the pitch. Key persons (your board members, community leaders, or other prominent people) can also help you in answering questions and filling in gaps.

Foundation program officers always ask probing questions and often play devil's advocate, so be ready to staunchly support your case (or cause). Yes, defend your proposal if you must, but be flexible and bend—a solid project won't break. Sometimes the foundation representative will inform you of similar projects. Instead of arguing that yours is different (avoid the label "unique" unless you can prove it), keep an open mind. These people probably get around more than you do. Check out their leads and, if warranted, come up with a revised plan that strengthens your previous efforts or provides additional services.

Here's a final tip on the type of behavior you should exhibit during this meeting. The vice-president of a major foundation recently stated that fund seekers should be *aggressive* when calling on funders. He's a nice person, bright, and a fine individual, but we disagree on terminology and tactics. *Assertive* action is far more appropriate and acceptable. This will also be more in character for the many nonprofit executives and development directors that we know. It would be better to err by being too polite than too pushy. There's always that next time around. It should go without saying that you must be on time for your appointment at the foundation offices. (We said it anyway for emphasis.)

The Follow-up Call

After the preliminary meeting, a follow-up phone call and/or note to your foundation contact is appropriate and offers another reminder of your project. Resist the temptation to overdo this because you can easily be perceived as a nuisance. Once again, remember that foundations are in business to help those eligible for their grants; so don't bow too deeply and don't beg. Hold your head up and display the confidence you have in your project and the respect you have for your personnel. If you have paid attention to details and have all the *bolts and nuts* in the proper places and fastened firmly, your chances for success will be greatly improved.

Taking the Plunge

Well, you've taken the plunge; you've submitted a grant proposal to a foundation. What happens next? How should you and others in your non-profit organization handle different responses such as "yes," "no," and "maybe"?

It all depends. This is not a dodge, but a pragmatic response. It depends on the type of foundation you approach and it depends on the restrictions or controls they place upon you. For instance, if you're dealing with a local foundation and you know the executive director or program officer, you might tactfully check into your progress within their process. Often this can occur through informal contact. However, you should be cautioned that foundation folks can be a lot like doctors, lawyers, bankers, et al.—they don't enjoy talking business at social events.

Most foundations (practically all regional and national organizations) have spelled out their procedures and probably yours for contacts after the proposal has been received. They will expect you to be responsible for reading and respecting their directives. For instance:

- A brief letter or card will be sent to you to acknowledge receipt of the grant request and possibly to tell you when it will be considered by the foundation board.
- Printed guidelines might state "don't call us, we'll call you." Nevertheless, things do get lost in the mail, and a telephone inquiry after a reasonable wait for a reply is acceptable. Keep a reminder file to alert you when it may be appropriate to make this call.

- Unfortunately, you might receive a letter from a point of entry staffer who informs you that your proposal does not meet the guidelines, policies, or priorities of a grantor. If this occurs, you are probably guilty of a "shotgun approach" in your request. That is, you've either asked for too many things that are not specific concerns of the foundation, or you have used a somewhat generic proposal which you send to almost everyone and doesn't focus on the interests of the recipient. It's also possible that the amount requested is beyond the limits of practicality and good judgment. In any event, you obviously didn't do your homework and you didn't follow to the letter the procedures of the potential grantor.

Take heart, occasionally the message you receive will offer you a second chance, even if your written proposal hasn't provided the foundation with all the details it needs. For example:

- You will receive a form letter or checklist which indicates that information sought by the grant-making organization was not included in the proposal you submitted. If you can still meet its deadlines, they'll probably keep your file active and allow you to supply the specifics needed. However, some foundations will eliminate your organization from consideration if your proposal is incomplete. Or,
- A program officer will call your office to seek clarification on matters related to goals, procedures, personnel, budgeting, or evaluation. Your verbal response could be all that is needed, although a follow-up in writing might be requested. Paper trails are a fact of life in fundraising and can save many of us, on both sides of the table, from disagreements or other discomforts in the future.

In many cases, the letter from the foundation that acknowledges that your proposal is complete and states that its directors will take action on your request at a meeting on a specific date, will be the last contact until you receive the official decision of the board.

Believers/Achievers

Previously we described a preliminary get-acquainted visit to a foundation. Some foundations might also invite you to visit them later in the game for a formal presentation of your proposal. We strongly urge you to bring a team to this session and not try to go it alone. You'll want to include one of your board officers and at least one key volunteer. Select persons of authority and/or influence. Perhaps these individuals know one or more of the foundation's directors and this could bring greater credibility to your project. A word of caution—what is traditionally referred to as "the old boy network," that is, your key person knowing and contacting one of theirs, can help you in your efforts to get the grant, but the "end run" can also disturb the foundation's staff members who follow closely the foundation's written regulations, and they might decide to tackle you. You take a chance when you go around the staff. One foundation official we know compared it to rolling the dice while another proffered that in most cases of circumventing the system, the dice will be loaded against you.

The Formal Presentation to the Foundation

A formal presentation to foundation executives and/or program officers calls for a clear understanding of your mission, the vital need for the project, your plan and potential for meeting the need, a sensible and specific budget, a proposed method of evaluating the program, and an idea of how your work might be replicated by other nonprofits. You should also be ready to share your concepts for the continuation of the program after the grant money has been expended.[1] Although your presentation isn't expected to be slick, it should be sincere and at least semiprofessional. By all means let the listeners know that you have a positive attitude about your endeavors and that you believe in what you are doing and what you are proposing. There's a lot to be said about a self-fulfilling prophecy. We're convinced that believers are achievers and officials at most foundations probably agree.

Since this meeting can be somewhat intimidating for almost anyone seeking a grant, you might try role playing with some of your staff members as a dress rehearsal a day or so prior to your presentation to the foundation professionals. Take heart, most foundation officials are conscientious, considerate, and caring folks just like yourselves. They will ask good questions and will be good listeners to your intelligent responses.

Some foundations invite applicants to make presentations directly to the board of directors. If they do, their literature and/or correspondence will be very specific regarding procedures to be followed by all parties. Don't try to persuade them to modify the rules for your benefit. At best you'll be perceived as ignorant, at worst arrogant. This presentation should be essentially the same type you would make to the foundation staff members, but you will probably feel a tad more pressure. Don't worry, board members are almost always very considerate in their deliberations with nonprofit organization representatives.

The Site Visit by the Foundation

A number of foundations will inform you that one or two members of their staff wish to conduct a site visit to become better acquainted with your present programs, the proposed project, and the personnel who will be responsible for directing the new program. If you are enthusiastic people with an innovative plan, for goodness sake display this spirit and excitement. In addition, if the foundation representatives are receptive, involve them in a special event that could be of interest to them or ask them to participate in one of your activities as a resource person, speaker, or panelist. Most foundation executives and program officers possess expertise in areas that could enlighten your publics and enrich your programs.

Responding to Rejection

Most grant requests submitted to foundations for consideration are denied. Many because the proposal is incomplete, inaccurate, or inappropriate for the grantmaker. The main reason foundations decline to fund proposals that meet their priorities and terms is that there is simply not enough money to go around. For instance, the Frost Foundation awards grants (not necessarily the full amount requested) to about one out of sixteen qualified applicants. The good news is that yours could be one of the winners. If not, be persistent. Remember the battle cry of the Chicago Cubs: "Wait 'Til Next Year!"

It's practically impossible for a foundation to reject a grant proposal in a manner that will not disappoint, annoy, or even anger those who are financially dependent on a project and deeply committed to it. Therefore, most grantors send a standard-type letter of declination (a softer term than "rejection") that explains clearly, concisely, and politely why your project was not awarded a grant. These letters are constructed so they can cover most situations.

Some foundations use a stock paragraph or two in a letter of declination and insert some comments directed to the specific grant applicant. In selected cases, personal comments might be offered. The reasons for a "canned memo" are readily understandable. Since many grantors receive from hundreds to thousands of requests annually (the majority of which will be turned down), it would be very time consuming and extremely difficult to write individual letters to each applicant. Besides, since almost no letter of refusal will completely soften the blow, it makes sense to decide on one that comes close and use it almost exclusively. By the way, even the letters of award usually follow a standard format.

Next Steps

O.K., your fears have been confirmed. The grantor has said "no." Now what? You should consider these steps.

1. Study the letter of declination to find the reasons why you didn't make it. Often it will be because there wasn't enough money to fund all the worthwhile requests. If so, don't be reluctant to try again with an improved and updated version of your proposal that incorporates suggestions made by the foundation staff. Remember that when a foundation says no, it may mean "not now."

2. If you and others at your organization are convinced that your proposal is in concert with the priorities and philosophy of the grantor, then a calm and discreet telephone call to the appropriate grant officer is definitely in order. When you call:

- Conduct yourself in a pleasant and professional manner.
- Ask questions directly related to the foundation's decision.

- Give the grant officer a chance to recall or retrieve the proposal and to respond to your queries. You're almost certain to get useful information that will serve you in the future. The program officer has the responsibility to be helpful and in most cases will be sensitive to your concerns.
- Don't ask for a written copy of reviewers' comments concerning your proposal unless providing such information is a standard procedure of the foundation.
- Should your call elicit additional specifics in writing, respond with a simple "thank you" and don't try to engage in another exchange of letters on a dead issue. Playing ping-pong with pen and paper is a no-win contest for you.

3. Reassess your prospect list.

- There must be other potential donors you can contact.
- There may also be other important contacts you haven't yet called on who could help you become better acquainted with foundations.

4. Reassess the capacity of your organization to carry out the program described in your proposal and react accordingly.

5. Follow effective marketing procedures in your future presentation(s).

- Have a well-organized and attractive packet.
- Use visuals to your advantage.
- Include carefully selected key person endorsements in support of your organization's ability to meet the needs and goals described in your proposal.

6. A great challenge to you is how you cope with the many rejections you will receive from funding organizations.

- Don't cry "foul play!" Foundation directors are required to perform the unpleasant task of saying no to a number of good programs and great people, don't make them feel sadder (or madder).
- Understand that over 90 percent of your proposals and requests could be unsuccessful.
- Don't internalize these rejections.
- Rebound and keep trying to develop new ideas and better approaches.

Allow us to share a story that illustrates a negative and foolish reaction by a rejected grant applicant contrasted with a positive and intelligent response by a prospective grant applicant. One wasted his time while the other invested his.

A friend (we'll call him Lou, because that's his name), an administrator at a state college, was at his state's department of higher education awaiting a conference with a program officer as a preliminary step to submitting a formal grant request. While in the waiting room, Lou observed an obviously angry individual bothering a secretary with boisterous charges that the grants were awarded unfairly because his college's proposal was denied while a smaller and, in his opinion, less prestigious institution received funding for two projects. Lou chuckled to himself about the behavior of the irritated individual for several obvious reasons. First, he was amused because the secretary was not in a position to help the individual although she certainly could hinder him in his quest if she wished to do so (Lou's guess is she wished it and did it). Second, and more important, Lou was overjoyed to receive a hot tip from the boor. After his appointment with the grant officer, Lou went directly to the telephone to call one of his contacts at the small college that had received the two grant awards. After the obligatory small talk, he proceeded to make appointments with the appropriate project directors in order to receive copies of the "winning proposals" and to learn about their projects and their successful presentations to the grants committee of the department of higher education. Does the story have a happy ending for Lou? Of course, why else would he be so willing to tell it? Based on the "insider" information he received from the successful grantseekers and, no doubt, a first-rate formal proposal, his institution received a six-figure award from the higher education department. What happened to the disgruntled chap who spewed his invective at the secretary? Based on his rude and raucous behavior, a reasonable hunch is that he embarked on a long losing streak.

Beating the Odds

An important statistic for you to consider is that in 1987, gifts to charitable organizations in the U.S. totaled $93.7 billion. Less than 11 percent of this amount was donated by corporations and private foundations. Most of the remainder was due to the generosity of individual donors. Based on these figures, fundraisers might quite justifiably question the wisdom of working so hard and bucking high odds to procure a foundation grant when it could be a wiser investment of time and talent to solicit gifts from individuals. You'll get no argument here. However, it must be stressed that if you're smart, all the steps you followed in the preparation of a proposal which could qualify for consideration by a private or corporate foundation should be used for your preparation and presentation when asking for gifts from individual donors.

If at First...

Because foundations work according to their deadlines and priorities and not yours, be ready to dig in for a long campaign. If you are turned down by a foundation (or individuals), but you're still convinced that your project is right for the funder, try again even if you must repeat most or all of the cycle outlined above.

Maybe?

Occasionally a foundation will defer a definitive response and give a "definite maybe." A "maybe" from a foundation is, in a sense, a "no for now" short-term delay. Often you are placed on hold because the donor likes the "doers," but lacks the dollars. If so, you could soon receive good news. However, a reply of "maybe" means just that. Don't assume it's a "done deal."

A Sure Thing

In the world of philanthropy, it can be legitimately argued that there is no such thing as a sure thing. There are countless examples of "guaranteed" grants that have slipped through a crack or were unceremoniously bounced at a foundation board meeting. About the closest thing to a cinch was an award of $100,000,000 (yes, eight zeroes) in 1986 by the Danforth Foundation to Washington University in St. Louis.

This was the largest single foundation gift ever awarded to a university. Even though the Danforth Foundation is one of the most prestigious in the country and Washington University is an outstanding institution, a few eyebrows were raised when the grant was announced because the chancellor of the university, William H. Danforth, also serves as chairman of the foundation board. Was it a sure thing? About a year after the record-setting award was made, executives from some of America's major private foundations were engaged in some informal bantering when one of the group turned to a vice-president of Danforth and slyly slipped in the needle when he asked, "Tell me, what did the chairman of your board, William H. Danforth, say to himself as the chancellor of Washington University, when he awarded the $100 million grant?" The response was almost instantaneous and a classic. He replied enthusiastically, "You wrote a really great proposal!"

T.G.I.F. (Thank God It's Funded)—Now Deliver the Goods

Since many institutions and organizations do qualify for grants and receive thumbs-up from foundations, let's assume that you have beaten the odds and been awarded a grant. You have every reason to feel proud, but also be humble. Thank God it's funded and don't become careless. Make the funding organization feel good about selecting your project from the large stack of competitive proposals. Here's how:

1. Follow all the rules of the grantor. Unilateral changes on your part could be costly.
2. Be proper stewards of the funds entrusted to you. Most nonprofit workers we know excel in this area.
3. Present periodic written and verbal reports to grant officers even when they don't require the feedback. (Avoid going to extremes.)
4. Show the grantor the same courtesy, enthusiasm, and consideration that you did when seeking the grant: People you have wooed and won will be disappointed if you ignore them after the award.
5. Encourage representatives of the foundation to become involved in the project.

- Often they can provide expertise and insight that will be beneficial; occasionally, they might help you avoid pitfalls.
- In addition, you will have given them the opportunity to be participants.
- Besides, even though most funding organizations readily accept the role of junior partner, few are satisfied with the role of silent partner.
- Once you demonstrate that you have utilized the grant effectively and ethically, your credibility in the funding community will be greatly enhanced and this could help you receive favorable decisions on other requests.

6. Provide a detailed accounting of your expenditures (your formal agreement will probably require this).
7. Provide a careful and honest evaluation of your project. You don't have to achieve all your goals to satisfy the grantor. Success is seldom guaranteed. Many foundations support a project because it breaks new ground. When dealing with innovation, a funder expects to take some risks and anticipates some failures.
8. Demonstrate your appreciation in an appropriate manner. For example:

- Thank you letters from the development officer, your chief administrative officials, your ranking board members, and the project director must be sent to donors. Personal visits to the donor(s) office by any of the aforementioned NPO representatives would be proper. Needless to say, make an appointment, don't just drop in.
- Gifts to donors, which would be anything from a paperweight to a plaque, are appropriate. Keep this within limits of propriety.
- A special event to honor donors such as an awards banquet or recognition luncheon, could be held at your project site.

Essentially, the key to pleasing a funder and, perhaps, cultivating future opportunities for support from a foundation, is to make every effort to meet the terms of the grant and to keep the donor informed and, within limits, involved. In other words, deliver the goods or give it your best effort.

Summary—A Dozen Tips

The following list represents a concise summary of the narrative and should serve as a ready guide for the steps to take in qualifying for a foundation grant and satisfying the donor.

I. Define your mission.
II. Devise your plan.
III. Describe the most critical need(s).
IV. Determine your priorities.
V. Delve into the library stacks; it takes lots of homework to identify potential donors with similar priorities.
VI. Develop a formal proposal.
VII. Don't overlook involving key persons in your presentation.
VIII. Defend your position if you must, but bend if you can.
IX. Display a positive attitude.
X. Do it their way if foundation staff members make a site visit.
XI. Dig in—be patient, persistent, and prepared to keep trying if rejected.
XII. Deliver the goods.

Note

1. These are also the salient features of your formal written proposal and, in fact, you might use the finished proposal (subject to modification after this session) as your script for the presentation.

CHAPTER SEVEN
Philanthropy and Voluntarism in American Society

Introduction

Chapter Seven brings the subject of nonprofit organizations full-circle, back to the most fundamental reasons why the nonprofit sector exists—to the benevolent donation of money, property, and time or effort to eliminate or prevent the causes of social problems and injustices. It is about the pros and cons of our society's chosen ways to "form a more perfect union" and to "secure the blessings of liberty to ourselves and our posterity." Although the spirit of philanthropy and voluntarism has been implicitly addressed and is infused through most of the readings, we conclude this anthology with an explicit exploration of philanthropy and voluntarism as topics in their own right. The subject of philanthropy is the subject of value preferences, individualism, pluralism, and applied moral values. Its historical roots extend at least as far back as the founding of the Republic. Thus, this book begins with philanthropy and ends with philanthropy and voluntarism.

Philanthropy is a broader term than *charity* in that a return is expected from the donation in terms of some form of improvement in the public's welfare or general benefit. Philanthropy is the effort to eliminate the causes of problems that charity seeks to alleviate (Ott & Shafritz, 1986, p. 284).

Until recently, philanthropy was largely limited to a leisure-time activity of the rich. In the last century, the great industrialists/robber barons and their families, after making their fortunes, might have donated funds for this or that public improvement. Andrew Carnegie was the most systematic example of this variety of traditional philanthropist. But this century's differing attitudes toward social responsibilities and tax laws have transformed philanthropy from the altruistic concern of a single individual or family to a huge enterprise that affects and sustains a major portion of our economy and our society.

To be sure, wealthy people as well as people of all economic means contribute money, time, energy, and property for socially desirable purposes. But the largest share of the available philanthropic dollar goes to endow foundations. There are tax advantages to the donor in doing this, and the income earned from the principal is taxed at a reduced rate. Therefore, using a foundation helps to multiply the total amount of philanthropic funds available for good works.

Philanthropy has been undergoing fundamental changes since 1969. The early 1970s were difficult years. The Tax Reform Act of 1969 severely weakened private foundations and threatened the continued existence of much of the nonprofit sector. New foundation formations ceased. The federal government was outspending private foundations by an estimated ratio of 30 to 1, thus rendering foundation grantmaking potentially irrelevant (Friedman, 1973).

But despite the difficult years of the 1970s, philanthropy survived its worst times and entered the 1980s optimistically and on an upswing. The national sentiment shifted away from big government domestic programs to solutions by local private voluntary organizations. A new administration in the White House advocated privatization of government functions to a strengthened nonprofit sector. Philanthropy was to become a pillar in a new philosophy leading to social progress. However, by 1984 it became evident that the promises were not to be. Changes in tax policy again reduced the incentives to contribute at the same time that government funding for programs typically operated by nonprofits was slashed. Foundations were besieged by starving nonprofits but were weakened in their ability to respond.

At issue is the very nature of our society's values, public and private initiatives, and our ability to implement community-based programs. After all, it was philanthropy that initially supported such movements as innovative children's television programming, birth control research and information dissemination, and the development of high yield food grains when the government sought to dispose of agricultural surpluses (Heimann, 1973, pp. 262–272). Yet the growing overlap in functions and influence of private foundations and governmental activity clearly points to the urgent need to avoid wasteful duplication—for more effective patterns of communication and cooperation between the private and public sectors.

The United States is an aggregation of attitudes, politics, policies, and people. Understanding the ethos of giving is important to understanding the nonprofit sector. Financial stability is crucial to the success of nonprofit operating organizations. Although philanthropy may represent only a small amount of funds in comparison with governmental social expenditures, it is the single most visible activity in our society that indicates public–private partnership and private support for the commonweal.

Now that philanthropy has to a large extent been institutionalized, its role has changed from random charitable or community developmental efforts to systematic efforts to find causes for focused efforts: to alleviate poverty in certain regions, control world population growth, or preserve rare artifacts, to state only three examples (O'Connell, 1987). The large-scale nature of philanthropy has caused it to become bureaucratized. No longer will an emotional charitable appeal suffice. A systematic proposal must be written and maneuvered through the various levels of approval of the requesting organization to the granting organization's often equally elaborate bureaucracy.

The focus of this final chapter is on the system of philanthropy that embodies the democratic spirit of economic independence. Here we try to demonstrate that philanthropy and voluntarism are manifested in many ways and for many reasons. They may result from different emotional causes: caring, concern, fear, community/social responsibility, and religious obligation. In individual cases a mix of motivations probably contributes. The theory of grants economy suggests that making a financial contribution is necessary in order to satisfy some inner need of "status, identity, community, or legitimacy" (Boulding, 1981). The readings that follow suggest that philanthropy and voluntarism are vital parts of secondary power, ever changing and adjusting in order to meet new questions. They attempt to document philanthropy and voluntarism in the United States by portraying the history, modes, and predicaments.

The chapter's first reading is Merle Curti's (1973) enduring philosophical/historical definition of philanthropy reprinted from *The Dictionary of the History of Ideas*. Curti describes the pre-Grecian origins of personal generosity and the influence of religion on the individual virtue of charitable giving. Of particular interest are Curti's account of the transition of philanthropic ideas into modern times, and the tracing of the changes in attitudes and beliefs from the feudal times through the rise of the middle class. The definition describes the onset of large-scale philanthropy, the need for greater social reform, and the leadership provided by citizens of great wealth.

David Horton Smith's paper, "The Impact of the Volunteer Sector on Society," describes ten characteristics of voluntary groups. Written in 1973, its emphasis is on the nature of nonprofit organizations in a three-sector environment: its capacity to provide for social risk capital, ideological innovation, social buffering, preservation of old ideas, and more.

Defining the role of voluntarism as Smith has done here is conceptually valuable because it expands our understanding of individual motivations for involvement in the sector. Smith explains that in the 1970s, nonprofits were a safe haven for post 1960s change and reform and, at the same time, keepers of American tradition. The article provides impetus for continued observation of voluntary organizations and the growth of the nonprofit sector. Smith also argues for more evaluation of voluntary action to determine the effectiveness of voluntary organizations and movements.

The role of foundations in the United States and the use of private resources to further the public good are the subjects of Merrimon Cuninggim's thoughtful 1972 article, "Caught in the Act of Helping." Cuninggim suggests that foundations are approaching a new era in which suspicion and distrust of private giving are changing attitudes toward philanthropy. Cuninggim presents a snapshot of attitudes during a period when distrust of institutions—particularly, but not exclusively, private foundations—was widespread in this country. (See Stephen Block's historical article in Chapter One.) Times of transition signal periods of growth in ideas and changes in values, and the early 1970s was such a period of transition; of changing sentiments about donors and changing attitudes of donors.

An example of changing attitudes is expressed in Robert F. Arnove's (1980) critical view of philanthropy. He states that it has a "corrosive influence on a democratic society; they [foundations and corporations] represent relatively unregulated and unaccountable concentrations of power and wealth which buy talent, promote causes, and in effect, establish an agenda of what merits society's attention." To demonstrate Arnove's contention, Slaughter and Silva's article on the influence of the Rockefeller Foundation on the Colorado coal field is included here.

Elizabeth Boris's "Philanthropy and the Future" surfaces the important trends within and around philanthropy that provide glimpses of the future of philanthropy, and examines several of them in depth. Boris echoes the definitional argument Payton poses in the Foreword: Philanthropy must be viewed broadly if it is "to include the diversity of initiatives that make up the nonprofit arena." Boris's wide-ranging piece sounds thoughtful warnings about the future vitality of philanthropy and the nonprofit sector. She concludes that encouraging the tradition of philanthropy in the upcoming years is an important challenge. "Young people and new immigrants will need to be cultivated as donors and participants in the philanthropic process. The success of that effort will help to determine the role that philanthropy will play in America's future."

References

Arnove, R. (Ed.). (1980). *Philanthropy and cultural imperialism.* Boston: G.K. Hall.

Bellah, R. N., Madsen, R., Sullivan, W. M., Swider, A., & Tipon, S. M. (1985). *Habits of the heart: Individualism and commitment in American life.* Berkeley: University of California Press.

Boris, E., & Brody, D. (1988). *1988 Foundation management report.* Washington, DC: Council on Foundations.

Boulding, K. E. (1981). *A preface to grants economics: The economy of love and fear.* New York: Praeger.

Bremner, R. H. (1988). *American philanthropy* (2d ed.). Chicago: University of Chicago Press.

Cuninggim, M. (1972). *Private money and public service: The role of foundations in American society.* New York: McGraw-Hill.

Curti, M. (1973). *The dictionary of the history of ideas.* New York: Scribner's.

Fisher, J. L. (Winter, 1986). The growth of heartlessness: The need for studies on philanthropy. *Educational Record*, 25–28.

Friedman, R. E. (1973). Private foundation–government relationships. In F. F. Heimann (Ed.), *The future of foundations* (pp. 166–167). Englewood Cliffs, NJ: Prentice-Hall.

Gladden, W. (1895). Tainted money. *Outlook*, 52, 886–887.

Heimann, F. F. (1973). Foundations and government: Perspectives for the future. In F. F. Heimann (Ed.), *The future of foundations* (pp. 262–273). Englewood Cliffs, NJ: Prentice-Hall.

Hodgkinson, V. A., & Weitzman, M. S. (1986). *Dimensions of the independent sector: A statistical profile.* Washington, DC, Independent Sector.

Hodgkinson, V. A., & Lyman, R. W. (Eds.). (1989). *The future of the nonprofit sector.* San Francisco: Jossey-Bass.

National Charities Information Bureau. (1988). *Standards in philanthropy.* New York: National Industrial Conference Board.

Nielsen, W. (1979). *The endangered sector.* New York: Columbia University Press.

O'Connell, B. (1987). *Philanthropy in action.* Washington, DC: The Foundation Center.

O'Connell, B. (September/October 1989). What voluntary activity can and cannot do for America. *Public Administration Review*, 49(5), 486–491.

Odendahl, T. (Ed.). (1987). *America's wealthy and the future of foundations.* New York: The Foundation Center.

Odendahl, T. (Fall 1989). The culture of elite philanthropy in the Reagan years. *Nonprofit and Voluntary Sector Quarterly*, 18(3), 237–248.

Ott, J. S. & Shafritz, J. M. (1986). *Dictionary of nonprofit organization management.* New York: Facts on File.

Panas, J. (1984). *Megagifts: Who gives them, who gets them.* Chicago, IL: Pluribus Press.

Payton, R. L. (1987). *The ethics of corporate grantmaking.* Washington, DC: Council on Foundations.

Payton, R. L. (1988). *Philanthropy: Voluntary action for the public good.* New York: American Council on Education and MacMillan.

Payton, R. L., Novak, N., O'Connell, B., & Hall, P. D. (1988). *Philanthropy: Four views.* New Brunswick: Social Philosophy and Policy Center.

Pifer, A. (1984, 1967). *Philanthropy in an age of transition: The essays of Alan Pifer.* New York: The Foundation Center.

Reeves, T. C. (1970). *Foundations under fire.* Ithica, NY: Cornell University Press.

Salamon, L. M. (Spring 1989). The voluntary sector and the future of the welfare state. *Nonprofit and Voluntary Sector Quarterly*, 18(1), 11–24.

Smith, B. L. R. (Ed.). (1975). *The new political economy: The public use of the private sector.* New York: Wiley.

Smith, D. H. (1973). *Voluntary action research: 1973.* Lexington, MA: Lexington Books.

Strom, M. S., & Stoskopf, A. L. (1989). Fostering philanthropic values in a modern democracy. In V. A. Hodgkinson & R. W. Lyman (Eds.), *The future of the nonprofit sector.* San Francisco: Jossey-Bass.

Tocqueville, A. de. (1840). *Democracy in America* Vol. II. New York: Knopf.

Van Til, J. (1988). *Mapping the third sector: Voluntarism in a changing social economy.* New York: The Foundation Center.

ARTICLE 27 ————————————
Philanthropy
Merle Curti

Philanthropy

The term "philanthropy," which entered the English language in the seventeenth century as a translation of the Greek φιλανθροπία and the Latin *philanthropia* ("the love of mankind"), has denoted various values and institutions. It has been related to many ethical and religious systems, movements of thought, and social contexts. Associated with charity, civic spirit, humanitarianism, social control, and social work, it has come in the twentieth century to mean, in the main, private and voluntary giving, individually and collectively, for public purposes. Its complex history can best be understood in terms of the related ideas that have characterized its evolution in time and place.

Pre-Greek Foundations

In the nineteenth century, when travelers and early ethnologists reported examples of mutual helpfulness among pre-literate peoples, the widening spectrum of thought about philanthropy was extended backward into prehistoric time. These reports gave support to Peter Kropotkin's contention in *Mutual Aid* (1890–96) that such behavior, whether innate or acquired, had been an indispensable factor in the evolution and survival of the human race and in the development of civilization. Without ignoring this movement in thought, the discussion of the ideas associated with philanthropy in the broadest sense may properly be confined to religious, ethical, and other firsthand written evidences. These, to be sure, can be understood only in relation to changing social, cultural, and institutional (and thus often nonverbal) contexts.

Chinese classical thought exhibited some sophistication and some differences in points of

SOURCE: Reprinted with permission of Charles Scribner's Sons, an imprint of Macmillan Publishing Company, from "Philanthropy" in THE DICTIONARY OF THE HISTORY OF IDEAS, Philip P. Wiener, editor-in-chief. Copyright © 1973 by Charles Scribner's Sons.

view toward philanthropy. Confucius and Mencius exalted universal benevolence as a personal virtue (Legge, I, 405; II, 485). Hsüntze in his *Essay on Human Nature*, regarded spontaneous sympathy with others as an acquired, rather than as an innate, human quality, but seemed to imply that this trait is within the capacity of all human beings (Dubs, p. 312). On the other hand, the Taoist Chuang-Tzŭ denounced philanthropy as a false outgrowth of human nature that disturbed human well-being (Giles, pp. 165–67). In practice, the maxim "love mankind" seems to have been largely operative in the extended family and in the institution of friendship until the early nineteenth century.

Personal generosity to those in need, especially to strangers, widows, and orphans, was commended or enjoined in the sacred writings and ethical teachings of pre-Greek civilizations. In some instances the practice of charity was advocated as a personal virtue, in others it was enjoined as a religious duty pleasing in the eyes of the gods. In some cases, notably in the Hindu scriptures, giving to the needy, especially to holy men dependent on alms, was an imperative duty, the fulfillment of which also rewarded the donor in a future state of existence. The general tone of admonition suggested that the emphasis was on the effect of giving on the donor, rather than on the recipient, except insofar as poverty was often identified with holiness. The teachings of Gautama, the Buddha (ca. 450 B.C.) not only sanctioned giving as a personal virtue but associated it with self-restraint as an evidence of rectitude. Buddhist institutionalization of philanthropy was evident in the establishment of hospitals, and in the example of King Aśoka in generous giving for the sake of spreading Buddhist truth. References, in more or less general terms, to a concern for the unfortunate appear in the Hammurabic Code (ca. 2000? B.C.), and in the Egyptian *Book of the Dead* in which a good man is identified as one who had given bread to the hungry, water to the thirsty, raiment to the naked, and a boat to one who had none. Egyptian inscriptions indicate that pharaohs regarded acts of benevolence and tomb-building as means of propitiating the gods in the interest of immortality and of insuring their own identity in the minds of succeeding generations.

Greek and Roman Philanthropy

Mercy, regard for others, hospitality and kindness beyond the limits of family, friends, and ethnocentric bounds found some expression in Homer, Hesiod, Herodotus, Thucydides, and the Attic orators, but the word "philanthropy," destined to have so long a history, makes almost its first appearance in Aeschylus' *Prometheus Bound*. Broadly speaking, in Greek thought the word connoted good citizenship and democratic, humanitarian inclinations. Xenophon called Socrates "democratic and philanthropic," that is to say, a friend of mankind. Demosthenes declared that "the laws ordain nothing that is cruel or violent or oligarchic, but on the contrary, all their provisions are made in a democratic and philanthropic spirit" (Macurdy, p. 98). With the Stoics the concept clearly transcended the dominant, ethnocentric emphasis on the rights and privileges of citizenship by emphasizing a kind and compassionate behavior toward all fellow human beings as a necessary corollary of a common humanity. In concrete terms and in an institutional implementation, however, the idea of love of mankind did not take among the Greeks the form of private charitable giving to the needy poor; guiding policy preferred the idea of public responsibility in the form of work relief projects or doles. When a man of wealth gave of his substance for public purposes, the objective was largely civic and cultural, as Alexander's gift of the library in Egypt, and as the endowment of the Academy and Lyceum indicate.

Roman concepts and practices did not greatly differ from Greek precedents although institutions for the sick and needy sometimes enjoyed private as well as public support. The custom of subsidies (*sportula*) by the wealthy and powerful to clients for political and personal reasons was not truly philanthropic in the original sense of the term, love of mankind.

Jewish Philanthropy

The age-old and possibly ubiquitous compassionate impulse to relieve suffering through personal service and the giving of personal substance to the needy, whenever a society developed marked inequality in possessions, found its most notable exemplification among the ancient Hebrews. In marked contrast with the permissiveness of charity in most early religious and ethical systems, and with the relegation to the state of responsibility for the poor in Greco-Roman civilization, Judaism made charity a central and imperative duty for each believer. In the fifth book of Moses (Deuteronomy 14:22) tithing was made a compulsory obligation: "For the poor shall never cease out of the land; therefore I command thee, saying, Thou shalt open thine hand wide unto thy brother, to thy poor, and to thy needy, in thy land." Similarly, it was an obligation to give one's bread to the hungry, to take the outcast into one's home, to clothe the naked (Isaiah 58:7). In making charity to all needy Jews an obligation (however gladly it was executed), Judaism identified charity and justice (*Zedakah*). Amos, Isaiah, and Micah severely attacked the exploitation of the weak by the strong, thus taking an innovating stand in attacking the problem of poverty at its root: a sense of social justice as well as humanitarian feeling is especially evident in the Psalms and in the Wisdom Literature of the Bible. Although the sense of justice was the animating note in the concept of charity, love of one's fellow men as the children of God was a fervent and even passionately expressed value—contrary to the contention of some Christian writers, such as Gehrhard Uhlhorn (*Christian Charity in the Ancient World*, New York [1883], Ch. 2). The idea of righteousness in the interest of ultimate salvation figured only in later Jewish thought. In addition to emphasizing duty, obligation, and ethical love, Judaism very early stressed the organization of charity as a principal institution of the synagogue. Jewish adherence to the religious duty of charity was reinforced by historical experience as an "out-group" in need of social cohesion, a need that was to continue through the Middle Ages and modern times.

The ethical and emotional distinctions in giving were explicated in a voluminous post-biblical, rabbinical literature. The best known medieval writer was Moses Maimonides, who in 1201 codified the Talmudic rules in the Eight Degrees of Charity. The highest sanction was that given to the kind of helpfulness that anticipated charity by preventing poverty: "He who aids the poor to support himself by advancing funds or by helping him to some lucrative occupation" fulfilled a high degree of charity, "than which there is no higher." Charity in which the donor did not know the recipient or the recipient the donor, was more meritorious than types of giving in which the donor could take satisfaction from the appreciation of the recipient. Giving before being asked, was preferable to giving after being asked; and he who gave inadequately but with good grace, was less blameworthy than he who gave with bad grace (Frisch, pp. 62–63). Maimonides as well as other writers were aware of the complexity of motives in giving and, while recognizing utilitarianism and enlightened self-interest, attached supreme importance to religious, ethical, and humanitarian considerations.

The institutionalization of these ideas reflected the problems of the Jews in specific historical contexts. Thus in the Middle Ages particular attention was given to the care of orphans and the ransoming of captives. Jewish philanthropy was adapted to concrete needs by mass-scale efforts and constructive thinking. The far-reaching program of the Baron de Hirsch Fund (1885) in reducing the incidence of persecution of the Jews in Russia by assisted emigration is only one example of the preventive and resourceful quality of modern Jewish philanthropic thought and activity. Another example is the response of worldwide Jewry to the tragedy of coreligionists in Germany and German-controlled areas during the Nazi persecutions. Most striking of all examples is the creative role of philanthropy in the making of the state of Israel with its distinctive civilization.

Semitic influences may in part explain Muslim admonitions to charity in the Koran and, possibly, the establishment of hospitals at Bagdad and other centers. Nevertheless, philanthropy in Muslim cultures did not develop an ideology and an institutionalization comparable in any sense to that in Judaic culture.

Christianity

The influence of Judaism on early Christian concepts and practices in philanthropy was positive and direct. Saint Paul developed the Hebrew idea of stewardship, which assumed that the rich man was not the owner but merely the steward of the

wealth in his hand, and must therefore use it in accordance with God's commands (I Corinthians 13; II Corinthians 8, 9). Many of the ideas in one of the passages in the New Testament (Matthew 25:35–46) most relevant to Christian philanthropy are closely related to if not identical with Hebrew antecedents. Certain ideas in this passage and in others in the New Testament may, however, be regarded as striking a somewhat new emphasis. One is the idea of reward and punishment in future life for the fulfillment of, or for the failure to fulfill, charitable commands. At the same time Christianity emphasizes the idea that charity enhances life in this world by bringing the giver into closer spiritual relationship with God. If acts of charity, including personal service, were not executed for the most lowly and for those in greatest need, then they were not being executed for God the King.

It might seem that the millennial expectations of the early Christians and the resulting emphasis on the imperative need of readiness for the Coming, would de-emphasize the Jewish tradition of charity as a duty to those in immediate physical distress and need. But such was not the case. The bias of Jesus toward the poor and disinherited, as those most apt to receive the message of God's kingdom, and the feeling that wealth endangers the soul provided an undertone for early Christian precepts and practices in the sphere of charity. The early commitments to those in need, to the equalization of wealth, and to enhancing the sense of fellowship in the community of believers were regarded as expressions of Christian love. At the same time the emphasis on the sanctity and dignity of each individual encouraged the development of the fraternal implications of the doctrine of Christian love. The early appearance of Christian hostels for wayfarers and the incapacitated, and arrangements for mutual aid and group security indicate that the idea of the supreme importance of the care of souls was not entirely disassociated from the care and cure of bodies. This idea was further implemented in A.D. 321 when the emperor Constantine recognized the validity of gifts and bequests for Christian institutions, including charities.

Thus as early as the fourth century the concept of *philanthropia* was well established in Christendom. In the Eastern or Byzantine empire public philanthropy, which owed something to Greek classical tradition, and private charity, largely Christian in inspiration, achieved a notable record in charitable institutions, including monasteries. Yet the Byzantine concept did not include concern for the prevention of poverty; constant almsgiving perpetuated poverty and tended to maintain the status quo in the social structure (Constantelos, p. 284).

In the West the disappearance of the state in the Greek and Roman sense left a vacuum in which no purely secular feudal agency was equipped to provide relief for poverty and disability. Thus the Church found ample scope for institutionalizing the doctrine of love of fellow men by encouraging and sponsoring gifts for charitable hospitals, colleges, and monasteries with well-defined functions for the care of the poor.

The dominance of theology and casuistry as intellectual interests, together with the magnitude of medieval philanthropy, insured the probing of its ethical assumptions and implications. It was undeniable that certain scriptural texts, indicating that generous bestowal of alms is a Christian duty the fulfilment of which would insure heavenly reward, opened the door to self-regard in acts of pious charity. Theologians and canonists held, however, that giving, in order to be pleasing to God, must be an outward manifestation of a genuine feeling of justice and a true act of love. Despite this emphasis, much giving was impulsive, indiscriminate, and perfunctory. Some was motivated by mechanically measured considerations of self-interest: this gift was equal to so much merit, that gift, to so much more or less. It was against all this that Saint Francis of Assisi protested, insisting on the importance, indeed the necessity, of sacrifice, disinterested love, and the dignity and worth of poverty.

According to Church canon, giving was also qualified by consideration of how the donor came by that which he gave. In the thirteenth century, canonists held it meritorious to give property even if it had been improperly acquired, provided that legal title had passed to the donor and that no party was left to claim restitution. Long after the Reformation the ethical criterion of the ways in which wealth flowing into charity had been obtained continued to be a thorny matter. In the twentieth century, Washington Gladden, a Protestant theologian of the Social Gospel, argued, in regard to Rockefeller gifts to Church missions and other charities, that the Church could not properly accept ill-gotten gains or "tainted wealth" no matter how pious the donor nor how worthy the object of donation. This, however, was a minority view.

Finally, contrary to later contentions, medieval canonists considered the effects of charity on recipients. In general, it is true that canonists favored generosity in the execution of the command, 'feed the hungry, clothe the naked." But Gratian's *Decretum* (1471), the great summing up of pros and cons on disputed theological points, noted that Saint Ambrose had suggested an order of preference among applicants for charity and that Saint Augustine had opposed donations to able-bodied beggars and vagrants. Thus in theory, if not in practice, medieval charity struck a balance between the interests and spiritual well-being of all concerned—donor, recipient, and community (Tierney, pp. 57–58).

The Transition to Modern Philanthropic Ideas

While Christianity continued to exert great influence during and after the transition from medieval to modern times, secular conditions altered and finally transformed traditional ideas about charity and philanthropy. What may be regarded as the beginnings of modern philanthropic ideas can be explained in large part by the interlocking of traditional attitudes and values with new social, economic, political, and religious conditions. These included the decline of feudalism, the rise of cities and the middle class, the dislocation of populations resulting from the enclosure movement and other economic changes, and the Reformation itself, related, as it was, to the emergence of national states. The religious foundations, especially after the dissolution of the monasteries in Tudor England, were no longer able to perform their older functions or to meet newer social, economic, and vocational needs. All these changes account in part for the extraordinary development of private philanthropy in Tudor and Stuart England. The merchant and gentry classes poured wealth into charitable and educational institutions, in effect accepting the Tudor policy of shifting to localities and to private donors responsibility for poor relief, and the development of schools and other charitable agencies.

Among the ideas that intermeshed with changing conditions, special importance is to be given to the Protestant rejection, or at least de-emphasis on the doctrine of salvation by good works or individual acts of charity, and the emphasis rather on salvation by faith—the reception of the holy spirit suffusing the entire personality of those worthy of it in God's eyes. This de-emphasized traditional medieval charity. It is true that Calvin, in Reformation Geneva, found biblical warrant for voluntary gifts to the laicized and rationalized welfare agencies previously controlled by the Catholic Church; he also involved himself in the operation of the *Bourse française*, a private fund for helping French refugees. The Calvinistic re-emphasis on the stewardship of riches encouraged giving to needy persons and to Christian charities. Thus Thomas Fuller's *History of the Worthies of England* (1662) provided a special category of donors to public causes. The reliance in England, and to some extent in other Protestant countries, on philanthropy to meet major new social and economic needs was accompanied by the idea of public control over private charitable donations, other current bequests and gifts, and trusts. The Elizabethan Statute of Charitable Uses (1601) summed up much earlier experiment with public supervision. While in England and other Protestant countries the new idea of private responsibility under public supervision for social and economic needs was developing, in Catholic countries the Church in general continued to function in charitable and educational roles with minimal state supervision.

The social as distinct from the personal and religious character of the new philanthropy was exemplified in its nationalistic and class overtones. Fear of the effects of an apparently declining population on the supply of cheap labor inspired greater attention to the establishment of orphanages for foundlings and hospitals (in the modern sense) for the poor. The need of the Royal Navy for personnel was met in part by greater concern for waifs who were salvaged from the dregs of society and given proprietary care and training for national service. To reduce tax costs and to accord with the idea of self-help, philanthropy encompassed a wide spectrum of innovations designed to maintain the class structure. These included various schemes for putting the poor to work rather than permitting them to receive relief for which they rendered no service.

The idea of voluntary organization in charity devoloped with new social and economic forces associated with overseas commercial expansion, including the slave trade, the industrial revolution, and the need for a cheap but stable and reliable labor force. The prevailing idea that poverty is the result, not of social and economic dislocations, but of a failure of character, the vogue of classical economics with its emphasis on laissez-faire, and the rise of evangelical Christianity with its strong impulse toward social reform, all contributed to the dominance of the idea of voluntary association in philanthropy which, perhaps, was also suggested by the joint stock company. Contributions to voluntary societies that were addressed to specific social problems were now often made in small sums and anonymously. These, together with larger gifts and bequests, were directed to the relief of distress, to hospitals, orphanages, schools for poor scholars, and agencies for training apprentices. The Society for the Promotion of Christian Knowledge, founded in 1698, which established over two thousand charity schools in the first century of its existence, was typical of the new emphasis on organized, voluntary philanthropy. So was the Society for the Propagation of the Gospel in Foreign Parts. Toward the end of the eighteenth century, with a mounting tide of conservative reaction against the French Revolution, new charity schools, organized by Robert Raikes and Hannah More and supported by voluntary, organized efforts, emphasized moral instruction as a means of reducing crime, and promoted religious teaching as a means of combatting radical innovation and "atheistic" Jacobinism.

Yet social control in associated, voluntary philanthropy was not the only idea underlying the proliferation of eighteenth-century philanthropy. Robert Eden, in *The Harmony of Benevolence: a Sermon on Psalm CXXXVI* (London, 1755), expounded the idea that benevolence is largely instinctive and emotional and that the satisfaction of this instinct is pleasurable. Oliver Goldsmith wrote that "the luxury of doing good" enhanced self-esteem. And the traditional idea of humanitarian compassion was sometimes expressed with an ironical twist, as in William Blake's poems entitled "Holy Thursday" and "The Human Abstract":

Is this a holy thing to see,
In a rich and fruitful land
Babes reduced to misery,
Fed with cold and usurous hand?
    ("Holy Thursday").

Pity would be no more,
If we did not make somebody poor,
And mercy no more could be
If all were as happy as we
    ("The Human Abstract").

Modern philanthropic ideas were given worldwide connotations when the Catholic religious orders undertook to Christianize and civilize indigenous peoples overseas, and to support French, Portuguese, and Spanish colonial empires. The Anglican, Lutheran, Moravian, and Quaker efforts to Christianize Indians and African slaves was the Protestant counterpart. Yet these and other overseas philanthropic interests were not always self-consciously "imperialistic" or even religious. Such considerations, while present in Oglethorpe's venture in founding Georgia, were subordinated to his humanitarian aim of rehabilitating unfortunates who had been imprisoned for debt. Another example of the impact of the new philanthropic spirit on overseas expansion was the comment of Benjamin Franklin, on learning in 1771 of the proposed colonization of New Zealand, that "a voyage is now proposed, to visit a distant people on the other side of the globe; not to cheat them, not to rob them . . . but merely to do them good, and make them, as far as in our power lies, to live as comfortably as ourselves" (*Writings*, ed. A. H. Smyth, V, 342).

The secular and civic tone of Franklin's remarks characterized the newer ideas of philanthropy which he brought to fruit in Philadelphia. In organizing voluntary associations for promoting self-help, such as libraries and discussion groups, in furthering the fortunes of the College of Philadelphia (the University of Pennsylvania) and the Pennsylvania Hospital, Franklin devoted both his means and his services to philanthropy. He also developed practical techniques for fund-raising. These included the listing of prospective donors, personally visiting them and presenting persuasive arguments, following up the visits when results were not forthcoming, and using the new media of communication, especially the public press. In effect he was secularizing and democratizing the Christian concept of the stewardship of wealth, to which his attention had been drawn in his youth in Boston by Cotton Mather's *Essays to do Good* (1710). Franklin's innovating ideas for fund-raising were used throughout the nineteenth century, especially for enlisting support for colleges, and provided the basis for further amplification and refinement by the new professional fund-raising organizations of twentieth-century America.

Humanitarian Reform

While the pecuniary element in philanthropy, both in concept and practice, was always an essential and sometimes the central emphasis, the term philanthropy was used in the late eighteenth and early nineteenth centuries in both England and America as a synonym for social and humanitarian reform. This identification was in part explicable by reason of the supporting pillars of social reform: evangelicism, humanitarianism, the idea of progress, and a middle-class awareness of the need for the maintenance of social order. No idea, however, was as important as the conviction that society has no right to advance its own aims and well-being at the expense of the disadvantaged individual. In the sense of social reform, philanthropy expressed itself mainly in the English-speaking countries in the movement for the abolition of the slave trade and, finally, of slavery itself; in the demand for the abolition of capital punishment and the reform of the penal code; in the concern for helpless and exploited children; in the battle for the political, legal, and social rights of women; in the more humane treatment of animals, the mentally ill, and others suffering from inherited or acquired handicaps; and in the elimination of war as a means for solving disputes among nations.

Philanthropy as social reform also expressed itself in charity societies, voluntary agencies for supplementing or even replacing inadequate public provisions for the care of the indigent poor. In both England and America the charity organization movement drew strength from the middle-class conviction that poverty is largely a matter of personal shortcoming and that the bestowal of relief or charity deteriorates the character of the recipient still further. "Human nature is so constituted," wrote a leading figure in the American charity organization movement, "that no man can receive as a gift what he should earn by his own labor without a moral deterioration" (Lowell, pp. 66, 76).

Thus the movement emphasized ways of making the unemployed poor self-supporting. The charity organization movement also sought to eliminate the wasteful duplication of agencies and the prevailing inefficiency in their operation. The idea of efficiency also figured in the emphasis on the careful investigation of the needs of each recipient. But this emphasis was also a function of the feeling that the problems of the poor and needy must be regarded in individual, personal, rather than class terms. To counteract the impersonal, even heartless treatment of those in distress by public agencies, the charity organization movement developed "friendly visiting," in which volunteers not only offered advice to the needy but showed personal interest and understanding. The related social-settlement idea also sought to bring the privileged and underprivileged into mutually rewarding human contacts. When the modern profession of social work developed from the charity organizations and the social settlements, scientific specialization and "expertise" largely supplanted the voluntary character of older practice. The first schools for training professional social workers were called schools of philanthropy.

The New Rationale of Large-Scale Giving

In the later decades of the nineteenth century and in the early years of the twentieth, ideas, in the main new, initiated an almost unprecedented chapter in the intellectual history of philanthropy. While a great deal of giving, both during the lives of donors and in provisions in their wills, continued to be directed toward charitable and religious institutions and causes, an increasing

emphasis was put on the use of philanthropy for the prevention of shortcomings in the social order, and for the general improvement of the quality of civilization, especially through the extension of knowledge, the increase of scientific understanding and control through research, and through the enhancement of health and the aesthetic and recreational components of everyday life. This emphasis was expressed in the magnitude of donations by Americans of great wealth for new programs and improvements in existing colleges and universities, and for the establishment of new schools and universities associated with the benefactions of Cornell, Johns Hopkins, Vanderbilt, Vassar, Eastman, Stanford, and Rockefeller. It was also expressed in philanthropic support for art museums, symphony orchestras, parks, and other recreational facilities. Not since the Renaissance and Tudor England had wealth been used on such a scale for the improvement of cultural values.

No less important was the rationale for this philanthropy. In an article in the *North American Review* (1889), Andrew Carnegie, a "self-made" multimillionaire, argued that men of great wealth should, during their lifetime, allocate most of it to purposes other than the relief of individual misfortunes or incompetence, a relief which might be left to the state. Assuming that those who had made great fortunes had demonstrated their competence in the struggle for survival, Carnegie contended that these men had a social obligation to use their acquired wealth to provide opportunities for hardworking, competent, and ambitious youths and adults to advance themselves. This, he felt, could best be done by the use of private wealth for stimulating communities to support public libraries, baths, and recreational and vocational training including that offered, as yet inadequately, for Negro youth. The millionaire, Carnegie concluded, should be ashamed to die rich. This rationale quickly came to be known as "The Gospel of Wealth." While in a sense a further secularization of the Christian doctrine of stewardship, it also emphasized prevention rather than cure, efficiency, and the equalization of opportunity.

Carnegie, together with the Rockefellers and the later Fords, was also a pioneer in the development of the modern foundation. This institution, to be sure, had a long history stretching back into ancient, medieval, and early modern times. But in its American form it differed from its predecessors, not only in the magnitude of its resources and in its use of specialized personnel for the allocation of grants, but in its emphasis less on specific purposes (though these continued to find expression) than on the general prevention of human suffering at home and abroad and on the enrichment of life through the improvement of educational standards, medical and social science research, and city planning, or through the support and dissemination of aesthetic values and opportunities. The promoters of the new foundations were in the main influenced by philanthropic interest and, to some extent, by the value of the foundation for creating a favorable public image of the donor. After 1917 and more particularly 1936, legal provisions in income-tax legislation, exempting gifts from taxation, stimulated much foundation activity, particularly in the case of the so-called family foundations, and in the new development of corporation foundations that directed their largess toward welfare programs, education, and local charities.

The foundation met with a mixed public response. At first, at the high tide of the Progressive movement, fear was expressed that its power and influence might become a bulwark for "conservatism," and inhibit the public assumption of social responsibilities deemed imperative by most liberals. In the early 1950's, during the "McCarthy period," foundations were attacked in some circles as supporters of subversive, "un-American" causes, particularly in the field of social welfare, and in grants given to liberal and radical scholars and other intellectuals. The use and abuse of tax-exemption privileges by many foundations, together with the secretive bookkeeping arrangements in some cases, led to Congressional investigations after mid-century, and to demands for a greater measure of public control.

The development of the welfare state in England, together with the new and large benefactions of the Wellcomes, Nuffields, and others that supplemented venerable trusts, raised again the issue of social efficiency or inefficiency of endowments, and the relation of these to public responsibility for social welfare and education. On the whole, in England and America, a consensus seemed to hold that by pioneering in needed fields in which government was

reluctant to experiment, the foundation at its best had an important and creative role to play in supplementing the state as an agent for social well-being. Although in some noncommunist countries in Europe, Latin America, and Asia philanthropy in the Anglo-American sense showed signs of developing in the mid-twentieth century, in modern times its importance in the history of ideas has largely been confined to Great Britain and the United States, where individual responsibility and the principle of voluntary cooperation for personal and social well-being have been significant values in the culture. Yet, a caveat expressed in the 1930's by Reinhold Niebuhr summed up a criticism almost as old as philanthropy itself: "The effort to make voluntary charity solve the problems of a major social crisis. . . results only in monumental hypocrisies and tempts selfish people to regard themselves as unselfish" (Niebuhr, p. 29).

Bibliography

The most satisfactory, comprehensive account of pre-Christian philanthropy is Hendrik Bolkestein, *Wohltätigkeit und Armpflege im Vorchristlichen Altertum* (Utrecht, 1939). James Legge's celebrated translations, *The Chinese Classics*, 5 vols. (Oxford, 1938–95), was reissued in Hong Kong in 1960. For Hsüntze's essay, see Homer H. Dubs, *The Works of Hsüntze* (London, 1928). Special studies include Yu-Yue Tsü, *The Spirit of Chinese Philanthropy. A Study in Mutual Aid* (New York, 1912). The literature on Jewish philanthropy is extensive; the best introduction is Ephraim Frisch, *An Historical Survey of Jewish Philanthropy* (New York, 1924). Translations from relevant Greek texts are conveniently accessible in Grace H. Macurdy, *The Quality of Mercy: the Gentler Virtues in Greek Literature* (New Haven, 1940). A sociological approach to the complex and developing ideas in the Christian tradition distinguishes Ernst Troeltsch's *Die Soziallehren der christlichen Kirchen und Gruppen* (Tübingen, 1922), trans. O. Wyon as *The Social Teaching of the Christian Churches*, 2 vols. (London and New York, 1931; reprint New York, 1960). It should, however, be read in connection with Michel Riquet, *Christian Charity in Action*, trans. from the French by P. J. Hepburne-Scott, in a series, *The Twentieth Century Encyclopedia of Catholicism*, Sec. ix

(New York, 1961). The first comprehensive study of the subject in the Eastern Church is Demetrios J. Constantelos, *Byzantine Philanthropy and Social Welfare* (New Brunswick, N.J., 1968). A corresponding study for medieval charity in the Roman Church is Brian Tierney, *Medieval Poor Law. A Sketch of Canonical Theory and its Application to England* (Berkeley and Los Angeles, 1959).

The earliest modern, and still useful, survey of the whole development of English philanthropy is B. K. Gray, *A History of English Philanthropy* (London, 1905). It has been corrected at many points and enormously enriched by the indispensable studies of W. K. Jordan, *Philanthropy in England 1480–1660* (London, 1960) and *The Charities of London* (London and New York, 1960), and by David Owen's *English Philanthropy* (Cambridge, Mass., 1964).

The best general introduction to American philanthropy is Robert H. Bremner, *American Philanthropy* (Chicago, 1960). Two basic sources for ideas about early American philanthropy are *The Apologia of Robert Keayne. The Self-Portrait of a Puritan Merchant*, ed. Bernard Bailyn (New York, 1965), and *The Writings of Benjamin Franklin*, ed. Albert Henry Smyth, 12 vols. (New York, 1907). Josephine Shaw Lowell's *Public Relief and Private Charity* (New York, 1884), and Frank D. Watson's *The Charity Organization Movement in the United States* (New York, 1894, and subsequent editions) are standard works. Special aspects of American philanthropy are treated in Roy Lubove, *The Professional Altruist. The Emergence of Social Work as a Career 1880–1930* (Cambridge, Mass., 1965); Merle Curti, *American Philanthropy Abroad* (New Brunswick, N.J., 1963); and Merle Curti and Roderick Nash, *Philanthropy in the Shaping of American Higher Education* (New Brunswick, N.J., 1965). An early critical work on American foundations is Eduard C. Lindeman, *Wealth and Culture* (New York, 1936). More objective is F. Emerson Andrews, *Philanthropic Foundations* (New York, 1956). Andrews' *Corporation Giving* (New York, 1952) is the first and still useful study of a new development in American philanthropy. The comprehensive survey edited and in part written by Warren Weaver, *United States Philanthropic Foundations* (New York, 1967), needs to be supplemented by monographic studies of specific foundations, relatively few having yet been undertaken.

Among the few philosophical analyses of the idea of philanthropy special mention is to be made of T. V. Smith, "George Herbert Mead and the Philosophy of Philanthropy," *Social Service Review*, 6 (March 1932), 37–54, and the study of Pitirim A. Sorokin, *Altruistic Love. A Study of American "Good Neighbors" and Christian Saints* (Boston, 1956).

ARTICLE 28 ——————————————————

The Impact of the Volunteer Sector on Society

David Horton Smith

The "voluntary sector" refers to all those persons, groups, roles, organizations, and institutions in society whose goals involve primarily voluntary action. The term "voluntary action" is treated at length in the first volume of this series (*Voluntary Action Research: 1972*), so that we shall not elaborate on its meaning here. Suffice it to say that, roughly speaking, it includes what one is neither made to nor paid to do, but rather what one does out of some kind of expectation of psychic benefits or commitment to some value, ideal, or common interest. The voluntary sector may be roughly delineated in a negative way by contrasting it with the commercial or business sector (sometimes called the "private sector") and with the government or public sector. Another way of describing the voluntary sector is by saying that it is the total persisting social embodiment (in the form of norms, expectations, customs, and ways of behaving) of voluntary action in society.

Our question here is, simply, what impact does the voluntary sector as a whole have on society? There is not sufficient research information to permit one to do an aggregate analysis, building up a picture of the whole by systematically combining the parts—the kinds of impacts of voluntary action at different system levels we

SOURCE: *Voluntary Action Research* by D. H. Smith. Copyright © 1973 by Lexington Press. Reprinted by permission of the author.

have been examining in part in prior chapters. Instead, we can only do the very sketchiest global analysis, based on a loose inductive logic and general theoretical considerations. In making this very brief and simplistic analysis, we are again more interested in suggesting some lines of possible future research and theory than in being exhaustive or thorough.

Another way of looking at what we are calling these impacts of the voluntary sector is to see the processes behind the impacts and to term them the "functions" or "roles" of the voluntary sector. These processes are not necessary features of the voluntary sector in any given nation, let alone in all nations. But they do represent what the voluntary sector can do and often has done in the past in particular societies at particular times. This is an attempt to help delineate more clearly why there is a voluntary sector in society, much as one might elsewhere discuss the role of government institutions or business or even the family in society. Like all of the latter, of course, the role of the voluntary sector changes over time in a given society and even in human society as a whole. Nevertheless, the impacts of the voluntary sector we discuss briefly below are suggested as very general aspects of the voluntary sector in human society, and hence they are present to at least some degree as long as there is a voluntary sector.

First, one of the most central impacts of the voluntary sector is to provide society with a large variety of partially tested social innovations, from which business, government, and other institutions can select and institutionalize those innovations which seem most promising. The independent voluntary sector is thus the prototyping test bed of many, perhaps most, new social forms and modes of human relations. Where business and government, science and technology are active in the creation and testing of technological innovations, the independent voluntary sector specializes in the practical testing of social ideas. Nearly every function currently performed by governments at various levels was once a new social idea and the experiment of some voluntary group, formal or informal—this is true of education, welfare, care for the aged, building roads, even fighting wars (volunteer citizen militias).

In sum, the voluntary sector has tended to provide the social risk capital of human society.

It has been sufficiently free of the kinds of constraints that bind business (the constant need to show a profit) and government (the need to maintain control, and, in societies with effective democracies, the need to act in accord with a broad consensus) so that its component elements (particular voluntary groups or even individuals) can act simply out of commitment to some value or idea, without needing to wait until the payoffs for that kind of activity can be justified in terms appropriate to mobilizing economic or governmental institutions. It is thus the most "error-embracing" and experimental component of society (see Smith with Dixon 1973).

Second, another central impact of the voluntary sector on society has been the provision of countervailing definitions of reality and morality —ideologies, perspectives, and worldviews that frequently challenge the prevailing assumptions about what exists and what is good and what should be done in society. The voluntary sector is that part of society which, collectively, is most likely to say that "the emperor has no clothes." Voluntary groups of various kinds are distinctive among human groups in the extent to which they develop their own ideologies and value systems. If these definitions of reality and morality are sufficiently compelling to people, voluntary groups grow into huge social movements and can change the course of history, both within a given nation (e.g., the abolitionist movement in the early and middle nineteenth century of the United States) and across human society as a whole (e.g., Christianity, Buddhism, democracy, communism).

This kind of impact of the voluntary sector is related to the previous one, but where the former kind of impact emphasized experimentation with social innovation in practice, the present impact emphasizes instead ideological and moral innovation. Where the previous point focused on the social risk capital role of the voluntary sector in society, the present point focuses on the role of the voluntary sector as a gadfly, dreamer, and moral leader in society. Voluntary groups of various kinds are concerned with the generation and allocation of human commitment in the deepest sense. In the process of doing this, the voluntary sector as a whole provides moral and ideological leadership to the majority of human society, and often calls into question the existing legitimacy structures and accepted social definitions of reality of particular societies.

A third major impact of the voluntary sector on society is to provide the play element in society, especially as the search for novelty, beauty, recreation, and fun for their own sake may be collectively organized. Again because the voluntary sector is not constrained generally by such values as profit, control, and broad social consensus, voluntary groups can form in terms of literally thousands of different kinds of common interests. A full array of common interest groups (especially expressive rather than instrumental ones) in an elaborated but still evolving voluntary sector permits (in principle) nearly all individuals to find at least one group that will be satisfying to them. If there is no such group, one or more individuals may form one, if they wish, to reflect their own needs and vision of the play element. Such a group may be formal or informal, large or small, permanent or transient, open or closed, and so forth.

To speak of the play element here is not to speak of something trivial and unimportant. As society becomes increasingly complex and work activity is increasingly structured in terms of large bureaucracies, people's unsatisfied needs for play, novelty, new experience, and all manner of recreation tend to increase. The kind of easy interchange and blending of play and work that could be present in more traditional economies tends to be lost. Under such circumstances, voluntary groups often provide a window of variety and intrinsic satisfaction in an otherwise rather boring or at least psychically fatiguing world of work and responsibility.

Fourth, the voluntary sector also has a major impact on the level of social integration in society. Partly through directly expressive groups, whose aims are explicitly to provide fellowship, sociability and mutual companionship, and partly through the sociability aspects of all other kinds of collective and interpersonal forms of voluntary action, the voluntary sector helps in a very basic way to satisfy some of the human needs for affiliation, approval, and so on. In advanced industrial and urbanized societies, where the family and kinship as well as the local community and neighborhood play a markedly reduced role in providing social integration, affiliations based

on common interests can become very important to the individual. Indeed, without the latter kind of voluntary-sector-based common interest affiliations, the resulting rates of individual social isolation in society would lead to even more anomie, alienation, and a variety of attendant social and psychological problems than are now the case. Obviously, the voluntary sector has not been the whole solution to the root problem of social isolation in modern society, yet voluntary groups do play a demonstrable and important part in the solution. And with the feeling of being accepted as a person that the voluntary sector provides (or can provide) to a significant proportion of the population in modern societies goes the correlative provision of positive affect, a major component of human happiness and the quality of human life.

Another aspect of the role of the voluntary sector in providing social integration is the social adjustment "buffering" function that many kinds of voluntary groups provide. When numerous individuals of a certain social and cultural background are for some reason uprooted from their customary societal niches, new voluntary groups frequently emerge to provide these individuals with an insulated or "buffered" special environment for part of their time. Typical examples would be the numerous immigrant associations that sprang up in the United States as a result of successive waves of immigration from various countries (Handlin 1951) or the kinship-oriented associations that emerged to ease the adjustment of rural West Africans to life in large cities (Little 1965).

These kinds of social-adjustment-oriented voluntary groups do not, however, emerge only in the case of physical/geographical changes on a large scale. The voluntary sector also provides a social adjustment "mechanism" to ease the shocks of social dislocations and rapid social changes of all sorts. The voluntary groups involved may cater to a former elite that has been disenfranchised or deprived of its former holdings (e.g., the association of maharajahs of India, which arose to fight for "maharajah's rights" when the Indian Congress stripped them of their traditional privileges and land, substituting a moderate annual stipend). Or the voluntary groups involved may represent a deprived category of persons who are attempting to adjust to changed social conditions that are more conducive to their sharing equitably in the good life as lived in their society (e.g., the early labor unions or black power groups, striving for recognition of their right to exist and to fight for the betterment of the conditions of their constituencies).

On another level, the voluntary sector plays an important integrative role by linking together individuals, groups, institutions and even nations that otherwise would be in greater conflict, or at least competition, with each other. (This and other impacts of voluntary groups are discussed further in Smith, 1966.) At the community level, a variety of voluntary associations will each tend to have as members a set of two or more individuals representing differing and often opposing political, religious, cultural, or social perspectives and backgrounds. The coparticipation of this set of individuals in the same voluntary association can have significant moderating effects on the relationships among these individuals. Similar integrative effects can be found at national levels where several groups from different parts of the country and/or different social and cultural perspectives participate together in a common federation or other national voluntary organization. And at the international level, the joint participation of voluntary groups from otherwise conflicting nations in some transnational federative organization may well have important long-range effects on the relations between the countries involved and on the possibilities of peace in the world.

A fifth kind of general impact of the voluntary sector involves the opposite of the first one, which dealt with the social innovation role of voluntarism. In addition to providing a wide variety of *new* ideas about social behavior, the voluntary sector also is active in preserving numerous *old* ideas. Voluntary action and voluntary organizations have played a major role in history in preserving values, ways of life, ideas, beliefs, artifacts, and other productions of the mind, heart, and hand of man from earlier times so that this great variety of human culture is not lost to future generations. For example, there are in the United States numerous local historical societies that specialize in preserving the history of particular towns and areas. There are nonprofit voluntary organizations that run local museums,

libraries, and historical sites. And there are a number of voluntary organizations whose primary function it is to preserve the values of cultures or subcultures that no longer have any substantial power or importance in American society, but that nevertheless represent a way of life of significant numbers of people at some period in history or somewhere around the world (e.g., American Indian groups, in some instances, or immigrant ethnic associations that persist long after the ethnic group involved has been thoroughly assimilated into American culture). The role of municipal, state, and national governments in supporting museums and historical sites grows from the roots of earlier nonprofit, nongovernmental support of such "islands of culture."

Another aspect of the belief/value preservation role of the voluntary sector involves voluntary associations as educational experiences, especially where these associations are attempting to pass on to their members or to the public at large some body of beliefs and values originating in the past. In part this would include many of the activities of most religious sects and denominations, especially insofar as one focuses upon their socialization and indoctrination activities (e.g., catechism classes, "Sunday schools," Hebrew day schools, etc.). In part this function also includes all manner of more strictly educational voluntary organizations, from Plato's Academy (see Peterson and Peterson 1973) to modern Great Books Discussion Groups and so-called "Free Universities."

The various levels of government in the contemporary world have largely taken over the task of education on a broad scale, yet voluntary organizations still are active in supplementing government-run educational systems by filling in the gaps and by prodding these systems to improve or take on responsibility for the preservation of additional knowledge or values. For instance, voluntary civil rights and black liberation organizations have taken the lead in educating both blacks and whites in the United States regarding black history and accomplishments. Gradually, under the pressure of such voluntary associations in the past several years, the public educational system in the United States has been changing to accommodate a more accurate and complete picture of black history, although the process is by no means finished yet. Similar examples could be given with regard to other content areas as well (women's history, American Indian history, etc.).

A sixth major impact of the voluntary sector is its embodiment and representation in society of the sense of mystery, wonder, and the sacred. Neither the business nor government sectors in modern society have much tendency to be concerned with such matters. Many would say that religion today *is* very much a big business; and both business and government support science in a substantial way. Yet precisely in those areas where religion and science almost meet, where the borders of religion are receding under the pressure of an ever-expanding science, the business and government sectors are often *least* involved. Voluntary associations and nonprofit foundations/research organizations are the only groups experimenting seriously with new forms of worship, non-drug-induced "consciousness expansion" and the "religious experience," the occult, investigation of flying saucers, extrasensory perception, etc.

The "heretics" of both science and religion are seldom supported in their work directly and consciously by the business or government sectors. Only through voluntary action and the support of the voluntary sector have the major changes in man's view of the supernatural and its relation to the natural tended to come about in the past. The same has also been true, by and large, for major changes in man's view of himself and of the natural universe in the past. The dominant economic and political (and religious) systems of any given epoch are seldom very receptive to the really new visions of either the natural or supernatural world (e.g., Galileo and Copernicus; Jesus). Voluntary action is thus the principal manner in which a sense of the sacred, the mysterious, and the weird can be preserved and permitted some measure of expression in our otherwise hyper-rational contemporary society.

A seventh impact of the voluntary sector results from its ability to liberate the individual and permit him or her the fullest possible measure of expression of personal capacities and potentialities within an otherwise constraining social environment. All societies have their systems of laws, customs, roles, and organizations that box people in and limit their opportunities for personal expression and personal development. The full extent of societal limitation on people has just begun to be realized in recent decades, spurred in part by the "liberation" movement of women, blacks, the poor, the "Third World" and other disadvantaged or disenfranchised groups. The primary embodiments of the societal barriers and boxes have generally been the economic and governmental systems, although other major institutions of society have played a role as well (e.g., education, the family, religion, etc.).

Voluntary associations and groups, on the other hand, have long been a primary means of at least partially escaping these barriers and boxes. Through participation in voluntary action a wide variety of people have been able to find or to create special social groups that would permit them to grow as individuals. This kind of personal growth has many relevant aspects, but can be summed up generally as "self-actualization," to use a term from Maslow (1954). For some this means intellectual development, the process of becoming increasingly analytical, informed, and self-conscious about the nature of one's life situation and problems. When this occurs for a whole category or group of people, the process is often referred to as "group conscienticization" or "consciousness-raising" (e.g., among blacks, women, the poor). Seldom does such special personal growth occur on a broad scale outside voluntary groups and movements.

For others, self-actualization through voluntary action takes the form of developing otherwise unused capacities, talents, skills or potentials of a more active and practical sort. For many kinds of people, depending on the stage of social, economic, and political development of a society, voluntary associations and voluntary action offer the only feasible opportunity for leadership, for learning to speak in public, for practicing the fine art of management, for exercising analytical judgment, etc. Until very recently in American society, for instance, neither blacks nor women nor the members of certain other disadvantaged groups could hope to develop fully their capacities through the occupational system of the economic or government sectors. Only in voluntary groups of their own making could they seek any kind of fulfillment and self-expression, bound as they were (and in part continue to be) by the prejudices and discrimination of the dominant white, male, Anglo-Saxon Protestants in our society. However, this situation is not unique to the United States. There are similar and even different forms of prejudice and discrimination in *all* other societies, varying only in degree and the particular social groups singled out for attention. And in all societies voluntary associations also offer the disadvantaged some chance of enhanced self-development, though these associations must sometimes meet in secret as underground groups if the society in which they are operating is oppressive and does not respect the right of free association.

Voluntary action potentially offers unique opportunities for personal growth and realization of personal potentials not only for those people whom society otherwise deprives, but also for *all* the members of society in certain directions. No matter how free, open, egalitarian, and highly developed the society, there are always limitations of some sort placed on the development of each person by his particular social environment. Any major decision to follow a certain line of personal occupational or educational development, for instance, automatically forecloses a number of other alternatives, or at least makes them highly unlikely. Voluntary associations, however, exist (or can exist) in such profusion and variety that they can provide otherwise missed personal development opportunities to almost any person at almost any stage of life. This is as true for the school teacher who always wanted to learn to fly (and who can join a flying club to do so even at age 60), as it is for the airline pilot who always wanted to write novels (and who can join a writer's club to work toward this end).

Of course, not every person will find the appropriate voluntary association for his or her personal growth needs to be available at the time it is needed. But the voluntary sector as a whole, nevertheless, still serves in some significant degree this general role of providing substantial numbers of individuals in society with otherwise unavailable opportunities for self-actualization and self-fulfillment.

An eighth major impact of the voluntary sector in society is one of overriding importance, relating directly to the first and second impacts discussed above. We are referring to the impact of the voluntary sector as a source of "negative feedback" for society as a whole, especially with regard to the directions taken by the major institutions of society such as government and business. Without "negative feedback," any system is dangerously vulnerable to destroying itself through excesses in one direction or another. Thus, however uncomfortable and irritating they may be at times, voluntary associations and the voluntary sector are absolutely vital to the continuing development of a society.

This systemic corrective role of the voluntary sector is, of course, not carried out by *all* voluntary associations, any more than all voluntary associations are concerned with the play element, value preservation, or the sacred. Yet the small cutting edge of the voluntary sector that does perform the role of social critic is extremely important, usually bearing the responsibility for the continued existence and future growth of the rest of the voluntary sector. In societies where a sufficient number and variety of voluntary groups are *unable* to play effectively their roles as social critics, the dominant governmental and economic institutions may well take over and suppress the entire voluntary sector (e.g., Allen 1965).

In the contemporary United States there are numerous examples of voluntary associations and groups playing this systemic corrective role. All of the cause oriented, advocacy, and issue-oriented groups tend to fall into this category, from the environmental movement to the civil rights movement and women's liberation. The tactics and strategy of such groups cover a broad range from rather traditional lobbying through demonstrations and "be-ins," to direct remedial action such as "ecotage" (sabotage of notable corporate polluters and other "environmental undesirables").

Some of the more imaginative and innovative approaches have been developed in an attempt to modify the business sector, rather than focusing solely on the government sector. For instance, there have been in-depth investigations by Ralph Nader and his associates of particular companies' practices and their relationship to the public interest (e.g., for First National City Bank of New York and for DuPont), counter-management stockholder activity in the public interest (e.g., Project G.M.), dissenting annual reports written to present a full public accounting of a corporation's activities harmful to the general public interest and welfare, class action suits brought by voluntary groups against manufacturers and developers, etc.

When looked at in the particular, such activities (which vary markedly in their success) often seem fruitless and doomed to failure, given the power of the organizations and systems being challenged. Yet when we see these activities of voluntary groups in a larger context, when we sum up these numerous activities attempting to modify and improve the dominant systems and organizations of our society, they take on a very important general meaning. Even if many or most of such system correction attempts by voluntary groups should fail, the continual and expanding pressure being brought to bear by the voluntary sector on the central institutions of society is still likely to have a salutary long-term modifying influence. When the leaders of the business and governmental sectors *know* that "someone is watching," that they will eventually have to account to the public interest for their actions, this awareness encourages greater attention to the public interest rather than merely to narrow, private interests.

When for one reason or another the voluntary sector is not able to operate effectively as a systemic corrective (either because of its own inadequacies or the failure of the leaders of dominant institutions to listen and change accordingly), the usual result in human history has been a broad social revolution (not just a palace revolution or simple coup). When the dominant institutions of any society have ignored for too long or too often the voices of the public interest as expressed by elements of the voluntary sector, revolutionary and usually underground voluntary groups arise and make concrete plans to overthrow the existing system completely. The American, French, Russian, Chinese, Cuban, and other revolutions all attest to this pattern.

Thus, when the voluntary sector cannot make itself heard adequately through the permissible communication and influence channels in a society, certain voluntary groups and movements tend to arise to revamp the whole system, establishing whole new institutional arrangements with their corresponding new channels of influence and communications. Not surprisingly, these new channels generally favor those kinds of persons and groups who were

unable to be heard previously (although the kinds of people formerly dominant often end up in as bad a position or worse than that faced by the formerly disadvantaged prior to the revolution). This cycle will tend to repeat itself until a society reaches a point where it is effectively and continuously self-correcting, through the activities of a strong and social-change-oriented voluntary sector, and where its major institutions are basically operating primarily in the public interest of *all* of its citizens (not just its white, male, Anglo-Saxon Protestants, or their equivalents in some societies other than the United States and the British Commonwealth).

The ninth major impact of the voluntary sector worth mentioning here is the support given by the voluntary sector specifically to the economic systems of a society, especially a modern industrial society. Voluntary associations of many kinds provide crucial kinds of social, intellectual, and technical linkages among works in numerous occupations: professional associations increase the effectiveness of most kinds of scientists, engineers, technicians, etc., just as manufacturers' and trade associations support the growth of whole industries. And various kinds of labor unions play their part as well, although many businessmen would question the degree to which they "support" the economic system. But labor unions only seem nonsupportive of the economic system when the latter is viewed narrowly from the point of view of an employer interested solely in profit maximization. Labor unions ultimately have to be deeply concerned with the viability of the economic system and productivity of their own members if they are to survive.

This economic support role of the voluntary sector is usually lost sight of because so many people tend to view all kinds of economic self-interest and occupationally related voluntary associations as integral parts of the business sector. In fact, these kinds of voluntary organizations are quite distinct from the business sector itself, however close their relationship might be to business corporations and occupational activities. The primary purpose of business corporations is to make a profit for their owners, whether they are actually involved in running the corporation or not. On the other hand, economic self-interest voluntary associations have as their primary purpose the enhancement of the long-term occupational and economic interests of their member-participants. While corporation employees and professionals are *paid* in salaries, wages or fees for their participation, the members of economic self-interest voluntary associations themselves *pay* for the privilege of belonging to and benefiting from these associations.

The tenth major impact of the voluntary sector we shall note is a rather subtle one: the voluntary sector constitutes an important *latent* resource for all kinds of goal attainment in the interests of the society as a whole. Put another way, the voluntary sector represents a tremendous reservoir of potential energy that can be mobilized under appropriate circumstances for broad societal goals. The role of the voluntary sector in revolutionary situations is but one example of this latent potential. The activity of voluntary association networks in more limited disaster situations is a more common example (Barton 1970). The voluntary sector and its component associations, groups, and channels of communication and influence make possible the mobilization of large numbers of people on relatively short notice for special purposes (usually in the common interest) without resorting to economic rewards or legal coercion as activating forces. Such a latent potential in the voluntary sector is especially important when neither economic nor political–legal forces can feasibly be brought to bear to resolve some widespread problem situation.

The latent potential of the voluntary sector can be viewed in another way as well. Voluntarism is based on a *charitable grants economy* (donations of time, money, etc.) as contrasted with the coercive grants economy (taxation) on which the government sector operates or the market economy on which the business sector operates. Both of the latter types of economy work well for certain kinds of purposes, but neither works well for the accomplishment of all kinds of purposes in society. In the same way, there are many kinds of purposes and activities (several of which are implicit in the nine major impacts of the voluntary sector reviewed above) for which the charitable grants economy tends to work best.

Now the important latent potential of the voluntary sector is that, under appropriately compelling circumstances (i.e., for the "right" value, goal or ideal), the money, goods, real property,

and services mobilized by the voluntary sector through the charitable grants economy can completely overwhelm all considerations of the coercive grants economy and the market economy. For certain goals and ideals, a large majority of society can be induced to "give their all" and to do so gladly, willingly, and voluntarily. This does not occur very often, to be sure, nor does it last very long. But the latent potential is there in any society at any time. With the right spark—usually a charismatic leader with an idea and an ideal—the course of history can be changed in these brief, rare periods of almost total societal mobilization through the leadership of the voluntary sector.

The Negative Side

In describing the foregoing ten types of impact that the voluntary sector tends to have in some degree in any society, we have emphasized the positive contributions that voluntary action makes to society. However, as with any form of human group or activity, voluntary action and the voluntary sector are by no means always positive in their impacts. For every one of the ten types of impact we have noted, there can be negative consequences in certain circumstances and with regard to certain values. Thus, when voluntary associations experiment with new social forms, the failures can often be harmful to specific people and organizations. When alternative definitions of reality and morality are offered, these can be evil as in the case of Nazi Germany and its ideology as generated by the Nazi party, a voluntary association. When voluntary groups focus on the play element, their fun can become mischievous as in the case of a boys' gang that wrecks a school "just for kicks." When social clubs provide a warm and close sense of belonging to their members, they can also create deep dissatisfaction in people who would dearly like to belong but are excluded from a particular club or kind of club.

In the same way, voluntary groups striving to preserve some beliefs or values from the past may be holding on to anachronisms that would be better left to the pages of history books. Clubs whose members chase around seeking flying saucers and little green men from Mars might more profitably spend their time and energy elsewhere with more satisfying results. Organizations that arouse the full potentials of black people—who must then go out into the real world and face a harsh reality of bigotry and discrimination—may or may not be doing them a favor. The kinds of systemic corrections being suggested by cause-oriented and advocacy groups may not be conducive to the greatest good of the greatest number. Economic self-interest voluntary groups often tend to ignore the public interest in favor of an exclusive and selfish private interest. And the latent potentials of the voluntary sector can be mobilized to do evil as well as to do good for one's fellow man.

Conclusion

What then? Our answer is clear: All the more reason to begin a thorough study of the impact of the voluntary sector and voluntary action at all system levels, in all kinds of societies, in terms of all kinds of possible value standards. What we have suggested as major impacts of the voluntary sector only scratch the surface of a very large area for research. We have tried harder to demonstrate what voluntary action *might* do in various areas, rather than what it actually *does* do. We have done more to illustrate the breadth of the present topic than to present a definitive synthesis of the way things are, based upon empirical research. In most areas and for most types of voluntary action we simply do not know what the impacts are because no relevant research exists.

Yet at many levels and in many topical areas the possible impacts are extremely important to human society, past, present and future. Therefore, we would argue that evaluation of the impact and effectiveness/ineffectiveness of all types of voluntary action is one of the highest priority areas for future research on voluntary action. We seem to have much less empirical evidence bearing on such impact questions than we have for almost any other area or subfield of voluntary action research. This situation can be remedied only by a great deal more future commitment to impact/effectiveness research on the part of voluntary action scholars (including the Association of Voluntary Action Scholars itself), voluntary organizations and movements, and funding agencies of all kinds. We sincerely hope this joint commitment will be forthcoming in the next few years.

Readings

1. Allen, William Sheridan. *The Nazi Seizure of Power.* Chicago: Quadrangle Books, 1965.
2. Barton, Allen H. *Communities in Disaster.* Garden City, New York: Anchor Books, Doubleday Company, 1970.
3. Handlin, Oscar. *The Uprooted.* New York: Grosset and Dunlap, 1951.
4. Little, Kenneth. *West African Urbanization: A Study of Voluntary Associations in Social Change.* Cambridge, England: Cambridge University Press, 1965.
5. Maslow, Abraham H. *Motivation and Personality.* New York: Harper and Row, 1954.
6. Peterson, Sophia, and Virgil Peterson. "Voluntary Associations in Ancient Greece." *Journal of Voluntary Action Research,* 2, no. 1: 2–16.
7. Smith, David Horton. "The Importance of Formal Voluntary Organizations for Society." *Sociology and Social Research* 50, (1966): 483–92.
8. Smith, David Horton, with John Dixon. "The Voluntary Sector." Chapter 7 in Edward Bursk, ed., *Challenge to Leadership: Managing in a Changing World.* New York: The Free Press, Macmillan and Co., 1973.
9. Smith, David Horton, Richard D. Reddy, and Burt R. Baldwin. "Types of Voluntary Action: A Definitional Essay." Chapter 10 in David Horton Smith et al., eds., *Voluntary Action Research: 1972.* Lexington, Mass.: Lexington Books, D.C. Heath and Co., 1972.

ARTICLE 29 _____
Caught in the Act of Helping
Merrimon Cuninggim

A. Introduction

Foundations are in serious trouble.

To whatever extent it may once have existed, the era of good feeling seems to be over.

Foundations are said to be "under fire," and the loss in public confidence, either hailed or deplored, is generally proclaimed. Whether they deserve to have a poor reputation or their faults are as bad as alleged or their accomplishments have been fully appreciated are matters for careful examination in the body of this book. But the point of beginning must be the recognition that foundations are suspect.

Of all the kinds of benevolence practiced in our society, the sort that seems to be in most disrepute is the activity of the large foundations. The giving of individual donors and the work of small foundations, company and community funds and charitable trusts may also be criticized from time to time. But these agencies are less visible, whereas the large foundations are inescapably in the public eye.

The Local Family Fund of Anytown, U.S.A., may do something to displease the good citizens of the town and its environs, but very few others ever hear of it. Let the big foundations seem to misbehave, however, and the press is bound to pick it up. The news travels across the country, and the outraged reaction is registered with the foundations themselves and with congressmen. Even the local merchant, going about his innocent business, may feel the pinch when he tries to sell Ford's cars, Kellogg's corn flakes, Lilly's pills or Purina's Dog Chow.

This essay is intended to examine the phenomenon of attack and defense: of widespread criticism on the one hand, and on the other, something less than widespread rejoinder. Why are the foundations in such bad odor? What, specifically, are the charges? Are they justified? Why have the foundations not made systematic, persuasive answers?

Other questions must be faced: Shorn of all boasting and glory language, what is the record of foundation achievement? Does the Tax Reform Act of 1969 help or hinder the foundations from performing their legitimate tasks? Foundations profess the support of humane values, and join with other such institutions—churches, universities, hospitals, courts of justice—in attempting to serve mankind. When their legitimate efforts are encumbered, or even proscribed, then by that much the effectiveness of the values they affirm is lessened. Do the regulations that Congress has imposed, or the attitudes that critics have expressed, prevent foundations from accomplishing their proper purpose?

Finally, what *are* their proper functions? What is the basic rationale for foundations? For philanthropy as a whole?

Before proceeding to a discussion of these questions in turn, we should pause to recognize some of the inherent difficulties. Hardly any agency in society is as poorly prepared to defend itself against attack as is a philanthropic foundation. This grows partly out of its history and partly out of its essential nature.

As for history, foundations have never been accustomed to think or act as a group, and only lately has it appeared that they need to do so. In the past it was generally felt that philanthropy was a private act, and even when one's philanthropy had come to be organized into a foundation, it had until recently been thought to be the donor's personal exercise of benevolence. If on rare occasion some other foundation were to receive unfavorable publicity, then this was obviously that other foundation's concern. Up until fairly recent times, foundations as a group simply did not recognize that their common activity of philanthropy was under more general suspicion, for the individual good name that each of them thought it possessed was felt to be sufficient protection against any possibility of public clamor.

The essential nature of foundations has also made it hard to fend off or reply to charges leveled against them. Other types of tax-exempt institutions have their built-in defenders and protagonists, usually in considerable numbers. When, say, a church or a university incurs the displeasure of some segment of the public, its parishioners or alumni, as the case may be, are ready at hand to do battle. For a church or a university the battle may turn out to be, of course, a civil war, for attack as well as defense may come from inside the institution. But the point is, such organizations have their own well-defined and numerous constituencies, whereas a foundation, even one of the very large ones, is composed of a quite small group of people.

Moreover, the very nature of the foundation's work makes it extremely awkward for the institution to call upon the support of those who have received benefit from it. None of us as children ever liked our parents' reminder, "Now say thank you." Furthermore, if recipients were to be mindful of the need for coming to the support of their benefactors without having their memory jogged, they would still feel a certain awkwardness in doing so. Wouldn't it inevitably be interpreted as an effort to ingratiate oneself further into the good graces of the foundation?

So it is that because of the very nature of a foundation's activity it has no automatic cheering section, no easy occasion for celebration, no ritual of thanksgiving or praise. When a foundation is attacked, it is all alone. Tears are not called for. All that is of moment here is to note the fact that when foundations are criticized, they often find it hard, by history and nature, to reply.

B. Definition and Diversity

Before we begin to examine the nature of the trouble in which foundations find themselves, a brief word should be said about the kind of organization we are considering. All sorts of things are called foundations, and no one type of institution has exclusive use of the word. If some agency of government or some program of community action, or some point of beginning, or some article of clothing, or some building stone, calls itself a foundation, each is within its linguistic rights.

For the purposes of this essay, however, the term "foundation" is being used to denote a non-governmental agency existing to serve the public good. Usually it is an endowed agency, its resources having been set aside as an endowment by some original donor or group of donors. But on occasion it may receive as well as disburse regular contributions, and may possess little or no endowment. Usually its way of serving the public is through the making of grants or subventions to recipients of various sorts and sizes, either individuals or organizations. On occasion, however, a foundation may support an action program of its own design, administered by its own staff. Rarely will a foundation be able to tackle anything as grandiose as "the general welfare"; it will normally choose some particular segment for its special area of concern. But most foundation charters are written in language sufficiently expansive to give room for change in direction.

Foundations of the sort that this essay considers are often modified by the adjective "private," but it is something of a misnomer and one ought to be chary about using the word. Their funds are not private, for the money no longer belongs to the original donor, whoever he is. Rather, it is public money, set aside to be so by an uncommon act of stewardship on the part of the donor. Correspondingly, the activities of foundations are not private, for a catalogue of them must be reported to the government as the representative of the people, and anyone is privileged to have a look. Their field of operation is not limited to the so-called private sector, for grants of many foundations have traditionally been made to a wide variety of governmental units and programs, large and small.

The only sense in which "private" applies is that the decisions of foundations are not in the hands of the general public or of Government. This is, of course, an immensely important distinction; and the trouble is, we simply do not have a suitable word to describe the peculiar mixture of public and private that characterizes a foundation—a combination of public interest and public service with private judgment. It is for this reason that in the simplified definition above, the modifier is "non-governmental." To say it in that way may be more illuminating than simply to call foundations unmodifiedly "private." A fuller definition might run to such a complicated, jawbreaking sentence as the following: Foundations are non-governmental agencies, privately established and managed, but in which the public has a stake and which are answerable to Government, possessing financial resources, usually in the form of endowment, and existing to serve the general welfare or some chosen segment of it, usually in the form of grants.

Even this grab bag of a definition, with hedges and possibilities for exceptions, may give the impression that foundations as a group are pretty much of a piece, each member of the group having a great deal in common with all its fellows, more in common than in contrast. The actual fact, however, is that the diversity among foundations is immense, and one of the first things that the general public needs to know about them is that they are not all alike. Their diversity is stretched across a broader spectrum than is perhaps the case for any other category of charitable or humane institution. All churches, no matter what their great differences, exist for the common purpose of worshipping God or some God-substitute. All colleges, again no matter what their great differences, engage in the common function of teaching and learning. But for foundations there is no overarching goal or program, stated in even the most general terms, that is accepted or practiced by all. It is the outside observer trying to compose a normative description, who says foundations exist, or at least should, to "serve the general welfare. . . ." Unfortunately, many foundations own to no such aim.

Size is one mark of their diversity. The range runs all the way from the colossus of the group, the Ford Foundation, with the market value of its holdings over $3 billion, down to funds whose assets are literally zero, or maybe even a few that have liabilities and nothing else. From time to time commentators have set various categories of size, so that the total mass can be divided into manageable and describable groups. Among the common dividing lines are the figures ten million and one hundred million, those falling below the ten million being "small" foundations, those between the two figures being "medium-sized," and those above the one-hundred-million mark being "large." In this essay, those will be the meanings given to those adjectives.

It must be noted, however, that such a pattern is quite unsatisfactory. A foundation whose assets are $15 million is likely to be an entirely different kind of philanthropic agency from one whose assets are $90 million; yet both are in the medium category.

Moreover, the two ends of the scale are unusually imprecise. In respect to the large foundations there are probably somewhere around thirty-five whose assets are over the line of $100 million. Figures fluctuate, up-to-date information is often not available, and thus no one can say for sure at any particular time. The chief trouble with the category, however, is the size of Ford, for it is over three times larger than the next largest, which is either Rockefeller or Lilly or the recently aggrandized Robert Wood Johnson Foundation. Ford's comparative immensity poses problems and opens up opportunities of which other foundations, even other large ones, are only dimly aware. Perhaps there ought to be another dividing line at this end of the scale,

$1 billion, with only the Ford Foundation above that line in solitary splendor.[1]

Certainly there needs to be another dividing line, perhaps two, at the other end of the scale. Foundations of $8-, $6-, or $4-million are able to undertake programs and make grants on a systematic basis, in pursuit of some well-defined aim, whereas foundations of less than a million in size may be tempted to disburse their income in less thoughtful ways. Foundations of less than $100,000 in size may be simply instruments for personal benevolence, though the recipients could be equally as worthy as those of the large foundations. One million and $100,000, therefore, might be further dividing lines in trying to set up reasonable categories of foundations. Size is no determinant of quality of work, of course, but some understanding of the wide disparity in size among foundations is important in the consideration of problems that face the field.

This question is complicated by the fact that market value of assets is not the only way, perhaps not the most accurate way, of measuring the relative size of foundations. Surely what a foundation does is a better indicator than how much its resources add up to, especially when its resources are measured in the imprecise terms of an ever-changing market value of its portfolio. If the criterion is the annual dollar activity of the foundation, then the breakdown of the group would be quite different. We shall return to this matter in other connections having to do with policy on annual expenditures and requirements as to pay-out. Suffice it now to say that the scale in this regard would be equally extensive with, though quite different from, the spectrum based on market value of assets. The two ends, however, might look much the same, for at one end would be the Ford Foundation, with annual dollar activity something over $200 million, and at the other some few foundations whose annual "activity" is zero.

Size is only the beginning of the various factors that make up the huge diversity among foundations. Take, for example, the tremendous differences in respect to ways in which foundations make decisions on their grants and other activities. At one end of this workload scale would be a considerable number of foundations, most of them large, that are able to make affirmative response to less than 5 percent, in a few cases considerably less, of the multitude of requests that come their way. At the other end of the scale are foundations, most of them small, that don't receive any requests at all. Some foundations, large and small, work at their job of philanthropy throughout the entire year, and try to space their work so as to be able to deal with program and grant possibilities in a conscientious and evenhanded way. Other foundations, not all of them small, are whimsical and sometimes frantic operations, and may end up the year in a flurry of December grant-making, to be sure that they have spent all that the law requires.

Size, however measured, is necessarily a chief factor in professional staffing, but even among the large foundations there are great differences in the number, experience and overall quality of the staff members. Size is not a reliable guideline in regard to the extent to which a foundation calls upon competent experts for advice in the chosen field of activity, but the use of wise counsel is itself another important factor in the determination of differences among foundations.

Still other factors are relevent. For example, sponsorship differs greatly: most foundations were established by an individual or a family, but they may retain for only a few years, or for a generation, or forever, the prevailing traits of a family fund. Those traits themselves will differ hugely in their effect on the foundation's activity. Though being a family fund will mean in general that one person or a small group of people will set the guidelines and dominate the decisions of the foundation, those guidelines and decisions can be narrow or broad, selfish or selfless, poorly or well conceived and executed.

Foundations are often sponsored by companies and corporations, as extensions of their regular programs of benevolence, and by communities—groups of like-minded people from various families and businesses, by towns, cities, regions. Again, geography is a factor of large disparity. In few other areas of activity does New York bestride the world to the extent it does in organized philanthropy. A majority of the large foundations have their offices there, and an immense number of the smaller ones as well. The latest edition of the *Foundation Directory* shows that out of the 5,454 listed for the country as a whole (according to special size eligibilities

for inclusion, to be noted hereafter), 1,161 are in New York City. This has its effect on the activity of foundations in other parts of the country, for it tends to increase the temptation to become parochial in interest and activity. It is not pertinent to the point at issue to explore the pros and cons of this problem now. All that is intended is to point out that one further mark of difference among foundations grows out of the geography of the field, for the locations of foundations explain some part of the huge diversity in outlook and program.

Almost nothing has been said about the diversity in program itself, which may be the largest single factor in explaining the differences among foundations and the most difficult one in arriving at a precise definition of the field. Hardly an area that man has ever explored, certainly none that is legal and moral, has been omitted from the catalogue of foundations' concerns. In succeeding pages, and especially in Chapter IV [not reprinted here], illustrations of the tremendous variety of foundation activities will be given, but they will be necessarily selective, and thus only barely suggestive of the cornucopia of philanthropic work.

The marks of difference are so numerous and broadly applicable that, once realized, they tend to obscure a couple of characteristics that nearly all foundations possess in common. Foundations do not hold sole ownership of the purpose to serve the general welfare. They share their humane intentions with many other kinds of tax-exempt and charitable organizations. But two things do indeed separate them from these other institutions. First, foundations do not have to raise money for their operating budgets or for the support of their various activities. By definition, they have the money to start with. Second, their money is relatively uncommitted. That is, a church must use its income to be a church, a school to be a school, whereas a foundation can exercise a considerable amount of freedom in determining what it will do. It possesses the capacity to change its mind about what it shall do without changing its essential nature as a foundation. These marks of distinctiveness are of considerable importance in enabling us to separate foundations from other types of non-profit institutions, and as far as they go, they are useful descriptives of the field of our inquiry.[2]

In light of their diversity how can one presume to throw all foundations into a single pot? The result is indigestible. In any effort to understand foundations the first thing to say is that everybody, supporters and critics alike, must learn to discriminate among the various kinds and types of foundations. The achievement of one doesn't tell anything at all about the record of another. By the same token, the misbehavior of one should not be allowed to throw suspicion on another. The American public has learned to discriminate between Harvard and Podunk—and this is not to say that Podunk may not also have its achievements or its problems. All of us know the difference between General Motors and the local repair shop, between the Library of Congress and the book collection of the junior high school, between the Metropolitan Opera and the benefit musicale. No disparagement of either end of any of those pairings is intended. In days of cynicism toward prestigious institutions, perhaps special assurance should be given that no finger of scorn is being pointed at Harvard, General Motors, the Library of Congress or the Metropolitan Opera. It is needful to look at foundations for what they are, in much the way that the public has already begun to learn to discriminate among individual specimens in other fields of activity.

In this essay I shall focus upon the large foundations. The first thing to be said about them, therefore, is that not even all the large ones are alike. They differ greatly among themselves as well as from foundations of other sizes.

C. A Note on History and Motivation

Foundations are largely a creation of the twentieth century. Historians of organized philanthropy put its beginnings in the post-Civil War period of the nineteenth century, and even into earlier times; and the history of benevolence, of course, goes back for centuries. Foundations as we know them today, however, are a relatively new development.

This is not the place for a detailed record of the history of American foundations. Such information is readily available,[3] and all we need to do is to note a few facts as background for the present scene. Yet even the most cursory reference to the past must take note of the two

big names in the establishment of philanthropic funds in this country, Andrew Carnegie and John D. Rockefeller. Their central agencies of benevolence were the Carnegie Corporation, established in 1911, and the Rockefeller Foundation, established in 1913. Each man set up a constellation of other funds for special purposes, such as the Carnegie Endowment for International Peace and the General Education Board, and other men of large wealth followed suit around the same time. In the first two decades of this century such foundations as Commonwealth, Milbank Memorial, Julius Rosenwald, Russell Sage and Surdna were started.

The twenties and thirties saw a considerable extension of the practice whereby families of means set aside assets in charitable trusts. Among the funds established during these decades were the Danforth, Duke, John Simon Guggenheim, Hartford, Hazen, Hill, Juilliard, Kellogg, Kettering, Kresge, Markle, Rosenberg and Woodruff foundations.

A new surge of development took place after World War II and has only now begun to subside. Many of today's largest foundations, even though some may have been established at an earlier time, have received the greatest proportion of their funds in these recent decades. Among this number are Ford, Robert Wood Johnson, Kaiser, Lilly, A. W. Mellon, R. K. Mellon, Moody, Mott, Pew, Sid Richardson, Rockefeller Brothers, Scaife and Sloan.

From the beginning the growth in number and resources of foundations has been hard to document. The first listing made in 1915, had twenty-seven names. It is likely that as late as 1930 the number was still less than two hundred. Thereafter a series of volumes entitled *American Foundations and Their Fields* slowly built up a body of fairly reliable data. Volume VI in 1948 contained information about 899 foundations; Volume VII, 1955, the last of the series, listed 4,162. Raw growth was not the sole explanation. The most important event was the opening of tax returns to public inspection in 1950. From then on statistics became somewhat more reliable.[4]

The first *Foundation Directory* was published in 1960. It proposed to include only those foundations above $50,000 in assets or $10,000 in annual grants, and found 5,202 foundations that qualified for inclusion. Its estimate as to the total number of foundations in existence at that time was 12,000.[5]

Four years later the second edition of the *Foundation Directory* adjusted its standard of eligibility to $100,000 in assets, and the number that then qualified was 6,007. The overall estimate of foundations in existence was thought to be 15,000.[6]

The criterion for inclusion was again changed for the third edition of the *Directory*, published in 1967. Foundations at that time had to be $200,000 in size of assets, and 6,803 were listed, with the estimate for the overall number being 18,000.[7]

The fourth edition of the *Foundation Directory* came off the press late in 1971. Once again changes were made in the eligibilities for inclusion, so as to keep the compilation from getting too large. The minimum standards were set at $500,000 in assets and/or $25,000 in annual grants, and 5,454 foundations qualified for inclusion on this basis.[8]

Such figures tell us that the number of foundations is large, is probably still growing and is unknown. The latter fact is at least as important as the other two, for the embarrassing truth about the field is that nobody, not even the Internal Revenue Service, knows how many foundations there are. The IRS published its first list, containing 30,262 entries, in 1968; but since it had no sound definition as to what a foundation is, its list is not fully acceptable. Even higher estimates, such as Representative Patman's oft-repeated figure of 45,124[9] are made by those not directly connected with the field who have some critical axe to grind. The Foundation Center, whose only axe is the furnishing of reliable information, estimates that there may have been somewhere around 26,000 in 1971, over 95 percent of which have been established since World War II.[10]

Figures in some of the categories of size are a little easier to come by. It was noted above that probably only one foundation is larger than one billion in assets and that around thirty-five are larger than one hundred million. Even here, however, the numbers are subject to guesswork and shifting fortunes. In categories of smaller size the Foundation Center estimates that there are approximately 300 foundations between ten and one hundred million, and around 1,850 between

one and ten million. This leaves somewhere between thirty-two and thirty-three hundred of less than a million in assets but still large enough to be included in the latest *Directory*. Those of even smaller size amount to over twenty thousand.[11]

The overall size of the assets held by foundations is subject to similar uncertainty. This should not be a matter of large surprise when one remembers that any individual foundation is likely not to know from day to day what the size of its own portfolio happens to be. Sums, therefore, are bound to be rough. The best guess as to the aggregate of foundation assets is that the figure is somewhere over twenty-six billion. It is reliably known that assets of all foundations larger than one million each in size total just about twenty-four billion. Thus the imbalance in the field becomes clear even though precise figures cannot be secured: less than 10 percent of the foundations hold over 90 percent of the assets.[12]

Trouble is, on the 990-A forms that foundations use in reporting to the Internal Revenue Service, some list assets at cost or at book value rather than at current market value. The lack of uniform reporting and of thorough governmental auditing means that totals taken from 990-A's are not reliable. The Commission on Foundations and Private Philanthropy (hereafter to be referred to as the Peterson Commission, for its chairman Peter Peterson) reported the example of the Irvine Foundation, "which until 1969 carried its assets at approximately $6 million. In 1969 it filed a form 990-A which reflected assets in excess of $100 million, and there have been estimates that the market value of that foundation's property is considerably higher."[13]

Though the large foundations, those over one hundred million in size, constitute less than 2 percent of the total number of philanthropic funds in this country, justification for centering attention on them in this essay grows out of the fact that they possess a disproportionate share of all foundation assets. The thirty-five or so in the large category hold something over $10 billion in assets, perhaps around two-fifths of the total, and all the thousands of smaller foundations share the remaining approximately three-fifths. The disproportion carries over into grant-making. Of the estimated $1.8 billion in annual grant-making by all foundations, something around one-third comes from the large foundations, and as small a number as "the hundred largest foundations account for roughly half of the total annual grants of all foundations." [14]

Lest these figures throw the full picture out of balance, however, it should be noted that the $1.8 billion in grants of all foundations represents less than 10 percent of the $18.3 billion total for American philanthropic giving in 1969, as estimated by the American Association of Fund-Raising Council.[15] Foundation resources and activity are concentrated in the large foundations, but even their comparatively sizeable annual benevolences account for probably less than 3 percent of the amount expended in philanthropy each year.

How did people of wealth come to use the instrument of the foundation as the expression for their philanthropic activity? What are the motives that account for the tremendous proliferation in numbers and the remarkable increase in assets of foundations during this century, especially since World War II? If in areas susceptible of statistical analysis we are ultimately reduced to guesswork, even more so in the area of motivation must we rely on opinion, inference and hunch. This has not kept people, both admirers and critics, from expressing themselves, and like everything else connected with foundations, variety is the rule.[16]

All sorts of reasons are given by donors for establishing foundations. Perhaps other reasons that donors would rather not have publicized were also present. Many of these unsavory motivations have been charged against donors by critics, both mild and muckraking. To some of these we shall return in later chapters, when we deal with the criticisms that have been levelled against foundations and with their response.

But let it be recorded now as one man's opinion that the most widely prevalent reason for the establishment of foundations has been the decent philanthropic urge on the part of the donor. Many people of means, including some of very great wealth, have been sensitive to the preferred economic status they have achieved or inherited, sensitive also to the needs of people of less privilege all around them, and have thus wanted to share their good fortune (double-entendre, if you wish) with others.

These same people, of course, have often been subject to selfish as well as to selfless

motives. The gamut runs from relatively innocent expressions of ego all the way to criminal acts of self-dealing. A donor may simply want to see his name in lights, at least the dignified lights of an incorporated foundation. He may want to escape the annoyance of answering hosts of personal appeals himself. He may wish to get appropriate tax deductions. He may want to retain some continuing control over the way in which his charitable donations will be used. He may take advantage of whatever loopholes continue to exist. He may skirt the edges of the law, or even transgress it. In other words, various degrees of selfishness have undoubtedly been present in the establishment of foundations through the years.

This is about what one would have to say in respect to the motivations of almost any person going into almost any line of activity. For the doctor or the businessman, for the minister or the lawyer, or for that matter, for the housewife, he or she could be expected to pursue the self-chosen task with a combination of selflessness and selfishness. From person to person high-minded idealism and personal advantage are mixed together in varying proportions—and so it undoubtedly is with philanthropists. Only the gullible will adopt the positions at either extreme, that the motive for establishing a foundation is either pure, unsullied benevolence, calling for unqualified approbation, or unrelieved venality, calling for complete condemnation. To the extent to which evidence of motivation is available in the life stories of donors and the histories of foundations, the self-denying and self-asserting reasons are mixed in ways that reflect accurately the ambivalent human condition of all of us.

D. Appreciation of Foundations

In a day when attacks on foundations are rife, one must go out of his way to register the conviction that a genuine philanthropic urge has existed and continues to exist. Criticism is not the only attitude toward foundations that the public displays. Other feelings prevail. To put censure into its proper perspective, we should take note of some of the other attitudes current in our society.

First is ignorance. The American public knows very little about foundations. Not even

Ford is a household word, at least when it applies to philanthropy. To the great mass of citizens, foundations are vague, fuzzy entities that go about doing, or thinking they do, good. But what, how, when and where are generally unknown.

Moreover, most Americans don't particularly care. Apathy is the oft-paired partner of ignorance. Those somewhat mysterious agencies, the foundations, may affect the lives of a chosen few, but their benefactions seldom touch, at least directly, the everyday existence of the faceless many. Foundations would do well to realize, and might sometimes be delighted, that the public views them with considerable indifference.

But more positive attitudes also exist. Next is awe. Foundation officials often have to put up with the embarrassment of unearned respect. Their offices are thought to be distant, thickly carpeted and hushed. They themselves are the next thing to God Almighty, and are either about to accept a high, nonelective post in Government or planning to turn it down because the job isn't good enough—unless, of course, they've just come from Washington. When a foundation official takes such reverence seriously, his shirt does indeed get stuffed. Even if he escapes this unjustified self-esteem, he can't escape the absurdity that laymen sometimes look upon him and his institution as Olympian. It is a notion as ridiculous as Mt. Olympus of old, and as much a psychological fact.

If there is any logic at all to such an attitude, it grows out of another which is occasionally forgotten by foundation people themselves when pressed by unfavorable circumstance. I refer to the feeling of admiration with which foundations are often viewed. Awe can be associated with fear, of course, or dread, but it can also be partner to honor and appreciation. The latter attitudes, in fact, are widely current among that portion of the American public not characterized by ignorance or apathy toward foundations. In other words, among those who know and those who care, a considerable host seem genuinely to admire the work of the large philanthropic funds. Praise and approbation are generously expressed, not alone to individual foundations themselves but to the world around.[17]

Here one must be on guard. *God Bless You, Mr. Rosewater* is more than the inspired and satirical title of a Kurt Vonnegut novel.[18] It is also the actual pose of the sycophant whom every foundation runs into now and again. In my experience, small family funds are more likely to be fooled by servile flattery than are large foundations, and trustees are more susceptible than staff members—but this judgment may mean no more than that I am a staff member of a large foundation. In any event, small or large, trustee or staff, most foundation people learn to tell the difference between artful compliments and sincere, disinterested commendation. The latter exists in encouraging measure, and constitutes one of the major reactions of the public toward organized philanthropy.

But everybody wants something. Even the truly disinterested may want something for someone else. To the extent to which this is an accurate appraisal of the human condition, it suggests a third positive attitude taken by the public toward foundations. Alongside awe and admiration is expectancy.

The lower level is well represented by the mendicant, hat in hand. It might be of interest to others to know that foundation people occasionally play this game with each other. An officer of Foundation A may approach Foundation B for some cause of personal concern, especially if his own organization is not supporting that cause. Like his non-foundation friends he will look expectantly to other foundations for support of some institution or project in which he believes; he may even look to his own, often in vain. By definition, a foundation is the place to which one goes for cash-lined succor. It is the American adult's Santa Claus. We all make out our lists and live in hope.

But this is not the kind of expectancy of which I speak. There is a higher form, with less of self and self-interest in it. It comes from knowing a person or an institution quite well over a period of time. Such knowledge gives one a feel for that person's or institution's character and a confidence that future actions will be consistent with it. The confidence may be misplaced, of course, for men and institutions change character from time to time. But that is ex post facto thinking. The point is, at any one time in the life of a person or an institution, the observer comes to expect a continuation of activity consistent with the known past.

Most people who are knowledgeable about foundations seem to have a generous expectation of them of this sort. They know that foundations have addressed themselves to serious social problems; they expect that such social concerns will continue. They know that foundations have done a lot of good; they assume that such work will be carried on. They credit foundations with substantial accomplishments in the past; they anticipate further achievements. The world of foundations is often the beneficiary of this kind of affirmative attitude, something more than backward-looking admiration, a happy antidote for all the criticism that comes their way.

E. The Attack on Foundations

Criticism, however, is the newsworthy attitude. Ignorance and perhaps apathy are understandable. Awe, admiration and a generous expectation of continuing good works should occasion no surprise. What catches the eye is the suspicion now visited upon foundations by a considerable segment of the public. The current attack has made foundations more visible than their good works ever managed to do, more visible than at any time in the history of organized philanthropy in this country.

But attacks on foundations are not a new phenomenon. Ever since some of the titans of industry began to organize their philanthropies in the early years of this century, critics have been present to raise questions about the sincerity of their efforts, the benefits that were likely to accrue to the public and the disinterestedness of those who praised the development.[19]

The first hullabaloo to catch the attention of the public was the effort to secure a Federal charter for the Rockefeller Foundation in 1910–1912. Objections arose in Congress and elsewhere, for this was the Progressive Era, when trust-busting and the fear of big business were wide concerns. Since the Rockefeller Foundation's initial resources consisted in $50 million worth of Jersey Standard stock, cries of "tainted money" and "creeping capitalism" were raised to prevent the Foundation's receiving a Federal charter, though it easily secured one from the state of New York in 1913.[20] A first congressional

investigation, that of the Walsh Commission, followed soon thereafter. Though it warned the public about foundations because they were tied up with big business, Congress gave scant heed to the Walsh report in 1915.[21]

This early criticism made little impression on the public mind, for foundations were few in number and most people were delighted to think that some of the fortunes of big industrialists might be put to the benefit of the general public. For the next thirty-five years or so, foundations grew substantially in numbers and resources, and their uncontroversial good deeds began to be more widely known and generally applauded. Occasionally the chronicler of the business career of some tycoon or, closer home, the executive of some foundation would raise the question about whether the finances or programs of the foundations were as beneficial as they ought to be to American society.[22] But until about 1950, few serious criticisms of foundations were voiced, and foundations themselves were lulled into an easy acceptance of the approbation that the general public seemed to give.

With the coming of Senator Joseph McCarthy, foundations along with universities, churches and other organizations for the service of society found themselves under suspicion and attack. An article in the *American Legion Magazine* charged that foundations were supporting "outright communists, fellow travelers, socialists, do-gooders, one-worlders, wild-eyed Utopians and well-meaning dupes." [23] Obviously a Congressional investigation was in order, and accordingly in 1952 the House of Representatives set up the Cox Committee to track down the subversion. Rare for those excitable times, the Committee failed to find substantiation of the wild charges being made and, with suggestions for some improvements here and there, gave the foundations a generally clean report.[24]

The final statement of the Cox Committee was published in 1953, but Representative Reece, a nominal member who had attended only one committee meeting, was not satisfied. He persuaded Congress to embark upon the same investigation again, only this time he meant for it to reach a different conclusion. Both the content and the method of the Reece Committee's investigation were roundly condemned, and the result would have been laughable if the country had not been caught in the grip of the McCarthy hysteria. Only one foundation representative appeared before the Committee, and the whole sorry show, involving public discord among its members and staff, was called off before it had run its appointed course. In its final report, issued in 1954, the majority asserted but did not substantiate the "diabolical conspiracy" that foundations were said to be engaged in, and the minority accused the majority of having made an "unseemly effort to reach a predetermined conclusion." [25]

Needless to say, no legislation resulted, and some commentators felt that little harm was done. But even when an investigation turns out to be a farce, the impression is left that there must be something there to investigate. With the Reece Committee's following so soon on the heels of the Cox Committee, foundations occupied the center stage of public attention, and the legitimacy of criticism seemed upheld.

The last of the four Congressional investigations to date is the sporadic inquiry by Representative Wright Patman, begun in 1961 and seemingly not yet concluded. Whereas the Walsh Committee thought that foundation programs might be reactionary and the Cox Committee questioned whether they were engaged in subversive activities, with the Reece Committee doing a delirious repeat of the same line, the focus of attention for Patman has been the alleged financial misbehavior of foundations. As Chairman of the House Select Committee on Small Business he has used the device of issuing published reports to the members of his own committee as a way of calling attention to a number of abuses that he and his staff have uncovered. In his various reports he has made sweeping charges about the business activities and fiscal policies of foundations; he has castigated the Internal Revenue Service for not having policed the situation adequately; and he has recommended drastic changes in the law for the closer regulation of foundation behavior. [26]

It is not easy to arrive at a fair summary of such a broad and unsystematic investigation. On the one hand, Patman has performed a public service by calling attention to some misdeeds and

naming a few names, and by raising the issue as to whether foundations are observing proper standards in their financial affairs and whether legislation to require them to do so is adequate. On the other hand, sloppy staff work, scarehead publicity, the technique of taking the minute part for the massive whole, the unwillingness to confess to or retract patent error—all these things have been flaws in the Patman story and have undoubtedly hurt the reputation of foundations in general. Whatever the balance to be drawn between benefit and harm, the Patman investigation, together with numerous other treatments that it provoked, succeeded in keeping the spotlight on foundations during the sixties. [27]

Building on the interest that Patman had aroused, the Treasury Department appointed a special committee to have a careful look at foundations and their behavior, and to make recommendations as to desirable legislative or executive action. The Treasury Department Report on Private Foundations came out in 1965 with a group of balanced judgments and constructive proposals. The work of this committee does not really belong under the heading of an attack of foundations, but its existence was undoubtedly due to the fact that Patman's and other attacks were widespread, and its report laid solid groundwork for the deliberations leading up to the Tax Reform Act of 1969. [28] Ever since the Cox and Reece committees, and especially since Patman's outbursts, foundations have received an immense amount of public attention, much of it critical, some of it hostile. Numerous books and magazine articles have taken foundations to task. Politicians such as Governor Wallace have discovered that their supporters are prepared to cheer when foundations are attacked. [29] The time when the American public blandly assumed their virtues, or ignored them, or when they could afford to ignore the public, is done, and foundations are having to get used to the new experience of being highly visible, distrusted and condemned.

Criticism is of varying degrees, of course. It can be mild in tone and constructive in spirit. It can be virulent and destructive. It can be anything in between. Today's attack on foundations is not a uniform assault, with an inner consistency of vigor or passion. Nor does it possess a harmony of content, . . .we simply take note at this point that the attack is widespread and real.[30]

F. The Disrepute of Giving

It is not foundations alone, however, that feel the opprobrium of the critic. Suspicion has come to be visited upon the individual donor, especially if he has the capacity and inclination to make large gifts. Suspicion is directed also at both profit-making and non-profit institutions—industries or universities, corporations or churches—especially if their contributions seem to be at the expense of the self-interest of shareholders, parishioners or other members of the institutions' immediate constituencies.

The attack on foundations is only one aspect of the general disrepute into which benevolence of any sort and size seems to have fallen. This attitude toward giving is sufficiently pervasive to require a special look, for even if foundations were to be completely successful in fending off the attacks directed at them, the problem in its deeper form of the suspicion of benevolence in general might make the foundations' efforts of little account.

Once there was a time when benevolence was listed high in the catalogue of American virtues.[31] The early American aphorism "Earn all you can, save all you can, give all you can" was a neat and widely accepted summary of the Puritan and capitalist ethic. For an earlier day Ben Franklin was its promulgator and embodiment. At a later time Andrew Carnegie, among many other hard-driving philanthropists, preached the doctrine most persuasively.[32]

The ethic of work was related, of course, to the ethic for everything else. Life was seamless, and if in one sense Sunday was set aside, in another sense its temper was consistent with the rest of the week. Work hard. Get ahead. This is, of course, a vale of tears, but God helps those who help themselves. For most of its citizens America was the Promised Land.

So, earn all you can. Nothing wrong with that. Nobody is suggesting that one cheat in order to do so. Fundamental to any such advice is the acceptance of the basic moral principles of honesty and fair play. The maxim is shorthand, of course. A more complete version would read:

Earn all you can as long as you don't gouge or swindle; play the game straight but play it hard.

To this day the proposition has the seal of much public approval. In Western society those at either end of the economic spectrum are looked at askance—the fellow who won't work because he doesn't want to ("lazy, shiftless, no-good"), and the fellow who won't work because he doesn't have to ("pampered darling, silver spoon in his mouth"). The great mass in the middle get on with it. Even those who, like the housewife, are once removed from the pay-window know that life is not meant to be either pecunious or impecunious leisure. All may not earn in the precise sense, but nearly all submit to the spirit of the advice. All of them may not earn all they can, but most of them have a grudging admiration for the big earners. Even envy is inverted admiration. Today's frantic scramble of human effort, in which all but the drop- and cop-outs are engaged, is proof that at least this part of the old ethic has survived.

But left to itself alone the saying is clearly incomplete. Earn, and that's an end to it? What for? The doctrine of work for work's sake may have a hard splendor about it, but it is never going to win any popularity prize.

So, save all you can. Rainy day. Waste is sinful. Who knows what the future will bring? You may need it, or somebody close to you. Be prepared.

The aphorism now begins to sound moral. For most people there is an inevitability to earning, or at least working; and to pretend that it has much of an ethical quality is to give it unjustified airs. One has no choice. But saving is something else. It has an oughtness and a rightness about it. However often one disobeys, one knows it to be disobedience. Less practiced than its predecessor maxim, it is more enjoined as a moral imperative. Down to the present time it has kept its high standing as a folkway involving some measure of ethical sensitivity. The opprobrium still visited upon its opposites—squandering, dissipating one's resources, wasting one's substance in riotous living—is sufficient sign that putting some part of one's earnings aside is the right and righteous thing to do, however much one dislikes it.

But the nagging bite of personal dissatisfaction begins almost at once. Saving, too, is incomplete. Less fun because it is more high-minded, it is still not high-minded enough to save it from its own exaggerations of hoarding and downright parsimony. Nobody can live to himself alone. At least, nobody ought to try it. Every great ethical system has admonished man to recognize his human relatedness; and even those who have no God to love, as well as those who do, give lip-service to loving one's neighbor.

So, give all you can. Give time. Give consideration. Not least, give money. Stop and have a look at the poor traveller. Bind up his wounds. Send him on his way with a purse. It is not he who is good. It is you who must be Good to the Samaritan. The challenging scriptural question, Who is my neighbor? received a testing answer, as if the question had been, What is neighborly behavior? It is the act of giving.

And so nobility entered the economic commandment. Earning points inward, toward self. Saving stays inward, with self. Giving turns outward, toward somebody else or something other. The third is the maxim that redeems the other two, purging them of selfishness, putting them in a social perspective.

To stop short with the first, or even with the first and second, is to be crass and, perhaps worse, aimless—or at least to appear to be aimless. Even one who gives nary a damn about anybody else somehow hates to say so. If he cares anything at all about his fellows' opinions of him, he needs some sort of justification for piling asset on asset and stashing it all away. To give all one can—that's the ticket. He may not do so, of course, but that's another story. What matters is that he has latched on to a noble purpose that somehow sanctifies his acquisitiveness. He has a reason for his earning and saving, one that enhances his own self-esteem and casts an aura of unctuous rectitude around his daily routine. Give—or at least express the intent.

It is easy to be snide. Yet I do not mean to suggest that only the first two were taken seriously and the third was always a cynical addendum. On the contrary, in the economic ethic of an earlier day the three went together. That is, all three were well thought of, and probably in ascending order. He who earned all he could was commended. If he managed to hang onto it, the admiration increased. And if he took the third step and used his earnings and savings

for the benefit of those around him, then the community responded with its highest accolades. For it was within the understanding of even the ethically obtuse that free-will, selfless giving was the most demanding of the approved disciplines; according to the Bible, "more blessed" than always to be on the receiving end. It took stamina to earn all one could. It took self-denial to save. But giving required on top of those virtues the unusual disposition to care.

Another reason that the three were regarded in ascending order of esteem was that, apart from their relative priority in moral splendor, they were identifiably unequal in their comparative frequency. Most men earned only some of what they could. Fewer managed to save. Rarest of all were those who, earning and saving in superlative fashion, possessed the seemingly contradictory capacity to turn it loose.

So the threefold precept worked its way into the life of our society. All three propositions were interrelated in that the second built upon the first and the third depended upon the other two. Giving was morally superior, less frequently practiced and thus more highly acclaimed than earning or saving. But they all went hand in hand.

Can we say as much now? I think not. In the American society of today something has happened to the practice and spirit of giving that bids fair to drive a wedge of separation between it and its two partners. To be more accurate, the change that has taken place is in the attitude of Americans toward giving, especially large-scale giving; that is, toward philanthropy. In this one regard at least, the value system that Americans believe in seems to have shifted, and we as a people may be in the process of doubting, perhaps even disavowing, a heretofore honored part of our ethical heritage.

It is important not to exaggerate the situation. Most individual Americans continue to make their modest contributions to worthy institutions and causes. Comparative statistics of annual benevolence are confusing—some agencies are up in their receipts and some are down. Particularities of time and circumstance affect such figures in ways that are beyond the interest of this essay. I do not mean that the mythical average American citizen is less generous than he used to be. I have no knowledge that this is so, and personally I don't believe it.

But what I do believe is that the attitude of the ordinary citizen toward those who, earning much and saving much, also give much has shifted from an earlier admiration to a present-day suspicion. This seems to me to be true whether the big donor is an individual, a family, a corporation or a foundation—or, for that matter, the Federal Government. Earning and saving continue to be widely praised if not as widely practiced. Small-scale giving is well regarded, especially if the recipient is tax-exempt. But large-scale giving is in disrepute.

Signs of the disrepute in which philanthropy is presently held are all around us. It would be easy at this point to back-track on our argument by referring to the various attacks on foundations, in Congress and out, to which we have already referred. But I invite the reader, instead, to cast an eye internally, to find within himself tokens of the attitude that seems to have invaded us all. My own exercise runs like this:

First, I feel that we Americans tend to greet the act of the large donor, whether personal or corporate, with the jaundiced question, What is he trying to buy? Something relatively harmless, perhaps, such as an honorary degree—and we are mildly amused. Or something insidious, such as a preferential stake in a business deal or a Government contract—and we are not amused. That he is buying something often goes without question. Why else would he spend the money?

Again, we hear of the large gift and immediately the question comes to mind, What is he trying to hide? There is more here than meets the eye, of course. What has somebody got on him? What guilt is he attempting to erase? Crossing the palm with silver is a time-honored way of reducing the heat. Big heat, big silver. We know we don't know all the pressures the donor feels, for surely his own explanation of the gift cannot be trusted. But we do know he feels them. Why else would he spend the money?

Or the reaction may be that he is putting on a show of generosity at our expense. Why does the Government let him get away with it? If he had not had some kind of favored position at the hands of Government—tax exemption, unlimited charitable deduction, opportunity to write off business losses—he wouldn't be able to play Galahad. The taxes we pay are higher than they ought to be. One reason is that we have to pay his share, because he is allowed to escape. He gets the glory but we foot the bill. How else would he have had that much money to spend?

The next reflex feeling has two versions, depending upon our political stripe. Both are summarized in the position: He is trying to change the social order and we don't like it. He wants to force his notions on all the rest of us. This is a democracy, isn't it? By what right does he manipulate things to his liking, masquerading as benevolent, when our view and our vote, supposedly equal to his, don't count? If he didn't mean his money to be effective on behalf of his own wrong-headed desires, why else would he spend it?

One version of this attitude points rightward, the other looks off to the left. The first says, That big donor is a reactionary, turning the clock back to an outmoded time. He supports this radio station, that college and the other community organization because he knows they will preach his gospel of laissez faire, fundamentalism or Communists-under-the-bed. The second says, That big donor is a revolutionary, tearing down our system and soiling our flag. He supports this TV program, that university and the other social agency because he knows they will spout his line of socialism, modernism or Birchites-under-the-bed. The two reactions amount to pretty much the same thing: when the gift doesn't go down our own ideological alley, we resist its nefarious overtones and resent its being made.

It all adds up to the querulous attitude: By what right does one wealthy person or one well-heeled trust have the chance to be charitable? Because of his or its money, that's all. Does that possession automatically bestow on him or it the liberty of being benevolent? If the factual answer is Yes, the atmospheric answer of much of the public is, We don't like it. We don't like a situation in which someone else, just because he has more money than we do, gets to exercise his generosity.

Moreover, we don't like the rich man's expectation that we will applaud him. Maybe he had earned and saved his money in meticulous fulfillment of the old, selfish ethic, but that is no assurance that he has gained and maintained a sufficient store of wisdom to support his now trying to become unselfish.

Such a line of thought is fashionable these days. The disrepute into which philanthropy, especially large philanthropy, has fallen is a fact of our times.

G. The Changing Attitudes of Donors

This disrepute can be seen, by reflection, in the changing attitudes of donors themselves, whether they are individuals, foundations or other organizations. Not long ago giving on a large scale was likely to be, in general, almost as routine as small-scale, personal donations. In a particular case, of course, a large gift was a circumstance of special import for both donor and recipient. But the overall pattern of philanthropy, large as well as small, followed a relatively unvarying formula, consisting of a combination of predictable actions and attitudes:

— the decision of the donor, made on his best understanding of the merits of the case;
— the gift itself, with very few extraneous considerations and conditions;
— sincere appreciation on the part of the recipient;
— genuine satisfaction on the part of the donor;
— and unmixed approbation on the part of the public.

Times are no longer so simple. Attitudes of the general public and even of recipients have come to be adulterated with doubt and criticism, both of the terms of the gift and of the intentions of the donor. Thus the donor, unsure of the gift and its reception, begins to make his decisions on factors other than just the merits of the case and to surround the gift with various kinds of protective understandings. His whole attitude toward the transaction may change.

Take his feeling about publicity, for example. The norm has always been, and still is, that most gifts of unusual size are appropriately announced, at least by the recipient if not by the donor. But ever since philanthropy began to be a fairly common practice among people of wealth, some donors have tried to eschew the limelight. Why? Put yourself in their place, if you can, and you will begin to sense something of what they have come to feel.

Let us play the game. The imaginary time is the teens of this century, and you want to make a donation of a million dollars to establish some high schools for (as you probably call them) "colored people." Schools for them are awfully poor, everybody knows, and they badly need education. But you don't want the gift publicized because you are a genuinely modest person. You don't want to be lionized, so you make it anonymously.

That's all right. We understand that. And if we happen to find out about your gift, we admire you all the more.

Now it's the forties. You plan to give two million dollars to a group of what are called "Negro" colleges. Everybody knows that separate isn't equal, and Negroes ought to have a chance at higher education, too. But those who can make that size of gift run the risk of being called "malefactors of great wealth," and you'd prefer not to be thought of in that category. You want secrecy not because you are doing anything wrong, but just because you don't want to be misunderstood and bothered.

That's all right, too. We accept your feeling. Anyway, it's your money and you ought to be able to do with it as you please, without interference.

But it's not the teens or the forties. It's the seventies. This time you want to give five million dollars to the "blacks." They need an opportunity to go to good schools and colleges, of course, but they need a lot more too. So you may spread it around a bit: some to fellowships earmarked for black students in professional schools, some to a black medical school, some for voter registration drives, some for financing black business enterprises, some for rehabilitation of the ghettos and fair housing programs.

But the last thing you want is publicity. Not because you are unduly modest, and certainly not because you hope not to be bothered—for if you've got that kind of money to give, you know you're going to be bothered anyway. Rather, because you simply don't relish the idea of being criticized for your efforts.

You are aware that the criticism will come from all points of the opinionated compass: segregationists will be livid, seeing all that money go to the blacks. Integrationists will also be irate, feeling that you are contributing to continued separatism. You can't win. So if you are still determined to put your money to good use on behalf of those who need it, you may tread softly, welcome silence and hope that some other philanthropic outfit draws the fire. You just don't want to put up with the inevitable flak.

This time it is not quite all right. Modesty and privacy are values to be prized, but a desire to escape criticism sounds craven. We who are your public, then, are likely to be doubly critical if we think you can't stand for us to be critical. All you want is praise? You'll get none of it from us.

The trouble with imaginary illustrations is just that: they are not real. All that they are meant to be, however, is suggestive. Anybody who ever wanted to give a million dollars was impelled by more than a sense of modesty; two million dollars, by more than a desire for privacy; five million dollars, by something quite different from a fear of criticism. These feelings are peripheral to the act of giving itself, and may even be antithetical to the impulse of generosity. That is, one makes the gift notwithstanding his modesty, at the risk of his loss of privacy, and in spite of his distaste for being criticized.

Somewhere along the line, however, these peripheral emotions may develop sufficient force to cut the donor's nerve of endeavor. When a potential benefactor comes to understand the negative reactions that his gift is likely to provoke—what's he trying to buy? to hide? to manipulate? and all the rest—his prudential stance of self-protection may well override his philanthropic impulse. If he doesn't lose the urge entirely, at least his joy in giving is considerably muted. Sooner or later he may begin to ask himself, Why bother?

Such a feeling on the part of today's philanthropists is not imaginary. As far as I am aware, no systematic research into a donor's shifting degrees of personal satisfaction has ever been undertaken. Graphs that tried to depict the changing patterns of a benefactor's attitudes would be silly. Such things are hardly susceptible to questionnaires, charts and the paraphernalia of analysis. But one cannot escape the impression gained from several decades of contact with donors and donations. As both recipient of and surrogate for philanthropy, I have watched at close range its moods and tempers as well as its acts and achievements.

And the summary impression I have gained is this: the benefactor today, large or small, is likely to be unhappy about his giving. In comparative terms, he is almost certain to be less starry-eyed, less sanguine about his gift's beneficent results, less glad, than was his predecessor of fifty or even fifteen years ago. Self-interest aside—and to the cynic it needs to be said that self-interest could indeed be often put aside—he feels less sure than he once did that his gift will accomplish anything worthwhile. Church treasurers, secretaries of college alumni funds, financial officers of hospitals, museums and symphony orchestras, can all testify to this fact, for their money-raising efforts and their daily mail give evidence of it.

Something of this sort is true, I believe, not only for individual donors but also for organized philanthropy; that is, for foundations, family and community funds and corporation charitable trusts. The money is there to be given, and so it is. But the dream of what it could help to do has lost some of its luster, and the pleasure in the doing is tempered. Rumors are not to be trusted, of course, but the fact of their currency tells something about the atmosphere of the times. In the last few years in the foundation field, rumors have been rife that the X Foundation intended to spend itself out of existence immediately, or that the Y Charitable Trust of the Z Corporation was going to give up its incorporated status and revert to being simply an annual benevolence program of its parent business. Rumor outruns fact, to be sure, but some such transformations have already taken place, more may be in the offing, and the moods of uncertainty and unhappiness becloud the scene.[33]

Short of dissolution, or giving up the war without a battle, foundations take a number of tacks in their response to criticism. Answers to specific charges will be discussed in the succeeding two chapters [not reprinted here]; now we mean simply to note some of the general reactions.

First is silence. But the immediate thing that must be said about it is that it is seldom practiced. "The public be damned" was once thought to be the attitude of more than one tycoon, but swashbuckling has gone out of style, and though answers to the attack occupy a broad spectrum of reaction, almost nobody emulates the ostrich.

But a number of big donors, including foundations, are genuinely surprised. Who, me? The era of good feeling toward philanthropists and foundations lasted so long that many were ill prepared for the suspicion and even censure with which they have recently been visited. How could anyone possibly say that they were feathering their own nests? Isn't it obvious that their only desire was to do good?

Lest the surprise be thought to be ingenuous, even feigned, we need to be mindful of the self-image of a person or organization engaged in philanthropic pursuits, a self-image that is undoubtedly one of the occupational hazards. Like the minister, the teacher, the doctor or the lawyer, he accepts as a premise of his work the belief that it is disinterested, patently directed toward the welfare of others. When his vocation is attacked, therefore, and when his selfless practice of it is questioned, his surprise is genuine.

He is likely to protest his innocence. Surely a foundation's protestation is a justified as well as predictable reaction, when the charges are blanket and free-swinging in character and when the foundation knows that they don't legitimately apply to it.

Confession is also an occasional reaction. Those few who are indeed guilty of serious wrongdoing are not likely to admit it, of course, any more than any other kind of criminal. But the confession of having transgressed the less serious levels of proper behavior is sometimes expressed. The most popular form of confession among foundations is the recognition that they have failed to keep the public completely informed about their doings and that they have practiced poor public relations.

Two further types of reaction, seemingly contradictory in nature, often go hand in hand. First is resignation, the recognition that criticism is the price a foundation must pay for operating in the public sector. If one is to do anything worthwhile, it is bound to make some people unhappy. Foundations are in the business of making people unhappy, for those whose appeals are turned down far outnumber those whose projects get supported. Even if some of the critics are not among the company of those who have been rebuffed, their attacks are to be expected, and sooner or later they will be made.

But nobody has to like it. The partner to resignation is indignation, and foundations increasingly express themselves, often in private, sometimes in public, in feelings of outrage at the terms of the attack upon them. On rare occasion the anger may be only faintly concealed and may even descend to ad hominem types of argument. Consider the source! What is the critic really after? Economic, social or political gain of his own? Even if such questions are sometimes in order, the flint shows through, and the resentment and exasperation of foundations at what they take to be unprovoked and undeserved attacks are among the responses now being made.

Self-examination is a reaction of an entirely different kind of which we shall take note in succeeding chapters [not reprinted here].

One way or another, all of these reactions add up to a defensive and dispirited posture.

It is rare indeed that second- or third-generation members of a family take as much delight in their fund's activity as did its founder. In many corporations chief executive officers turn over the chore of supervising the benevolence programs to junior personnel. Board memberships and positions on the staffs of large foundations are not the sinecures they were once thought to be. Annual reports of such organizations tell more than they once did, but much of what they tell is not merely reportorial but in a tone of self-justification. Let it be clearly stated: Those who are in any way intimately connected with philanthropy are now being disabused of the earlier notions of its splendor, its public approbation and its fun.

H. Conclusion

We find ourselves, then, in a strange time. As non-governmental endowed agencies devoted to the general welfare, foundations have grown remarkably in numbers, size of resources and diversity of structure and program. They have a right to be genuinely proud of their brief history. Motivations that explain their founding and have inspired their functioning are, like those of all other organizations, both selfish and selfless, and both kinds need to be credited and observed.

The work of foundations has inspired a variety of feelings and attitudes, many of them appreciative. But man-bites-dog is always the newsworthy item, and the charge that foundations are biting the public hand that feeds them is the attitude that has caught much of Congressional and general attention. It is of a piece with the general disrepute into which giving of all sorts and sizes seems to have fallen, and this widespread suspicion of decent reflexes, generous impulses and good works may represent a serious shift in American values. As agents for much of American philanthropy, foundations are victim to this suspicion. They have been caught in the act of helping, and their effectiveness in so doing will be seriously proscribed if they cannot make persuasive answer to the charges leveled against them. Among the attitudes to which they must respond are those that philanthropists have themselves begun to feel—a distaste for being criticized, a loss of satisfaction in the work of benevolence, a retreat into a defensive posture.

To whatever extent this brief outline of fact and feeling is true, it behooves us to ask why. The purpose of this book is to participate in that inquiry and, further, to postulate as to ways in which philanthropy may come again, deservedly, into the good graces of the public. My chief interest is in organized rather than personal philanthropy, not only because my experience in the latter is so modest, necessarily, as to be of no moment to anyone else, but also because my employment is with the former. As a foundation executive I am concerned about what has happened to foundations in recent years and, more, what their future may be. But beyond foundations I am interested in the survival of the American spirit of magnanimity and the strengthening of the American urge to face problems squarely and seek to solve them. Though foundations are only one type of institution that can manifest that spirit and that urge, an analysis of their current state of mind and manner may be suggestive for other institutions and for the citizenry in general.

Notes

1. For information on individual foundations, see Marianna O. Lewis and Patricia Bowers, eds., *The Foundation Directory*, Edition 4, New York, Columbia University Press, 1971. (Hereafter referred to as FD-4.) For news about the Robert Wood Johnson Foundation, see *Foundation News*, January–February, 1972, p. 39.

2. See *Foundations, Private Giving and Public Policy: Report and Recommendations of the Commission on Foundations and Private*

Philanthropy (Peter G. Peterson, Chairman), Chicago, University of Chicago Press, 1970, pp. 39–41. (Hereafter referred to as Report of Peterson Commission.)

3. See F. Emerson Andrews, *Philanthropic Foundations*, New York, Russell Sage Foundation, 1956; Warren Weaver, *U.S. Philanthropic Foundations: Their History, Structure, Management, and Record,* New York, Harper and Row, 1967; Abraham Flexner, *Funds and Foundations*, New York, Harper & Brothers, 1952.

4. F. Emerson Andrews, "Introduction," in Ann D. Walton and Marianna O. Lewis, eds., *The Foundation Directory*, Edition 2, New York, Russell Sage Foundation, 1964, pp. 11–16. (Hereafter referred to as FD-2.) See also periodic volumes of *American Foundations and Their Fields*, with various editors and publishers, from 1931 to 1955.

5. Ann D. Walton, *et. al.*, eds., "Introduction," *The Foundation Directory*, Edition 1, New York, Russell Sage Foundation, 1960. (Hereafter referred to as FD-1.)

6. FD-2, pp. 9–16.

7. Marianna O. Lewis, ed., *The Foundation Directory*, Edition 3, New York, Russell Sage Foundation, 1967, pp. 7–13. (Hereafter referred to as FD-3.)

8. FD-4, pp. vii–x.

9. Weaver, *op. cit.*, p. 57; F. Emerson Andrews, *Patman and Foundations: Review and Assessment*, New York, The Foundation Center, 1968, p. 8.

10. FD-4, p. viii.

11. *Ibid.*, pp. viii–x.

12. *Ibid.*, pp. viii–xii. In April, 1972, the Editor of FD-4 estimated the current assets at $28 billion, because of recent advances in the stock market and the new money received by the Robert Wood Johnson Foundation.

13. Report of Peterson Commission, *op. cit.*, p. 49.

14. *Ibid.*, p. 51. Figure of $1.8 billion comes from FD-4, p. xiv.

15. *Giving USA*, New York, American Association of Fund-Raising Council, Inc., 1971, p. 7. (Incidentally, the AAFRC's estimate for foundation grants in 1970 is only $1.7 billion; pp. 8, 21.)

16. For discussion of motives in establishing foundations; see Weaver, *op. cit.*, chap. 8;

Andrews, *Philanthropic Foundations, op. cit.*, chap. 2; Report of the Peterson Commission, *op. cit.*, pp. 45–47; Joseph C. Kiger, *Operating Principles of the Larger Foundations*, New York, Russell Sage Foundation, 1954, chap. 1.

17. See, for example, Whitney M. Young, Jr., "Foundations Under Attack," in Thomas C. Reeves, ed., *Foundations Under Fire*, Ithaca, Cornell University Press, 1970; Robert D. Calkins, *The Role of the Philanthropic Foundation*, Washington, Cosmos Club, 1969; Irwin Ross, "Let's Not Fence in the Foundations," in *Fortune*, June 1969; statements of Herman Wells, Theodore M. Hesburgh, Frank C. Erwin, Jr., John Cooper, Felix Robb, W. Russell Arrington, Carl Kaysen, O. Meredith Wilson, Kermit Gordon, and others in *Foundations and the Tax Bill*, New York, The Foundation Center, 1969; and various authors, Part II, "Judgments Concerning the Value of Foundation Aid," in Weaver, *op. cit.*, pp. 221–457.

18. Kurt Vonnegut, Jr., *God Bless You, Mr. Rosewater*, New York, Dell Publishing Co., 1965.

19. See Ferdinand Lundberg, *The Rich and the Super-Rich*, New York, Bantam Books, 1968, chap. 10; Eduard C. Lindeman, *Wealth and Culture*, New York, Harcourt Brace, 1936; Joseph C. Goulden, *The Money Givers*, New York, Random House, 1971, chap. 2.

20. See Report of Peterson Commission, *op. cit.*, p. 63; Goulden, *op. cit.*, pp. 32–37.

21. See Weaver, *op. cit.*, pp. 170–171; Kiger, *op. cit.*, pp. 85–88; Harold M. Keele, *Unpublished Proceedings of New York University's Ninth Biennial Conference on Charitable Foundations: An Exercise in Censorship*, Chicago, 1970, pp. 7–9.

22. See Kiger, *op. cit.*, pp. 88-91.

23. Quoted in Report of Peterson Commission, *op. cit.*, p. 65.

24. See *Final Report of the Select Committee to Investigate Foundations and Other Organizations*, U.S. House, 82d Congress, 2d Session, House Report No. 2514, Washington, D.C., Government Printing Office, 1953; Kiger, *op. cit.*, pp. 91–97; Keele, *op. cit.*, pp. 9–14; Helen Hill Miller, "Investigating the Foundations," *The Reporter*, November 24, 1953, pp. 37–40.

25. See Weaver, *op.cit.*, pp. 174–179; Report of Peterson Commission, *op. cit.*, pp. 66–67;

Robert M. Hutchins, *Freedom, Education and the Fund*, New York, Meridian, 1956, pp. 201–207, quoted in Reeves, *op. cit.*, pp. 112–120.

26. See various Installments of *Tax-Exempt Foundations and Charitable Trusts: Their Impact on Our Economy*, Washington, D.C., Government Printing Office, beginning in 1962, the widely publicized series of Reports, six to date, of Mr. Patman, to his own Subcommittee. (Hereafter referred to as Patman Reports, with number and date.)

27. For a variety of points of view on the Patman investigations, see Lundberg, *op. cit.*, pp. 470–497; Weaver, *op. cit.*, pp. 179–185; Keele, *op. cit.*, pp. 17–20; Goulden, *op. cit.*, pp. 229–237; Wright Patman, "The Free-Wheeling Foundations," *The Progressive*, June, 1967, pp. 27–31; Andrews, *Patman and Foundations: Review and Assessment, op.cit.*

28. See *Treasury Department Report on Private Foundations*, Committee on Finance, United States Senate, Washington, D.C., Government Printing Office, 1965. (Hereafter, referred to as Treasury Department Report.) See also Weaver, *op. cit.*, pp. 185–186; Staff of the Russell Sage Foundation, "Views of the Treasury Report," in *Foundation News*, March, 1968, pp. 29–33.

29. See Stephan Lesher, "Who knows what frustrations lurk in the hearts of X million Americans? George Wallace knows—and he's off and running," *New York Times Magazine*, January 2, 1972; Richard Fitzgerald, "In Re: Gov. Wallace vs. Foundations," *Non-Profit Report*, December, 1971, pp. 7–8, and "Governor Wallace's Foundation Targets," *Ibid.*, January, 1972, p. 15.

30. See, for example, Lundberg, *op. cit.*, chap. 10; Goulden, *op. cit.*; Reeves, *op. cit.*, pp. 1–35; quotations in *Ibid.* from Fred J. Cook, pp. 127–133 and Burton Raffel, pp. 86–93; Taylor Branch, "The Case Against Foundations," *The Washington Monthly*, July, 1971, pp. 3–18.

31. See Herbert W. Schneider, *A History of American Philosophy*, New York, Columbia University Press, 1946, chap. IV, "Benevolence"; Robert H. Bremner, *American Philanthropy*, Chicago, University of Chicago Press, 1960.

32. See Andrew Carnegie, *The Gospel of Wealth*, New York, Century Company, 1900.

33. The uncertain and unhappy mood is reflected in the tables of contents of recent issues of both *Foundation News* and *Non-Profit Report*; the latter has begun to run a fairly regular listing of "Terminated Foundations" (e.g., November, 1971, p. 8; December, 1971, p. 12; January, 1972, p. 15). It is reflected also in the agendas of nearly all the host of conferences on and for foundations that take place regularly.

ARTICLE 30 ———————————

Looking Backwards: How Foundations Formulated Ideology in the Progressive Period
Sheila Slaughter and Edward T. Silva

In looking backwards to the progressive period (1900–1920) and the part played by the first foundations in the systematic shaping of ideas, it is necessary to recall that the era was turbulent with a new material reality. In the years following the Civil War, radical changes in the mode of production shifted the United States from an agrarian to an industrial nation in which the exploitation of the technical developments that made industrialization possible depended on a landless, polyglot, urban proletariat whose only stake in existing social arrangements was the inadequate hourly wage. The resulting conflicts between capital and labor often flared into violence of such proportions that these struggles were referred to as labor wars and treated, with armed troops and martial law, as civil insurrections. Imperfect coordination of a newly national economy created frequent economic breakdowns— virtually half the years between the Civil War and World War I were beset with depression— that shook the confidence of the rapidly growing white-collar sector as to the stability of industrial capital. Finally, the emerging role of the farming hinterland as an internal colony—as a market for manufactured goods and a cheap food and fiber supplier for an increasingly urbanized labor force—gave rise to years of virulent and sustained

SOURCE: Copyright 1980 and reprinted with the permission of G. K. Hall & Co., Boston.

regional opposition to the centralizing thrust of eastern finance capital.[1]

Rapid post-Civil War industrialization created a series of national crises as conflict followed conflict across the American political-economic stage. Continued crises called forth new ideologies to compete with established ones. Each ideology, new or old, was a more or less coherent set of ideas explaining the problematic issues of the day somewhat differently and offering its own solution to them. These ideologies helped organize their adherents' beliefs and hopes about their world's present and future, giving structure to citizens' perceptions in three ways.

First, each ideology outlined the way the political economy operated, clearly delineating who exercised power and on what grounds. This provided a framework for interpreting the wide variety of problematic social issues and conflicts encountered in daily life, in media, and in the political arena.

Second, ideology offered criteria for a moral evaluation of the ongoing political economy. In particular, it helped focus attention on the propriety of power arrangements and their consequences—on who got what, when, where, and how. Were these arrangements and their consequences basically just or fundamentally unfair? Were they good or bad?

Third, the descriptive and evaluative elements in these ideologies combined to supply citizens with imperatives to collective action. Ideologies mandated either a defense of the status quo—if it was seen as just and good—or an attack on those structures requiring change. Ideologies either inhibited or inspired social movements. In the progressive period, then, ideologies supplied a variety of solutions to the social problems that plagued industrializing America, explaining the way society worked and offering blueprints for the future.

While individual citizens were free to construct their own idiosyncratic analysis of current conditions and design programs for the future, they might also choose from those offered by a variety of groups—socialists, populists, urban reformers, business leaders, anarchists, conservative unionists, and radical workers— responding to the agreed-upon issues of the day: urban poverty, industrial concentration, the decay of the democratic process, and the role of state in mediating relationships between private capital and public welfare. How citizens constructed and chose blueprints for the future was of considerable interest to those satisfied with existing power arrangements and well rewarded by their consequences. Since ideologies supplied the social cement for collective political action, these satisfied resource holders concerned themselves with influencing the process of ideology formation—the production, dissemination, and consumption of ideas. Inasmuch as philanthropic foundations in the progressive period were created and controlled by satisfied resource holders, they vigorously intervened in the era's vibrant marketplace of ideas, putting their vast resources at the disposal of only some of the groups promulgating ideologies, furthering only these groups' capacities to produce and disseminate world-views supportive of the status quo. The foundations, in effect, subsidized the manufacture and distribution of some ideologies and not others, eventually to the extent of trying to create a consuming public for their subsidized wares.

In this chapter, we examine the work of three of the first foundations—Carnegie (1903), Russell Sage (1907), and the Rockefeller Foundation (1913). We present case studies of their deployment of resources to professionals and experts engaged in the examination and amelioration of social problems. By inspecting funding patterns, project expectations, and the product professionals and experts were able to deliver, we begin to understand how foundations attempted to shape ideas. Our last section shows the problems foundations faced when attempting to influence ideology formation in the progressive period.[2]

Russell Sage and Social Service

On July 22, 1906, Russell Sage, a noted robber baron,[3] died, leaving $65 million to his seventy-seven year old wife, Margaret Olivia Sage. During the last dozen years of her life, she donated $35 million and willed $36 million to charitable, educational, and religious organizations. One of her earliest and largest beneficiaries was the Russell Sage Foundation. Chartered in New York in 1907, the foundation began with $10 million and was heir to another $5 million. Its charter empowered the foundation to use its resources for "the improvement of social and living conditions in the USA" by "any means...including research, publication, education," and the support and creation of social service organizations. Equipped with vast resources and a broad mandate, the foundation invested in ideology production.[4]

Sage's involvement in ideology production is best seen through its founding personages and their common vision of social improvement. They shared, in the words of the foundation's official historians, "the fresh enthusiasm of the early years of the twentieth century for hunting down the causes of poverty, disease and crime, and discovering what could be done to eliminate or at least control those causes." [5] However, this enthusiasm and discovery was limited by a reluctance to explore to the left. Thus, the Sage's vision was blind to the many anticapitalist alternatives abroad during the progressive period. In general, Sage funded the tacit opponents of the left and helped them contain proponents of alternative ideologies, especially socialistic ideologies, by supporting social amelioration that took capitalist economic development for granted. In particular, the foundation joined hands with a "charity organization" movement that assumed industrial capitalism was a necessary framework for progress. Sage supplied resources to help nationally coordinate and centralize the charity organization movement and in so doing countered more radical approaches to social problems.

The charity organization movement arose after the Civil War. Before that war, the amelioration of social ills was often in the hands of individual citizens—the Lady Bountifuls—of the communities who took care of the poorly educated, the blind, the halt, and the lame as a matter of religious stewardship, ethical humanism, noblesse oblige, and the like. There was little sense of collective obligation for the "unfortunates" of the community. Indeed, given the laissez-faire ethos of the time, even such ad hoc amelioration was the due only of those who through no fault of their own could not compete in the Social Darwinian struggle of the fit.

After 1865, such unsystematic and unorganized relief began to reveal its limits in the face of accelerating, unplanned industrialization. In large urban areas, where social ills became most apparent, new charity organizations emerged to provide services beyond the scope of Lady

Bountifuls. These local organizations, often headed by community political and economic elites, sought systematic and more efficient means to deliver "social improvement" to those they saw as deserving and worthy victims of misfortune. They concerned themselves particularly with economic poverty and its social and physical attendants: pauperism (the culture of poverty), family disruption, child labor, poor housing, lack of recreation opportunities, and so on.[6]

With such efforts, the local "charity organization societies" (COSs) began to modify their received laissez-faire ideologies in a reform direction. But their ideas of reform possibilities were limited by a strong and binding commitment to the very social process that underlay the poverty that so concerned them—accelerating industrial capitalism. Thus they saw poverty as an individual problem involving personal limitations—improper education, physical disabilities, bad work habits—and not as a structural problem inherent in capitalistic development. They did not see low wages as the other side of capital formation, nor did they view wageless unemployment as the result of widespread mechanization. Further, they were blind to the broader social problems that illuminated other movements. They did not see the problems inherent in the vast, socially irresponsible wealth such as that held in the hands of the robber barons, in the unprecedented concentration of social power in the corporate economy, and in the expression of that extraordinary wealth and power in rigged elections, purchased legislation, and, indeed, the wholesale corruption of liberal democratic political forms. In their selection of only some of the consequences of capitalist development as social problems worthy of efficient ameliorative reform, the COSs revealed their ideological commitment to capitalism per se.[7]

The charity organization movement spread rapidly across urban America. By the 1890s, ninety-odd local units were operating. COS representatives became dominant in the National Conference of Charities and Corrections (NCCC), asserting a claim to central leadership of the emerging profession of social work.[8] The NCCC, however, was unable to unify social service ideology and delivery because its internal coherence was limited by the persistence of strong factions, the inherently localistic focus of

many participants, and a lack of resources. Thus, factions advocating working-class self-help organizations (workingmen's benevolent societies, five-cent savings banks, and the like) competed with those supporting limited union organization; and both these groups were opposed by champions of local and limited aid in crisis situations. Further, popular acceptance of professionally controlled social service was still tenuous. At this critical juncture, the newly organized Russell Sage Foundation put its resources behind professionalizing COS operatives, thereby tipping the scales toward a nationwide ideology of efficient, systematic social amelioration directed by trained social workers.

When Mrs. Sage decided to spend her husband's fortune on charity, her attention was turned to social work by her lawyers, one of whom—Robert W. deForest—had been president of the New York City COS for eighteen years as well as a past president of NCCC. DeForest drew heavily on his connections in the charity organization movement to help Mrs. Sage see the need for a foundation that would centralize and coordinate that movement. He was aided by Daniel Coit Gilman, a past president of the Baltimore COS and a founding Sage trustee, and John M. Glenn, another Baltimore COS leader, founding trustee, and Sage's chief executive officer. In fact, so successful was deForest that the foundation's self-perpetuating board was composed mainly of well-known charity movement activists.[9]

The Sage board, heavy with COS partisans, began immediately to support the movement's effort to disseminate its views. It granted the Charities Publication Committee of the New York COS sufficient funds to complete its efforts to establish a national journal. The initial grant to the committee was $20,000 in 1907, given in expectation of increasing the "circulation and educational influence" of its magazine. This level of support was continued over the next decade, during which $223,000 was advanced. This amounted to 12.4 percent—one dollar in eight—of the $1.8 million granted by the Sage in that first decade. Perhaps Sage's understanding of the need for such increased "circulation and educational influence" was made clearer by deForest, Gilman, and Glenn, who sat on both the New York City COS Publication Committee and

Sage's board. Thus Sage helped *Charities and the Commons,* which was already a combination of Chicago and New York City COS-based journals, become *Survey,* a vehicle with a more nationally representative editorial board and audience. The charity movement then had a national periodical to spread an ideology of professionally directed reform aimed at solving problems within the parameters set by existing power arrangements.[10]

Beyond subsidizing *Survey* as a means of ideological dissemination for the charity organization movement, Sage funded various educational efforts whose activities were publicized in *Survey* and other social service journals. In effect, it funded the activities reported in these magazines, in a sense creating "copy" for their pages. These educational activities offered detailed and continuing instruction in ameliorative reforms providing the emerging white-collar sector—the clerks and secretaries, state officials and schoolteachers, managers and professionals—with a more palatable solution to the problems posed by rapid industrialization than the drastic structural solutions offered by socialism. They informed citizens that their part-time, volunteeristic efforts would solve their community's most pressing problems: "poverty, disease and crime."

The flavor of these well-publicized educational efforts is nicely captured in Sage's own use of the community survey. Upon invitation from a community's leaders, Sage would send staff to identify local needs. Then the community leaders would supply local citizens to tramp about documenting the exact extent of the identified ill, be it housing, TB, or loansharking.[11] Finally Sage would help orchestrate a festival of publicity and exhibits to more fully inform the populace about the unmet needs of their locale.[12] The hoped-for outcome of such surveys, publicity, and exhibits was a sense of informed social outrage which would be channelled into "constructive" volunteer work to solve social ills as defined by Sage and documented by the community.

At nub, both the educational efforts and Sage's own surveys were forms of ideology-in-action. Participation concretized ideological commitment to the notion that aroused citizens could and should solve the ills of the day by ad hoc volunteer work directed by social service

professionals. Community mobilization was intended to create ideological consensus among the white-collar middle strata then coming to some sense of self-consciousness. Volunteer work with the urban poor confirmed the merit of its donors and identified members of the emerging white-collar strata to each other, while promising the perfection of industrial capitalism without structural change. Thus Sage by its own efforts in its surveys as well as through its broad support of other educational activities funded what amounted to procapitalist agitation and propaganda. And what it supported at the local level, it also gifted at the state and national levels. In sum, foundation sponsorship of these educational activities helped to construct the curricula that filled the pages of the Sage-funded *Survey,* the charity organization movement's self-conscious means of nationwide ideological instruction.

In addition to providing resources for a national journal and educational activities that supplied copy for that journal, Sage helped create a permanent work force to implement and maintain its ideology of ameliorative reform within capitalistic development by actively supporting the professionalization of social work. Sage made direct grants to emerging organizations engaged in creating social work, notably occupational associations and the new urban social service schools linked to the COS movement. Sage's contributions to social work occupational associations included providing office space in its building and $1,000 to the Intercollegiate Bureau of Occupations in 1913 to establish a department placing social service graduates in professional positions, and continuing grants from 1914 forward to the National Social Worker Exchange, another employment bureau. Its support to urban social service schools, which later became major social work schools, included gifts to the Boston School for Social Workers ($70,100), the Chicago Institute of Social Science ($71,100), and the St. Louis School of Social Economy ($50,500), all between 1908 and 1915. Substantial aid was also given the New York School of Philanthropy. All told, some $246,700 was given the new schools—roughly one-eighth of the foundation's grants before World War I.[13]

Financial assistance was also given to agencies for demonstration as well as routine work. Innovative social service teaching and technical advances were fostered, results written up, and publications subsidized. Hundreds of pamphlets and books were produced with the aid of Sage resources, often with technical help from *Survey* staff. Particularly important innovators were put on foundation payrolls. Among them was Mary Richmond, who systematized social work's distinctive individualistic, not structural, case work theory and method. Sage also created a leading social work library in its ambition to become a national clearing house for professional social service information.[14]

The foundation, then, acted to faciliate the growth and development of a profession that would control, even monopolize, employment opportunities in the sector the COSs had long tried to organize. Sage funds enabled COS leaders and professionals to manufacture and distribute an ideology that buttressed both their leadership in the field of social service and ameliorative reform as an alternative to more basic structural changes.

In sum, Mrs. Sage's foundation contributed to ideology manufacture in a variety of ways. *Survey* was a vehicle for the dissemination of a set of ideas purporting to offer solutions to the problem of urban poverty: data collection, education, mitigation of the eyesores of city life (unsanitary and overcrowded housing, the lack of recreational space, "street arabs" —apparently abandoned or improperly supervised children) through the volunteered effort of the emerging white-collar strata directed by professional social workers. Sage was concerned not only with dissemination of this ideology, but also with its pragmatic demonstration. Monies from the Sage coffers provided for community surveys, the results of which were used to inform the responsible classes of the issues at hand as well as to guide their efforts at amelioration. These projects served the additional purpose of providing copy for *Survey* and other social service magazines. Finally, Sage contributed heavily to the establishment of social work, which supplied a permanent cadre of professionals to supervise implementation of the ideological line developed in *Survey*. Thus Sage funds worked to join together the COS's ideas and practice into a social work profession with an ideology that narrowly structured ways of thinking about the relation of social service to human needs in the

progressive era. Some consequences of the structural poverty generated by industrial capitalism were treated, while fundamental problematics even within that system (socially irresponsible wealth, industrial concentration, political corruption) remained unchallenged.

The Carnegie Institute and the Economic History of the United States

The Carnegie Institute of Washington, D.C. (CIW) provides perhaps the earliest example of sustained resource support for a specific group of academics and public service professionals engaged in producing ideas that addressed clearly defined social issues. Founded in 1903, the business of the institute was to "conduct, endow and assist investigation" in all learned fields in conjunction with formal agencies of higher education in order to secure for the United States "leadership in the domain of discovery and the utilization of new forces for the benefit of mankind."[15] The method by which the potential of original investigation would be unleashed was through "the substitution of organized for unorganized effort" in the domain of intellectual production.[16] Carnegie's general desire was to rationalize the production of new knowledge focused on a wide variety of problems confronting an industrializing society. By supplying resources for the production of knowledge to solve social and economic problems, the Carnegie Institute funded the construction of a pragmatic ideology of ameliorative reform that justified the perpetuation of industrial capitalism.

The successful construction of this ideology required locating and recruiting trained intellectual workers, and the CIW's board numbered among its trustees several university managers with a sense of such things. One such trustee was Carroll D. Wright, president of Clark University, who had helped select and train knowledge[able] workers while serving as United States Commissioner of Labor (1885–1905). Another trustee, Andrew D. White, a past president of Cornell University, had acted as a foreign minister and diplomat who routinely evaluated knowledge and information producers. Finally, Daniel Coit Gilman had molded Johns Hopkins University while its president and had helped shape the

Russell Sage Foundation as its trustee. Gilman became the CIW's first president.

The institute's main instrument of ideological production was its Department of Economics and Sociology. This department was concerned with the analysis of industrial production, the distribution of wealth, the relation of capital and labor, and the relation of private capital to the state.[17] These broad categories were broken down into a series of specific research problems that would yield solutions upon systematic investigation.[18] The institute trustees delegated the selection of manpower to advisory committees of experts chosen on the basis of shared friendship and acceptable past work. The chairman of the Economics Advisory Committee was Trustee Carroll D. Wright. The other two members of the institute's Advisory Committee on Economics were Henry W. Farnam of Yale and John Bates Clark of Columbia, both of whom shared the upperclass background of the majority of institute trustees, had worked with them in policymaking forums such as the Chicago Conference on Trusts, and would eventually act as foundation managers themselves.[19]

These three economists turned to an organization they themselves had helped create—the American Economic Association (AEA)—to recruit the manpower necessary to solve the problems identified by the Department. The Advisory Committee used the mediating efforts of AEA president E. R. A. Seligman, Columbia professor and son of the New York banking family, to secure recommendations from the AEA Council for personnel suitable to deal with the controversial subject matter under the department's investigation.[20] After expressing gratitude to the Carnegie Institute for providing research monies in the area of economics, the AEA Council nominated seven of eleven initial section heads from its own number.[21] Work in these eleven areas would result in a new, standard economic history of the United States, one drawing upon the past to create a future for the benefit of the "public welfare."[22] The project managers' understanding of the public welfare is suggested by a remark in Seligman's AEA Presidential Address: "the aim of economics is to show the reconciliation of private wealth with public welfare...."[23]

The Carnegie Institute, then, saw new knowledge as raw material that could be exploited for ideological purposes if producers of intellectual goods could be efficiently mobilized. To that end, the trustees turned through its advisory committee to a specialized national organization of competent academics—the AEA—with an offer for resource support. The particular economics professors with whom they then negotiated resource agreements were ideologically "safe." They shared with the trustees a definition of the parameters within which problems of power arrangements must be solved: the public welfare can be served while private wealth is preserved.

Although the general problems for investigation (development of industrial production, distribution of wealth, the relationship of capital and labor, the relation of private capital to the state) were set for them, the AEA economics professors were given wide latitude in mapping areas of study and in choosing the form of the final product. They divided the department into eleven sections: population and immigration, agriculture and forestry, mining, manufactures, transportation, domestic and foreign commerce, money and banking, labor movement, industrial organization, social legislation, and federal and state financing, including taxation. The results of investigation in each section would be packaged in books, the entire project in a set of volumes that would account for the economic history of the United States. They were also well funded. CIW doubled their first-year allocation request ($15,000), providing $30,000 in start-up funds. When the department's work was not completed in the initially projected five-year period (1904–1909), CIW continued support, granting a quarter of a million dollars over a dozen years (1904–1916).[24]

The arrangement between professors and trustees was mutually beneficial. Trustees chose professors with a shared sense of problem to investigate the ideologically relevant issues of the day, and provided them with resources and the autonomy to arrange their own work. Economists of the progressive period defined themselves as scientists able to intervene in the course of history if they could secure the opportunities necessary to full development of the discipline.[25] In return for such support, the institute expected organization of a data base that would permit "a forecast of American social and economic development," a reasonable expectation since institute president Gilman saw "the goal of science" as "a capacity for prediction" and held that "economic and social science are. . .plainly destined to play an increasingly important role in the progress of mankind." [26]

Social scientists, then, were asked to develop predictive capacity while organizing data in ways that pointed to solutions of current social problems. Knowledge of the future gave leverage for control. As E. R. A. Seligman said, "as the science itself becomes more complete, it. . .will be in a better position. . .to explain. . .the true method of making the real conform to the ideal." The application of theory to economic practice would result in stabilizing command; "industrial capital correctly analyzed and rightly controlled" would insure continued economic and social progress.[27] Moreover, as the Department of Economics and Sociology gathered data, it would "put the matter before the people in a way so much needed at the present time." [28] This would accomplish one of the ideological functions of CIW's social science research. It would show that U.S. capitalistic development was understandable, controllable, and reformable.

In sum, the research undertaken by the Department of Economics and Sociology was intended to serve several purposes: (1) the production of the tools for prediction; (2) the use of these tools in stabilizing an economy that was based on highly concentrated, privately controlled industrial capital; (3) the presentation of information to the public that legitimated an economic order based on a capitalism open to the process of incremental reform.

The project, however, was more easily negotiated than delivered. In the first several years, the economists began to appreciate the immensity of the task they had defined. No provision had been made for leaves of absence or permanent staff. Under the press of academic and civic duties, the eminent professors who functioned as section heads were forced to subcontract to graduate students in need of research support.[29] The graduate students in turn redefined areas of research to meet degree requirements; this fragmented a unified treatment of problem areas. Therefore, more professors and more graduate students were funded, with over 200 persons receiving subsidies at one point.[30] Yet by 1909,

the date initially scheduled for project completion, there was not a single completed volume.[31]

During this period, CIW trustees developed a more systematic policy of resource support. The gentleman's agreement that had marked the inauguration of the Institute was replaced by more accountable management that was aimed at maximum knowledge production with minimum resource outlay. The CIW ceased funding individual researchers, concentrated capital in large programs, and selected projects that promised demonstrable, easily publicized results. The new resource disbursement policy of the trustee was restated in the metaphor of the marketplace: they wanted "sure returns." [32] Indeed, after the first general project audit in 1910, the department was very nearly disbanded. The economists had not produced the promised volumes, let alone a basis from which to predict the industrial future. The project was refunded on a temporary basis only when Henry Farnam of Yale, one of the original advisors, agreed to become project manager—department chairman —and made a pledge of reorganization, efficiency, and production.[33]

With the new resource policy, the trustee's expectation of the economic history of the United States changed. "A capacity for prediction," [34] which President Gilman had recognized early on as the identifying mark of a science, was no longer mentioned as a project goal. Emphasis was placed on technical competence in designing ameliorative strategies of social and economic intervention: economists produced material on protective labor legislation, railroad and securities regulatory commissions, arbitration of capital-labor disputes.[35] As Farnam said in an annual report, "our studies in economic history . . .have an important bearing upon practical questions. In these days of rapidly increasing governmental regulation of business and labor, the one safe guide is the experience of the past." [36]

But while funding policy and some trustee project expectations shifted, the bedrock ideological function of the CIW's economic history continued as a vehicle for legitimating industrial capital by erecting a scientific bulwark against socialism. In expressing his conviction as to the importance and utility of the project, Farnam said, "Since we began our work, not a few books in American economic history have been published by writers under the influence of the Marxian doctrine of class conflict." After belaboring these writers for their undue emphasis on "material and egotistic motives," he offered instead, as the raison d'être of the department, "the scientific spirit...[that] will have an authority which cannot be possessed by the work of those who write with a theory to prove."[37] Farnam refused to recognize that Marxian economics made the same claim to science as did economists committed to incremental change. He ignored also the contradiction of a scientific social science that automatically rejected socialist solutions. Thus Farnam underscored the Carnegie Department of Economics and Sociology's commitment to the manufacture of an ideology justifying American capitalistic development while providing for the systematic and incremental amelioration of the social chaos and structural imbalances arising during industrialization. However, despite Farnam's sincerely given promises, his CIW Department of Economics and Sociology never did complete their new economic history. To understand fully why the history was not brought to fruition, we turn now to the Rockefeller Foundation's efforts at ideology manufacture.

Rockefeller and Industrial Relations

Limited and experimental foundation support of procapitalistic ideology manufacture and ameliorative reform, such as we have documented above, could not still industrial unrest. At the height of the progressive era, intense ideological conflict mirrored bloody clashes between capital and labor. According to the closest students of labor disorders, the years from 1911–1916 were "the most violent in American history except for the Civil War."[38] During these years, the Rockefeller Foundation (RF) was established and began planning to expend resources to combat the challenge militant labor presented to capitalist control of American industrialization in general and to the Rockefeller business group's antiunion stand in particular.

Both the Rockefeller industries and the RF held ideological and managerial positions at variance with many of their peers: the nation's largest corporations and foundations. The

Rockefeller business enterprises, long led by John D. Rockefeller, Senior and Junior, were opposed to union recognition in principle and vigorously upheld the right of robber barons to control their industrial fiefdoms absolutely. This was a markedly more laissez-faire policy than that taken by many "enlightened" corporate leaders, such as the Morgan group and many financial and industrial leaders in the National Civic Federation. The more liberal corporate leaders held that recognition of conservative unions was not objectionable since it permitted organized labor and large-scale industry to negotiate a division of efficiently produced wealth within a framework of mutually accepted capitalism.[39]

As the Rockefeller group was at odds with many "corporate liberal" leaders on the labor issue, so the Rockefeller Foundation was operated differently than were other major foundations. Since Sage was dead and Carnegie had sold his steel-making operations to Morgan, their foundations could be offered to the public as gifts by principals putatively no longer active in finance or industry. It was therefore difficult to link up their foundations' granting to any financially interested Sage or Carnegie business enterprise. But the Rockefellers—JDR, Sr., and JDR, Jr.—were alive and well, running both their far-flung corporate empire and their philanthropic ventures. While the RF and the corporations were legally separated, the foundation shared offices, staff, and, most importantly, key decision-makers with the business group. Indeed, the foundation and the corporate empire were very closely interlocked at their tops, where all crucial resource decisions were made.[40] Accordingly, while Sage and Carnegie managers might argue with some plausibility that the separation of their funds from industrial production permitted them to deploy their resources in the widest public interest, the RF found it difficult to counter convincingly critics linking their grants to the private interests of its associated business group.

This lack of separable interests helped place the RF at the very center of major public debate on the proper role of foundations in United States life. In the fall of 1913, at about the time Rockefeller decision-makers began to discuss possible projects for their newly chartered foundation, miners in Colorado went on strike, in part for union recognition. The key firm was

Colorado Fuel and Iron, an enterprise employing 6,000 of the 30,000 miners in the region and owned 40 percent by Rockefeller.[41] Interestingly, Jerome Greene, the foundation secretary, identified economic "research and propaganda," to quiet social and political unrest, as an area demanding philanthropic attention.[42] Apparently, public opinion on the labor question could be shaped through the foundation in order to counter leftist and populist attacks on both the Rockefeller business enterprises and on capitalism.

When looking for methods of approaching the public, Rockefeller Foundation officials had to contend with many other ideological producers, including an increasingly popular method of ideology manufacture—the nonpartisan investigating commission. The commission concept depended on the notion that social problems were technical problems. If the scientific facts on controversial subjects could be established, then the solution that best served the public interest would present itself and bring consensus to conflicting interest groups. Commissions were used in the progressive era by both government and business groups. In general, they operated through the appointment of representatives of capital, labor, and the public by a sponsoring agency: together these interest blocks investigated social problems with the support of professionals, often academics.[43] Both the process of investigation, which brought together contending groups, and wide publication of results were thought to resolve conflict over power arrangements in society.

In preparing to manufacture ideology on the labor problem, the Rockefeller Foundation had to take particular account of the U.S. Commission on Industrial Relations, or the Walsh Commission. This commission was the most popular, largest, and longest lived of the many commissions in the progressive era. It was conceived by a group of intellectual and social reformers (centered around the Sage subsidized *Survey*) after a 1910 dynamite blast destroyed the plant of the militantly antiunion *Los Angeles Times*. The *Survey* group helped President Taft draft a proposal for the commission which became part of his 1912 State of the Union message. Its commissioners were appointed days before miners struck in the Colorado coal fields on September 23, 1912.[44] The strike and the Rockefeller group's involvement became one of the Walsh Commission's broadest targets.

In fact, the Colorado coal wars and the part played by the Rockefeller group in fueling violence between capital and labor called forth a host of investigating groups, each bent on manufacturing and distributing its own variety of ideology. After state mediation efforts failed, a congressional (the Foster) subcommittee on mines and mining looked at the conflict in January 1914. Heightened violence culminating in the Ludlow Massacre stunned the nation in April 1914, leading President Wilson to appoint the Davis-Fairley Commission, which began work in May 1914. The Rockefeller Foundation itself presented plans for a study of Industrial Peace in October 1914, shortly after the Davis-Fairley Commission issued findings and recommendations that were extremely critical of, and unacceptable to, the Rockefeller enterprises. The Walsh Commission suspected the proposed Rockefeller Foundation study as a potential whitewash of the Rockefeller business group's role in the coal wars. It immediately subpoenaed the foundation officials involved and also intensified its own formal investigations in Colorado. With the Rockefeller Foundation and the Walsh Commission at odds over their investigations, President Wilson appointed a final commission headed by Seth Low to provide yet another viewpoint.[45] Thus a congressional committee, three federal commissions, and the RF were all engaged in competitive ideology formation, investigating violence between labor and capital in general and the Colorado coal wars in particular, between 1913–1916.

Putatively, these investigating groups were to articulate the national and the public interest, to make no prior assumptions about the rights and wrongs or possible solutions to the problem under investigation. In practice, interest groups engaged in elaborate manipulations of the appointment process, each striving to have appointments awarded to persons who accepted their frame of reference. For example, when Louis Brandeis was suggested by President Wilson as a possible head of the Industrial Relations Commission, Ralph Easley, director of the business-dominated National Civic Federation, exhorted Wilson to change his mind. Easley found Brandeis objectionable because Brandeis had suggested allowing representatives of the radical Industrial Workers of the World (IWW) to participate on the commission while Easley was prepared to tolerate only members of the more conservative American Federation of Labor (AFL).[46]

The four federal investigating groups— headed by Walsh, Foster, Davis-Fairley, and Low—were all led by people who accepted industrial capital as an economic system while recognizing a need for reform. These bodies, however, did take distinct positions on the degree of reform needed to establish peace in industrial relations. The Low Commission, for example, favored reforms wrought without benefit of union recognition. The Walsh Commission went so far as to solicit the testimony of Socialists and IWW representatives, and pushed, in its final report, for far-reaching reforms that anticipated the labor laws of the 1930s.[47] These federal bodies, then, produced and disseminated various brands of reform ideology, and suggest some of the "competition" the RF faced in its efforts.

The Rockefeller Foundation was a belated, privately sponsored entry into the ideological debate over industrial relations. The Rockefeller's most ideologically sensitive advisors, like Jerome Greene, were new recruits to the Rockefeller enterprises and worked closely with JDR, Jr., to modify the well-established conservative, even reactionary, image associated with JDR, Sr. Still, the small, closely knit staff was able to plot the foundation's ideological course with much greater control than the more democratically organized investigating bodies with whom the foundation would compete in presenting industrial ideology to the public.[48] And its $100 million resource base guaranteed a certain impact.

The foundation officials considered their options carefully. About the time that the Walsh Commission began operations, members of the Rockefeller group considered joining forces with other corporate leaders interested in ideology formation. They attended

> a conference...held between representatives of some of the largest financial interests of this country, in order to see whether something might be done to relieve the general unrest through some well-organized agency of investigation and publicity.[49]

At this conference two approaches emerged, each designed to educate the citizenry in procapitalistic ideology and thus relieve unrest. One view saw the difficulty rooted in the poor quality of facts

and interpretation available on social and economic issues. Accordingly, "what was needed was a constant stream of correct information, put before the public by a sort of publicity bureau" to reach "the middle and lower classes upon whom the demagogues chiefly preyed." This bureau would support prompt and detailed information on current topics of controversy: labor disputes, rail rates, tariffs, and the like.[50]

The Rockefeller representatives at the conference proposed an alternative strategy of public enlightenment. Although they accepted the usefulness of such a publicity organization, they also wanted a permanent research organization to manufacture knowledge on these subjects. While a publicity organization would "correct popular misinformation," the research institution would study the "causes of social and economic evils," using its reputation for disinterestedness and scientific detachment to "obtain public confidence and respect," for its findings. And, of course, the research findings could be disseminated through the publicity bureau as well as other outlets. However, the conference "came to naught because of the fundamental difference of opinion" among these large financial interests.[51]

Operating by themselves, Rockefeller Foundation officials continued to discuss plans for ideology production. In 1914 they considered a Department of Social Work that paralleled Sage efforts and an Institute for Economic Research similar to the Carnegie Institute of Washington.[52] However, events that touched the Rockefeller business operations suggested the project on which the foundation finally settled.

The Colorado strike lasted through the winter of 1913–1914. The miners endured the hardship and privation of life in tent cities after they were evicted from company towns. Violence between the coal firms' private armies and the strikers was without end. As a major owner, John D. Rockefeller, Jr., was called to explain to the Foster congressional subcommittee why his firm—Colorado Fuel and Iron—had not agreed to arbitration. In testimony he later compromised when confronted with documents subpoenaed by the Walsh Commission, Rockefeller argued that he had no personal part in his managers' actions. In effect, he took the position of an absentee owner out of touch with the local management, unable to influence them on a technical matter: arbitration.[53]

Two weeks after Rockefeller testified before the Foster subcommittee, the Colorado situation exploded into open warfare. On April 20, 1914, the Colorado militia called up by the governor to contain violence attacked a tent city, looted, and fired on tents in what has come to be known as the Ludlow Massacre. Colorado's union leaders retaliated by asking its membership to move by force of arms against the coal companies' armies and the state guard. President Wilson declared a state of insurrection and sent in federal troops.[54]

With the Ludlow Massacre, the Rockefeller group found itself at the very center of a national ideological conflict, for the violence repelled the nation and the insurrection threatened the social order. Further, many correctly suspected that JDR, Jr., had been less than forthright before the Foster subcommittee on his role in the Colorado coal wars. In fact, the eastern officials of the Rockefeller group had actively supported the strategy and tactics developed by the company's western managers, who had pressured the Colorado governor on the state guard's use, with Ludlow as the result.[55] To deal with the heated ideological climate, President Wilson appointed another commission, this one headed by Hywell Davis, a Kentucky coal capitalist, and W. R. Fairley, a former United Mine Worker (UMW) official, to ease the Colorado situation, if at all possible.[56] The Walsh Commission was also stepping up its investigations in Colorado. The Rockefeller interests at this point were clearly vulnerable to serious ideological attack.

To meet the crisis after Ludlow, the Rockefeller group planned an ideological offensive mounted by both the corporation and the foundation. They sought out experts to give the Rockefeller empire an image that stressed its concern with public welfare as well as private gain. Ivy Lee, one of the first professional public relations men, was paid out of corporate coffers. He was joined by William Lyon Mackenzie King, a Canadian labor specialist, who served initially as a consultant and later as an employee of the Rockefeller enterprises. But not the least of King's major contributions to meet the Ludlow crisis was his agreement to engage in a foundation-funded solo study presented to the public as an impartial "Investigation of Industrial Relations to Promote Industrial Peace," while

doing what he could to defend the Rockefeller business interests.[57]

King and his industrial relations work were well known in the United States. Indeed, he testified as a labor expert before the Walsh Commission.[58] In Canada, King had served as minister of labor and had dealt with hundreds of labor disputes. His approach explicitly emphasized the structural depolarization of conflict between capital and labor, while implicitly limiting labor's strike strength and revolutionary potential. For example, he favored "compulsory investigation" which forbade employer lockouts or worker strikes until government investigators had found the facts of the dispute and offered them to the public for its advice and opinion. Compulsory investigation was designed to bring an informed public opinion to bear on the dispute, placing the economic struggle of worker and owner within the political order of the community. However, since industrial production continued while the facts were placed before the public, workers lost their most effective weapon —the strike.

Subjection of economic and potential class conflict to regulation in the name of the community's will was complemented by King's views on union recognition. He thought union recognition should not stand in the way of improving the workers' lot. He accepted company unions as potentially more realistic and democratic than autonomous unions, since they avoided the creation of "union tyrants." Of course, company unions also dampened the potential of autonomous unions to broaden any particular industrial dispute into wider class conflict. In sum, King favored defensive unions within capitalism to offensive unions testing the limits of the established economic order.[59]

After Ludlow, King was asked to join the Rockefeller group. During the summer of 1914, King was in close contact with Rockefeller, offering expert, confidential advice on how to resolve the conflict in Colorado without granting union recognition, a fact not widely known to the public at the time. In August of 1914, the Rockefeller Foundation voted to appoint King formally, effective October 1. King, who had earlier and privately advised Rockefeller on how to handle the Colorado conflict, was now to conduct his "Investigation of Industrial Relations" as an impartial third party representing the public and the foundation.[60]

In September, shortly before King's appointment was announced to the public, the Davis-Fairley Commission issued its report on the Colorado strike. The report viewed the strike as a war and called for a three-year truce, after which new negotiations would begin. The UMW accepted the Davis-Fairley scheme, even though it meant the union would not be recognized. However, Colorado Fuel and Iron Company rejected the Davis-Fairley report, indicating they had another plan. The announcement of King as director of Rockefeller Foundation's "Investigation of Industrial Relations" was made on October 1, 1914. Eight days later, Walsh subpoenaed JDR, Jr., King, and Greene, the foundation's secretary. He was convinced that King's investigation was being funded by the Rockefeller Foundation to whitewash the Rockefeller enterprises. Before the foundation even started its "Industrial Peace" work, it stood suspect of intent to produce ideology favorable to the Rockefeller empire.[61]

During the winter of 1914–15, King devoted his energies to helping the RF deal with the Walsh Commission's inquiries about the propriety of the foundation's project. He helped write the foundation's answers to the commission's many written questions. He also undertook the tutelage of JDR, Jr., preparing him for his appearance before the commission. King "advised, and even preached, in season and out of season, at meal time, in the office, in walks along New York streets, in the subway and in the family car." He also supervised JDR, Jr.'s, series of appearances with union activists, designed to further the Rockefeller's liberalizing public image. JDR, Jr., was an apt pupil. He passed his examination before the Walsh Commission in January 1915 with flying colors.[62] It seemed that the Rockefeller ideological offensive was succeeding.

However, on April 23, 1915, one year after Ludlow, the Walsh Commission released subpoenaed Rockefeller papers to the press that documented JDR, Jr.'s close personal involvement in directing the events that led to Ludlow. In the furor that ensued, foundation operatives were called before the Industrial Relations Commission once again. Walsh—a maverick

Wilsonian Democrat and an expert Kansas City trial lawyer—put JDR, Jr., King, and others into the witness box. Walsh was particularly interested in the relationship between the Rockefeller Foundation and the Rockefeller business empire. In his examinations of JDR, Jr., and Mackenzie King, he pointed out to the public the potential of the Rockefeller Foundation to produce ideology that defended the Rockefeller enterprises. Under questioning, JDR, Jr., maintained his position taken at the Foster subcommittee hearings, namely that the foundation was separate from the corporation, that it was established for the common good rather than Rockefeller's private interest, and that King was an impartial investigator. Walsh then produced correspondence from summer 1914 between King, now director of the Rockefeller Foundation Industrial Peace study, and Rockefeller, owner and director of the corporation, that spelled out King's plan for containing militant labor in Colorado without union recognition. While JDR, Jr., compromised his earlier testimony, Walsh hammered home the interlocking relationship between foundation and corporation again and again, pointing to the impossibility of the foundation's impartiality, and labeling the King project as an exercise in ideology rather than a scientific investigation.[63]

When King testified, he took the position that he had functioned as a technical expert advising Rockefeller on modern means of industrial peace in Colorado while conducting a more general study of the same phenomena worldwide. He argued that his work for Rockefeller was technical and did not affect his impartiality. However, when Walsh asked if the technical expert in a democracy should use his talents by placing the facts as he sees them before the public, or by advising those with power and influence, King indicated his preference for serving power: "More will come about" more quickly "than...years spent...trying to focus [popular] opinion" on "industrial conditions." King betrayed the propensity of the period's social science experts to serve power rather than public, and confirmed Walsh's point that social scientists working for foundations might well have a proclivity for gathering facts most useful to the men and women who endowed the foundations.[64]

In its *Final Report*, the Walsh Commission addressed the issue of the service of experts and social scientists to their resource suppliers. The *Report* denounced foundation support for social science research. It questioned the researchers' ability to maintain scientific integrity while investigating social problems when their work was begin paid for by those who had interests in the conclusions reached. The *Report* asked if foundations set up by corporate capitalists should fund research on socially controversial issues, issues that in a democracy should be decided by a public unswayed by interpretations manufactured by social scientists on foundation payrolls.[65]

The Walsh Commission's critique of social science funding culminated in recommendations for federal regulatory legislation for foundations; this was not enacted. However, the Walsh Commission seems to have had some effect on the manufacture of ideology in the progressive era. Shortly after the *Final Report* was issued, the CIW shut down the Department of Economics and Sociology, abruptly ending thirteen years of funding. Only a year previously the institute had seriously entertained plans to make the department permanent rather than issuing funds on an annual basis. At the RF, King continued on the foundation payroll, producing a highly personal book, *Industry and Humanity*,[66] at the end of four years. But his previously announced full-dress investigation of worldwide industrial conditions never took place.

The Walsh Commission, then, raised the question as to whether foundations magnificently endowed by great capitalists produced objective research or ideology. The *Final Report* suggested that ideology was more likely than objectivity. The principal foundations engaged in direct support of social research on ideology-determining issues (Carnegie and Rockefeller) seemed initially to withdraw their resources. However, they did not cease funding social research altogether. After the hiatus caused by the Great War, the learned foundations—perhaps taking their cue from Walsh's insistence that mixing funding with direct project management automatically invalidated results—began jointly funneling their resources through academic holding companies such as the Social Science Research Council (SSRC) and the American Council of Learned Societies (ACLS).

The SSRC was formed in 1924 and acted as a conduit for foundation funds to social science

projects, fellows, conferences, and publications. Run by the disciplinary associations, the SSRC was granted $28 million between 1924 and 1960. Most of this funding came from three sources: $14.6 million from Rockefeller, $5.5 million from Carnegie, and $6.4 million from Ford (for further discussion see Seybold chapter) [not reprinted here]. The ACLS was formed in 1919 to represent several learned societies in an International Union of Academics. It evolved into a mechanism for channeling foundation monies to support foreign language and area studies in the main. From 1925–1960 it received $20 million from foundations, of which $11.5 million came from the Rockefeller, the Carnegie, and the Ford.[67] By such arrangements, the foundations tacitly met one of the tests set out by the Walsh Commission: funds were now given through intermediaries. Whether such mediation answers the basic question of objective research versus ideology is a topic for another occasion.

Looking Backwards: Why the Foundations' Experiments in Ideology Formation Failed in the Progressive Period

In the progressive era foundations such as Carnegie, Russell Sage, and Rockefeller tried to bring their resources to bear on ideology formation in the public sector. Foundation leaders and managers fully realized the problems presented by a free marketplace of ideas in a democratic society undergoing rapid capitalistic industrialization. Concentrated wealth and power coexisted uneasily with widespread poverty and alienation in a political democracy that gave the masses a voice in government. As representatives of capital, they clearly saw the potential threat posed to their control of the economy by popular, organized anticapitalist groups offering alternative ideological interpretations of power arrangements. Accordingly, they began using their resources to experiment with methods of producing, distributing, and, indeed, imposing an ideology that justified industrial capital.

Surely Jerome Greene, secretary of the Rockefeller Foundation, was speaking to such problems, when in a memo to the foundation's directors, he wrote:

The early demonstration that the Foundation was seeking the best possible way of keeping alive its sense of responsibility to the people and of keeping in touch with the varied and changing needs of the country, would have a moral effect on the public that would greatly strengthen the Foundation's position and enlarge its influence. This is a vitally important consideration at a time when large aggregations of capital, even for philanthropic purposes, are regarded with suspicion—a suspicion which might lead to dissolution and the enforced distribution of funds in ways that might greatly injure their productiveness.[68]

Fears like Greene's about the dissolution and enforced distribution of great aggregations of capital were not simply upper-class paranoia. The *Final Report* of the Walsh Commission contained a full section devoted to what it styled "the concentration of wealth and influence." This section painstakingly and clearly linked together the large aggregations of capital so legitimate in Greene's mind and the enormous potential influence of foundations like the Rockefeller. It damned this link as corrosive to American democracy and called for further government investigation directed toward eventual popular control of philanthropic foundations via legislation.[69]

But as the Walsh Commission's Final Report recommendations fell on barren soil, so too did the foundations' first experiments at ideology formation during the progressive period. Looking backwards to understand this failure of serious and well-funded capitalists to realize their will, it is clear that foundation trustees and managers were fundamentally concerned with abolishing competition among political-economic ideologies. In a sense, the open and diversified marketplace of ideas mirrored the problems of inefficiency and instability industrial capitalists faced in the national economy. When the Sage, Carnegie, and Rockefeller Foundations entered into the process of ideology formation, they were faced with a threefold task: (1) the design and production of a new standardized industrial ideology, one justifying the power arrangements making possible the previously unthinkable accumulation of capital, such as that used to endow the foundations; (2) the marketing and dissemination of

such an ideology; and (3) the creation of a unified public to consume that ideology.

Since the genius of industrial capitalists and their managers—men such as those who sat on the foundation boards—lay not in creation, whether technical or ideational, but in organization, they applied these talents to the tasks of ideological formation. Rather than attempting to invent ideology anew, the foundations initially used their resources to organize and rationalize existing knowledge production groups already engaged in approaching the issues of the day from a position favorable to their interests. Thus, the CIW provided funding for established AEA economists who had been working piecemeal on uncoordinated research that embodied wholehearted and shared acceptance of the newly emerging organizational forms of industrial capital. Russell Sage poured resources into those professionalizing groups able to convert local and idiosyncratic charity organizations into more systematic services. The Rockefeller Foundation, before the Ludlow crisis, hoped to orchestrate its proposed publicity bureau and research institute in a systematic counterpoint against socialist, populist, and other oppositional critics of capitalism, creating a great chord of ideological containment and consensus.

The foundations' initial approach to ideology manufacture was not formal. Trustees and managers were not interested in construction of a theoretical statement of a set of interrelated ideas that systematically explained and projected the dynamics of existing and future power arrangements in society. Formal development of ideology systems was elitist in tradition; foundation decision-makers recognized this was unsuited to the tenets and workings of a democratic society. Instead, foundation trustees and managers were pragmatic with regard to ideology. They looked for what worked and hoped to see a viable ideology emerge from this process.

To illustrate, the resources Carnegie and Russell Sage devoted to the support of economic research and social service were initially directed toward the examination and solution of controversial issues around which ideology coalesced. Thus in 1904 CIW-AEA economists began investigating the development of manufacturing, the organization of the economy, social legislation, and the role of the state in mediating between private capital and public welfare; all were issues that underlined power arrangements in society. Russell Sage in 1907 began engaging in a variety of practices designed to ameliorate poverty, an obvious manifestation of such power structures.

As the projects funded by these foundations materialized, the possibilities and limitations of expert intellectual and professional workers were revealed. The Russell Sage Foundation, from its 1907 beginning, emphasized word as well as deed, uniting its subsidized media—the *Survey*, books, pamphlets—with community action under the direction of professionals. The Carnegie Institute, after 1910, no longer asked economists to develop predictive capabilities. It accepted instead the economists' own union of ideology and technique; the experts who wrote on railroad regulation also served on the Interstate Commerce Commission. The Rockefeller Foundation, drawing upon these and its creators' previous philanthropic experiences, was able by 1913 to formulate demands upon intellectual workers with somewhat greater clarity and precision. As we have seen, the RF's managers were alive to the potential of expert professionals like Mackenzie King to shape public opinion. However, these managers also hoped their funded authorities would ground their efforts in practical problem solving. As John D. Rockefeller, Jr., said in his testimony before the Industrial Relations Commission,

> ...merely scientific investigation, an academic study, simply the collection of facts would not seem...sufficiently worthwhile to the board of directors of the Rockefeller Foundation. Their hope is that under Mr. King's leadership [in the Industrial Peace study] something that will appeal to the labor interests of the country, to the capitalist interests of the country, may result. If it does not appeal to both these groups, if the result of the study is not something practical that both desire to try and many find to work, that is the end of it; nothing will have been accomplished.[70]

In sum, the foundations came to identify ideology manufacture as a major purpose underlying resource deployment, and its production was joined to the pragmatic solution of specific problems. This resulted in three related but distinct modes of ideology manufacture. First, ideologies of practice arose out of the confrontation and amelioration of actual, concrete social problems within industrializing capitalism. This occurred, for example, in social work. Second, ideologies of technique developed from the concentrated energies of intellectual workers on the rationalization of technical problems within existing social arrangements. Such was the case in academic economics. Third, ideologies of structure emerged to describe and value a political economy, midway between the extremes of laissez-faire capitalism and socialism. Typical producers included university-based sociologists and Protestant theologians sympathetic to, but not deeply involved in, "the Social Gospel." Since each of these three modes of ideology production created its own separate ideological content, the foundations ended up subsidizing an overall ideology with two main characteristics: (1) it was aggressively pragmatic and intellectually inconsistent, while (2) consistently defending capitalism. Foundations were not concerned with theoretical elegance; they sponsored a tactical ideology whose very lack of structure gave strategic advantage by rendering meaningful critiques extremely difficult.

Beyond production, foundations—through professors and other professionals who claimed objectivity and value neutrality in their practice and publications—marketed ideology that justified industrial capital. Professionals were sought out to mediate the idea flow from corporate capital to public in their role as experts representing no constituency other than science, since, as Jerome Greene, a secretary of the Rockefeller Foundation, noted, "this generation has, in large measure, accepted the principle that exact knowledge of underlying facts must be the basis of all movements looking toward betterment and progress."[71] Professionals willing to serve foundation goals were not hard to find, for once industrial capital was accepted by professionals as the framework in which betterment and progress would occur, social issues became technical problems with these ideational assumptions embedded therein. Then the professions could perform latent ideological functions while correctly claiming a manifest value neutrality.

However, the foundations' efforts in manufacturing and marketing ideology were not enough to eliminate competing products. The always complex problems of ideology distribution were intensified because media lagged behind other industries in terms of the technical sophistication, centralization, and national integration that facilitate control by groups in possession of significant amounts of capital. In the progressive era, well before the advent of electronic media, almost any organized and determined group, sect, or party could command significant means of ideology production by running a printing press, renting a headquarters and meeting hall, speaking on the labyrinth lecture circuit, and otherwise moving into the marketplace of ideas. Ideological variety was manifested in the myriad daily and weekly newspapers and in the plethora of journals of the period, and fed by an ever-rising literacy level, most dramatically attested to by the growth of public high schools. In 1870 there were 500 secondary schools; in 1920, 10,000. Increasing ease of access to the means of ideology production combined with rising literary sophistication to enable competing groups both to proselytize and maintain their own internal cohesion. This sharpened rather than blunted ideological struggles, and also created a public of considerable diversity in taste, style, and thought. This diversity made it difficult to create a simple and direct ideology distribution mechanism.[72]

The creation of a unified public to consume ideology was a still more difficult issue. Given the decentralized media, the readily accessible means of ideological production, and the resulting diversity of publics, the foundations directed their efforts toward the increasingly self-conscious white-collar sector. An emerging consensus and common purpose might be strengthened by mobilizing the middle sector to pay attention to, and even participate in, ameliorative reforms sponsored by foundations. Further, such social action might also provide industrial workers with a sense that reform was a possibility. As we have seen, foundations created publications and filled them with copy oriented in this direction. In addition, the university classroom and the professional school were increasingly tied into this process. Professors disseminated and elaborated reformist ideas to a captive student audience already committed, by their very presence in college, to vaguely white-collar, even capitalistic, values and norms.

By the close of the progressive era with World War I, the foundations' experiment at pragmatic ideology formation had borne little fruit. While they did succeed at manufacturing some ideology, they could not solve the problems of distribution and consumption. The nub was that while they could deploy their own resources, they could not deny other groups the use of competing resources. Socialists, populists, and all sorts of oppositional anticapitalist groups continued their own ideological production, distribution, and consumption. In addition, a great variety of ideology poured out of investigating bodies where class-conscious representatives of workers' interests refused to endorse amelioration in which limits were set by industrial capital. For such reasons, as well as a desire to make a contribution to the war effort, the foundations by 1917 had temporarily withdrawn from ideology formation.

The Great War, however, served to create the unified public with some sense of consensus and common purpose that foundation leaders had earlier sought. After the war, while many Americans were still moved by nationalist sentiment, groups holding deviant ideologies were decimated through the use of wartime statutes (the Red Scare, the Palmer Raids, mass deportations).[73] In the 1920s foundations returned to funding research on social issues. However, this time foundations worked in a field from which many deviant ideologies had been uprooted, where the consensus of normality obtained, fostered by the rapid rise of centralized electronic media, and where the idea structure of professionals already supported industrial capital. Foundations were now able to direct their resources toward ideological formation unbothered by a free marketplace of ideas, and with a much greater probability of success.

Notes

1. For documentation of the period's economic turbulence, see Robert Wiebe, *The Search for Order, 1877–1920* (New York: Hill and Wang, 1967); and William Appleman Williams, *Contours of American History* (Chicago: Quadrangle, 1966); as well as the more specialized studies of Gabriel Kolko, *The Triumph of Conservatism: A Reinterpretation of American History* (Chicago: Quadrangle, 1967); Philip Foner, *A*

History of the Labor Movement in the United States, Vols. 3 and 4 (New York: International, 1963, 1964); and James Weinstein, *The Corporate Ideal in the Liberal State, 1900-1918* (Boston: Beacon, 1968). Consult Samuel P. Hays, *The Response to Industrialism, 1885-1914* (Chicago: University of Chicago Press, 1957), on the farming hinterland as internal colony; and Michael Meeropol, "W. A. Williams' Historiography," *Radical America* (July–August 1970): 29–49, for a careful review of the period's depression statistics.

2. Our sense of "ideology" follows that advanced in Kenneth M. Dolbeare and Patricia Dolbeare, *American Ideologies* (Chicago: Markham, 1971). In selecting the Sage, Rockefeller and Washington Institute of the Carnegie Foundations for examination, we make no claim for statistical representativeness. Indeed, American foundations as they now exist were largely invented and institutionalized in the progressive period, and their explosive growth defies the usual sampling methodologies. See, for details, Barbara Howe, "The Emergence of the Philanthropic Foundation as an American Social Institution, 1900-1920," Ph.D. Thesis, Department of Sociology, Cornell University, 1976, and her chapter in this [original] book; on growth, Ernest V. Hollis, *Philanthropic Foundations and Higher Education* (New York: Columbia University Press, 1938).

However, we do claim that Sage, Rockefeller, and Carnegie were the leading creative foundations of the time. This view was common in the period itself. See, for example, the comments of the Socialist leader Morris Hillquit, *Industrial Relations: Final Report and Testimony Submitted to Congress by the U. S. Commission on Industrial Relations*, United States Senate, Doc. 415, 64th Congress, 1st Session (Washington, D.C.: USGPO, 1916), Vol. 8, pp. 8263–8275 (hereafter cited as *Final Report*) as well as comments in the *New York Times* by Rev. Joseph H. Rockwell, President of Brooklyn College, cited in "Summary of Criticism Directed against the Rockefeller Foundation," Dept. of Surveys and Exhibits, International Health Board, January 1919, pp. 2, 4 (available at the Rockefeller Foundation Archives, Hillcrest, Pocantico Hills, North Tarrytown, N.Y.; hereafter RFA). Accordingly, we present our analysis as not at all

statistically representative of foundations operating in the period, but rather as an examination of the leading edge of their ideological work, work that cut the pattern for other foundations and later times.

3. For Sage as robber baron, see Matthew Josephson, *The Robber Barons* (New York: Harcourt, Brace & World, 1962), pp. 209-211 and elsewhere.

4. John M. Glenn, Lilian Brandt, and F. Emerson Andrews, *Russell Sage Foundation, 1907-1946* (New York: Russell Sage Foundation, 1974), pp. 3–13.

5. Ibid., p. 5.

6. On the organization of nineteenth-century social service, see Robert Bremner, *From the Depths: The Discovery of Poverty in the U.S.* (New York: NYU Press, 1956); and Robert Trattner, *From Poor Law to Welfare State* (New York: Free Press, 1974).

7. For analysis of the dilemma of consumption—and hence wages and poverty versus capital formation during industrialization, consult Karl de Schweimitz, *Industrialization and Democracy* (New York: Free Press, 1964), pp. 56–186. For data on wealth, power, and political corruption, see Wiebe, *Search for Order*, and Hays, *Response to Industrialism*.

8. Blanche D. Coll, *Perspectives in Public Welfare* (Washington, D.C.: USGPO, 1969), pp. 44–62 documents the growth of COSs in the late nineteenth century, and Trattner, *Welfare State*, p. 195, notes the COS takeover of the NCCC.

9. The founding board is listed in Glenn et. al., *Russell Sage Foundation*, pp. 9–10.

10. Ibid., pp. 27–28, 222–224, 685–701.

11. Ibid., p. 181. Apparently participation was not always voluntary, as when Prof. W. F. Willcox seems to have offered his students to the Ithaca Survey.

12. Ibid., pp. 177–196, 93–96.

13. Ibid., pp. 224–225, 685–686, 689–690.

14. For Sage support of the emerging social work profession, see ibid., p. 223*ff.*, as well as pp. 685–691, which lists the Foundation's first fifty-six grants made between 1907 and 1920, almost all furthering the cause.

15. "Remarks by Mr. Carnegie on Presenting the Trust Deed," *Carnegie Institute of Washington Yearbook* (*CIWY* hereafter) 1 (January 1903): xiv.

16. "Proceedings of the Executive Committee," *CIWY* 1 (January 1903): xxxviii.

17. "Report of the Advisory Committee on Economics," Appendix A—Reports of Advisory Committees, *CIWY* 1 (January 1903): 1–2.

18. C. D. Wright, "Report of the Department of Economics and Sociology," *CIWY* 3 (January 1905): 55–64.

19. "Memorial—Carroll Davidson Wright, 1840–1909," *CIWY* 8 (February 1910): 13. Farnam's father was president of the Chicago and Rock Island Railroad; Clark's father was a manufacturer of milling machinery in Providence, R.I. Both were educated at Ivy League schools, received Ph.D.s in Germany, became economics professors at Yale and Columbia, respectively, leaders of the AEA, and served as foundation managers with Carnegie: Farnam as chairman of the Department of Economics and Sociology after Wright's death, and Clark as director of the Division of Economics and History of the Carnegie Endowment for International Peace, 1911–1923. Farnam was active in national Civil Service reform work at the time of his appointment to the Advisory Board of the CIW; Clark had recently served as Governor Theodore Roosevelt's representative to the Chicago Conference on Trusts.

20. For the importance of Clark and Seligman in the organization of the AEA, see Joseph Dorfman, *The Economic Mind in American Civilization*, vol. 3, 1865–1918 (New York: Viking, 1949), pp. 205–208. Wright was also a charter member (1885), while Farnam joined in 1890 and was active throughout the progressive era. See also A. W. Coates, "The First Two Decades of the AEA," *American Economic Review* 50 (September 1960): 555–574. For Seligman as negotiator between CIW and the AEA see "Report of the Secretary," *Publications of the American Economics Association* (hereafter *PAEA*) Part 1, 3rd ser. 5 (December 1903): 42.

21. For AEA expressions of gratitude, see "Report of the Secretary," *PAEA* Part 1, 3rd ser. 5 (December 1903): p. 42. The seven AEA leaders were Wright, W. F. Willcox, W. Z. Ripley, D. R. Dewey, J. W. Jenks, H. W. Farnam, and H. B. Gardner. Many other prominent AEA economists were assigned subsections of investigation under these section heads; see C. D.

Wright, "Report of the Department of Economics and Sociology," *CIWY* 3 (January 1905): 55–64.

22. C. D. Wright, "An Economic History of the United States," *PAEA* Part 1, 3rd ser. 4 (May 1905): 390–409.

23. E. R. A. Seligman, "Social Aspects of Economic Law," *PAEA* Part 1, 3rd ser. 5 (December 1904): 73.

24. The original concept of the project is most clearly stated by H. W. Farnam, when he reviewed the department on taking over as chairman in 1909. See H. W. Farnam, chairman, "Department of Economics and Sociology," *CIWY* 8 (February 1910): 81–83. The estimate of total project cost is first given in "Report of the Advisory Committee on Economics," *CIWY* 1 (January 1903): 1–2. The total figure is cumulated from the annual amounts given in the yearbooks.

25. See for example, E. R. A. Seligman, "Economic and Social Progress," *PAEA* 3rd ser. 4 (February 1903): 70, 64.

26. D. C. Gilman, "Report of the President of the Institute," *CIWY* 4 (January 1906): 23.

27. E. R. A. Seligman, "Economic and Social Progress," p. 70.

28. C. D. Wright, "Economics and Sociology: Report of the Director," *CIWY* 5 (January 1907): 163.

29. H. W. Farnam, "Department of Economics and Sociology," *CIWY* 8 (February 1910): 81–93.

30. C. D. Wright, "Department of Economics and Sociology," *CIWY* 7 (February 1909): 74–85.

31. "Report of the President," *CIWY* 8 (February 1910): 30–31. The department did produce eight volumes of "Indexes of Economic Material in the Documents of the States of the U.S." by 1909. However, the department received a separate allocation for this project, which was not regarded as fulfilling the economic history of the United States for which the collaborators had contracted.

32. "Report of the President of the Institute," *CIWY* 4 (January 1906): 17, 23, 31.

33. See H. W. Farnam, "Department of Economics and Sociology," *CIWY* 8 (February 1910): 71–83, for his plans for organization. For the CIW's reaction see "Report of the President 1910," *CIWY* 9 (January 1911): 22, in which the

president of the institute indicates the department will get no more funds. Due to Farnam's efforts, the institute reconsidered and plans for a permanent department were underway by 1913. See "Report of the President," *CIWY* 12 (January 1913): 18.

34. "Proceedings of Executive Committee," *CIWY* 1 (January 1903): xiv.

35. The same men who wrote with Carnegie funds on labor legislation, railroads and securities commissions, arbitration of capital and labor disputes also aided in implementing the intervention strategies they participated in designing. Indeed, one of Farnam's constant complaints was that his section heads were unable to complete their work because they were called to public service. See H. W. Farnam, "Department of Economics and Sociology," *CIWY* 8 (February 1910): 82. In brief illustration of the interrelationship of research and practice, the work done by D. R. Dewey, head of the CIW money and banking section, was slated to be published by the National Monetary Commission; H. W. Farnam, head of the section on social legislation as well as chairman of the department, was also president of the American Association of Labor Legislation; J. R. Commons, who took over the section on labor after Wright's death, pooled his Carnegie funds with other monies to support his ongoing work on labor history. He largely turned over this effort to Selig Perlman and other University of Wisconsin graduate students because his energies were occupied by his appointments to the U.S. Industrial Relations Commission and the Wisconsin Industrial Commission. B. M. Meyer, head of the section on transportation, was called to the Interstate Commerce Commission. V. S. Clark, head of the section of manufacturing, had to turn his work over to Francis Walker of the U.S. Bureau of Corporations because he was engaged on census work in Hawaii, and on government missions in Japan and Manchuria. Some also entered private service; E. Parker, head of the mining section, gave up his U.S. Geological Survey position to become director of the Anthracite Bureau of Information for mining corporations in Pennsylvania. See H. W. Farnam, "Department of Economics and Sociology," *CIWY* 8–15 (February 1910–February 1916).

36. H. W. Farnam, "Department of Economics and Sociology," *CIWY* 15 (February 1916), pp. 101–102.

37. Ibid.

38. Philip Taft and Philip Ross, "American Labor Violence: Its Causes, Character and Outcome," in Hugh D. Graham and Ted R. Gurr (eds.), *A History of Violence in America* (New York: Praeger, 1969), pp. 281–395; quotation at p. 320.

39. On differences in corporate ideology and tactics in the period, see Weinstein, *Corporate Ideal*; Marguerite Green, *The National Civic Federation and the American Labor Movement, 1900–1925* (Washington, D.C.: Catholic University of America Press, 1956); Albert K. Steigerwalt, *The National Association of Manufacturers, 1895–1914* (Ann Arbor: University of Michigan Bureau of Business Research, 1964); and Foner, *History Labor Movement*.

40. "Testimony of John D. Rockefeller, Jr., *Final Report*, Vol. 8, p. 7776.

41. For a discussion of Rockefeller holdings in Colorado Fuel and Iron, see Peter Collier and David Horowitz, *The Rockefellers: An American Dynasty* (New York: NAL, 1977), pp. 106–107, 128n.

42. Jerome Greene, Secretary of the Foundation, Memo RFDR No. 12, October 22, 1913, "To the Members of the Rockefeller Foundation," p. 10ff. (RFA).

43. On the composition of such commissions, see Weinstein, *Corporate Ideal*, p. 7; and Foner, *History Labor Movement*, pp. 61–66.

44. Graham Adams, Jr., *Age of Industrial Violence 1910–1915: The Activities and Findings of the U.S. Commission on Industrial Relations* (New York: Columbia University Press, 1966). See also Weinstein, *Corporate Ideal*, pp. 172–213.

45. Fred A. McGregor, *The Fall and Rise of Mackenzie King: 1911–1919* (Toronto: Macmillan of Canada, 1962), pp. 121–130.

46. Green, *National Civic Federation*, pp. 349–350.

47. On the Low Report see McGregor, *Mackenzie King;* on the Walsh Commission see Weinstein, *Corporate Ideal*, pp. 211–212.

48. Collier and Horowitz, *Rockefellers*, pp. 95–133; and McGregor, *Mackenzie King*, pp. 143–144.

49. Jerome Greene, Memo RFDR, No. 12, p. 15. Such conferences were not unusual, at least so far as philanthropic funding was concerned. . . . Unfortunately, Greene's account of this conference does not name the "largest financial interests" it mentions.

50. Greene, Memo RFDR, No. 12, p. 16.

51. Ibid., pp. 16–17.

52. Jerome Greene, Memo DR 32, "Future Organization of the Rockefeller Foundation," 1914, pp. 2–9 (RFA).

53. Adams, *Industrial Violence*, pp. 154–167, contains an account of JDR, Jr's, conflicting testimonies before the Walsh Commission; McGregor, *Mackenzie King*, pp. 121–122.

54. Taft and Ross, *American Labor Violence*, pp. 330–332.

55. The fullest published narrative account of the role of the Rockefeller Eastern officials in the Colorado coal wars is George P. West, *Report on the Colorado Strike* (Washington, D.C.: U.S. Commission on Industrial Relations, 1915). It is based on subpoenaed documents.

56. McGregor, *Mackenzie King*, pp. 120–124.

57. Collier and Horowitz, *Rockefellers*, pp. 109–133; Henry Ferns and Bernard Ostry, *The Age of Mackenzie King* (Toronto: James Lorimer, 1976), pp. 187*ff.*

58. In addition, the Foundation knew King at least via Director Eliot and Secretary Greene. King was a favorite of Harvard's President Charles Eliot, who twice sought King for posts: first in the Economics Department and then as founding head of what evolved into the Harvard Business School. Jerome Greene, then Harvard advisor to Eliot, dissuaded the latter appointment, stressing King's Canadian citizenship. See Herbert Heaton, *A Scholar in Action: Edwin F. Gay* (Cambridge, Mass.: Harvard University Press, 1952), p. 67, and R. MacGregor Dawson, *William Lyon Mackenzie King: A Political Biography, 1874–1923* (Toronto: University of Toronto Press, 1958).

59. On King's approach to industrial relations, see Ferns and Ostry, *Age of Mackenzie King*; and Paul Craven, "An Impartial Umpire: Industrial Relations and the Canadian State, 1900–1911" (Ph.D. thesis, Department of Sociology, University of Toronto, 1978).

60. Dawson, *A Political Biography*, pp. 235–255.

61. McGregor, *Mackenzie King*, pp. 123–124, 129–130.

62. Ibid., pp. 130–143; quotation at p. 131.

63. Adams, *Industrial Violence*, pp. 161–168; Collier and Horowitz, *Rockefellers*, pp. 119, 123–125.

64. McGregor, *Mackenzie King*, pp. 165–174; quotation at pp. 169–170.

65. *Final Report*, Vol. 1, Section V.

66. William L. M. King, *Industry and Humanity* (Toronto: University of Toronto Press, 1973), contains a very useful "Introduction" by David Jay Bercuson, one that reviews reactions to the work, pp. v–xxiv.

67. On the return of the foundations to social science funding in the 1920s, see Ernest Victor Hollis, *Foundations and Higher Education*, p. 248 and elsewhere. For details on SSRC and ACLS funding, see Joseph C. Kiger, "Foundation Support of Educational Innovation by Learned Societies, Councils, and Institutes," in Mathew B. Miles (ed.), *Innovation in Education* (New York: Teachers College Press, 1964), pp. 533–561. For a brief account of the ACLS, consult Whitney J. Oates, "The Humanities and Foundations," in Warren Weaver (ed.), *U.S. Philanthropic Foundations* (New York: Harper and Row, 1967), pp. 300–303.

68. Jerome Greene, 1913, Memo RDFR No. 12, p. 9.

69. *Final Report*, Vol. 1, Section V.

70. Ibid., Vol. 8, p. 7893.

71. Greene, 1913, Memo RFDR, No. 12, pp. 10–11.

72. For an account of the ways in which books could be published before the consolidation of the industry during and after World War II, see Bill Henderson, "Introduction: A Tradition of Do-It-Yourself Publishing," in the *Publish-It-Yourself Handbook: Literary Tradition and How-To*, ed. Bill Henderson (New York: The Pushcart Book Press, 1973), pp. 11–36; Bill Henderson, "Independent Publishing: Today and Yesterday," in *Perspectives on Publishing*, eds. Philip G. Altbach and Sheila McVey (Lexington, Mass.: Lexington Books, 1976), pp. 217–229; Scott Nearing discusses the great accessibility of media in the progressive era in his *The Making*

of a Radical: A Political Autobiography (New York: Harper and Row, Torchbook Library Edition, 1972), especially Chapter 4, "A Teacher Must Communicate," pp. 52–75. On the growth of the public comprehensive secondary school, see Martin Trow, "The Second Transformation of American Secondary Education," in Sam D. Sieber and David E. Wilder (eds.), *The School in Society* (New York: Free Press, 1973), pp. 45–61.

73. For details on repression of this sort during World War I, consult Harry N. Schreiber, *The Wilson Administration and Civil Liberties, 1917–1921* (Ithaca, N.Y.: Cornell University Press); and Robert Justin Goldstein, *Political Repression in Modern America* (Cambridge, Mass., and New York: Schenkman and Two Continents, 1978), pp. 137–163, 547–574.

ARTICLE 31 ⎯⎯⎯⎯⎯⎯⎯⎯⎯⎯
Philanthropy and the Future
Elizabeth T. Boris

Philanthropy means many things to many people. In its broadest sense it covers giving and volunteering for the public good and includes the activities of individual givers, nonprofit institutions and service providers as well as funding intermediaries such as federated fundraising organizations and foundations. Understanding the relationships of this diverse group of institutions to each other and to the wider economic and political system is a challenge that is only beginning to be met. The future of philanthropy hinges on developing a deeper knowledge base and using this knowledge to enhance the ability of nonprofit organizations to serve the public.

With a better knowledge base, we can begin to disentangle the definitional confusion about the boundaries of philanthropy. Traditional charity, defined as personal gifts to the poor, is sometimes understood as the proper sphere of philanthropy. Yet the term "philanthropy" also may mean the search for root causes of social problems and is used to refer to the grantmaking of philanthropic foundations. Neither of the limited definitions covers the advocacy and community based efforts that the nonprofit sector also includes. The definition of philanthropy must be broadened to include the diversity of initiatives that make up the nonprofit arena. Only then can we begin to talk realistically about activities that range from church daycare centers, homeless shelters, and soup kitchens, to environmental groups, advocacy for and against issues such as gun control and abortion, and art museums, dance groups, and others. The organizations, large and small, that conduct these activities reflect the desire of private citizens to have an impact, solve problems and contribute to the quality of life in this society. In the following pages I will briefly mention the trends that I think will have an important impact on philanthropy, broadly defined, and I will elaborate on several of those.

Trends Within Philanthropy

A crystal ball is not necessary to discern the major trends that are currently giving shape to the philanthropy of the future. They include the following:

• First, philanthropy is becoming more visible, both to the public and to scholars. Increased visibility has helped to raise public consciousness about the sector, but coming at a time of government cutbacks in spending on social programs, recognition of philanthropic work has also led to unrealistic expectations of its capacity to meet pressing needs.

• Second, the financial status of many nonprofits has weakened. The loss of government revenues and the slowdown in the growth of giving combined with increased demand for services has led many nonprofits to focus increasing attention on developing revenue for their activities. The growth of the foundation sector of the nonprofit economy has also not kept pace with inflation and thus provides a lower proportion of nonprofit support than in the past.

• Third, within philanthropy there is growing professionalism including an increased emphasis on accountability and a rising concern with ethical conduct. Partly as a result of the financial squeeze, higher priority is being given to management efficiency and organizational effectiveness.

- Fourth, the regulatory climate is becoming more critical as policy makers take on issues of great importance to the sector: tax deductibility of charitable gifts; nonprofit competition with small businesses; taxes on unrelated business income; limits on nonprofit lobbying activities; ceilings on allowable fundraising expenditures, and limitations on foundation grant administrative expenses.
- Fifth, nonprofits are confronting these challenges through cooperative efforts. National, regional, and citywide efforts are being developed to tell the philanthropic story, increase the funding base, improve the management skills, and work with public officials.

These are five major trends internal to philanthropy that will continue to shape the character of the sector through the end of the century. But, they do not operate in a vacuum. The demands of the changing society create the context in which the trends in philanthropy will play out.

External Trends that Will Affect Philanthropy

In the wider society, events are unfolding that will result in an even greater need for the services of the nonprofit sector. Among the many forces that will affect philanthropy, six seem particularly important to mention here.

- First, the demographics of the population are changing dramatically. The population is aging and becoming more ethnically and racially diverse.
- Second, there are greater numbers of women, children, and entire families who are living in poverty. Many are homeless.
- Third, AIDS, crime, and drugs are claiming increasing numbers of victims, thus increasing the need for services, advocacy, and research.
- Fourth, proposed reforms of the educational system, welfare, and medical coverage are gaining momentum and the revitalization of the nation's cities is slowly advancing.
- Fifth, the economy is undergoing a major restructuring through business mergers and acquisitions. These changes will have a major impact on jobs, productivity, and on the performance of the economy as a whole. They will also affect corporate contributions.

- Sixth, environmental issues are generating a newfound sense of urgency as the scope and severity of the problems become evident. These include disposing of toxic wastes, pollution of the oceans and groundwater, acid rain, the degenerating ozone layer and climatic warming, increasing desertification of the land, and the destruction of rainforests.

These are only a few of the forces that are shaping the future. They are not driven by any one sector of society, and the responses to and channeling of these forces will, of necessity, require involvement of a wide spectrum of institutions. Nonprofit service providers, often dealing closely with individuals affected by such unfolding trends, will continue to have a recognized role in meeting human needs. Foundations, universities, and others will be needed to support and conduct research, develop new approaches, and facilitate the exchange of information. But philanthropy will also have a role in the public policy debates that will determine how, as a society, we will confront and manage these challenges.

The future of philanthropy lies at the intersection of these internal and external trends. How well will philanthropy anticipate the coming needs and opportunities for public service? Will there be outreach to the newly emerging groups in society, not only to provide services or grants, but as board and staff members? Will policy makers come to a realistic appreciation of the capacity and potential of philanthropy? Will the field be able to fulfill its role as facilitator of public discussion on major issues? Most fundamentally, will philanthropy and the values of community, commitment, and service that sustain it, survive and flourish in the years to come?

The answers to these questions are not certain. Almost ten years after the publication of Waldemar Nielsen's book, *The Endangered Sector* (1979), there is still justifiable concern about the level of public understanding of the philanthropic sector, the depth of commitment to the existence of that sector, and the survival of the values underlying voluntary giving and service. The vulnerability of philanthropy came as a surprise to many, but since no one posited the existence of an invisible hand to assure its optimal functioning, calculated efforts to improve it and ensure its survival are underway. Increasing the visibility of the field, developing a strong financial base, promoting effective management, and anticipating the changing demographics of the country are among the major strategies.

Visibility

The trend toward increased visibility of philanthropy is healthy and desirable, indeed vital, if philanthropy is to achieve its potential. Many organizations are endeavoring to provide more information to the media and to the public. New nonprofit publications like the *Chronicle of Philanthropy* and the *Nonprofit Times* have emerged and major newspapers are assigning reporters to cover philanthropy. Yet progress is slow. There is still the feeling in some quarters that philanthropy is a private matter, and much individual philanthropy is understandably anonymous.

It is necessary for the public to understand and appreciate the work that is going on. The information flow promotes accountability and provides feedback that has an impact on the internal operations of agencies. Perhaps the greatest immediate benefit is that visibility provides a context for realistic public policy toward nonprofit organizations. Visibility will not, however, always bring positive reactions. Successes and failures, as well as scandals will come to light. But the news, good and bad, will be viewed increasingly in the context of greater knowledge of and appreciation for the accomplishments of nonprofits.

An important challenge confronting this area of American life is not only conveying the idea that important civic work is being done by nonprofit organizations, but that those activities are part of a somewhat distinctive tradition of nonbusiness, nongovernmental efforts to solve problems and promote community. Many people do volunteer and give money to causes they care about, but it is not often that they make the connection between those activities and the existence of a nonprofit, philanthropic, or independent sector. Those names do not convey meaning for most of the population. Often, people think that nonprofits are run by governments, or that they are for-profit businesses. For example, most of

the interns enrolled in a new program designed to place college students in independent sector organizations for a semester of work had no idea what the independent sector was.

Even people who work in nonprofit organizations—hospitals, colleges, museums, and other agencies—may not identify themselves as employees in the philanthropic sector. In reality, the diversity of the institutions is so great that it is difficult to identify a common interest. In recent years, the unifying element has been provided by legislative proposals that would affect the ability of such groups to raise money or put their ideas before the Congress.

These and other legislative issues became the focal point for nonprofits who joined together to address their common needs. The potential negative impacts of such proposals helped to make the sector more visible and more cohesive. The birth of the Independent Sector, a national association of nonprofits with membership from all parts of this field, has provided a unified voice. Regional groups and those with members from subsectors such as health, education, museums, or foundations have also contributed to the public policy debate and initiated communications with the media and policy makers.

Increased visibility and interaction in the legislative arena quickly illuminated the need for better statistics and more in-depth studies of the whole sector as well as the various parts. Laws and regulations were being proposed with little or no information on the present situation or on the potential impact of the changes. Studies commissioned by national organizations filled in the gaps while an active effort to increase scholarly interest in and attention to philanthropy and nonprofit issues was undertaken. Scholars have responded to this vacuum. At present count there are four academic centers devoted to research and hundreds of studies in progress at colleges and universities across the country.[1]

The future of philanthropy will be affected by the research that is being conducted. Lester Salamon has helped to delineate the interdependence of nonprofits, government, and business in the provision of services and enhancement of the quality of American life (1987). Myths about the independence of these institutions from government and from business are being dispelled. Government accounts for about 36 percent of nonprofit revenue, though the proportion varies greatly by area. In addition, the degree to which nonprofit human service agencies depend on fees to help finance their activities (28 percent) puts into perspective the limited role that individual gifts (20 percent)—traditional philanthropy—play in this part of the nonprofit economy. Data from Gallup polls commissioned by the Independent Sector are helping to chart more precisely the extent of giving and volunteer service. This information is vital to our understanding of the importance of such service to the giver as well as to the receiving organization (Independent Sector, 1988). In sum, recent research is permitting us to draw a better picture of the operation of voluntary initiatives today.

That the national and state governments contract with nonprofits to deliver services in our unique version of the welfare state is a surprise to some. But bringing that fact to light invites informed debate on who should be delivering services. Is this mixed system of government, nonprofits, and for-profits an efficient, effective, and humane way to proceed? Where does it work best? Where is it not working? Who is being served? Who is being left out? These questions can now be raised with some assurance that informed answers are possible.

Prospects for Growth in Philanthropy

The financial health of the sector is at risk. Government funding was reduced during the last eight years, just as the demand for services peaked. While fees for services and individual, foundation, and corporate giving continued to grow during most of that period, they did not offset those lost revenues. But, according to the latest estimates in *Giving USA* (1988), the growth rate of giving declined significantly in 1987 for all givers, falling from 9.43 percent in 1985–1986 to 6.45 percent from 1986–1987. Corporate giving, which grew at high rates in the early 1980s, started to level off in 1984 and failed to grow at all in 1987. The factors that affected philanthropic giving are a slowdown in the growth of personal income, the restructuring of the business sector through mergers and acquisitions, the stock market crash which affected some foundations and wealthy donors, the elimination of the non-itemizer deduction for gifts to charity, and the

lowering of the income tax rate which made the tax deductibility of contributions less advantageous to donors.

Philanthropic foundations are also affected. Research reported in *America's Wealthy and the Future of Foundations* (Odendahl, 1987) shows that the rate of formation of new foundations declined over the last twenty years and that foundation assets have not grown relative to the overall economy. In a survey of existing foundations and in over 135 interviews with wealthy donors, we tried to identify the factors that caused them to form foundations. Altruistic concern for the welfare of others and a desire to use wealth to make a difference, as well as the advantages of having a vehicle that facilitates systematic giving are among the major motivations for forming a foundation. Inhibiting factors are the regulations of the 1969 Tax Reform Act and the interpretation of those regulations by attorneys and others who advise wealthy persons about their charitable giving. We found that after 1969 many attorneys would not recommend the formation of a foundation to their clients. They regarded the tax advantages of forming a foundation as less favorable than those found in other charitable vehicles. Advisors placed more emphasis on the tax implications of giving than the donors did. The Council on Foundations, cosponsor of the research, has worked to remove the disincentives to foundation formation, and developed a series of programs to promote the formation of new private foundations, to encourage giving to community foundations, and to strengthen corporate foundations and giving programs (Yankelovitch Group, 1988).

Other recent studies of giving and volunteering also suggest that individuals can be expected to give more to philanthropic activities. Many people believe they should be doing more but have not been asked, or do not know how much they should give (Yankelovitch, 1986). Two national organizations, Independent Sector and United Way of America, have developed programs to encourage more people to participate in philanthropic giving. Independent Sector's campaign promotes the idea that each person should give five percent of yearly income and five hours of volunteer time per week. The impact of these efforts to increase the donor base will probably not be apparent for several years.

Meanwhile, driven by the immediate need to raise additional funds and pressed by increasing competition among nonprofits for gifts, campaigns using direct mail, door to door, and telephone solicitations are expanding. These are expensive and intrusive, but effective. However, the impact of the more aggressive tactics may be counterproductive in the long run. Local efforts to keep out or control solicitors, legislate appropriate levels of fund-raising costs, and otherwise protect the public from the excesses of nonprofit fundraising zeal, whether successful or not, are indications of the negative impact.

Despite the growing sophistication of fundraising techniques and efforts to broaden the donor base, the sector needs a larger and more stable revenue base. Entrepreneurial activities, unrelated businesses, "cause related marketing" (a term copyrighted by the American Express Company), are some of the new approaches, but they are raising fears that the sector is becoming commercialized by its close relationship with businesses. Should nonprofits become identified with certain companies and their products? Will the popular, noncontroversial causes be strengthened at the expense of less popular ones? Will donors become cynical about such "philanthropic" appeals? These questions are being raised with increasing frequency. Of course, when nonprofits began accepting substantial government grants during the late 1960s and 1970s, many feared that government would take over nonprofits, make them dependent, and subvert their missions.

Whether a massive increase over the estimated $93.68 billion given to philanthropy in 1987 is possible is open to question. How much further nonprofits can raise dues and fees is another. Unrelated business income seemed to be one answer before small businesses began to press the issue of unfair competition. Other avenues are being explored by the Exploratory Project on Financing the Nonprofit Sector. That project has sifted through hundreds of ideas looking for some viable sources of additional income. While some models working in a few states have potential, there are no easy solutions, and the ideas that have come forward, for example, the use of surplus bond reserves, special taxing districts, and semi-postal stamps, will require a great deal of cooperation among and between the three sectors to bear fruit (Exploratory Project, 1988).

One small part of improving the financing of the sector is to enhance the ability of the sector to manage the endowments and resources it commands. In the foundation sector, for example, a recent study of investments conducted by Lester Salamon (1988) concluded that while the large foundations are generally obtaining a reasonable return on their investments, the smaller foundations might benefit from a common investment fund like the one that exists for colleges and universities. That idea has also been advanced as a possibility for other endowed institutions. A common fund would reduce investment expenses while increasing, in most cases, the level of professional expertise available to manage the funds.

Raising the level of individual and foundation giving may be successful and if so, will help to meet the financial needs of the sector. But it is doubtful that this will be sufficient. If the sector is to meet the challenges of the future, other sources of income are needed, whether from government grants and contracts, fees for services, or business related activities. A central unknown for the future is how active a role government will take in activities related to the sector. Unfortunately, the desperate need for revenue has the potential to undermine the values that philanthropy espouses. Some fundamental questions must be resolved: Who will be served by nonprofits? Only those able to pay? Who will serve those who cannot afford to pay? What role should government play? Is this country headed toward a system where government serves the poor, nonprofits serve the middle class, and for-profits serve the wealthy?

Efficiency and Effectiveness

Efficiency and effectiveness are two of the most popular buzz words in philanthropy today. Partly as a result of financial necessity and partly as a result of the emphasis in the society during the 1980s on business and profit oriented solutions, nonprofits have had to tighten up their procedures and pay more attention to the way they are doing their jobs. The common stereotype of a "do gooder" or program specialist at the head of an organization that does the best possible work in its field, but has no financial records or management expertise, is becoming a thing of the past.

Donors, both individuals and institutions (foundations, federated campaigns, and governments) want to know that their funds are well-spent. In the competitive environment for grants, and for revenue of all types, nonprofits have had to develop better management and accounting systems. And as the realization dawned that there are 1.2 million nonprofits that employ as many people as the automobile industry and contribute 5.5 percent of the GNP (Hodgkinson and Weitzman, 1986), colleges and universities began to take a greater interest in providing management courses and degree granting programs that address the special needs of nonprofit managers. Currently about 300 colleges and universities offer a concentration in nonprofit management, up from thirty-six just four years ago.

This sudden popularity of nonprofit management courses occurred before a consensus developed on what should be taught. The quest for efficiency was often translated into methods to cut costs. Management theories from business and public administration were taught, sometimes with little knowledge of how those theories should be applied to the somewhat different realities of nonprofit financial and governance structures. Out of this confusion a literature of nonprofit management and research is developing. In time, it will have an important impact on the theory and practice of nonprofit management.[2]

Employees in some parts of the field are beginning to think of themselves as, for example, professional fundraisers or grantmakers and are seeking credentials that certify their expertise. Unions are gaining strength in fields such as higher education and hospitals, but even among institutions that are not unionized, there is growing concern about salary levels, benefits, and working conditions. The long-held notion that individuals who work in nonprofit organizations should accept lower wages than workers in other sectors of the economy is being challenged. It is an issue that will surface with greater frequency in the next few years. What are reasonable salaries for those who work in nonprofits? Should salaries be lower than those paid for comparable positions in business? Should they be higher than government salaries? Is it ethical to pay workers

poverty-level wages? Like business and government, nonprofit surveys that compare salaries across a field of activity or a metropolitan area are becoming more common. The public, including donors and regulators, is interested in the costs of running entities; board and staff executives need to know how much they must pay to attract and retain good workers; and employees want to know if they are being paid a competitive wage.

Among foundations a series of foundation management surveys track salary levels, the demographics of employees and board members, and other issues. Over the past eight years those surveys have documented the rise in the number of women who work in foundations, an increase in the number of women who serve on foundation boards, and a decreasing salary gap between men and women.[3] These trends may reflect the success of the pressure exerted by women through their organization, Women and Foundations/Corporate Philanthropy. It may also be a further reflection of the societywide trend of women entering the labor force in greater numbers. While philanthropy as a whole employs a greater proportion of women and minorities than other sectors of the economy, certain fields that have not been hospitable to these groups, will experience pressure to change. And, given the strong emphasis on efficiency and cost consciousness, women and minorities, who command lower salaries, will be hired in even greater numbers.

Effectiveness, the second key word current in the sector, finds expression in concern with the quality of the services, from college educations to medical care. Are the organizations delivering the appropriate level of service? Could other entities do the job better? Often it seems that organizations do not know what the impact of their work is. Evaluation, comparison with other organizations and with other sectors of the economy, will become more commonplace as the demand for effectiveness accelerates. The early temptation to equate evaluation with counting will give way to more sophisticated qualitative and quantitative analyses. But evaluation can be expensive. It is important to learn when to use it. Unfortunately, those that need such information most may be the ones least able to afford it.

Effectiveness also relates to standards. In higher education there are accrediting bodies that evaluate the degree granting programs. Similar programs exist in the health field. But most other types of institutions operate without such accountability. Standard setting bodies such as the National Charities Information Bureau and the Philanthropic Advisory Service of the Council of Better Business Bureaus have each developed a set of principles that they use to evaluate nonprofits for the benefit of potential donors who subscribe to their services.[4] And some associations have their own codes for their particular members. For example, the Council on Foundations has Recommended Principles and Practices for Effective Grantmaking that all members must subscribe to on their membership application form (Viscusi, 1985).

The concern with effectiveness and with appropriate or ethical behavior will continue to grow. Pressure to clean up abuses in the wake of widely publicized scandals involving televangelists (and others), will result in more attempts to provide self-regulation both to avoid government regulation and to improve the climate of trust among donors and clients.

Ethics is the third term gaining currency. *Foundation News* has been running a section on ethics since January 1983. More recently, national and local philanthropic meetings have been featuring discussions about ethical dilemmas (Johnston, 1988). A renewed concern with ethics in fundraising, in grantmaking, and in governance is coming to the fore. The reasons for renewed attention to ethics are not just related to recent scandals. The impetus to consider ethical questions has deeper roots. As institutions grow and become effective, they have the potential for greater impact—on people and on the society. Increased professionalization, and the lack of formal accountability mechanisms has intensified the need of those engaged in this work to question not only how they do their work, but their values, priorities, and goals (Boris and Odendahl, 1988). Philanthropy will continue to wrestle with ethical issues in the future. The struggle to reach consensus and to delineate the values involved will strengthen the field.[5]

The Changing Demographics of American Society

Of all the external trends that will affect philanthropy, the changing demographics of the nation will necessitate the greatest adjustment and response. The dynamics of American society are changing as the demographics begin to reflect an aging population with a majority of the youth coming from what are now minority ethnic and racial groups. These changes will have an impact on the donor and client base of philanthropy. The trend toward two-earner families that need basic childcare services as well as help to care for aging parents will accelerate. The aging population is already living longer and as that group expands there will be increased demand not only for healthcare and in-home services, but for leisure activities, learning opportunities, cultural events, and meaningful volunteer service programs. The need for youth programs designed for those with limited facility in English will grow as will the demand for nontraditional educational offerings.

Although the level of government involvement in meeting social needs will wax and wane with the temper of the times and the party in power, it is probably safe to say that in many communities, nonprofits will be among the primary service providers or advocates for social services. Of necessity, nonprofits must become more sophisticated about looking ahead to anticipate how the upcoming trends will affect the needs in their communities. An encouraging step is being taken by United Way of America which is helping its members to assess upcoming community needs and develop the planning skills to anticipate effective responses.

Changing demographics are also prompting leaders in this field to think about ways to ensure that the philanthropic tradition is carried on to the next generation. An analysis of textbooks showed that almost none mention the role of nonprofits or philanthropic activities in this country's history. This lack of acknowledgment of individual efforts has led several organizations to promote the teaching of philanthropy in our schools. For example, the American Association of Fund Raising Counsel's Trust for Philanthropy is supporting the development of college courses in philanthropy through a competitive grant process. The Council on Foundations has developed a special project to study the philanthropic heritage and traditions among Americans of Black, Hispanic, and Asian backgrounds. Illuminating the philanthropic traditions within those communities may help to preserve and extend knowledge of them in the wider community.

Philanthropy has always been a major integrating factor in American communities. Self-help projects from volunteer fire fighters and parent–teacher associations to community recreation and redevelopment groups have made neighborhoods livable and created a sense of participation and belonging. Encouraging that tradition in the upcoming years is an important challenge. Young people and new immigrants will need to be cultivated as donors and participants in the philanthropic process. The success of that effort will help to determine the role that philanthropy will play in America's future.

Notes

1. The Program on Non-Profit Organizations at Yale University was started in 1977 under the leadership of John G. Simon. It was the first center for philanthropic research and has been responsible for the publication of several books, over a hundred papers, a seminar series, graduate fellowships, and summer internships. Not until 1986 did the second academic center begin when City University of New York started the Center for the Study of Philanthropy with Kathleen McCarthy at its head. In short order, centers were also started by Duke University and Indiana University. A compilation of research underway in all of these centers and in other organizations throughout the country and abroad are in *Research in Progress* by Virginia Hodgkinson (1988).

2. The literature of nonprofit management is expanding rapidly and is too broad to be reviewed here. Of particular interest, however, is a new collection by Michael O'Neill and Dennis R. Young, *Educating Managers of Nonprofit Organizations* (1988) which explores the question of what nonprofit managers need to know. Other resources are often "how-to" handbooks, for example, the new series of nine booklets by Brian O'Connell. Still others take the unique characteristics of nonprofits and try to apply appropriate management techniques, for example, *Voluntary Nonprofit Enterprise Management* by David Mason (1984). A different type of resource is illustrated by the *Facts on File Dictionary of Nonprofit Organization Management*, by J. Steven Ott and Jay M. Shafritz (1986).

3. Surveys of the foundation field began in 1976 and were slowly expanded until by 1980 they included information on gender and minority characteristics of staff and board positions. Some of this information was analyzed in the book *Working in Foundations: Career Patterns of Women and Men* by Teresa Odendahl, Elizabeth Boris, and Arlene Daniels (1985). This analysis revealed an increase in the number of women working in foundation philanthropy since 1970 and also documented a salary gap between men and women and the small number of women who headed the largest foundations. Eight years later, the *1988 Foundation Management Report* reveals that 56 percent of foundation professional staff is female and that more women are running the largest foundations.

4. The National Charities Information Bureau revised its standards in 1988 after a long review (1988). A commentary on the standards is presented by Henry Shurke "Some Limitations of Standard Setting" (1988). Somewhat similar standards are used by the Philanthropic Advisory Service of the Council of Better Business Bureaus (1982).

5. Ethics was the topic of a major meeting in California sponsored by the Josephson Institute, the subject of an article by David Johnston, "Looking for an Honest Answer" (1988). The Ethics feature has been running since 1983 in *Foundation News*. In that series grantmakers give their reactions to ethical situations they might confront in their work. Robert Payton led a discussion on ethics in corporate giving which resulted in the paper, *The Ethics of Corporate Grantmaking* (1987). Paul Ylvisaker is well known for his thinking and teaching on the subject of ethics in grantmaking. His speech to the Associated Grantmakers of Massachusetts reflects his thoughtful approach (1982).

References

Boris, Elizabeth, and Deborah Brody. (1988). *1988 Foundation Management Report*. Washington DC: Council on Foundations.

Boris, Elizabeth and Teresa Odendahl. (1988). "Ethics and Philanthropy." In Jon Van Til, (Ed.), *Cutting Edge Issues in Philanthropy*. (Forthcoming)

Council of Better Business Bureaus. (1982). *Standards for Charitable Solicitations*.

Arlington, VA: Council of Better Business Bureaus, Inc.

Exploratory Project on Financing the Nonprofit Sector. (1988). *Part of the Solution: Innovative Approaches to Nonprofit Funding.* (Forthcoming). Washington, DC: Institute for Public Policy and Administration, Union for Experimenting Colleges and Universities.

Fund Raising Management, 18 (1987, July).

Hodgkinson, Virginia Ann and Murray S. Weitzman. (1986). *Dimensions of the Independent Sector: A Statistical Profile.* Washington, DC: Independent Sector.

Giving and Volunteering in the United States: Findings of a National Survey. (1988). Washington, DC: Survey Conducted by the Gallup Organization for Independent Sector.

Independent Sector. (1988). *Research in Progress.* Washington, DC: Independent Sector.

Johnston, David. (1988, January/February). "Looking for an Honest Answer." *Foundation News, 29*(i): 54–56.

Mason, David. (1984). *Voluntary Nonprofit Enterprise Management.* New York: Plenum Press.

National Charities Information Bureau. (1988). *Standards in Philanthropy.* New York: NCIB.

Nielsen, Waldemar. (1979). *The Endangered Sector.* New York: Columbia University Press.

O'Connell, Brian. (1988). 9-part Nonprofit Management Series. Washington, DC: Independent Sector.

Odendahl, Teresa. (Ed.). (1987). *America's Wealthy and the Future of Foundations.* New York: The Foundation Center.

Odendahl, Teresa, Elizabeth Boris, and Arlene Daniels. (1985). *Working in Foundations: Career Patterns of Women and Men.* New York: The Foundation Center.

O'Neill, Michael, and Dennis R. Young. (Eds.). (1988). *Educating Managers of Nonprofit Organizations.* Westport, CT: Praeger.

Ott, J. Steven, and Jay M. Shafritz. (1986). *The Facts on File Dictionary of Nonprofit Organization Management.* New York: Facts on File.

Payton, Robert. (1987). *The Ethics of Corporate Grantmaking.* Washington, DC: Council on Foundations.

Salamon, Lester M. (1987). "Partners in Public Service: The Scope and Theory of Government–Nonprofit Relations." In Walter W. Powell, (Ed.), *The Nonprofit Sector: A Research Handbook.* New Haven: Yale University Press.

Salamon, Lester M., and Kenneth P. Voytek. (1988). *Managing Foundation Assets: An Analysis of Foundation Investment and Payout Procedures and Performance.* New York: The Foundation Center. (Forthcoming)

Shurke, Henry. (1987, October). "Some Limitations of Standard Setting." *Philanthropy Monthly, 20* (9): 5–16.

Viscusi, Margo. (1985, May/June). "Coming of Age." *Foundation News, 26* (3): 26–35.

Weber, Nathan. (Ed.). (1988). *Giving USA: The Annual Report on Philanthropy for the Year 1987.* New York: AAFRC Trust for Philanthropy.

Yankelovitch Group. (1988). *The Climate for Giving: The Outlook of Current and Future CEOs.* Washington, DC: Council on Foundations.

Yankelovitch, Skelly and White, Inc. (1986). *The Charitable Behavior of Americans: A National Survey.* Washington, DC: Independent Sector.

Ylvisaker, Paul. (1982). "Ethics and Philanthropy." Adapted from a speech delivered to the Associated Grantmakers of Massachusetts, Inc. March 18, 1982. (Unpublished)